THE

SACRED WRITINGS

of the

WORLD'S

GREAT RELIGIONS

Selected and edited by

S. E. FROST, Jr.

McGraw-Hill Book Company

New York • St. Louis • San Francisco • London • Düsseldorf
Kuala Lumpur • Mexico • Montreal • Panama • Rio de Janeiro
Sydney • Toronto • Johannesburg • New Delhi • Singapore

PREFACE

THE SELECTIONS from the sacred writings of the thirteen religions included in this book reveal how often religions, originating in very different cultures and in ages far apart, teach similar doctrines and similar principles of ethics and morals. This similarity is pointedly indicated in a topical index at the end of the volume. Here a number of beliefs and doctrines have been listed and reference made to chapter and verse where the different religious teachings on these subjects may be found. This volume is therefore not only a treasure house of living religious literature but also a guide to the understanding of the fundamental similarity among religions.

In this volume of selected sacred writings we have reproduced passages of appreciable length rather than brief excerpts, so that the reader may have the context and appreciate the full message or teaching. A line or verse torn from its context seldom carries to the reader the meaning which the author intended. Within its context the teaching conveys not only what is said but what is implied. This, we believe, is the only fair and accurate way to quote from the scriptures.

In making our selections of the sacred writings, we have been fortunate in having access to the most authoritative translations available to modern scholars.

The material dealing with the sacred writings of the Church of Jesus Christ of Latter-day Saints has been prepared with the aid of the Church Publicity and Mission Literature Committee of that body and has its complete approval. Also the section dealing with Christian Science was written largely by especially appointed members of the Christian Science Committee on Publications and carries the approval of the church. We take this opportunity of thanking these committees, and all those who have been helpful with suggestions and criticisms during the preparation of the other sections of this book.

S. E. FROST, JR.

CONTENTS

INTRODUCTION

THE STUDY of man from primitive times to the present day discloses no people without some belief in a power or powers ruling the universe, some form of worship, and some code of conduct or morals. This universal nature of religion is an outstanding fact in the history of mankind. There have been many religions, many beliefs about the gods and many ways of worshiping them. A number of great historical religions have risen, flourished for a time, and then died out; among them: the religions of ancient Egypt, Babylonia, the Hittites, the cult of the sun god called Mithraism, and Manichaeism which saw life as a conflict of light and darkness, the beliefs of the ancient Greeks, the Romans, the Celts, the Scandinavians, and the Teutons, and in the Americas the religions of the Incas, Mayas, and Aztecs.

There are eleven great "living" religions and several smaller religions today. Four of these, Christianity, Mohammedanism, Confucianism, and Hinduism, are maintaining their growth. Four, Judaism, Buddhism, Sikhism, and Taoism, show neither gain nor loss over a long period of time. Three of the world's great religions, Zoroastrianism, Jainism, and Shinto, are definitely on the decline.

Among the lesser religious bodies of today are two of particular interest to people of the United States. These are the Latter Day Saints, or Mormons, and the Church of Christ, Scientist, usually referred to as Christian Science. Mormonism is a relatively small organization having the greater part of its membership in Utah. The Church of Christ, Scientist, founded in Massachusetts, is steadily growing.

The world's "living" religions differ from the "dead" religions in that they cherish certain definite writings as sacred. The religions which have ceased to exist have left no sacred canon or body of scriptures. Their literature was scattered, most of it being handed down from father to son, or "priest" to worshiper, by word of mouth. A little of it was collected much later and written down in such books as the *Iliad* and the *Odyssey* of Homer. But most of the lore about the gods and their doings, the nature of the universe and of life after death, the laws and moral precepts of the religion, were never brought together into anything that could be called a canon.

The sacred writings, or scriptures of the world's living religions are:

CHRISTIANITY: *The Bible,* consisting of the Old and New Testaments, and certain books known as the Apocrypha.

CONFUCIANISM: *The Five Classics* and *The Four Books.* Included in the former are the *Shu King* or *Canon of History,* the *Shih King* of *Canon of Poetry,* the *I King* or *Canon of Changes,* the *Li Ki* or *Book of Rites,* and the *Chun Chiu* or *Spring and Autumn Annals.* Some authorities add a sixth Classic, the *Hsiao King* or *Book of Filial Piety.* The latter consist of the *Ta Hsio* or *Great Learning,* the *Chung Yung* or *Doctrine of the Mean,* the *Lun Yu* or *Analects of Confucius,* and the *Meng-tze* or *Works of Mencius.*

MOHAMMEDANISM: *The Koran,* consisting of 114 chapters or *Suras.* The first chapter is a short opening prayer, the famous *Fatihah.* The other 113 chapters are arranged in the order of their length from one of 286 verses to one of three verses.

HINDUISM: *The Vedas* or *Books of Knowledge.* These have their origin sometime before 1000 B.C. and form the basis for all Hinduism. There are four of these *Vedas:* The *Rig-Veda* or *Veda of Verses,* the *Yajur Veda* or *Veda of Sacred Formulas,* the *Sama Veda* or the *Veda of Chants,* and the *Atharva Veda* or *Veda of Charms.* During the long period between the writing of these books and the beginning of the Christian era, Hinduism went through several changes affecting groups within the main body of the religion. Out of each change there came a literature which was accepted as sacred by the groups concerned. The *Satapatha Brahmana* is an outgrowth of the priestly development of Hinduism during the period from 1000 B.C. to 800 B.C. This development was followed, between 800 and 600 B.C., by a philosophic interest out of which came the *Upanishads* or books of philosophic discussion. In about 250 B.C. Hinduism developed a strong legalistic tone and from this was produced the *Laws of Manu* or code of Hindu law. Then, at the beginning of the Christian era a great many Hindus began to place considerable emphasis upon prayer and devotion. These produced the *Bhagavad Gita,* a dramatic poem of great beauty and high moral precepts. While these documents constitute the sacred books of Hinduism, there are two *Epics* and eighteen *Puranas,* dating from the beginning of the Christian era to about 250 A.D., which have had considerable influence upon popular Hinduism. The *Epics* are the *Mahabharata* or *The Great Bharata War* and the *Ramayana* or *The Career of the God Rama.* Of the *Puranas* the *Vishnu, Garuda,* and *Markandeya* are most important.

BUDDHISM: *The Tripitaka* or *Three Baskets* of teachings. These consist of the *Vinaya Pitaka* or *Discipline Basket,* the *Sutta Pitaka* or *Teaching Basket,* and the *Abhidhamma Pitaka* or *Metaphysical Basket.* Also *The Dhammapada* or *Way of Virtue.*

TAOISM: *The Tao-Teh-King* or *Canon of Reason and Virtue.* This book consists of a number of generalizations and wise sayings gathered together with no system or plan. In addition to this basic sacred text, Taoists revere the *Tai-Shang Kang-Ying Pien* or *Tractate of Actions and Their Retributions.* This volume contains many very crude and primitive teachings along with passages which rival anything in the best of moral literature. A third book, classified as non-canonical, is the *Kwang-Tze* or *Works of Kwang-Tze.*

SHINTO: *Ko-ji-ki* or *Records of Ancient Matters* and *Nihon-gi* or *Chronicles of Japan.* The first is the story of deeds and conversations in the "age of the gods" before men existed on this earth. The second tells of the creation of Japan and the rule of the Emperors. Neither book is historically reliable. A third sacred document of Shinto is the *Yengi-shiki* or *Institutes of the Period of Yengi.* This book consists of 50 chapters, dating from about the 10th century A.D. Its text is a series of prayers for various occasions. A fourth among the sacred Shinto writings is the *Manyo-shiu* or *Collection of Ten Thousand Leaves,* an anthology of 4496 poems dating from the 5th to the 8th centuries A.D.

JUDAISM: *The Old Testament* and the *Talmud.* The former consists of three sections: The Law, The Prophets, and The Sacred Writings. The latter is divided into the *Mishna* or text and the *Gemara* or Commentary on the text. In addition some scholars include the *Old Testament Apocrypha* as part of the Jewish sacred scriptures. This consists of a group of writings produced by Jews of ancient times but not officially admitted to the sacred canon.

SIKHISM: *Granth* or *The Book.* This is a collection of poems totaling about 29,480 verses dealing with meditation about God and exhortation to a moral life. There are several *Granths* composed at different times and containing differences in material. The *Adi Granth* is the oldest, dating from 1604 A.D. The orthodox Sikhs recognize the authority of the *Dasam Granth* or the *Granth of the Tenth Guru,* a later compilation.

JAINISM: The *Agamas* or *Precepts.* Another name often used for these writings is *Siddhantas* or *Treatises.* This consists of an undetermined number of sacred documents. One sect, the Sthanakvasi, recognizes 33 documents as canonical while another sect, the Svetambara, recognizes 45 documents. Some Jains hold that there are actually 84 sacred documents to be included in the canon. The first section of the *Agamas* consisted of 12 *Angas* or bodies, of which only 11 are known, the 12th having been lost. Four important *Agamas* are: *Akaranga, Kalpa, Uttaradhyayana,* and *Sutrakritanga.*

ZOROASTRIANISM: *Avesta* or *Knowledge.* This consists of four main groups. The *Yasna* deals with worship and sacrifice and contains the 17 *Gathas* or *Psalms.* The *Visperad* is a collection of invocations to all the gods. The *Vendidad* is a priestly code of ceremonial laws dealing with methods of fighting demons. The *Yashts* is an anthology of religious poetry or worship hymns. A fifth document, sometimes included as part of the *Avesta,* is the *Khorda-Avesta* or *Little Avesta,* a devotional handbook of litanies and prayers used by all Zoroastrians as a daily guide to worship and prayer.

MORMONISM: *Book of Mormon* offers a history of the Lost Tribes of Israel, connecting them with the ancestors of the American aborigines. The Mormons also accept the Bible, "if correctly translated," as sacred.

CHURCH OF CHRIST, SCIENTIST: The Bible is the sacred book of this religious group. *Science and Health with Key to the Scriptures,* a commentary by Mary Baker Eddy, is the volume around which the church is organized and is held by the members to have a special religious value.

Although each religion is distinct from all others in much that is essential, there are certain basic teachings which are common to all. Every religion has some individual possessing divine qualities and claiming the veneration of all its adherents. Early Buddhism and early Jainism denied the existence of a Supreme Being, but later both developed a worship of the founder. Judaism has always worshiped one God, Jehovah. Before the exile it admitted that other gods existed and might be worshiped by other people. After the exile it came to deny the existence of any other god than Jehovah. While Confucianism teaches the worship of one Supreme Ruler, popular Confucianism worships a great host of nature spirits and also the spirits of dead ancestors.

In Zoroastrianism we find two powerful forces, Ahura Mazda, supremely worshipful, and Angra Mainyu, the spirit of evil. Many other good spirits are also worshiped. In both Hinduism and Taoism we find the doctrine of a Supreme Being. For the Hindu this power is Brahma and for the Taoist it is the Tao or Way. Neither is worshiped in any real sense of the term. In the popular phases of both religions there are many deities which command worship. In Christianity, Sikhism, and Mohammedanism there is definite belief in a Supreme Power who deserves complete worship.

In many of the world's living religions is to be found the idea that the Supreme Being has become flesh and dwelt among men. Philosophic Hinduism holds that every object is in some degree a manifestation of the Brahma. Popular Hinduism is full of gods who have taken the form of men. Vishnu is held to have visited the earth many times in various forms, including the forms of animals. Buddhism teaches that the Buddha was one of 24 incarnations of "The Buddha" and that there is to be another incarnation. The Mohammedan sect, Shiite, broke from the Sunnite sect on the Belief that Ali, fourth caliph, was a divine incarnation of Allah and thus the real successor of the prophet Mohammed. Some members of the sect hold that there have been other incarnations. Christianity holds that Jesus Christ was actually God living for a time in the form of man.

The belief that the founder of a religion was of supernatural origin is to be found in many of the world's living religions. Christianity teaches that Jesus was the Son of God born of a virgin through divine conception. The Buddha is held to have been the divine child of a queen and to have had a pre-existence in heaven. Lao-tze is represented as having been born fully matured after being carried in his mother's womb for 72 or 81 years, according to different translations of the scripture. At his birth he was a "Wise Old Boy" or "Wise Old Philosopher" with white hair.

The founder of Jainism, Mahavira, is believed to have lived in heaven before being supernaturally placed in his mother's womb and then born after his mother had 14 prophetic dreams about him and his coming. The mother of Zoroaster is believed to have been "glorified" when she was a virgin of only 15 years, consequently Zoroastrians hold that all future saviors will be born of a virgin mother of 15 years.

Each religion lays claim to being the avenue of some divine revelation of truth. The Supreme Being and the founder or early leader of the religion is believed to have had some supernatural access to Truth and has shown this Truth to his followers. As a result, those who follow the religion and read its sacred writings are believed to be in possession of this Truth. For example, Hinduism teaches that the divine is in the world and that the society of men and women is a divinely built structure. As members of society, each follower of Hinduism is part of this divine structure and has access to the divine. As he becomes one with the divine, he moves toward the goal of all life. Thus, people must return to life again and again until they have become completely united with the divine that is in the universe. When this state is reached, people cease to exist as individuals, and live forever as the divine.

Further, all the living religions believe firmly that their sacred scriptures are divinely inspired, that is, that they have come directly from the Supreme Being believed in by the followers of the religion. Since they originate in this way, it is held that they reveal divine truth that is not to be questioned. The *Rig-Veda* and the *Koran* are held to be the exact words dictated by the Supreme Being and taken down without change; thus one who reads them reads the actual words of the god. Many Christians hold to this same theory as regards the Bible.

In many other respects the world's living religions agree. Among these is the contention that the founder and the especially sainted men and women in the religion's history were workers of miracles, that the followers of the religion constitute an especially sacred community or "church" which has peculiar protection from the god or Supreme Being, and that belief in the religion and careful obedience to its laws and precepts will insure rewards in the life after death.

But these religions differ in many respects. And this is to be expected when it is recognized that every religion has its origin in the racial experiences of a people. Each religion has a history, and the history of each differs from that of all the others. This history is the history of the people who gradually, through hundreds or thousands of years, have built up their belief out of their needs and experiences, their sufferings and successes, their defeats and victories.

A careful study of any religion will reveal how it has changed as the life of the people has changed. For example, when the early Hebrews were nothing more than a tribe of nomads wandering over the land from Ur of the Chaldees to Egypt, their religion was a crude form of worship of nature gods. These gods were cruel and had particular concern with the welfare of this nomadic people. Later their religion became that of a settled, cattle-raising and farming people. As the nation grew, the religion became such as fitted the needs of the nation.

And when the Hebrews began to think in terms of other peoples, their religion, during the period of the prophets, became more and more universal. Thus it was possible eventually for Christianity, a world religion, to grow out of the Hebrew religion. In this we see a religion growing and developing from a small tribal affair to a worldwide gospel as the people developed and changed.

It is natural, then, that each religion should take on the characteristics of the people around whose culture it developed. The surprising thing is that the world's living religions are so much alike in many respects. Considering the great diversity of cultural developments throughout the world, it is a wonder that the religions of mankind are at all alike. The only possible explanation is that the religions of present-day mankind were cradled in the East and began with people who were much alike. Then too, religion is one of the most conservative factors in human history. While people will change their political and social life radically over a period of time, they change their religious beliefs slowly. Add to this the fact that these religions have sacred documents believed to be inspired and handed down from early times with the halo of the divine about them, it becomes evident that there will be many similarities among the religions of the world.

In this volume we shall come to know the sacred writings of the world's great living religions. We shall read from the sacred books passages which give the flavor of the writings and suggest the doctrines taught by them. For here are selected masterpieces of the world's great religious literature, which have given to countless millions comfort, guidance, and inspiration.

I

HINDUISM

HINDUISM is the oldest living organized religion in the world, dating from a time between 2000 and 1500 B.C. From its beginnings to the present it has been changing and growing so that few of the beliefs and doctrines of the earliest Hindus are accepted in their original form by present-day adherents of the religion.

Although confined almost wholly to India, Hinduism has been adding steadily to its membership through a natural increase of the population. Some estimates place the annual increase at a little over 1,000,000. The present membership is slightly more than 240,000,000.

Fundamental to Hinduism, and the one factor which is to be found throughout the history of this religion from its earliest beginnings to the present, is strict adherence to a caste system. Hindus differ widely in their beliefs about theological matters while remaining Hindus just the same, yet they all agree regarding the caste system. Indeed, it has been said, "No one is interested in what his neighbor believes, but he is very much interested in knowing whether he can eat with him or take water from his hands."

There are four chief castes in Hinduism. Members of each are required by strict religious laws to follow certain hereditary occupations and to refrain from intermarriage or eating with members of the other castes. The highest, or priestly and intellectual, caste is that of the Brahmans. Next to this in rank is the Kshatriya, or ruling and warrior caste. The Vaisya, or common artisan and agricultural caste, is below the Kshatriya. At the very bottom of the caste system are the Sudras, or low-caste people. Within each of these four castes there are numerous subdivisions, so that there are now more than 2,000 castes, each living largely to itself and excluding all others.

There are strict religious laws keeping each caste out of contact with all others, and the penalties for disregarding these laws are, in many cases, most severe. However, there is today some agitation in India for an abandonment of these hard and fast lines. This movement is confined to a few intellectuals and has made little or no impression upon the vast millions of devout Hindus.

Within the general area known as Hinduism, considered historically, there have been at least six very different religions or "types of religions." Each developed its own library of sacred writings and, in many instances, an earlier type made a substantial contribution to later developments. Although each type has its distinctive features, it is possible to trace a clear line of growth and development from the earliest nature-worship to the latest philosophic and theological teachings of recent reformers.

The most primitive type, characterized by a crude nature-worship, was given literary form in the *Vedas* or *Books of Knowledge.* There are four of these *Vedas:* the *Rig-Veda,* or *Veda of Verses;* the *Yajur-Veda,* or *Veda of Sacred Formulas;* the *Sama-Veda,* or *Veda of Chants;* and the *Atharva-Veda,* or *Veda of Charms.* In these writings is to be found "a poetic testament of a people's collective reaction to the wonder and awe of existence." They are books of the childhood of Hinduism and are full of childhood's simple faith and enchantment with life, a faith that is not as yet burdened with intellectual brooding. The Vedas date from some period between 2000 and 1000 B.C.

After the Hindus moved into India and conquered the country, their religion began to harden into a vast system of laws and sacred formulae which were interpreted and enforced by a religious group of priests. Out of this grew the *Brahmanas* or *Priestlies,* extensive prose writings on religion. Here are many religious legends mixed with detailed instructions as to sacrifices and religious observances. This development took place between 1000 and 800 B.C. and was characterized by the rising power of the priests as a class and a decided lessening of the authority of the old Vedic gods.

But Hinduism was not to remain long in the shackles of the priests. Gradually the Hindus' love for philosophic speculation asserted itself, so that between 800 and 600 B.C. there was developed a group of writings in which this love for speculation was given free rein. These writings have become known as the *Upanishads* or *Seances.* Here are found the results of deep "brooding on the meaning of existence," of calm meditation and keenness of spiritual insight. The early childlike faith and the later trust in ceremonies are both gone, and in their place has come the earnest desire to explore "the infinite depths of the Soul in which the central principle of creation is reflected."

As in so many religions, the philosophic movement within Hinduism was followed by a strong legalistic movement around 250 B.C. Thus, in the *Laws of Manu* is to be found a code of Hindu law which aimed at setting up an institution which would be effective throughout generations. This code is full of commandments and prohibitions for daily living through all the stages of life as well as a great number of wise sayings and maxims.

One of the greatest eras of Hinduism, in the estimation of many, was around 1 A.D. when there appeared the *Bhagavad Gita*, or *Lord's Song*. This work is an expression of the devotional strain in Hinduism, a reformulation of the religion in terms of devotion to a personal god who will take care of everything if the worshiper will do his duty according to his caste and trust in God.

After the beginning of the Christian era, Hinduism entered a period during which many attempts were made to reinterpret the fundamental doctrines and beliefs in popular form. These attempts gave rise to the final literary work of the Hindu sacred writings, the two epics: *Mahabharata*, or the *Great Bharata War*, and the *Ramayana*, or the *Career of the God Rama*, and eighteen *Puranas*, or *Ancient Tales*. These documents are an indiscriminate mixture of many features of earlier Hinduism with modern doctrines picked up from many sources. They date from the period 1 to 250 A.D. Within the pattern of popular Hinduism are to be found laws and regulations regarding caste, eating, idolatry, sacred places and festivals, and much superstition.

Many attempts have been made since the beginning of the Christian era to reform Hinduism and numerous leaders have come forward as spearheads of these attempts. In most cases the result of their work has been little more than the establishment of a small sect varying only slightly from the vast body of the religion. These small movements have had little or no effect upon the great stream of the religion.

THE RIG–VEDA

OF THE FOUR *Vedas,* or *Books of Knowledge,* which constitute the sacred writings of ancient Hinduism, the *Rig-Veda,* or *Veda of Verses,* is the most important. In fact, this document is the oldest writing among the world's living religions, dating from 2000 to 1000 B.C. Nevertheless, it reveals a people who have progressed far in building a civilization and developing a culture. In it is little or nothing of the primitive beliefs of savage or semi-savage people. The gods and the beliefs expressed here compare favorably to those of the Homeric Greeks.

The *Rig-Veda* consists of 10 books comprising a total of 1,028 hymns or psalms. These hymns are most certainly the result of a long period of development during which the people sang or recited them and often added to them as their beliefs changed. Consequently, although the general trend is that of nature-worship, there are many varieties of belief and worship among the hymns. Prayers to some 70 objects, each serving as a deity, are to be found, along with affirmations of a high ethical idealism and psalms which equal anything in the Old Testament.

We also find mention of the caste system, with a definite statement comparing the four groups of human beings to parts of the human body.

I. 1. TO AGNI

1. I LAUD Agni, the chosen priest,
   god, minister of sacrifice,
   The hotar, lavishest of wealth.
2. Worthy is Agni to be praised by
   living as by ancient seers:
   He shall bring hitherward the
   gods.
3. Through Agni man obtaineth
   wealth, yea, plenty, waxing day
   by day,
   Most rich in heroes, glorious.
4. Agni, the perfect sacrifice which
   thou encompassest about
   Verily goeth to the gods.
5. May Agni, sapient-minded priest,
   truthful, most gloriously great,
   The god, come hither with the
   gods.

6. Whatever blessing, Agni, thou wilt
   grant unto thy worshipper,
   That, Angiras, is indeed thy truth.
7. To thee, dispeller of the night,
   O Agni, day by day with prayer
   Bringing thee reverence, we come;
8. Ruler of sacrifices, guard of law
   eternal, radiant one,
   Increasing in thine own abode.
9. Be to us easy of approach, even as
   a father to his son;
   Agni, be with us for our weal.

I. 25. TO VARUNA

1. WHATEVER law of thine, O god,
   O Varuna, as we are men,
   Day after day we violate,
2. Give us not as a prey to death, to
   be destroyed by thee in wrath,

To thy fierce anger when displeased.

3. To gain thy mercy, Varuna, with
hymns we bind thy heart, as
binds

The charioteer his tethered horse.

4. They flee from me dispirited, bent
only on obtaining wealth,

As to their nests the birds of air.

5. When shall we bring, to be ap-
peased, the hero, lord of warrior
might,

Him, the far-seeing Varuna?

6. This—this with joy they both accept in common: never do they
fail

The ever-faithful worshipper.

7. He knows the path of birds that
fly through heaven, and, sovran
of the sea,

He knows the ships that are
thereon.

8. True to his holy law, he knows the
twelve moons with their prog-
eny;

He knows the moon of later birth.

9. He knows the pathway of the
wind, the spreading, high, and
mighty wind;

He knows the gods who dwell
above.

10. Varuna, true to holy law, sits
down among his people; he,

Most wise, sits there to govern all.

11. From thence perceiving, he beholds all wondrous things, both
what hath been

And what hereafter will be done.

12. May that Aditya, very wise, make
fair paths for us all our days;

May he prolong our lives for us.

13. Varuna, wearing golden mail,
hath clad him in a shining robe;

His spies are seated round about.

14. The god whom enemies threaten
not, nor those who tyrannize
o'er men,

Nor those whose minds are bent
on wrong.

15. He who gives glory to mankind,
not glory that is incomplete,

To our own bodies giving it.

16. Yearning for the wide-seeing one,
my thoughts move onward unto
him

As kine unto their pastures move.

17. Once more together let us speak,
because my meath is brought;
priest-like

Thou eatest what is dear to thee.

18. Now saw I him whom all may see;
I saw his car above the earth;
He hath accepted these my songs.

19. Varuna, hear this call of mine: be
gracious unto us this day,

Longing for help I cry to thee.

20. Thou, O wise god, art lord of all,
thou art the king of earth and
heaven;

Hear, as thou goest on thy way.

21. Release us from the upper bond,
untie the bond between, and
loose

The bonds below, that I may live.

II. 28. To Varuna

1. This laud of the self-radiant wise
Aditya shall be supreme o'er all
that is in greatness.

I beg renown of Varuna the
mighty, the god exceeding kind
to him who worships.

2. Having extolled thee, Varuna,
with thoughtful care may we
have high fortune in thy service.

Singing thy praises like the fires
at coming, day after day, of
mornings rich in cattle.

3. May we be in thy keeping, O thou
leader, wide ruling Varuna,
Lord of many heroes.

O sons of Aditi, for ever faithful,
pardon us, gods, admit us to
your friendship.

4. He made them flow, the Aditya,
the sustainer: the rivers run by
Varuna's commandment.

These feel no weariness, nor cease
from flowing: swift have they
flown like birds in air around
us.

5. Loose me from sin as from a band
   that binds me: may we swell,
   Varuna, thy spring of order.
   Let not my thread, while I weave
   song, be severed, nor my work's
   sum, before the time, be shat-
   tered.

6. Far from me, Varuna, remove all
   danger: accept me graciously,
   thou holy sovran.
   Cast off, like cords that hold a
   calf, my troubles: I am not even
   mine eyelid's lord without thee.

7. Strike us not, Varuna, with those
   dread weapons which, Asura, at
   thy bidding wound the sinner.
   Let us not pass away from light to
   exile. Scatter, that we may live,
   the men who hate us.

8. O mighty Varuna, now and hereafter, even as of old, will we
   speak forth our worship.
   For in thyself, invincible god, thy
   statutes ne'er to be moved are
   fixed as on a mountain.

9. Move far from me what sins I
   have committed: let me not
   suffer, King, for guilt of others.
   Full many a morn remains to
   dawn upon us: in these, O
   Varuna, while we live direct us.

10. O king, whoever, be he friend or
    kinsman, hath threatened me
    affrighted in my slumber—
    If any wolf or robber fain would
    harm us, therefrom, O Varuna,
    give thou us protection.

11. May I not live, O Varuna, to wit-
    ness my wealthy, liberal, dear
    friend's destitution.
    King, may I never lack well-
    ordered riches. Loud may we
    speak with heroes in assembly.

III. 62.   TO INDRA AND
OTHERS

1. YOUR well-known prompt activities aforetime needed no impulse from your faithful servant.
   Where, Indra-Varuna, is now that
   glory wherewith ye brought support to those who loved you?

2. This man, most diligent, seeking
   after riches, incessantly invokes
   you for your favour.
   Accordant, Indra-Varuna, with
   Maruts, with heaven and earth,
   hear ye mine invocation.

3. O Indra-Varuna, ours be this
   treasure, ours be wealth, Maruts, with full store of heroes.
   May the Varutris with their
   shelter aid us, and Bharati and
   Hotra with the mornings.

4. Be pleased with our oblations,
   thou loved of all gods, Brihaspati:
   Give wealth to him who brings
   thee gifts.

5. At sacrifices, with your hymns
   worship the pure Brihaspati—I
   pray for power which none may
   bend—

6. The bull of men, whom none deceive, the wearer of each shape
   at will,
   Brihaspati most excellent.

7. Divine, resplendent Pushan, this
   our newest hymn of eulogy
   By us is chanted forth to thee.

8. Accept with favour this my song,
   be gracious to the earnest
   thought,
   Even as a bridegroom to his bride.

9. May he who sees all living things,
   sees them together at a glance—
   May he, may Pushan be our help.

10. May we attain that excellent glory
    of Savitar the god:
    So may he stimulate our prayers.

11. With understanding, earnestly, of
    Savitar the god we crave
    Our portion of prosperity.

12. Men, singers worship Savitar the
    god with hymn and holy rites,
    Urged by the impulse of their
    thoughts.

13. Soma, who gives success, goes
    forth, goes to the gathering-
    place of gods,
    To seat him at the seat of Law.

14. To us and to our cattle may Soma
    give salutary food,
    To biped and to quadruped.
15. May Soma, strengthening our
    power of life, and conquering
    our foes,
    In our assembly take his seat.
16. May Mitra-Varuna, sapient pair,
    bedew our pasturage with oil,
    With meath the regions of the air.
17. Far-ruling, joyful when adored, ye
    reign through majesty of might,
    With pure laws everlastingly.
18. Lauded by Jamadagni's song, sit
    in the place of holy Law:
    Drink soma, ye who strengthen
    Law.

v. 85.　　To Varuna

1. Sing forth a hymn sublime and
   solemn, grateful to glorious
   Varuna, imperial ruler,
   Who hath struck out, like one who
   slays the victim, earth as a skin
   to spread in front of Surya.
2. In the tree-tops the air he hath
   extended, put milk in kine and
   vigorous speed in horses,
   Set intellect in hearts, fire in the
   waters, Surya in heaven and
   Soma on the mountain.
3. Varuna lets the big cask, opening
   downward, flow through the
   heaven and earth and air's mid-
   region.
   Therewith the universe's sovran
   waters earth as the shower of
   rain bedews the barley.
4. When Varuna is fain for milk, he
   moistens the sky, the land, and
   earth to her foundation.
   Then straight the mountains
   clothe them in the raincloud:
   the heroes, putting forth their
   vigour, loose them.
5. I will declare this mighty deed of
   magic, of glorious Varuna, the
   lord immortal,
   Who, standing in the firmament,
   hath meted the earth out with
   the sun as with a measure.

6. None, verily, hath ever let or hin-
   dered this the most wise god's
   mighty deed of magic,
   Whereby with all their flood, the
   lucid rivers fill not one sea
   wherein they pour their waters.
7. If we have sinned against the man
   who loves us, have ever
   wronged a brother, friend, or
   comrade,
   The neighbour ever with us, or a
   stranger, O Varuna, remove
   from us the trespass.
8. If we, as gamesters cheat at play,
   have cheated, done wrong un-
   wittingly or sinned of purpose,
   Cast all these sins away like
   loosened fetters, and, Varuna,
   let us be thine own beloved.

x. 117.　　To Liberality

1. The gods have not ordained
   hunger to be our death: even to
   the well-fed man comes death
   in varied shape.
   The riches of the liberal never
   waste away, while he who will
   not give finds none to comfort
   him.
2. The man with food in store who,
   when the needy comes in miserable case begging for bread to
   eat,
   Hardens his heart against him—
   even when of old he did him
   service—finds not one to comfort him.
3. Bounteous is he who gives unto
   the beggar who comes to him in
   want of food and feeble.
   Success attends him in the shout
   of battle. He makes a friend of
   him in future troubles.
4. No friend is he who to his friend
   and comrade who comes im-
   ploring food, will offer nothing.
   Let him depart—no home is that
   to rest in—and rather seek a
   stranger to support him.

5. Let the rich satisfy the poor im-
plorer, and bend his eye upon a
longer pathway.
Riches come now to one, now to
another, and like the wheels of
cars are ever rolling.

6. The foolish man wins food with
fruitless labour: that food—I
speak the truth—shall be his
ruin.
He feeds no trusty friend, no man
to love him. All guilt is he who
eats with no partaker.

7. The ploughshares ploughing makes
the food that feeds us, and with
its feet cuts through the path it
follows.
Better the speaking than the silent
Brahman: the liberal friend
outvalues him who gives not.

8. He with one foot hath far outrun
the biped, and the two-footed
catches the three-footed.
Four-footed creatures come when
bipeds call them, and stand and
look where five are met together.

9. The hands are both alike: their
labour differs. The yield of sister milch-kine is unequal.

Twins even differ in their strength
and vigour: two, even kinsmen,
differ in their bounty.

x. 151.   TO FAITH

1. By faith is Agni kindled, through
faith is oblation offered up.
We celebrate with praises faith
upon the height of happiness.

2. Bless thou the man who gives, O
Faith; Faith, bless the man who
fain would give.
Bless thou the liberal worshippers;
bless thou the word that I have
said.

3. Even as the deities maintained
faith in the mighty Asuras,
So make this uttered wish of mine
true for the liberal worshippers.

4. Guarded by Vayu, gods and men
who sacrifice draw near to faith.
Man winneth faith by yearnings of
the heart, and opulence by
faith.

5. Faith in the early morning, Faith
at noonday will we invocate,
Faith at the setting of the sun. O
Faith, endow us with belief.

THE UPANISHADS

THE *Upanishads* come from a people who have settled in permanent cities and have developed a high degree of civilization. They date from possibly 800 to 600 B.C. and are the finest results of Hindu speculation upon the fundamental problems that have challenged philosophic minds throughout the ages.

The word *Upanishad* is derived from the root meaning "to sit". The Hindu had time to sit and discuss these problems with his fellows. Thus the writings are connected discourses, or rather conversations, participated in by men whose hair had grown white and who had seen their sons' sons,—the old and very wise men. One gets the impression as one reads these books that much of the conversation was punctuated by long periods of silence when the speakers remained quiet, lost in thought too deep for words.

The chief problem of the *Upanishads,* dominating and casting its glow over almost every page, is the relationship of the outer world to the inner self of man. And the conclusion reached is that they are identical, that the outer world is spiritual. "All is Self" is the constant theme of the *Upanishads,* and in it the Hindu believed that he had found a solution of all his deepest problems. The spirit which was himself was also the essence of the outer world.

There are many *Upanishads,* or philosophic writings of this period, that are considered sacred by the Hindus. Only a few of these have been translated into English or are available for study by Western scholars. Of those available, we have chosen the *Brihad-Aranyaka,* the *Chandogya,* the *Katha,* the *Isa,* and the *Svetasvatara* as representative of the general tenor of the entire development of philosophic Hinduism.

The Brihad-Aranyaka Upanishad

FIRST ADHYAYA

THIRD BRAHMANA

1. There were two kinds of descendants of Prajapati, the Devas and the Asuras. Now the Devas were indeed the younger, the Asuras the elder ones. The Devas, who were struggling in these worlds, said: "Well, let us overcome the Asuras at the sacrifices (the Jyotishtoma) by means of the udgitha."

2. They said to speech (Vach): "Do thou sing out for us (the udgitha)." "Yes," said speech, and sang (the udgitha). Whatever delight there is in speech, that she obtained for the Devas by singing (the three pavamanas); but that she pronounced well (in the other nine pavamanas), that was for herself. The Asuras knew: "Verily, through this singer they will overcome us." They therefore rushed at the singer and pierced her with evil.

17

That evil which consists in saying what is bad, that is that evil.

3. Then they (the Devas) said to breath (scent): "Do thou sing out for us." "Yes," said breath, and sang. Whatever delight there is in breath (smell), that he obtained for the Devas by singing; but that he smelled well, that was for himself. The Asuras knew: "Verily, through this singer they will overcome us." They therefore rushed at the singer, and pierced him with evil. That evil which consists in smelling what is bad, that is that evil.

4. Then they said to the eye: "Do thou sing out for us." "Yes," said the eye, and sang. Whatever delight there is in the eye, that he obtained for the Devas by singing; but that he saw well, that was for himself. The Asuras knew: "Verily, through this singer they will overcome us." They therefore rushed at the singer, and pierced him with evil. That evil which consists in seeing what is bad, that is that evil.

5. Then they said to the ear: "Do thou sing out for us." "Yes," said the ear, and sang. Whatever delight there is in the ear, that he obtained for the Devas by singing; but that he heard well, that was for himself. The Asuras knew: "Verily, through this singer they will overcome us." They therefore rushed at the singer, and pierced him with evil. That evil which consists in hearing what is bad, that is that evil.

6. Then they said to the mind: "Do thou sing out for us." "Yes," said the mind, and sang. Whatever delight there is in the mind, that he obtained for the Devas by singing; but that he thought well, that was for himself. The Asuras knew: "Verily, through this singer they will overcome us." They therefore rushed at the singer, and pierced him with evil. That evil which consists in thinking what is bad, that is that evil.

Thus they overwhelmed these deities with evils, thus they pierced them with evil.

7. Then they said to the breath in the mouth: "Do thou sing for us." "Yes," said the breath, and sang. The Asuras knew: "Verily, through this singer they will overcome us." They therefore rushed at him and pierced him with evil. Now as a ball of earth will be scattered when hitting a stone, thus they perished, scattered in all directions. Hence the Devas rose, the Asuras fell. He who knows this, rises by his Self, and the enemy who hates him falls.

8. Then they (the Devas) said: "Where was he then who thus stuck to us?" It was (the breath) within the mouth (asye 'ntar), and therefore called Ayasya; he was the sap (rasa) of the limbs (anga), and therefore called Angirasa.

9. That deity was called Dur, because death was far (duran) from it. From him who knows this, death is far off.

10. That deity, after having taken away the evil of those deities, viz. death, sent it to where the end of the quarters of the earth is. There he deposited their sins. Therefore let no one go to a man, let no one go to the end (of the quarters of the earth), that he may not meet there with evil, with death.

11. That deity, after having taken away the evil of those deities, viz. death, carried them beyond death.

12. He carried speech across first. When speech had become freed from death, it became (what it had been before) Agni (fire). That Agni, after having stepped beyond death, shines.

13. Then he carried breath (scent) across. When breath had become freed from death, it became Vayu (air). That Vayu, after having stepped beyond death, blows.

14. Then he carried the eye across. When the eye had become freed from death, it became Aditya (the sun).

That Aditya, after having stepped beyond death, burns.

15. Then he carried the ear across. When the ear had become freed from death, it became the quarters (space). These are our quarters (space), which have stepped beyond death.

16. Then he carried the mind across. When the mind had become freed from death, it became the moon (Chandramas). That moon, after having stepped beyond death, shines. Thus does that deity carry him, who knows this, across death.

17. Then breath (vital), by singing, obtained for himself eatable food. For whatever food is eaten, is eaten by breath alone, and in it breath rests.

The Devas said: "Verily, thus far, whatever food there is, thou hast by singing acquired it for thyself. Now therefore give us a share in that food." He said: "You, there, enter into me." They said "Yes," and entered all into him. Therefore whatever food is eaten by breath, by it the other senses are satisfied.

18. If a man knows this, then his own relations come to him in the same manner; he becomes their supporter, their chief leader, their strong ruler. And if ever anyone tries to oppose one who is possessed of such knowledge among his own relatives, then he will not be able to support his own belongings. But he who follows the man who is possessed of such knowledge, and who with his permission wishes to support those whom he has to support, he indeed will be able to support his own belongings.

19. He was called Ayasya Angirasa, for he is the sap (rasa) of the limbs (anga). Verily, breath is the sap of the limbs. Yes, breath is the sap of the limbs. Therefore from whatever limb breath goes away, that limb withers, for breath verily is the sap of the limbs.

20. He (breath) is also Brihaspati, for speech is Brihati (Rigveda), and

he is her lord; therefore he is Brihaspati.

21. He (breath) is also Brahmanaspati, for speech is Brahman (Yajurveda), and he is her lord; therefore he is Brahmanaspati.

He (breath) is also Saman (the Udgitha), for speech is Saman (Samaveda), and that is both speech (sa) and breath (ama). This is why Saman is called Saman.

22. Or because he is equal (sama) to a grub, equal to a gnat, equal to an elephant, equal to these three worlds, nay, equal to this universe, therefore he is Saman. He who thus knows this Saman, obtains union and oneness with Saman.

23. He (breath) is Udgitha. Breath verily is Ut, for by breath this universe is upheld (uttabdha); and speech is Githa, song. And because he is ut and githa, therefore he (breath) is Udgitha.

24. And thus Brahmadatta Chaikitaneya (the grandson of Chikitana), while taking Soma (rajan), said: "May this Soma strike my head off, if Ayasya Angirasa sang another Udgitha than this. He sang it indeed as speech and breath."

25. He who knows what is the property of this Saman, obtains property. Now verily its property is tone only. Therefore let a priest, who is going to perform the sacrificial work of a Sama-singer, desire that his voice may have a good tone, and let him perform the sacrifice with a voice that is in good tone. Therefore people (who want a priest) for a sacrifice, look out for one who possesses a good voice, as for one who possesses property. He who thus knows what is the property of that Saman, obtains property.

26. He who knows what is the gold of that Saman, obtains gold. Now verily its gold is tone only. He who thus knows what is the gold of that Saman, obtains gold.

27. He who knows what is the support of that Saman, he is supported. Now verily its support is speech only. For, as supported in speech, that breath is sung as that Saman. Some say the support is in food.

Next follows the Abhyaroha (the ascension) of the Pavamana verses. Verily the Prastotri begins to sing the Saman, and when he begins, then let him (the sacrificer) recite these (three Yajus-verses):

"Lead me from the unreal to the real! Lead me from darkness to light! Lead me from death to immortality!"

Now when he says, "Lead me from the unreal to the real," the unreal is verily death, the real immortality. He therefore says, "Lead me from death to immortality, make me immortal."

When he says, "Lead me from darkness to light," darkness is verily death, light immortality. He therefore says, "Lead me from death to immortality, make me immortal."

When he says, "Lead me from death to immortality," there is nothing there, as it were, hidden (obscure, requiring explanation).

28. Next come the other Stotras with which the priest may obtain food for himself by singing them. Therefore let the sacrificer, while these Stotras are being sung, ask for a boon, whatever desire he may desire. An Udgatri priest who knows this obtains by his singing whatever desire he may desire either for himself or for the sacrificer. This (knowledge) indeed is called the conqueror of the worlds. He who thus knows this Saman, for him there is no fear of his not being admitted to the worlds.

Second Adhyaya

First Brahmana

1. There was formerly the proud Gargya Balaki, a man of great reading. He said to Ajatasatru of Kasi, "Shall I tell you Brahman?" Ajatasatru said: "We give a thousand (cows) for that speech (of yours), for verily all people run away, saying, Janaka (the king of Mithila) is our father (patron)."

2. Gargya said: "The person that is in the sun, that I adore as Brahman." Ajatasatru said to him: "No, no! Do not speak to me on this. I adore him verily as the supreme, the head of all beings, the king. Whoso adores him thus, becomes supreme, the head of all beings, a king."

3. Gargya said: "The person that is in the moon (and in the mind) that I adore as Brahman." Ajatasatru said to him: "No, no! Do not speak to me on this. I adore him verily as the great, clad in white raiment, as Soma, the king. Whoso adores him thus, Soma is poured out and poured forth for him day by day, and his food does not fail."

4. Gargya said: "The person that is in the lightning (and in the heart), that I adore as Brahman." Ajatasatru said to him: "No, no! Do not speak to me on this. I adore him verily as the luminous. Whoso adores him thus, becomes luminous, and his offspring becomes luminous."

5. Gargya said: "The person that is in the ether (and in the ether of the heart), that I adore as Brahman." Ajatasatru said to him: "No, no! Do not speak to me on this. I adore him as what is full, and quiescent. Whoso adores him thus, becomes filled with offspring and cattle, and his offspring does not cease from this world."

6. Gargya said: "The person that is in the wind (and in the breath), that I adore as Brahman." Ajatasatru said to him: "No, no! Do not speak to me on this. I adore him as Indra Vaikuntha, as the unconquerable arm (of the Maruts). Whoso adores him thus, becomes victorious, unconquerable, conquering his enemies."

7. Gargya said: "The person that is in the fire (and in the heart), that I

adore as Brahman." Ajatasatru said to him: "No, no! Do not speak to me on this. I adore him as powerful. Whoso adores him thus, becomes powerful, and his offspring becomes powerful."

8. Gargya said: "The person that is in the water (in seed, and in the heart), that I adore as Brahman." Ajatasatru said to him: "No, no! Do not speak to me on this. I adore him as likeness. Whoso adores him thus, to him comes what is likely (or proper), not what is improper; what is born from him is like unto him."

9. Gargya said: "The person that is in the mirror, that I adore as Brahman." Ajatasatru said to him: "No, no! Do not speak to me on this. I adore him verily as the brilliant. Whoso adores him thus, he becomes brilliant, his offspring becomes brilliant, and with whomsoever he comes together, he outshines them."

10. Gargya said: "The sound that follows a man while he moves, that I adore as Brahman." Ajatasatru said to him: "No, no! Do not speak to me on this. I adore him verily as life. Whoso adores him thus, he reaches his full age in this world, breath does not leave him before the time."

11. Gargya said: "The person that is in space, that I adore as Brahman." Ajatasatru said to him: "No, no! Do not speak to me on this. I adore him verily as the second who never leaves us. Whoso adores him thus, becomes possessed of a second, his party is not cut off from him."

12. Gargya said: "The person that consists of the shadow, that I adore as Brahman." Ajatasatru said to him: "No, no! Do not speak to me on this. I adore him verily as death. Whoso adores him thus, he reaches his whole age in this world, death does not approach him before the time."

13. Gargya said: "The person that is in the body, that I adore as Brahman." Ajatasatru said to him: "No, no! Do not speak to me on this. I

adore him verily as embodied. Whoso adores him thus, becomes embodied, and his offspring becomes embodied." Then Gargya became silent.

14. Ajatasatru said: "Thus far only?" "Thus far only," he replied. Ajatasatru said: "This does not suffice to know it (the true Brahman)." Gargya replied: "Then let me come to you, as a pupil."

15. Ajatasatru said: "Verily, it is unnatural that a Brahmana should come to a Kshatriya, hoping that he should tell him the Brahman. However, I shall make you know him clearly"; thus saying, he took him by the hand and rose.

And the two together came to a person who was asleep. He called him by these names, "Thou, great one, clad in white raiment, Soma, king." He did not rise. Then rubbing him with his hand, he woke him, and he arose.

16. Ajatasatru said: "When this man was thus asleep, where was then the person (purusha), the intelligent? and from whence did he thus come back?" Gargya did not know this.

17. Ajatasatru said: "When this man was thus asleep, then the intelligent person (purusha), having through the intelligence of the senses (pranas) absorbed within himself all intelligence, lies in the ether, which is in the heart. When he takes in these different kinds of intelligence, then it is said that the man sleeps (svapiti). Then the breath is kept in, speech is kept in, the ear is kept in, the eye is kept in, the mind is kept in.

18. "But when he moves about in sleep (and dream), then these are his worlds. He is, as it were, a great king; he is, as it were, a great Brahmana; he rises, as it were, and he falls. And as a great king might keep in his own subjects, and move about, according to his pleasure, within his own domain, thus does that person (who is endowed with intelligence) keep in the various senses (pranas) and move about, ac-

cording to his pleasure, within his own body (while dreaming).

19. "Next, when he is in profound sleep, and knows nothing, there are the seventy-two thousand arteries called Hita, which from the heart spread through the body. Through them he moves forth and rests in the surrounding body. And as a young man, or a great king, or a great Brahmana, having reached the summit of happiness, might rest, so does he then rest.

20. "As the spider comes out with its thread, or as small sparks come forth from fire, thus do all senses, all worlds, all Devas, all beings come forth from that Self. The Upanishad (the true name and doctrine) of that Self is 'the True of the True.' Verily the senses are the True, and he is the True of the True."

FOURTH BRAHMANA

1. Now when Yajnavalkya was going to enter upon another state, he said: "Maitreyi, verily I am going away from this my house (into the forest). Forsooth, let me make a settlement between thee and that Katyayani (my other wife)."

2. Maitreyi said: "My lord, if this whole earth, full of wealth, belonged to me, tell me, should I be immortal by it?"

"No," replied Yajnavalkya; "like the life of rich people will be thy life. But there is no hope of immortality by wealth."

3. And Maitreyi said: "What should I do with that by which I do not become immortal? What my lord knoweth (of immortality), tell that to me."

4. Yajnavalkya replied: "Thou who art truly dear to me, thou speakest dear words. Come, sit down, I will explain it to thee, and mark well what I say."

5. And he said: "Verily, a husband is not dear, that you may love the husband; but that you may love the Self, therefore a husband is dear.

"Verily, a wife is not dear, that you may love the wife; but that you may love the Self, therefore a wife is dear.

"Verily, sons are not dear, that you may love the sons; but that you may love the Self, therefore sons are dear.

"Verily, wealth is not dear, that you may love wealth; but that you may love the Self, therefore wealth is dear.

"Verily, the Brahman-class is not dear, that you may love the Brahman-class; but that you may love the Self, therefore the Brahman-class is dear.

"Verily, the Kshatra-class is not dear, that you may love the Kshatra-class; but that you may love the Self, therefore the Kshatra-class is dear.

"Verily, the worlds are not dear, that you may love the worlds; but that you may love the Self, therefore the worlds are dear.

"Verily, the Devas are not dear, that you may love the Devas; but that you may love the Self, therefore the Devas are dear.

"Verily, creatures are not dear, that you may love the creatures; but that you may love the Self, therefore are creatures dear.

"Verily, everything is not dear, that you may love everything; but that you may love the Self, therefore everything is dear.

"Verily, the Self is to be seen, to be heard, to be perceived, to be marked, O Maitreyi! When we see, hear, perceive, and know the Self, then all this is known.

6. "Whosoever looks for the Brahman-class elsewhere than in the Self, was abandoned by the Brahman-class. Whosoever looks for the Kshatra-class elsewhere than in the Self, was abandoned by the Kshatra-class. Whosoever looks for the worlds elsewhere than in the Self, was abandoned by the worlds. Whosoever looks for the Devas elsewhere than in the Self, was

abandoned by the Devas. Whosoever looks for creatures elsewhere than in the Self, was abandoned by the creatures. Whosoever looks for anything elsewhere than in the Self, was abandoned by everything. This Brahman-class, this Kshatra-class, these worlds, these Devas, these creatures, this everything, all is that Self.

7. "Now as the sounds of a drum, when beaten, cannot be seized externally (by themselves), but the sound is seized, when the drum is seized or the beater of the drum;

8. "And as the sounds of a conch-shell, when blown, cannot be seized externally (by themselves), but the sound is seized, when the shell is seized or the blower of the shell;

9. "And as the sounds of a lute, when played, cannot be seized externally (by themselves), but the sound is seized, when the lute is seized or the player of the lute;

10. "As clouds of smoke proceed by themselves out of a lighted fire kindled with damp fuel, thus, verily, O Maitreyi, has been breathed forth from this great Being what we have as Rigveda, Yajur-veda, Sama-veda, Atharvangirasas, Itihasa (legends), Purana (cosmogonies), Vidya (knowledge), the Upanishads, Slokas (verses), Sutras (prose rules), Anuvyakhyanas (glosses), Vyakhyanas (commentaries). From him alone all these were breathed forth.

11. "As all waters find their centre in the sea, all touches in the skin, all tastes in the tongue, all smells in the nose, all colours in the eye, all sounds in the ear, all percepts in the mind, all knowledge in the heart, all actions in the hands, all movements in the feet, and all the Vedas in speech—

12. "As a lump of salt, when thrown into water, becomes dissolved into water, and could not be taken out again, but wherever we taste (the water) it is salt—thus verily, O Maitreyi, does this great Being, endless, unlimited, consisting of nothing but knowledge, rise from out these elements, and vanish again in them. When he has departed, there is no more knowledge (name), I say, O Maitreyi." Thus spoke Yajnavalkya.

13. Then Maitreyi said: "Here thou has bewildered me, Sir, when thou sayest that having departed, there is no more knowledge."

But Yajnavalkya replied: "O Maitreyi, I say nothing that is bewildering. This is enough, O beloved, for wisdom.

"For when there is as it were duality, then one sees the other, one smells the other, one hears the other, one salutes the other, one perceives the other, one knows the other; but when the Self only is all this, how should he smell another, how should he see another, how should he hear another, how should he salute another, how should he perceive another, how should he know another? How should he know him by whom he knows all this? How, O beloved, should he know (himself), the Knower?"

Third Adhyaya

NINTH BRAHMANA

1. Then Vidagdha Sakalya asked him: "How many gods are there, O Yajnavalkya?" He replied with this very Nivid: "As many as are mentioned in the Nivid of the hymn of praise addressed to the Visvedevas, viz. three and three hundred, three and three thousand."

"Yes," he said, and asked again: "How many gods are there really, O Yajnavalkya?"

"Thirty-three," he said.

"Yes," he said, and asked again: "How many gods are there really, O Yajnavalkya?"

"Six," he said.

"Yes," he said, and asked again:

"How many gods are there really, O Yajnavalkya?"

"Three," he said.

"Yes," he said, and asked again: "How many gods are there really, O Yajnavalkya?"

"Two," he said.

"Yes," he said, and asked again: "How many gods are there really, O Yajnavalkya?"

"One and a half (adhyardha)," he said.

"Yes," he said, and asked again: "How many gods are there really, O Yajnavalkya?"

"One," he said.

"Yes," he said, and asked: "Who are these three and three hundred, three and three thousand?"

2. Yajnavalkya replied: "They are only the various powers of them, in reality there are only thirty-three gods."

He asked: "Who are those thirty-three?"

Yajnavalkya replied: "The eight Vasus, the eleven Rudras, the twelve Adityas. They make thirty-one, and Indra and Prajapati make the thirty-three."

3. He asked: "Who are the Vasus?"

Yajnavalkya replied: "Agni (fire), Prithivi (earth), Vayu (air), Antariksha (sky), Aditya (sun), Dyu (heaven), Chandramas (moon), the Nakshatras (stars), these are the Vasus, for in them all that dwells (this world) rests; and therefore they are called Vasus."

4. He asked: "Who are the Rudras?"

Yajnavalkya replied: "These ten vital breaths (pranas, the senses, i.e. the five jnanendriyas, and the five karmendriyas), and Atman, as the eleventh. When they depart from this mortal body, they make us cry (rodayanti), and because they make us cry, they are called Rudras."

5. He asked: "Who are the Adityas?"

Yajnavalkya replied: "The twelve months of the year, and they are Adityas, because they move along (yanti), taking up everything (adadana). Because they move along, taking up everything, therefore they are called Adityas."

6. He asked: "And who is Indra, and who is Prajapati?"

Yajnavalkya replied: "Indra is thunder, Prajapati is the sacrifice."

He asked: "And what is the thunder?"

Yajnavalkya replied: "The thunderbolt."

He asked: "And what is the sacrifice?"

Yajnavalkya replied: "The (sacrificial) animals."

7. He asked: "Who are the six?"

Yajnavalkya replied: "Agni (fire), Prithivi (earth), Vayu (air), Antariksha (sky), Aditya (sun), Dyu (heaven), they are the six, for they are all this, the six."

8. He asked: "Who are the three gods?"

Yajnavalkya replied: "These three worlds, for in them all these gods exist."

He asked: "Who are the two gods?"

Yajnavalkya replied: "Food and breath."

He asked: "Who is the one god and a half?"

Yajnavalkya replied: "He that blows."

9. Here they say: "How is it that he who blows like one only, should be called one and a half (adhyardha)?" And the answer is: "Because, when the wind was blowing, everything grew (adhyardhnot)."

He asked: "Who is the one god?"

Yajnavalkya replied: "Breath (prana), and he is Brahman (the Sutratman), and they call him That (tyad)."

10. Sakalya said: "Whosoever knows that person (or god) whose dwelling (body) is the earth, whose

sight (world) is fire, whose mind is light—the principle of every (living) self, he indeed is a teacher, O Yajnavalkya."

Yajnavalkya said: "I know that person, the principle of every self, of whom thou speakest. This corporeal (material, earthy) person, 'he is he.' But tell me, Sakalya, who is his devata (deity)?"

Sakalya replied: "The Immortal."

11. Sakalya said: "Whosoever knows that person whose dwelling is love (a body capable of sensual love), whose sight is the heart, whose mind is light—the principle of every self, he indeed is a teacher, O Yajnavalkya."

Yajnavalkya replied: "I know that person, the principle of every self, of whom thou speakest. This love-made (loving) person, 'he is he.' But tell me, Sakalya, who is his devata?"

Sakalya replied: "The women."

12. Sakalya said: "Whosoever knows that person whose dwelling are the colours, whose sight is the eye, whose mind is light—the principle of every self, he indeed is a teacher, O Yajnavalkya."

Yajnavalkya replied: "I know that person, the principle of every self, of whom thou speakest. That person in the sun, 'he is he.' But tell me, Sakalya, who is his devata?"

Sakalya replied: "The True."

13. Sakalya said: "Whosoever knows that person whose dwelling is ether, whose sight is the ear, whose mind is light—the principle of every self, he indeed is a teacher, O Yajnavalkya."

Yajnavalkya replied: "I know that person, the principle of every self, of whom thou speakest. The person who hears and answers, 'he is he.' But tell me, Sakalya, who is his devata?"

Sakalya replied: "Space."

14. Sakalya said: "Whosoever knows that person whose dwelling is darkness, whose sight is the heart, whose mind is light—the principle of

every self, he indeed is a teacher, O Yajnavalkya."

Yajnavalkya replied: "I know that person, the principle of every self, of whom thou speakest. The shadowy person, 'he is he.' But tell me, Sakalya, who is his devata?"

Sakalya replied: "Death."

15. Sakalya said: "Whosoever knows that person whose dwelling is (bright) colours, whose sight is the eye, whose mind is light—the principle of every self, he indeed is a teacher, O Yajnavalkya."

Yajnavalkya replied: "I know that person, the principle of every self, of whom thou speakest. The person in the looking-glass, 'he is he.' But tell me, Sakalya, who is his devata?"

Sakalya replied: "Vital breath (asu)."

16. Sakalya said: "Whosoever knows that person whose dwelling is water, whose sight is the heart, whose mind is light—the principle of every self, he indeed is a teacher, O Yajnavalkya."

Yajnavalkya replied: "I know that person, the principle of every self, of whom thou speakest. The person in the water, 'he is he.' But tell me, Sakalya, who is his devata?"

Sakalya replied: "Varuna."

17. Sakalya said: "Whosoever knows that person whose dwelling is seed, whose sight is the heart, whose mind is light—the principle of every self, he indeed is a teacher, O Yajnavalkya."

Yajnavalkya replied: "I know that person, the principle of every self, of whom thou speakest. The filial person, 'he is he.' But tell me, Sakalya, who is his devata?"

Sakalya replied: "Prajapati."

18. Yajnavalkya said: "Sakalya, did those Brahmanas (who themselves shrank from the contest) make thee the victim?"

Sakalya said: "Yajnavalkya, because thou hast decried the Brahmanas of the Kuru-Panchalas, what Brahman dost thou know?"

19. Yajnavalkya said: "I know the quarters with their deities and their abodes."

Sakalya said: "If thou knowest the quarters with their deities and their abodes,

20. "Which is thy deity in the eastern quarter?"

Yajnavalkya said: "Aditya (the sun)."

Sakalya said: "In what does that Aditya abide?"

Yajnavalkya said: "In the eye."

Sakalya said: "In what does the eye abide?"

Yajnavalkya said: "In the colours, for with the eye he sees the colours."

Sakalya said: "And in what then do the colours abide?"

Yajnavalkya said: "In the heart, for we know colours by the heart, for colours abide in the heart."

Sakalya said: "So it is indeed, O Yajnavalkya."

21. Sakalya said: "Which is thy deity in the southern quarter?"

Yajnavalkya said: "Yama."

Sakalya said: "In what does that Yama abide?"

Yajnavalkya said: "In the sacrifice."

Sakalya said: "In what does the sacrifice abide?"

Yajnavalkya said: "In the Dakshina (the gifts to be given to the priests)."

Sakalya said: "In what does the Dakshina abide?"

Yajnavalkya said: "In Sraddha (faith), for if a man believes, then he gives Dakshina, and Dakshina truly abides in faith."

Sakalya said: "And in what then does faith abide?"

Yajnavalkya said: "In the heart, for by the heart faith knows, and therefore faith abides in the heart."

Sakalya said: "So it is indeed, O Yajnavalkya."

22. Sakalya said: "Which is thy deity in the western quarter?"

Yajnavalkya said: "Varuna."

Sakalya said: "In what does that Varuna abide?"

Yajnavalkya said: "In the water."

Sakalya said: "In what does the water abide?"

Yajnavalkya said: "In the seed."

Sakalya said: "And in what does the seed abide?"

Yajnavalkya said: "In the heart. And therefore also they say of a son who is like his father, that he seems as if slipt from his heart, or made from his heart; for the seed abides in the heart."

Sakalya said: "So it is indeed, O Yajnavalkya."

23. Sakalya said: "Which is thy deity in the northern quarter?"

Yajnavalkya said: "Soma."

Sakalya said: "In what does that Soma abide?"

Yajnavalkya said: "In the Diksha."

Sakalya said: "In what does the Diksha abide?"

Yajnavalkya said: "In the True; and therefore they say to one who has performed the Diksha, Speak what is true, for in the True indeed the Diksha abides."

Sakalya said: "And in what does the True abide?"

Yajnavalkya said: "In the heart, for with the heart do we know what is true, and in the heart indeed the True abides."

Sakalya said: "So it is indeed, O Yajnavalkya."

24. Sakalya said: "Which is thy deity in the zenith?"

Yajnavalkya said: "Agni."

Sakalya said: "In what does that Agni abide?"

Yajnavalkya said: "In speech."

Sakalya said: "And in what does speech abide?"

Yajnavalkya said: "In the heart."

Sakalya said: "And in what does the heart abide?"

25. Yajnavalkya said: "O Ahallika, when you think the heart could be anywhere else away from us, if it were away from us, the dogs might eat it, or the birds tear it."

26. Sakalya said: "And in what dost thou (thy body) and the Self (thy heart) abide?"

Yajnavalkya said: "In the Prana (breath)."

Sakalya said: "In what does the Prana abide?"

Yajnavalkya said: "In the Apana (down-breathing)."

Sakalya said: "In what does the Apana abide?"

Yajnavalkya said: "In the Vyana (back-breathing)."

Sakalya said: "In what does the Vyana abide?"

Yajnavalkya said: "In the Udana (the out-breathing)."

Sakalya said: "In what does the Udana abide?"

Yajnavalkya said: "In the Samana. That Self (atman) is to be described by No, no! He is incomprehensible, for he cannot be (is not) comprehended; he is imperishable, for he cannot perish; he is unattached, for he does not attach himself; unfettered, he does not suffer, he does not fail.

"These are the eight abodes (the earth, etc.), the eight worlds (fire, etc.), the eight gods (the immortal food, etc.), the eight persons (the corporeal, etc.). He who after dividing and uniting these persons, went beyond (the Samana), that person, taught in the Upanishads, I now ask thee (to teach me). If thou shalt not explain him to me, thy head will fall."

Sakalya did not know him, and his head fell, nay, thieves took away his bones, mistaking them for something else.

27. Then Yajnavalkya said: "Reverend Brahmanas, whosoever among you desires to do so, may now question me. Or question me, all of you. Or whosoever among you desires it, I shall question him, or I shall question all of you."

But those Brahmanas durst not (say anything).

28. Then Yajnavalkya questioned them with these Slokas:

"As a mighty tree in the forest, so in truth is man, his hairs are the leaves, his outer skin is the bark.

"From his skin flows forth blood, sap from the skin (of the tree); and thus from the wounded man comes forth blood, as from a tree that is struck.

"The lumps of his flesh are (in the tree) the layers of wood, the fibre is strong like the tendons. The bones are the (hard) wood within, the marrow is made like the marrow of the tree.

"But, while the tree, when felled, grows up again more young from the root, from what root, tell me, does a mortal grow up, after he has been felled by death?

"Do not say, 'from seed,' for seed is produced from the living; but a tree, springing from a grain, clearly rises again after death.

"If a tree is pulled up with the root, it will not grow again; from what root then, tell me, does a mortal grow up, after he has been felled by death?

"Once born, he is not born (again); for who should create him again?

"Brahman, who is knowledge and bliss, he is the principle, both to him who gives gifts, and also to him who stands firm, and knows."

FOURTH ADHYAYA

FOURTH BRAHMANA

1. Yajnavalkya continued: "Now when that Self, having sunk into weakness, sinks, as it were, into unconsciousness, then gather those senses (pranas) around him, and he, taking with him those elements of light, descends into the heart. When that person in the eye turns away, then he ceases to know any forms.

2. " 'He has become one,' they say, 'he does not see.' 'He has become one,' they say, 'he does not smell.' 'He has become one,' they say, 'he does not taste.' 'He has become one,' they say, 'he does not speak.' 'He has become one,' they say, 'he does not hear.' 'He has become one,' they say, 'he does not think.' 'He has become one,' they say, 'he does not touch.' 'He has become one,' they say, 'he does not know.' The point of his heart becomes lighted up, and by that light the Self departs, either through the eye, or through the skull, or through other places of the body. And when he thus departs, life (the chief prana) departs after him, and when life thus departs, all the other vital spirits (pranas) depart after it. He is conscious, and being conscious he follows and departs.

"Then both his knowledge and his work take hold of him, and his acquaintance with former things.

3. "And as a caterpillar, after having reached the end of a blade of grass, and after having made another approach (to another blade), draws itself together towards it, thus does this Self, after having thrown off this body and dispelled all ignorance, and after making another approach (to another body), draw himself together towards it.

4. "And as a goldsmith, taking a piece of gold, turns it into another, newer and more beautiful shape, so does this Self, after having thrown off this body and dispelled all ignorance, make unto himself another, newer and more beautiful shape, whether it be like the fathers, or like the Gandharvas, or like the Devas, or like Prajapati, or like Brahman, or like other beings.

5. "That Self is indeed Brahman, consisting of knowledge, mind, life, sight, hearing, earth, water, wind, ether, light and no light, desire and no desire, anger and no anger, right or wrong, and all things. Now as a man is like this or like that, according as he acts and according as he behaves, so will he be—a man of good acts will become good, a man of bad acts, bad. He becomes pure by pure deeds, bad by bad deeds.

"And here they say that a person consists of desires. And as is his desire, so is his will; and as is his will, so is his deed; and whatever deed he does, that he will reap.

6. "And here there is this verse: 'To whatever object a man's own mind is attached, to that he goes strenuously together with his deed; and having obtained the end (the last results) of whatever deed he does here on earth, he returns again from that world (which is the temporary reward of his deed) to this world of action.'

"So much for the man who desires. But as to the man who does not desire, who, not desiring, freed from desires, is satisfied in his desires, or desires the Self only, his vital spirits do not depart elsewhere—being Brahman, he goes to Brahman.

7. "On this there is this verse: 'When all desires which once entered his heart are undone, then does the mortal become immortal, then he obtains Brahman.'

"And as the slough of a snake lies on an ant-hill, dead and cast away, thus lies this body; but that disembodied immortal spirit (prana, life) is Brahman only, is only light."

Janaka Vaideha said: "Sir, I give you a thousand."

8. "On this there are these verses:

" 'The small, old path stretching far away has been found by me. On it sages who know Brahman move on to the Svargaloka (heaven), and thence higher on, as entirely free.

9. " 'On that path they say that there is white, or blue, or yellow, or green, or red; that path was found by Brahman, and on it goes whoever knows Brahman, and who has done good, and obtained splendour.

10. " 'All who worship what is not knowledge (avidya) enter into blind darkness: those who delight in knowledge, enter, as it were, into greater darkness.

11. " 'There are indeed those unblessed worlds, covered with blind darkness. Men who are ignorant and not enlightened go after death to those worlds.

12. " 'If a man understands the Self, saying, "I am He," what could be wish or desire that he should pine after the body?

13. " 'Whoever has found and understood the Self that has entered into this patched-together hiding-place, he indeed is the creator, for he is the maker of everything, his is the world, and he is the world itself.

14. " 'While we are here, we may know this; if not, I am ignorant, and there is great destruction. Those who know it become immortal, but others suffer pain indeed.

15. " 'If a man clearly beholds this Self as God, and as the lord of all that is and will be, then he is no more afraid.

16. " 'He behind whom the year revolves with the days, him the gods worship as the light of lights, as immortal time.

17. " 'He in whom the five beings and the ether rest, him alone I believe to be the Self—I who know, believe him to be Brahman; I who am immortal, believe him to be immortal.

18. " 'They who know the life of life, the eye of the eye, the ear of the ear, the mind of the mind, they have comprehended the ancient, primeval Brahman.

19. " 'By the mind alone it is to be perceived, there is in it no diversity. He who perceives therein any diversity, goes from death to death.

20. " 'This eternal being that can never be proved, is to be perceived in one way only; it is spotless, beyond the ether, the unborn Self, great and eternal.

21. " 'Let a wise Brahmana, after he has discovered him, practise wisdom. Let him not seek after many words, for that is mere weariness of the tongue.'

22. "And he is that great unborn Self, who consists of knowledge, is surrounded by the Pranas, the ether within the heart. In it there reposes the ruler of all, the lord of all, the king of all. He does not become greater by good works, nor smaller by evil works. He is the lord of all, the king of all things, the protector of all things. He is a bank and a boundary, so that these worlds may not be confounded. Brahmanas seek to know him by the study of the Veda, by sacrifice, by gifts, by penance, by fasting, and he who knows him becomes a Muni. Wishing for that world (for Brahman) only, mendicants leave their homes.

"Knowing this, the people of old did not wish for offspring. What shall we do with offspring, they said, we who have this Self and this world (of Brahman). And they, having risen above the desire for sons, wealth, and new worlds, wander about as mendicants. For desire for sons is desire for wealth, and desire for wealth is desire for worlds. Both these are indeed desires only. He, the Self, is to be described by No, no! He is incomprehensible, for he cannot be comprehended; he is imperishable, for he cannot perish; he is unattached, for he does not attach himself; unfettered, he does not suffer, he does not fail. Him (who knows), these two do not overcome, whether he says that for some reason he has done evil, or for some reason he has done good—he overcomes both, and neither what he has done, nor what he has omitted to do, burns (affects) him.

23. "This has been told by a verse (Rich): 'This eternal greatness of the Brahmana does not grow larger by work, nor does it grow smaller. Let

man try to find (know) its trace, for having found (known) it, he is not sullied by any evil deed.'

"He therefore that knows it, after having become quiet, subdued, satisfied, patient, and collected, sees self in Self, sees all as Self. Evil does not overcome him, he overcomes all evil. Evil does not burn him, he burns all evil. Free from evil, free from spots, free from doubt, he becomes a (true) Brahmana; this is the Brahma-world, O king"—thus spoke Yajnavalkya.

Janaka Vaideha said: "Sir, I give you the Videhas, and also myself, to be together your slaves."

24. This indeed is the great, the unborn Self, the strong, the giver of wealth. He who knows this obtains wealth.

25. This great, unborn Self, undecaying, undying, immortal, fearless, is indeed Brahman. Fearless is Brahman, and he who knows this becomes verily the fearless Brahman.

FIFTH ADHYAYA

SECOND BRAHMANA

1. The threefold descendants of Prajapati, gods, men, and Asuras (evil spirits), dwelt as Brahmacharins (students) with their father Prajapati. Having finished their studentship the gods said: "Tell us (something), Sir." He told them the syllable da. Then he said: "Did you understand?" They said: "We did understand. You told us 'Damyata,' Be subdued." "Yes," he said, "you have understood."

2. Then the men said to him: "Tell us something, Sir." He told them the same syllable da. Then he said: "Did you understand?" They said: "We did understand. You told us, 'Datta,' Give." "Yes," he said, "you have understood."

3. Then the Asuras said to him: "Tell us something, Sir." He told them

the same syllable da. Then he said: "Did you understand?" They said: "We did understand. You told us, 'Dayadham,' Be merciful." "Yes," he said, "you have understood."

The divine voice of thunder repeats the same, Da da da, that is, Be subdued, Give, Be merciful. Therefore let that triad be taught, Subduing, Giving, and Mercy.

The Chandogya Upanishad

FIRST PRAPATHAKA

FIRST KHANDA

1. Let a man meditate on the syllable Om, called the udgitha; for the udgitha (a portion of the Sama-veda) is sung, beginning with Om.

The full account, however, of Om is this:

2. The essence of all beings is the earth, the essence of the earth is water, the essence of water the plants, the essence of plants man, the essence of man speech, the essence of speech the Rigveda, the essence of the Rigveda the Sama-veda, the essence of the Sama-veda the udgitha (which is Om).

3. That udgitha (Om) is the best of all essences, the highest, deserving the highest place, the eighth.

4. What then is the Rig? What is the Saman? What is the udgitha? This is the question.

5. The Rig indeed is speech, Saman is breath, the udgitha is the syllable Om. Now speech and breath, or Rig and Saman, form one couple.

6. And that couple is joined together in the syllable Om. When two people come together, they fulfil each other's desire.

7. Thus, he who knowing this, meditates on the syllable (Om), the udgitha, becomes indeed a fulfiller of desires.

8. That syllable is a syllable of permission, for whenever we permit anything, we say Om, yes. Now permission is gratification. He who knowing this meditates on the syllable (Om), the udgitha, becomes indeed a gratifier of desires.

9. By that syllable does the threefold knowledge (the sacrifice, more particularly the soma-sacrifice, as founded on the three vedas) proceed. When the Adhvaryu priest gives an order, he says Om. When the Hotri priest recites, he says Om. When the Udgatri priest sings, he says Om—all for the glory of that syllable. The threefold knowledge (the sacrifice) proceeds by the greatness of that syllable (the vital breaths), and by its essence (the oblations).

10. Now therefore it would seem to follow, that both he who knows this (the true meaning of the syllable Om), and he who does not, perform the same sacrifice. But this is not so, for knowledge and ignorance are different. The sacrifice which a man performs with knowledge, faith, and the upanishad is more powerful. This is the full account of the syllable Om.

THIRD PRAPATHAKA

FOURTEENTH KHANDA

1. All this is Brahman (n.). Let a man meditate on that (visible world) as beginning, ending, and breathing in it (the Brahman).

Now man is a creature of will. According to what his will is in this world, so will he be when he has departed this life. Let him therefore have this will and belief:

2. The intelligent, whose body is spirit, whose form is light, whose thoughts are true, whose nature is like ether (omnipresent and invisible), from whom all works, all desires, all sweet odours and tastes proceed; he who embraces all this, who never speaks, and is never surprised,

3. He is my self within the heart, smaller than a corn of rice, smaller than a corn of barley, smaller than a mustard seed, smaller than a canary seed or the kernel of a canary seed. He also is my self within the heart, greater than the earth, greater than the sky, greater than heaven, greater than all these worlds.

4. He from whom all works, all desires, all sweet odours and tastes proceed, who embraces all this, who never speaks and who is never surprised, he, my self within the heart, is that Brahman (n.). When I shall have departed from hence, I shall obtain him (that Self). He who has this faith has no doubt; thus said Sandilya, yea, thus he said.

SEVENTH PRAPATHAKA

SIXTH KHANDA

1. "Reflection (dhyana) is better than consideration. The earth reflects, as it were, and thus does the sky, the heaven, the water, the mountains, gods and men. Therefore those who among men obtain greatness here on earth, seem to have obtained a part of the object of reflection (because they show a certain repose of manner). Thus while small and vulgar people are always quarrelling, abusive, and slandering, great men seem to have obtained a part of the reward of reflection. Meditate on reflection.

2. "He who meditates on reflection as Brahman, is lord and master, as it were, as far as reflection reaches—he who meditates on reflection as Brahman."

"Sir, is there something better than reflection?"

"Yes, there is something better than reflection."

"Sir, tell it me."

EIGHTH PRAPATHAKA

SEVENTH KHANDA

1. Prajapati said: "The Self which is free from sin, free from old age, from death and grief, from hunger and thirst, which desires nothing but what it ought to desire, and imagines nothing but what it ought to imagine, that it is which we must search out, that it is which we must try to understand. He who has searched out that Self and understands it, obtains all worlds and all desires."

2. The Devas (gods) and Asuras (demons) both heard these words, and said: "Well, let us search for that Self by which, if one has searched it out, all worlds and all desires are obtained."

Thus saying Indra went from the Devas, Virochana from the Asuras, and both, without having communicated with each other, approached Prajapati, holding fuel in their hands, as is the custom for pupils approaching their master.

3. They dwelt there as pupils for thirty-two years. Then Prajapati asked them: "For what purpose have you both dwelt here?"

They replied: "A saying of yours is being repeated, viz. 'the Self which is free from sin, free from old age, from death and grief, from hunger and thirst, which desires nothing but what it ought to desire, and imagines nothing but what it ought to imagine, that it is which we must search out, that it is which we must try to understand. He who has searched out that Self and understands it, obtains all worlds and all desires.' Now we both have dwelt here because we wish for that Self."

Prajapati said to them: "The person that is seen in the eye, that is the Self. This is what I have said. This is the immortal, the fearless, this is Brahman."

They asked: "Sir, he who is perceived in the water, and he who is perceived in a mirror, who is he?"

He replied: "He himself indeed is seen in all these."

The Katha Upanishad

FIRST ADHYAYA

FIRST VALLI

1. Vajasravasa, desirous (of heavenly rewards), surrendered (at a sacrifice) all that he possessed. He had a son of the name of Nachiketas.

2. When the (promised) presents were being given (to the priests), faith entered into the heart of Nachiketas, who was still a boy, and he thought:

3. "Unblessed, surely, are the worlds to which a man goes by giving (as his promised present at a sacrifice) cows which have drunk water, eaten hay, given their milk, and are barren."

4. He (knowing that his father had promised to give up all that he possessed, and therefore his son also) said to his father: "Dear father, to whom wilt thou give me?"

He said it a second and a third time. Then the father replied (angrily):

"I shall give thee unto Death."

(The father, having once said so, though in haste, had to be true to his word and to sacrifice his son.)

5. The son said: "I go as the first, at the head of many (who have still to die); I go in the midst of many (who are now dying). What will be the work of Yama (the ruler of the departed) which to-day he has to do unto me?

6. "Look back how it was with those who came before, look forward how it will be with those who come hereafter. A mortal ripens like corn, like corn he springs up again."

(Nachiketas enters into the abode of Yama Vaivasvata, and there is no one to receive him. Thereupon one of the attendants of Yama is supposed to say:)

7. "Fire enters into the houses, when a Brahmana enters as a guest. That fire is quenched by this peace-offering—bring water, O Vaivasvata!

8. "A Brahmana that dwells in the house of a foolish man without receiving food to eat, destroys his hopes and expectations, his possessions, his righteousness, his sacred and his good deeds, and all his sons and cattle."

(Yama, returning to his house after an absence of three nights, during which time Nachiketas had received no hospitality from him, says:)

9. "O Brahmana, as thou, a venerable guest, hast dwelt in my house three nights without eating, therefore choose now three boons. Hail to thee! and welfare to me!"

10. Nachiketas said: "O Death, as the first of the three boons I choose that Gautama, my father, be pacified, kind, and free from anger towards me; and that he may know me and greet me, when I shall have been dismissed by thee."

11. Yama said: "Through my favour Auddalaki Aruni, thy father, will know thee, and be again towards thee as he was before. He shall sleep peacefully through the night, and free from anger, after having seen thee freed from the mouth of death."

12. Nachiketas said: "In the heaven-world there is no fear; thou art not there, O Death, and no one is afraid on account of old age. Leaving behind both hunger and thirst, and out of the reach of sorrow, all rejoice in the world of heaven.

13. "Thou knowest, O Death, the fire-sacrifice which leads us to heaven; tell it to me, for I am full of faith. Those who live in the heaven-world reach immortality—this I ask as my second boon."

14. Yama said: "I tell it thee, learn it from me, and when thou understandest that fire-sacrifice which leads

to heaven, know, O Nachiketas, that it is the attainment of the endless worlds, and their firm support, hidden in darkness."

15. Yama then told him about fire-sacrifice, the beginning of all the worlds, and what bricks are required for the altar, and how many, and how they are to be placed. And Nachiketas repeated all as it had been told to him. Then Mrityu, being pleased with him, said again:

16. The generous, being satisfied, said to him: "I give thee now another boon; that fire-sacrifice shall be named after thee, take also this many-coloured chain.

17. "He who has three times performed this Nachiketa rite, and has been united with the three (father, mother, and teacher), and has performed the three duties (study, sacrifice, almsgiving) overcomes birth and death. When he has learnt and understood this fire, which knows (or makes us know) all that is born of Brahman, which is venerable and divine, then he obtains everlasting peace.

18. "He who knows the three Nachiketa fires, and knowing the three, piles up the Nachiketa sacrifice, he, having first thrown off the chains of death, rejoices in the world of heaven, beyond the reach of grief.

19. "This, O Nachiketas, is thy fire which leads to heaven, and which thou hast chosen as thy second boon. That fire all men will proclaim. Choose now, O Nachiketas, thy third boon."

20. Nachiketas said: "There is that doubt, when a man is dead—some saying, he is; others, he is not. This I should like to know, taught by thee; this is the third of my boons."

21. Death said: "On this point even the gods have doubted formerly; it is not easy to understand. That subject is subtle. Choose another boon, O Nachiketas, do not press me, and let me off that boon."

22. Nachiketas said: "On this point

even the gods have doubted indeed, and thou, Death, hast declared it to be not easy to understand, and another teacher like thee is not to be found—surely no other boon is like unto this."

23. Death said: "Choose sons and grandsons who shall live a hundred years, herds of cattle, elephants, gold, and horses. Choose the wide abode of the earth, and live thyself as many harvests as thou desirest.

24. "If you can think of any boon equal to that, choose wealth, and long life. Be (king), Nachiketas, on the wide earth. I make thee the enjoyer of all desires.

25. "Whatever desires are difficult to attain among mortals, ask for them according to thy wish; these fair maidens with their chariots and musical instruments—such are indeed not to be obtained by men—be waited on by them whom I give to thee, but do not ask me about dying."

26. Nachiketas said: "These things last till to-morrow, O Death, for they wear out this vigour of all the senses. Even the whole of life is short. Keep thou thy horses, keep dance and song for thyself.

27. "No man can be made happy by wealth. Shall we possess wealth, when we see thee? Shall we live, as long as thou rulest? Only that boon (which I have chosen) is to be chosen by me.

28. "What mortal, slowly decaying here below, and knowing, after having approached them, the freedom from decay enjoyed by the immortals, would delight in a long life, after he has pondered on the pleasures which arise from beauty and love?

29. "No, that on which there is this doubt, O Death, tell us what there is in that great hereafter. Nachiketas does not choose another boon but that which enters into the hidden world."

SECOND VALLI

1. Death said: "The good is one thing, the pleasant another; these two, having different objects, chain a man. It is well with him who clings to the good; he who chooses the pleasant, misses his end.

2. "The good and pleasant approach man: the wise goes round about them and distinguishes them. Yea, the wise prefers the good to the pleasant, but the fool chooses the pleasant through greed and avarice.

3. "Thou, O Nachiketas, after pondering all pleasures that are or seem delightful, hast dismissed them all. Thou hast not gone into the road that leadeth to wealth, in which many men perish.

4. "Wide apart and leading to different points are these two, ignorance, and what is known as wisdom. I believe Nachiketas to be one who desires knowledge, for even many pleasures did not tear thee away.

5. "Fools dwelling in darkness, wise in their own conceit, and puffed up with vain knowledge, go round and round, staggering to and fro, like blind men led by the blind.

6. "The hereafter never rises before the eyes of the careless child, deluded by the delusion of wealth. 'This is the world,' he thinks, 'there is no other'—thus he falls again and again under my sway.

7. "He (the Self) of whom many are not even able to hear, whom many, even when they hear of him, do not comprehend; wonderful is a man, when found, who is able to teach him (the Self); wonderful is he who comprehends him, when taught by an able teacher.

8. "That (Self), when taught by an inferior man, is not easy to be known, even though often thought upon; unless it be taught by another, there is no way to it, for it is inconceivably smaller than what is small.

9. "That doctrine is not to be obtained by argument, but when it is declared by another, then, O dearest, it is easy to understand. Thou hast

obtained it now; thou art truly a man of true resolve. May we have always an inquirer like thee!"

10. Nachiketas said: "I know that what is called a treasure is transient, for that eternal is not obtained by things which are not eternal. Hence the Nachiketa fire (-sacrifice) has been laid by me (first); then, by means of transient things, I have obtained what is not transient (the teaching of Yama)."

11. Yama said: "Though thou hadst seen the fulfilment of all desires, the foundation of the world, the endless rewards of good deeds, the shore where there is no fear, that which is magnified by praise, the wide abode, the rest, yet being wise thou hast with firm resolve dismissed it all.

12. "The wise who, by means of meditation on his Self, recognises the Ancient, who is difficult to be seen, who has entered into the dark, who is hidden in the cave, who dwells in the abyss, as God, he indeed leaves joy and sorrow far behind.

13. "A mortal who has heard this and embraced it, who has separated from it all qualities, and has thus reached the subtle Being, rejoices, because he has obtained what is a cause for rejoicing. The house (of Brahman) is open, I believe, O Nachiketas."

14. Nachiketas said: "That which thou seest as neither this nor that, as neither effect nor cause, as neither past nor future, tell me that."

15. Yama said: "That word (or place) which all the Vedas record, which all penances proclaim, which men desire when they live as religious students, that word I tell thee briefly, it is Om.

16. "That (imperishable) syllable means Brahman, that syllable means the highest (Brahman); he who knows that syllable, whatever he desires, is his.

17. "This is the best support, this is the highest support; he who knows

that support is magnified in the world of Brahma.

18. "The knowing (Self) is not born, it dies not; it sprang from nothing, nothing sprang from it. The Ancient is unborn, eternal, everlasting; he is not killed, though the body is killed.

19. "If the killer thinks that he kills, if the killed think that he is killed, they do not understand; for this one does not kill, nor is that one killed.

20. "The Self, smaller than small, greater than great, is hidden in the heart of that creature. A man who is free from desires and free from grief, sees the majesty of the Self by the grace of the Creator.

21. "Though sitting still, he walks far; though lying down, he goes everywhere. Who, save myself, is able to know that God who rejoices and rejoices not?

22. "The wise who knows the Self as bodiless within the bodies, as unchanging among changing things, as great and omnipresent, does never grieve.

23. "That Self cannot be gained by the Veda, nor by understanding, nor by much learning. He whom the Self chooses, by him the Self can be gained. The Self chooses him (his body) as his own.

24. "But he who has not first turned away from his wickedness, who is not tranquil, and subdued, or whose mind is not at rest, he can never obtain the Self (even) by knowledge.

25. "Who then knows where He is, He to whom the Brahmans and Kshatriyas are (as it were) but food, and death itself a condiment?

THIRD VALLI

1. "There are the two, drinking their reward in the world of their own works, entered into the cave (of the heart), dwelling on the highest summit

(the ether in the heart). Those who know Brahman call them shade and light; likewise, those householders who perform the Trinachiketa sacrifice.

2. "May we be able to master that Nachiketa rite which is a bridge for sacrifices; also that which is the highest, imperishable Brahman for those who wish to cross over to the fearless shore.

3. "Know the Self to be sitting in the chariot, the body to be the chariot, the intellect (buddhi) the charioteer, and the mind the reins.

4. "The senses they call the horses, the objects of the senses their roads. When he (the Highest Self) is in union with the body, the senses, and the mind, then wise people call him the Enjoyer.

5. "He who has no understanding and whose mind (the reins) is never firmly held, his senses (horses) are unmanageable, like vicious horses of a charioteer.

6. "But he who has understanding and whose mind is always firmly held, his senses are under control, like good horses of a charioteer.

7. "He who has no understanding, who is unmindful and always impure, never reaches that place, but enters into the round of births.

8. "But he who has understanding, who is mindful and always pure, reaches indeed that place, from whence he is not born again.

9. "But he who has understanding for his charioteer, and who holds the reins of the mind, he reaches the end of his journey, and that is the highest place of Vishnu.

10. "Beyond the senses there are the objects, beyond the objects there is the mind, beyond the mind there is the intellect, the Great Self is beyond the intellect.

11. "Beyond the Great there is the Undeveloped, beyond the Undeveloped there is the Person (purusha).

Beyond the Person there is nothing—this is the goal, the highest road.

12. "That Self is hidden in all beings and does not shine forth, but it is seen by subtle seers through their sharp and subtle intellect.

13. "A wise man should keep down speech and mind; he should keep them within the Self which is knowledge; he should keep knowledge within the Self which is the Great; and he should keep that (the Great) within the Self which is the Quiet.

14. "Rise, awake! having obtained your boons, understand them! The sharp edge of a razor is difficult to pass over; thus the wise say the path (to the Self) is hard.

15. "He who has perceived that which is without sound, without touch, without form, without decay, without taste, eternal, without smell, without beginning, without end, beyond the Great, and unchangeable, is freed from the jaws of death.

16. "A wise man who has repeated or heard the ancient story of Nachiketas told by Death, is magnified in the world of Brahman.

17. "And he who repeats this greatest mystery in an assembly of Brahmans, or full of devotion at the time of the Sraddha sacrifice, obtains thereby infinite rewards."

SECOND ADHYAYA

FOURTH VALLI

1. Death said: "The Self-existent pierced the openings (of the senses) so that they turn forward: therefore man looks forward, not backward into himself. Some wise man, however, with his eyes closed and wishing for immortality, saw the Self behind.

2. "Children follow after outward pleasures, and fall into the snare of widespread death. Wise men only, knowing the nature of what is immortal, do not look for anything stable here among things unstable.

3. "That by which we know form, taste, smell, sounds, and loving touches, by that also we know what exists besides. This is that (which thou hast asked for).

4. "The wise, when he knows that that by which he perceives all objects in sleep or in waking is the great omnipresent Self, grieves no more.

5. "He who knows this living soul which eats honey (perceives objects) as being the Self, always near, the Lord of the past and the future, henceforward fears no more. This is that.

6. "He who (knows) him who was born first from the brooding heat (for he was born before the water), who, entering into the heart, abides therein, and was perceived from the elements. This is that.

7. "(He who knows) Aditi also, who is one with all deities, who arises with Prana (breath or Hiranyagarbha), who, entering into the heart, abides therein, and was born from the elements. This is that.

8. "There is Agni (fire), the allseeing, hidden in the two fire-sticks, well-guarded like a child (in the womb) by the mother, day after day to be adored by men when they awake and bring oblations. This is that.

9. "And that whence the sun rises and whither it goes to set, there all the Devas are contained, and no one goes beyond. This is that.

10. "What is here (visible in the world), the same is there (invisible in Brahman); and what is there, the same is here. He who sees any difference here (between Brahman and the world), goes from death to death.

11. "Even by the mind this (Brahman) is to be obtained, and then there is no difference whatsoever. He goes from death to death who sees any difference here.

12. "The person (purusha), of the size of a thumb, stands in the middle of the Self (body?), as lord of the past and the future, and henceforward fears no more. This is that.

13. "That person, of the size of a thumb, is like a light without smoke, lord of the past and the future, he is the same to-day and to-morrow. This is that.

14. "As rain-water that has fallen on a mountain-ridge runs down the rocks on all sides, thus does he, who sees a difference between qualities, run after them on all sides.

15. "As pure water poured into pure water remains the same, thus, O Gautama, is the Self of a thinker who knows.

FIFTH VALLI

1. "There is a town with eleven gates belonging to the Unborn (Brahman), whose thoughts are never crooked. He who approaches it, grieves no more, and liberated (from all bonds of ignorance) becomes free. This is that.

2. "He (Brahman) is the swan (sun), dwelling in the bright heaven; he is the Vasu (air), dwelling in the sky; he is the sacrificer (fire), dwelling on the hearth; he is the guest (Soma), dwelling in the sacrificial jar; he dwells in men, in gods (vara), in the sacrifice (rita), in heaven; he is born in the water, on earth, in the sacrifice (rita), on the mountains; he is the True and the Great.

3. "He (Brahman) it is who sends up the breath (prana), and who throws back the breath (apana). All the Devas (senses) worship him, the adorable (or the dwarf), who sits in the centre.

4. "When that incorporated (Brahman), who dwells in the body, is torn away and freed from the body, what remains then? This is that.

5. "No mortal lives by the breath that goes up and by the breath that goes down. We live by another, in whom these two repose.

6. "Well then, O Gautama, I shall tell thee this mystery, the old Brahman, and what happens to the Self, after reaching death.

7. "Some enter the womb in order to have a body, as organic beings, others go into inorganic matter, according to their work and according to their knowledge.

8. "He, the highest Person, who is awake in us while we are asleep, shaping one lovely sight after another, that indeed is the Bright, that is Brahman, that alone is called the Immortal. All worlds are contained in it, and no one goes beyond. This is that.

9. "As the one fire, after it has entered the world, though one, becomes different according to whatever it burns, thus the one Self within all things becomes different, according to whatever it enters, and exists also without.

10. "As the one air, after it has entered the world, though one, becomes different according to whatever it enters, thus the one Self within all things becomes different, according to whatever it enters, and exists also without.

11. "As the sun, the eye of the whole world, is not contaminated by the external impurities seen by the eyes, thus the one Self within all things is never contaminated by the misery of the world, being himself without.

12. "There is one ruler, the Self within all things, who makes the one form manifold. The wise who perceive him within their Self, to them belongs eternal happiness, not to others.

13. "There is one eternal thinker, thinking non-eternal thoughts, who, though one, fulfils the desires of many. The wise who perceive him within their Self, to them belongs eternal peace, not to others.

14. "They perceive that highest indescribable pleasure, saying, This is that. How then can I understand it? Has it its own light, or does it reflect light?

15. "The sun does not shine there, nor the moon and the stars, nor these lightnings, and much less this fire. When he shines, everything shines after him; by his light all this is lighted."

The Isa Upanishad

Sometimes called
The Vajasaneyi-Samhita Upanishad

1. All this, whatsoever moves on earth, is to be hidden in the Lord (the Self). When thou hast surrendered all this, then thou mayest enjoy. Do not covet the wealth of any man!

2. Though a man may wish to live a hundred years, performing works, it will be thus with him; but not in any other way: work will thus not cling to a man.

3. There are the worlds of the Asuras covered with blind darkness. Those who have destroyed their self (who perform works, without having arrived at a knowledge of the true Self), go after death to those worlds.

4. That one (the Self), though never stirring, is swifter than thought. The Devas (senses) never reached it, it walked before them. Though standing still, it overtakes the others who are running. Matarisvan (the wind, the moving spirit) bestows powers on it.

5. It stirs and it stirs not; it is far, and likewise near. It is inside of all this, and it is outside of all this.

6. And he who beholds all beings in the Self, and the Self in all beings, he never turns away from it.

7. When to a man who understands, the Self has become all things, what sorrow, what trouble can there be to him who once beheld that unity?

8. He (the Self) encircled all, bright, incorporeal, scatheless, without muscles, pure, untouched by evil; a seer, wise, omnipresent, self-existent,

he disposed all things rightly for eternal years.

9. All who worship what is not real knowledge (good works), enter into blind darkness: those who delight in real knowledge, enter, as it were, into greater darkness.

10. One thing, they say, is obtained from real knowledge; another, they say, from what is not knowledge. Thus we have heard from the wise who taught us this.

11. He who knows at the same time both knowledge and not-knowledge, overcomes death through not-knowledge, and obtains immortality through knowledge.

12. All who worship what is not the true cause, enter into blind darkness; those who delight in the true cause, enter, as it were, into greater darkness.

13. One thing, they say, is obtained from (knowledge of) the cause; another, they say, from (knowledge of) what is not the cause. Thus we have heard from the wise who taught us this.

14. He who knows at the same time both the cause and the destruction (the perishable body), overcomes death by destruction (the perishable body), and obtains immortality through (knowledge of) the true cause.

15. The door of the True is covered with a golden disk. Open that, O Pushan, that we may see the nature of the True.

16. O Pushan, only seer, Yama (judge), Surya (sun) son of Prajapati, spread thy rays and gather them! The light which is thy fairest form, I see it. I am what He is (viz. the person in the sun).

17. Breath to air, and to the immortal! Then this my body ends in ashes. Om! Mind, remember! Remember thy deeds! Mind, remember! Remember thy deeds!

18. Agni, lead us on to wealth (beatitude) by a good path, thou, O God, who knowest all things! Keep far from us crooked evil, and we shall offer thee the fullest praise!

The Svetasvatara Upanishad

First Adhyaya

1. The Brahma-students say: Is Brahman the cause? Whence are we born? Whereby do we live, and whither do we go? O ye who know Brahman, (tell us) at whose command we abide, whether in pain or in pleasure?

2. Should time, or nature, or necessity, or chance, or the elements be considered as the cause, or he who is called the person (purusha, vijnanatma)? It cannot be their union either, because that is not self-dependent, and the self also is powerless, because there is (independent of him) a cause of good and evil.

3. The sages, devoted to meditation and concentration, have seen the power belonging to God himself, hidden in its own qualities (guna). He, being one, superintends all those causes, time, self, and the rest.

4. We meditate on him who (like a wheel) has one felly with three tires, sixteen ends, fifty spokes, with twenty counter-spokes, and six sets of eight; whose one rope is manifold, who proceeds on three different roads, and whose illusion arises from two causes.

5. We meditate on the river whose water consists of the five streams, which is wild and winding with its five springs, whose waves are the five vital breaths, whose fountain head is the mind, the course of the five kinds of perceptions. It has five whirlpools, its rapids are the five pains; it has fifty kinds of suffering, and five branches.

6. In that vast Brahma-wheel, in which all things live and rest, the bird flutters about, so long as he thinks that the self (in him) is different from the

mover (the god, the lord). When he has been blessed by him, then he gains immortality.

7. But what is praised (in the upanishads) is the Highest Brahman, and in it there is the triad. The Highest Brahman is the safe support, it is imperishable. The Brahma - students, when they have known what is within this (world), are devoted and merged in the Brahman, free from birth.

8. The Lord (isa) supports all this together, the perishable and the imperishable, the developed and the undeveloped. The (living) self, not being a lord, is bound, because he has to enjoy (the fruits of works); but when he has known the god (deva), he is freed from all fetters.

9. There are two, one knowing (isvara), the other not-knowing (jiva), both unborn, one strong, the other weak; there is she, the unborn, through whom each man receives the recompense of his works; and there is the infinite Self (appearing) under all forms, but himself inactive. When a man finds out these three, that is Brahma.

10. That which is perishable is the Pradhana (the first), the immortal and imperishable is Hara. The one god rules the perishable (the pradhana) and the (living) self. From meditating on him, from joining him, from becoming one with him there is further cessation of all illusion in the end.

11. When that god is known, all fetters fall off, sufferings are destroyed, and birth and death cease. From meditating on him there arises, on the dissolution of the body, the third state, that of universal lordship; but he only who is alone, is satisfied.

12. This, which rests eternally within the self, should be known; and beyond this not anything has to be known. By knowing the enjoyer, the enjoyed, and the ruler, everything has been declared to be threefold, and this is Brahman.

13. As the form of fire, while it exists in the under-wood, is not seen, nor is its seed destroyed, but it has to be seized again and again by means of the stick and the under-wood, so it is in both cases, and the Self has to be seized in the body by means of the pranava (the syllable Om).

14. By making his body the under-wood, and the syllable Om the upper-wood, man, after repeating the drill of meditation, will perceive the bright god, like the spark hidden in the wood.

15. As oil in seeds, as butter in cream, as water in (dry) river-beds, as fire in wood, so is the Self seized within the self, if man looks for him by truthfulness and penance;

16. (If he looks) for the Self that pervades everything, as butter is contained in milk, and the roots whereof are self-knowledge and penance. That is the Brahman taught by the upanishad.

Third Adhyaya

1. The snarer who rules alone by his powers, who rules all the worlds by his powers, who is one and the same, while things arise and exist—they who know this are immortal.

2. For there is one Rudra only, they do not allow a second, who rules all the worlds by his powers. He stands behind all persons, and after having created all worlds he, the protector, rolls it up at the end of time.

3. That one god, having his eyes, his face, his arms, and his feet in every place, when producing heaven and earth, forges them together with his arms and his wings.

4. He, the creator and supporter of the gods, Rudra, the great seer, the lord of all, he who formerly gave birth to Hiranyagarbha, may he endow us with good thoughts.

5. O Rudra, thou dweller in the mountains, look upon us with that most blessed form of thine which is

auspicious, not terrible, and reveals no evil!

6. O lord of the mountains, make lucky that arrow which thou, a dweller in the mountains, holdest in thy hand to shoot. Do not hurt man or beast!

7. Those who know beyond this the High Brahman, the vast, hidden in the bodies of all creatures, and alone enveloping everything, as the Lord, they become immortal.

8. I know that great person (purusha) of sunlike lustre beyond the darkness. A man who knows him truly, passes over death; there is no other path to go.

9. This whole universe is filled by this person (purusha), to whom there is nothing superior, from whom there is nothing different, than whom there is nothing smaller or larger, who stands alone, fixed like a tree in the sky.

10. That which is beyond this world is without form and without suffering. They who know it, become immortal, but others suffer pain indeed.

11. That Bhagavat exists in the faces, the heads, the necks of all, he dwells in the cave (of the heart) of all beings, he is all-pervading, therefore he is the omnipresent Siva.

12. That person (purusha) is the great lord; he is the mover of existence, he possesses that purest power of reaching everything; he is light, he is undecaying.

13. The person (purusha), not larger than a thumb, dwelling within, always dwelling in the heart of man, is perceived by the heart, the thought, the mind; they who know it become immortal.

14. The person (purusha) with a thousand heads, a thousand eyes, a thousand feet, having compassed the earth on every side, extends beyond it by ten fingers' breadth.

15. That person alone (purusha) is all this, what has been and what will

be; he is also the lord of immortality; he is whatever grows by food.

16. Its hands and feet are everywhere, its eyes and head are everywhere, its ears are everywhere, it stands encompassing all in the world.

17. Separate from all the senses, yet reflecting the qualities of all the senses, it is the lord and ruler of all, it is the great refuge of all.

18. The embodied spirit within the town with nine gates, the bird, flutters outwards, the ruler of the whole world, of all that rests and of all that moves.

19. Grasping without hands, hasting without feet, he sees without eyes, he hears without ears. He knows what can be known, but no one knows him; they call him the first, the great person (purusha).

20. The Self, smaller than small, greater than great, is hidden in the heart of the creature. A man who has left all grief behind, sees the majesty, the Lord, the passionless, by the grace of the creator (the Lord).

21. I know this undecaying, ancient one, the self of all things, being infinite and omnipresent. They declare that in him all birth is stopped, for the Brahma-students proclaim him to be eternal.

FOURTH ADHYAYA

1. He, the sun, without any colour, who with set purpose by means of his power (sakti) produces endless colours, in whom all this comes together in the beginning, and comes asunder in the end—may he, the god, endow us with good thoughts.

2. That (Self) indeed is Agni (fire), it is Aditya (sun), it is Vayu (wind), it is Chandramas (moon); the same also is the starry firmament, it is Brahman (Hiranyagarbha), it is water, it is Prajapati (Viraj).

3. Thou art woman, thou art man; thou art youth, thou art maiden; thou, as an old man, totterest along on thy

staff; thou art born with thy face turned everywhere.

4. Thou art the dark-blue bee, thou art the green parrot with red eyes, thou art the thunder-cloud, the seasons, the seas. Thou art without beginning, because thou art infinite, thou from whom all worlds are born.

5. There is one unborn being (female), red, white, and black, uniform, but producing manifold offspring. There is one unborn being (male) who loves her and lies by her; there is another who leaves her, while she is eating what has to be eaten.

6. Two birds, inseparable friends, cling to the same tree. One of them eats the sweet fruit, the other looks on without eating.

7. On the same tree man sits grieving, immersed, bewildered, by his own impotence (an-isa). But when he sees the other lord (isa) contented, and knows his glory, then his grief passes away.

8. He who does not know that indestructible being of the Rigveda, that highest ether-like (Self) wherein all the gods reside, of what use is the Rigveda to him? Those only who know it, rest contented.

9. That from which the maker (mayin) sends forth all this—the sacred verses, the offerings, the sacrifices, the panaceas, the past, the future, and all that the Vedas declare —in that the other is bound up through that maya.

10. Know then Prakriti (nature) is Maya (art), and the great Lord the Mayin (maker); the whole world is filled with what are his members.

11. If a man has discerned him, who being one only, rules over every germ (cause), in whom all this comes together and comes asunder again, who is the lord, the bestower of blessing, the adorable god, then he passes for ever into that peace.

12. He, the creator and supporter of the gods, Rudra, the great seer, the lord of all, who saw Hiranyagarbha being born, may he endow us with good thoughts.

13. He who is the sovereign of the gods, he in whom all the worlds rest, he who rules over all two-footed and four-footed beings, to that god let us sacrifice an oblation.

14. He who has known him who is more subtile than subtile, in the midst of chaos, creating all things, having many forms, alone enveloping everything, the happy one (Siva), passes into peace for ever.

15. He also was in time the guardian of this world, the lord of all, hidden in all beings. In him the Brahmarshis and the deities are united, and he who knows him cuts the fetters of death asunder.

16. He who knows Siva (the blessed) hidden in all beings, like the subtile film that rises from out the clarified butter, alone enveloping everything—he who knows the god, is freed from all fetters.

17. That god, the maker of all things, the great Self, always dwelling in the heart of man, is perceived by the heart, the soul, the mind;—they who know it become immortal.

18. When the light has risen, there is no day, no night, neither existence nor non-existence; Siva (the blessed) alone is there. That is the eternal, the adorable light of Savitri—and the ancient wisdom proceeded thence.

19. No one has grasped him above, or across, or in the middle. There is no image of him whose name is Great Glory.

20. His form cannot be seen, no one perceives him with the eye. Those who through heart and mind know him thus abiding in the heart, become immortal.

21. "Thou art unborn," with these words some one comes near to thee, trembling. O Rudra, let thy gracious face protect me for ever!

22. O Rudra! hurt us not in our

offspring and descendants, hurt us not in our own lives, nor in our cows, nor in our horses! Do not slay our men in thy wrath, for, holding oblations, we call on thee always.

FIFTH ADHYAYA

1. In the imperishable and infinite Highest Brahman, wherein the two, knowledge and ignorance, are hidden, the one, ignorance, perishes, the other, knowledge, is immortal; but he who controls both, knowledge and ignorance, is another.

2. It is he who, being one only, rules over every germ (cause), over all forms, and over all germs; it is he who, in the beginning, bears in his thoughts the wise son, the fiery, whom he wishes to look on while he is born.

3. In that field in which the god, after spreading out one net after another in various ways, draws it together again, the Lord, the great Self, having further created the lords, thus carries on his lordship over all.

4. As the car (of the sun) shines, lighting up all quarters, above, below, and across, thus does that god, the holy, the adorable, being one, rule over all that has the nature of a germ.

5. He, being one, rules over all and everything, so that the universal germ ripens its nature, diversifies all natures that can be ripened, and determines all qualities.

6. Brahma (Hiranyagarbha) knows this, which is hidden in the upanishads, which are hidden in the Vedas, as the Brahma-germ. The ancient gods and poets who knew it, they became it and were immortal.

7. But he who is endowed with qualities, and performs works that are to bear fruit, and enjoys the reward of whatever he has done, migrates through his own works, the lord of life, assuming all forms, led by the three Gunas, and following the three paths.

8. That lower one also, not larger than a thumb, but brilliant like the sun, who is endowed with personality and thoughts, with the quality of mind and the quality of body, is seen small even like the point of a goad.

9. That living soul is to be known as part of the hundredth part of the point of a hair, divided a hundred times, and yet it is to be infinite.

10. It is not woman, it is not man, nor is it neuter; whatever body it takes, with that it is joined (only).

11. By means of thoughts, touching, seeing, and passions the incarnate Self assumes successively in various places various forms, in accordance with his deeds, just as the body grows when food and drink are poured into it.

12. That incarnate Self, according to his own qualities, chooses (assumes) many shapes, coarse or subtile, and having himself caused his union with them, he is seen as another and another, through the qualities of his acts, and through the qualities of his body.

13. He who knows him who has no beginning and no end, in the midst of chaos, creating all things, having many forms, alone enveloping everything, is freed from all fetters.

14. Those who know him who is to be grasped by the mind, who is not to be called the nest (the body), who makes existence and non-existence, the happy one (Siva), who also creates the elements, they have left the body.

SIXTH ADHYAYA

1. Some wise men, deluded, speak of Nature, and others of Time (as the cause of everything); but it is the greatness of God by which this Brahma-wheel is made to turn.

2. It is at the command of him who always covers this world, the knower, the time of time, who assumes qualities and all knowledge, it is at his command that this work (creation) unfolds itself, which is called earth, water, fire, air, and ether;

3. He who, after he has done that work and rested again, and after he has brought together one essence (the self) with the other (matter), with one, two, three, or eight, with time also and with the subtile qualities of the mind,

4. Who, after starting the works endowed with (the three) qualities, can order all things, yet when, in the absence of all these, he has caused the destruction of the work, goes on, being in truth different (from all he has produced);

5. He is the beginning, producing the causes which unite (the soul with the body), and, being above the three kinds of time (past, present, future), he is seen as without parts, after we have first worshipped that adorable god, who has many forms, and who is the true source (of all things), as dwelling in our own mind.

6. He is beyond all the forms of the tree (of the world) and of time, he is the other, from whom this world moves round, when one has known him who brings good and removes evil, the lord of bliss, as dwelling within the self, the immortal, the support of all.

7. Let us know that highest great lord of lords, the highest deity of deities, the master of masters, the highest above, as god, the lord of the world, the adorable.

8. There is no effect and no cause known of him, no one is seen like unto him or better; his high power is revealed as manifold, as inherent, acting as force and knowledge.

9. There is no master of his in the world, no ruler of his, not even a sign of him. He is the cause, the lord of the lords of the organs, and there is of him neither parent nor lord.

10. That only god who spontaneously covered himself, like a spider, with threads drawn from the first cause (pradhana), grant us entrance into Brahman.

11. He is the one God, hidden in all beings, all-pervading, the self within all beings, watching over all works, dwelling in all beings, the witness, the perceiver, the only one, free from qualities.

12. He is the one ruler of many who (seem to act, but really) do not act; he makes the one seed manifold. The wise who perceive him within their self, to them belongs eternal happiness, not to others.

13. He is the eternal among eternals, the thinker among thinkers, who, though one, fulfils the desires of many. He who has known that cause which is to be apprehended by Samkhya (philosophy) and Yoga (religious discipline), he is freed from all fetters.

14. The sun does not shine there, nor the moon and the stars, nor these lightnings, and much less this fire. When he shines, everything shines after him; by his light all this is lightened.

15. He is the one bird in the midst of the world; he is also (like) the fire (of the sun) that has set in the ocean. A man who knows him truly, passes over death; there is no other path to go.

16. He makes all, he knows all, the self-caused, the knower, the time of time (destroyer of time), who assumes qualities and knows everything, the master of nature and of man, the lord of the three qualities (guna), the cause of the bondage, the existence, and the liberation of the world.

17. He who has become that, he is the immortal, remaining the lord, the knower, the ever-present guardian of this world, who rules this world for ever, for no one else is able to rule it.

18. Seeking for freedom I go for refuge to that God who is the light of his own thoughts, he who first creates Brahman (m.) and delivers the Vedas to him;

19. Who is without parts, without actions, tranquil, without fault, without taint, the highest bridge to im-

mortality—like a fire that has consumed its fuel.

20. Only when men shall roll up the sky like a hide, will there be an end of misery, unless God has first been known.

21. Through the power of his penance and through the grace of God has the wise Svetasvatara truly proclaimed Brahman, the highest and holiest, to the best of ascetics, as approved by the company of Rishis.

22. This highest mystery in the Vedanta, delivered in a former age, should not be given to one whose passions have not been subdued, nor to one who is not a son, or who is not a pupil.

23. If these truths have been told to a high-minded man, who feels the highest devotion for God, and for his Guru as for God, then they will shine forth—then they will shine forth indeed.

THE BHAGAVAD–GITA

THIS document is the high point of Hindu religion. Here the long history of Hinduism culminates in a great devotional poem, teaching complete surrender to the will of Krishna, the God. Although it is tied closely to the Hindu religious tradition, the *Bhagavad-Gita* moves out beyond this to a deeper and more universal religious consciousness.

The book took form near the beginning of the Christian era from the work of many Hindu religious minds and gathered together their thinking and many traditional beliefs and doctrines which had come from far back in Hindu history. In it we find a definite doctrine of the immortality of the soul, the idea that the God is able to assume the form of man to teach men His ways, an offer of universal salvation to sinners, even to low-caste women, and at the same time strict adherence to the ancient caste system.

The *Bhagavad-Gita* has been translated by more than a half hundred scholars and as we come to understand its message, its place among the masterpieces of devotional literature becomes more and more secure.

LESSON THE FIRST

ARJUNA SPAKE:—

28. "As I look, O Krishna, upon these kinsfolk meeting for battle,

29. My limbs fail and my face withers. Trembling comes upon my body, and upstanding of the hair;

30. Gandiva falls from my hand, and my skin burns. I cannot stand in my place; my mind is as if awhirl.

31. Contrary are the omens that I behold, O long-haired one. I see no blessing from slaying of kinsfolk in strife;

32. I desire not victory, O Krishna, nor kingship, nor delights. What shall avail me kingship, O lord of the herds, or pleasures, or life?

33. They for whose sake I desired kingship, pleasures, and delights stand here in battle-array, offering up their lives and substance—

34. Teachers, fathers, sons, likewise grandsires, uncles, fathers-in-law, grandsons, brothers-in-law, kinsmen also.

35. These though they smite me I would not smite, O Madhu-slayer, even for the sake of empire over the three worlds, much less for the sake of the earth.

36. What pleasure can there be to us, O troubler of the folk, from slaughter of Dhritarashtra's folk? Guilt in sooth will lodge with us for doing these to death with armed hand.

37. Therefore it is not meet that we slay Dhritarashtra's folk, our kinsmen; for if we do to death our own kith how can we walk in joy, O lord of Madhu?

38. Albeit they, whose wits are stopped by greed, mark not the guilt of destroying a stock and the sin of treason to friends,

39. Yet how, O troubler of the folk, shall not we with clear sight see the sin of destroying a stock, so that we be stayed from this guilt?

40. In the destruction of a stock

perish the ancient laws of the stock; when law perishes, lawlessness falls upon the whole stock.

41. When lawlessness comes upon it, O Krishna, the women of the stock fall to sin; and from the women's sinning, O thou of Vrishni's race, castes become confounded.

42. Confounding of caste brings to hell alike the stock's slayers and the stock; for their fathers fall when the offerings of the cake and the water to them fail.

43. By this guilt of the destroyers of a stock, which makes castes to be confounded, the everlasting laws of race and laws of stock are overthrown.

44. For men the laws of whose stock are overthrown, O troubler of the folk, a dwelling is ordained in hell; thus have we heard.

45. Ah me! a heavy sin have we resolved to do, that we strive to slay our kin from lust after the sweets of kingship!

46. It were more comfortable to me if Dhritarashtra's folk with armed hand should slay me in the strife unresisting and weaponless."

LESSON THE SECOND

THE LORD SPAKE:—

11. "Thou hast grieved over them for whom grief is unmeet, though thou speakest words of understanding. The learned grieve not for them whose lives are fled nor for them whose lives are not fled.

12. Never have I not been, never hast thou and never have these princes of men not been; and never shall time yet come when we shall not all be.

13. As the body's tenant goes through childhood and manhood and old age in this body, so does it pass to other bodies; the wise man is not confounded therein.

14. It is the touchings of the senses' instruments, O Kunti's son, that beget cold and heat, pleasure and pain; it is they that come and go, that abide not; bear with them, O thou of Bharata's race.

15. Verily the man whom these disturb not, indifferent alike to pain and to pleasure, and wise, is meet for immortality, O chief of men.

16. Of what is not there cannot be being; of what is there cannot be aught but being. The bounds of these twain have been beheld by them that behold the Verity.

17. But know that That which pervades this universe is imperishable; there is none can make to perish that changeless being.

18. It is these bodies of the everlasting, unperishing, incomprehensible body-dweller that have an end, as it is said. Therefore fight, O thou of Bharata's race.

19. He who deems This to be a slayer, and he who thinks This to be slain, are alike without discernment; This slays not, neither is it slain.

20. This never is born, and never dies, nor may it after being come again to be not; this unborn, everlasting, abiding ancient is not slain when the body is slain.

21. Knowing This to be imperishable, everlasting, unborn, changeless, O son of Pritha, how and whom can a man make to be slain, or slay?

22. As a man lays aside outworn garments and takes others that are new, so the body-dweller puts away outworn bodies and goes to others that are new.

23. Weapons cleave not This, fire burns not This, waters wet not This, wind dries it not.

24. Not to be cleft is This, not to be burned, nor to be wetted, nor likewise to be dried; everlasting is This, dwelling in all things, firm, motionless, ancient of days.

25. Unshown is This called, unthinkable This, unalterable This;

therefore, knowing it in this wise, thou dost not well to grieve.

26. So though thou deemest it everlastingly to pass through births and everlastingly through deaths, nevertheless, O strong of arm, thou shouldst not grieve thus.

27. For to the born sure is death, to the dead sure is birth; so for an issue that may not be escaped thou dost not well to sorrow.

28. Born beings have for their beginning the unshown state, for their midway the shown, O thou of Bharata's race, and for their ending the unshown; what lament is there for this?

29. As a marvel one looks upon This; as a marvel another tells thereof; and as a marvel another hears of it; but though he hear of This none knows it.

30. This body's tenant for all time may not be wounded, O thou of Bharata's stock, in the bodies of any beings. Therefore thou dost not well to sorrow for any born beings.

31. Looking likewise on thine own law, thou shouldst not be dismayed; for to a knight there is no thing more blest than a lawful strife.

32. Happy the knights, O son of Pritha, who find such a strife coming unsought to them as an open door to Paradise.

33. But if thou wilt not wage this lawful battle, then wilt thou fail thine own law and thine honour, and get sin.

34. Also born beings will tell of thee a tale of unchanging dishonour; and to a man of repute dishonour is more than death.

35. The lords of great chariots will deem thee to have held back from the strife through fear; and thou wilt come to be lightly esteemed of those by whom thou wert erstwhile deemed of much worth.

36. They that seek thy hurt will say many words of ill speech, crying out upon thee for thy faintness; now what is more grievous than this?

37. If thou be slain, thou wilt win Paradise; if thou conquer, thou wilt have the joys of the earth; therefore rise up resolute for the fray, O son of Kunti.

38. Holding in indifference alike pleasure and pain, gain and loss, conquest and defeat, so make thyself ready for the fight; thus shalt thou get no sin.

39. This understanding has been told to thee according to the School of the Count; now hear of that understanding according to the School of the Rule, by rule of which, O son of Pritha, thou shalt cast off the bond of works.

40. Herein there is no failing of enterprise, nor backsliding. Even a very little of this law saves from the great dread.

41. One and sure is the understanding that is herein, O son of the Kurus; but many-branched and endless are the understandings of the unsure.

42. That flowery speech, O son of Pritha, which is spoken by the undiscerning, who hold fast to the words of the Veda, and say 'There is naught else,'

43. Whose spirit is all lust, whose supreme end is Paradise—(speech) appointing births as meed of works, and dwelling much on various rites for reaching pleasure and empire—

44. That (speech) steals away the wit of such lusters after pleasure and empire, and their understanding, being not sure, cannot be brought to concent.

45. The Vedas' realm is the three moods (gunas). Be thou not of the three moods, O Arjuna, be without the pairs, abiding in everlasting goodness, neither winning nor hoarding, possessed of Self.

46. As much profit as is in a pool of waters gathered from all sides lies in

all the Vedas, for the discerning Brahman.

47. In works be thine office; in their fruits must it never be. Be not moved by the fruits of works; but let not attachment to worklessness dwell in thee.

48. Abiding under the Rule and casting off attachment, O wealth-winner, so do thy works, indifferent alike whether thou gain or gain not. Indifference is called the Rule.

49. For work is far lower than the Rule of the understanding, O wealth-winner. Seek refuge in the understanding; base are they who are moved by fruits.

50. Under the Rule of the understanding a man leaves behind him here alike good deeds and ill. Therefore set thyself to the Rule; skill in works is the Rule.

51. For under the Rule of the understanding prudent men regard not fruits of works, and loose themselves from the bond of birth, and go to a land where no sickness is.

52. When thine understanding shall have passed through the broil of confusion, then thou wilt come into discontent with the things that thou shalt hear and hast heard.

53. When thine understanding, that erstwhile swayed unbalanced by reason of what thou hast heard, shall stand firm and moveless in concent, then shalt thou come into the Rule."

ARJUNA SPAKE:—

54. "What are the words for the man of abiding wisdom who stays in concent, O long-haired one? What will the man of abiding wisdom say? How shall he sit or walk?"

THE LORD SPAKE:—

55. "When one leaves all the loves that dwell in the mind, O son of Pritha, and is gladdened only in his Self by his Self, then he is said to be of abiding wisdom.

56. He whose mind is undismayed in pain, who is freed from longings for pleasure, from whom passion, fear, and wrath have fled, is called a man of abiding prudence, a saintly man.

57. He who is without affection for aught, and whatever fair or foul fortune may betide neither rejoices in it nor loathes it, has wisdom abidingly set.

58. When such a one draws in his sense-instruments altogether from the objects of the sense-instruments, as a tortoise draws in its limbs, he has wisdom abidingly set.

59. The ranges of sense vanish away from a body-dweller who haunts them not, save only relish; and at sight of the Supreme the relish likewise passes away from him.

60. For though the prudent man strive, O son of Kunti, his froward instruments of sense carry away his mind perforce.

61. Let him hold all these in constraint and sit under the Rule, given over to me; for he who has his sense-instruments under his sway has wisdom abidingly set.

62. In the man whose thoughts dwell on the ranges of sense arises attachment to them; from attachment is born love; from love springs wrath.

63. From wrath is confusion born; from confusion wandering of memory; from breaking of memory wreck of understanding; from wreck of understanding a man is lost.

64. But he who walks through the ranges of sense with sense-instruments severed from passion and hatred and obedient to the Self, and possesses his Self in due order, comes to clearness.

65. In clearness it comes about that all pains in him vanish away; for in them whose minds are clear the understanding is utterly steadfast.

66. In him who is not under the Rule is no understanding; in him who is not under the Rule is no inspiration; in him who feels no inspiration peace

is not; in him who has not peace whence can there be joy?

67. For if a man's mind move under the sway of errant sense-instruments, it sweeps away his enlightenment, as the wind a ship on the waters.

68. Therefore he only who utterly holds back his sense-instruments from sense-objects, O mighty-armed one, has wisdom abidingly set.

69. In the night of all born beings the austere man is awake; the time when born beings are awake is night to the saintly man who has vision.

70. He whom all loves enter as waters enter the full and immovably established ocean wins to peace; not so the lover of loves.

71. The man who casts off all desires and walks without desire, with no thought of a *Mine* and of an *I,* comes unto peace.

72. This is the state of abiding in Brahma, O son of Pritha. He that has come therein is not confounded; if even at his last hours he dwell in it, he passes to extinction in Brahma."

Lesson the Third

THE LORD SPAKE:—

3. "In this world is a twofold foundation declared of old by me, O sinless one, in the knowledge-rule of the School of the Count and the work-rule of the School of the Rule.

4. Without undertaking works no man may possess worklessness, nor can he come to adeptship by mere casting-off of works.

5. For no man ever, even for a moment, abides workless; everyone is perforce made to do work by the moods born of nature.

6. He who sits with his sense-instruments of action restrained but with his mind dwelling on the objects of the sense-instruments is said to be a deluded soul, a walker in vain ways.

7. But he is more excellent who, having the sense-instruments under control of the mind, engages his sense-instruments of action on the Rule of works, free from attachment, O Arjuna.

8. Do thine ordained work; for work is more excellent than no-work. Even the subsistence of thy body cannot be won from no-work.

9. This world is fettered by works, save in the work that has for its end the sacrifice. Work to this end do thou fulfil, O son of Kunti, freed from attachment.

10. The lord of beings aforetime, creating beings together with the sacrifice, spake thus: 'By this increase your kind; be this the milch-cow of your desires.

11. With this comfort ye the gods, and let the gods comfort you; comforting one another, ye shall get supreme bliss.

12. For the gods, comforted by the sacrifice, shall give to you the pleasures of your desire. He that enjoys these their gifts without giving to them is a thief.

13. Good folk that eat what is left over from the sacrifice are released from all defilements; but they that dress food only for themselves are evil-doers, and eat sin.'

14. From food are born beings; from rain arises food; from sacrifice comes rain; and from works does sacrifice arise.

15. Know that works arise from Brahma; Brahma is born of the imperishable; therefore Brahma, the everlasting, who abides in all things, has his seat in the sacrifice.

16. Thus is the cycle made to revolve, and he who joins not in its course here, O son of Pritha, lives in vain, his life being sin and his delight being from the sense-instruments.

17. But for the man whose delight is in Self, who is contented with Self, and is glad of Self, there is naught for which he should work.

18. He has indeed no object here either in work or no-work, nor do his purposes lie with any of born beings.

19. Therefore fulfil ever without attachment the work that thou hast to do; for the man that does his work without attachment wins to the supreme.

20. For it was with works that Janaka and others came unto adeptship; thou too shouldst do them, considering the order of the world.

21. Whatsoever the noble man does, that same the other folk do; whatever he makes his standard, that the world obeys.

22. There is naught in the three worlds, O son of Pritha, that I must needs do, naught that I have not gotten or that I shall not get; yet do I abide in work.

23. For if I should not abide ever unwearying in work, O son of Pritha, men would altogether follow in my way;

24. These worlds would perish, if I should not do works; I should make confusion, and bring these beings to harm.

25. As do the unwise, attached to works, O thou of Bharata's race, so should the wise do, but without attachment, seeking to establish order in the world.

26. He should not bring about a rift in the understanding of the unwise who are attached to works; the sage should approve all works, fulfilling them under the Rule.

27. Works are done altogether by the moods of nature; but he whose Self is confounded by the thought of an *I* imagines '*I* am the doer thereof.'

28. But he that knows the verity of the two orders of moods and works, O mighty-armed one, judges that moods dwell in moods, and has no attachment.

29. Confounded by the moods of nature, men are attached to the works of the moods; the man of perfect knowledge should not shake these dull men of imperfect knowledge.

30. Casting off all thy works upon me with thy mind on the One over Self, be thou without craving and without thought of a *mine*, and put away thy fever and fight.

31. The men who ever fulfil this my teaching, possessed of faith and unmurmuring, are released from works.

32. But know that they who murmur at this my teaching and fulfil it not are confounded in all knowledges, mindless, and lost.

33. Even the man of knowledge does acts like to his own nature; all born beings follow nature; what can repression do?

34. Passion and loathing are appointed to the object of each several sense-instrument; one should not come under the sway of these twain, for they are foes in his path.

35. There is more happiness in doing one's own law without excellence than in doing another's law well. It is happier to die in one's own law; another's law brings dread."

Lesson the Fourth

THE LORD SPAKE:—

5. "Many births of me and thee have passed, O Arjuna. I know them all; but thou knowest them not, O affrighter of the foe.

6. Though birthless and unchanging of essence, and though lord of born beings, yet in my sway over the Nature that is mine own I come into birth by my own magic.

7. For whensoever the law fails and lawlessness uprises, O thou of Bharata's race, then do I bring myself to bodied birth.

8. To guard the righteous, to destroy evildoers, to establish the law, I come into birth age after age.

9. He who knows in verity my divine birth and works comes not

again to birth when he has left the body; he comes to me, O Arjuna.

10. Many, freed from passion, fear, and wrath, instinct with me, making their home in me, and cleansed by the mortifications of knowledge, have come into my Being.

11. With them that seek me I deal in like measure; mortals altogether follow in my path, O son of Pritha.

12. In desire for their works to bear fruit do men here offer sacrifice to gods; for speedily is fruit born of works in the world of mortality.

13. The four castes were created by me according to the orders of moods and works; know that I am indeed the doer of that work, yet no worker, unchanging.

14. Works defile me not; in me is no longing for fruit of works. He who recognizes me as such is not fettered by works.

15. With such knowledge works were done by former seekers after deliverance; therefore do thou likewise works as were done by former men in former days.

16. What is work, what no-work? Herein even seers are bewildered. That work I will declare to thee, by knowledge whereof thou shalt be delivered from ill.

17. For of work there should be heed, and of ill-work there should be heed, and of no-work there should be heed; devious is the course of work.

18. He who beholds in work no-work, and in no-work work, is the man of understanding among mortals; he is in the Rule, a doer of perfect work.

19. The man whose every motion is void of love and purpose, whose works are burned away by the fire of knowledge, the enlightened call 'learned.'

20. Free from attachment to fruit of works, everlastingly contented, unconfined, even though he be engaged in work he does not work at all.

21. Whoso, being without craving, restrained of mind, surrendering all possessions, does but work of the body's office, gets no defilement.

22. Happy in what chance brings him, beyond the pairs, void of envy, indifferent alike whether he gain or gain not, even in working he becomes not fettered.

23. In one who, being void of attachment, delivered, and possessing a mind established in knowledge, yet fulfils the sacrifice, all works vanish away.

24. Brahma is the deed of sacrifice; Brahma is the oblation, by Brahma offered in the fire that is Brahma; and to Brahma shall he go who dwells in concent with the works that are Brahma.

25. Some there be, men of the Rule, that worship the sacrifice to the gods; some with the sacrifice offer sacrifice in the fire which is Brahma.

26. Some offer the ear and other sense-instruments in the fires of constraint; others offer sound and other ranges of sense in the fires of the sense-instruments.

27. Others offer the works of all sense-instruments and works of breath in the knowledge-kindled fire of the Rule that is constraint in Self.

28. Other anchorites there are, strict of vows, who make offering of substance, or of mortification, or of the Rule, or of the knowledge of their scripture-reading.

29. Others offer the outward breath in the inward breath, or the inward breath in the outward breath; or they set themselves to constraint of breath by staying the course alike of outward and inward breath.

30. Others, restricting their food, offer breaths in breaths. All these, knowers of sacrifice, cleanse away their defilements by sacrifice.

31. Feeding on the ambrosial remains of sacrifice, they come to the ancient Brahma. This world is not for him who offers no sacrifice; how then

should another be for him, O best of Kurus?

32. Thus manifold are the sacrifices set forth in the mouth of Brahma. Know that they are all born of works; with this knowledge shalt thou be delivered.

33. There is more bliss in sacrifice of knowledge than in sacrifice of substance, O wealth-winner; all works without limit, O son of Pritha, are contained in knowledge.

34. Know thou that for reverence, for asking, and for service men of knowledge who behold the verity will teach thee this knowledge.

35. Knowing that, thou wilt never again fall into such bewilderment, O son of Pandu; by that thou wilt see born beings altogether in thy self, and likewise in me.

36. Even though thou shouldst be of all sinners the greatest evildoer, thou shalt be by the boat of knowledge carried over all evil.

37. As a kindled fire makes its fuel into ashes, O Arjuna, so the fire of knowledge makes into ashes all works.

38. For there is naught here that is like in power of cleansing to knowledge; this the adept of the Rule himself finds after many days in his Self.

39. Knowledge he wins who has faith, who is devoted, who restrains the instruments of sense; having won knowledge, he speedily comes to supreme peace.

40. He perishes who has not knowledge or faith, who is all unbelief; neither this world nor the world beyond nor pleasantness is for him who is unbelieving.

41. But works fetter not him who has cast off works under the Rule, who has cleft unbelief by knowledge, and possesses his Self, O wealth-winner.

42. Therefore arise, O thou of Bharata's race, and set thyself to the Rule, cleaving with the sword of knowledge this unbelief in Self, born of ignorance, that lodges in thy heart."

LESSON THE FIFTH

THE LORD SPAKE:—

2. "Casting-off of works and Rule of works both lead to bliss; but of these the Rule of works is higher than casting-off of works.

3. He who hates not and desires not should be deemed to have everlastingly cast off works; for he who knows not the pairs, O mighty-armed one, is easily delivered from the fetter.

4. The simple speak of the School of the Count and the School of the Rule as diverse, but not so the learned; he that has meetly set himself thereto finds the same fruit from either.

5. The place won by the men of the Count is likewise reached by the Rule-men; he who sees the School of the Count and the School of the Rule to be one sees indeed.

6. But it is hard to win to casting-off of works without the Rule, O mighty-armed one. The holy man who follows the Rule speedily comes to Brahma.

7. Following the Rule, cleansed of spirit, victorious over himself, holding the sense-instruments under his sway, his Self become the Self of all born beings, he is not defiled though he do works.

8. The knower of the verity following the Rule will wot well that he does not works at all, though he see, hear, touch, smell, eat, walk, sleep, breathe,

9. Speak, loose, seize, open or close his eyes; or he bears in mind that the sense-instruments dwell in the objects of the sense-instruments.

10. He who in doing works lays his works on Brahma and puts away attachment is not defiled, as the lotus-leaf is unsullied by the water.

11. With body, mind, understanding, and bare sense-instruments, the men of the Rule do their works to purify the Self, putting away attachment.

12. Following the Rule, putting aside the fruit of works, one wins to fundamental peace; following not the Rule, attached by the workings of desire to fruits, one becomes bound.

13. When one has cast off by power of mind all works, the body-dweller abides in pleasantness and mastery in the nine-gated city, neither working nor moving to work.

14. The lord creates not for the world either power of work, or works, or union of fruit with works; it is its own nature that moves.

15. The supreme takes unto himself no sin of any man, and likewise no good deed. Knowledge is covered over by ignorance, whereby creatures are confounded.

16. But to them in whom this ignorance of Self is by knowledge dispelled, knowledge sun-like reveals the supreme verity.

17. With understanding set on That, with Self at one with That, with heart in That, with That for their supreme path, cleansed of defilement by knowledge, they return never again.

18. The learned look with indifference alike upon a wise and courteous Brahman, a cow, an elephant, a dog, or an outcast man.

19. They are victorious over birth in this world whose minds abide in indifference; for Brahma is stainless and indifferent, and therefore they abide in Brahma.

20. Firm of understanding, unbewildered, the knower of Brahma, who abides in Brahma, will not rejoice when pleasant things befall nor be dismayed when things unpleasing betide him.

21. His spirit unattached to outward touch, he finds in his Self pleasantness; his spirit following the Brahma-Rule, he is fed with undying pleasantness.

22. For the delights born of touch, having beginning and end, are in truth founts of pain, O son of Kunti; the enlightened man has no joy in them.

23. He who has strength to bear here ere release from the body the passion born of love and wrath, is of the Rule, he is a happy man.

24. The man of the Rule that has joy within, pleasance within, and light within becomes Brahma and wins to extinction in Brahma.

25. Extinction in Brahma do saints win in whom impurity is destroyed, that have cleft unbelief, strict of soul, delighting in the weal of all born beings.

26. Strict-minded saintly men, who have cast away love and wrath, and know the Self, are compassed around by extinction in Brahma.

27. Putting outward touchings without and the eyes in the midst of the brows, making the outward and the inward breaths equal in their course within the nostrils,

28. The saintly man subdued in sense-instruments, mind, and understanding, who has made deliverance his supreme goal and is ever void of desire, fear, and wrath, is in truth delivered.

29. Knowing that I am he whom sacrifice and austerity touch, the great lord of all worlds, the friend of all born beings, he wins to peace."

Lesson the Sixth

THE LORD SPAKE:—

1. "One that does his appointed works without heed to fruit of works is both a caster-off of works and a man of the Rule; not so the fireless, workless man.

2. Know thou, O son of Pandu, that what men call casting-off is the Rule; for none becomes a man of the Rule without he cast off purpose.

3. For the saintly man who seeks to rise on the Rule, works are said to be the means; after he has risen on the Rule, calm is said to be the means.

4. For when one clings not to the objects of the sense-instruments and to works, and has cast off all purposes, then is he said to have *risen on the Rule*.

5. He shall by Self lift up himself, nor let himself sink; for a man's self has no friend but Self, no foe but Self.

6. The Self is friend to that self that has by self conquered self; but Self will be a very foe warring against him who possesses not his self.

7. In him that has conquered self and come to peace, the supreme Self abides in concent, alike in cold and heat, in joy and sorrow, in honour and dishonour.

8. With spirit contented in knowledge and discernment, set on high, victorious over the sense-instruments, the man of the Rule to whom clods, stones, and gold are alike is said to be *under the Rule*.

9. Most excellent is he whose understanding is indifferent alike to the friend, the lover, the enemy, the indifferent, the one facing both ways, the hateful, and the kinsman, alike to the good and the evil.

10. The man of the Rule shall ever hold himself under the Rule, abiding alone in a secret place, utterly subdued in mind, without craving and without possessions.

11. On a pure spot he shall set for himself a firm seat, neither over-high nor over-low, and having over it a cloth, a deer's skin, and *kusa* grass.

12. On this couch he shall seat himself with thought intent and the workings of mind and sense-instruments restrained, and shall for purification of spirit labour on the Rule.

13. Firm, holding body, head, and neck in unmoving equipoise, gazing on the end of his nose, and looking not round about him,

14. Calm of spirit, void of fear, abiding under the vow of chastity, with mind restrained and thought set on me, so shall he sit that is under the Rule, given over to me.

15. In this wise holding himself ever under the Rule, the strict-minded man of the Rule comes to the peace that ends in extinction and that abides with me.

16. The Rule is not with him that eats overmuch nor with him that eats not at all, not with him that is given to overmuch sleep nor with him that sleeps not, O Arjuna.

17. The sorrow-slaying Rule is with him whose eating and walking are by rule, whose action in works is by rule, whose sleeping and waking are by rule.

18. When he, void of longing for any loves, sets his restrained mind upon his Self, then is he said to be *under the Rule*.

19. As a lamp in a windless spot flickers not, such is the likeness that is told of the strict-minded man of the Rule who labours upon the Rule of the Self.

20. When the mind, held in check by service of the Rule, comes to stillness, and when from beholding Self by Self he has joy in Self,

21. And when he knows the boundless happiness that lies beyond sense-instruments and is grasped by understanding, and in steadfastness swerves not from the verity,

22. Than which, once gotten, he deems no other boon better; wherein he abides, and is not shaken even by sore pain;

23. This severance from union with pain, be it known to him, bears the name of the *Rule;* on this Rule he should resolutely labour, with unwearied mind.

24. Putting away utterly all the loves born of purpose, by force of mind compassing with restraint the group of sense-instruments,

25. Little by little he shall win stillness by understanding ruled in firmness; making his mind abide in the

Self, he shall ponder upon nothing whatsoever.

26. Wheresoever the fickle and unsteady mind wanders off, there he shall check it and bring it into obedience to the Self.

27. For to this peaceful-minded man of the Rule, who has stilled the mood of fieriness, who is stainless, one with Brahma, there comes exceeding joy.

28. Thus the man of the Rule, void of stain, who ever labours upon the Self, has easy enjoyment of boundless happiness in touch with Brahma.

29. With spirit following the Rule, with vision indifferent towards all things, he beholds the Self dwelling in all born beings and all born beings in the Self.

30. If one sees me in all things and all things in me, I am not lost to him nor is he lost to me.

31. The man of the Rule, who, setting himself to union, worships me as dwelling in all born beings, abides in me, wheresoever he may abide.

32. He who sees indifferently all things in the likeness of Self, O Arjuna, whether joy or sorrow betide, is deemed the supreme Man of the Rule."

ARJUNA SPAKE:——

33. "Thou hast declared this Rule to be of indifference, O Madhu-slayer; but I see not how it may be firmly established, by reason of fickleness.

34. For fickle is the mind, O Krishna, froward, forceful, and stiff; I deem it as hard to check as is the wind."

THE LORD SPAKE:——

35. "Doubtless the mind is ill to check and fickle, O mighty armed one; but by constant labour and passionlessness, O son of Kunti, it may be held.

36. For one of unrestrained spirit the Rule is hard of attainment, I trow; but by one of obedient spirit who strives it may be won by the means thereto."

ARJUNA SPAKE:——

37. "If one possessed of faith mortify himself not, and his mind swerve from the Rule, so that he wins not to accomplishment of the Rule, into what ways comes he, O Krishna?

38. Falls he not from both paths, and perishes he not like a riven cloud, O mighty-armed one, unestablished and bewildered in the road to Brahma?

39. This is my doubt, O Krishna, it is meet for thee to resolve altogether; there is no resolver of this doubt beside thee."

THE LORD SPAKE:——

40. "Son of Pritha, neither here nor in the other world is there destruction for him; for none that does righteousness, beloved, comes to evil estate.

41. He that is fallen from the Rule wins to the worlds of them that do godly deeds, and dwells there changeless years; then he is born in the house of pure and prosperous folk.

42. Or haply he may be born in the race of wise men of the Rule; but such birth as this is very hard to win in the world.

43. There he is given that Rule of the understanding which he had in his former body, O child of the Kurus, and therefore he strives further for adeptship.

44. For he is led onward, without will of his own, by that former striving; if he have even the wish to know the Rule, he passes beyond the Word-Brahma.

45. But the man of the Rule who labours stoutly, when cleansed of defilements and brought to adeptship through many births, goes thence by the way supreme.

46. Greater than mortifiers of the flesh is deemed the man of the Rule, greater also than men of knowledge, and greater than doers of works; therefore be thou a man of the Rule, O Arjuna.

47. Of all men of the Rule I deem him who worships me in faith with his inward Self dwelling in me to be most utterly *under the Rule.*"

Lesson the Seventh

THE LORD SPAKE:—

1. "Hear, son of Pritha, how, if thou labourest upon the Rule with mind clinging to me and with me for thy dwelling-place, thou shalt surely know me in my fullness.

2. I will tell thee of the knowledge and discernment which if thou possessest there shall remain naught else to know.

3. Of thousands of men, but few strive for adeptship; of the adepts that strive, but few know me in verity.

4. A nature have I of eight orders— Earth, Water, Fire, Wind, Ether, Mind, Understanding, and Thought of an *I.*

5. This is the lower. But know that I have another and higher nature than this, one of Elemental Soul, O mighty-armed one, and thereby is upheld this universe.

6. Learn that from these twain are sprung all born beings; the source of the whole universe and its dissolution am I.

7. There is naught higher than I, O wealth-winner; all this universe is strung upon me, as rows of gems upon a thread.

8. I am the taste in water, O son of Kunti; I am the light in moon and sun, the Om in all the Vedas, sound in the ether, manhood in men.

9. The pure scent in earth am I, and the light in fire; the life in all born beings am I, and the mortification of them that mortify the flesh.

10. Know me to be the ancient seed of all born beings, O son of Pritha; I am the understanding of them that understand, the splendour of the splendid.

11. The might of the mighty am I, void of love and passion; I am the desire in born beings which the law bars not, O Bharata-prince.

12. Know that from me are the existences alike of the goodness-mood, the fiery-mood, and the gloom-mood; I am not in them, but they are in me.

13. Bewildered by these three existences of mood, this whole universe perceives not that I am higher than they, and changeless.

14. For this my divine magic of mood is hard to fathom; but they who make their refuge in me pass beyond this magic.

15. But not to me come for refuge besotted workers of evil, basest of men; being through the magic bereft of knowledge, they come into dæmonic existence.

16. Four orders of doers of righteousness worship me, O Arjuna—the afflicted, the seeker after knowledge, the desirer of substance, and the man of knowledge, O Bharata-prince.

17. Of these most excellent is the man of knowledge, everlastingly under the Rule, worshipping me alone; for exceeding dear am I to the man of knowledge, and he to me.

18. High in rank are all these, but the man of knowledge I deem to be my very Self; for he with spirit under the Rule sets himself to the supreme way—and that am I.

19. At the end of many births, the man of knowledge finds refuge in me, knowing Vasudeva to be the all; very rare is such a great-hearted man.

20. But they whose knowledge is swept away by this and that love make other gods their refuge, holding by this

and that rule, and bound by their own nature."

Lesson the Ninth

THE LORD SPAKE:—

11. "Misguided men despise me when I enter a mortal frame, not knowing my higher being as the great lord of born beings;

12. Vain of hope, vain of works, vain of knowledge, void of mind, they fall into a wildering devilish or dæmonic nature.

13. But into a godlike nature, O son of Pritha, enter great-hearted men who worship me with undivided mind, knowing me to be the beginning of born beings, the unchanging;

14. Ever singing my praises, labouring firm in their vows, devoutly doing homage, everlastingly under the Rule, men wait on me.

15. Others again there are that wait on me, offering the sacrifice of knowledge, according to my unity, or my severalty, or my manifold aspects that face all ways.

16. The sacrifice am I, the offering am I, the father's oblation am I, the herb am I, the spell am I, the butterlibation am I, the fire am I, the rite of oblation am I;

17. Father of this universe am I, mother, ordainer, grandsire, the thing that is known and the being that makes clean, the word Om, the Rich, the Sama, and the Yajus;

18. The way, the supporter, the lord, the witness, the dwelling, the refuge, the friend, the origin, the dissolution, the abiding-place, the house of ward, the changeless seed.

19. I give heat; I arrest and let loose the rain; I am likewise power of immortality and death, being and nobeing, O Arjuna.

20. Men of the threefold lore that drink the soma and are cleansed of sin, worshipping me with sacrifices, pray for the way to paradise; winning as meed of righteousness the world of the lord of gods, they taste in heaven the heavenly delights of the gods.

21. When they have enjoyed that wide world of paradise and their wage of righteousness is spent, they enter into the world of mortals; thus the lovers of loves who follow the Law of the Three Books win but a going and a coming.

22. But to the men everlastingly under the Rule, who in undivided service think and wait on me, I bring power to win and to maintain.

23. They also who worship other gods and make offering to them with faith, O son of Kunti, do verily make offering to me, though not according to ordinance.

24. For I am he that has enjoyment and lordship of all sacrifices; but they recognize me not in verity, and therefore they fall.

25. They whose vows are to the gods go to the gods, they whose vows are to the fathers go to the fathers; they who offer to ghosts go to ghosts; but they that offer to me go to me.

26. If one of earnest spirit set before me with devotion a leaf, a flower, fruit, or water, I enjoy this offering of devotion.

27. Whatever be thy work, thine eating, thy sacrifice, thy gift, thy mortification, make thou it an offering to me, O son of Kunti.

28. Thus shalt thou be released from the bonds of works, fair or foul of fruit; thy spirit inspired by castingoff of works and following the Rule, thou shalt be delivered and come unto me.

29. I am indifferent to all born beings; there is none whom I hate, none whom I love. But they that worship me with devotion dwell in me, and I in them.

30. Even though he should be a doer of exceeding evil that worships me with undivided worship, he shall

be deemed good; for he is of right purpose.

31. Speedily he becomes righteous of soul, and comes to lasting peace. O son of Kunti, be assured that none who is devoted to me is lost.

32. For even they that be born of sin, O son of Pritha—women, traffickers, and serfs—if they turn to me, come to the supreme path;

33. How much more then shall righteous Brahmans and devout kingly sages? As thou hast come into this unstable and joyless world, worship me.

34. Have thy mind on me, thy devotion toward me, thy sacrifice to me, do homage to me. Thus guiding thyself, given over to me, so to me shalt thou come."

LESSON THE TENTH

THE LORD SPAKE:—

1. "Again, O strong-armed one, hearken to my sublime tale, which in desire for thy weal I will recite to thy delighted ear.

2. The ranks of the gods and the saints know not my origin; for I am altogether the beginning of gods and saints.

3. He who unbewildered knows me to be the unborn, the one without beginning, great lord of worlds, is released from all sins amidst mortals.

4. Understanding, knowledge, unconfounded vision, patience, truth, restraint of sense and spirit, joy and sorrow, origination and not-being, fear and fearlessness,

5. Harmlessness, indifference, delight, mortification, almsgiving, fame, and infamy—these are the forms of born beings' existence severally dispensed by me.

6. The seven great saints, the four ancients, and the Manus had their spirit of me, and were born of my mind; of them are these living creatures in the world.

7. He that knows in verity my power and rule is assuredly ruled by unwavering Rule.

8. I am the origin of the All; from me the All proceeds; with this belief the enlightened, possessed of the spirit, pay worship to me.

9. With mind on me, with lifebreath in me instructing one another and telling of me, they are in everlasting delight and content.

10. On these, who are ever under the Rule, worshipping me with love, I bestow the Rule of understanding, whereby they come to me.

11. Present in their spirit's mood, I for pity's sake dissipate with the radiant lamp of knowledge the darkness born in them of ignorance."

ARJUNA SPAKE:—

12. "Supreme Brahma, supreme glory, power of highest purity art thou. The male, unchanging, heavenly, primal of gods, unborn, all-pervading—

13. Thus have all the saints named thee, and the god-saint Narada, Asita, Devala, and Vyasa, and so thou tellest me thyself.

14. All this that thou tellest me, O long-haired one, I believe true; for neither gods nor Danavas, O lord, know thine apparition.

15. Thou of thyself knowest Self by Self, O male supreme, inspirer of born beings, lord of born beings, god of gods, master of the universe.

16. So I pray thee to tell to me fully thine own divine powers, wherewith thou abidest pervading these worlds.

17. How, O ruler, may I know thee in constant meditation; and in what forms of existence art thou to be conceived, my lord, by me?

18. Relate again to me in fullness thy Rule and powers, O troubler of the folk; for I am not sated with hearing that immortal tale."

Lesson the Eleventh

ARJUNA SPAKE:—

15. "I behold in thy body, O god, all the gods and hosts of the orders of born beings, lord Brahman sitting on the lotus-throne, and all the saints and heavenly serpents.

16. I behold thee of many arms, bellies, faces, and eyes, on all sides endless; I behold in thee no end nor midst nor beginning, O all-sovereign of all forms;

17. I behold thee bearing diadem, mace, and disk, massed in radiance, on all sides glistening, hardly discernible, shining round about as gleaming fire and sun, immeasurable.

18. Thou art to my thought the supreme imperishable, the one to be known; thou art this universe's supreme place of ward; thou art the warden of everlasting law, thou art the ancient male.

19. I see thee without beginning or midst or end, boundless in potency, boundless of arms, with mouth of gleaming fire, giving of thine own radiance heat to this All.

20. For this mid-space between heaven and earth and all the quarters of the sky are filled with thee alone. Seeing this thy fearful and wonderful form, O great-hearted one, the three-fold world quakes.

21. These hosts of Suras come unto thee; some, affrighted, praise with clasped hands. With cries of "Hail!" the hosts of great saints and adepts sing to thee hymns of abounding praise.

22. Rudras, Adityas, Vasus, and Sadhyas all, the Asvins, Maruts, drinkers of the warm draught, the hosts of Gandharvas, fairies, Asuras, and adepts all gaze on thee in amazement.

23. Looking upon thy mighty form of many mouths and eyes, of many arms and thighs and feet, of many bellies, and grim with many teeth, O mighty-armed one, the worlds and I quake.

24. For as I behold thee touching the heavens, glittering, many-hued, with yawning mouths, with wide eyes agleam, my inward soul trembles, and I find not constancy nor peace, O Vishnu.

25. Seeing thy mouths grim with teeth, like to the fire of the Last Day, I recognize not the quarters of the heavens, and take no joy; lord of gods, home of the universe, be gracious!

26. These sons of Dhritarashtra all with the hosts of kings, Bhishma, Drona, and the charioteer's son yonder, and likewise the chief of our warriors

27. Hasting enter into thy mouths grim with fangs and terrible; some, caught between the teeth, appear with crushed heads.

28. As many currents of rivers flow to meet the sea, so these warriors of the world of mankind pass into thy blazing mouths.

29. As moths with exceeding speed pass into a lighted fire to perish, so pass the worlds with exceeding speed into thy mouths to perish.

30. Thou devourest and lickest up all the worlds around with flaming mouths; filling the whole universe with radiance, grim glow thy splendours, O Vishnu.

31. Relate to me who thou art in this grim form. Homage to thee, chief of gods; be gracious! I would fain know thee as first being, for I understand not thy way of action."

THE LORD SPAKE:—

32. "I am time that makes worlds to perish away, waxed full and working here to compass the worlds' destruction. Even without thee, there shall live none of all the warriors that are arrayed in confronting ranks.

33. Therefore rise up and get thee glory; by conquest of thy foes enjoy ample empire. By me have they al-

ready been given to death; be thou the mere occasion thereto, O left-handed archer.

34. Drona, Bhishma, Jayadratha, Karna, and other mighty men of war smite thou, for I have smitten them. Quail not, but fight; thou shalt overcome thine adversaries in the fray."

SANJAYA SPAKE:—

35. Hearing this word of the long-haired one, the diadem-wearer trembling clasped his hands, and with obeisance again spake thus bowing to Krishna, faltering in voice, and all afraid.

ARJUNA SPAKE:—

36. "Meetly, O high-haired one, is the world at thy praise moved to delight and love; goblins in terror flee on all sides; and all the hosts of the adepts do homage.

37. And wherefore shall they not bow to thee, O great-hearted one, most reverend first creator even of Brahman? O boundless lord of gods, dwelling-place of the universe! thou art the imperishable, being and no-being, the supreme verity.

38. Thou art the first of gods, the ancient male; thou art the universe's supreme place of ward; thou art the knower and the known, the supreme abode; by thee, O boundless of form, is the all filled.

39. Thou art wind, yama, fire, moon, lord of beings, and the grandsire's sire. Homage, homage to thee a thousand times, and yet again homage, homage to thee!

40. Homage before and after thee, homage be to thee on all sides, O all-being! Thou art of boundless potency and immeasurable prowess; thou fillest all, therefore art thou the all-being.

41. Whatever rude word I have spoken, thinking of thee as a friend, and hailing thee as "Krishna," "Ya-dava," or "comrade" in ignorance of this thy majesty, through heedlessness or affection,

42. And whatever deed of unkindness for the sake of mirth has been done to thee, whether alone or in sight of men, in ranging abroad, lying, sitting, or eating—for these, O never-falling, I crave mercy of thee, who art immeasurable.

43. Thou art the father of this world, moving and unmoving, and its worshipful and most reverend teacher. There is no peer to thee; how should there be a greater in all the three worlds, O being of power beyond likeness?

44. Therefore with obeisance and prostration of body I crave grace of thee, the adorable lord; as father with son, as comrade with comrade, as lover with mistress, mayst thou bear with me, O god!

45. I am rejoiced with seeing what none before has seen. But my mind is quaking with fear; show me the same form [as before]; be gracious, O lord of gods, home of the universe!

46. I would fain see thee in the same guise [as erstwhile], with diadem, with mace, with disk in hand; assume that same four-armed shape, O thousand-armed universal-bodied being."

LESSON THE TWELFTH

ARJUNA SPAKE:—

1. "Of them that in everlasting obedience to the Rule worship thee with devotion and of them that worship thee as the imperishable and unshown, which know best the Rule?"

THE LORD SPAKE:—

2. "I deem them to be right well under the Rule who lay their minds on me and do service to me everlastingly under the Rule, possessed of supreme faith.

3. But they who worship the im-

perishable, indefinable, unshown, that is everywhere present, inconceivable, set on high, unmovable, steadfast,

4. And who by suppression of the group of sense-instruments hold everywhere their understanding in indifference—they, rejoicing in the weal of all born beings, win to me.

5. Exceeding great is the toil of these whose mind is attached to the unshown; for the unshown way is painfully won by them that wear the body.

6. But as for them who, having cast all works on me and given themselves over to me, worship me in meditation with undivided Rule,

7. I lift them up speedily from the ocean of deathly life-wanderings, O son of Pritha, as their mind is laid on me.

8. On me then set thy mind, in me let thine understanding dwell; so shalt thou assuredly abide afterward in me.

9. If so thou canst not set thy mind on me in steadfastness, then with rule of constant labour seek to win to me, O wealth-winner.

10. If thou hast not strength even for constant labour, give thyself over to works for me; if thou doest even works for my sake, thou shalt win to adeptship.

11. If likewise thou hast not strength to do this, then come thou unto my Rule and with restrained spirit surrender the fruit of all works.

12. For knowledge has more happiness than constant labour; meditation is more excellent than knowledge, surrender of fruits of works than meditation; after surrender, peace comes straightway.

13. Hateless toward all born beings, friendly, and pitiful, void of the thought of a *Mine* and an *I*, bearing indifferently pain and pleasure, patient.

14. Ever content, the man of the Rule subdued of spirit and steadfast of purpose, who has set mind and understanding on me and worships me, is dear to me.

15. He before whom the world is not dismayed and who is not dismayed before the world, who is void of joy, impatience, fear, and dismay,

16. Desireless, pure, skilful, impartial, free from terrors, who renounces all undertakings and worships me, is dear to me.

17. He who rejoices not, hates not, grieves not, desires not, who renounces alike fair and foul, and has devotion, is dear to me.

18. One indifferent to foe and to friend, indifferent in honour and in dishonour, in heat and in cold, in joy and in pain, free of attachment,

19. Who holds in equal account blame and praise, silent, content with whatsoever befall, homeless, firm of judgment, possessed of devotion, is a man dear to me.

20. Truly the worshippers possessed of faith and given over to me, who do service to this lawful power of immortality whereof I have told, are exceedingly dear to me."

LESSON THE SIXTEENTH

THE LORD SPAKE:—

1. "Fearlessness, purity of the goodness-mood, abiding in knowledge and the Rule, almsgiving, restraint of sense, sacrifice, scripture-reading, mortification, uprightness,

2. Harmlessness, truth, wrathlessness, renunciation, restraint of spirit, lack of malice, pity towards born beings, unwantoning sense, tenderness, modesty, steadfastness,

3. Heroic temper, patience, constancy, purity, innocence, and lack of overweening spirit are in him that is born to gods' estate, O thou of Bharata's race.

4. Hypocrisy, haughtiness, overweening spirit, wrath, rudeness, and

ignorance are in him that is born to dæmons' estate, O son of Pritha.

5. The gods' estate is deemed to lead to deliverance, the dæmons' estate to bondage. Grieve not; thou art born to gods' estate, O son of Pandu.

6. Two orders of born beings there are in this world, the godlike and the dæmonic. The godlike order has been fully declared; hear from me touching the dæmonic, O son of Pritha.

7. Dæmonic men have understanding neither of action nor of inaction; in them are found not purity, right conduct, or truth.

8. They say the universe is without truth, without foundation, without sovereign, arising in no serial order, with nothing but desire for its motive force.

9. Perverted in spirit, mean of understanding, cruel in works, they that uphold this creed arise as foes for the destruction of the world.

10. Turned to insatiable desire, possessed of hypocrisy, pride, and lust, they seize in bewilderment upon false convictions and walk in foul rites.

11. Turned to unbounded imaginations issuing in ruin, given over to enjoyment of desires, assured that this is all,

12. Bound by hundreds of the bonds of hope, given over to desire and wrath, they seek to gather substance unrighteously for the enjoyment of their desires.

13. 'This desire to-day have I won; this will I attain; this wealth is mine, this likewise shall afterward be mine.

14. 'This foe have I slain; others likewise will I slay. I am sovereign; I am in enjoyment; I am successful, strong, happy.

15. 'I am wealthy, noble; what other man is like to me? I will make offerings and give alms; I will rejoice' —thus they say, bewildered by ignorance.

16. Erring in many imaginations, covered over with the mesh of bewilderment, attached to the enjoyments of desire, they fall into a foul hell.

17. Self-conceited, stiff, possessed of pride and lust from their wealth, they make sacrifices that are sacrifices but in name, with hypocrisy and not in accord with ordinance.

18. Turned to thought of an *I*, to force, pride, desire, and wrath, they jealously bear hate against me in their own and in others' bodies.

19. These that hate me, cruel, basest of men and foul, I unceasingly hurl as they wander through life into dæmonic wombs.

20. Falling into dæmonic wombs and bewildered in birth after birth, they win never to me, O son of Kunti, and thence they come to the lowest way.

21. Desire, wrath, and greed, these are the triple gate of hell that destroys the Self; therefore should one forsake these three.

22. Released from these three gates of darkness, O son of Kunti, a man works bliss for his Self; thence he goes to the supreme way.

23. He who walks under the guidance of desire, forsaking the ordinance of teaching-books, wins not to adeptship, nor to happiness, nor to the supreme way.

24. Therefore thou shouldst know the teaching-book to be the standard for determining right and wrong, and do here the works whereof the ordinance of the teaching-book tells."

LESSON THE SEVENTEENTH

THE LORD SPAKE:—

2. "Threefold is faith in body-dwellers; it is born of their natures, and is of the mood of goodness, or of fieriness, or of gloom. As such, hear it.

3. The faith of everyone is according to his condition, O thou of Bharata's race. Man is composed of faith;

he is indeed as that wherein he has faith.

4. Men of the goodness-mood sacrifice to gods, they of the fiery mood to elves and goblins; men of the gloom-mood make offerings to the spirits of the dead and the ghostly bands.

5. The folk who rack themselves with grim mortifications not ordained by teaching-books, who are inspired by hypocrisy and thought of the *I*, possessed by the forces of desire and passion,

6. Mindless, wasting away the sum of born things dwelling in their bodies and me likewise that dwell within their bodies—these, know thou, are of dæmonic conviction.

7. Now threefold is the food that is dear to each, also the sacrifice, the mortification, and the gift. Hearken to this their distinction.

8. The foods that are dear to men of the goodness-mood are moist, oily, firm, and cordial, such as foster vitality, life, strength, health, comfort, and pleasure.

9. The foods dear to men of the mood of fieriness are bitter, sour, salty, overhot, sharp, rough, and scorching, such as bring pain, grief, and sickness.

10. The fare dear to men of the gloom-mood is such as has been spoilt, which has lost its moisture and is stinking and stale, also food left from meals or unfit for sacrifice.

11. The sacrifice is of the goodness-mood that is observed according to ordinance and offered by men desiring not fruit thereof, whose mind is set in concert, in the knowledge that sacrifice must be done.

12. But know, O noblest of Bharatas, that the sacrifice is of the mood of fieriness which is offered with a purpose to get fruit therefrom, or because of hypocrisy.

13. The sacrifice is declared to be of the gloom-mood, which is without ordinance, without gift of food, lacking the spell and the fee, and void of faith.

14. Reverence to gods, Brahmans, elders, and sages, purity, uprightness, chastity, and harmlessness are called the mortification of the body.

15. Speech that gives no pain, true, pleasant, and wholesome, likewise practice of scripture-reading, are called the mortification of speech.

16. Clearness of the mind, pleasantness, silence, suppression of self, and cleanness of spirit, these are called the mortification of the mind.

17. This triple mortification fulfilled in supreme faith by men under the Rule, who desire not fruit, they declare to be of the goodness-mood.

18. Mortification done for the sake of entertainment, honour, and reverence, and in hypocrisy, is said here to be of the mood of fieriness, and is unstable and unsure.

19. Mortification done from a crazed conviction, with self-torment, or for the sake of destroying another, is pronounced to be of the gloom-mood.

20. The gift that is given as a duty to one who cannot make return, with fitness of place, time, and person, is known as a gift of the goodness-mood.

21. But that which is for the sake of reward or in view of fruit hereafter, or is grudged in the giving, is known as a gift of the mood of fieriness.

22. That which is given in an unfit place or time, or to unfit persons, or is given without entertainment or with disdain, is pronounced to be of the gloom-mood.

23. *Om Tat Sat* is known as the triune definition of Brahma; by it were ordained aforetime Brahmans, Vedas, and sacrifices.

24. Therefore it is with utterance of *Om* that the works of sacrifice, alms-giving, and mortification by expounders of Brahma are ever carried on, as declared by ordinance.

25. With *Tat* and with no heed of fruit are divers works of sacrifice and

mortification and works of almsgiving done by seekers after deliverance.

26. The word *Sat* is applied to existence and goodness; moreover, the word *Sat* is used for a felicitous work, O son of Pritha.

27. Engagement in sacrifice, mortification, and almsgiving is likewise called *Sat;* and also works with these purposes are said to be *Sat.*

28. Libations offered, almsgiving bestowed, and mortification exercised without faith are called *Asat,* O son of Pritha, and avail neither hereafter nor here."

Lesson the eighteenth

the lord spake:——

45. "According as each man devotes himself to his own proper work does he attain to consummation. Hear how by devotion to his proper work he wins consummation.

46. A mortal wins consummation by worshipping with his proper work him whence comes the energy of born beings and by whom this universe is filled.

47. There is more happiness in doing one's own law without excellence than in doing another's law well. In doing the work assigned by nature one gets no stain.

48. The work to which one is born he should not forsake, O son of Kunti, faulty though it be; for all undertakings are involved in faultiness, as fire in smoke.

49. He whose understanding is without attachment, who has wholly conquered self, and from whom longings have passed away, wins by casting-off [of works] to the supreme consummation of worklessness.

50. Learn from me briefly, O son of Kunti, how he that has won consummation wins to Brahma, which is the supreme foundation of knowledge.

51. Possessed of purified understanding, restraining self by constancy, forsaking sound and other ranges of sense, and casting aside passion and hatred,

52. Haunting the wilderness, eating little, restraining speech, body, and mind, given over to the Rule of meditation, turned everlastingly to passionlessness.

53. Free from thought of an *I,* from force, pride, desire, wrath, and possession, without thought of a *Mine,* and at peace, one becomes fit for Brahmahood.

54. Becoming Brahma, he is clear of spirit, he grieves not and desires not; indifferent towards all born beings, he wins to supreme devotion toward me.

55. By devotion he recognizes in verity who and what I am; then, knowing me in verity, he speedily enters into me.

56. Doing always all works, making his home in me, one attains by my grace to the everlasting changeless region.

57. Casting off with thy mind all works upon me, be thou given over to me; turned to Rule of the understanding, keep thy thought ever on me.

58. If thou hast thy thought on me, thou shalt by my grace pass over all hard ways; but if from thought of the *I* thou hearken not, thou shalt be lost.

59. Turned to thought of the *I,* thou art minded to fight not; but this thy resolve is vain, nature will drive thee.

60. Bound by thine own nature-born works, O son of Kunti, that which from bewilderment thou seekest not to do thou shalt do perforce.

61. The lord dwells in the heart of all born beings, O Arjuna, and with magic makes all born beings spin about as though set upon a whirligig.

62. In him seek refuge with thy whole soul, O thou of Bharata's race; by his grace thou shalt win supreme peace, the everlasting realm.

63. Thus have I set forth to thee

deepest of deep knowledge; ponder upon it in its fullness, and do as thou wilt.

64. Hear again my supreme word, deepest of all; for that thou art exceedingly beloved of me, therefore I will say what is for thy weal.

65. Have thy mind on me, thy devotion toward me, thy sacrifice to me, do homage to me. To me shalt thou come. I make thee a truthful promise; thou art dear to me.

66. Surrendering all the laws, come for refuge to me alone. I will deliver thee from all sins; grieve not.

67. This thou mayst never tell to one doing not mortification, to one without devotion, to one that obeys not, or to one that murmurs against me.

68. He who in supreme devotion toward me shall recite this supreme secret among my worshippers shall assuredly come to me.

69. None of men shall be to me more acceptable of works than he; none shall be dearer to me on earth than he.

70. And by him that shall read this lawful communion of us twain I shall be worshipped with the offering of knowledge; thus is my thought.

71. The believing and unmurmuring man that shall but hear it shall be delivered, and win to the happy worlds of the workers of holiness.

72. Hast thou heard this, O son of Pritha, with wholly intent mind? has thy bewilderment of ignorance vanished away, O wealth-winner?"

ARJUNA SPAKE:—

73. "My bewilderment has vanished away; I have gotten remembrance by thy grace, O never-falling. I stand freed from doubt; I will do thy word."

SANJAYA SPAKE:—

74. Thus was this wondrous, hair-stirring communion of Vasudeva and the great-hearted son of Pritha that I heard.

75. By the grace of Vyasa I heard this supreme secret from Krishna, the lord of the Rule, himself reciting his Rule.

76. O king, as often as I remember this wondrous and holy communion of the long-haired one and Arjuna, I rejoice time after time.

77. And as often as I remember the exceedingly wondrous form of Hari, great astonishment comes upon me, O king, and I rejoice again and again.

78. Whereso is Krishna the lord of Rule, whereso is the archer, Pritha's son, there, I trow, are fortune, victory, sure weal, and policy.

II

ZOROASTRIANISM

ZOROASTRIANISM may be classified as a dying religion, although its history reveals the fact that it has had an influence over other religions, particularly Christianity, far in excess of its individual importance. Today only about 100,000 followers of Zoroaster are in existence, scattered throughout Persia and India.

A great many of the concepts found both in the Old and the New Testament stem directly from Zoroastrianism, though the religion itself is not mentioned anywhere in the Bible. Many of the kings of Persia mentioned in the Old Testament were Zoroastrians. Among these are Josiah, Cyrus, Artaxerxes, Ahasuerus, and Darius. The Magi, wise men from the East, who came to the manger to see the new-born Jesus, were Zoroastrian priests. Although many early religions exerted influence over the religion of the Old and New Testaments, Zoroastrianism is the only one remaining alive today.

Satan, as described and accepted in the Bible, was introduced from Zoroastrianism, as was also the whole elaborate scheme of angels and demons, of the Saviour who was to come, and the doctrines of resurrection and final judgment as well as the conception of a future life to be lived in "Paradise".

Zoroastrianism was the first religion to teach universality. It held that the salvation offered by its god, Ahura Mazda, was not to be confined to the few, but was for everyone who would come to its knowledge and understanding. However, this universality has been abandoned by the more modern followers of Zoroaster so that today the religion is hereditary, a fact which accounts for the shrinking number of its adherents.

Zoroaster, (also known as Zarathustra) the founder of Zoroastrianism, or the religion of the Parsis, probably lived in the Seventh Century B.C. However, in Zoroastrianism tradition there are stories that would date his birth as early as 6000 B.C. This tradition is also filled with stories of miracles and of divine prophecies of his birth and deeds. At 15 years of age Zoroaster dedicated himself to the religious life and, when 30, he is believed to have had a direct call into the presence of Ahura Mazda to receive his blessing and instructions for founding the religion. From this time the young man continued to confer with Ahura Mazda and to preach a universal progressive religion among the agricultural communities of Pars in Persia.

The story of Zoroaster's life is filled with accounts of his magnetic preaching, temptations which he successfully resisted, miracles, and constant sacrifies. During middle life Zoroaster was able to convert the king, Vistaspa, and his brother, a counsellor, and the grand vizier. This gave his work official sanction and led to his marriage to the daughter of the king's counsellor. Throughout the remainder of his life Zoroaster worked in close harmony with the government and was able to use its power to spread his teachings and obtain converts. The religion became the official faith of the government and was employed to sanction the militaristic nationalism of Persia during these years.

The sacred books of Zoroastrianism are known under the general title of *Avesta*, meaning "knowledge". Those parts of the Avesta remaining today are arranged in five large groups. The earliest and most important section is the *Yasna*, meaning worship or sacrifice. Interlaced within the *Avesta* are 17 psalms, or *Gathas*. These psalms are believed to have been written by Zoroaster himself. Another small section of the *Avesta* is the *Visperad*, a less important liturgical work often employed in worship services. The *Vendidad* is a priestly code of laws governing ceremonies and contains much material about the history, cosmology, and theology of the religion. Other sections of the Zoroastrian scriptures are the *Yashts*, or worship hymns, and the *Khorda-Avesta*, or *Little Avesta*, a devotional handbook used by all true Zoroastrians.

Although Persia began a period of conquest and expansion under kings devoted to Zoroastrianism and continued this for some time, eventually it was conquered by the Arabs, followers of Mohammed, and most of the Zoroastrians were converted to this new religion after 650 A.D. Today Zoroastrians are a small group scattered throughout the world. Many of the most influential citizens of India are Zoroastrians, and the charitable works of these people are great.

THE YASNA

THE *Yasna* is the most important liturgy of the followers of Zoroaster. Here is to be found confession, invocation, prayer, exhortation, and praise combined, as in any series of liturgies. The various fragments composing this work were selected from writings of many ages and are composed in many different literary forms. The present arrangement of these fragments is of very ancient origin; however, the work as it now stands was not in existence during the earliest periods of Zoroastrianism but took form much later as the religion began to crystallize into a set pattern. The word *Yasna* means "worship including sacrifice".

1,21: If I have offended thee, whether by thought, or word, or deed, whether by act of will, or without intent or wish, I earnestly make up the deficiency of this in praise to thee. If I have caused decrease in that which is Thy Yasna, and Thy homage, I announce (and celebrate) to thee (the more for this)!

10,16: To five do I belong, to five others do I not; of the good thought am I, of the evil am I not; of the good word am I, of the evil am I not; of the good deed am I, and of the evil, not.
To Obedience am I given, and to deaf disobedience, not; to the saint do I belong, and to the wicked, not; and so from this on to the ending shall be the spirits' parting.

11,17–18: I celebrate my praise for good thoughts, good words, and good deeds for my thoughts, my speeches, and (my) actions. With chanting praises I present all good thoughts, good words, and good deeds, and with rejection I repudiate all evil thoughts, and words, and deeds. Here I give to you, O ye Bountiful Immortals! sacrifice and homage with the mind, with words, deeds, and my entire person; yea, (I offer) to you the flesh of my very body (as your own). And I praise

Righteousness. A blessing is Righteousness (called) the Best, &c.

12,1: I drive the Daevas hence; I confess as a Mazda-worshipper of the order of Zarathustra, estranged from the Daevas, devoted to the lore of the Lord, a praiser of the Bountiful Immortals; and to Ahura Mazda, the good and endowed with good possessions, I attribute all things good, to the holy One, the resplendent, to the glorious, whose are all things whatsoever which are good; whose is the Kine, whose is Asha (the righteous order pervading all things pure), whose are the stars, in whose lights the glorious beings and objects are clothed.

28,4: O (thou Divine) Righteousness, and thou Benevolent Mind (of Deity)! I will worship you, and Ahura Mazda the first, for all of whom the Pious ready mind (within us) is causing the imperishable Kingdom to advance. (And while I thus utter my supplications to You), come Ye to my calls to help!

28,11: And therefore do Thou, O Lord, the Great Creator! fill up and satisfy (my) desire with these attainments (of the grace) of Thy Good Mind, which Thou dost know to be derived from Righteousness (and) which (are verily) sublime, for I have known Thine instructions to be never void of their effect (in the struggles) for our (daily) food, and therefore worthy objects of desire.

29,11: And when shall the (Divine) Righteousness, the Good Mind (of the Lord, and His) Sovereign Powers (come) hastening to me (to give me strength for my task and mission), O Great Creator, the Living Lord! (For without him I cannot advance to undertake my toil.) Do ye now therefore assign unto us your aid and in abundance for our great cause. May we be (partakers) of the bountiful grace of these your equals (your counsellors and servants)!

30,2-4: Hear ye then with your ears; see ye the bright flames with the (eyes of the) Better Mind. It is for a decision as to religions, man and man, each individually for himself. Before the great effort of the cause, awake ye (all) to our teaching!

Thus are the primeval spirits who as a pair (combining their opposite strivings), and (yet each) independent in his action, have been famed (of old). (They are) a better thing, they two, and a worse, as to thought, as to word, and as to deed. And between these two let the wisely acting choose aright. (Choose ye) not (as) the evil-doers!

(Yea) when the two spirits came together at the first to make life, and life's absence, and to determine how the world at the last shall be (ordered), for the wicked (Hell) the worst life, for the holy (Heaven) the Best Mental State.

30,11: Wherefore, O ye men! ye are learning (thus) these religious incitations which Ahura gave in (our) happiness and (our) sorrow. (And ye are also learning) what is the long wound-

ing for the wicked, and the blessings which are in store for the righteous. And when these (shall have begun their course), salvation shall be (your portion)!

31,11-13: (And this doctrine was the first of rules to regulate our actions. Yet the opposer speaks beside Thee.) For when first, O Ahura Mazda! Thou didst create the (holy) settlements, and didst reveal the religious laws; and when Thou gavest (us) understanding from Thine own mind, and madest our (full) bodily life, and (didst thus determine) actions (by Thy power), and didst moreover deliver to us (nearer) injunctions whereby (as by a rule) the wisher may place his choices.

(There strife at once arose, and still is raging.) There (beside Thy prophet) the truthful or liar, the enlightened or unenlightened, lifts his voice (to utter his faith), and with devoted mind and heart. (But without hindrance from this striving, or pausing with feeble search, our) Piety steadily questions the two spirits (not here on earth) but (there in the spirit-world) where (they dwell as) in their home.

(Yea, my Piety questions searchingly, for Thou, O Maker! hast Thy view on all; we cannot question lightly.) What questions are asked which are open (permitted to our thoughts), or what questions (are asked) which are furtive (hiding themselves from the light), or (what decision soever we may make, and the man) who for the smallest sin binds on the heaviest penance, on all with Thy glittering eye(s) as a righteous guard Thou art gazing!

31,21-22: But Ahura Mazda will give both Universal Weal and Immortality in the fulness of His Righteous Order, and from himself as the head of Dominion (within His saints). And he will likewise give the Good Mind's vigorous might to him who in spirit and deeds is His friend, (and with faith fulfils his vows).

And to the wise are these things clear as to the one discerning with his mind (not blinded by the perverter). With Thy Good Mind and Thy (holy) Kingdom he follows the Righteous Order both in his words and his actions. And to Thee, O Ahura Mazda! such a man shall be the most helpful and vigorous being (for he serves with every power)!

33,2: Yea, (he will act with justice but with vengeance, for) he who does evil to the wicked by word, or with thought (and plan), and (who therein does not dally, but toils labouring as) with both the hands, or he (again) who admonishes one for his good, such as these are offering (a gift) to their religious faith in the love (and with the approving view) of Ahura Mazda; (they are offering to conscience).

33,10–11: (And not for these alone do I pray, but for us as well.) All prosperous states in being which have been enjoyed in the past, which men are now enjoying, and which shall be known in the future, do Thou grant (me) these in Thy love. (Yea), cause (our) bodily and personal life to be blest with salvation through (Thy) Good Mind, (Thy) Sovereign Power, and (Thy) Sanctity.

And, O Thou who art the most beneficent Ahura Mazda! and thou who art Aramaiti (our piety), and also the Righteous Order who dost further on the settlements; and Thou, the Good Mind, and the Sovereign Power! hear ye me all, and have mercy for every deed which I do whatsoever!

34,8: Through these our deeds (of sacrifice and zeal), they are terrified among whom there was (once) destruction, and for many (at the time)

when the oppressor of Thy holy vows was as the stronger oppressing the weaker. They who have not thought (in consonance) with Thy Righteous Order, from these Thy Good Mind abideth afar.

36,1–5: We would approach You two, O (Ye) primeval ones in the house of this Thy holy Fire, O Ahura Mazda, Thou most bounteous Spirit! Who brings pollutions to this (Thy flame) him wilt Thou cover with pollutions (in his turn). But as the most friendly do Thou give us zeal, O Fire of the Lord! and approach us, and with the loving blessing of the most friendly, with the praise of the most adored. Yea, may'st thou approach to aid us in this our greatest (undertaking) among the efforts of our zeal.

The Fire of Ahura Mazda art thou verily; yea, the most bounteous one of His Spirit, wherefore Thine is the most potent of all names (for grace), O Fire of the Lord! And therefore we should approach Thee, (O Ahura!) with the help of Thy Good Mind (which Thou dost implant within us), with Thy (good) Righteousness, and with the actions and the words inculcated by Thy good wisdom!

We therefore bow before Thee, and we direct our prayers to Thee with confessions of our guilt, O Ahura Mazda! with all the good thoughts (which Thou dost inspire), with all the words well said, and the deeds well done, with these would we approach Thee.

37,1–4: Thus therefore do we worship Ahura Mazda, who made the Kine (the living creation), and the (embodied) Righteousness (which is incarnate in the clean), and the waters, and the wholesome plants, the stars, and the earth, and all (existing) objects that are good. Yea, we worship Him for His Sovereign Power and His greatness, beneficent (as they are), and with priority among the Yazads who abide beside the Kine (and care for her protection and support).

And we worship Him under His name as Lord, to Mazda dear, the most beneficent (of names). We worship him with our bones, and with our flesh, (with our bodies and our life). And we worship the Fravashis of the saints, of holy men, and holy women; and Righteousness the Best do we worship, the most beauteous, the Bountiful Immortal and that which is endowed with light in all things good.

41,1–6: Praises, and songs, and adorations do we offer to Ahura Mazda, and to Righteousness the Best; yea, we offer and we ascribe them, and proclaim them. And to Thy good Kingdom, O Ahura Mazda! may we attain for ever, and a good King be Thou over us; and let each man of us, and so each woman, thus abide, O Thou most beneficent of beings, and for both the worlds! Thus do we render Thee, the helpful Yazad, endowed with good devices, the friend of them (who worship Thee) with (well-adjusted) ritual; so may'st Thou be to us our life, and our body's vigour, O Thou most beneficent of beings, and that for both the worlds.

Aye, let us win and conquer (?) long life, O Ahura Mazda! in Thy grace, and through Thy will may we be powerful. May'st Thou lay hold on us to help, and long, and with salvation, O Thou most beneficent of beings!

Thy praisers and Mathra-speakers may we be called, O Ahura Mazda! so do we wish, and to this may we attain. What reward most meet for our deserving Thou hast appointed for the souls, O Ahura Mazda! of that do Thou bestow on us for this life, and for that of mind. Of that reward (do Thou Thyself grant this advantage), that we may come under Thy protecting guardianship, and that

of Righteousness for ever. We sacrifice to that brave Yasna, the Yasna Haptanghaiti, the holy, the ritual chief!

43,1–5: Salvation to this man, salvation to him whosoever (he may be)! Let the absolutely ruling Great Creator grant (us, He) the living Lord, the two eternal powers. Yea, verily, I ask it of Thee (O Ahura) for the maintaining Righteousness. And may'st Thou also give it to me, (O inspiring) Piety! splendour (as it is), holy blessings, the Good Mind's life.

Yea, to this one may the man endowed with glory give the best of all things, the (spiritual) glory. And do Thou likewise (Thyself) reveal Thine own (gifts) through Thy most bountiful spirit, O Mazda! (And do Thou teach us) Thy wonderful thoughts of wisdom, those of Thy Good Mind, which Thou hast revealed (to us) by Thy Righteousness (within us) with the happy increase of (our joy), and on a long life's every day.

And may that (holy man) approach toward that which is the better than the good, he who will show to us the straight paths of (spiritual) profit, (the blessings) of this corporeal life, and of that the mental, in those veritably real (eternal) worlds, where dwells Ahura; (that holy man) an offerer of Thine, O Mazda! a faithful citizen, and bountiful of (mind).

Yea, I will regard Thee as mighty and likewise bountiful, O Ahura Mazda! when (I behold) those aids of grace (approach me), aids which Thou dost guard and nurture as (Thy) just awards to the wicked (to hold him far from us), as well as to the righteous (for our help), Thy Fire's flame, therewith so strong through the Holy Order, and when to me the Good Mind's power comes.

(For) so I conceived of Thee as bountiful, O Great Giver, Mazda! when I beheld Thee as supreme in the generation of life, when, as rewarding deeds and words, Thou didst establish evil for the evil, and happy blessings for the good, by Thy (great) virtue (to be adjudged to each) in the creation's final change.

43,8–11: Then to him I, Zarathustra, as my first answer, said: To the wicked (would that I could be) in very truth a strong tormentor and avenger, but to the righteous may I be a mighty help and joy, since to preparations for Thy Kingdom, and in desire (for its approach), I would devote myself so long as to Thee, O Mazda! I may praise, and weave my song.

Yea, I conceive of Thee as bountiful, O Ahura Mazda! when (Thine herald) with Thy Good Mind near approached me, and asked me thus: For what dost thou desire that thou may'st gain, and that thou may'st know it? Then for Thy Fire an offering of praise and holiness (I desired. And on that offering for myself) as long as I have the power, will I meditate, (and for its holy power among Thy people will I plan).

And may'st Thou likewise grant me (Thy) Righteousness (within me), since I earnestly invoke that perfect readiness (of mind), joining in my prayer with Aramaiti (our Piety toward Thee. Yea, pray Thou Thyself within me through these holy powers). Ask Thou (Thyself) our questions, those which shall be asked by us of Thee; for a question asked by Thee (as its inspirer), is as the question of the mighty, when'er Thy (?) ruler speaks his potent wish.

Yea, I conceived of Thee as bountiful, O Ahura Mazda! when (Thy messenger) with Thy Good Mind near approached me, and with your words I first impressed (my soul). Woes then 'midst men Thy heart-devoted ones declared (to be) my (portion); but that will I do which Thou did'st say was best.

43,15–16: Yea, I conceived of Thee as bounteous, O Ahura Mazda! when with the Good Mind's grace Thy Sraosha (Obedience) approached me, (and said): Let the quiet and long-enduring better mind with understanding teach (thee); let not a foremost man conciliate the wicked (as sycophant desiring aid), for with that (quiet mind of faith), Thy saints have brought full many a sinner unto Thee (as convert, and in penitence).

Thus, O Ahura Mazda! this Zarathustra loves the Spirit, and every man most bounteous prays (beside him): Be Righteousness life-strong, and clothed with body. In that (holy) Realm which shines (with splendour) as the sun, let Piety be present; and may she through the indwelling of Thy Good Mind give us blessings in reward for deeds!

44,7–8: This I ask Thee, O Ahura! tell me aright; who fashioned Aramaiti (our piety) the beloved, together with Thy Sovereign Power? Who, through his guiding wisdom, hath made the son revering the father? (Who made him beloved?) With (questions such as) these, so abundant, O Mazda! I press Thee, O bountiful Spirit, (Thou) maker of all!

This I ask Thee, O Ahura! tell me aright, that I may ponder these which are Thy revelations, O Mazda! and the words which were asked (of Thee) by Thy Good Mind (within us), and that whereby we may attain, through Thine Order, to this life's perfection. Yea, how may my soul with joyfulness increase in goodness? Let it thus be.

45,4–10: Thus I will declare forth this world's best (being). From (the insight of His) Righteous Mazda, who hath appointed these (things), hath known (what He utters to be true; yea, I will declare) Him the father of the toiling Good Mind (within us). So is His daughter through good deeds (our) Piety. Not to be deceived is the all-viewing Lord.

Yea, I will declare that which the most bountiful One told me, that word which is the best to be heeded by mortals. They who therein grant me obedient attention, upon them cometh Weal to bless, and the Immortal being, and in the deeds of His Good Mind cometh the Lord.

Aye, thus I will declare forth Him who is of all the greatest, praising through my Righteousness, I who do aright, those who (dispose of all as well aright). Let Ahura Mazda hear with His bounteous spirit, in whose homage (what I asked) was asked with the Good Mind. Aye, let Him exhort me through His wisdom (which is ever) the best.

(Yea, I will declare Him) whose blessings the offerers will seek for, those who are living now, as well as those who have lived (aforetime), as will they also who are coming (hereafter. Yea, even) the soul(s) of the righteous (will desire) them in the eternal Immortality. (Those things they will desire which are blessings to the righteous) but woes to the wicked. And these hath Ahura Mazda (established) through His kingdom, He, the creator (of all).

Him in our hymns of homage and of praise would I faithfully serve, for now with (mine) eye, I see Him clearly, Lord of the good spirit, of word, and action, I knowing through my Righteousness Him who is Ahura Mazda. And to Him (not here alone, but) in His home of song, His praise we shall bear.

Yea, Him with our better Mind we seek to honour, who desiring (good), shall come to us (to bless) in weal and sorrow. May He, Ahura Mazda, make us vigorous through Khshathra's royal power, our flocks and men in thrift to further, from the good support and bearing of His Good Mind, (itself born in us) by His Righteousness.

Him in the Yasnas of our Piety we seek to praise with homage, who in His persistent energy was famed to be (in truth) the Lord Ahura Mazda, for He hath appointed in His kingdom, through His holy Order and His Good Mind, both Weal and Immortality, to grant the eternal mighty pair to this our land (and the creation).

46,16: (And to the Hvogvas would I likewise speak.) Thou Frashaostra Hvogva (whom I see); go thou (forth) with the generous helpers, with those whom we are praying for as for salvation to the land. Go thou where Piety joins hand in hand with the Righteous Order, where are the wished-for Realms of Good Mind, where Mazda in His most honoured home abides.

48,10: When, Mazda! shall the men of mind's perfection come? And when shall they drive from hence, the soil of this (polluted) drunken joy, whereby the Karpans with (their) angry zeal would crush us, and by whose inspiration the tyrants of the provinces (hold on) their evil rule?

49,8: (And I do not ask in vain, for such an one is found for us, and near at hand.) To Fraṣhaostra hast Thou given that most favouring guardian p wer, the headship of the Holy Order (for us), O Ahura! This therefore would I pray of Thee (to confirm to him that gracious gift), and for myself likewise, would I now seek as well that sheltering headship which is within Thy Realm; yea, most blest and foremost may we both for ever be within it.

50,6: (Therefore will I incite him to his task the more. Let him indeed proclaim the righteous way) he who already lifts his voice in Mathras, O Ahura Mazda! he, Zarathustra, the faithful friend in accordance with the

Holy Order, and with self-abasing worship, giver of understanding for this land, voice-guider (of the way to glory), let him indeed proclaim and teach my regulations, and in accordance with Thy Good Mind (as his law).

50,10: (Mine every wish and prayer is this), then therefore whatsoever I shall do, and whatsoever deeds (of ritual and truth I shall yet further do) on account of, (and to make full) these (prior deeds of worship), yea, whatsoever (holy works) shine bright as having worth in (all) men's eyes through Thy Good Mind (whose character they share; these as) the stars, suns, and the Aurora which brings on the light of days, are all, through their Righteous Order, (the speakers) of Thy praise, O Thou Great Giver, Lord!

51,7: (And as Thou wilt bestow thus graciously on him) so grant me also, O Thou most bountiful Spirit Mazda, Thou who hast made both the Kine and the waters and the plants (for her support)! both Immortality and Welfare, those two eternal powers, and through Thy Good Mind in the doctrine (which is revealed through his inspired words).

52,1–4: I pray with benedictions for a benefit, and for the good, even for the entire creation of the holy (and the clean); I beseech for them for the (generation which is) now alive, for that which is just coming into life, and for that which shall be hereafter. And (I pray for that) sanctity which leads to prosperity, and which has long afforded shelter, which goes on hand in hand with it, which joins it in its walk, and of itself becoming its close companion as it delivers forth its precepts, bearing every form of healing virtue which comes to us in waters, appertains to cattle, or is found in plants, and overwhelming all the harmful malice of the Daevas, (and their servants) who might harm this dwelling and its lord, bringing good gifts, and better blessings, given very early, and later (gifts), leading to successes, and for a long time giving shelter. And so the greatest, and the best, and the most beautiful benefits of sanctity fall likewise to our lot for the sacrifice, homage, propitiation, and the praise of the Bountiful Immortality, for the bringing prosperity to this abode, and for the prosperity of the entire creation of the holy, and the clean, (and as for this, so) for the opposition of the entire evil creation. (And I pray for this) as I praise through Righteousness, I who am beneficent, those who are (likewise of a better mind).

53,3: And him will they give Thee, O Pourukista, Haekat-aspid and Spitami! young (as thou art) of the daughters of Zarathustra, him will they give thee as a help in the Good Mind's true service, of Asha's and Mazda's, as a chief and a guardian. Counsel well then (together), with the mind of Armaiti, most bounteous and pious; and act with just action.

53,5–7: Monitions for the marrying I speak to (you) maidens, to you, I who know them; and heed ye my (sayings): By these laws of the faith which I utter obtain ye the life of the Good Mind (on earth and in heaven). (And to you, bride and groom), let each one the other in Righteousness cherish; thus alone unto each shall the home-life be happy.

[Thus real are these things, ye men and ye women!] from the Lie-demon protecting, I guard o'er my (faithful), and so (I) grant progress (in weal and in goodness). And the hate of the Lie (with the hate of her) bondsmen (?) I pray from the body, (and so would expel it). For to those who bear Vayu, (and bring him to power), his shame mars the glory. To these evil truth-harmers by these means he reaches. Ye thus slay the life mental (if ye follow his courses).

But yours be the recompense, (O ye righteous women!) of this great cause. For while lustful desire heart-inflamed from the body there beyond goeth down where the spirit of evil reaches (to ruin, still) ye bring forth the champion to help on the cause, (and thus conquer temptation). So your last word is "Vayu"; (ye cry it in triumph).

57,4: We worship Sraosha, Obedience the blessed, and that lofty Lord who is Ahura Mazda Himself, Him who has attained the most to this our ritual, Him who has approached the nearest to us in our celebrations. And we worship all the words of Zarathustra, and all the deeds well done (for him), both those that have been done (in times gone by) and those which are yet to be done (for him in times to come).

60,1–5: Thus that better than the good may he approach, who shows to us straight paths of profit appertaining to this bodily life and to the mental likewise, in the eternal (?) realms where dwells Ahura; yea, may he approach it, who is Thy worthy servant, and good citizen, O Great giver Lord!

May these blessings approach this house, which are the wise perceptions of the saints, the sacred blessings bestowed through the ritual, their guileless characteristics, together with their recognition of what is due; and may the Righteous Order appear for this village, and the Divine Sovereign Power, together with the benefit and glorious welfare (which ensues),

And with these the long enduring prominence of this Religion of Ahura's, the Zarathustrian Faith. And may the Kine be now with greatest speed within (the farm-yard of) this house, most speedily may the rewarded sanctity and the strength of the holy man be here, most speedily as well Ahura's lore. And may the good and heroic and bountiful Fravashis of the saints come here, and may they go hand in hand with us with the healing virtues of (their) blessed gifts as widespread as the earth, as far-spread as the rivers, as high-reaching as the sun, for the furtherance of the better men, for the hindrance of the hostile, and for the abundant growth of riches and of glory.

May Sraosha (Obedience) conquer disobedience within this house, and may peace triumph over discord here, and generous giving over avarice, reverence over contempt, speech with truthful words over lying utterance. May the Righteous Order gain the victory over the Demon of the Lie.

71,13–14: Let the holy Zarathustra himself seek out a friend and a protector. And I say to thee (O Zarathustra!) to make to thee a friend holy beyond the holy, and truer than the true, for that is the better thing; for he is evil who is the best to the evil, and he is holy to whom the holy is a friend, for these are the best of words, those which Ahura Mazda spoke to Zarathustra.

And do thou, O Zarathustra! pronounce these words at the last ending of (thy) life.

THE VENDIDAD

THE *Vendidad* is one section of the *Zend-Avesta*, or sacred book of the Parsis. According to Parsi tradition, it is the only *Nask*, or book, out of twenty-one, which has been preserved in its entirety, although it gives the impression of being merely a collection of fragments. Often described as the code of laws of the Parsis, the *Vendidad* is devoted largely to laws of purification. However, it does contain laws regarding both religious and civil matters. The book contains 22 chapters or *fargards* and was composed sometime after the middle of the fifth century B.C.

3,33: "Then let people learn by heart this holy saying: 'No one who does not eat, has strength to do heavy works of holiness, strength to do works of husbandry, strength to beget children. By eating every material creature lives, by not eating it dies away.' "

3,40–42: When is it so?
"It is so, if the sinner be a professor of the Religion of Mazda, or one who has been taught in it.

"But if he be not a professor of the Religion of Mazda, nor one who has been taught in it, then his sin is taken from him, if he makes confession of the Religion of Mazda and resolves never to commit again such forbidden deeds.

"The Religion of Mazda indeed, O Spitama Zarathustra! takes away from him who makes confession of it the bonds of his sin; it takes away (the sin of) breach of trust; it takes away (the sin of) murdering one of the faithful; it takes away (the sin of) burying a corpse; it takes away (the sin of) deeds for which there is no atonement; it takes away the worst sin of usury; it takes away any sin that may be sinned.

"In the same way the Religion of Mazda, O Spitama Zarathustra! cleanses the faithful from every evil thought, word, and deed, as a swift-rushing mighty wind cleanses the plain.

"So let all the deeds he doeth be henceforth good, O Zarathustra! a full atonement for his sin is effected by means of the Religion of Mazda."

4,43–45: And they shall thenceforth in their doings walk after the way of holiness, after the word of holiness, after the ordinance of holiness.

If men of the same faith, either friends or brothers, come to an agreement together, that one may obtain from the other, either goods, or a wife, or knowledge, let him who desires goods have them delivered to him; let him who desires a wife receive and wed her; let him who desires knowledge be taught the holy word,

During the first part of the day and the last, during the first part of the night and the last, that his mind may be increased in intelligence and wax strong in holiness. So shall he sit up, in devotion and prayers, that he may be increased in intelligence; he shall rest during the middle part of the day, during the middle part of the night, and thus shall he continue until he can say all the words which former Aethrapaitis have said.

5,21: With these words the holy Ahura Mazda rejoiced the holy Zarathustra: "Purity is for man, next to life, the greatest good, that purity, O Zarathustra, that is in the Religion of Mazda for him who cleanses his own self with good thoughts, words, and deeds."

8,19: "An Athravan shall first go along the way and shall say aloud these victorious words: 'Yatha ahu vairyo:—The will of the Lord is the law of righteousness.

" 'The gifts of Vohu-mano to the deeds done in this world for Mazda.

" 'He who relieves the poor makes Ahura king.' "

10,19: "Make thy own self pure, O righteous man! any one in the world here below can win purity for his own self, namely, when he cleanses his own self with good thoughts, words, and deeds."

18,27: " 'May herds of oxen and sons accrue to thee; may thy mind be master of its vow, may thy soul be master of its vow, and may'st thou live on in the joy of thy soul all the nights of thy life.'

"This is the blessing which Atar speaks unto him who brings him dry wood, well examined by the light of the day, well cleansed with godly intent."

19,10: Zarathustra chanted aloud the Ahuna-Vairya.

The holy Zarathustra said aloud: "This I ask thee: teach me the truth, O Lord! . . ."

19,22: "He shall recite a hundred Ashen vohu: 'Holiness is the best of all good: it is also happiness. Happy the man who is holy with perfect holiness!'

"He shall chant two hundred Ahuna-Vairya: 'The will of the Lord is the law of righteousness. The gifts of Vohu-mano to the deeds done in this world for Mazda! He who relieves the poor makes Ahura king.'

"He shall wash himself four times with the gomez from the ox, and twice with the water made by Mazda."

III

TAOISM

TAOISM is the oldest of the personally founded religions of China, being one of the "Three Religions" of that vast land. The other two are Confucianism and Buddhism. However, there are many who maintain that it should not be classed as a religion at all. Others point out that it was originally simply a way of ethical living and was not organized as a religion until late in its history, near the opening of the Christian era.

Today there are approximately forty million adherents of this faith, most of them being in China. Japan and a few other areas of the East have felt its influence slightly, but its most vital influence remains among the Chinese, where it has become mingled with other religions and doctrinal teachings.

Taoism, according to tradition, was founded by a humble Chinese known at Lao-tze, who lived between 604 and 517 B.C. Scholars point out, however, that Lao-tze was actually the crystallizer of a philosophy which had existed in China for many centuries before his birth.

Lao-tze was born about fifty years before Confucius, in Honan province of Central China. He was a contemporary of Zoroaster, Mahavira, Buddha, Jeremiah, and Ezekiel. His was indeed an age of great religious movements in the East. It is recorded that when Confucius was about thirty years of age he visited the "Venerable Philosopher" and was greatly influenced by his wealth of knowledge and understanding.

Lao-tze held various public offices, chief of which was keeper of the archives at the court of the Chinese dynasty of Chou. However, his chief concern was with teaching and attaining to the virtues of the *Tao*. Fundamental to all his teaching was the idea that the highest life consisted in following the divine Way, or *Tao*, of the universe. He was constantly emphasizing, both through his teachings and his living, that a person should return good for evil at all times. But, though passionately concerned with the *Tao*, Lao-tze did nothing about the world, seeking rather to retire from it and spend his time in contemplation.

It was long after Lao-tze's death that his followers began to look upon him as worthy of worship. But gradually this man became the symbol of divinity, and miracle stories grew up about his memory. In 156 A.D. state sacrifices were made to him. There arose a theory of his immaculate conception, of his being born an old man with white hair and great wisdom after being carried in his mother's womb for seventy years.

Of the sacred writings of Taoism, we have chosen for consideration the *Tao Teh King* and the *Writings of Kwang-Tze*. The former is the chief literary treasure of the religion, whereas the latter illustrates the type of writing which was done by later followers of Lao-tze. Both works give one the flavor of Taoism and something of its teachings.

The history of Taoism reveals it in constant antagonism to Confucianism. It also was violently opposed to Buddhism when the latter came on the Chinese scene. Although several Chinese Emperors have been favorable to Taoism, it has never been the dominant faith of this vast nation. In 212 B.C. the Emperor Shi Hwang-ti accepted Taoism, burned Confucian books, and sent an expedition to fairy islands to search for the herb of immortality. This was followed about two hundred years later by the attempt on the part of leading Taoists to compound a pill of immortality. Then, in the seventh century of the Christian era, Lao-tze was made a saint and his works were included among subjects for government examinations. Throughout all this time Taoism was producing a group of doctors who claimed to cure diseases by magic. These came into conflict with the government and were often condemned by official decree.

Modern Taoism is a very different religion. Most of the fine teachings of Lao-tze and his followers have been disregarded and in their place have come polytheism, demonology, witchcraft, and occultism.

THE TAO TEH KING

THIS document is the most important literary treasure of the Taoists. Most scholars agree that the material comes direct from Lao-tze and was possibly written by him in much the same form as we now have it.

Translating the *Tao Teh King* has proved to be a most difficult and yet fascinating task, and many attempts have been made to give the meaning of the text in various languages. Very often, however, alien influences have crept in to distort the true meaning. We have chosen here a translation that seeks to divest the work of any Confucian or other antagonistic influences and render into English the exact meanings as Taoist scholars believe they should be given.

The work is a series of wise sayings and generalizations arranged with no idea of order. It was written sometime during the first half of the sixth century B.C.

2. The Beautiful being once recognised as such by the world, the Repulsive appears. Goodness being once recognised as such, Evil appears in like manner. Thus existence and non-existence produce each other; the difficult and the easy bring about each other; the long and the short impart form to each other; the high and low comply with each other; sounds and voices harmonize with each other; priority and sequence alternate with each other.

Wherefore the Sage pursues a policy of inaction, and teaches men in silence;

He forms all things without shrinking; produces them without claiming the possession (of virtue); acts without presuming on (his ability); and completes his achievements without taking any credit to himself. It is only he who thus does not stand upon his merit; and therefore his merit does not depart from him.

4. The Tao is full; yet in operation as though not self-elated. In its origin it is as it were the Ancestor of All Things. It chastens asperity; it unravels confusion; it moderates the radiance (proceeding from those in whom Tao is embodied); and it identifies itself with the sordid ones (of the earth). Pellucid (as a spreading ocean) it yet has the semblance of permanence. I know not whose offspring it is. Its "idea" existed before God was.

7. Heaven is everlasting; Earth endures. The reason of the endurance of Heaven and Earth is that they were not self-produced. Therefore it is that they are able to endure for ever. Thus, though the sage regards the cultivation of his body as of secondary importance, his body still progresses; he discards his body, and yet his body is preserved. Is not this because he has no selfishness? Wherefore he is able to realize all his wishes.

8. The goodness of the Ruler resembles water. The goodness of water is beneficial to all things, and that without struggling.

The abiding-place (of the Imperial

goodness) is despised by the multitude; and therefore it is near to Tao. Wherever it dwells, it sanctifies the spot. In the heart, its sanctifying properties are unfathomable. In bestowing, it sanctifies benevolence; in speaking, it sanctifies trustworthiness; in administration, it sanctifies government; in the fulfillment of daily work, it sanctifies ability; in the adoption of public measures it sanctifies acting seasonably. It alone never strives against any one; and therefore it gives rise to no resentful feelings.

9. It is better to desist altogether, than, having once grasped (the Tao) to pride oneself on one's self-sufficiency. Research, if carried on to too keen a point, prevents the preservation of the body. When a hall is filled up with gold and jewels, it cannot be guarded intact. When wealth and honours are combined with arrogance, they themselves invoke calamity. To keep oneself in the background when merit has been achieved and fame has followed in its wake; this is the way of Heaven.

12. The five colours blind the eyes of men. The five tones deafen their ears. The five flavours vitiate their palates. Galloping and hunting induce derangement of the mind. Objects that are difficult of attainment lead them to incur obstacles.

Thus the Sage cares for his inner self, and not for that which his eye can see; for which reason he discards the latter and preserves the former.

16. When the extreme of emptiness is reached, and quiescence rigidly preserved, then all things are simultaneously produced; and by this I observe their revolutions. All things, after flourishing like the herb yun, return each to what it sprang from. Returning to this source is called quiescence, and this implies a reversion to the original ordinance (of Heaven). Reversion to the original ordinance (of Heaven) is called the basis or pivot of Tao. Knowledge of this may be called enlightenment, while ignorance of it leads to a reckless working-out of one's own ruin. He who knows it, bears with others. Bearing with others, he is just; being just, he is fit to be a king; being a king, he is the associate of Heaven (whose decree he holds and whose ordinances he carries out). Heaven is (the offspring of) the Tao; and Tao survives the death of him who is the embodiment of it, living on unharmed for ever.

17. Those of pre-eminent wisdom and purity knew (this Tao) intuitively from their birth, and so possessed it. Those of the second rank—the men of virtue—approached it nearly, and eulogised it. Those of the third rank— who were still above the commonalty —stood in awe of it. Those of the lowest rank held it in light esteem. Their belief in it was superficial, or imperfect; while there were even some who did not believe in it at all.

(The first) spoke only with forethought and calculation, as though honouring their words. When their (public) labours were achieved, and affairs progressed unimpeded, the people all said, "This is our natural and spontaneous condition."

19. When Sages are rejected as rulers, and the services of the wise are discarded, the people's wealth will increase a hundredfold; (for their hearts will all be set on covetousness). When benevolence and rectitude (in government) are abjured, (such will be the height of disorder that) the people will revert to their natural qualities of filial piety and compassion (by sheer force of reaction). When ingenuities of luxury and eagerness for gain are renounced, there will be no more robbers —(for there will be no more accumulations

of wealth to be worth stealing). These three propositions show that mere externals are insufficient for good government, and therefore each man should be ordered to confine himself to performing his own special work in life.

21. The appearance of Virtue in its fullest exuberance is no more than the result of compliance with the Tao. Tao, considered as an entity, is obscure and vague. Vague and obscure! yet within it there is Form. Obscure and vague! yet within it there is Substance. Vacuous and unfathomable! yet within it there is Quintessential Energy—and this is supremely real. Within it, too, there is Trustworthiness; from ancient down to modern times its name has never been lost; by it I can include in the range of my observation the whole of animate nature. How am I cognizant of the acquiescence of animate nature (in Tao)?—By Tao itself.

22. (In cultivating Tao) there are first the sprouts; then perfection. First, there is perversion; then rectification. First there is hollowness; then plenitude. First there is destruction (of the old); then renovation. First there is humility; then acquisition. Self-sufficiency is followed by suspicion (on the part of others). Therefore the Sage preserves unity (in his heart) and becomes a pattern to the whole world. He does not say himself that he can see, and therefore he is perspicacious. He does not say himself that he is right, and therefore he is manifested to all. He does not praise himself, and therefore his merit is recognized. He is not self-conceited, and therefore he increases (in knowledge). And as he never strives with anybody, so the world does not strive with him.

Can that saying of the olden times— "First the sprout, then perfection"—be called meaningless? The attainment of genuine perfection implies a reversion (to the original nature of man).

24. A man who raises himself on tiptoe cannot remain firm. A man with crooked legs cannot walk (far).

He who says himself that he can see is not enlightened. He who says himself that he is right is not manifested to others. He who praises himself has no merit. He who is self-conceited will not increase (in knowledge).

Such men may be said to search after Tao that they may gorge themselves in feeding, and act the parasite; moreover, they are universally detested. Therefore those who are possessed of Tao do not act thus.

27. The conduct of the virtuous leaves neither trace nor clue. The words of the virtuous afford no ground for fault-finding. The projects of the virtuous require no intrigue.

When the virtuous are obstructed (in their policy), though there be no bolt to the door which shuts them in, it yet cannot be opened. When the virtuous enter into relations with others, though they be not bound by the ties of contract, they yet may not release themselves (from their obligations).

Thus the Sage ever uses his goodness in saving others; and therefore there are none who are abandoned. He ever uses his goodness in saving the inanimate creation; and therefore there are none of these who are abandoned. This is called being doubly enlightened.

Wherefore the virtuous man is the teacher, or patron, of the bad man, while the bad man is employed as material, on which to work, by the virtuous man. If the bad man does not reverence the other as his teacher, nor the good man love the former as his material; then, in spite of any wisdom either may possess, they are both greatly blinded. This doctrine is both important and sublime.

28. He who, conscious of manly strength, guards a womanly weakness, becomes the channel of the whole Empire. Being thus the channel of the whole Empire, the cardinal virtues will never depart from him, and he will revert to a condition of childlike innocence.

He who, conscious of light, keeps in obscurity, will become a model for the whole Empire. Being a model for the whole Empire, the cardinal virtues will never fail him, and he will revert to the Unconditioned.

He who, conscious of his glory, guards humility, will become the valley of the whole Empire. Being the valley of the Empire, he will revert to his original simplicity. When this simplicity is distributed, the man becomes a thing of utility (to the State). The Sage employs men of this simplicity, and advances them to high rank; therefore his administration is on a grand scale, and never comes to an end.

30. Those who use Tao in assisting their Sovereign do not employ soldiers to force the Empire. The methods of government they adopt are such as have a tendency to react upon themselves. Where garrisons are quartered, briars and thorns spring up. Disastrous years inevitably follow in the wake of great armies.

Wise rulers act with decision, and nothing more. They do not venture to use overbearing measures. They are decided without self-conceit, or boasting, or pride. They are decided in spite of themselves, and without presuming on brute force.

After a man has arrived at the prime of his strength, he begins to age. This is attributable to his not possessing Tao. Those who do not possess Tao die before their time.

33. They who know others are shrewd; self-knowers are enlightened. Those who overcome others have bodily strength; self-vanquishers have determination. Those who know when they have enough are rich. Those who act with determination or perseverance have strength of will. Those who lose not what they have learnt—the Tao—retain it always. Those who, up till death, are not lost, enjoy posthumous activity.

34. The Great Tao is all-pervasive; it may be seen on the right and on the left.

All things depend upon it, and are produced; it denies itself to none.

It achieves its works of merit, but has no name or reputation. With tenderness it nourishes all things, yet claims no lordship over them.

It is ever passionless, and may be named among the smallest things.

All things submit to it, yet it claims no lordship over them; it may be called great.

Thus the Sage to the end of his life never exalts himself; and thus he is able to achieve great things.

43. The weakest things in the world subjugate the strongest.

There are no men who persevere uninterruptedly (in the culture of Tao). I know from this that in inaction there is advantage. There are few in the world who attain to teaching without words, or to the advantage that results from inaction.

44. Which is the more important—one's reputation or one's body?

Which is the more valuable—one's body or one's goods?

Which is the greatest evil—getting or losing?

Inordinate love cannot but result in utter abandonment of its object (through eventual disgust); and over-hoarding cannot but result in heavy loss.

He who knows when he has enough does not lay himself open to shame. He who knows when to stop, will not incur danger. These two contain the elements of endurance.

49. The Sage's heart is not immutable; he regards the people's heart as his own.

The virtuous I encourage, or approve; the unvirtuous I would incite to virtue. The virtue (of the Sage) makes others virtuous. The trustworthy I trust; the untrustworthy I would make trustworthy. The virtue (of the Sage) engenders trust.

When the Sage occupies the throne of the Empire, he is anxiously bent on making it all of one mind. The people all fix their ears and eyes on him; and the Sage treats them as his children.

51. What Tao produces, its Energy nourishes. The things (so produced and nourished) have form, which is determined by the nature of their surroundings; so that there is nothing in the whole world that does not reflect honour upon Tao and reverence upon its Energy.

The honour thus paid to the one, and the reverence paid to the other, is the result of no command; it is the ordinary and natural condition of things. Therefore what Tao produces, Energy nourishes. Everything is nurtured as it grows; is brought to maturity when complete; is protected while being fed.

(Tao) produces without claiming merit; it works without presuming; it causes increase without destroying. This is called Sublime Virtue.

52. In the beginning of the world there was that which became the world's Mother.

If one knows the Mother, he will likewise recognize the offspring; and to the end of his days he will incur no danger.

If one represses his lustful inclinations and closes his door, he will be in quietude all his life; but if he gives rein to voluptuousness and indulges in desires, there will never be any salvation for him.

He who can perceive things that are minute is called clear-sighted. He who husbands his weakness is called resolute, or strongminded. He who uses the light that is in him will revert to his native perspicacity. Not exposing the body to disaster implies the practice of ethical morality.

53. Given that I am possessed of all-embracing knowledge, I act in accordance with the great Tao. Only, there is danger in conferring (this privilege) on others; for the great Tao is far removed, and the common people are addicted to walking in cross-roads.

When the Imperial Court is devoid (of virtuous ministers), the fields will be entirely neglected, and the granaries entirely empty.

To dress in rich embroideries, to carry a sharp sword, to be wasteful in food and drink, and to have a super-abundance of wealth and goods; this is to be what may be called a robber-chief; this is not Tao, indeed!

62. Tao is the deep reservoir of all things. It is the jewel of the good man, the guardian of the bad.

Virtuous words are marketable; honourable deeds may be made over to the credit of others. What reason is there for casting a man off on account of his being unvirtuous?

Wherefore, though the Emperor be enthroned, and his Ministers appointed, holding their jade badges of office in front of them and riding in a chariot and four; it would be better to remain seated in quiet, and to adopt, or enter into, this Tao.

It was this Tao that the ancients reverenced. Why do not (the rulers of to-day) strive daily to acquire it? The ancients taking the national sins upon themselves, their subjects put away their depravity; and therefore they were honoured by the whole Empire.

63. (The Sage) acts as though not acting. He occupies himself as though having nothing to do. He relishes that which is insipid—the Tao.

The great, the small, the many, the few, (are all equal in his sight). He recompenses injury with kindness. In setting about difficult tasks, he begins with what is easy. In performing great things, he begins with little ones.

The difficult affairs of the world must be begun from what is easy; the great things of the world must be begun from what is small. That is why the Sage never sets about great undertakings and yet is able to accomplish great things.

Lightly made promises lead to very little faith (being placed in the promiser). He to whom most things are very easy at first will certainly find many difficulties afterwards. Thus the Sage always recognizes the existence of difficulty, and by this means he never experiences any difficulty in practice.

67. The inhabitants of the world all say that I am great, although I have the appearance of incompetence. This apparent incompetence is the result of my very greatness. In the case of one who is possessed of more than ordinary ability, he sets his mind constantly upon even the smallest matters.

Now there are three things which I regard as precious, which I grasp and prize.

The first is compassion; the second is frugality; the third is not venturing to take precedence of others—modesty.

I prize compassion; therefore I am able to be fearless. I prize frugality; therefore I am able to be liberal. I prize modesty; therefore I am able to become a leader of men. But men of the present day abandon compassion, yet aim at valiancy; they abandon frugality, yet aim at being liberal; they abandon modesty, yet aim at leadership. This is death to them.

Now when one is compassionate in battle, he will be victorious. When one is compassionate in defending, his defences will be strong. When Heaven intends to deliver men, it employs compassion to protect them.

68. Those eminent for scholarly virtues are not fighting men. Those eminent in war do not lose their temper. Those eminent for victory do not struggle. Those eminent for making use of others descend to their level.

This may be called the virtue which does not contend; the power of utilising men; the utmost limit that can be reached in equalling Heaven and the men of old.

79. When peace is made after a great quarrel, there is always a feeling of resentment left behind. How can this be regarded as right?

Wherefore the Sage, unwilling to shift responsibility upon others, keeps, on his left hand, an officer to make record (of his obligations). The virtuous man keeps a record of his compacts; the unprincipled man repudiates them.

The Tao of Heaven has no favorites; its practice is simply to reward the virtuous.

THE WRITINGS OF KWANG–TZE

THIS document appeared sometime between the middle of the fourth and third centuries B.C., a work attributed to one of the most outstanding followers of Lao-tze, Kwang-tze. This writer was a native of the duchy of Sung, being born in what was then called the district of Mang, a section of the state or kingdom of Liang. He held an official post in his city but devoted most of his time to religious duties.

The work is divided into 33 books separated into three parts: the *Nei* or "Inner", the *Wai* or "Outer", and the *Ta* or "Miscellaneous". The first part is made up of 7 books, the second of 15, and the last of 11. The "Inner" is concerned with the "more important" doctrines or the esoteric teachings of the saint. The second part is supplementary and is often referred to as the "wings" of the first seven books. The remaining eleven books are also supplementary and of less importance than the others.

1,3: Thus it is that men, whose wisdom is sufficient for the duties of some one office, or whose conduct will secure harmony in some one district, or whose virtue is befitting a ruler so that they could efficiently govern some one state, are sure to look on themselves in this manner (like the quail), and yet Yung-tze of Sung would have smiled and laughed at them. (This Yung-tze), though the whole world should have praised him, would not for that have stimulated himself to greater endeavour, and though the whole world should have condemned him, would not have exercised any more repression of his course; so fixed was he in the difference between the internal (judgment of himself) and the external (judgment of others), so distinctly had he marked out the bounding limit of glory and disgrace. His place in the world indeed had become indifferent to him, but still he had not planted himself firmly (in the right position).

There was Lieh-tze, who rode on the wind and pursued his way, with admirable indifference (to all external things), returning, however, after fifteen days (to his place). In regard to the things that (are supposed to) contribute to happiness, he was free from all endeavours to obtain them; but though he had not to walk, there was still something for which he had to wait. But suppose one who mounts on (the ether of) heaven and earth in its normal operation, and drives along the six elemental energies of the changing (seasons), thus enjoying himself in the illimitable,—what has he to wait for? Therefore it is said, "The Perfect man has no (thought of) self; the Spirit-like man, none of merit; the Sagely-minded man, none of fame."

2,7: The Great Tao does not admit of being praised. The Great Argument does not require words. Great Benevolence is not (officiously) benevolent. Great Disinterestedness does not vaunt its humility. Great Courage is not seen in stubborn bravery.

3,1: There is a limit to our life; but to knowledge there is no limit. With what is limited to pursue after what is unlimited is a perilous thing; and when, knowing this, we still seek the increase of our knowledge, the peril cannot be averted. There should not be the practice of what is good with any thought of the fame (which it will bring), nor of what is evil with any approximation to the punishment (which it will incur) :—an accordance with the Central Element (of our nature) is the regular way to preserve the body, to maintain the life, to nourish our parents, and to complete our term of years.

4,2: Not to move a step is easy; to walk without treading on the ground is difficult. In acting after the manner of men, it is easy to fall into hypocrisy; in acting after the manner of Heaven, it is difficult to play the hypocrite. I have heard of flying with wings; I have not heard of flying without them. I have heard of the knowledge of the wise; I have not heard of the knowledge of the unwise.

5,3: In Lu there was a cripple, called Shu-shan the Toeless, who came on his heels to see Kung-ni. Kung-ni said to him, "By your want of circumspection in the past, Sir, you have incurred such a calamity;—of what use is your coming to me now?" Toeless said, "Through my ignorance of my proper business and taking too little care of my body, I came to lose my feet. But now I am come to you, still possessing what is more honourable than my feet, and which therefore I am anxious to preserve entire. There is nothing which Heaven does not cover, and nothing which Earth does not sustain; you, Master, were regarded by me as doing the part of Heaven and Earth;—how could I know that you would receive me in such a way?" Confucius rejoined, "I am but a poor creature. But why, my master, do you not come inside, where

I will try to tell you what I have learned?" When Toeless had gone out, Confucius said, "Be stimulated to effort, my disciples. This toeless cripple is still anxious to learn to make up for the evil of his former conduct;—how much more should those be so whose conduct has been unchallenged!"

5,5: The sagely man . . . has the bodily form of man, but not the passions and desires of (other) men. He has the form of man, and therefore he is a man. Being without the passions and desires of men, their approvings and disapprovings are not to be found in him. How insignificant and small is (the body) by which he belongs to humanity! How grand and great is he in the unique perfection of his Heavenly (nature)!

Hui-tze said to Kwang-tze, "Can a man indeed be without desires and passions?" The reply was, "He can." "But on what grounds do you call him a man, who is thus without passions and desires?" Kwang-tze said, "The Tao gives him his personal appearance (and powers); Heaven gives him his bodily form; how should we not call him a man?" . . .

11,7: Therefore the sages contemplated Heaven, but did not assist it. They tried to perfect their virtue, but did not allow it to embarrass them. They proceeded according to the Tao, but did not lay any plans. They associated benevolence (with all their doings), but did not rely on it. They pursued righteousness extensively, but did not try to accumulate it. They responded to ceremonies, but did not conceal (their opinion as to the troublesomeness of them). They engaged in affairs as they occurred, and did not decline them. They strove to render their laws uniform, but (feared that confusion) might arise from them. They relied upon the people, and did not set light by them. They depended on things as their instruments, and did not discard them.

They did not think things equal to what they employed them for, but yet they did not see that they could do without employing them. Those who do not understand Heaven are not pure in their virtue. Those who do not comprehend the Tao have no course which they can pursue successfully. Alas for them who do not clearly understand the Tao!

12,2: The Master said, "It is the Tao that overspreads and sustains all things. How great It is in Its overflowing influence! The Superior man ought by all means to remove from his mind (all that is contrary to It). Acting without action is what is called Heaven(-like). Speech coming forth of itself is what is called (a mark of) the (true) Virtue. Loving men and benefiting things is what is called Benevolence. Seeing wherein things that are different yet agree is what is called being Great. Conduct free from the ambition of being distinguished above others is what is called being Generous. The possession in himself of a myriad points of difference is what is called being Rich. Therefore to hold fast the natural attributes is what is called the Guiding Line (of government); the perfecting of those attributes is what is called its Establishment; accordance with the Tao is what is called being Complete; and not allowing anything external to affect the will is what is called being Perfect.

13,2: . . . The clear understanding of the virtue of Heaven and Earth is what is called "The Great Root," and "The Great Origin";—they who have it are in harmony with Heaven, and so they produce all equable arrangements in the world;—they are those who are in harmony with men. Being in harmony with men is called the Joy of men; being in harmony with Heaven is called the Joy of Heaven.

14,5: "Those who think that wealth is the proper thing for them cannot give up their revenues; those who seek distinction cannot give up the thought of fame; those who cleave to power cannot give the handle of it to others. While they hold their grasp of those things, they are afraid (of losing them). When they let them go, they are grieved; and they will not look at a single example, from which they might perceive the (folly) of their restless pursuits:—such men are under the doom of Heaven."

15,1: Ingrained ideas and a high estimate of their own conduct; leaving the world, and pursuing uncommon ways; talking loftily and in resentful disparagement of others;—all this is simply symptomatic of arrogance. This is what scholars who betake themselves to the hills and valleys, who are always blaming the world, and who stand aloof like withered trees, or throw themselves into deep pools, are fond of.

Discoursing of benevolence, righteousness, loyalty, and good faith; being humble and frugal, self-forgetful and courteous;—all this is simply symptomatic of (self-)cultivation. This is what scholars who wish to tranquillise the world, teachers and instructors, men who pursue their studies at home and abroad, are fond of.

15,3: . . . Hence it is said (once again), "To be guileless and pure, and free from all admixture; to be still and uniform, without undergoing any change; to be indifferent and do nothing; to move and yet to act like Heaven:—this is the way to nourish the spirit. Now he who possesses a sword made at Kan-yue preserves it carefully in a box, and does not dare to use it;—it is considered the perfection of valuable swords. But the human spirit goes forth in all directions, flowing on without limit, reaching to heaven above, and wreathing round the earth beneath. It transforms and nourishes all things, and cannot be represented by any form. Its name is 'the Divinity (in man).' It is only the path of pure simplicity which guards and preserves the Spirit. When this path is preserved and not lost, it becomes one with the Spirit; and in this ethereal amalgamation, it acts in harmony with the orderly operation of Heaven."

16,1: Those who would correct their nature by means of the vulgar learning, seeking to restore it to its original condition, and those who would regulate their desires, by the vulgar ways of thinking, seeking thereby to carry their intelligence to perfection, must be pronounced to be deluded and ignorant people. The ancients who regulated the Tao nourished their faculty of knowledge by their placidity, and all through life abstained from employing that faculty in action;—they must be pronounced to have (thus also) nourished their placidity by their knowledge.

When the faculty of knowledge and the placidity (thus) blend together, and they nourish each other, then from the nature there comes forth harmony and orderly method. The attributes (of the Tao) constitute the harmony; the Tao (itself) secures the orderly method. When the attributes appear in a universal practice of forbearance, we have Benevolence; when the path is all marked by orderly method, we have Righteousness; when the righteousness is clearly manifested, and (all) things are regarded with affection, we have Leal-heartedness; when the (heart's) core is thus (pure) and real, and carried back to its (proper) qualities, we have Music; when this sincerity appears in all the range of the capacity, and its demonstrations are in accordance with what is elegant, we have Ceremony. If Ceremonies and Music are carried out in an imperfect and one-sided manner, the world is thrown into confusion. When men would rectify others, and their own virtue is beclouded, it is not sufficient to extend itself to them. If an attempt be made so to extend it, they also will lose their (proper) nature.

IV

CONFUCIANISM

TODAY there are more than 250,000,000 adherents of Confucianism, the official religion of China. However, Confucius never thought of his work as that of a founder of a religion but rather as that of a social and administrative reformer.

China had been religious long before Confucius. In fact, from its earliest days, about 2356 B.C., China has had an official religion. During the latter part of the sixth century B.C., however, the government was falling into decay and the moral life of the people was not good. It was at that time that the young Confucius became famous as a teacher. This success was followed by success in political office and then as an itinerant preacher. As a result of his works and life, the religion of China, which had existed for centuries unnamed, became known as Confucianism.

Confucius lived between 551 and 478 B.C. in the province of Shantung, China, an area which has since been regarded as the Chinese Holy Land. The youngest of eleven children, Confucius had to work hard during his youth because of the early death of his father. He married at 19 and had one son and several daughters. Between 21 and 51 he was a successful teacher and a generous helper of the poor so that locally he became a famous figure. This led to several official appointments, the highest of which was Chief Justice of his state. After 55 he devoted himself largely to preaching and reform of the moral and religious life of the people. In later years he compiled "The Classics", writing little himself. He died at 72, feeling that his life had not been a success.

But his work, and his great ability to win loyal disciples, resulted in his becoming the "founder" of Confucianism, although this was the last thing of which he dreamed.

Gradually the Chinese people developed a system of worship, a theology, and a body of doctrines centered about the belief in the divinity of Confucius. Today popular Confucianism is a religion in every sense of the term. Temples for worship are to be found in all parts of China and Confucius is venerated along with founders of other religions.

The sacred scriptures of Confucianism are divided into two groups. The first group, "The Classics", was compiled by Confucius out of the sacred lore of the ancient Chinese religion. There are six books in this group, as follows:

1. The *Shu King* or *Book of History,*
2. The *Shih King* or *Book of Poetry,*
3. The *I King* or *Book of Changes,*
4. The *Li Ki* or *Book of Rites,*
5. The *Ch'un Ch'iu* or *Spring and Autumn Annals,*
6. The *Hsiao King* or *Book of Filial Piety.*

Of these, the first two are most important and most interesting to the average reader.

The second group of Confucian scriptures is "The Four Books", as follows:

1. The *Ta Hsio* or *Great Learning,* a book of teachings concerning virtue,
2. The *Chung Yung* or *Doctrine of the Mean,*
3. The *Lun Yu* or the *Analects,*
4. The *Meng-tze* or *Book of Mencius.*

The best known and most often read is the *Lun Yu,* commonly called *The Analects of Confucius.* This book contains a group of sayings supposedly by Confucius.

Although these writings are not claimed to be inspired in any supernatural way, they have actually exerted great influence upon the Chinese character. In them we find much that reminds us of Christianity as well as of other great religions.

THE SHU KING

THE *Shu King* (*Book of History*) is the oldest of the Chinese classical books known to man. It is concerned with the history of China and contains historical documents relating to the period from 2357 to 627 B.C., and bears the subtitle *Book of History*. Although some late scholars gave the impression that this book was written by Confucius, it is most definitely known now that the book existed before his time. Originally it consisted of approximately 100 books, but some of these were lost before the time of Confucius and others have been lost since. The *Shu* was very early accepted as one of the sacred books of Confucianism and holds a high place in the religion today.

2,1,5: The Ti said, "Khwei, I appoint you to be Director of Music, and to teach our sons, so that the straightforward shall yet be mild; the gentle, dignified; the strong, not tyrannical; and the impetuous, not arrogant. Poetry is the expression of earnest thought; singing is the prolonged utterance of that expression; the notes accompany that utterance, and they are harmonized themselves by the standard-tubes. . . ."

2,2,1: Yu said, "Accordance with the right leads to good fortune; following what is opposed to it, to bad;—the shadow and the echo." Yi said, "Alas! be cautious! Admonish yourself to caution, when there seems to be no occasion for anxiety. Do not fail to observe the laws and ordinances. Do not find your enjoyment in idleness. Do not go to excess in pleasure. In your employment of men of worth, let none come between you and them. Put away evil without hesitation. Do not carry out plans, of (the wisdom of) which you have doubts. Study that all your purposes may be with the light of reason. Do not go against what is right, to get the praise of the people. Do not oppose the people's (wishes), to follow your own desires. (Attend to these things) without idleness or omission, and the barbarous tribes all around will come and acknowledge your sovereignty."

2,2,2: The Ti said, "Kao-yao, that of these my ministers and all (my people) hardly one is found to offend against the regulations of the government is owing to your being Minister of Crime, and intelligent in the use of the five punishments, thereby assisting (the inculcation of) the five cardinal duties, with a view to the perfection of my government, and that through punishment there may come to be no punishment, but the people accord with (the path of) the Mean. (Continue to) be strenuous." Kao-yao replied, "Your virtue, O Ti, is faultless. You condescend to your ministers with a kindly ease; you preside over the multitudes with generous forbearance. Punishments do not extend to (the criminal's) heirs, while rewards reach to (succeeding) generations. You pardon inadvertent faults, however great, and punish purposed crimes, however small. In case of doubtful crimes, you deal with them lightly; in case of doubtful merit, you prefer the high estimation. Rather than put an innocent person to death, you will run the risk of irregularity and error. This life-loving virtue has penetrated the minds of the people, and this is why they do not render themselves liable to be punished by your officers." The Ti said, "That I am able to follow and obtain what I desire in my government, the people responding everywhere as if moved by the wind,—this is your excellence."

2,2,3: At the end of three decades, the people of Miao continued rebellious against the commands (issued to them), when Yi came to the help of Yu, saying, "It is virtue that moves Heaven; there is no distance to which it does not reach. Pride brings loss, and humility receives increase;—this is the way of heaven. In the early times of the Ti, when he was living by mount Li, he went into the fields, and daily cried with tears to compassionate Heaven, and to his parents, taking to himself all guilt, and charging himself with (their) wickedness. (At the same time) with respectful service he appeared before Ku-sau, looking grave and awe-struck, till Ku also became transformed by his example. Entire sincerity moves spiritual beings,—how much more will it move this lord of Miao!" Yu did homage to the excellent words, and said, "Yes." (Thereupon) he led back his army, having drawn off the troops. The Ti set about diffusing on a grand scale the virtuous influences of peace;—with shields and feathers they danced between the two staircases (in his courtyard). In seventy days, the lord of Miao came (and made his submission).

2,4,1: Yu said, "So far good! But let your light shine, O Ti, all under heaven, even to every grassy corner of the sea-shore, and throughout the myriad regions the most worthy of the people will all (wish) to be your ministers. Then, O Ti, you may advance them to office . . ."

4,2,3: " . . . Our king did not approach to (dissolute) music and women; he did not seek to accumulate property and wealth. To great virtue he gave great offices, and to great merit great reward. He employed others as if (their excellences) were his own; he was not slow to change his errors. Rightly indulgent and rightly benevolent, from the display (of such virtue), confidence was reposed in him by the millions of the people."

4,2,4: " . . . I have heard the saying, 'He who finds instructors for himself, comes to the supreme dominion; he who says that others are not equal to himself, comes to ruin. He who likes to put questions, becomes enlarged; he who uses only his own views, becomes smaller (than he was).' Oh! he who would take care for the end must be attentive to the beginning. There is establishment for the observers of propriety, and overthrow for the blinded and wantonly indifferent. To revere and honour the path prescribed by Heaven is the way ever to preserve the favouring appointment of Heaven."

4,3,2: The king said, "Ah! ye multitudes of the myriad regions, listen clearly to the announcement of me, the One man. The great God has conferred (even) on the inferior people a moral sense, compliance with which would show their nature invariably right. To make them tranquilly pursue the course which it would indicate is the work of the sovereign.

. . . Then I sought for the great Sage, with whom I might unite my strength, to request the favour (of Heaven) for you, my multitudes. High Heaven truly showed its favour to the inferior people, and the criminal has been degraded and subjected. What Heaven appoints is without error;—brilliantly (now), like the blossoming of plants and trees, the millions of the people show a true reviving."

4,3,3: "It is given to me, the One man, to secure the harmony and tranquillity of your states and clans; and now I know not whether I may not offend against (the Powers) above and below. I am fearful and trembling, as if I were in danger of falling into a deep abyss. Throughout all the regions that enter on a new life under me, do not, (ye princes), follow lawless ways; make no approach to insolence and dissoluteness; let everyone be careful to keep his statutes;—that so we may receive the favour of Heaven. The good in you I will not dare to keep concealed; and for the evil in me I will not dare to forgive myself. I will examine these things in harmony with the mind of God. When guilt is found anywhere in you who occupy the myriad regions, let it rest on me, the One man. When guilt is found in me, the One man, it shall not attach to you who occupy the myriad regions.

"Oh! let us attain to be sincere in these things, and so we shall likewise have a (happy) consummation."

4,4,2: " . . . Our king of Shang brilliantly displayed his sagely prowess; for oppression he substituted his generous gentleness; and the millions of the people gave him their hearts. Now your Majesty is entering on the inheritance of his virtue;—all depends on (how) you commence your reign. To set up love, it is for you to love (your relations); to set up respect, it is for you to respect (your elders). The commencement is in the family and the state; the consummation is in (all within) the four seas."

4,6,2: " . . . Where (the sovereign's) virtue is pure, his enterprises are all fortunate; where his virtue is wavering and uncertain, his enterprises are all unfortunate. Good and evil do not wrongly befall men, but Heaven sends down misery or happiness according to their conduct."

4,8,2,1: "For all affairs let there be adequate preparation;—with preparation there will be no calamitous issue. Do not open the door for favorites, from whom you will receive contempt. Do not be ashamed of mistakes, and (go on to) make them crimes. Let your mind rest in its proper objects, and the affairs of your government will be pure. Officiousness in sacrificing is called irreverence; and multiplying ceremonies leads to disorder. To serve the spirits acceptably (in this way) is difficult."

5,1,1: "Heaven, for the help of the inferior people, made for them rulers, and made for them instructors, that they might be able to be aiding to God, and secure the tranquillity of the four quarters (of the kingdom). In regard to who are criminals and who are not, how dare I give any allowance to my own wishes?"

5,1,2: "Heaven loves the people, and the sovereign should reverently carry out (this mind of) Heaven. Kieh, the sovereign of Hsia, would not follow the example of Heaven, but sent forth his poisonous injuries through the states of the kingdom:— Heaven therefore gave its aid to Thang the Successful, and charged him to make an end of the appointment of Hsia. . . ."

5,1,3: The time was on the morrow, when the king went round his six hosts in state, and made a clear declaration to all his officers. He said, "O! my valiant men of the west, from Heaven are the illustrious courses of duty, of which the (several) requirements are quite plain. And now Shau, the king of Shang, treats with contemptuous slight the five regular (virtues), and abandons himself to wild idleness and irreverence. He has cut himself off from Heaven, and brought enmity between himself and the people."

" . . . (It is said again), 'In planting (a man's) virtue, strive to make it great; in putting away (a man's) wickedness, strive to do it from the roots.' . . ."

5,4,1: In the thirteenth year, the king went to enquire of the count of Khi, and said to him, "Oh! count of Khi, Heaven, (working) unseen, secures the tranquillity of the lower people, aiding them to be in harmony with their condition. I do not know how the unvarying principles (of its method in doing so) should be set forth in due order."

5,4,3,5: "Among all the multitudes of the people there will be those who have ability to plan and to act, and who keep themselves (from evil) : —do you keep such in mind; and there will be those who, not coming up to the highest point of excellence, yet do not involve themselves in evil: let the sovereign receive such. And when a placid satisfaction appears in their countenances, and they say, 'Our love is fixed on virtue,' do you then confer favours on them;—those men will in this way advance to the perfection of the sovereign. Do not let him oppress the friendless and childless, nor let him fear the high and distinguished. When men (in office) have ability and administrative power, let them be made still more to cultivate their conduct; and the prosperity of the country will be promoted. . . ."

5,5,2: "Oh! early and late never be but earnest. If you do not attend jealously to your small actions, the result will be to affect your virtue in great matters; in raising a mound of nine fathoms, the work may be unfinished

for want of one basket (of earth). If you really pursue this course (which I indicate), the people will preserve their possessions, and the throne will descend from generation to generation."

5,9,2: The king says, "Oh! Fang, the little one, be respectfully careful, as if you were suffering from a disease. Awful though Heaven be, it yet helps the sincere. The feelings of the people can for the most part be discerned; but it is difficult to preserve (the attachment of) the lower classes. Where you go, employ all your heart. Do not seek repose, nor be fond of ease and pleasure. I have read the saying,— 'Dissatisfaction is caused not so much by great things, or by small things, as by (a ruler's) observance of principle or the reverse, and by his energy of conduct or the reverse.' Yes, it is yours, O little one,—it is your business to enlarge the royal (influence), and to protect the people of Yin in harmony with their feelings. Thus also shall you assist the king, consolidating the appointment of Heaven, and renovating the people."

5,9,4: The king said, "Oh! Fang, be reverent! Do not what will cause murmurings; and do not use bad counsels and uncommon ways. With the determination of sincerity, give yourself to imitate the active virtue (of the ancients). Hereby give repose to your mind, examine your virtue, send far forward your plans; and thus by your generous forbearance you will make the people repose in what is good, and I shall not have to blame you or cast you off."

5,10,1: "King Wan admonished and instructed the young nobles, who were charged with office or in any employment, that they should not ordinarily use spirits; and throughout all the states, he required that such should drink spirits only on occasion of sacrifices, and that then virtue should preside so that there might be no drunkenness."

5,10,2: " . . . and above all, do you strictly keep yourself from drink."

5,12,2: "Oh! it is as on the birth of a son, when all depends on (the training of) his early life, through which he may secure his wisdom in the future, as if it were decreed to him. Now Heaven may have decreed wisdom (to the king); it may have decreed good fortune or bad; it may have decreed a (long) course of years; —we only know that now is with him the commencement of his duties. Dwelling in this new city, let the king now sedulously cultivate the virtue of reverence. When he is all devoted to this virtue, he may pray to Heaven for a long-abiding decree in his favour."

5,14,2: "I have heard the saying, 'God leads men to tranquil security,' but the sovereign of Hsia would not move to such security, whereupon God sent down corrections, indicating his mind to him . . ."

5,15,1: The duke of Kau said, "Oh! the superior man rests in this,— that he will indulge in no luxurious ease. He first understands how the painful toil of sowing and reaping conducts to ease, and thus he understands how the lower people depend on this toil (for their support). I have observed among the lower people, that where the parents have diligently laboured in sowing and reaping, their sons (often) do not understand this painful toil, but abandon themselves to ease, and to village slang, and become quite disorderly. Or where they do not do so, they (still) throw contempt on their parents, saying, 'Those old people have heard nothing and know nothing.' "

5,15,2: " . . . The kings that arose after these, from their birth enjoyed ease. Enjoying ease from their birth, they did not know the painful toil of sowing and reaping, and had not heard of the hard labours of the lower people. They sought for nothing but excessive pleasure; and so not one of them had long life. They (reigned) for ten years, for seven or eight, for five or six, or perhaps (only) for three or four."

5,17,2: "The king speaks to this effect:—' . . . Great Heaven has no partial affections; it helps only the virtuous. The people's hearts have no unchanging attachment;—they cherish only the kind. Acts of goodness are different, but they contribute in common to good order. Acts of evil are different, but they contribute in common to disorder. Be cautious!

'In giving heed to the beginning think of the end;—the end will then be without distress. If you do not think of the end, it will be full of distress, even of the greatest.

'Exert yourself to achieve your proper merit. Seek to be in harmony with all your neighbours. Be a fence to the royal House. Live in amity with your brethren. Tranquillize and help the lower people.

'Follow the course of the Mean, and do not by aiming to be intelligent throw old statutes into confusion. Watch over what you see and hear, and do not for one-sided words deviate from the right rule. Then I, the One man, will praise you.' "

5,18,2: " 'The wise, through not thinking, become foolish, and the foolish, by thinking, become wise. Heaven for five years waited kindly, and forbore with the descendant (of Thang), to see if he would indeed prove himself the ruler of the people; but there was nothing in him deserving to be regarded. . . .' "

5,20,4: The king said, "Oh! all ye men of virtue, my occupiers of office, pay reverent attention to your charges. Be careful in the commands you issue; for, once issued, they must be carried into effect, and cannot be retracted. Extinguish all selfish aims by your public feeling, and the people will have confidence in you, and be gladly obedient. Study antiquity as a preparation for entering on your offices. . . ."

5,21,13: "Do not cherish anger against the obstinate, and dislike them. Seek not every quality in one individual. You must have patience, and you will be successful; have forbearance, and your virtue will be great. Mark those who discharge their duties well, and also mark those who do not do so, (and distinguish them from one another). Advance the good, to induce those who may not be so to follow (their example)."

5,26. "Now I appoint you to be High Chamberlain, to see that all the officers in your department and my personal attendants are upright and correct, that they strive to promote the virtue of their sovereign, and together supply my deficiencies. Be careful in selecting your officers. Do not employ men of artful speech and insinuating looks, men whose likes and dislikes are ruled by mine, one-sided men and flatterers; but employ good men. When these household officers are correct, the sovereign will be correct; when they are flatterers, the sovereign will consider himself a sage. His virtue or his want of it equally depends on them. Cultivate no intimacy with flatterers, nor get them to do duty for me as my ears and eyes;—they will lead their sovereign to disregard the statutes of the former kings. If you choose the men not for their personal goodness, but for the sake of their bribes, their offices will be made of no effect, your great want of reverence for your sovereign will be apparent, and I will hold you guilty."

5,27,5: "When there are doubts as to the infliction of any of the five punishments, that infliction should be forborne. When there are doubts as to the infliction of any of the five fines, it should be forborne. Do you carefully examine, and prove yourselves equal to overcome (every difficulty). When you have examined and many things are clear, yet form a judgment from studying the appearance of the parties. If you find nothing out on examination, do not listen (to the case any more). In everything stand in awe of the dread majesty of Heaven."

THE SHIH KING

THE *Shih King (Book of Poetry)* is the second oldest of the Chinese classical books. This work contains 305 poems, and there are extant the titles of six others which have been lost. The poems probably date from 1766 to 586 B.C. It is believed that possibly some of the earliest verses may date as far back as the nineteenth century B.C. Although only a few of these poems are strictly religious, the book as a whole has been included within the sacred books of Confucianism, somewhat as *The Song of Solomon* was included in The Old Testament in the Bible. Some of the poems are ballads, some are songs, hymns, while still others have no English equivalent. For lack of a better name, they are referred to as "odes," meaning lyric poems that were set to music.

The entire collection is divided into four parts, as follows:

Part 1, *The Kwo Fang,* 15 books and 160 pieces;

Part 2, *The Hsiao Ya,* 8 books and 74 pieces plus the titles of six others;

Part 3, *The Ta Ya,* 3 books and 31 pieces;

Part 4, *The Sung,* 3 books and 40 pieces.

I. Odes of the Temple and the Altar

1. THE SACRIFICIAL ODES OF SHANG

ODE 1. THE NA.

How admirable! how admirable!
Here are set our hand-drums and drums.
The drums resound harmonious and loud,
To delight our meritorious ancestors.

The descendant of Thang invites him with this music,
That he may soothe us with the realization of our thoughts.
Deep is the sound of our hand-drums and drums;
Shrilly sound the flutes;
All harmonious and blending together,

According to the notes of the sonorous gem.
Oh! majestic is the descendant of Thang;
Very admirable is his music.

The large bells and drums fill the ear;
The various dances are grandly performed.
We have the admirable visitors,
Who are pleased and delighted.

From of old, before our time,
The former men set us the example;—
How to be mild and humble from morning to night,
And to be reverent in discharging the service.
May he regard our sacrifices of winter and autumn,
(Thus) offered by the descendant of Thang!

2. The Sacrificial Odes of Kau

(The First Decade, or that of Khing Miao.)

ODE 1. THE KHING MIAO.

Oh! solemn is the ancestral temple in
its pure stillness.
Reverent and harmonious were the
distinguished assistants;
Great was the number of the of-
ficers:—
(All) assiduous followers of the virtue
of (king Wan).
In response to him in heaven,
Grandly they hurried about in the
temple.
Distinguished is he and honoured,
And will never be wearied of among
men.

ODE 7. THE WO KIANG

I have brought my offerings,
A ram and a bull.
May Heaven accept them!

I imitate and follow and observe the
statutes of king Wan,
Seeking daily to secure the tranquillity
of the kingdom.
King Wan, the Blesser, has descended
on the right, and accepted (the
offerings).
Do I not, night and day,
Revere the majesty of Heaven,
Thus to preserve (its favour)?

(The Second Decade, or that of Khan Kung.)

ODE 3. THE KAU LU.

A flock of egrets is flying,
About the marsh there in the west.
My visitors came,
With an (elegant) carriage like those
birds.

There, (in their states), not disliked,
Here, (in Kau), never tired of;—

They are sure, day and night,
To perpetuate their fame.

(The Third Decade, or that of Min Yu Hsiao Tsze.)

ODE 1. THE MIN YU.

Alas for me, who am a little child,
On whom has devolved the unsettled
state!
Solitary am I and full of distress.
Oh! my great Father,
All my life long, thou wast filial.

Thou didst think of my great grandfather,
(Seeing him, as it were) ascending
and descending in the court,
I, the little child,

Day and night will be as reverent.
Oh! ye great kings,
As your successor,
I will strive not to forget you.

ODE 3. THE KING KIH.

Let me be reverent!
Let me be reverent!
(The way of) Heaven is evident,
And its appointment is not easily pre-
served.
Let me not say that it is high aloft
above me.
It ascends and descends about our
doings;
It daily inspects us wherever we are.

I am a little child,
Without intelligence to be reverently
(attentive to my duties);
But by daily progress and monthly
advance,
I will learn to hold fast the gleams (of
knowledge), till I arrive at bright
intelligence.
Assist me to bear the burden (of my
position),
And show me how to display a virtuous conduct.

II. The Minor Odes of the Kingdom

(First Decade, or that of Lu-ming.)

ODE 9, STANZA 4. THE TI TU.

They have not packed up, they do not come.
My sorrowing heart is greatly distressed.
The time is past, and he is not here,
To the multiplication of my sorrows.
Both by the tortoise-shell and the reeds have I divined,
And they unite in saying he is near.
My warrior is at hand.

(Fourth Decade, or that of Khi fu.)

ODE 6, STANZA 4. THE WU YANG.

Your herdsmen shall dream,
Of multitudes and then of fishes,
Of the tortoise-and-serpent, and then of the falcon, banners.
The chief diviner will divine the dreams;—
How the multitudes, dissolving into fishes,
Betoken plentiful years;
How the tortoise-and-serpent, dissolving into the falcon, banners,
Betoken the increasing population of the kingdom.

(Eighth Decade, or that of Po Hwa.)

ODE 5, STANZAS 1 AND 2. THE PO HWA.

The fibres from the white-flowered rush
Are bound with the white grass.
This man's sending me away makes me dwell solitary.

The light and brilliant clouds
Bedew the rush and the grass.
The way of Heaven is hard and difficult;—
This man does not conform (to good principle).

III. The Major Odes of the Kingdom

(Second Decade, or that of Shang Min.)

ODE 5, STANZA 1. THE KIA LO.

Of our admirable, amiable sovereign
Most illustrious is the excellent virtue.
He orders rightly the people, orders rightly the officers,
And receives high dignity from Heaven,
Which protects and helps him, and (confirms) his appointment,
By repeated acts of renewal from Heaven.

ODE 10. THE PAN.

God has reversed (his usual course of procedure),
And the lower people are full of distress.
The words which you utter are not right;
The plans which you form are not far-reaching.
As there are not sages, you think you have no guidance;—
You have no real sincerity.
(Thus) your plans do not reach far,
And I therefore strongly admonish you.

Heaven is now sending down calamities;—
Do not be so complacent.
Heaven is now producing such movements;—
Do not be so indifferent.
If your words were harmonious,
The people would become united.
If your words were gentle and kind,
The people would be settled.

Though my duties are different from yours,
I am your fellow-servant.
I come to advise with you,

And you hear me with contemptuous indifference.
My words are about the (present urgent) affairs;—
Do not think them matter for laughter.
The ancients had a saying:—
"Consult the gatherers of grass and firewood."

. . . .

Good men are a fence;
The multitudes of the people are a wall;
Great states are screens;
Great families are buttresses;
The cherishing of virtue secures repose;
The circle of (the king's) relatives is a fortified wall.
We must not let the fortified wall get destroyed;
We must not let (the king) be solitary and consumed with terrors.

Revere the anger of Heaven,
And presume not to make sport or be idle.
Revere the changing moods of Heaven,
And presume not to drive about (at your pleasure).
Great Heaven is intelligent,
And is with you in all your goings.
Great Heaven is clear-seeing,
And is with you in your wanderings and indulgences.

IV. Lessons From the States

BOOK 2, ODE 2, THE ZHAI FAN.

She gathers the white southernwood,
By the ponds, on the islets.
She employs it,
In the business of our prince.

She gathers the white southernwood,
Along the streams in the valleys.
She employs it,
In the temple of our prince.

With head-dress reverently rising aloft,
Early, while yet it is night, she is in the prince's (temple).
In her head-dress, slowly retiring,
She returns (to her own apartment).

BOOK 10. ODE 11. THE KO SHANG.

The dolichos grows, covering the thorn trees;
The convolvulus spreads all over the waste.
The man of my admiration is no more here;—
With whom can I dwell?
I abide alone.

The dolichos grows, covering the jujube trees;
The convolvulus spreads all over the tombs.
The man of my admiration is no more here;—
With whom can I dwell?
I rest alone.

How beautiful was the pillow of horn!
How splendid was the embroidered coverlet!
The man of my admiration is no more here;—
With whom can I dwell?
Alone (I wait for) the morning.
Through the (long) days of summer,
Through the (long) nights of winter (shall I be alone),
Till the lapse of a hundred years,
When I shall go home to his abode.
Through the (long) nights of winter,
Through the (long) days of summer (shall I be alone),
Till the lapse of a hundred years,
When I shall go home to his chamber.

THE LUN YU

The *Lun Yu,* more commonly called *The Analects of Confucius,* is a collection of "conversations" or "discourses." In it Confucius, referred to as "The Master," replies to questions put to him on moral and personal matters by various disciples. These "sayings" were not written down when spoken, but were passed from disciple to disciple for possibly 50 years after the Master's death. Then they were gathered together and written down for preservation.

These sayings, in very much the same form as they appear in the written work, are to be found in many places throughout the lands inhabited by followers of Confucius so that scholars are led to believe that here is a fairly accurate expression of the thinking of the Master.

There is no order of arrangement, but the sayings are scattered throughout the book without reason or plan. The essence of the entire book, however, may be summed up in two phrases: duty to oneself and charity to one's neighbor.

1,2,2: "The superior man bends his attention to what is radical. That being established, all practical courses naturally grow up. Filial piety and fraternal submission!—are they not the root of all benevolent actions?"

1,5: The Master said, "To rule a country of a thousand chariots, there must be reverent attention to business, and sincerity; economy in expenditure, and love for men; and the employment of the people at the proper seasons."

1,6: The Master said, "A youth, when at home, should be filial, and, abroad, respectful to his elders. He should be earnest and truthful. He should overflow in love to all, and cultivate the friendship of the good. When he has time and opportunity, after the performance of these things, he should employ them in polite studies."

1,8,1–4: The Master said, "If the scholar be not grave, he will not call forth any veneration, and his learning will not be solid.

"Hold faithfulness and sincerity as first principles.

"Have no friends not equal to yourself.

"When you have faults, do not fear to abandon them."

1,13: The philosopher Yu said, "When agreements are made according to what is right, what is spoken can be made good. When respect is shown according to what is proper, one keeps far from shame and disgrace. When the parties upon whom a man leans are proper persons to be intimate with, he can make them his guides and masters."

1,14: The Master said, "He who aims to be a man of complete virtue in his food does not seek to gratify his appetite, nor in his dwelling place does he seek the appliances of ease; he is earnest in what he is doing, and careful in his speech; he frequents the company of men of principle that he may be rectified:—such a person may be said indeed to love to learn."

2,2: The Master said, "In the Book of Poetry are three hundred pieces, but the design of them all may be embraced in one sentence—'Having no depraved thoughts!' "

2,3,1–2: The Master said, "If the people be led by laws, and uniformity sought to be given them by punishments, they will try to avoid the punishment, but have no sense of shame.

"If they be led by virtue, and uniformity sought to be given them by the rules of propriety, they will have the sense of shame, and moreover will become good."

2,14: The Master said, "The superior man is catholic and no partisan. The mean man is a partisan and not catholic."

2,22: The Master said, "I do not know how a man without truthfulness is to get on. How can a large carriage be made to go without the crossbar for yoking the oxen to, or a small carriage without the arrangement for yoking the horses?"

2,24,1–2: The Master said, "For a man to sacrifice to a spirit which does not belong to him is flattery.

"To see what is right and not to do it is want of courage."

4,11: The Master said, "The superior man thinks of virtue; the small man thinks of comfort. The superior man thinks of the sanctions of law; the small man thinks of favors *which he may* receive."

4,12: The Master said, "He who acts with a constant view to his own advantage will be much murmured against."

4,15,1–2: The Master said, "Shan, my doctrine is that of an all-pervading unity." The disciple Tsang replied, "Yes."

The Master went out, and the *other* disciples asked, saying, "What do his words mean?" Tsang said, "The doctrine of our master is to be true to the principles of our nature and the benevolent exercise of them to others, —this and nothing more."

4,16: The Master said, "The mind of the superior man is conversant with righteousness; the mind of the mean man is conversant with gain."

4,25: The Master said, "Virtue is not left to stand alone. *He who practices it* will have neighbors."

5,4,1–2: Some one said, "Yung is truly virtuous, but he is not ready with his tongue."

The Master said, "What is the good of being ready with the tongue? They who encounter men with smartnesses of speech for the most part procure themselves hatred. I know not whether he be truly virtuous, but why should he show readiness of the tongue?"

5,11: Tsze-kung said, "What I do not wish men to do to me, I also wish not to do to men." The Master said, "Ts'ze, you have not attained to that."

5,25,1–4: Yen Yuan and Chi Lu being by his side, the Master said to them, "Come, let each of you tell his wishes."

Tsze-lu said, "I should like, having chariots and horses, and light fur dresses, to share them with my friends, and though they should spoil them, I would not be displeased."

Yen Yuan said, "I should like not to boast of my excellence, nor to make a display of my meritorious deeds."

Tsze-lu then said, "I should like, sir, to hear your wishes." The Master said,

"They are, in regard to the aged, to give them rest; in regard to friends, to show them sincerity; in regard to the young, to treat them tenderly."

6,3,2: The Master said, "When Ch'ih was proceeding to Ch'i, he had fat horses to his carriage, and wore light furs. I have heard that a superior man helps the distressed, but does not add to the wealth of the rich."

6,18: The Master said, "They who know *the truth* are not equal to those who love it, and they who love it are not equal to those who delight in it."

6,28,1–3: Tsze-kung said, "Suppose the case of a man extensively conferring benefits on the people, and able to assist all, what would you say of him? Might he be called perfectly virtuous?" The Master said, "Why speak only of virtue in connection with him? Must he not have the qualities of a sage? Even Yao and Shun were still solicitous about this.

"Now the man of perfect virtue, wishing to be established himself, seeks also to establish others; wishing to be enlarged himself, he seeks also to enlarge others.

"To be able to judge *of others* by what is nigh *in ourselves;*—this may be called the art of virtue."

7,15: The Master said, "With coarse rice to eat, with water to drink, and my bended arm for a pillow;—I have still joy in the midst of these things. Riches and honors acquired by unrighteousness are to me as a floating cloud."

7,22: The Master said, "Heaven produced the virtue that is in me. Hwan T'ui—what can he do to me?"

7,36: The Master said, "The superior man is satisfied and composed; the mean man is always full of distress."

8,13,1–3: The Master said, "With sincere faith he unites the love of learning; holding firm to death, he is perfecting the excellence of his course.

"Such a one will not enter a tottering state, nor dwell in a disorganized one. When right principles of government prevail in the kingdom, he will show himself; when they are prostrated, he will keep concealed.

"When a country is well governed, poverty and a mean condition are things to be ashamed of. When a country is ill governed, riches and honor are things to be ashamed of."

9,4: There were four things from which the Master was entirely free. He had no foregone conclusions, no arbitrary predeterminations, no obstinacy, and no egoism.

9,5,1–3: The Master was put in fear in K'wang.

He said, "After the death of King Wan, was not the cause of truth lodged here *in me?*

"If Heaven had wished to let this cause of truth perish, then I, a future mortal, should not have got such a relation to that cause. While Heaven does not let the cause of truth perish, what can the people of K'wang do to me?"

12,2: Yen Yuan said, "I beg to ask the steps of that process." The Master replied, "Look not at what is contrary to propriety; listen not to what is contrary to propriety; speak not what is contrary to propriety; make no movement which is contrary to propriety." Yen Yuan *then* said, "Though I am deficient in intelligence and vigor, I will make it my business to practice this lesson."

12,5,1–4: Sze-ma Niu, full of anxiety, said, *"Other* men all have their brothers, I only have not."

Tsze-hsia said to him, "There is the

following saying which I have heard—
" 'Death and life have their determined appointment; riches and honors depend upon Heaven.'

"Let the superior man never fail reverently to order his own conduct, and let him be respectful to others and observant of propriety:—then all within the four seas will be his brothers. What has the superior man to do with being distressed because he has no brothers?"

12,24: The philosopher Tsang said, "The superior man on grounds of culture meets with friends, and by their friendship helps his virtue."

14,1: Hsien asked what was shameful. The Master said, "When good government prevails in a state, *to be thinking only of* salary; and, when bad government prevails, *to be thinking, in the same way, only of* salary;—this is shameful."

14,5: The Master said, "The virtuous will be sure to speak *correctly*, but those whose speech is good may not always be virtuous. Men of principle are sure to be bold, but those who are bold may not always be men of principle."

14,29: The Master said, "The superior man is modest in his speech, but exceeds in his actions."

15,5,1–4: Tsze-chang asked how a man should conduct himself, *so as to be everywhere appreciated.*
The Master said, "Let his words be sincere and truthful, and his actions honorable and careful;—such conduct may be practiced among the rude tribes of the South or of the North. If his words be not sincere and truthful, and his actions not honorable and careful, will he, with such conduct, be appreciated, even in his neighborhood?

"When he is standing, let him see those two things, as it were, fronting him. When he is in a carriage, let him see them attached to the yoke. Then may he subsequently carry them into practice."
Tsze-chang wrote these counsels on the end of his sash.

15,9: Tsze-kung asked about the practice of virtue. The Master said, "The mechanic, who wishes to do his work well, must first sharpen his tools. When you are living in any state, take service with the most worthy among its great officers, and make friends of the most virtuous among its scholars."

15,14: The Master said, "He who requires much from himself and little from others, will keep himself from *being the object of* resentment."

15,31: The Master said, "The object of the superior man is truth. Food is not his object. There is plowing;—even in that there is *sometimes* want. So with learning;—emolument may be found in it. The superior man is anxious lest he should not get truth; he is not anxious lest poverty should come upon him."

16,4: Confucius said, "There are three friendships which are advantageous, and three which are injurious. Friendship with the upright; friendship with the sincere; and friendship with the man of much observation:—these are advantageous. Friendship with the man of specious airs; friendship with the insinuatingly soft; and friendship with the glib-tongued: these are injurious."

17,6: Tsze-chang asked Confucius about perfect virtue. Confucius said, "To be able to practice five things everywhere under heaven constitutes perfect virtue." He begged to ask what they were, and was told, "Gravity, generosity *of soul,* sincerity, earnestness, and kindness. If you are grave, you will not be treated with disrespect. If you are generous, you will win all. If you are sincere, people will repose trust in you. If you are earnest, you will accomplish much. If you are kind, this will enable you to employ the services of others."

17,8,1–3: The Master said, "Yu, have you heard the six words to which are attached six becloudings?" Yu replied, "I have not."

"Sit down, and I will tell them to you.

"There is the love of being benevolent without the love of learning;— the beclouding here leads to a foolish simplicity. There is the love of knowing without the love of learning;—the beclouding here leads to dissipation of mind. There is the love of being sincere without the love of learning;— the beclouding here leads to an injurious disregard of consequences. There is the love of straightforwardness without the love of learning;—the beclouding here leads to rudeness. There is the love of boldness without the love of learning;—the beclouding here leads to insubordination. There is the love of firmness without the love of learning;—the beclouding here leads to extravagant conduct."

20,3,1–3: The Master said, "Without recognizing the ordinances (of Heaven), it is impossible to be a superior man.

"Without an acquaintance with the rules of Propriety, it is impossible for the character to be established.

"Without knowing (the force of) words, it is impossible to know men."

THE CHUNG YUNG

THIS is one of the so-called "Four Books" written about Confucius and his doctrines by faithful disciples, and is to be distinguished from "The Classics" which are attributed to Confucius himself. The English title is, *The Doctrine of the Mean.* Tradition has it that K'ung Chi, grandson of Confucius, fearing that errors would creep into the sayings of the master if they were not written down, put this group into written form. However, scholars are convinced that he added some of his own thoughts to those of his grandfather. Nevertheless, this short book gives us one of the clearest pictures of Confucius' mind and thoughts and is one of the most highly prized books of Confucianism. It is one of those generally known as the *Catechism of the Confucian Teaching.* The other is the *Ta Hsueh* or *The Great Learning.*

1,1: The ordinance of God is what we call the law of our being. To fulfil the law of our being is what we call the moral law. The moral law when reduced to a system is what we call religion.

1,2: The moral law is a law from whose operation we cannot for one instant in our existence escape. A law from which we may escape is not the moral law. Wherefore it is that the moral man watches diligently over what his eyes cannot see and is in fear and awe of what his ears cannot hear.

1,3: There is nothing more evident than that which cannot be seen by the eyes and nothing more palpable than that which cannot be perceived by the senses. Wherefore the moral man watches diligently over his secret thoughts.

1,4: When the passions, such as joy, anger, grief, and pleasure, have not awakened, that is our true self, or moral being. When these passions awaken and each and all attain due measure and degree, that is the moral order. Our true self or moral being is the great reality (*lit.* great root) of existence, and moral order is the universal law in the world.

1,5: When true moral being and moral order are realised, the universe then becomes a cosmos and all things attain their full growth and development.

10,1: Tzu-lu asked what constituted force of character.

10,2-3: Confucius said: "Do you mean force of character of the people of the southern countries or force of character of the people of the northern countries; or do you mean force of character in an absolute sense? To be patient and gentle, ready to teach, returning not evil for evil: that is the force of character of the people of the southern countries. It is the ideal of the moral man."

10,4: "To lie under arms and meet death without regret: that is the force of character of the people of the northern countries. It is the ideal of the brave man."

10,5: "But force of character in an absolute sense is another thing. Wherefore the man with the true force of moral character is one who is easy and accommodating and yet without weakness or indiscrimination. How unflinchingly firm he is in his strength! He is independent without any bias. How unflinchingly firm he is in his strength! When there is moral social order in the country, if he enters public life he does not change from what he was when in retirement. When there is no moral social order in the country he holds on his way without changing even unto death. How unflinchingly firm he is in his strength!"

12,1: The moral law is to be found everywhere, and yet it is a secret.

12,2: The simple intelligence of ordinary men and women of the people may understand something of the moral law; but in its utmost reaches there is something which even the wisest and holiest of men cannot understand. The ignoble natures of ordinary men and women of the people may be able to carry out the moral law; but in its utmost reaches even the wisest and holiest of men cannot live up to it.
Great as the Universe is, man with the infinite moral nature in him is never satisfied. For there is nothing so great but the mind of the moral man can conceive of something still greater which nothing in the world can hold. There is nothing so small but the mind of moral man can conceive of something still smaller which nothing in the world can split.

12,3: The Book of Songs says:

"The hawk soars to the heavens above and fishes dive to the depths below."

That is to say, there is no place in the highest heavens above nor in the deepest waters below where the moral law does not reign.

12,4: The moral law takes its rise in the relation between man and woman; but in its utmost reaches it reigns supreme over heaven and earth.

13,1: Confucius remarked: "The moral law is not something away from the actuality of human life. When men take up something away from the actuality of human life as the moral law, that is not the moral law."

13,2: The Book of Songs says:

"In hewing an axe handle, the pattern is not far off."

"Thus, when we take an axe handle in our hand to hew the other and glance from one to the other there is still some distance between them as compared with the relation between the moral law and the man himself. Wherefore the moral man in dealing with men appeals to the common human nature and changes the manner of their lives and nothing more.

13,3: "When a man carries out the principles of conscientiousness and reciprocity he is not far from the moral law. What you do not wish others should do unto you, do not do unto them.

13,4: "There are four things in the moral life of a man, not one of which I have been able to carry out in my life. To serve my father as I would expect my son to serve me: that I have not been able to do. To serve my sovereign as I would expect a minister under me to serve me: that I have not been able to do. To act towards my elder brother as I would expect my younger brother to act towards me: that I have not been able to do. To be the first to behave towards friends as I would expect them to behave towards me: that I have not been able to do.

"In the discharge of the ordinary duties of life and in the exercise of care in ordinary conversation, whenever there is shortcoming, never fail to strive for improvement, and when there is much to be said, always say less than what is necessary; words having respect to actions and actions having respect to words. Is it not just this thorough genuineness and absence of pretence which characterises the moral man?"

14,1: The moral man conforms himself to his life circumstances; he does not desire anything outside of his position.

14,2: Finding himself in a position of wealth and honour, he lives as becomes one living in a position of wealth and honour. Finding himself in a position of poverty and humble circumstances, he lives as becomes one living in a position of poverty and humble circumstances. Finding himself in uncivilized countries, he lives as becomes one living in uncivilized countries. Finding himself in circumstances of danger and difficulty, he acts according to what is required of a man under such circumstances. In one word, the moral man can find himself in no situation in life in which he is not master of himself.

14,3: In a high position he does not domineer over his subordinates. In a subordinate position he does not court the favours of his superiors. He puts in order his own personal conduct and seeks nothing from others; hence he has no complaint to make. He complains not against God nor rails against men.

14,4: Thus it is that the moral man lives out the even tenor of his life, calmly waiting for the appointment of God, whereas the vulgar person takes to dangerous courses, expecting the uncertain chances of luck.

14,5: Confucius remarked: "In the practice of archery we have something resembling the principle in a moral man's life. When the archer misses the centre of the target he turns round and seeks for the cause of his failure within himself."

17,1: Confucius remarked: "The Emperor Shun might perhaps be considered in the highest sense of the word a pious man. In moral qualities he was a saint. In dignity of office he was the ruler of the empire. In wealth all that the wide world contained belonged to him. After his death his spirit was sacrificed to in the ancestral temple, and his children and grandchildren preserved the sacrifice for long generations.

17,2: "Thus it is that he who possesses great moral qualities will certainly attain to corresponding high position; to corresponding great prosperity; to corresponding great name; to corresponding great age.

17,3: "For God in giving life to all created things is surely bountiful to them according to their qualities. Hence the tree that is full of life He fosters and sustains, while that which is ready to fall He cuts off and destroys."

17,4: The Book of Songs says:

"That great and noble Prince displayed
   The sense of right in all he wrought;
Adjusting justly, grade by grade,
   The spirit of his wisdom swayed
Peasant and peer; the crowd, the court.
So Heav'n, that crowned his sires, restored

The countless honours they had known;
For Heav'n aye keepeth watch and ward,
And through the son renews the throne."

17,5: "It is therefore true that he who possesses exceedingly great moral qualities will certainly receive the divine call to the Imperial throne."

22,1: It is only he, in the world, who possesses absolute truth who can get to the bottom of the law of his being. He who is able to get to the bottom of the law of his being will be able to get to the bottom of the law of being of other men. He who is able to get to the bottom of the law of being of men will be able to get to the bottom of the laws of physical nature. He who is able to get to the bottom of the laws of physical nature will be able to influence the forces of creation of the Universe. He who can influence the forces of creation of the Universe is one with the Powers of the Universe.

26,1–5: Thus absolute truth is indestructible. Being indestructible, it is eternal. Being eternal, it is self-existent. Being self-existent, it is infinite. Being infinite, it is vast and deep. Being vast and deep, it is transcendental and intelligent. It is because it is vast and deep that it contains all existence. It is because it is transcendental and intelligent that it embraces all existence. It is because it is infinite and eternal that it fills all existence. In vastness and depth it is like the Earth. In transcendental intelligence it is like Heaven. Infinite and eternal, it is Infinitude itself.

26,6: Such being the nature of absolute truth, it manifests itself without being evident; it produces effects without action; it accomplishes its ends without being conscious.

26,7: The principle in the course and operation of nature may be summed up in one word: it exists for its own sake without any double or ulterior motive. Hence the way in which it produces things is unfathomable.

26,8–9: Nature is vast, deep, high, intelligent, infinite, and eternal. The heaven appearing before us is only this bright, shining spot; but when taken in its immeasurable extent, the sun, moon, stars, and constellations are suspended in it, and all things are embraced under it. The earth, appearing before us, is but a handful of soil; but taken in all its breadth and depth, it sustains mighty Himalayas without feeling their weight; rivers and seas dash against it without causing it to leak. The mountain appearing before us is only a mass of rock; but taken in all the vastness of its size, grass and vegetation grow upon it, birds and beasts dwell on it, and treasures of precious stones are found in it. The water appearing before us is but a ladleful of liquid; but taken in all its unfathomable depths, the largest crustaceans, fishes, and reptiles are produced in them, and all useful products abound in them.

26,10: In the Book of Songs it is said:

"The ordinance of God,
How inscrutable it is and goes on for ever."

That is to say, this is the attribute of God. It is again said:

"How excellent it is,
The moral perfection of King Wen."

That is to say, this is the characteristic of the nobleness of the Emperor Wen. Moral perfection also never dies.

27,1–5: Oh, how great is the divine moral law in man! Vast and illimitable, it gives birth and life to all created things. It towers high up to the very heavens. How wonderful and great it is! All the institutions of human society and civilisation—laws, customs, and usages—have their origin there. All these institutions wait for the man before they can be put into practice. Hence it is said: Unless there be highest moral power, the highest moral law cannot be realised.

27,6: Wherefore the moral man, while honouring the greatness and power of his moral nature, yet does not neglect inquiry and pursuit of knowledge. While widening the extent of his knowledge, he yet seeks to attain utmost accuracy in the minutest details. While seeking to understand the highest things, he yet lives a plain, ordinary life in accordance with the moral order. Going over what he has already acquired, he keeps adding to it new knowledge. Earnest and simple, he respects and obeys the laws and usages of social life.

27,7: Therefore, when in a position of authority, he is not proud; in a subordinate position, he is not insubordinate. When there is moral social order in the country, what he speaks will be of benefit to the nation; and when there is no moral social order in the country his silence will ensure forbearance for himself.

In the Book of Songs it is said:

"With wisdom and good sense,
He guards his life from harm."

That is the description of the moral man.

28,1: Confucius remarked: "A man who is foolish, and yet is fond of using his own judgment; who is in humble circumstances, and yet is fond of assuming authority; who, while living in the present age, reverts to the ways of antiquity: such a man is one who will bring calamity upon himself."

28,2–3: To no one but the supreme head of the empire does it belong to disturb the established religious and social institutions, to introduce new forms of government, to change the form and use of language. At the present day throughout the empire carriage wheels all have the same standard form and size, all writing is written with the same characters, and in all the relations of life all recognise the same established principles.

28,4: Although a man may occupy the position of the supreme head of the empire, yet, unless he possesses the moral qualities fitting him for the task, he may not take upon himself to make changes in the established moral and religious institutions. Although one may possess the moral qualities fitting him for the task, yet, unless he occupies the position of the supreme head of the empire, he may not take upon himself to make changes in the established moral and religious institutions.

28,5: Confucius remarked: "I have tried to understand the moral and religious institutions of the Hsia dynasty, but what remains of those institutions in the present state of Ch'i is not sufficient to give me a clue. I have studied the moral and religious institutions of the Yin dynasty; the remains of them are still preserved in the present state of Sung. I have studied the moral and religious institutions of the present Chow dynasty, which are now in use. In practice I follow the forms of the present Chow dynasty."

THE MENG–TZE

The *Meng-tze,* or as it is called in English, *The Works of Mencius,* is the writing of "The Philosopher Meng," or Mencius. He was born about 372 B.C. amidst much political corruption and dictatorial rule. It was against such government that Meng threw himself in an attempt to discover a ruler who would adopt a more humane and moral method of ruling his people than that in general use. Most of his work was done in Ch'i, the one of the three great Chinese kingdoms toward the east. But, because of his independence and tactlessness, he was not a great success and, in 309 B.C., received a rebuff which convinced him of the futility of his efforts. For the remaining 20 years of his life he lived in retirement.

The philosophy of Meng is contained in seven books of some 260 chapters and 35,000 characters. The book itself was written after Meng's retirement and with the help of some of his disciples. The sayings and wise observations and advice have no logical arrangement, but are scattered about at random. But, they express the philosopher's interpretation of the teachings of Confucius so clearly that the book has been chosen as one of the "Four Books" of Confucianism and is reverenced deeply by the modern disciples of the saint.

1,1,1,1–2: Mencius went to visit King Hui of Liang. The King said to him: You are an old man, yet you have not shrunk from a journey of a thousand *li* in order to come hither. Doubtless you have something in your mind which will profit my kingdom?

1,1,1,3–6: Mencius replied: Why must your Majesty use that word "profit"? My business is with benevolence and righteousness and nothing else. If the King says, How shall I profit my kingdom? the great officers will say, How shall we profit our families? and the petty officers and common people will say, How shall we profit ourselves? And while upper and lower are thus engaged in a fierce struggle for profits, the State will be brought into peril. If the ruler of ten thousand chariots is slain, it will be by a family of a thousand; if the ruler of a thousand chariots is slain, it will be by a family of a hundred. A thousand out of ten thousand, or a hundred out of one thousand, is no small proportion of the whole. But if righteousness be considered of less importance than profit, people will never · be satisfied without grasping more than they possess. As benevolence is incompatible with neglect of one's parents, so righteousness never puts the interests of one's sovereign last. Let me, then, hear your Majesty speak only of benevolence and righteousness. There is no need to use the word "profit" at all.

2,1,2,1–4: Kung-sun Ch'ou asked, saying: If, Sir, you were appointed Chancellor of the Ch'i State, you would be able to put your principles into practice; and it would not be at all surprising if you thereby succeeded in obtaining the hegemony, or the royal dignity itself, for your prince. In such circumstances, would you feel agitated in mind?—No, replied Mencius; by the age of forty I had achieved imperturbability of mind. In that case, you are far superior to Meng Pen.—It is not hard to acquire. The philosopher Kao achieved the same result before I did. Is there any special method of acquiring it?—Oh, yes. Pei-kung Yu trained himself in physical courage so as not to flinch from a blow or to relax the steadiness of his gaze. He would resent the slightest push from anybody as fiercely as a thrashing in the market-place; he would not stomach an insult either from a coarsely clad man of the people or from a lord of ten thousand chariots. When it came to stabbing, prince and pauper were all the same to him. He stood in no awe of the feudal princes, and if an abusive word was addressed to him, he would be sure to retort.

2,1,2,5–8: Meng Shih-she had another method of fostering his courage. He used to say: "I care not whether I win or lose. One who weighs up the enemy before he advances, and plans for victory before he joins battle, is in reality afraid of the army he is fighting. How can I make certain of victory? All I can do is to have no fear." Meng Shih-she was like Tseng Tzu, and Pei-kung Yu was like Tzu Hsia. Which of the two was the more courageous I do not know, but Meng Shih-she held to the essential point. Tseng Tzu once said to his disciple Tzu Hsiang: "Do you admire courage? On the subject of courage in its highest form I once heard our Master say: If on self-examination I find that I am not in the right, shall I not be afraid even of the humblest yokel? But if I find that I am in the right, I will face the enemy in his thousands and tens of thousands." After all, Meng Shih-she's hold on his spirit was not so good as Tseng Tzu's hold on the essential point.

2,1,3,1–2: Mencius said: He is a tyrant who uses force while making a show of benevolence. To be a tyrant, one must have a large kingdom at one's command. He is a true king who practises benevolence in a virtuous spirit. To be a true king, one need not wait for a large kingdom. T'ang ruled over seventy square *li*, and King Wen over a hundred. When men are subdued by force, it is not their hearts that are won but their strength that gives out. When men are won by goodness, their hearts are glad within them and their submission is sincere. Thus were the seventy disciples of Confucius won by their Master. This is what is meant in the *Book of Songs* where it says: "From east and west, from north and south, came no thought but of surrender."

2,1,4,1–6: Mencius said: Benevolence brings honour, without it comes disgrace. To hate disgrace and yet to be content to live without benevolence is like hating damp and yet living in a hollow. If a ruler hates disgrace, his best way is to prize virtue and do honour to the scholar. With worthy men in high places and able men in office, his country may enjoy a season of peace and quiet; and if he uses this opportunity to clarify law and government, even a great kingdom will be wary of him. It is said in the *Book of Songs*:

"Ere that the rain-clouds gathered,
I took the bark of the mulberry tree
And wove it into window and door.
Now, ye people below,
Which of you will dare to affront me?"

Confucius said of the maker of this ode that he knew the principles of statecraft; for who will dare to affront a ruler that can order his kingdom well? But, now that the State is enjoying a season of quiet, to use the opportunity for junketing and idle amusement is nothing less than seeking out misfortune. Happiness and misfortune are indeed always of man's own seeking. That is the lesson conveyed in the *Book of Songs:*

"Ever adjust thyself to the will of Heaven,
And great happiness will be thine;"

and in the *T'ai Chia:* "Heaven-sent calamities you may stand up against, but you cannot survive those brought on by yourself."

2,1,6,1–7: Mencius said: All men have a certain sympathy towards their fellows. The great monarchs of old had this human sympathy, and it resulted in their government being sympathetic. Having this feeling of sympathy for his fellows, he who acts upon it in governing the Empire will find that his rule can be conducted as it were in the palm of his hand. What I mean by this feeling of sympathy which all men possess is this: If anyone were to see a child falling into a well, he would have a feeling of horror and pity, not because he happened to be an intimate friend of the child's parents, nor because he sought the approbation of his neighbours and friends, nor yet because he feared to be thought inhumane. Looking at the matter in the light of this example, we may say that no man is devoid of a feeling of compassion, nor of a feeling of shame, nor of a feeling of consideration for others, nor of a feeling of plain right and wrong. The feeling of compassion is the origin of benevolence; the feeling of shame is the origin of righteousness; the feeling of consideration for others is the origin of good manners; the feeling of right and wrong is the origin of wisdom. The presence of these four elements in man is as natural to him as the possession of his four limbs. Having these four elements within

him, the man who says he is powerless to act as he should is doing a grave injury to himself. And the man who says the same of his prince is likewise doing him a grave injury. Let a man but know how to expand and develop these four elements existing in the soul, and his progress becomes as irresistible as a newly kindled fire or a spring that has just burst from the ground. If they can be fully developed, these virtues are strong enough to safeguard all within the Four Seas; if allowed to remain undeveloped, they will not suffice for the service due to one's parents.

4,1,4,1–2: Mencius said: If you love others but are not loved in return examine your own feeling of benevolence. If you try to govern others and do not succeed, turn inwards and examine your wisdom. If you treat others with courtesy but evoke no response, examine your inward feeling of respect. Whenever our actions fail to produce the effect desired, we should look for the cause in ourselves. For when a man is inwardly correct, the world will not be slow in paying him homage.

4,1,8,4: A man must insult himself before others will. A family must begin to destroy itself before others do so. A State must smite itself before it is smitten from without.

4,1,10,1–3: With one who does violence to his own nature words are of no avail. For one who throws himself away, nothing can be done. To discard decency and right feeling in one's speech is what I mean by doing violence to one's nature. To profess inability to abide in benevolence and follow the road of righteousness is what I mean by throwing oneself away. Benevolence is man's peaceful abode, and righteousness his true road. Alas for those who desert the peaceful abode, and dwell not therein! Alas for those who abandon the true road and follow it not!

4,1,11,1: The path of duty lies close at hand, yet we seek for it afar. Our business lies in what is simple, yet we seek for it in what is difficult. If every man would love his parents and treat his elders as they should be treated, the Empire would be at peace.

4,2,9,1: What trouble is he not laying up for himself who discourses on other people's faults!

4,2,11,1: The great man makes no effort to be sincere in his speech nor resolute in his acts: he simply does as his conscience prompts him.

4,2,12,1: The great man is one who has never lost the heart of a child.

4,2,13,1: Not the support of one's parents when alive but rather the performance of their obsequies after death, is to be accounted the great test of filial piety.

4,2,18,1–3: The disciple Hsü said: Confucius used to apostrophize water in terms of praise. What did he find to admire in it?—Mencius replied: A spring of water flows in a copious stream, never ceasing day and night, filling all cavities and, continuing its course, finding its way at last into the ocean. Such is the behaviour of water that flows from a spring, and this is what he admired. But where there is no spring, though channels and ditches are filled after rainfall in the seventh and eighth months, yet the water may soon be expected to dry up again. Thus the princely man is ashamed to enjoy a reputation which exceeds his real deserts.

4,2,28,1–6: The princely man is distinguished from others by the feelings laid up in his heart, and these are the feelings of benevolence and propriety. The benevolent man loves his fellows; the man of propriety respects his fellows. He who loves his fellows is loved by them in return; he who respects his fellows is respected by them in return. The nobler type of man, when treated by anybody in a rude and churlish manner, will turn his eyes inward and say: "I must have been lacking in benevolence; I must have shown a want of propriety; or how could this have happened?" Having examined himself thus, he may find that he has really been inspired by benevolence and propriety. If the other man is none the less rude and churlish, he will again subject himself to a searching examination, saying: "I cannot have been true to myself." But if he finds that he has been true to himself, and the rudeness of the other still persists, he will say to himself: "This must be an unreasonable sort of fellow after all. If he behaves thus, there is little to choose between him and a bird or beast. And why should I be unduly concerned about a bird or beast?"

4,2,28,7: Thus it is that the nobler type of man, while constantly solicitous, never suffers grief of any duration. Solicitude, indeed, he feels; for he will argue thus: "Shun was a man; I too am a man. But Shun was an example to the Empire, worthy of being handed down to posterity, whereas I have not yet risen above the level of an ordinary villager." This, then, causes him solicitude, which is nothing more than anxiety to become like Shun himself. But anything that would cause him real grief simply does not exist. He never acts without a feeling of benevolence, never moves without a sense of propriety. Even if some transient cause for grief were to come his way, he would not regard it as such.

6,1,2,1–3: The philosopher Kao said: Man's nature is like a current of water: deflected in an easterly direction, it will flow to the east; deflected in a westerly direction, it will flow to the west. And just as water has no predilection either for east or for west, so man's nature is not predisposed either to good or to evil.—Mencius replied: It is true that water has no predilection for east or west, but will it flow equally well up or down? Human nature is disposed towards goodness just as water flows downwards. There is no water but flows down, and no men but show this tendency to good. Now, if water is splashed up, it can be made to go right over your head; by forcing it along, it can be made to go uphill. But how can that be termed its natural bent? It is some external force that causes it to do so. And likewise, if men are made to do what is not good, their nature is being distorted in a similar way.

6,1,10,1–5: Mencius said: I am fond of fish, and I am also fond of bear's paws. If I cannot have both, I will give up the fish and take the bear's paws. Similarly, I hold life dear, and also hold righteousness dear. If I cannot have both, I will give up my life and keep my righteousness. Although I hold life dear, there are things which I hold dearer than life, therefore I will not keep it at the expense of what is right. Although I hate death, there are things which I hate more than death, therefore there are certain dangers from which I will not flee. If there was nothing that men desired more than life, would they not use any possible means of preserving it? And if there was nothing men hated more than death, would they not do anything to escape from danger? Yet there are means of preserving one's life which men will not use, ways of avoiding danger which men will not adopt. Thus it appears that men desire some things more than life, and hate some things more than death. And it is not only the virtuous man who has

such feelings; all men have them. What distinguishes the virtuous man is that he can keep those feelings from being stifled within him.

6,1,15,1–2: The disciple Kung-tu asked, saying: Human nature is common to us all. How is it, then, that some are great men and some are small men?—Mencius replied: Those that follow their higher nature are great men; those that follow their lower nature are small men.—Kung-tu said: Seeing that all alike are men, how is it that some follow their higher nature and some their lower nature?—Mencius replied: The function of the eye and the ear is not thought, but is determined by material objects; for when objects impinge on the senses, these cannot but follow wherever they lead. Thought is the function of the mind: by thinking, it achieves; by not thinking, it fails to achieve. These faculties are implanted in us by Nature. If we take our stand from the first on the higher part of our being, the lower part will not be able to rob us of it. It is simply this that constitutes the great man.

6,1,16,1–3: Mencius said: Heaven confers titles of nobility as well as man. Man's titles of nobility are duke, chancellor, great officer. Those of Heaven are benevolence, righteousness, true-heartedness and good faith, with unwearying delight in the practice of those virtues. The men of old cultivated the nobility of Heaven, and the nobility of man followed naturally in its wake. The men of to-day cultivate the nobility of Heaven only with an eye to the nobility of man, and when that has been won they cast away the other. But this is the height of delusion; for in the end they must surely lose the nobility of man as well.

6,1,18,1–2: Mencius said: Benevolence overcomes its opposite even as water overcomes fire. But those who practise benevolence nowadays are taking a cup of water, as it were, to quench a cart-load of burning fuel. Failing to extinguish the blaze, they say that water cannot overcome fire! This only helps the cause of those who are against benevolence altogether, and in the end their own benevolence will also disappear.

7,1,9,1–6: Mencius said to Sung Kou-chien: You are a great traveller, Sir, are you not? Let me speak to you on the subject. If your counsels are heeded, be content; if they are not heeded, still be content.—Kou-chien said: What should I do in order to have this feeling of contentment?—Honour virtue, was the reply, and take delight in righteousness; then this feeling will come to you. Poverty does not make the worthy scholar lose his righteousness, success does not make him swerve from the Way. Poor, yet not losing his righteousness, he remains master of himself; successful, yet not swerving from the Way, he will not disappoint the hopes of the people. The man of old who attained his ambition showered blessings upon the people; or if he failed, he made self-improvement his task and shone brightly before the world. If without means, he concentrated his efforts on his own virtue; if he rose to power, he made the whole Empire virtuous as well.

7,2,32,1–3: Words concerned with the near, yet pointing far away, are good words. Principles concentrating on the essential, yet wide of application, are good principles. The words of the princely man do not come from below the girdle, but the deeper principles are there. What the princely man sets his heart on is self-development, but the Empire thereby obtains peace. A sad failing in man is that he neglects his own field to weed his neighbour's; that his demands on others are heavy, while the burden he lays on himself is light.

7,2,33,1–3: Yao and Shun were naturally good; T'ang and Wu reverted to natural goodness. The highest degree of virtue is indicated in the man whose every act and gesture is dictated by right feeling. Wailing for the dead should be the expression of real grief, not done for the benefit of the living. The path of virtue should be pursued without turning back, and with no eye to emolument. The words one utters should be true, but with no eye to correctness of conduct. The nobler type of man simply acts according to the rule of right, and then awaits whatever may be ordained.

V

JAINISM

HINDUISM, as we have seen, was, in its earlier phases, dominated by unalterable caste distinctions, animal sacrifice, and other primitive practices. These offended a great many fine and sensitive spirits in India who eventually sought after reforms. Jainism was the first organized effort to effect such reform. It was followed about 30 years later by Buddhism, another similar movement. Both movements eventually became separate religions, growing out of Hinduism but developing into separate bodies of belief and doctrine.

Although Jainism has not spread outside of India and is not accepted by a large following, there being about 1,250,000 Jains today, it has had a tremendous influence over the development of India. Most Jains are merchants and, as such, have acquired considerable wealth with which to control much of the commercial life of the southern and western districts of India. Further, their architecture has played a prominent role in the country. The Jain memorial mound at Muthura is believed by many to be the oldest existing building in India. Further, among the architectural treasures of India are the beautiful monolithic Jain temple at Kaligamalai in southern India and the temples at Ahmedabad, Ellora, Ajmere, and Mount Abu in western India. It is to these places that travelers from all parts of the world go when they visit India.

The founder of Jainism was Mahavira, who lived between 599 and 527 B.C. This was a time of religious ferment throughout the East. It was the period when Confucius and Lao-tze were working in China, Zoroaster was preaching in Persia, the great prophets of the Babylonian exile, Jeremiah, Ezekiel, and Isaiah, were teaching and preaching to the Jews, and the early Greek philosophers were seeking for a reasoned explanation of the universe and man's relation to it.

As a youth Mahavira lived the life of a pampered prince who had

119

every opportunity for wealth and position. He married the daughter
of another princely family, and had one daughter. Then, upon the
death of his parents, Mahavira resolved to renounce the world and
become an ascetic. He is said to have given away all he possessed, pulled
out all his hair in five handfuls, and vowed absolute holiness. For a few
months he wore clothes, but soon gave them up and lived as a naked
ascetic, wandering about receiving injuries from men and beasts and
imposing all kinds of self-torture upon himself. This he did in an effort
to gain complete mastery over himself and his body.

When he believed that he had obtained this mastery, he returned
to social life and became a leader and teacher. He won many converts
and gained the favor of four kings. This work was continued the remainder of his life.

Although Mahavira taught that one should worship no man or object, but should live "a life quiet and unperturbed, self-denying and
harmless and prayerless," his followers came very soon to worship him
as divine. Later many stories of miracles grew up about his memory.
He was believed to have been omniscient, pre-existent, and a divine
saviour of men. Today he is idolized by his followers who worship
images of him.

The sacred scriptures of Jainism are usually called Agamas (precepts) or Siddhantas (treatises). The first Agama is called *Ayaranya
Sutra*. Originally this Agama consisted of twelve Angas (bodies), but
only eleven are extant at present, the twelfth having been lost. The
second Agama is called *Sutrakritanga*. Another Agama of importance
is the *Uttaradhyayana Sutra*. There are many other Agamas which
have not been translated into English. Indeed, Jains are broken into
sects due to disagreement as to the number of Agamas which are to be
accepted as authoritative. One sect, the Sthanakvasi, holds that only 33
are sacred. The Svetambara sect recognizes 45, while other sects accept
as many as 84. Nevertheless, regardless of the number of Agamas which
a particular sect accepts, very few Jains are acquainted with their scriptures due to the fact that most Jains know nothing of the Prakrit
vernacular of the documents or of Sanskrit, the language of the commentaries.

Today the Jains are a small religious group in India, self-centered
and exclusive. The two main sects came into being over the question of wearing clothes. Those living in the north where the climate
is cool, the Svetambara, wear clothes, and those further south, the
Digambara or "sky-clad," wear no clothes except where Mohammedan
invaders have forced them to wear a loin cloth. These Jains carry their
dispute to their idols. Those of the north clothe their idols in white gar-

ments while those of the south leave their idols naked. They also differ in their attitude toward women. In the north nuns are accepted as members of the sect; in the south women are held to be excluded from salvation until they are reborn as men.

THE AYARANYA SUTRA

THE *Ayaranya Sutra,* sometimes called the *Samayika,* is the first book of the Jain canon. It deals with problems of conduct.

This Agama consists of two sections. Of these, the first is a basic document, whereas the second is a grouping of four appendices. The basic section describes the progress of a faithful individual towards the highest perfection. Perhaps the last lesson, a popular ballad on the glorious suffering of the prophet, was added later.

A large part of both sections is written in the most bewildering prose. Many of the sentences are mere fragments and others are difficult for one to understand. Some scholars believe that this work is made up of quotations taken at random from other works which were well-known at the time but are unknown today.

The first section contains eight lectures, a ninth having been lost. The second section consists of four parts, the first and second stating rules of conduct. The third and fourth parts, according to Jain tradition, were revealed to the oldest sister of Sthulabhadra by Simandhara, a Jain, living in Purvavideha, a mythical continent. The third part gives some material about the life of Mahavira, the founder of Jainism.

1,1,6,6: He who injures these (animals) does not comprehend and renounce the sinful acts; he who does not injure these, comprehends and renounces the sinful acts. Knowing them, a wise man should not act sinfully toward animals, nor cause others to act so, nor allow others to act so. He who knows these causes of sin relating to animals, is called a reward-knowing sage. Thus I say.

1,2,2,1: A wise man should remove any aversion (to control); he will be liberated in the proper time. Some, following wrong instruction, turn away (from control). They are dull, wrapped in delusion. While they imitate the life of monks, (saying), "We shall be free from attachment," they enjoy the pleasures that offer themselves. Through wrong instruction the (would-be) sages trouble themselves (for pleasures); thus they sink deeper and deeper in delusion, (and cannot get) to this, nor to the opposite shore. Those who are freed (from attachment to the world and its pleasures), reach the opposite shore. Subduing desire by desirelessness, he does not enjoy the pleasures that offer themselves. Desireless, giving up the world, and ceasing to act, he knows, and sees, and has no wishes because of his discernment; he is called houseless.

1,2,2,3: Thus violence is done by these various acts, deliberately, out of fear, because they think "it is for the expiation of sins," or for some other hope. Knowing this, a wise man should neither himself commit violence by such acts, nor order others to commit violence by such acts, nor consent to the violence done by somebody else.

This road (to happiness) has been

declared by the noble ones, that a clever man should not be defiled (by sin). Thus I say.

1,2,3,2: Therefore a wise man should neither be glad nor angry (about his lot): thou shouldst know and consider the happiness of living creatures. Carefully conducting himself, he should mind this: blindness, deafness, dumbness, one-eyedness, hunchbackedness, blackness, variety of colour (he will always experience); because of his carelessness he is born in many births, he experiences various feelings.

1,2,3,4: Those who are of a steady conduct do not desire this (wealth). Knowing birth and death, one should firmly walk the path (i.e. right conduct), (and not wait for old age to commence a religious life),

For there is nothing inaccessible for death. All beings are fond of life, like pleasure, hate pain, shun destruction, like life, long to live. To all life is dear.

1,2,6,1: He who perfectly understands (what has been said in the preceding lesson) and follows the (faith) to be coveted, should therefore do no sinful act, nor cause others to do one. Perchance he meditates a sin (by an act against only) one (of the six aggregates of lives); but he will be guilty (of sin against) every one of the six. Desiring happiness and bewailing much, he comes ignorantly to grief through his own misfortune.

1,2,6,5: Thus understanding (and renouncing) acts, a man who recognizes the truth, delights in nothing else; and he who delights only in the truth, recognizes nothing else. As (the law) has been revealed for the full one, so for the empty one; as for the empty one, so for the full one. But he (to whom the faith is preached) will perhaps disrespectfully beat (the preacher). Yet know, there is no good in this (indiscriminate preaching). (But ascertain before) what sort of man he is, and whom he worships. He is called a hero who liberates the bound, above, below, and in the sideward directions. He always conforms to all knowledge (and renunciation); the hero is not polluted by the sin of killing. He is a wise man who perfectly knows the non-killing, who searches after the liberation of the bound. The clever one is neither bound nor liberated; he should do or leave undone (what the hero does or does not do); he should not do what (the hero) leaves undone:

Knowing (and renouncing) murder of any kind and worldly ideas in all respects.

He who sees himself, needs no instruction. But the miserable and afflicted fool who delights in pleasures and whose miseries do not cease, is turned round in the whirl of pains. Thus I say.

1,3,2,1–3: That man will be liberated from death; he is a sage who sees the danger, knowing the highest good in the world, leading a circumspect life, calm, guarded, endowed (with knowledge, &c.), always restrained, longing for death, he should lead a religious life. Manifold, indeed, appear sinful actions; therefore prove constant to truth! Delighting in it, a wise man destroys all karman.

Many, indeed, are the plans of this man (of the world); he will satisfy his desires; he (thereby causes) the slaughter of others, the pain of others, the punishment of others, the slaughter, the blame, the punishment of a whole province. Doing such things, some have exerted themselves.

Therefore the second (i.e. the wrong creed) is not adhered to. The knowing one seeing the vanity (of the world) [knowing the rise and fall of the souls], that Brahman follows the unrivalled (control of the Gainas). He should not kill, nor cause others to kill, nor consent to the killing of others. "Avoid gaiety, not delighting in creatures (i.e. women), having the highest intuition," keeping off from sinful acts.

1,3,4,1–2: That man (i.e. the liberated) conquers wrath, pride, deceit, and greed. This is the doctrine of the Seer who does not injure living beings and has put an end (to acts and to samsara). Preventing propensity to sin destroys former actions. He who knows one thing, knows all things; and he who knows all things, knows one thing. He who is careless in all respects, is in danger; he who is not careless in all respects, is free from danger.

He who conquers one (passion), conquers many; and he who conquers many, conquers one. "Knowing the misery of the world," rejecting the connection with the world, "the heroes go on the great journey," they rise gradually; "they do not desire life."

1,5,1,1: Many entertain cruel thoughts against the world, with a motive or without one; they entertain cruel thoughts against these (six classes of living beings). To him pleasures are dear. Therefore he is near death. Because he is near death, he is far (from liberation). But he who is neither near (death) nor far (from liberation), considers the life of a slow and ignorant fool as similar to a dewdrop trembling on the sharp point of the blade of Kusa grass which falls down when shaken by the wind. A fool, doing cruel acts, comes thereby ignorantly to grief. "Through delusion he is born, dies, &c." Being conversant with the deliberation about this delusion, one is conversant with the samsara; being not conversant with that deliberation, one is not conversant with the samsara. He who is clever, should not seek after sexual intercourse. But having done so, (it would

be) a second folly of the weak-minded not to own it. Repenting and excluding (from the mind) the begotten pleasures, one should instruct others to follow the commandment. Thus I say.

1,5,2,3–5: Those who are not given to sinful acts are (nevertheless) attacked by calamities; but then the steadfast will bear them. (He has to bear) them afterwards as (he has done) before (his conversion). (The body) is of a fragile, decaying nature, (it is) unstable, transient, uneternal, increasing and decreasing, of a changeable nature. Perceive this as its true character. For him who will understand this, who delights in the unique refuge, for the liberated and inactive there is no passage (from birth to death). Thus I say.

Many are attached to something in the world—be it little or much, small or great, sentient or non-sentient— they are attached to it (here) amongst these (householders). Thus some incur great danger. For him who contemplates the course of the world and does not acknowledge these attachments (there is no such danger). Knowing that that which is well understood is well practiced, man! with thy eyes on the highest good, be victorious (in control). Among such men only is real Brahmanhood. Thus I say.

I have heard this, and it is in my innermost heart; and the freedom from bonds is in your innermost heart. He who has ceased (to have worldly attachments), the houseless, suffer with patience a long time.

The careless stand outside, the careful lead a religious life.

Maintain rightly this state of a sage. Thus I say.

1,5,4,5: When strongly vexed by the influence of the senses, he should eat bad food, mortify himself, stand upright, wander from village to village, take no food at all, withdraw his mind from women. First troubles, then pleasures; first pleasures, then troubles: thus they are the cause of quarrels. Considering this and well understanding it, one should teach oneself not to cultivate (sensuality). Thus I say. He should not speak of women, nor look at them, nor converse with them, nor claim them as his own, nor do their work. Careful in his speech and guarding his mind, he should always avoid sin. He should maintain his sagedom. Thus I say.

1,6,4,2: Those who deserve to be called fools, are born again and again. Standing low (in learning or control) they will exalt themselves (and say) in their pride: I am learned. They speak harshly unto the passionless; they upbraid them with their former trades, or revile them with untrue reproaches. The wise, therefore, should know the law. Thou lovest unrighteousness, because thou art young, and lovest acts, and sayest: "Kill beings"; thou killest them or consent to their being killed by others. (Such a man) thinks contemptuously: A very severe religion has been proclaimed. Sinking in opposition to the law, he is called murderer. Thus I say.

1,8,2,12: (Sometimes to avoid greater troubles when asked), "Who is there within?" he answered, "It is I, a mendicant." But this is the best law: silently to meditate, even if badly treated.

2,16,5: As the lustre of a burning flame increases, so increase the austerity, wisdom, and glory of a steadfast sage who, with vanquished desires, meditates on the supreme place of virtue, though suffering pain.

THE SUTRAKRITANGA

This book is the second Agama of the Jain canon and is one of the oldest of the Jain scriptures. It begins with a refutation of heretical doctrines. This is followed by discussions of the holy life, the difficulties which monks have to overcome, punishments which befall the unholy, and praise of Mahavira. The document is divided into two sections, the first being the oldest and probably the original work while the second is a supplement intended for the guidance of young monks. Although the material in this document was probably circulated orally for many generations, it was gathered into this form sometime during the fifth century of the Christian era.

1,1,2,26–29: "There are three ways of committing sins: by one's own activity, by commission, by approval (of the deed).

"These are the three ways of committing sins. Thus by purity of the heart one reaches Nirvana.

"A layman may kill his son (during a famine) and eat him; a wise (monk) who partakes of the meat, will not be defiled by the sin."

The mind of those who sin in thoughts is not pure; they are wrong, they do not conduct themselves carefully.

1,2,1,20–21: Some people are (foolishly) attached to others, and are thereby deluded; the unrighteous make them adopt unrighteousness, and they exult in their wickedness.

Therefore a worthy and wise man should be careful, ceasing from sin and being entirely happy. The virtuous heroes of faith (have chosen) the great road, the right and certain path to perfection.

1,2,3,13–19: The man also who still lives in the house, should, in accordance with his creed, be merciful to living beings; we are bidden to be fair and equal with all; (thereby even a

householder) goes to the world of the gods.

Being instructed in the creed of the Lord, exert yourself in the truth (i.e. in control)! A monk who has thoroughly subdued his selfishness should collect pure alms.

Knowing the truth, one should live up to it, seeking the Law, earnest in the performance of austerities, possessing the Guptis, being accomplished, one should always exert oneself, intent on the soul's benefit, and desiring the highest good (viz. liberation).

The fool thinks that his wealth, cattle, and relations will save him; they him, or he them. But they are no help, no protection.

When calamity befalls him, or the end of his life draws near, he must go and come alone; the wise believe that there is nothing to protect him.

All living beings owe their present form of existence to their own Karman; timid, wicked, suffering latent misery, they err about (in the Circle of Births), subject to birth, old age, and death.

He should know that the present time is the best opportunity to mend, and that an awakening is difficult to obtain. A wise man should be aware of this. The (first) Gina has said this, and so the remaining ones (will) say it.

1,3,1,14: Some low people who lead a life of iniquity, and entertain heretical opinions, being subject to love and hatred, injure a monk.

1,3,2,4: "Support your mother and father, thus you will win this world; it is a duty in this world to protect one's mother."

1,3,4,19–20: A monk who knows this, will live as a virtuous man guarded by the Samitis; he will abstain from untrue speech, and not take what is not freely given him.

He should cease to injure living beings whether they move or not, on high, below, and on earth. For this has been called the Nirvana, which consists in peace.

1,9,3,5: The iniquity of all these men who cling to property goes on increasing; for those who procure themselves pleasures by sinful acts will not get rid of misery.

After a man has done acts which cause the death of living beings, his pleasure-seeking relations take possession of his wealth, whilst the doer of the acts must suffer for them.

"Mother, father, daughter-in-law, brother, wife, and sons will not be able to help me, when I suffer for my own deeds."

1,9,30–33: Not desirous of fine things, he should wander about, exerting himself; not careless in his conduct, he should bear whatever pains he has to suffer.

If beaten, he should not be angry; if abused, he should not fly into a passion; with a placid mind he should bear everything and not make a great noise.

He should not enjoy pleasures though they offer themselves; for thus he is said (to reach) discernment. He should always practice what is right to do in the presence of the enlightened ones.

He should obey and serve a wise and pious teacher, (such teachers) as are heroes (of faith), who search for the benefit of their souls, are firm in control, and subdue their senses.

1,10,1–3: The wise (Arhat) having pondered on the Law proclaimed it; learn from me correctly what is carefulness. A monk who forms no resolutions and is possessed of carefulness, should wander about, giving no offence to any creature;

To no living beings, whether they move or not, whether above or below or on earth, by putting a strain upon them by his hands or feet. Nor should he take from householders anything that is not freely given.

Having mastered the Law and got rid of carelessness, he should live on allowed food, and treat all beings as he himself would be treated; he should not expose himself to guilt by his desire for life; a monk who performs austerities should not keep any store.

1,10,13: Abstain from sexual intercourse with women, do not acquire property; a man possessed of carefulness will, beyond doubt, be a savior (to others) in all circumstances.

1,10,18: Forgetting that his life will have an end, a rash and foolish man is full of selfishness; he toils day and night, greedy of wealth, as if he never should grow old or die.

1,11,9–11: A wise man should study them with all means of philosophical research. All beings hate pains; therefore one should not kill them.

This is the quintessence of wisdom: not to kill anything. Know this to be the legitimate conclusion from the principle of the reciprocity with regard to non-killing.

He should cease to injure living beings whether they move or not, on high, below, and on earth. For this has been called the Nirvana, which consists in peace.

1,15,9–10: Those men whom women do not seduce, value Moksha most; those men are free from bondage and do not desire life.

Turning from worldly life, they reach the goal by pious acts; by their pious acts they are directed (towards Liberation), and they show the way to others.

2,2,17: Now we treat of the ninth kind of committing sins, viz. through pride. This is the case when a man drunk (as it were) with pride of caste, family, beauty, piety, knowledge, success, power, intelligence, or any other kind of pride, slights, blames, abuses, reviles, despises somebody else and extols himself, (thinking:) "he is my inferior, I am of better caste or family, and possess greater power and other advantages." When he leaves this body and is only accompanied by his Karman, he, without a will of his own, goes forth from womb to womb, from birth to birth, from death to death, from hell to hell. He is cruel, stubborn, fickle, and proud. Thereby the bad Karman accrues to him. This is the ninth kind of committing sins, viz. through pride.

THE UTTARADHYAYANA SUTRA

THE purpose of this Jain scripture is to give instruction to a young monk in his duties, to praise the ascetic life through telling cases of such living, and to give him ample warning of the dangers which will confront him because of his career. The young monk must know animate and inanimate things and a long discussion of this subject is added at the end of the book. The material was taken from the traditional literature of the Jains. The book took final shape during the fifth century of the Christian era, although its material dates far back before this era.

1,7–9: Therefore be eager for discipline, that you may acquire righteousness; a son of the wise, who desires liberation, will not be turned away from anywhere.

One should always be meek, and not be talkative in the presence of the wise; one should acquire valuable knowledge, and avoid what is worthless.

When reprimanded a wise man should not be angry, but he should be of a forbearing mood; he should not associate, laugh, and play with mean men.

1,45: An intelligent man who has learned (the sacred texts) takes his duties upon himself, and he becomes renowned in the world; as the earth is the dwelling of all beings, so he will be a dwelling of all duties.

2,26: A monk should not be angry if beaten, nor should he therefore entertain sinful thoughts; knowing patience to be the highest good, a monk should meditate on the Law.

3,12: The pious obtain purity, and the pure stand firmly in the Law: (the soul afterwards) reaches the highest Nirvana, being like unto a fire fed with ghee.

4,2–5: Men who adhering to wrong principles acquire wealth by evil deeds, will lose it, falling into the snares (of their passions) and being held captive by their hatred.

As the burglar caught in the breach of the wall perishes by the work the sinner himself had executed, thus people in this life and the next cannot escape the effect of their own actions.

If a man living in the Samsara does an action for the sake of somebody else, or one by which he himself also profits, then, at the time of reaping the fruit of his actions, his relations will not act as true relations (i.e. will not come to his help).

Wealth will not protect a careless man in this world and the next. Though he had seen the right way, he does not see it, even as one in the dark whose lamp has suddenly been put out.

5,14–15: As a charioteer, who against his better judgment leaves the smooth highway and gets on a rugged road, repents when the axle breaks; so the fool, who transgresses the Law and embraces unrighteousness, repents in the hour of death, like (the charioteer) over the broken axle.

6,10: Clever talking will not work salvation; how should philosophical instruction do it? Fools, though sinking lower and lower through their sins, believe themselves to be wise men.

8,16–17: And if somebody should give the whole earth to one man, he would not have enough; so difficult is it to satisfy anybody.

The more you get, the more you want; your desires increase with your means. Though two mashas would do to supply your want, still you would scarcely think ten millions sufficient.

10,20: Though one believe in the Law, he will rarely practice it; for people are engrossed by pleasures; Gautama, be careful all the while!

13,27: "I, too, know just as well as you, O saint, what you have told me in your speech: pleasures will get a hold on men and are not easily abandoned by such as we are, sir."

14,25: "The day that goes by will never return; the days elapse with much profit to him who acts up to the Law."

14,32: "We have finished enjoying pleasures, my dear; our life is drawing to its close. I do not abandon pleasures for the sake of an unholy life; but looking with indifference on gain and loss, on happiness and suffering, I shall lead the life of a monk."

18,25–27: "Men who commit sins will go to hell; but those who have walked the road of righteousness, will obtain a place in heaven.

"All this delusive talk (of the heretics) is untrue and without any meaning; I live and walk about according to the rules of self-control.

"I know all these heresies to be contemptible; I know that there will be a life hereafter, and I know my Self."

18,33: "A wise man believes in the existence of the soul, he avoids the heresy of the non-existence of the soul; possessing true faith one should practice the very difficult Law according to the faith."

19,25: "Impartiality towards all beings in the world, whether friends or enemies, and abstention from injury to living beings throughout the whole life: this is a difficult duty."

23,38: "Self is the one invincible foe, (together with the four) cardinal passions, (viz. anger, pride, deceit, and greed, they are five) and the (five) senses (make ten). These (foes), O great sage, I have regularly vanquished."

29,14: By praise and hymns he obtains the wisdom consisting in knowledge, faith, and conduct; thereby he gains such improvement, that he will put an end to his worldly existence, (or) be born afterwards in one of the Kalpas and Vimanas.

29,17: By begging forgiveness he obtains happiness of mind; thereby he acquires a kind disposition towards all kinds of living beings; by this kind disposition he obtains purity of character and freedom from fear.

29,25–26: By concentration of his thoughts he obtains stability of the mind.

By control he obtains freedom from sins.

29,48–53: By simplicity he will become upright in actions, thoughts, and speech, and he will become veracious; thereby he will truly practice the Law.

By humility he will acquire freedom from self-conceit; thereby he will become of a kind and meek disposition, and avoid the eight kinds of pride.

By sincerity of mind he obtains purity of mind, which will cause him to exert himself for the fulfilment of the Law which the Ginas have proclaimed; and he will practice the Law in the next world too.

By sincerity in religious practice, he obtains proficiency in it; being proficient in it he will act up to his words.

By sincerity of acting he will become pure in his actions.

By watchfulness of the mind he concentrates his thoughts; thereby he truly practices control.

VI

BUDDHISM

BUDDHISM, at least in its earliest stages, cannot be called a religion in the true sense of the term. Founded by Gautama (B.C. 563–483), son of a rich Hindu rajah of the Sakya clan, it was merely a system of morality and philosophy based on the belief that life was too full of suffering to be worth living. For a long time its principles and moral code appealed to people of many and varied religious beliefs. Then, gradually, Gautama was deified as the Buddha, or the "Enlightened," miracle stories grew up about his life, and what was originally an important system of morals and philosophic thought became a religion.

Today Buddhism is regarded by scholars as the first of the great international religions, being followed later by Christianity and Mohammedanism. While hundreds of millions are tremendously influenced by the moral and philosophic teachings of Gautama, they cannot be truly classed as Buddhists. It is nearer the truth to say that those who worship Gautama, pray to him, and accept the doctrine of his divinity number near to 150,000,000.

Although beginning in India, Buddhism has practically ceased to exist in that vast country. Hindu Buddhists number today slightly over 2,500. It has spread, however, among the Mongolians. Nevertheless, as a religion it is not making great gains today.

Born amid wealth and destined to rulership, Gautama was so impressed by the poverty and suffering of mankind that he renounced his birth, his family, and his fortune, and turned to the life of a monk. After trying to find peace and a solution to the problems of universal suffering and misery through Hinduism and later Jainism, he experienced a "Great Enlightenment" at the age of 35. This consisted of a firm conviction that the only escape from suffering lay in complete renunciation of all desires. Immediately he began preaching this new doctrine and gathering disciples. This he continued until his death at the age of 80.

Buddhist scriptures consist of the "Three Baskets" of Wisdom and the *Dhammapada*. The first "Basket," the *Vinaya Pitaka,* or *Discipline Basket,* contains minute rules for those who are to be initiated into the order of high-class Buddhists. The second is the *Sutta Pitaka,* or *Teaching Basket.* This contains the sayings and teachings of the Buddha. The third is the *Abhidhamma Pitaka, or Metaphysical Basket.* Here are to be found detailed explanations of Buddhist doctrines and of Buddhist psychology. The *Dhammapada* is a collection of the sayings of the Buddha. There are also many Buddhist writings which have not been accepted as canonical by the Buddhists.

Not all the sacred writings of Buddhism have been translated into English. Indeed, much of the *Three Baskets* has never even been published in the original Pali, the dialect of the common people of north-central India. Although much work has been done by Western scholars on this material, only a small part is available for study.

THE VINAYA PITAKA

Mahavagga

The Mahavagga is a section of the Vinaya Pitaka (Discipline Basket) of Buddhism. Here are to be found numerous directions and teachings written for the instruction of initiates into the higher class of Buddhism. Rules are laid down and detailed directions for preparation and living are stated. The candidate must be fit and willing to live a clean, virtuous life. The book is often referred to as the "Greater Group."

5,1,10: And having seen the Truth, having mastered the Truth, having understood the Truth, having penetrated the Truth, having overcome uncertainty, having dispelled all doubts, having gained full knowledge, dependent on nobody else for the knowledge of the doctrine of the Teacher, they said to the Blessed One: "Glorious Lord! glorious, Lord! Just as if one should set up, Lord, what has been overturned, or should reveal what has been hidden, or should point out the way to one who has lost his way, or should bring a lamp into the darkness, in order that those who had eyes might see visible things, thus has the Blessed One preached the doctrine in many ways. We take our refuge, Lord, in the Blessed One, and in the Dhamma, and in the fraternity of Bhikkhus; may the Blessed One receive us from this day forth while our life lasts as his disciples who have taken their refuge in Him."

5,1,16: "Now what think you, Sona, —when the strings of your lute were too loose, had your lute then any sound, was it in a fit state to be played upon?"
"Not so, Lord!"

"Now what think you, Sona,—when the strings of your lute were neither too much stretched nor too loose, but fixed in even proportion, had your lute sound then, was it then in a fit state to be played upon?"
"Yes, Lord!"
"And just so, Sona, does too eager a determination conduce to self-righteousness, and too weak a determination to sloth."

5,1,17: "Do thou, therefore, O Sona, be steadfast in evenness of determination, press through to harmony of your mental powers. Let that be the object of your thought!"
"Even so, Lord!" said the venerable Sona, and hearkened to the word of the Blessed One.
And when the Blessed One had exhorted the venerable Sona with this exhortation, then, as quickly as a strong man can stretch forth his arm, or can draw it back again when it has been stretched forth, he vanished from the presence of the venerable Sona in the Sitavana grove, and reappeared on the hill of the Vulture's Peak.

5,1,25: "When a Bhikkhu, Lord, has thus become fully emancipated in heart, even though many objects visible to the sight should enter the path of his eye, yet they take not possession of his mind: undefiled is his mind, firm, immovable; and he sees into the (manner in which that impression) passes away—even though many objects audible to the ear, smellable to the nostrils, tastable to the tongue, feelable to the body, sensible to the intellect should enter upon the path of the ear, the nose, the tongue, the skin, the intellect, yet they take not possession of his mind: undefiled is his mind, firm, immovable, and he sees into the (manner in which that impression) passes away."

5,1,26: "Just, Lord, as if there be a mountain of rock, undivided, solid, one mass, and much wind and rain should fall upon it from the direction of the East, or of the West, or of the North, or of the South, yet they would not make it shake, or tremble, or quake; just so, Lord, when a Bhikkhu has thus become fully emancipated in heart . . ." [etc., as in 25, down to the end].

5,1,28: And the Blessed One addressed the Bhikkhus, and said: "Thus, brethren, do young men of worth make their insight known. The truth is spoken, and the self is not obtruded. But herein some foolish ones, methinks, make known their insight to be a thing ridiculous, and they, thereafter, fall into defeat!"

5,4,2: Then those Bhikkhus told this thing to the Blessed One.

"Is it true, what they say, O Bhikkhus, that the Khabbaggiya Bhikkhus walk shod, though the Master and the Elders walk unshod?"

"It is true, Lord."

The Blessed Buddha rebuked them, saying,

"How, O Bhikkhus, can these foolish persons walk shod, though the Master and the Elders walk unshod? For even the laymen, O Bhikkhus, who are clad in white, for the sake of some handicraft that may procure them a living, will be respectful, affectionate, hospitable to their teachers."

5,13,9: Then the Blessed One, after spending the greater part of the night in the open air, entered the Vihara. And also the venerable Sona, having spent the greater part of the night in the open air, entered the Vihara. And

the Blessed One rose up, early in the morning, towards dawn, and requested the venerable Sona, saying,

"May the Dhamma so become clear to you that you may speak."

"Even so, Lord!" said the venerable Sona in assent to the Blessed One; and he intoned all the verses in the Book of the Eights (Atthaka-vaggikani).

And the Blessed One, at the conclusion of the venerable Sona's recitation, expressed his pleasure, saying,

"Excellent, most excellent, O Bhikkhu! Well have the Eights been grasped by thee, well thought over, well learnt by heart: and with a fine voice art thou gifted, distinct, pleasant, able to make things understood. How many years is it since thou hast been ordained?"

"One year, my Lord!"

6,31,7: "And in which way is it, Siha, that one speaking truly could say of me: 'The Samana Gotama maintains annihilation; he teaches the doctrine of annihilation; and in this doctrine he trains his disciples?' I proclaim, Siha, the annihilation of lust, of ill-will, of delusion; I proclaim the annihilation of the manifold conditions (of heart) which are evil and not good. . . .

"And in which way is it, Siha, that one speaking truly could say of me: 'The Samana Gotama proclaims contemptibleness, &c.?' I deem, Siha, unrighteous actions contemptible, whether they be performed by deed, or by word, or by thought; I proclaim the doctrine of the contemptibleness of falling into the manifold conditions (of heart) which are evil and not good. . . ."

6,31,13: At that time a great number of Niganthas (running) through Vesali, from road to road and from cross-way to cross-way, with outstretched arms, cried: "To-day Siha, the general, has killed a great ox and has made a meal for the Samana Gotama; the Samana Gotama knowingly eats this meat of an animal killed for this very purpose, and has thus become virtually the author of that deed (of killing the animal)!"

Then a certain man went to the place where Siha, the general, was. Having approached him he said to Siha, the general, into his ear: "Please, Lord, have you noticed that a great number of Niganthas (running) through Vesali, . . . ?"

"Do not mind it, my good Sir. Long since those venerable brethren are trying to discredit the Buddha, the Dhamma, and the Sanggha; and those venerable brethren do not become tired of telling false, idle, vain lies of the Blessed One. Not for our life would we ever intentionally kill a living being."

8,1,35: And the Blessed One, after having delivered a religious discourse in consequence of that, thus addressed the Bhikkhus:

"I allow you, O Bhikkhus, to wear lay robes. He who likes may wear pamsukula robes; he who likes may accept lay robes. Whether you are pleased with the one or with the other sort of robes, I approve it."

Now the people of Ragagaha heard, "The Blessed One has allowed the Bhikkhus to wear lay robes." Then those people became glad and delighted (because they thought), "Now we will bestow gifts (on the Bhikkhus) and acquire merit by good works, since the Blessed One has allowed the Bhikkhus to wear lay robes." And in one day many thousands of robes were presented at Ragagaha (to the Bhikkhus).

And the people in the country heard, "The Blessed One has allowed the Bhikkhus to wear lay robes." Then those people became glad [etc., as above, down to:] And in one day many thousands of robes were presented through the country also (to the Bhikkhus).

8,15,13: "If they should reply to me, 'He had formerly been at Savatthi,' then shall I arrive at the conclusion, 'For a certainty did that brother enjoy either the robes for the rainy season, or the food for the incoming Bhikkhus, or the food for the outgoing Bhikkhus, or the food for the sick, or the food for those that wait upon the sick, or the medicine for the sick, or the constant supply of congey.' Then will gladness spring up within me on my calling that to mind; and joy will arise to me thus gladdened; and so rejoicing all my frame will be at peace; and being thus at peace I shall experience a blissful feeling of content; and in that bliss my heart will be at rest; and that will be to me an exercise of my moral sense, an exercise of my moral powers, an exercise of seven kinds of wisdom! This, Lord, was the advantage I had in view for myself in asking those eight boons of the Blessed One."

8,22,1: Now at that time a quantity of robes had come into the possession of a certain Bhikkhu, and he was desirous of giving those robes to his father and mother.

They told this matter to the Blessed One.

"Since they are his father and mother, what can we say, O Bhikkhus, though he give them to them. I allow you, O Bhikkhus, to give (robes, in such a case), to your parents. And a gift of faith is not to be made of no avail. Whosoever shall make it of no avail, he is guilty of a dukkata."

8,26,3: Then the Blessed One, on that occasion and in that connection, convened a meeting of the Bhikkhu-samgha, and asked the Bhikkhus, "Is there, O Bhikkhus, in such and such an apartment, a Bhikkhu who is sick?"

"There is, Lord."

"Then what, O Bhikkhus, is the matter with that Bhikkhu?"

"He has a disturbance, Lord, in his bowels."

"And is there any one, O Bhikkhus, to wait upon him?"

"No, Lord."

"Why, then, do not the Bhikkhus wait upon him?"

"That Bhikkhu, Lord, is of no service to the Bhikkhus; therefore do they not wait upon him."

"Ye, O Bhikkhus, have no mothers and no fathers who might wait upon you! If ye, O Bhikkhus, wait not one upon the other, who is there indeed who will wait upon you? Whosoever, O Bhikkhus, would wait upon me, he should wait upon the sick."

9,1,9: Then those Bhikkhus rose from their seats, adjusted their upper robes so as to cover one shoulder, prostrated themselves, inclined their heads to the feet of the Blessed One, and said to the Blessed One: "Transgression, O Lord, has overcome us like the foolish, like the erring, like the unhappy, in this that we have expelled a pure, guiltless Bhikkhu without any cause and reason. May, O Lord, the Blessed One accept (the confession of) our sin in its sinfulness, and we will refrain from it in future."

"Truly, O Bhikkhus, transgression has overcome you like the foolish, like the erring, like the unhappy, in that you have expelled a pure, guiltless Bhikkhu without any cause and reason. But as you see, O Bhikkhus, your sin in its sinfulness, and duly make amends for it, we accept it from you. For this, O Bhikkhus, is called progress in the discipline of the noble one, if one sees his sin in its sinfulness, and duly makes amends for it, and refrains from it in future."

10,2,20: "Then king Brahmadatta of Kasi, O Bhikkhus, thought: 'O wonderful! O Marvelous! How clever of

this young Dighavu, that he understands in its full extent the meaning of what his father spoke so concisely,'—and he gave him back his father's troops and vehicles, his realm, his treasuries and storehouses, and he gave him his daughter."

"Now, O Bhikkhus, if such is the forbearance and mildness of kings who wield the sceptre and bear the sword, so much more, O Bhikkhus, must you so let your light shine before the world that you, having embraced the religious life according to so well-taught a doctrine and a discipline, are seen to be forbearing and mild."

And for the third time the Blessed One thus addressed those Bhikkhus: "Enough, O Bhikkhus, no altercations, no contentions, no disunion, no quarrels!"

And for the third time that Bhikkhu who adhered to the party who were wrong, said to the Blessed One: "Lord, may the Blessed One, the king of Truth, be patient! Lord, may the Blessed One quietly enjoy the bliss he has obtained already in this life! The responsibility for these altercations and contentions, for this disunion and quarrel will rest with us alone." And the Blessed One thought: "Truly these fools are infatuate; it is no easy task to administer instruction to them,"—and he rose from his seat and went away.

10,4,3: And the venerable Anuruddha, the venerable Nandiya, and the venerable Kimbila went forth to meet the Blessed One; one took the bowl and the robe of the Blessed One, the other one prepared a seat, and the third one brought water for the washing of his feet, a foot-stool, and a towel. Then the Blessed One sat down on the seat they had prepared; and when he was seated, the Blessed One washed his feet. And also those venerable persons, having respectfully saluted the Blessed One, sat down near him. When the venerable Anuruddha was sitting near him, the Blessed One said to him: "Is it all well with you, O Anuruddhas? Do you find your living? Do you get food without too much trouble?"

"It is all well with us, Lord; we find our living, Lord; we get food, Lord, without too much trouble."

"And do you live, O Anuruddhas, in unity and concord, without quarrels, like milk and water (mixed together), and looking at each other with friendly eyes?"

"Certainly, Lord, do we live in unity and concord [etc., down to:] and looking at each other with friendly eyes."

"And in what way, O Anuruddhas, do you live in unity and concord, . . . ?"

10,4,4: "I think, Lord: 'It is all gain to me indeed, it is high bliss for me indeed, that I live in the companionship of brethren like these.' Thus, Lord, do I exercise towards these venerable brethren friendliness in my actions, both openly and in secret; I exercise (towards them) friendliness in my words, and friendliness in my thoughts, both openly and in secret. And I think thus, Lord: 'What if I were to give up my own will and to live only according to the will of these venerable brethren.' Thus, Lord, I give up my own will and live only according to the will of these venerable brethren. Our bodies, Lord, are different, but our minds, I think, have become one."

And also the venerable Nandiya . . . and also the venerable Kimbila . . . said to the Blessed One: "I think also, Lord: 'It is all gain to me' [etc., down to:] have become one."

"In this way, Lord, do we live in unity and concord, without quarrels, like milk and water (mixed together), and looking at each other with friendly eyes."

10,4,5: "And do you live, O Anuruddhas, in earnestness, zeal, and resolvedness?"

"Certainly, Lord, do we live in earnestness, zeal, and resolvedness."

"And in what way, O Anuruddhas, do you live in earnestness, zeal, and resolvedness?"

"He who first of us comes back, Lord, from the village, from his alms-pilgrimage, prepares seats, gets water for washing feet, a foot-stool, and a towel, cleans the slop-basin, and gets it ready, and puts there (water to) drink and food. He who comes back last from the village, from his alms-pilgrimage, eats, if there is any food left (from the dinner of the others) and if he desires to do so; and if he does not desire (to eat), he throws it away at a place free from grass, or pours it away into water in which no living things are; takes away the seat, puts away the water for washing the feet, the foot-stool, and the towel, cleans the slop-basin and puts it away, puts the water and the food away, and sweeps the dining-room. He who sees a water-pot, or a bowl for food, or an easing-chair, empty and void, puts it (into its proper place), and if he is not able to do so single-handed, he calls some one else, and thus we put it (into its place) with our united effort, but we do not utter a word, Lord, on that account. And every five days, Lord, we spend a whole night, sitting together, in religious discourse. In this way, Lord, do we live in earnestness, zeal, and resolvedness."

THE SUTTA PITAKA

Mahaparinibbana Sutta

This book is from among those writings known as the Sutta Pitaka (*Teaching Basket*) *of Buddhism. Its other title, an attempt to translate the original title into English, is the "Book of the Great Decease." It is also part of the* Digha Nikaya *or "Long Collection" of Buddhist teachings. Here the Buddha is seen teaching his disciples and developing his moral and philosophic position. There is much detail and a great deal of repetition as the teacher attempts to impress upon his followers the doctrines of the group.*

1,8: "Other seven conditions of welfare will I teach you, O brethren. Listen well, and attend, and I will speak."

And on their expressing their assent, he spake as follows:

"So long as the brethren shall be full of faith, modest in heart, afraid of sin, full of learning, strong in energy, active in mind, and full of wisdom, so long may the brethren be expected not to decline, but to prosper.

"So long as these conditions shall continue to exist among the brethren, so long as they are instructed in these conditions, so long may the brethren be expected not to decline, but to prosper."

1,9: "Other seven conditions of welfare will I teach you, O brethren. Listen well, and attend, and I will speak."

And on their expressing their assent, he spake as follows:

"So long as the brethren shall exercise themselves in the sevenfold higher wisdom, that is to say, in mental activity, search after truth, energy, joy, peace, earnest contemplation and equanimity of mind, so long may the brethren be expected not to decline, but to prosper.

"So long as these conditions shall continue to exist among the brethren, so long as they are instructed in these conditions, so long may the brethren be expected not to decline, but to prosper."

1,11: "Six conditions of welfare will I teach you, O brethren. Listen well, and attend, and I will speak."

And on their expressing their assent, he spake as follows:

"So long as the brethren shall persevere in kindness of action, speech, and thought amongst the saints, both in public and in private—so long as they shall decide without partiality, and share in common with the upright and the holy, all such things as they receive in accordance with the just provisions of the order, down even to the mere contents of a begging bowl—so long as the brethren shall live among the saints in the practice, both in public and in private, of those virtues which (unbroken, intact, unspotted, unblemished) are productive of freedom, and praised by the wise; which are untarnished by the desire of future life, or by the belief in the efficacy of outward acts; and which are conducive to high and holy thoughts—so long as the brethren shall live among the saints, cherishing, both in public and in private, that noble and saving faith which leads to the complete destruction of the sorrow of him who acts according to it—so long may the brethren be expected not to decline, but to prosper.

"So long as these six conditions shall continue to exist among the brethren, so long as they are instructed in these six conditions, so long may the brethren be expected not to decline, but to prosper."

1,12: And whilst the Blessed One stayed there at Ragagaha on the Vulture's Peak he held that comprehensive religious talk with the brethren on the nature of upright conduct, and of earnest contemplation, and of intelligence. "Great is the fruit, great the advantage of earnest contemplation when set round with upright conduct. Great is the fruit, great the advantage of intellect when set round with earnest contemplation. The mind set round with intelligence is freed from the great evils, that is to say, from sensuality, from individuality, from delusion, and from ignorance."

1,14: There the Blessed One stayed in the king's house and held that comprehensive religious talk with the brethren on the nature of upright conduct, and of earnest contemplation, and of intelligence. "Great is the fruit, great the advantage of earnest contemplation when set round with upright conduct. Great is the fruit, great the advantage of intellect when set round with earnest contemplation. The mind set round with intelligence is freed from the great evils, that is to say, from sensuality, from individuality, from delusion, and from ignorance."

1,31: And when they were thus seated the Blessed One gave thanks in these verses:—

"Wheresoe'er the prudent man shall
    take up his abode
Let him support there good and upright men of self-control.
Let him give gifts to all such deities
    as may be there.
Revered, they will revere him; honored, they honor him again;
Are gracious to him as a mother to
    her own, her only son.

And the man who has the grace of the
    gods, good fortune he beholds."

2,7: "The brother named Salha, Ananda, by the destruction of the great evils has by himself, and in this world, known and realized and attained to Arahatship, and to emancipation of heart and to emancipation of mind. The sister named Nanda, Ananda, has, by the complete destruction of the five bonds that bind people to this world, become an inheritor of the highest heavens, there to pass entirely away, thence never to return. The devout Sudatta, Ananda, by the complete destruction of the three bonds, and by the reduction to a minimum of lust, hatred, and delusion has become a Sakadagamin, who on his first return to this world will make an end of sorrow. The devout woman Sugata, Ananda, by the complete destruction of the three bonds, has become converted, is no longer liable to be reborn in a state of suffering, and is assured of final salvation. The devout Kukudha, Ananda, by the complete destruction of the five bonds that bind people to these lower worlds of lust, has become an inheritor of the highest heavens, there to pass entirely away, thence never to return . . . More than ninety devout men of Nadika, who have died, Ananda, have by the complete destruction of the three bonds, and by the reduction of lust, hatred, and delusion, become Sakadagamins, who on their first return to this world will make an end of sorrow."

2,33: "Therefore, O Ananda, be ye lamps unto yourselves. Be ye a refuge to yourselves. Betake yourselves to no external refuge. Hold fast to the truth as a lamp. Hold fast as a refuge to the truth. Look not for refuge to anyone besides yourselves. And how, Ananda, is a brother to be a lamp unto himself, a refuge to himself, betaking himself to no external refuge, holding fast to the truth as a lamp, holding fast as a refuge to the truth, looking not for refuge to anyone besides himself?"

2,34: "Herein, O Ananda, let a brother, as he dwells in the body, so regard the body that he, being strenuous, thoughtful, and mindful, may, whilst in the world, overcome the grief which arises from bodily craving—while subject to sensations let him continue so to regard the sensations that he, being strenuous, thoughtful, and mindful, may, whilst in the world, overcome the grief which arises from the sensations—and so, also, as he thinks, or reasons, or feels, let him overcome the grief which arises from the craving due to ideas, or to reasoning, or to feeling."

2,35: "And whosoever, Ananda, either now or after I am dead, shall be a lamp unto themselves, shall betake themselves to no external refuge, but holding fast to the truth as their lamp, and holding fast as their refuge to the truth, shall look not for refuge to anyone besides themselves—it is they, Ananda, among my bhikkhus, who shall reach the very topmost Height! —but they must be anxious to learn."

3,49: And when he had thus spoken the venerable Ananda addressed the Blessed One, and said: "Vouchsafe, Lord, to remain during the kalpa! live on through the kalpa, O Blessed One! for the good and the happiness of the great multitudes, out of pity for the world, for the good and the gain and the weal of gods and men!"

3,66: And the Blessed One exhorted the brethren, and said: "Behold now, O brethren, I exhort you, saying, 'All component things must grow old. Work out your salvation with diligence. The final extinction of the Tathagata will take place before long.

At the end of three months from this time the Tathagata will die!'"

"My age is now full ripe, my life draws to its close:
I leave you, I depart, relying on myself alone!
Be earnest then, O brethren! holy, full of thought!
Be steadfast in resolve! Keep watch o'er your own hearts!
Who worries not, but holds fast to this truth and law,
Shall cross this sea of life, shall make an end of grief."

5,35: Then the Blessed One said to the venerable Ananda, as he sat there by his side: "Enough, Ananda! Do not let yourself be troubled; do not weep! Have I not already, on former occasions, told you that it is in the very nature of all things most near and dear unto us that we must divide ourselves from them, leave them, sever ourselves from them? How, then, Ananda, can this be possible—whereas anything whatever born, brought into being, and organized, contains within itself the inherent necessity of dissolution—how, then, can this be possible, that such a being should not be dissolved? No such condition can exist! For a long time, Ananda, have you been very near to me by acts of love, kind and good, that never varies, and is beyond all measure. For a long time, Ananda, have you been very near to me by words of love, kind and good, that never varies, and is beyond all measure. For a long time, Ananda, have you been very near to me by thoughts of love, kind and good, that never varies, and is beyond all measure. You have done well, Ananda! Be earnest in effort, and you too shall soon be free from the great evils—from sensuality, from individuality, from delusion, and from ignorance!"

5,62: And the Blessed One spake: "In whatsoever doctrine and discipline,

Subhadda, the noble eightfold path is not found, neither in it is there found a man of true saintliness of the first or of the second or of the third or of the fourth degree. And in whatsoever doctrine and discipline, Subhadda, the noble eightfold path is found, is found the man of true saintliness of the first and the second and the third and the fourth degree. Now in this doctrine and discipline, Subhadda, is found the noble eightfold path, and in it alone, Subhadda, is the man of true saintliness. Void are the systems of other teachers—void of true saints. And in this one, Subhadda, may the brethren live the Life that's Right, so that the world be not bereft of Arahats.

"But twenty-nine was I when I renounced
The world, Subhadda, seeking after good.
For fifty years and one year more, Subhadda,
Since I went out, a pilgrim have I been
Through the wide realms of virtue and of truth,
And outside these no really true 'saint' can be!

"Yea, not of the first, nor of the second, nor of the third, nor of the fourth degree. Void are the systems of other teachers—void of true saints. But in this one, Subhadda, may the brethren live the perfect life, that the world be not bereft of those who have reached the highest fruit."

Tevigga Sutta

The Tevigga Sutta *is the final (the twelfth) Sutta of the first division of the "Long Collection," a part of the* Sutta Pitaka *(Teaching Basket). It is often called the "Knowledge of the Three Vedas." This book consists of 12 dialogues dealing with the problems of right conduct. Two earnest* young Brahmans are pictured as seeking the true path to union with God. The *Sutta is a lengthy argument to prove to them that right conduct is the only direct route to any real union with God.*

1,46: Then the Blessed One spake and said:

"Know, Vasettha, that (from time to time) a Tathagata is born into the world, a fully Enlightened One, blessed and worthy, abounding in wisdom and goodness, happy, with knowledge of the world, unsurpassed as a guide to erring mortals, a teacher of gods and men, a Blessed Buddha. He, by himself, thoroughly understands, and sees, as it were, face to face this universe—the world below with all its spirits, and the world above, of Mara and of Brahma—and all creatures, Samanas and Brahmans, gods and men, and he then makes his knowledge known to others. The truth doth he proclaim both in its letter and in its spirit, lovely in its origin, lovely in its progress, lovely in its consummation: the higher life doth he make known, in all its purity and in all its perfectness."

1,49: "When he has thus become a recluse he passes a life self-restrained according to the rules of the Patimokkha; uprightness is his delight, and he sees danger in the least of those things he should avoid; he adopts and trains himself in the precepts; he encompasses himself with holiness in word and deed; he sustains his life by means that are quite pure; good is his conduct, guarded the door of his senses; mindful and self-possessed, he is altogether happy!"

2,4: "Putting away lying, he abstains from speaking falsehood. He speaks truth, from the truth he never swerves; faithful and trustworthy, he injures not his fellow man by deceit.

"This, too, is the kind of goodness that he has."

2,5: "Putting away slander, he abstains from calumny. What he hears here he repeats not elsewhere to raise a quarrel against the people here: what he hears elsewhere he repeats not here to raise a quarrel against the people there. Thus he lives as a binder together of those who are divided, an encourager of those who are friends, a peacemaker, a lover of peace, impassioned for peace, a speaker of words that make for peace.

"This, too, is the kind of goodness that he has."

Maha-Sudassana Sutta

The English title of this Sutta *is "The Great King of Glory." The* Sutta *is a section of the Buddhist* Sutta Pitaka *(Teaching Basket), and is to be found in the* Digha Nikaya *or "Long Collection." Here is an attempt, by means of a beautiful fairy tale or poem, to describe the greatest possible king in all his majesty and wealth. The purpose is to prove that even this greatest of great possible things is all vanity and that only righteousness is abiding and valuable.*

1,16: "Thus spake the Great King of Glory:

" 'Ye shall slay no living thing.

" 'Ye shall not take that which has not been given.

" 'Ye shall not act wrongly touching the bodily desires.

" 'Ye shall speak no lie.

" 'Ye shall drink no maddening drink.

" 'Ye shall eat as ye have eaten.' "

1,67: "Now, Ananda, when Sakka, the king of the gods, became aware in his mind of the thoughts that were in the heart of the Great King of Glory, he addressed Vissakamma the god, and said:

" 'Come now, Vissakamma, create me a mansion for the Great King of Glory—a palace which shall be called Righteousness.' "

1,69: "Then, Ananda, Vissakamma the god said to the Great King of Glory:

" 'I would create for thee, O King, a mansion—a palace which shall be called Righteousness!'

"Then, Ananda, the Great King of Glory signified, by silence, his consent."

THE DHAMMAPADA

THE *Dhammapada* (Way of Virtue) was accepted in 240 B.C. by the Council of Asoka, the great Indian monarch, as a true collection of the sayings of Gautama. Nevertheless, it was not written until much later and, being transmitted largely by word of mouth, it undoubtedly was added to and changed from time to time. Regardless of this fact, the book is accepted by Buddhists as a true account of the Buddha and is used widely as a book of devotions and for meditation.

1. Mind it is which gives to things their quality, their foundation, and their being: whoso speaks or acts with impure mind, him sorrow dogs, as the wheel follows the steps of the draught-ox.

2. Mind it is which gives to things their quality, their foundation, and their being: whoso speaks or acts with purified mind, him happiness accompanies as his faithful shadow.

3. "He has abused me, beaten me, worsted me, robbed me"; those who dwell upon such thoughts never lose their hate.

4. "He has abused me, beaten me, worsted me, robbed me"; those who dwell not upon such thoughts are freed of hate.

5. Never does hatred cease by hating; by not hating does it cease: this is the ancient law.

10. He who has doffed his impurities, calm and clothed upon with temperance and truth, he wears the pure robe worthily.

11. Those who mistake the shadow for the substance, and the substance for the shadow, never attain the reality, following wandering fires [lit. followers of a false pursuit].

12. But if a man knows the substance and the shadow as they are, he attains the reality, following the true trail.

18. Here and hereafter the good man rejoices; rejoices as he thinks "I have done well": yea rather rejoices when he goes to a heaven.

19. If a man is a great preacher of the sacred text, but slothful and no doer of it, he is a hireling shepherd, who has no part in the flock.

20. If a man preaches but a little of the text and practises the teaching, putting away lust and hatred and infatuation; if he is truly wise and detached and seeks nothing here or hereafter, his lot is with the holy ones.

21. Zeal is the way to Nirvana. Sloth is the day of death. The zealous die not: the slothful are as it were dead.

22. The wise who know the power of zeal delight in it, rejoicing in the lot of the noble.

23. These wise ones by meditation and reflection, by constant effort reach Nirvana, highest freedom.

24. Great grows the glory of him who is zealous in meditation, whose actions are pure and deliberate, whose life is calm and righteous and full of vigour.

25. By strenuous effort, by self-control, by temperance, let the wise man make for himself an island which the flood cannot overwhelm.

26. Fools in their folly give themselves to sloth: the wise man guards his vigour as his greatest possession.

27. Give not yourselves over to sloth, and to dalliance with delights:

he who meditates with earnestness attains great joy.

28. When the wise one puts off sloth for zeal, ascending the high tower of wisdom he gazes sorrowless upon the sorrowing crowd below! Wise himself, he looks upon the fools as one upon a mountain-peak gazing upon the dwellers in the valley.

29. Zealous amidst the slothful, vigilant among the sleepers, go the prudent, as a racehorse outstrips a hack.

35. Good it is to tame the mind, so difficult to control, fickle, and capricious. Blessed is the tamed mind.

36. Let the wise man guard his mind, incomprehensible, subtle, and capricious though it is. Blessed is the guarded mind.

42. Badly does an enemy treat his enemy, a foeman his foe: worse is the havoc wrought by a misdirected mind.

43. Not mother and father, not kith and kin can so benefit a man as a mind attentive to the right.

50. Be not concerned with other men's evil words or deeds or neglect of good: look rather to thine own sins and negligence [lit. "sins of commission and omission": things done and undone].

51. As some bright flower—fair to look at, but lacking fragrance—so are fair words which bear no fruit in action.

52. As some bright flower, fragrant as it is fair, so are fair words whose fruit is seen in action.

53. As if from a pile of flowers one were to weave many a garland, so let mortals string together much merit.

54. No scent of flower is borne against the wind, though it were sandal, or incense or jasmine: but the fragrance of the holy is borne against the wind: the righteous pervade all space (with their fragrance).

55. More excellent than the scent of sandal and incense, of lily and jasmine, is the fragrance of good deeds.

56. A slight thing is this scent of incense and of sandal-wood, but the scent of the holy pervades the highest heaven.

61. If on a journey thou canst not find thy peer or one better than thyself, make the journey stoutly alone: there is no company with a fool.

62. "I have sons and wealth," thinks the fool with anxious care; he is not even master of himself, much less of sons and wealth.

63. The fool who knows his folly is so far wise: but the fool who reckons himself wise is called a fool indeed.

64. Though for a lifetime the fool keeps company with the wise, yet does he not learn righteousness, as spoon gets no taste of soup.

65. If but for a moment the thoughtful keep company with the wise, straightway he learns righteousness, as tongue tastes soup.

66. Fools and dolts go their way, their own worst enemies: working evil which bears bitter fruit.

67. That is no good deed which brings remorse, whose reward one receives with tears and lamentation.

68. But that is the good deed which brings no remorse, whose reward the doer takes with joy and gladness.

69. Honey-sweet to the fool is his sin—until it ripens: then he comes to grief.

76. Look upon him who shows you your faults as a revealer of treasure: seek his company who checks and chides you, the sage who is wise in reproof: it fares well and not ill with him who seeks such company.

77. Let a man admonish, and advise, and keep others from strife! So will he be dear to the righteous, and hated by the unrighteous.

103. If one were to conquer a thousand thousand in the battle—he who conquers self is the greatest warrior.

104,105. Self-conquest is better than

other victories: neither god nor demi-god, neither Mara nor Brahma, can undo the victory of such a one, who is self-controlled and always calm.

106. If month by month throughout a hundred years one were to offer sacrifices costing thousands, and if for a moment another were to reverence the self-controlled—this is the better worship.

107. If one for a hundred years tended the sacred fire in the glade, and another for a moment reverenced the self-controlled, this is the better worship.

108. Whatsoever sacrifice or offering a man makes for a full year in hope of benefits, all is not worth a quarter of that better offering—reverence to the upright.

109. In him who is trained in constant courtesy and reverence to the old, four qualities increase: length of days, beauty, gladness, and strength.

117. If one offends, let him not repeat his offence; let him not set his heart upon it. Sad is the piling up of sin.

118. If one does well, let him repeat his well-doing: let him set his heart upon it. Glad is the storing up of good.

119. The bad man sees good days, until his wrong-doing ripens; then he beholds evil days.

120. Even a good man may see evil days till his well-doing comes to fruition; then he beholds good days.

121. Think not lightly of evil "It will not come nigh me." Drop by drop the pitcher is filled: slowly yet surely the fool is saturated with evil.

122. Think not lightly of good "It will not come nigh me." Drop by drop the pitcher is filled: slowly yet surely the good are filled with merit.

129. All fear the rod, all quake at death. Judge then by thyself, and forbear from slaughter, or from causing to slay.

130. To all is life dear. Judge then by thyself, and forbear to slay or to cause slaughter.

131. Whoso himself desires joy, yet hurts them who love joy, shall not obtain it hereafter.

132. Whoso himself desires joy and hurts not them who love it, shall hereafter attain to joy.

133. Speak not harshly to any one: else will men turn upon *you*. Sad are the words of strife: retribution will follow them.

142. If even a fop fosters the serene mind, calm and controlled, pious and pure, and does no hurt to any living thing, he is the Brahmin, he is the Samana, he is the Bhikkhu.

143. Is there in all the world a man so modest that he provokes no blame, as a noble steed never deserves the whip? As a noble steed stung by the whip, be ye spirited and swift.

144. By faith, by righteousness, by manliness, by meditation, by just judgment, by theory and practice, by mindfulness, leave aside sorrow—no slight burden.

145. Engineers control the water, fletchers fashion their shafts, carpenters shape the wood: it is themselves that the pious fashion and control.

157. If a man love himself, let him diligently watch himself: the wise will keep vigil for one of the three watches of the night.

158. Keep first thyself aright: then mayest thou advise others. So is the wise man unblameable.

159. If one so shapes his own life as he directs others, himself controlled, he will duly control others: self, they say, is hard to tame.

160. A man is his own helper: who else is there to help? By self-control man is a rare help to himself.

161. The ill that is begun and has its growth and its being in self, bruises the foolish one, as the diamond pierces its own matrix.

162. As the creeper overpowers the tree, so he whose sin is great, works

for himself the havoc his enemy would wish for him.

163. Ill is easy to do; it is easy to do harm: hard indeed it is to do helpful and good deeds.

164. Whoso fondly repudiates the teaching of the noble and virtuous Arahats, following false doctrine, is like the bamboo which bears fruit to its own destruction.

165. Thou art brought low by the evil thou hast done thyself: by the evil thou hast left undone art thou purified. Purity and impurity are things of man's inmost self; no man can purify another.

166. Even for great benefit to another let no man imperil his own benefit. When he has realised what is for his own good, let him pursue that earnestly.

173. He who covers his idle deeds with goodness lights up the world as the moon freed of clouds.

174. Blinded are the men of this world; few there are who have eyes to see: few are the birds which escape the fowler's net; few are they who go to heaven.

175. Through the sky fly the swans: Rishis too pass through the air. The wise leave the world altogether, deserting Mara and his hosts.

176. There is no wrong he would not do who breaks one precept, speaking lies and mocking at the life to come.

177. Misers go not to the realm of gods: therefore he is a fool who does not delight in liberality. The wise delighting in liberality come thereby with gladness to the other world.

178. Good is kingship of the earth; good is birth in heaven; good is universal empire; better still is the fruit of conversion.

183. "Eschew all evil: cherish good: cleanse your inmost thoughts" —this is the teaching of Buddhas.

184. "Patience and fortitude is the supreme asceticism: Nirvana is above

all," say the Buddhas. He is no recluse who harms others: nor is he who causes grief an ascetic (samana).

194. A blessing is the arising of Buddhas, a blessing is the true preaching. Blessed is the unity of the Sangha, blessed is the devotion of those who dwell in unity.

195, 196. Immeasurable is the merit of him who does reverence to those to whom reverence is due, Buddha and his disciples, men who have left behind them the trammels of evil, and crossed beyond the stream of sorrow and wailing, calmed and free of all fear.

197. O Joy! We live in bliss; amongst men of hate, hating none. Let us indeed dwell among them without hatred.

198. O Joy! In bliss we dwell; healthy amidst the ailing. Let us indeed dwell amongst them in perfect health.

199. Yea in very bliss we dwell: free from care amidst the careworn. Let us indeed dwell amongst them without care.

200. In bliss we dwell possessing nothing: let us dwell feeding upon joy like the shining ones in their splendour.

201. The victor breeds enmity; the conquered sleeps in sorrow. Regardless of either victory or defeat the calm man dwells in peace.

202. There is no fire like lust; no luck so bad as hate. There is no sorrow like existence: no bliss greater than Nirvana (rest).

203. Hunger is the greatest ill: existence is the greatest sorrow. Sure knowledge of this is Nirvana, highest bliss.

204. Health is the greatest boon; content is the greatest wealth; a loyal friend is the truest kinsman; Nirvana is the Supreme Bliss.

205. Having tasted the joy of solitude and of serenity, a man is freed

from sorrow and from sin, and tastes the nectar of piety.

206. Good is the vision of the Noble; good is their company. He may be always happy who escapes the sight of fools.

207. He who consorts with fools knows lasting grief. Grievous is the company of fools, as that of enemies; glad is the company of the wise, as that of kinsfolk.

208. Therefore do thou consort with the wise, the sage, the learned, the noble ones who shun not the yoke of duty: follow in the wake of such a one, the wise and prudent, as the moon follows the path of the stars.

222. Whoso controls his rising anger as a running chariot, him I call the charioteer: the others only hold the reins.

223. By calmness let a man overcome wrath; let him overcome evil by good; the miser let him subdue by liberality, and the liar by truth.

224. Speak the truth, be not angry, give of thy poverty to the suppliant: by these three virtues a man attains to the company of the gods.

231. Guard against evil deeds: control the body. Eschew evil deeds and do good.

232. Guard against evil words; control the tongue. Eschew evil words and speak good ones.

233. Guard against evil thoughts; control the mind. Eschew evil thoughts and think good ones.

234. The wise, controlled in act, in word, in thought, are well controlled indeed.

235. Thou art withered as a sere leaf: Death's messengers await thee. Thou standest at the gate of death, and hast made no provision for the journey.

236. Make to thyself a refuge; come, strive and be prudent: when thy impurities are purged, thou shalt come into the heavenly abode of the Noble.

237. Thy life is ended; thou art come into the Presence of Death: there is no resting-place by the way, and thou hast no provision for the journey.

238. Make for thyself a refuge; come, strive and play the sage! Burn off thy taints, and thou shalt know birth and old age no more.

239. As a smith purifies silver in the fire, so bit by bit continually the sage burns away his impurities.

245. Hard it is for the modest, the lover of purity, the disinterested and simple and clean, the man of insight.

246, 247. The murderer, the liar, the thief, the adulterer, and the drunkard—these even in this world uproot themselves.

256, 257. Hasty judgment shows no man just. He is called just who discriminates between right and wrong, who judges others not hastily, but with righteous and calm judgment, a wise guardian of the law.

258. Neither is a man wise by much speaking: he is called wise who is forgiving, kindly, and fearless.

268, 269. Not by silence (mona) is a man a sage (muni) if he be ignorant and foolish: he who holds as it were the balance, taking the good and rejecting the bad, he is the sage: he who is sage for both worlds, he is the true sage.

270. A man is no warrior who worries living things: by not worrying is a man called warrior.

303. The faithful, upright man is endowed with (the true) fame and wealth, and is honoured wherever he goes.

304. Far off are seen the Holy Ones, like the Himalayas: the unholy pass unseen as arrows shot in the darkness.

305. Alone when eating, alone when sleeping, alone when walking, let a man strongly control himself and take his pleasure in the forest glade.

313. If a duty is to be done, do it

with thy might: a careless recluse scatters contagion broadcast.

314. Better leave undone a bad deed; one day the doer will lament: good it is to do the good deed which brings no remorse.

315. As a fortress guarded within and without, so guard thyself. Leave no loophole for attack! They who fail at their post mourn here, and hereafter go to hell.

316. Some are ashamed at what is not shameful, and blush not at deeds of shame: these perverse ones go to hell.

317. They who see fear where there is no fear, and tremble not at fearful things: these perverse ones go to hell.

318. They who think evil where there is no evil, and make light of grievous sin: these perverse ones go to hell.

319. But whoso calls sin sin, and innocence innocence: these right-minded ones go to happiness.

327. Be ye zealous: guard your thoughts. As an elephant sunk in the mud extricate yourselves from the clutches of evil.

328. If you can find a dutiful friend to go with you, a righteous and prudent man not caring for hardships, go with him deliberately.

329. If you cannot find such a one, travel alone as a king leaving a conquered realm, or as the elephant in the jungle.

330. It is better to be alone; there is no companionship with a fool: travel alone and sin not, forgetting care as the elephant in the jungle.

331. Good are companions in time of need; contentment with thy lot is good; at the hour of death, merit is a good friend, and good is the leaving of all sorrow.

332. Good is reverence for mother and father: good, too, reverence for recluses and sages.

333. Good is lifelong righteousness; and rooted faith is good: good is the getting of wisdom, and good the avoiding of sin.

334. As the "maluwa" creeper, so spreads the desire of the sluggard. From birth to birth he leaps like a monkey seeking fruit.

335. Whoso is subdued by this sordid clinging desire, his sorrows wax more and more, like "birana" grass after rain.

336. But *his* sorrows drop off like water from the lotus leaf, who subdues this sordid, powerful desire.

372. There is no meditation apart from wisdom; there is no wisdom apart from meditation. Those in whom wisdom and meditation meet are not far from Nirvana.

373. Divine pleasure is his who enters into solitude, the Bhikkhu who is calmed and sees the law with the seeing eye:

374. Whenever he ponders the beginning and the end of the elements of being, he finds joy and bliss; nectar it is to those who know.

375. This is the beginning in my teaching for a wise Bhikkhu; self-mastery, contentment, and control by the precepts: to cultivate those who are noble, righteous, and zealous friends;

376. To be hospitable and courteous, this is to be glad and to make an end of sorrow.

377. As jasmine sheds its withered blossoms so, O Bhikkhus, do you put away lust and hatred.

378. He who is controlled in act, in speech, in thought, and altogether calmed, having purged away worldliness, that Bhikkhu is called calm.

379. Come, rouse thyself! Examine thine own heart. The Bhikkhu who is thus self-guarded and mindful will live in happiness.

380. Each man is his own helper, each his own host; therefore curb thyself as the merchant curbs a spirited horse.

381. The glad Bhikkhu who puts

his trust in Buddha's Preaching goes to Nirvana, calm and blissful end of rebirth.

382. Let the young Bhikkhu apply himself to Buddha's Preaching: so will he light up the world as the moon escaped from the clouds.

390. It is no slight benefit to a Brahmin when he learns to hold his impulses in check; from whatever motive evil temper is controlled, by that control grief is truly soothed.

391. By whomsoever no evil is done in deed, or word, or thought, him I call a Brahmin who is guarded in these three.

392. As the Brahmin honours the burnt-sacrifice, so do thou honour him, from whomsoever is learnt the law of the true Buddha.

393. Not by matted locks, nor by lineage, nor by caste is one a Brahmin; he is the Brahmin in whom are truth and righteousness and purity.

394. What boots your tangled hair, O fool, what avails your garment of skins? You have adorned the outer parts, within you are full of uncleanness.

395. A man clothed in cast-off rags, lean, with knotted veins, meditating alone in the forest, him I call a Brahmin.

396. Not him do I call Brahmin who is merely born of a Brahmin mother; men may give him salutation as a Brahmin, though he be not detached from the world: but him I call a Brahmin who has attachment to nothing.

397. Him I call a Brahmin who has cut the bonds, who does not thirst for pleasures, who has left behind the hindrances.

398. Whoso has cut the cable, and the rope and the chain with all its links, and has pushed aside the bolt, this wise one I call a Brahmin.

399. Whoever bears patiently abuse and injury and imprisonment, whose bodyguard is fortitude, he is the Brahmin.

400. He is the Brahmin who does not give way to anger, who is careful of religious duties, who is upright, pure, and controlled, who has reached his last birth.

401. He who clings not to pleasures as water clings not to the lotus leaf, nor mustard-seed to the needle-point, him I call Brahmin.

402. He is the Brahmin who in this very world knows the end of sorrow, who has laid the burden aside and is free.

403. Whoso is wise with deep wisdom, seeing the right way and the wrong, and has reached the goal, him I call Brahmin.

404. He is the Brahmin who is not entangled either with householders or with recluses, who has no home and few wants.

405. He who lays down the rod, who neither kills, nor causes the death of creatures, moving or fixed, he is the Brahmin.

406. Not opposing those who oppose, calm amidst the fighters, not grasping amidst men who grasp, he is the Brahmin.

407. He is the Brahmin from whom anger, and hatred, and pride, and slander have dropped away, as the mustard-seed from the needle-point.

VII

JUDAISM

JUDAISM is the name for the religion of the Hebrews.

This religion, in its long development from before 1200 B.C., has borrowed a great deal from other religions, but has also contributed greatly to many religious systems, particularly Christianity and Mohammedanism. Indeed, Christianity grew out of Judaism and includes the sacred writings of Judaism among its own sacred literature.

The sacred scriptures of Judaism consist of 39 "books" or writings which are generally known as the Old Testament. These books are usually divided by the Jews into three groups as follows:

I.   TORAH or Law: *Genesis, Exodus, Leviticus, Numbers,* and *Deuteronomy.*

II. NEBIIM or The Prophets: *Joshua, Judges, I Samuel, II Samuel, I Kings, II Kings, Isaiah, Jeremiah, Ezekiel, Hosea, Joel, Amos, Obadiah, Jonah, Micah, Nahum, Habakkuk, Zephaniah, Haggai, Zachariah, Malachi.*

III. KETHUBIM or Sacred Writings: *Psalms, Proverbs, Job, Song of Solomon, Ruth, Lamentations, Ecclesiastes, Esther, Daniel, Ezra, Nehemiah, I Chronicles, II Chronicles.*

All of these books were originally composed in Hebrew, except approximately half of *Daniel,* some parts of *Ezra,* and a verse of *Jeremiah.* These latter were written in Aramaic.

There are other documents read by the Hebrews and held to have special religious value even though they are not included in the canon of scriptures. Chief among these is the *Talmud,* which is divided into the *Mishna,* or text, and the *Gemara,* or commentary.

Several writings have been grouped together and are known as the *Apocrypha.* These books formed part of the sacred writings of the Alexandrian Jews and are to be found as part of the Hebrew scriptures in early manuscripts. However, most authorities reject them.

Although the Council of Trent, defining the doctrines of Catholicism, declared them to be canonical and ordered them included in the Bible, the books are usually omitted from the Protestant Bible.

The sacred scriptures of Judaism represent a literary activity spreading over more than 1,000 years. The earlier books were produced in a semi-savage, nomadic culture and reflect the crude, war-infested thinking of these early people, who were polytheistic, believed in polygamy, and practiced many religious rites that seem strange to us today. Chief among these was human sacrifice. However, during the period of development which is reflected in these writings, the Hebrews rose from this semi-savage state to a highly moral and ethical civilization. Their leaders preached a code of human relationships that reach beyond much that we have been able to attain even in our own day. By so doing, they repudiated the teachings and practices of their primitive ancestors. There is a great difference between the god of the early Hebrews who ordered his followers to destroy their enemies even to dashing the heads of babies against rocks and the God of Isaiah and Hosea who taught men to love their enemies.

The literature of the Hebrews reflects this development from primitive life to civilization, from crude beliefs of nomadic tribesmen to the high ethical idealism of the prophets, from the nature worship of Abraham to the spiritual insight of Isaiah. Thus the Old Testament is a history of Hebrew literature and of Hebrew moral and ethical development.

As the Hebrews roamed about and came into contact with other peoples and other religious beliefs and practices, they borrowed much, adding what they borrowed to their religion and dropping some of their own rites and beliefs. It is possible to find much of Egyptian, Babylonian, and other religious beliefs mixed into Judaism.

One of the great ideas running through much of Hebrew sacred literature is belief in a coming Messiah who would restore a traditional and often imaginary glory of the Jewish race. God is believed to be, in a peculiar way, the God of the Jews and to have a special place for them in the scheme of things. Thus the Jew looked for a Messiah who would carry out God's plan for them.

Jesus was acclaimed by many as the promised Messiah at a time when the Jews were greatly interested in the coming of a Messiah. The Maccabees and others had attempted to stir up revolt against the Roman overlords so that the Jews might attain a position of renewed pride and honor. In Jesus a great many saw the fulfilment of this hope. But Jesus failed the militant Jews and they turned from him. He did not attempt an armed revolt against the Romans, but rather preached peace and subjection. He taught that all men were brothers and equal in the sight of God.

Thus the Jews continue to look for this "Coming One" who will restore their ancient glory.

THE OLD TESTAMENT

THE "books" or writings contained in the Old Testament, 39 of them, are the canonical works sacred to the Jews. This is, of course, a small selection of the great mass of literature which has come down to us from the early centuries of Hebrew life. But this group of books contains history and legend, poetry, drama, wise sayings, polemic writing, sermons and tracts written for special purposes.

The first five books of the Old Testament, attributed to Moses, are a composite of many documents which have unknown origins. Gradually these documents, along with stories and legends of the early days of the race, were brought together by some unknown author or authors and became the books that we know.

The prophetic books of the Old Testament deal with the preaching of a number of individuals who were attempting to awaken the people to their mistakes and shortcomings. The Hebrews lived among enemies, both without and within the nation. Unless the Hebrews continued to be vigilant, these enemies would destroy them. The prophets associated this situation with religion and held such mistakes and shortcomings to be sins. Further, they preached that God was on their side if they would only use him. The prophets were wise men who saw the social and political dangers threatening the nation and attempted to awaken the people, calling them to a religious crusade that would save them.

The Sacred Writings are a large group of books written for many purposes, some religious and others not. Ruth, for example, is a tract written to show that the grandmother of the great King David was not a Jewess. The Song of Solomon is a collection of wedding songs. Psalms are songs which the Jews sang in their synagogues or at other religious gatherings. Job is a drama dealing with the problem of the good man who suffers. The religious value of these books varies from book to book. To meet this problem and make all the books of equal religious value, some ancient scholars used the allegorical approach. They argued that the writings did not mean what they said, but were to be interpreted as allegories. However, this approach is not approved by most of the modern scholars.

Genesis

Genesis, meaning generation or origin, is the title of this book as it appears in the Septuagint, an early Greek translation of the Bible. The Hebrew name for this book is Bereshith, meaning "in the beginning." The book was first put into written form from early documents in about

156

the eighth century B.C. It deals with the origin and early history and legends of the Israelites.

CHAPTER 1

1. In the beginning God created the heaven and the earth.

2. And the earth was without form, and void; and darkness was upon the face of the deep. And the Spirit of God moved upon the face of the waters.

3. And God said, Let there be light: and there was light.

4. And God saw the light, that it was good: and God divided the light from the darkness.

5. And God called the light Day, and the darkness he called Night. And the evening and the morning were the first day.

6. And God said, Let there be a firmament in the midst of the waters, and let it divide the waters from the waters.

7. And God made the firmament, and divided the waters which were under the firmament from the waters which were above the firmament: and it was so.

8. And God called the firmament Heaven. And the evening and the morning were the second day.

9. And God said, Let the waters under the heaven be gathered together unto one place, and let the dry land appear: and it was so.

10. And God called the dry land Earth; and the gathering together of the waters called he Seas: and God saw that it was good.

11. And God said, Let the earth bring forth grass, the herb yielding seed, and the fruit tree yielding fruit after his kind, whose seed is in itself, upon the earth: and it was so.

12. And the earth brought forth grass, and herb yielding seed after his kind, and the tree yielding fruit, whose seed was in itself, after his kind: and God saw that it was good.

13. And the evening and the morning were the third day.

14. And God said, Let there be lights in the firmament of the heaven to divide the day from the night; and let them be for signs, and for seasons, and for days, and years:

15. And let them be for lights in the firmament of the heaven to give light upon the earth: and it was so.

16. And God made two great lights; the greater light to rule the day, and the lesser light to rule the night: he made the stars also.

17. And God set them in the firmament of the heaven to give light upon the earth,

18. And to rule over the day and over the night, and to divide the light from the darkness: and God saw that it was good.

19. And the evening and the morning were the fourth day.

20. And God said, Let the waters bring forth abundantly the moving creature that hath life, and fowl that may fly above the earth in the open firmament of heaven.

21. And God created great whales, and every living creature that moveth, which the waters brought forth abundantly, after their kind, and every winged fowl after his kind: and God saw that it was good.

22. And God blessed them, saying, Be fruitful, and multiply, and fill the waters in the seas, and let fowl multiply in the earth.

23. And the evening and the morning were the fifth day.

24. And God said, Let the earth bring forth the living creature after his kind, cattle, and creeping thing, and beast of the earth after his kind: and it was so.

25. And God made the beast of the earth after his kind, and cattle after their kind, and every thing that creep-

eth upon the earth after his kind: and God saw that it was good.

26. And God said, Let us make man in our image, after our likeness: and let them have dominion over the fish of the sea, and over the fowl of the air, and over the cattle, and over all the earth, and over every creeping thing that creepeth upon the earth.

27. So God created man in his own image, in the image of God created he him; male and female created he them.

28. And God blessed them, and God said unto them, Be fruitful, and multiply, and replenish the earth, and subdue it: and have dominion over the fish of the sea, and over the fowl of the air, and over every living thing that moveth upon the earth.

29. And God said, Behold, I have given you every herb bearing seed, which is upon the face of all the earth, and every tree, in the which is the fruit of a tree yielding seed; to you it shall be for meat.

30. And to every beast of the earth, and to every fowl of the air, and to every thing that creepeth upon the earth, wherein there is life, I have given every green herb for meat: and it was so.

31. And God saw every thing that he had made, and, behold, it was very good. And the evening and the morning were the sixth day.

Exodus

This book gets its title from its contents. These tell of the departure of the Hebrews from Egypt and their wanderings through the lands between Egypt and Mount Sinai. The story covers the time between the death of Joseph and the giving of the law at Sinai. The first 18 chapters tell of the persecution endured by the Jews in Egypt and their escape to Sinai. The last 22 chapters tell of the giving of the law at Sinai and the building of the tabernacle and its dedication. This is the story of how the Jews, believers in many crude nature gods, gave these up to follow a new god, the Jehovah who dwelt on Sinai. It is a story of a great religious revolution and of a people turning to a new divinity.

Chapter 20

1. And God spake all these words, saying,

2. I am the Lord thy God, which have brought thee out of the land of Egypt, out of the house of bondage.

3. Thou shalt have no other gods before me.

4. Thou shalt not make unto thee any graven image, or any likeness of any thing that is in heaven above, or that is in the earth beneath, or that is in the water under the earth:

5. Thou shalt not bow down thyself to them, nor serve them: for I the Lord thy God am a jealous God, visiting the iniquity of the fathers upon the children unto the third and fourth generation of them that hate me;

6. And shewing mercy unto thousands of them that love me, and keep my commandments.

7. Thou shalt not take the name of the Lord thy God in vain; for the Lord will not hold him guiltless that taketh his name in vain.

8. Remember the sabbath day, to keep it holy.

9. Six days shalt thou labour, and do all thy work:

10. But the seventh day is the sabbath of the Lord thy God; in it thou shalt not do any work, thou, nor thy son, nor thy daughter, thy manservant, nor thy maidservant, nor thy cattle, nor thy stranger that is within thy gates:

11. For in six days the Lord made heaven and earth, the sea, and all that in them is, and rested the seventh day:

wherefore the LORD blessed the sabbath day, and hallowed it.

12. Honour thy father and thy mother: that thy days may be long upon the land which the LORD thy God giveth thee.

13. Thou shalt not kill.

14. Thou shalt not commit adultery.

15. Thou shalt not steal.

16. Thou shalt not bear false witness against thy neighbour.

17. Thou shalt not covet thy neighbour's house, thou shalt not covet thy neighbour's wife, nor his manservant, nor his maidservant, nor his ox, nor his ass, nor any thing that is thy neighbour's.

CHAPTER 23

1. Thou shalt not raise a false report: put not thine hand with the wicked to be an unrighteous witness.

2. Thou shalt not follow a multitude to do evil; neither shalt thou speak in a cause to decline after many to wrest judgment:

3. Neither shalt thou countenance a poor man in his cause.

4. If thou meet thine enemy's ox or his ass going astray, thou shalt surely bring it back to him again.

5. If thou see the ass of him that hateth thee lying under his burden, and wouldest forbear to help him, thou shalt surely help with him.

6. Thou shalt not wrest the judgment of thy poor in his cause.

7. Keep thee far from a false matter; and the innocent and righteous slay thou not: for I will not justify the wicked.

8. And thou shalt take no gift: for the gift blindeth the wise, and perverteth the words of the righteous.

9. Also thou shalt not oppress a stranger: for ye know the heart of a stranger, seeing ye were strangers in the land of Egypt.

10. And six years thou shalt sow thy land, and shalt gather in the fruits thereof:

11. But the seventh year thou shalt let it rest and lie still; that the poor of thy people may eat: and what they leave the beasts of the field shall eat. In like manner thou shalt deal with thy vineyard, and with thy oliveyard.

12. Six days thou shalt do thy work, and on the seventh day thou shalt rest: that thine ox and thine ass may rest, and the son of thy handmaid, and the stranger, may be refreshed.

13. And in all things that I have said unto you be circumspect: and make no mention of the name of other gods, neither let it be heard out of thy mouth.

14. Three times thou shalt keep a feast unto me in the year.

15. Thou shalt keep the feast of unleavened bread: (thou shalt eat unleavened bread seven days, as I commanded thee, in the time appointed of the month Abib; for in it thou camest out from Egypt: and none shall appear before me empty:)

16. And the feast of harvest, the firstfruits of thy labours, which thou hast sown in the field: and the feast of ingathering, which is in the end of the year, when thou hast gathered in thy labours out of the field.

17. Three times in the year all thy males shall appear before the Lord GOD.

18. Thou shalt not offer the blood of my sacrifice with leavened bread; neither shall the fat of my sacrifice remain until the morning.

19. The first of the firstfruits of thy land thou shalt bring into the house of the LORD thy God. Thou shalt not seethe a kid in his mother's milk.

20. Behold, I send an Angel before thee, to keep thee in the way, and to bring thee into the place which I have prepared.

21. Beware of him, and obey his voice, provoke him not; for he will

not pardon your transgressions: for my name is in him.

22. But if thou shalt indeed obey his voice, and do all that I speak; then I will be an enemy unto thine enemies, and an adversary unto thine adversaries.

23. For mine Angel shall go before thee, and bring thee in unto the Amorites, and the Hittites, and the Perizzites, and the Canaanites, the Hivites, and the Jebusites: and I will cut them off.

24. Thou shalt not bow down to their gods, nor serve them, nor do after their works: but thou shalt utterly overthrow them, and quite break down their images.

25. And ye shall serve the Lord your God, and he shall bless thy bread, and thy water; and I will take sickness away from the midst of thee.

26. There shall nothing cast their young, nor be barren, in thy land: the number of thy days I will fulfil.

27. I will send my fear before thee, and will destroy all the people to whom thou shalt come, and I will make all thine enemies turn their backs unto thee.

28. And I will send hornets before thee, which shall drive out the Hivite, the Canaanite, and the Hittite, from before thee.

29. I will not drive them out from before thee in one year; lest the land become desolate, and the beast of the field multiply against thee.

30. By little and little I will drive them out from before thee, until thou be increased, and inherit the land.

31. And I will set thy bounds from the Red sea even unto the sea of the Philistines, and from the desert unto the river: for I will deliver the inhabitants of the land into your hand; and thou shalt drive them out before thee.

32. Thou shalt make no covenant with them, nor with their gods.

33. They shall not dwell in thy land, lest they make thee sin against me:

for if thou serve their gods, it will surely be a snare unto thee.

Chapter 34

1. And the Lord said unto Moses, Hew thee two tables of stone like unto the first: and I will write upon these tables the words that were in the first tables, which thou brakest.

2. And be ready in the morning, and come up in the morning unto mount Sinai, and present thyself there to me in the top of the mount.

3. And no man shall come up with thee, neither let any man be seen throughout all the mount; neither let the flocks nor herds feed before that mount.

4. And he hewed two tables of stone like unto the first; and Moses rose up early in the morning, and went up unto mount Sinai, as the Lord had commanded him, and took in his hand the two tables of stone.

5. And the Lord descended in the cloud, and stood with him there, and proclaimed the name of the Lord.

6. And the Lord passed by before him, and proclaimed, The Lord, The Lord God, merciful and gracious, longsuffering, and abundant in goodness and truth,

7. Keeping mercy for thousands, forgiving iniquity and transgression and sin, and that will by no means clear the guilty; visiting the iniquity of the fathers upon the children, and upon the children's children, unto the third and to the fourth generation.

8. And Moses made haste, and bowed his head toward the earth, and worshipped.

9. And he said, If now I have found grace in thy sight, O Lord, let my Lord, I pray thee, go among us; for it is a stiffnecked people; and pardon our iniquity and our sin, and take us for thine inheritance.

10. And he said, Behold, I make a covenant: before all thy people I will

do marvels, such as have not been done in all the earth, nor in any nation: and all the people among which thou art shall see the work of the LORD: for it is a terrible thing that I will do with thee.

11. Observe thou that which I command thee this day: behold, I drive out before thee the Amorite, and the Canaanite, and the Hittite, and the Perizzite, and the Hivite, and the Jebusite.

12. Take heed to thyself, lest thou make a covenant with the inhabitants of the land whither thou goest, lest it be for a snare in the midst of thee:

13. But ye shall destroy their altars, break their images, and cut down their groves:

14. For thou shalt worship no other god: for the LORD, whose name is Jealous, is a jealous God:

15. Lest thou make a covenant with the inhabitants of the land, and they go a whoring after their gods, and do sacrifice unto their gods, and one call thee, and thou eat of his sacrifice;

16. And thou take of their daughters unto thy sons, and their daughters go a whoring after their gods, and make thy sons go a whoring after their gods.

17. Thou shalt make thee no molten gods.

18. The feast of unleavened bread shalt thou keep. Seven days thou shalt eat unleavened bread, as I commanded thee, in the time of the month Abib: for in the month Abib thou camest out from Egypt.

19. All that openeth the matrix is mine; and every firstling among thy cattle, whether ox or sheep, that is male.

20. But the firstling of an ass thou shalt redeem with a lamb: and if thou redeem him not, then shalt thou break his neck. All the firstborn of thy sons thou shalt redeem. And none shall appear before me empty.

21. Six days thou shalt work, but on the seventh day thou shalt rest: in earing time and in harvest thou shalt rest.

22. And thou shalt observe the feast of weeks, of the firstfruits of wheat harvest, and the feast of ingathering at the year's end.

23. Thrice in the year shall all your menchildren appear before the LORD God, the God of Israel.

24. For I will cast out the nations before thee, and enlarge thy borders: neither shall any man desire thy land, when thou shalt go up to appear before the LORD thy God thrice in the year.

25. Thou shalt not offer the blood of my sacrifice with leaven; neither shall the sacrifice of the feast of the passover be left unto the morning.

26. The first of the firstfruits of thy land thou shalt bring unto the house of the LORD thy God. Thou shalt not seethe a kid in his mother's milk.

27. And the LORD said unto Moses, Write thou these words: for after the tenor of these words I have made a covenant with thee and with Israel.

28. And he was there with the LORD forty days and forty nights; he did neither eat bread, nor drink water. And he wrote upon the tables the words of the covenant, the ten commandments.

Leviticus

The name of this book, Leviticus, is a Latinized form of the title as it appears in the Septuagint, meaning "pertaining to the Levites." For the most part, it contains laws and decrees designed to govern the people of Israel. The first seven chapters deal with laws relating to sacrifice. The next three tell of the consecration of Aaron and his sons to the priesthood. Chapters 11 to 16 state the laws relative to cleanliness while the remainder of the book deals with laws in general.

CHAPTER 19

1. And the LORD spake unto Moses, saying,

2. Speak unto all the congregation of the children of Israel, and say unto them, Ye shall be holy: for I the LORD your God am holy.

3. Ye shall fear every man his mother, and his father, and keep my sabbaths: I am the LORD your God.

4. Turn ye not unto idols, nor make to yourselves molten gods: I am the LORD your God.

5. And if ye offer a sacrifice of peace offerings unto the LORD, ye shall offer it at your own will.

6. It shall be eaten the same day ye offer it, and on the morrow: and if ought remain until the third day, it shall be burnt in the fire.

7. And if it be eaten at all on the third day, it is abominable; it shall not be accepted.

8. Therefore every one that eateth it shall bear his iniquity, because he hath profaned the hallowed thing of the LORD: and that soul shall be cut off from among his people.

9. And when ye reap the harvest of your land, thou shalt not wholly reap the corners of thy field, neither shalt thou gather the gleanings of thy harvest.

10. And thou shalt not glean thy vineyard, neither shalt thou gather every grape of thy vineyard; thou shalt leave them for the poor and stranger: I am the LORD your God.

11. Ye shall not steal, neither deal falsely, neither lie one to another.

12. And ye shall not swear by my name falsely, neither shalt thou profane the name of thy God: I am the LORD.

13. Thou shalt not defraud thy neighbour, neither rob him: the wages of him that is hired shall not abide with thee all night until the morning.

14. Thou shalt not curse the deaf, nor put a stumbling block before the blind, but shalt fear thy God: I am the LORD.

15. Ye shall do no unrighteousness in judgment: thou shalt not respect the person of the poor, nor honour the person of the mighty: but in righteousness shalt thou judge thy neighbour.

16. Thou shalt not go up and down as a talebearer among thy people: neither shalt thou stand against the blood of thy neighbour: I am the LORD.

17. Thou shalt not hate thy brother in thine heart: thou shalt in any wise rebuke thy neighbour, and not suffer sin upon him.

18. Thou shalt not avenge, nor bear any grudge against the children of thy people, but thou shalt love thy neighbour as thyself: I am the LORD.

CHAPTER 26

1. Ye shall make you no idols nor graven image, neither rear you up a standing image, neither shall ye set up any image of stone in your land, to bow down unto it: for I am the LORD your God.

2. Ye shall keep my sabbaths, and reverence my sanctuary: I am the LORD.

3. If ye walk in my statutes, and keep my commandments, and do them;

4. Then I will give you rain in due season, and the land shall yield her increase, and the trees of the field shall yield their fruit.

5. And your threshing shall reach unto the vintage, and the vintage shall reach unto the sowing time: and ye shall eat your bread to the full, and dwell in your land safely.

6. And I will give peace in the land, and ye shall lie down, and none shall make you afraid: and I will rid evil beasts out of the land, neither shall the sword go through your land.

7. And ye shall chase your enemies,

and they shall fall before you by the sword.

8. And five of you shall chase an hundred, and an hundred of you shall put ten thousand to flight: and your enemies shall fall before you by the sword.

9. For I will have respect unto you, and make you fruitful, and multiply you, and establish my covenant with you.

10. And ye shall eat old store, and bring forth the old because of the new.

11. And I will set my tabernacle among you: and my soul shall not abhor you.

12. And I will walk among you, and will be your God, and ye shall be my people.

13. I am the LORD your God, which brought you forth out of the land of Egypt, that ye should not be their bondmen; and I have broken the bands of your yoke, and made you go upright.

14. But if ye will not hearken unto me, and will not do all these commandments;

15. And if ye shall despise my statutes, or if your soul abhor my judgments, so that ye will not do all my commandments, but that ye break my covenant:

16. I also will do this unto you; I will even appoint over you terror, consumption, and the burning ague, that shall consume the eyes, and cause sorrow of heart: and ye shall sow your seed in vain, for your enemies shall eat it.

17. And I will set my face against you, and ye shall be slain before your enemies: they that hate you shall reign over you; and ye shall flee when none pursueth you.

18. And if ye will not yet for all this hearken unto me, then I will punish you seven times more for your sins.

19. And I will break the pride of your power; and I will make your

heaven as iron, and your earth as brass:

20. And your strength shall be spent in vain: for your land shall not yield her increase, neither shall the trees of the land yield their fruits.

21. And if ye walk contrary unto me, and will not hearken unto me; I will bring seven times more plagues upon you according to your sins.

22. I will also send wild beasts among you, which shall rob you of your children, and destroy your cattle, and make you few in number; and your high ways shall be desolate.

23. And if ye will not be reformed by me by these things, but will walk contrary unto me;

24. Then will I also walk contrary unto you, and will punish you yet seven times for your sins.

25. And I will bring a sword upon you, that shall avenge the quarrel of my covenant: and when ye are gathered together within your cities, I will send the pestilence among you; and ye shall be delivered into the hand of the enemy.

26. And when I have broken the staff of your bread, ten women shall bake your bread in one oven, and they shall deliver you your bread again by weight: and ye shall eat, and not be satisfied.

27. And if ye will not for all this hearken unto me, but walk contrary unto me;

28. Then I will walk contrary unto you also in fury; and I, even I, will chastise you seven times for your sins.

29. And ye shall eat the flesh of your sons, and the flesh of your daughters shall ye eat.

30. And I will destroy your high places, and cut down your images, and cast your carcases upon the carcases of your idols, and my soul shall abhor you.

31. And I will make your cities waste, and bring your sanctuaries unto

desolation, and I will not smell the savour of your sweet odours.

32. And I will bring the land into desolation: and your enemies which dwell therein shall be astonished at it.

33. And I will scatter you among the heathen, and will draw out a sword after you: and your land shall be desolate, and your cities waste.

34. Then shall the land enjoy her sabbaths, as long as it lieth desolate, and ye be in your enemies' land; even then shall the land rest, and enjoy her sabbaths.

35. As long as it lieth desolate it shall rest; because it did not rest in your sabbaths, when ye dwelt upon it.

36. And upon them that are left alive of you I will send a faintness into their hearts in the lands of their enemies; and the sound of a shaken leaf shall chase them; and they shall flee, as fleeing from a sword; and they shall fall when none pursueth.

37. And they shall fall one upon another, as it were before a sword, when none pursueth: and ye shall have no power to stand before your enemies.

38. And ye shall perish among the heathen, and the land of your enemies shall eat you up.

39. And they that are left of you shall pine away in their iniquity in your enemies' lands; and also in the iniquities of their fathers shall they pine away with them.

40. If they shall confess their iniquity, and the iniquity of their fathers, with their trespass which they trespassed against me, and that also they have walked contrary unto me;

41. And that I also have walked contrary unto them, and have brought them into the land of their enemies; if then their uncircumcised hearts be humbled, and they then accept of the punishment of their iniquity:

42. Then will I remember my covenant with Jacob, and also my covenant with Isaac, and also my covenant with Abraham will I remember; and I will remember the land.

43. The land also shall be left of them, and shall enjoy her sabbaths, while she lieth desolate without them: and they shall accept of the punishment of their iniquity: because, even because they despised my judgments, and because their soul abhorred my statutes.

44. And yet for all that, when they be in the land of their enemies, I will not cast them away, neither will I abhor them, to destroy them utterly, and to break my covenant with them: for I am the LORD their God.

45. But I will for their sakes remember the covenant of their ancestors, whom I brought forth out of the land of Egypt in the sight of the heathen, that I might be their God: I am the LORD.

46. These are the statutes and judgments and laws, which the LORD made between him and the children of Israel in mount Sinai by the hand of Moses.

Deuteronomy

The title of this book, Deuteronomy, comes from an incorrect translating of the Septuagint translation of an expression in chapter 17:18 which means "a copy of the law." It was believed that this phrase referred to the whole book and thus it became the title. Actually, the book is a collection of addresses which Moses, the great Hebrew leader, had made to the people. At the close of the book we have the story of the death and burial of Moses.

CHAPTER 5

6. I am the LORD thy God, which brought thee out of the land of Egypt, from the house of bondage.

7. Thou shalt have none other gods before me.

8. Thou shalt not make thee any graven image, or any likeness of any

thing that is in heaven above, or that is in the earth beneath, or that is in the waters beneath the earth:

9. Thou shalt not bow down thyself unto them, nor serve them: for I the LORD thy God am a jealous God, visiting the iniquity of the fathers upon the children unto the third and fourth generation of them that hate me,

10. And shewing mercy unto thousands of them that love me and keep my commandments.

11. Thou shalt not take the name of the LORD thy God in vain: for the LORD will not hold him guiltless that taketh his name in vain.

12. Keep the sabbath day to sanctify it, as the LORD thy God hath commanded thee.

13. Six days thou shalt labour, and do all thy work:

14. But the seventh day is the sabbath of the LORD thy God: in it thou shalt not do any work, thou, nor thy son, nor thy daughter, nor thy manservant, nor thy maidservant, nor thine ox, nor thine ass, nor any of thy cattle, nor thy stranger that is within thy gates; that thy manservant and thy maidservant may rest as well as thou.

15. And remember that thou wast a servant in the land of Egypt, and that the LORD thy God brought thee out thence through a mighty hand and by a stretched out arm: therefore the LORD thy God commanded thee to keep the sabbath day.

16. Honour thy father and thy mother, as the LORD thy God hath commanded thee; that thy days may be prolonged, and that it may go well with thee, in the land which the LORD thy God giveth thee.

17. Thou shalt not kill.

18. Neither shalt thou commit adultery.

19. Neither shalt thou steal.

20. Neither shalt thou bear false witness against thy neighbour.

21. Neither shalt thou desire thy neighbour's wife, neither shalt thou covet thy neighbour's house, his field, or his manservant, or his maidservant, his ox, or his ass, or any thing that is thy neighbour's.

CHAPTER 6

1. Now these are the commandments, the statutes, and the judgments, which the LORD your God commanded to teach you, that ye might do them in the land whither ye go to possess it:

2. That thou mightest fear the LORD thy God, to keep all his statutes and his commandments, which I command thee, thou, and thy son, and thy son's son, all the days of thy life; and that thy days may be prolonged.

3. Hear therefore, O Israel, and observe to do it; that it may be well with thee, and that ye may increase mightily, as the LORD God of thy fathers hath promised thee, in the land that floweth with milk and honey.

4. Hear, O Israel: the LORD our God is one LORD:

5. And thou shalt love the LORD thy God with all thine heart, and with all thy soul, and with all thy might.

6. And these words, which I command thee this day, shall be in thine heart:

7. And thou shalt teach them diligently unto thy children, and shalt talk of them when thou sittest in thine house, and when thou walkest by the way, and when thou liest down, and when thou risest up.

8. And thou shalt bind them for a sign upon thine hand, and they shall be as frontlets between thine eyes.

9. And thou shalt write them upon the posts of thy house, and on thy gates.

10. And it shall be, when the LORD thy God shall have brought thee into the land which he sware unto thy fathers, to Abraham, to Isaac, and to Jacob, to give thee great and goodly cities, which thou buildedst not,

11. And houses full of all good

things, which thou filledst not, and wells digged, which thou diggedst not, vineyards and olive trees, which thou plantedst not; when thou shalt have eaten and be full;

12. Then beware lest thou forget the LORD, which brought thee forth out of the land of Egypt, from the house of bondage.

13. Thou shalt fear the LORD thy God, and serve him, and shalt swear by his name.

14. Ye shall not go after other gods, of the gods of the people which are round about you;

15. (For the LORD thy God is a jealous God among you) lest the anger of the LORD thy God be kindled against thee, and destroy thee from off the face of the earth.

16. Ye shall not tempt the LORD your God, as ye tempted him in Massah.

17. Ye shall diligently keep the commandments of the LORD your God, and his testimonies, and his statutes, which he hath commanded thee.

18. And thou shalt do that which is right and good in the sight of the LORD: that it may be well with thee, and that thou mayest go in and possess the good land which the LORD sware unto thy fathers,

19. To cast out all thine enemies from before thee, as the LORD hath spoken.

20. And when thy son asketh thee in time to come, saying, What mean the testimonies, and the statutes, and the judgments, which the LORD our God hath commanded you?

21. Then thou shalt say unto thy son, We were Pharaoh's bondmen in Egypt; and the LORD brought us out of Egypt with a mighty hand:

22. And the LORD shewed signs and wonders, great and sore, upon Egypt, upon Pharaoh, and upon all his household, before our eyes:

23. And he brought us out from thence, that he might bring us in, to give us the land which he sware unto our fathers.

24. And the LORD commanded us to do all these statutes, to fear the LORD our God, for our good always, that he might preserve us alive, as it is at this day.

25. And it shall be our righteousness, if we observe to do all these commandments before the LORD our God, as he hath commanded us.

CHAPTER 7

9. Know therefore that the LORD thy God, he is God, the faithful God, which keepeth covenant and mercy with them that love him and keep his commandments to a thousand generations.

CHAPTER 10

12. And now, Israel, what doth the LORD thy God require of thee, but to fear the LORD thy God, to walk in all his ways, and to love him, and to serve the LORD thy God with all thy heart and with all thy soul,

13. To keep the commandments of the LORD, and his statutes, which I command thee this day for thy good?

14. Behold, the heaven and the heaven of heavens is the LORD'S thy God, the earth also, with all that therein is.

15. Only the LORD had a delight in thy fathers to love them, and he chose their seed after them, even you above all people, as it is this day.

16. Circumcise therefore the foreskin of your heart, and be no more stiffnecked.

17. For the LORD your God is God of gods, and LORD of lords, a great God, a mighty, and a terrible, which regardeth not 'persons, nor taketh reward:

18. He doth execute the judgment of the fatherless and widow, and loveth the stranger, in giving him food and raiment.

19. Love ye therefore the stranger: for ye were strangers in the land of Egypt.

20. Thou shalt fear the LORD thy God; him shalt thou serve, and to him shalt thou cleave, and swear by his name.

21. He is thy praise, and he is thy God, that hath done for thee these great and terrible things, which thine eyes have seen.

22. Thy fathers went down into Egypt with threescore and ten persons; and now the LORD thy God hath made thee as the stars of heaven for multitude.

CHAPTER 11

1. Therefore thou shalt love the LORD thy God, and keep his charge, and his statutes, and his judgments, and his commandments, alway.

18. Therefore shall ye lay up these my words in your heart and in your soul, and bind them for a sign upon your hand, that they may be as frontlets between your eyes.

19. And ye shall teach them your children, speaking of them when thou sittest in thine house, and when thou walkest by the way, when thou liest down, and when thou risest up.

20. And thou shalt write them upon the door posts of thine house, and upon thy gates:

21. That your days may be multiplied, and the days of your children, in the land which the LORD sware unto your fathers to give them, as the days of heaven upon the earth.

CHAPTER 15

7. If there be among you a poor man of one of thy brethren within any of thy gates in thy land which the LORD thy God giveth thee, thou shalt not harden thine heart, nor shut thine hand from thy poor brother:

8. But thou shalt open thine hand wide unto him, and shalt surely lend him sufficient for his need, in that which he wanteth.

9. Beware that there be not a thought in thy wicked heart, saying, The seventh year, the year of release, is at hand; and thine eye be evil against thy poor brother, and thou givest him nought; and he cry unto the LORD against thee, and it be sin unto thee.

10. Thou shalt surely give him, and thine heart shall not be grieved when thou givest unto him: because that for this thing the LORD thy God shall bless thee in all thy works, and in all that thou puttest thine hand unto.

11. For the poor shall never cease out of the land: therefore I command thee, saying, Thou shalt open thine hand wide unto thy brother, to thy poor, and to thy needy, in thy land.

CHAPTER 30

1. And it shall come to pass, when all these things are come upon thee, the blessing and the curse, which I have set before thee, and thou shalt call them to mind among all the nations, whither the LORD thy God hath driven thee,

2. And shalt return unto the LORD thy God, and shalt obey his voice according to all that I command thee this day, thou and thy children, with all thine heart, and with all thy soul;

3. That then the LORD thy God will turn thy captivity, and have compassion upon thee, and will return and gather thee from all the nations, whither the LORD thy God hath scattered thee.

4. If any of thine be driven out unto the outmost parts of heaven, from thence will the LORD thy God gather thee, and from thence will he fetch thee:

5. And the LORD thy God will bring thee into the land which thy fathers

possessed, and thou shalt possess it; and he will do thee good, and multiply thee above thy fathers.

6. And the LORD thy God will circumcise thine heart, and the heart of thy seed, to love the LORD thy God with all thine heart, and with all thy soul, that thou mayest live.

7. And the LORD thy God will put all these curses upon thine enemies, and on them that hate thee, which persecuted thee.

8. And thou shalt return and obey the voice of the LORD, and do all his commandments which I command thee this day.

9. And the LORD thy God will make thee plenteous in every work of thine hand, in the fruit of thy body, and in the fruit of thy cattle, and in the fruit of thy land, for good: for the LORD will again rejoice over thee for good, as he rejoiced over thy fathers:

10. If thou shalt hearken unto the voice of the LORD thy God, to keep his commandments and his statutes which are written in this book of the law, and if thou turn unto the LORD thy God with all thine heart, and with all thy soul.

11. For this commandment which I command thee this day, it is not hidden from thee, neither is it far off.

12. It is not in heaven, that thou shouldest say, Who shall go up for us to heaven, and bring it unto us, that we may hear it, and do it?

13. Neither is it beyond the sea, that thou shouldest say, Who shall go over the sea for us, and bring it unto us, that we may hear it, and do it?

14. But the word is very nigh unto thee, in thy mouth, and in thy heart, that thou mayest do it.

15. See, I have set before thee this day life and good, and death and evil;

16. In that I command thee this day to love the LORD thy God, to walk in his ways, and to keep his commandments and his statutes and his judgments, that thou mayest live and

multiply: and the LORD thy God shall bless thee in the land whither thou goest to possess it.

17. But if thine heart turn away, so that thou wilt not hear, but shalt be drawn away, and worship other gods, and serve them;

18. I denounce unto you this day, that ye shall surely perish, and that ye shall not prolong your days upon the land, whither thou passest over Jordan to go to possess it.

19. I call heaven and earth to record this day against you, that I have set before you life and death, blessing and cursing: therefore choose life, that both thou and thy seed may live:

20. That thou mayest love the LORD thy God, and that thou mayest obey his voice, and that thou mayest cleave unto him: for he is thy life, and the length of thy days: that thou mayest dwell in the land which the LORD sware unto thy fathers, to Abraham, to Isaac, and to Jacob, to give them.

CHAPTER 31

6. Be strong and of a good courage, fear not, nor be afraid of them: for the LORD thy God, he it is that doth go with thee; he will not fail thee, nor forsake thee.

Joshua

This book is actually the concluding part of the Pentateuch or first five books of the Bible. However, in the Hebrew canon it is the first of four books grouped under the title of "Former Prophets." It derives its name from the fact that early Jewish and Christian commentators believed it to have been written by Joshua who led the Jews into Canaan. But modern scholars hold that the author of the book is unknown. The book deals with the entrance of the Jews into Canaan and the division of the land among the tribes. It also contains the last speeches of Joshua and an account of his death.

Chapter 24

14. Now therefore fear the Lord, and serve him in sincerity and in truth: and put away the gods which your fathers served on the other side of the flood, and in Egypt; and serve ye the Lord.

15. And if it seem evil unto you to serve the Lord, choose you this day whom ye will serve; whether the gods which your fathers served that were on the other side of the flood, or the gods of the Amorites, in whose land ye dwell: but as for me and my house, we will serve the Lord.

16. And the people answered and said, God forbid that we should forsake the Lord, to serve other gods;

17. For the Lord our God, he it is that brought us up and our fathers out of the land of Egypt, from the house of bondage, and which did those great signs in our sight, and preserved us in all the way wherein we went, and among all the people through whom we passed:

18. And the Lord drave out from before us all the people, even the Amorites which dwelt in the land: therefore will we also serve the Lord; for he is our God.

First and Second Samuel

In the modern Bible we find two books of Samuel, usually entitled First and Second Samuel. In Hebrew manuscripts the two books are written as one but they are divided in the Septuagint and in the Vulgate, an early Latin translation. Samuel is mentioned in the title, not because he wrote the books, but because he is the most prominent figure in them. Much of the material contained in the books may have been gathered by him, but it probably dates originally from the separation of the kingdoms of Judah and Israel. Moreover, the writings have undergone much modification throughout the centuries. The books relate the activities of prophets contemporary with the early kings of the Hebrews, Samuel, Saul, and David. Three parts seem to stand out. In I Samuel 1–12 we have the story of Samuel and of Eli. The second part, I Samuel 13 to II Samuel 1, we have the story of Saul from his rise to the throne of Israel to his death. The third part, II Samuel 2–24, deals with the great reign of King David.

I Samuel

Chapter 2

1. And Hannah prayed, and said, My heart rejoiceth in the Lord, mine horn is exalted in the Lord: my mouth is enlarged over mine enemies; because I rejoice in thy salvation.

2. There is none holy as the Lord: for there is none beside thee: neither is there any rock like our God.

3. Talk no more so exceeding proudly; let not arrogancy come out of your mouth: for the Lord is a God of knowledge, and by him actions are weighed.

4. The bows of the mighty men are broken, and they that stumbled are girded with strength.

5. They that were full have hired out themselves for bread; and they that were hungry ceased: so that the barren hath born seven; and she that hath many children is waxed feeble.

6. The Lord killeth, and maketh alive: he bringeth down to the grave, and bringeth up.

7. The Lord maketh poor, and maketh rich: he bringeth low, and lifteth up.

8. He raiseth up the poor out of the dust, and lifteth up the beggar from the dunghill, to set them among princes, and to make them inherit

the throne of glory: for the pillars of the earth are the LORD's, and he hath set the world upon them.

9. He will keep the feet of his saints, and the wicked shall be silent in darkness; for by strength shall no man prevail.

10. The adversaries of the LORD shall be broken to pieces; out of heaven shall he thunder upon them: the LORD shall judge the ends of the earth; and he shall give strength unto his king, and exalt the horn of his anointed.

II Samuel

CHAPTER 22

1. And David spake unto the LORD the words of this song in the day that the LORD had delivered him out of the hand of all his enemies, and out of the hand of Saul:

2. And he said, The LORD is my rock, and my fortress, and my deliverer;

3. The God of my rock; in him will I trust: he is my shield, and the horn of my salvation, my high tower, and my refuge, my saviour; thou savest me from violence.

4. I will call on the LORD, who is worthy to be praised: so shall I be saved from mine.enemies.

5. When the waves of death compassed me, the floods of ungodly men made me afraid;

6. The sorrows of hell compassed me about; the snares of death prevented me;

7. In my distress I called upon the LORD, and cried to my God: and he did hear my voice out of his temple, and my cry did enter into his ears.

8. Then the earth shook and trembled; the foundations of heaven moved and shook, because he was wroth.

9. There went up a smoke out of his nostrils, and fire out of his mouth devoured: coals were kindled by it.

10. He bowed the heavens also, and came down; and darkness was under his feet.

11. And he rode upon a cherub, and did fly: and he was seen upon the wings of the wind.

12. And he made darkness pavilions round about him, dark waters, and thick clouds of the skies.

13. Through the brightness before him were coals of fire kindled.

14. The LORD thundered from heaven, and the most High uttered his voice.

15. And he sent out arrows, and scattered them; lightning, and discomfited them.

16. And the channels of the sea appeared, the foundations of the world were discovered, at the rebuking of the LORD, at the blast of the breath of his nostrils.

17. He sent from above, he took me; he drew me out of many waters;

18. He delivered me from my strong enemy, and from them that hated me: for they were too strong for me.

19. They prevented me in the day of my calamity: but the LORD was my stay.

20. He brought me forth also into a large place: he delivered me, because he delighted in me.

21. The LORD rewarded me according to my righteousness: according to the cleanness of my hands hath he recompensed me.

22. For I have kept the ways of the LORD, and have not wickedly departed from my God.

23. For all his judgments were before me: and as for his statutes, I did not depart from them.

24. I was also upright before him, and have kept myself from mine iniquity.

25. Therefore the LORD hath recompensed me according to my righteousness; according to my cleanness in his eye sight.

26. With the merciful thou wilt shew thyself merciful, and with the

upright man thou wilt shew thyself upright.

27. With the pure thou wilt shew thyself pure; and with the froward thou wilt shew thyself unsavoury.

28. And the afflicted people thou wilt save: but thine eyes are upon the haughty, that thou mayest bring them down.

29. For thou art my lamp, O LORD: and the LORD will lighten my darkness.

30. For by thee I have run through a troop: by my God have I leaped over a wall.

31. As for God, his way is perfect; the word of the LORD is tried: he is a buckler to all them that trust in him.

32. For who is God, save the LORD? and who is a rock, save our God?

33. God is my strength and power: and he maketh my way perfect.

34. He maketh my feet like hinds' feet: and setteth me upon my high places.

35. He teacheth my hands to war; so that a bow of steel is broken by mine arms.

36. Thou hast also given me the shield of thy salvation: and thy gentleness hath made me great.

37. Thou hast enlarged my steps under me; so that my feet did not slip.

38. I have pursued mine enemies, and destroyed them; and turned not again until I had consumed them.

39. And I have consumed them, and wounded them, that they could not arise: yea, they are fallen under my feet.

40. For thou hast girded me with strength to battle: them that rose up against me hast thou subdued under me.

41. Thou hast also given me the necks of mine enemies, that I might destroy them that hate me.

42. They looked, but there was none to save; even unto the LORD, but he answered them not.

43. Then did I beat them as small as the dust of the earth, I did stamp them as the mire of the street, and did spread them abroad.

44. Thou also hast delivered me from the strivings of my people, thou hast kept me to be head of the heathen: a people which I knew not shall serve me.

45. Strangers shall submit themselves unto me: as soon as they hear, they shall be obedient unto me.

46. Strangers shall fade away, and they shall be afraid out of their close places.

47. The LORD liveth; and blessed be my rock; and exalted be the God of the rock of my salvation.

48. It is God that avengeth me, and that bringeth down the people under me,

49. And that bringeth me forth from mine enemies: thou also hast lifted me up on high above them that rose up against me: thou hast delivered me from the violent man.

50. Therefore I will give thanks unto thee, O LORD, among the heathen, and I will sing praises unto thy name.

51. He is the tower of salvation for his king: and sheweth mercy to his anointed, unto David, and to his seed for evermore.

First and Second Kings

The two books of the Old Testament entitled I Kings and II Kings are considered as one book in Hebrew manuscripts. However, in the Septuagint and the Vulgate they bear the titles of Third Kings and Fourth Kings. The books were probably compiled sometime during the second half of the Babylonian Captivity of the Jews. In them we have the history of the northern kingdom after its separation from Judah, and the emphasis is religious rather than historical. The books fall into natural divisions as follows: I Kings 1–11 tells of the reign of Solomon; I Kings 12 to II Kings 17 tells the stories of both the kingdoms of Israel and of Judah until the former is destroyed; II Kings 18–25 is the story of the kingdom of Judah until the Babylonian Captivity.

I Kings

CHAPTER 8

44. If thy people go out to battle against their enemy, whithersoever thou shalt send them, and shall pray unto the LORD toward the city which thou hast chosen, and toward the house that I have built for thy name:

45. Then hear thou in heaven their prayer and their supplication, and maintain their cause.

46. If they sin against thee, (for there is no man that sinneth not,) and thou be angry with them, and deliver them to the enemy, so that they carry them away captives unto the land of the enemy, far or near;

47. Yet if they shall bethink themselves in the land whither they were carried captives, and repent, and make supplication unto thee in the land of them that carried them captives, saying, We have sinned, and have done perversely, we have committed wickedness;

48. And so return unto thee with all their heart, and with all their soul, in the land of their enemies, which led them away captive, and pray unto thee toward their land, which thou gavest unto their fathers, the city which thou hast chosen, and the house which I have built for thy name:

49. Then hear thou their prayer and their supplication in heaven thy dwelling place, and maintain their cause,

50. And forgive thy people that have sinned against thee, and all their transgressions wherein they have transgressed against thee, and give them compassion before them who carried them captive, that they may have compassion on them:

51. For they be thy people, and thine inheritance, which thou broughtest forth out of Egypt, from the midst of the furnace of iron:

52. That thine eyes may be open unto the supplication of thy servant, and unto the supplication of thy people Israel, to hearken unto them in all that they call for unto thee.

53. For thou didst separate them from among all the people of the earth, to be thine inheritance, as thou spakest by the hand of Moses thy servant, when thou broughtest our fathers out of Egypt, O Lord GOD.

54. And it was so, that when Solomon had made an end of praying all this prayer and supplication unto the LORD, he arose from before the altar of the LORD, from kneeling on his knees with his hands spread up to heaven.

55. And he stood, and blessed all the congregation of Israel with a loud voice, saying,

56. Blessed be the LORD, that hath given rest unto his people Israel, according to all that he promised: there hath not failed one word of all his good promise, which he promised by the hand of Moses his servant.

57. The LORD our God be with us, as he was with our fathers: let him not leave us, nor forsake us:

58. That he may incline our hearts unto him, to walk in all his ways, and to keep his commandments, and his statutes, and his judgments, which he commanded our fathers.

59. And let these my words, wherewith I have made supplication before the LORD, be nigh unto the LORD our God day and night, that he maintain the cause of his servant, and the cause of his people Israel at all times, as the matter shall require:

60. That all the people of the earth may know that the LORD is God, and that there is none else.

61. Let your heart therefore be perfect with the LORD our God, to walk in his statutes, and to keep his commandments, as at this day.

First and Second Chronicles

Although divided into two books, I Chronicles and II Chronicles, in the Vulgate and the Septuagint as well as in modern Bibles, in Hebrew manuscripts there is only one book of Chronicles with the title "Acts of the Days." Jewish tradition attributes the authorship of the book to Ezra. It seems more probable that the work was written by a Levite connected with the musical services of the second temple. His purpose seems to have been to write a historical book from the religious and Levitical point of view. The two books trace the history of the Jews from Adam to the Babylonian Captivity.

I Chronicles

CHAPTER 16

7. Then on that day David delivered first this psalm to thank the LORD into the hand of Asaph and his brethren.

8. Give thanks unto the LORD, call upon his name, make known his deeds among the people.

9. Sing unto him, sing psalms unto him, talk ye of all his wondrous works.

10. Glory ye in his holy name: let the heart of them rejoice that seek the LORD.

11. Seek the LORD and his strength, seek his face continually.

12. Remember his marvellous works that he hath done, his wonders, and the judgments of his mouth;

13. O ye seed of Israel his servant, ye children of Jacob, his chosen ones.

14. He is the LORD our God; his judgments are in all the earth.

15. Be ye mindful always of his covenant; the word which he commanded to a thousand generations;

16. Even of the covenant which he made with Abraham, and of his oath unto Isaac;

17. And hath confirmed the same to Jacob for a law, and to Israel for an everlasting covenant.

18. Saying, Unto thee will I give the land of Canaan, the lot of your inheritance;

19. When ye were but few, even a few, and strangers in it.

20. And when they went from nation to nation, and from one kingdom to another people;

21. He suffered no man to do them wrong: yea, he reproved kings for their sakes,

22. Saying, Touch not mine anointed, and do my prophets no harm.

23. Sing unto the LORD, all the earth; shew forth from day to day his salvation.

24. Declare his glory among the heathen; his marvellous works among all nations.

25. For great is the LORD, and greatly to be praised: he also is to be feared above all gods.

26. For all the gods of the people are idols: but the LORD made the heavens.

27. Glory and honour are in his presence; strength and gladness are in his place.

28. Give unto the LORD, ye kindreds of the people, give unto the LORD glory and strength.

29. Give unto the LORD the glory due unto his name: bring an offering, and come before him: worship the LORD in the beauty of holiness.

30. Fear before him, all the earth: the world also shall be stable, that it be not moved.

31. Let the heavens be glad, and let the earth rejoice: and let men say among the nations, The LORD reigneth.

32. Let the sea roar, and the fulness thereof: let the fields rejoice, and all that is therein.

33. Then shall the trees of the wood sing out at the presence of the LORD, because he cometh to judge the earth.

34. O give thanks unto the LORD; for he is good; for his mercy endureth for ever.

35. And say ye, Save us, O God of our salvation, and gather us together, and deliver us from the heathen, that we may give thanks to thy holy name, and glory in thy praise.

36. Blessed be the LORD God of Israel for ever and ever. And all the people said, A-men, and praised the LORD.

CHAPTER 29

10. Wherefore David blessed the LORD before all the congregation: and David said, Blessed be thou, LORD God of Israel our father, for ever and ever.

11. Thine, O LORD, is the greatness, and the power, and the glory, and the victory, and the majesty: for all that is in the heaven and in the earth is thine; thine is the kingdom, O LORD, and thou art exalted as head above all.

12. Both riches and honour come of thee, and thou reignest over all; and in thine hand is power and might; and in thine hand it is to make great, and to give strength unto all.

13. Now therefore, our God, we thank thee, and praise thy glorious name.

14. But who am I, and what is my people, that we should be able to offer so willingly after this sort? for all things come of thee, and of thine own have we given thee.

15. For we are strangers before thee, and sojourners, as were all our fathers: our days on the earth are as a shadow, and there is none abiding.

16. O LORD our God, all this store that we have prepared to build thee

an house for thine holy name cometh of thine hand, and is all thine own.

17. I know also, my God, that thou triest the heart, and hast pleasure in uprightness. As for me, in the uprightness of mine heart I have willingly offered all these things: and now have I seen with joy thy people, which are present here, to offer willingly unto thee.

18. O LORD God of Abraham, Isaac, and of Israel, our fathers, keep this for ever in the imagination of the thoughts of the heart of thy people, and prepare their heart unto thee:

19. And give unto Solomon my son a perfect heart, to keep thy commandments, thy testimonies, and thy statutes, and to do all these things, and to build the palace, for the which I have made provision.

Psalms

This is the first book of the "Writings," the third division of the Old Testament. Its title is derived from the Greek "psalmoi." The Hebrew title of the book is Sepher Tehillim (*Book of Praises). Although David is prominent in the book, the psalms were written by others as well as by this King. Other authors of writings in the Psalter were the sons of Korah, Asaph, Solomon, Ethan the Ezrahite, and a group of anonymous writers. Many religious subjects are treated in the Psalms. Among these are: supplication; gratitude; adoration; God's power, majesty, and glory; and other didactic and prophetic matters. This book is the poetic treasure house of the Hebrews.*

PSALM 1

1. Blessed is the man that walketh not in the counsel of the ungodly, nor standeth in the way of sinners, nor sitteth in the seat of the scornful.

2. But his delight is in the law of

the LORD; and in his law doth he meditate day and night.

3. And he shall be like a tree planted by the rivers of water, that bringeth forth his fruit in his season; his leaf also shall not wither; and whatsoever he doeth shall prosper.

4. The ungodly are not so: but are like the chaff which the wind driveth away.

5. Therefore the ungodly shall not stand in the judgment, nor sinners in the congregation of the righteous.

6. For the LORD knoweth the way of the righteous: but the way of the ungodly shall perish.

PSALM 8

1. O LORD our Lord, how excellent is thy name in all the earth! who hast set thy glory above the heavens.

2. Out of the mouth of babes and sucklings hast thou ordained strength because of thine enemies, that thou mightest still the enemy and the avenger.

3. When I consider thy heavens, the work of thy fingers, the moon and the stars, which thou hast ordained;

4. What is man, that thou art mindful of him? and the son of man, that thou visitest him?

5. For thou hast made him a little lower than the angels, and hast crowned him with glory and honour.

6. Thou madest him to have dominion over the works of thy hands; thou hast put all things under his feet:

7. All sheep and oxen, yea, and the beasts of the field;

8. The fowl of the air, and the fish of the sea, and whatsoever passeth through the paths of the seas.

9. O LORD our Lord, how excellent is thy name in all the earth!

PSALM 10

1. Why standest thou afar off, O LORD? why hidest thou thyself in times of trouble?

2. The wicked in his pride doth persecute the poor: let them be taken in the devices that they have imagined.

3. For the wicked boasteth of his heart's desire, and blesseth the covetous, whom the LORD abhorreth.

4. The wicked, through the pride of his countenance, will not seek after God: God is not in all his thoughts.

5. His ways are always grievous; thy judgments are far above out of his sight: as for all his enemies, he puffeth at them.

6. He hath said in his heart, I shall not be moved: for I shall never be in adversity.

7. His mouth is full of cursing and deceit and fraud: under his tongue is mischief and vanity.

8. He sitteth in the lurking places of the villages: in the secret places doth he murder the innocent: his eyes are privily set against the poor.

9. He lieth in wait secretly as a lion in his den: he lieth in wait to catch the poor: he doth catch the poor, when he draweth him into his net.

10. He croucheth, and humbleth himself, that the poor may fall by his strong ones.

11. He hath said in his heart, God hath forgotten: he hideth his face; he will never see it.

12. Arise, O LORD; O God, lift up thine hand; forget not the humble.

13. Wherefore doth the wicked contemn God? he hath said in his heart, Thou wilt not require it.

14. Thou hast seen it; for thou beholdest mischief and spite, to requite it with thy hand: the poor committeth himself unto thee; thou art the helper of the fatherless.

15. Break thou the arm of the wicked and the evil man: seek out his wickedness till thou find none.

16. The LORD is King for ever and ever: the heathen are perished out of his land.

17 LORD, thou hast heard the desire

of the humble: thou wilt prepare their heart, thou wilt cause thine ear to hear:

18. To judge the fatherless and the oppressed, that the man of the earth may no more oppress.

PSALM 15

1. LORD, who shall abide in thy tabernacle? who shall dwell in thy holy hill?

2. He that walketh uprightly, and worketh righteousness, and speaketh the truth in his heart.

3. He that backbiteth not with his tongue, nor doeth evil to his neighbour, nor taketh up a reproach against his neighbour.

4. In whose eyes a vile person is contemned; but he honoureth them that fear the LORD. He that sweareth to his own hurt, and changeth not.

5. He that putteth not out his money to usury, nor taketh reward against the innocent. He that doeth these things shall never be moved.

PSALM 16

1. Preserve me, O God: for in thee do I put my trust.

2. O my soul, thou hast said unto the LORD, Thou art my Lord: my goodness extendeth not to thee;

3. But to the saints that are in the earth, and to the excellent, in whom is all my delight.

4. Their sorrows shall be multiplied that hasten after another god: their drink offerings of blood will I not offer, nor take up their names into my lips.

5. The LORD is the portion of mine inheritance and of my cup: thou maintainest my lot.

6. The lines are fallen unto me in pleasant places; yea, I have a goodly heritage.

7. I will bless the LORD, who hath given me counsel: my reins also instruct me in the night seasons.

8. I have set the LORD always before me: because he is at my right hand, I shall not be moved.

9. Therefore my heart is glad, and my glory rejoiceth: my flesh also shall rest in hope.

10. For thou wilt not leave my soul in hell; neither wilt thou suffer thine Holy One to see corruption.

11. Thou wilt shew me the path of life: in thy presence is fulness of joy; at thy right hand there are pleasures for evermore.

PSALM 18

1. I will love thee, O LORD, my strength.

2. The LORD is my rock, and my fortress, and my deliverer; my God, my strength, in whom I will trust; my buckler, and the horn of my salvation, and my high tower.

3. I will call upon the LORD, who is worthy to be praised: so shall I be saved from mine enemies.

4. The sorrows of death compassed me, and the floods of ungodly men made me afraid.

5. The sorrows of hell compassed me about: the snares of death prevented me.

6. In my distress I called upon the LORD, and cried unto my God: he heard my voice out of his temple, and my cry came before him, even into his ears.

7. Then the earth shook and trembled; the foundations also of the hills moved and were shaken, because he was wroth.

8. There went up a smoke out of his nostrils, and fire out of his mouth devoured: coals were kindled by it.

9. He bowed the heavens also, and came down: and darkness was under his feet.

10. And he rode upon a cherub, and did fly: yea, he did fly upon the wings of the wind.

11. He made darkness his secret

place: his pavilion round about him were dark waters and thick clouds of the skies.

12. At the brightness that was before him his thick clouds passed, hail stones and coals of fire.

13. The LORD also thundered in the heavens, and the Highest gave his voice; hail stones and coals of fire.

14. Yea, he sent out his arrows, and scattered them; and he shot out lightnings, and discomfited them.

15. Then the channels of waters were seen, and the foundations of the world were discovered at thy rebuke, O LORD, at the blast of the breath of thy nostrils.

16. He sent from above, he took me, he drew me out of many waters.

17. He delivered me from my strong enemy, and from them which hated me: for they were too strong for me.

18. They prevented me in the day of my calamity: but the LORD was my stay.

19. He brought me forth also into a large place; he delivered me, because he delighted in me.

20. The LORD rewarded me according to my righteousness; according to the cleanness of my hands hath he recompensed me.

21. For I have kept the ways of the LORD, and have not wickedly departed from my God.

22. For all his judgments were before me, and I did not put away his statutes from me.

23. I was also upright before him, and I kept myself from mine iniquity.

24. Therefore hath the LORD recompensed me according to my righteousness, according to the cleanness of my hands in his eyesight.

25. With the merciful thou wilt shew thyself merciful; with an upright man thou wilt shew thyself upright;

26. With the pure thou wilt shew thyself pure; and with the froward thou wilt shew thyself froward.

27. For thou wilt save the afflicted people; but wilt bring down high looks.

28. For thou wilt light my candle: the LORD my God will enlighten my darkness.

29. For by thee I have run through a troop; and by my God have I leaped over a wall.

30. As for God, his way is perfect: the word of the LORD is tried: he is a buckler to all those that trust in him.

31. For who is God save the LORD? or who is a rock save our God?

32. It is God that girdeth me with strength, and maketh my way perfect.

33. He maketh my feet like hinds' feet, and setteth me upon my high places.

34. He teacheth my hands to war, so that a bow of steel is broken by mine arms.

35. Thou hast also given me the shield of thy salvation: and thy right hand hath holden me up, and thy gentleness hath made me great.

36. Thou hast enlarged my steps under me, that my feet did not slip.

37. I have pursued mine enemies, and overtaken them: neither did I turn again till they were consumed.

38. I have wounded them that they were not able to rise: they are fallen under my feet.

39. For thou hast girded me with strength unto the battle: thou hast subdued under me those that rose up against me.

40. Thou hast also given me the necks of mine enemies; that I might destroy them that hate me.

41. They cried, but there was none to save them: even unto the LORD, but he answered them not.

42. Then did I beat them small as the dust before the wind: I did cast them out as the dirt in the streets.

43. Thou hast delivered me from the strivings of the people; and thou hast made me the head of the

heathen: a people whom I have not known shall serve me.

44. As soon as they hear of me, they shall obey me: the strangers shall submit themselves unto me.

45. The strangers shall fade away, and be afraid out of their close places.

46. The LORD liveth; and blessed be my rock; and let the God of my salvation be exalted.

47. It is God that avengeth me, and subdueth the people under me.

48. He delivereth me from mine enemies: yea, thou liftest me up above those that rise up against me: thou hast delivered me from the violent man.

49. Therefore will I give thanks unto thee, O LORD, among the heathen, and sing praises unto thy name.

50. Great deliverance giveth he to his king; and sheweth mercy to his anointed, to David, and to his seed for evermore.

PSALM 19

1. The heavens declare the glory of God; and the firmament sheweth his handywork.

2. Day unto day uttereth speech, and night unto night sheweth knowledge.

3. There is no speech nor language, where their voice is not heard.

4. Their line is gone out through all the earth, and their words to the end of the world. In them hath he set a tabernacle for the sun,

5. Which is as a bridegroom coming out of his chamber, and rejoiceth as a strong man to run a race.

6. His going forth is from the end of the heaven, and his circuit unto the ends of it: and there is nothing hid from the heat thereof.

7. The law of the LORD is perfect, converting the soul: the testimony of the LORD is sure, making wise the simple.

8. The statutes of the LORD are right, rejoicing the heart: the commandment of the LORD is pure, enlightening the eyes.

9. The fear of the LORD is clean, enduring for ever: the judgments of the LORD are true and righteous altogether.

10. More to be desired are they than gold, yea, than much fine gold: sweeter also than honey and the honeycomb.

11. Moreover by them is thy servant warned: and in keeping of them there is great reward.

12. Who can understand his errors? cleanse thou me from secret faults.

13. Keep back thy servant also from presumptuous sins; let them not have dominion over me: then shall I be upright, and I shall be innocent from the great transgression.

14. Let the words of my mouth, and the meditation of my heart, be acceptable in thy sight, O LORD, my strength, and my redeemer.

PSALM 22

1. My God, my God, why hast thou forsaken me? why art thou so far from helping me, and from the words of my roaring?

2. O my God, I cry in the daytime, but thou hearest not; and in the night season, and am not silent.

3. But thou art holy, O thou that inhabitest the praises of Israel.

4. Our fathers trusted in thee: they trusted, and thou didst deliver them.

5. They cried unto thee, and were delivered: they trusted in thee, and were not confounded.

6. But I am a worm, and no man; a reproach of men, and despised of the people.

7. All they that see me laugh me to scorn: they shoot out the lip, they shake the head, saying,

8. He trusted on the LORD that he would deliver him: let him deliver him, seeing he delighted in him.

9. But thou art he that took me out of the womb: thou didst make me hope when I was upon my mother's breasts.

10. I was cast upon thee from the womb: thou art my God from my mother's belly.

11. Be not far from me; for trouble is near; for there is none to help.

12. Many bulls have compassed me: strong bulls of Bashan have beset me round.

13. They gaped upon me with their mouths, as a ravening and a roaring lion.

14. I am poured out like water, and all my bones are out of joint: my heart is like wax; it is melted in the midst of my bowels.

15. My strength is dried up like a potsherd; and my tongue cleaveth to my jaws; and thou hast brought me into the dust of death.

16. For dogs have compassed me: the assembly of the wicked have inclosed me: they pierced my hands and my feet.

17. I may tell all my bones: they look and stare upon me.

18. They part my garments among them, and cast lots upon my vesture.

19. But be not thou far from me, O Lord: O my strength, haste thee to help me.

20. Deliver my soul from the sword; my darling from the power of the dog.

21. Save me from the lion's mouth: for thou hast heard me from the horns of the unicorns.

22. I will declare thy name unto my brethren: in the midst of the congregation will I praise thee.

23. Ye that fear the Lord, praise him; all ye the seed of Jacob, glorify him; and fear him, all ye the seed of Israel.

24. For he hath not despised nor abhorred the affliction of the afflicted; neither hath he hid his face from him; but when he cried unto him, he heard.

25. My praise shall be of thee in the great congregation: I will pay my vows before them that fear him.

26. The meek shall eat and be satisfied: they shall praise the Lord that seek him: your heart shall live for ever.

27. All the ends of the world shall remember and turn unto the Lord: and all the kindreds of the nations shall worship before thee.

28. For the kingdom is the Lord's: and he is the governor among the nations.

29. All they that be fat upon earth shall eat and worship: all they that go down to the dust shall bow before him: and none can keep alive his own soul.

30. A seed shall serve him; it shall be accounted to the Lord for a generation.

31. They shall come, and shall declare his righteousness unto a people that shall be born, that he hath done this.

Psalm 23

1. The Lord is my shepherd; I shall not want.

2. He maketh me to lie down in green pastures: he leadeth me beside the still waters.

3. He restoreth my soul: he leadeth me in the paths of righteousness for his name's sake.

4. Yea, though I walk through the valley of the shadow of death, I will fear no evil: for thou art with me; thy rod and thy staff they comfort me.

5. Thou preparest a table before me in the presence of mine enemies: thou anointest my head with oil; my cup runneth over.

6. Surely goodness and mercy shall follow me all the days of my life: and I will dwell in the house of the Lord for ever.

Psalm 24

1. The earth is the Lord's, and the fulness thereof; the world, and they that dwell therein.

2. For he hath founded it upon the seas, and established it upon the floods.

3. Who shall ascend into the hill of the Lord? or who shall stand in his holy place?

4. He that hath clean hands, and a pure heart; who hath not lifted up his soul unto vanity, nor sworn deceitfully.

5. He shall receive the blessing from the Lord, and righteousness from the God of his salvation.

6. This is the generation of them that seek him, that seek thy face, O Jacob. Selah.

7. Lift up your heads, O ye gates; and be ye lift up, ye everlasting doors; and the King of glory shall come in.

8. Who is this King of glory? The Lord strong and mighty, the Lord mighty in battle.

9. Lift up your heads, O ye gates; even lift them up, ye everlasting doors; and the King of glory shall come in.

10. Who is this King of glory? The Lord of hosts, he is the King of glory. Selah.

Psalm 25

1. Unto thee, O Lord, do I lift up my soul.

2. O my God, I trust in thee: let me not be ashamed, let not mine enemies triumph over me.

3. Yea, let none that wait on thee be ashamed: let them be ashamed which transgress without cause.

4. Shew me thy ways, O Lord; teach me thy paths.

5. Lead me in thy truth, and teach me: for thou art the God of my salvation; on thee do I wait all the day.

6. Remember, O Lord, thy tender mercies and thy lovingkindnesses; for they have been ever of old.

7. Remember not the sins of my youth, nor my transgressions: according to thy mercy remember thou me for thy goodness' sake, O Lord.

8. Good and upright is the Lord:

therefore will he teach sinners in the way.

9. The meek will he guide in judgment: and the meek will he teach his way.

10. All the paths of the Lord are mercy and truth unto such as keep his covenant and his testimonies.

11. For thy name's sake, O Lord, pardon mine iniquity; for it is great.

12. What man is he that feareth the Lord? him shall he teach in the way that he shall choose.

13. His soul shall dwell at ease; and his seed shall inherit the earth.

14. The secret of the Lord is with them that fear him; and he will shew them his covenant.

15. Mine eyes are ever toward the Lord; for he shall pluck my feet out of the net.

16. Turn thee unto me, and have mercy upon me; for I am desolate and afflicted.

17. The troubles of my heart are enlarged: O bring thou me out of my distresses.

18. Look upon mine affliction and my pain; and forgive all my sins.

19. Consider mine enemies; for they are many; and they hate me with cruel hatred.

20. O keep my soul, and deliver me: let me not be ashamed; for I put my trust in thee.

21. Let integrity and uprightness preserve me; for I wait on thee.

22. Redeem Israel, O God, out of all his troubles.

Psalm 26

1. Judge me, O Lord; for I have walked in mine integrity: I have trusted also in the Lord; therefore I shall not slide.

2. Examine me, O Lord, and prove me; try my reins and my heart.

3. For thy lovingkindness is before mine eyes: and I have walked in thy truth.

4. I have not sat with vain persons, neither will I go in with dissemblers.

5. I have hated the congregation of evildoers; and will not sit with the wicked.

6. I will wash mine hands in innocency: so will I compass thine altar, O LORD:

7. That I may publish with the voice of thanksgiving, and tell of all thy wondrous works.

8. LORD, I have loved the habitation of thy house, and the place where thine honour dwelleth.

9. Gather not my soul with sinners, nor my life with bloody men:

10. In whose hands is mischief, and their right hand is full of bribes.

11. But as for me, I will walk in mine integrity: redeem me, and be merciful unto me.

12. My foot standeth in an even place: in the congregations will I bless the LORD.

PSALM 27

1. The LORD is my light and my salvation; whom shall I fear? the LORD is the strength of my life; of whom shall I be afraid?

2. When the wicked, even mine enemies and my foes, came upon me to eat up my flesh, they stumbled and fell.

3. Though an host should encamp against me, my heart shall not fear: though war should rise against me, in this will I be confident.

4. One thing have I desired of the LORD, that will I seek after; that I may dwell in the house of the LORD all the days of my life, to behold the beauty of the LORD, and to enquire in his temple.

5. For in the time of trouble he shall hide me in his pavilion: in the secret of his tabernacle shall he hide me; he shall set me up upon a rock.

6. And now shall mine head be lifted up above mine enemies round about me: therefore will I offer in his tabernacle sacrifices of joy; I will sing, yea, I will sing praises unto the LORD.

7. Hear, O LORD, when I cry with my voice: have mercy also upon me, and answer me.

8. When thou saidst, Seek ye my face; my heart said unto thee, Thy face, LORD, will I seek.

9. Hide not thy face far from me; put not thy servant away in anger: thou hast been my help; leave me not, neither forsake me, O God of my salvation.

10. When my father and my mother forsake me, then the LORD will take me up.

11. Teach me thy way, O LORD, and lead me in a plain path, because of mine enemies.

12. Deliver me not over unto the will of mine enemies: for false witnesses are risen up against me, and such as breathe out cruelty.

13. I had fainted, unless I had believed to see the goodness of the LORD in the land of the living.

14. Wait on the LORD: be of good courage, and he shall strengthen thine heart: wait, I say, on the LORD.

PSALM 28

1. Unto thee will I cry, O LORD my rock; be not silent to me: lest, if thou be silent to me, I become like them that go down into the pit.

2. Hear the voice of my supplications, when I cry unto thee, when I lift up my hands toward thy holy oracle.

3. Draw me not away with the wicked, and with the workers of iniquity, which speak peace to their neighbours, but mischief is in their hearts.

4. Give them according to their deeds, and according to the wickedness of their endeavours: give them after the work of their hands; render to them their desert.

5. Because they regard not the works of the Lord, nor the operation of his hands, he shall destroy them, and not build them up.

6. Blessed be the Lord, because he hath heard the voice of my supplications.

7. The Lord is my strength and my shield; my heart trusted in him, and I am helped: therefore my heart greatly rejoiceth; and with my song will I praise him.

8. The Lord is their strength, and he is the saving strength of his anointed.

9. Save thy people, and bless thine inheritance: feed them also, and lift them up for ever.

Psalm 31

1. In thee, O Lord, do I put my trust; let me never be ashamed: deliver me in thy righteousness.

2. Bow down thine ear to me; deliver me speedily: be thou my strong rock, for an house of defence to save me.

3. For thou art my rock and my fortress; therefore for thy name's sake lead me, and guide me.

4. Pull me out of the net that they have laid privily for me: for thou art my strength.

5. Into thine hand I commit my spirit: thou hast redeemed me, O Lord God of truth.

6. I have hated them that regard lying vanities: but I trust in the Lord.

7. I will be glad and rejoice in thy mercy: for thou hast considered my trouble; thou hast known my soul in adversities;

8. And hast not shut me up into the hand of the enemy: thou hast set my feet in a large room.

9. Have mercy upon me, O Lord, for I am in trouble: mine eye is consumed with grief, yea, my soul and my belly.

10. For my life is spent with grief, and my years with sighing: my strength faileth because of mine iniquity, and my bones are consumed.

11. I was a reproach among all mine enemies, but especially among my neighbours, and a fear to mine acquaintance: they that did see me without fled from me.

12. I am forgotten as a dead man out of mind: I am like a broken vessel.

13. For I have heard the slander of many: fear was on every side: while they took counsel together against me, they devised to take away my life.

14. But I trusted in thee, O Lord: I said, Thou art my God.

15. My times are in thy hand: deliver me from the hand of mine enemies, and from them that persecute me.

16. Make thy face to shine upon thy servant: save me for thy mercies' sake.

17. Let me not be ashamed, O Lord; for I have called upon thee: let the wicked be ashamed, and let them be silent in the grave.

18. Let the lying lips be put to silence; which speak grievous things proudly and contemptuously against the righteous.

19. Oh how great is thy goodness, which thou hast laid up for them that fear thee; which thou hast wrought for them that trust in thee before the sons of men!

20. Thou shalt hide them in the secret of thy presence from the pride of man: thou shalt keep them secretly in a pavilion from the strife of tongues.

21. Blessed be the Lord: for he hath shewed me his marvellous kindness in a strong city.

22. For I said in my haste, I am cut off from before thine eyes: nevertheless thou heardest the voice of my supplications when I cried unto thee.

23. O love the Lord, all ye his saints: for the Lord preserveth the

faithful, and plentifully rewardeth the proud doer.

24. Be of good courage, and he shall strengthen your heart, all ye that hope in the LORD.

PSALM 33

1. Rejoice in the LORD, O ye righteous: for praise is comely for the upright.

2. Praise the LORD with harp: sing unto him with the psaltery and an instrument of ten strings.

3. Sing unto him a new song; play skilfully with a loud noise.

4. For the word of the LORD is right; and all his works are done in truth.

5. He loveth righteousness and judgment: the earth is full of the goodness of the LORD.

6. By the word of the LORD were the heavens made; and all the host of them by the breath of his mouth.

7. He gathereth the waters of the sea together as an heap: he layeth up the depth in storehouses.

8. Let all the earth fear the LORD: let all the inhabitants of the world stand in awe of him.

9. For he spake, and it was done; he commanded, and it stood fast.

10. The LORD bringeth the counsel of the heathen to nought: he maketh the devices of the people of none effect.

11. The counsel of the LORD standeth for ever, the thoughts of his heart to all generations.

12. Blessed is the nation whose God is the LORD; and the people whom he hath chosen for his own inheritance.

13. The LORD looketh from heaven; he beholdeth all the sons of men.

14. From the place of his habitation he looketh upon all the inhabitants of the earth.

15. He fashioneth their hearts alike; he considereth all their works.

16. There is no king saved by the multitude of an host: a mighty man is not delivered by much strength.

17. An horse is a vain thing for safety: neither shall he deliver any by his great strength.

18. Behold, the eye of the LORD is upon them that fear him, upon them that hope in his mercy;

19. To deliver their soul from death, and to keep them alive in famine.

20. Our soul waiteth for the LORD: he is our help and our shield.

21. For our heart shall rejoice in him, because we have trusted in his holy name.

22. Let thy mercy, O LORD, be upon us, according as we hope in thee.

PSALM 34

1. I will bless the LORD at all times: his praise shall continually be in my mouth.

2. My soul shall make her boast in the LORD: the humble shall hear thereof, and be glad.

3. O magnify the LORD with me, and let us exalt his name together.

4. I sought the LORD, and he heard me, and delivered me from all my fears.

5. They looked unto him, and were lightened: and their faces were not ashamed.

6. This poor man cried, and the LORD heard him, and saved him out of all his troubles.

7. The angel of the LORD encampeth round about them that fear him, and delivereth them.

8. O taste and see that the LORD is good: blessed is the man that trusteth in him.

9. O fear the LORD, ye his saints: for there is no want to them that fear him.

10. The young lions do lack, and suffer hunger: but they that seek the LORD shall not want any good thing.

11. Come, ye children, hearken

unto me: I will teach you the fear of the LORD.

12. What man is he that desireth life, and loveth many days, that he may see good?

13. Keep thy tongue from evil, and thy lips from speaking guile.

14. Depart from evil, and do good: seek peace, and pursue it.

PSALM 37

1. Fret not thyself because of evildoers, neither be thou envious against the workers of iniquity.

2. For they shall soon be cut down like the grass, and wither as the green herb.

3. Trust in the LORD, and do good; so shalt thou dwell in the land, and verily thou shalt be fed.

4. Delight thyself also in the LORD; and he shall give thee the desires of thine heart.

5. Commit thy way unto the LORD; trust also in him; and he shall bring it to pass.

6. And he shall bring forth thy righteousness as the light, and thy judgment as the noonday.

7. Rest in the LORD, and wait patiently for him: fret not thyself because of him who prospereth in his way, because of the man who bringeth wicked devices to pass.

8. Cease from anger, and forsake wrath: fret not thyself in any wise to do evil.

9. For evildoers shall be cut off: but those that wait upon the LORD, they shall inherit the earth.

10. For yet a little while, and the wicked shall not be: yea, thou shalt diligently consider his place, and it shall not be.

11. But the meek shall inherit the earth; and shall delight themselves in the abundance of peace.

12. The wicked plotteth against the just, and gnasheth upon him with his teeth.

13. The Lord shall laugh at him: for he seeth that his day is coming.

14. The wicked have drawn out the sword, and have bent their bow, to cast down the poor and needy, and to slay such as be of upright conversation.

15. Their sword shall enter into their own heart, and their bows shall be broken.

16. A little that a righteous man hath is better than the riches of many wicked.

17. For the arms of the wicked shall be broken: but the LORD upholdeth the righteous.

18. The LORD knoweth the days of the upright: and their inheritance shall be for ever.

19. They shall not be ashamed in the evil time: and in the days of famine they shall be satisfied.

20. But the wicked shall perish, and the enemies of the LORD shall be as the fat of lambs: they shall consume; into smoke shall they consume away.

21. The wicked borroweth, and payeth not again: but the righteous sheweth mercy, and giveth.

22. For such as be blessed of him shall inherit the earth; and they that be cursed of him shall be cut off.

23. The steps of a good man are ordered by the LORD: and he delighteth in his way.

24. Though he fall, he shall not be utterly cast down: for the LORD upholdeth him with his hand.

25. I have been young, and now am old; yet have I not seen the righteous forsaken, nor his seed begging bread.

26. He is ever merciful, and lendeth; and his seed is blessed.

27. Depart from evil, and do good; and dwell for evermore.

28. For the LORD loveth judgment, and forsaketh not his saints; they are preserved for ever: but the seed of the wicked shall be cut off.

29. The righteous shall inherit the land, and dwell therein for ever.

30. The mouth of the righteous speaketh wisdom, and his tongue talketh of judgment.

31. The law of his God is in his heart; none of his steps shall slide.

32. The wicked watcheth the righteous, and seeketh to slay him.

33. The LORD will not leave him in his hand, nor condemn him when he is judged.

34. Wait on the LORD, and keep his way, and he shall exalt thee to inherit the land: when the wicked are cut off, thou shalt see it.

35. I have seen the wicked in great power, and spreading himself like a green bay tree.

36. Yet he passed away, and, lo, he was not: yea, I sought him, but he could not be found.

37. Mark the perfect man, and behold the upright: for the end of that man is peace.

38. But the transgressors shall be destroyed together: the end of the wicked shall be cut off.

39. But the salvation of the righteous is of the LORD: he is their strength in the time of trouble.

40. And the LORD shall help them, and deliver them: he shall deliver them from the wicked, and save them, because they trust in him.

PSALM 38

1. O LORD, rebuke me not in thy wrath: neither chasten me in thy hot displeasure.

2. For thine arrows stick fast in me, and thy hand presseth me sore.

3. There is no soundness in my flesh because of thine anger; neither is there any rest in my bones because of my sin.

4. For mine iniquities are gone over mine head: as an heavy burden they are too heavy for me.

5. My wounds stink and are corrupt because of my foolishness.

6. I am troubled; I am bowed down

greatly; I go mourning all the day long.

7. For my loins are filled with a loathsome disease: and there is no soundness in my flesh.

8. I am feeble and sore broken: I have roared by reason of the disquietness of my heart.

9. Lord, all my desire is before thee; and my groaning is not hid from thee.

10. My heart panteth, my strength faileth me: as for the light of mine eyes, it also is gone from me.

11. My lovers and my friends stand aloof from my sore; and my kinsmen stand afar off.

12. They also that seek after my life lay snares for me: and they that seek my hurt speak mischievous things, and imagine deceits all the day long.

13. But I, as a deaf man, heard not; and I was as a dumb man that openeth not his mouth.

14. Thus I was as a man that heareth not, and in whose mouth are no reproofs.

15. For in thee, O LORD, do I hope: thou wilt hear, O Lord my God.

16. For I said, Hear me, lest otherwise they should rejoice over me: when my foot slippeth, they magnify themselves against me.

17. For I am ready to halt, and my sorrow is continually before me.

18. For I will declare mine iniquity; I will be sorry for my sin.

19. But mine enemies are lively, and they are strong: and they that hate me wrongfully are multiplied.

20. They also that render evil for good are mine adversaries; because I follow the thing that good is.

21. Forsake me not, O LORD: O my God, be not far from me.

22. Make haste to help me, O Lord my salvation.

PSALM 41

1. Blessed is he that considereth the poor: the LORD will deliver him in time of trouble.

2. The LORD will preserve him, and keep him alive; and he shall be blessed upon the earth: and thou wilt not deliver him unto the will of his enemies.

3. The LORD will strengthen him upon the bed of languishing: thou wilt make all his bed in his sickness.

4. I said, LORD, be merciful unto me: heal my soul; for I have sinned against thee.

5. Mine enemies speak evil of me, When shall he die, and his name perish?

6. And if he come to see me, he speaketh vanity: his heart gathereth iniquity to itself; when he goeth abroad, he telleth it.

7. All that hate me whisper together against me: against me do they devise my hurt.

8. An evil disease, say they, cleaveth fast unto him: and now that he lieth he shall rise up no more.

9. Yea, mine own familiar friend, in whom I trusted, which did eat of my bread, hath lifted up his heel against me.

10. But thou, O LORD, be merciful unto me, and raise me up, that I may requite them.

11. By this I know that thou favourest me, because mine enemy doth not triumph over me.

12. And as for me, thou upholdest me in mine integrity, and settest me before thy face for ever.

13. Blessed be the LORD God of Israel from everlasting, and to everlasting. Amen, and Amen.

PSALM 46

1. God is our refuge and strength, a very present help in trouble.

2. Therefore will not we fear, though the earth be removed, and though the mountains be carried into the midst of the sea;

3. Though the waters thereof roar and be troubled, though the mountains shake with the swelling thereof. Selah.

4. There is a river, the streams whereof shall make glad the city of God, the holy place of the tabernacles of the most High.

5. God is in the midst of her; she shall not be moved: God shall help her, and that right early.

6. The heathen raged, the kingdoms were moved: he uttered his voice, the earth melted.

7. The LORD of hosts is with us; the God of Jacob is our refuge. Selah.

8. Come, behold the works of the LORD, what desolations he hath made in the earth.

9. He maketh wars to cease unto the end of the earth; he breaketh the bow, and cutteth the spear in sunder; he burneth the chariot in the fire.

10. Be still, and know that I am God: I will be exalted among the heathen, I will be exalted in the earth.

11. The LORD of hosts is with us; the God of Jacob is our refuge. Selah.

PSALM 51

1. Have mercy upon me, O God, according to thy lovingkindness: according unto the multitude of thy tender mercies blot out my transgressions.

2. Wash me throughly from mine iniquity, and cleanse me from my sin.

3. For I acknowledge my transgressions: and my sin is ever before me.

4. Against thee, thee only, have I sinned, and done this evil in thy sight: that thou mightest be justified when thou speakest, and be clear when thou judgest.

5. Behold, I was shapen in iniquity; and in sin did my mother conceive me.

6. Behold, thou desirest truth in the inward parts: and in the hidden part thou shalt make me to know wisdom.

7. Purge me with hyssop, and I shall be clean: wash me, and I shall be whiter than snow.

8. Make me to hear joy and gladness; that the bones which thou hast broken may rejoice.

9. Hide thy face from my sins, and blot out all mine iniquities.

10. Create in me a clean heart, O God; and renew a right spirit within me.

11. Cast me not away from thy presence; and take not thy holy spirit from me.

12. Restore unto me the joy of thy salvation; and uphold me with thy free spirit.

13. Then will I teach transgressors thy ways; and sinners shall be converted unto thee.

14. Deliver me from bloodguiltiness, O God, thou God of my salvation: and my tongue shall sing aloud of thy righteousness.

15. O Lord, open thou my lips; and my mouth shall shew forth thy praise.

16. For thou desirest not sacrifice; else would I give it: thou delightest not in burnt offering.

17. The sacrifices of God are a broken spirit: a broken and a contrite heart, O God, thou wilt not despise.

18. Do good in thy good pleasure unto Zion: build thou the walls of Jerusalem.

19. Then shalt thou be pleased with the sacrifices of righteousness, with burnt offering and whole burnt offering: then shall they offer bullocks upon thine altar.

PSALM 53

1. The fool hath said in his heart, There is no God. Corrupt are they, and have done abominable iniquity: there is none that doeth good.

2. God looked down from heaven upon the children of men, to see if there were any that did understand, that did seek God.

3. Every one of them is gone back: they are altogether become filthy; there is none that doeth good, no, not one.

4. Have the workers of iniquity no knowledge? who eat up my people as they eat bread: they have not called upon God.

5. There were they in great fear, where no fear was: for God hath scattered the bones of him that encampeth against thee: thou hast put them to shame, because God hath despised them.

6. Oh that the salvation of Israel were come out of Zion! When God bringeth back the captivity of his people, Jacob shall rejoice, and Israel shall be glad.

PSALM 62

1. Truly my soul waiteth upon God: from him cometh my salvation.

2. He only is my rock and my salvation; he is my defence; I shall not be greatly moved.

3. How long will ye imagine mischief against a man? ye shall be slain all of you: as a bowing wall shall ye be, and as a tottering fence.

4. They only consult to cast him down from his excellency: they delight in lies: they bless with their mouth, but they curse inwardly. Selah.

5. My soul, wait thou only upon God; for my expectation is from him.

6. He only is my rock and my salvation: he is my defence; I shall not be moved.

7. In God is my salvation and my glory: the rock of my strength, and my refuge, is in God.

8. Trust in him at all times; ye people, pour out your heart before him: God is a refuge for us. Selah.

9. Surely men of low degree are vanity, and men of high degree are a lie: to be laid in the balance, they are altogether lighter than vanity.

10. Trust not in oppression, and become not vain in robbery: if riches increase, set not your heart upon them.

11. God hath spoken once; twice have I heard this; that power belongeth unto God.

12. Also unto thee, O Lord, belongeth mercy: for thou renderest to every man according to his work.

PSALM 63

1. O God, thou art my God; early will I seek thee: my soul thirsteth for thee, my flesh longeth for thee in a dry and thirsty land, where no water is;

2. To see thy power and thy glory, so as I have seen thee in the sanctuary.

3. Because thy lovingkindness is better than life, my lips shall praise thee.

4. Thus will I bless thee while I live: I will lift up my hands in thy name.

5. My soul shall be satisfied as with marrow and fatness; and my mouth shall praise thee with joyful lips:

6. When I remember thee upon my bed, and meditate on thee in the night watches.

7. Because thou hast been my help, therefore in the shadow of thy wings will I rejoice.

8. My soul followeth hard after thee: thy right hand upholdeth me.

9. But those that seek my soul, to destroy it, shall go into the lower parts of the earth.

10. They shall fall by the sword: they shall be a portion for foxes.

11. But the king shall rejoice in God; every one that sweareth by him shall glory: but the mouth of them that speak lies shall be stopped.

PSALM 65

1. Praise waiteth for thee, O God, in Sion: and unto thee shall the vow be performed:

2. O thou that hearest prayer, unto thee shall all flesh come.

3. Iniquities prevail against me: as for our transgressions, thou shalt purge them away.

4. Blessed is the man whom thou choosest, and causest to approach unto thee, that he may dwell in thy courts: we shall be satisfied with the goodness of thy house, even of thy holy temple.

5. By terrible things in righteousness wilt thou answer us, O God of our salvation; who art the confidence of all the ends of the earth, and of them that are afar off upon the sea:

6. Which by his strength setteth fast the mountains; being girded with power:

7. Which stilleth the noise of the seas, the noise of their waves, and the tumult of the people.

8. They also that dwell in the uttermost parts are afraid at thy tokens: thou makest the outgoings of the morning and evening to rejoice.

9. Thou visitest the earth, and waterest it: thou greatly enrichest it with the river of God, which is full of water: thou preparest them corn, when thou hast so provided for it.

10. Thou waterest the ridges thereof abundantly: thou settlest the furrows thereof: thou makest it soft with showers: thou blessest the springing thereof.

11. Thou crownest the year with thy goodness; and thy paths drop fatness.

12. They drop upon the pastures of the wilderness: and the little hills rejoice on every side.

13. The pastures are clothed with flocks; the valleys also are covered over with corn; they shout for joy, they also sing.

PSALM 66

1. Make a joyful noise unto God, all ye lands:

2. Sing forth the honour of his name: make his praise glorious.

3. Say unto God, How terrible art

thou in thy works! through the greatness of thy power shall thine enemies submit themselves unto thee.

4. All the earth shall worship thee, and shall sing unto thee; they shall sing to thy name. Selah.

5. Come and see the works of God: he is terrible in his doing toward the children of men.

6. He turned the sea into dry land: they went through the flood on foot: there did we rejoice in him.

7. He ruleth by his power for ever; his eyes behold the nations: let not the rebellious exalt themselves. Selah.

8. O bless our God, ye people, and make the voice of his praise to be heard:

9. Which holdeth our soul in life, and suffereth not our feet to be moved.

10. For thou, O God, hast proved us: thou hast tried us, as silver is tried.

11. Thou broughtest us into the net; thou laidst affliction upon our loins.

12. Thou hast caused men to ride over our heads; we went through fire and through water: but thou broughtest us out into a wealthy place.

13. I will go into thy house with burnt offerings: I will pay thee my vows,

14. Which my lips have uttered, and my mouth hath spoken, when I was in trouble.

15. I will offer unto thee burnt sacrifices of fatlings, with the incense of rams; I will offer bullocks with goats. Selah.

16. Come and hear, all ye that fear God, and I will declare what he hath done for my soul.

17. I cried unto him with my mouth, and he was extolled with my tongue.

18. If I regard iniquity in my heart, the Lord will not hear me:

19. But verily God hath heard me; he hath attended to the voice of my prayer.

20. Blessed be God, which hath not turned away my prayer, nor his mercy from me.

Psalm 67

1. God be merciful unto us, and bless us; and cause his face to shine upon us; Selah.

2. That thy way may be known upon earth, thy saving health among all nations.

3. Let the people praise thee, O God; let all the people praise thee.

4. O let the nations be glad and sing for joy: for thou shalt judge the people righteously, and govern the nations upon earth. Selah.

5. Let the people praise thee, O God; let all the people praise thee.

6. Then shall the earth yield her increase; and God, even our own God shall bless us.

7. God shall bless us; and all the ends of the earth shall fear him.

Psalm 84

1. How amiable are thy tabernacles, O Lord of hosts!

2. My soul longeth, yea, even fainteth for the courts of the Lord: my heart and my flesh crieth out for the living God.

3. Yea, the sparrow hath found an house, and the swallow a nest for herself, where she may lay her young, even thine altars, O Lord of hosts, my King, and my God.

4. Blessed are they that dwell in thy house: they will be still praising thee. Selah.

5. Blessed is the man whose strength is in thee; in whose heart are the ways of them.

6. Who passing through the valley of Baca make it a well; the rain also filleth the pools.

7. They go from strength to

strength, every one of them in Zion appeareth before God.

8. O Lord God of hosts, hear my prayer: give ear, O God of Jacob. Selah.

9. Behold, O God our shield, and look upon the face of thine anointed.

10. For a day in thy courts is better than a thousand. I had rather be a doorkeeper in the house of my God, than to dwell in the tents of wickedness.

11. For the Lord God is a sun and shield: the Lord will give grace and glory: no good thing will he withhold from them that walk uprightly.

12. O Lord of hosts, blessed is the man that trusteth in thee.

Psalm 92

1. It is a good thing to give thanks unto the Lord, and to sing praises unto thy name, O most High:

2. To shew forth thy lovingkindness in the morning, and thy faithfulness every night,

3. Upon an instrument of ten strings, and upon the psaltery; upon the harp with a solemn sound.

4. For thou, Lord, hast made me glad through thy work: I will triumph in the works of thy hands.

5. O Lord, how great are thy works! and thy thoughts are very deep.

6. A brutish man knoweth not; neither doth a fool understand this.

7. When the wicked spring as the grass, and when all the workers of iniquity do flourish; it is that they shall be destroyed for ever:

8. But thou, Lord, art most high for evermore.

9. For, lo, thine enemies, O Lord, for, lo, thine enemies shall perish; all the workers of iniquity shall be scattered.

10. But my horn shalt thou exalt like the horn of an unicorn: I shall be anointed with fresh oil.

11. Mine eye also shall see my desire on mine enemies, and mine ears shall hear my desire of the wicked that rise up against me.

12. The righteous shall flourish like the palm tree: he shall grow like a cedar in Lebanon.

13. Those that be planted in the house of the Lord shall flourish in the courts of our God.

14. They shall still bring forth fruit in old age; they shall be fat and flourishing;

15. To shew that the Lord is upright: he is my rock, and there is no unrighteousness in him.

Psalm 97

1. The Lord reigneth; let the earth rejoice; let the multitude of isles be glad thereof.

2. Clouds and darkness are round about him: righteousness and judgment are the habitation of his throne.

3. A fire goeth before him, and burneth up his enemies round about.

4. His lightnings enlightened the world: the earth saw, and trembled.

5. The hills melted like wax at the presence of the Lord, at the presence of the Lord of the whole earth.

6. The heavens declare his righteousness, and all the people see his glory.

7. Confounded be all they that serve graven images, that boast themselves of idols: worship him, all ye gods.

8. Zion heard, and was glad; and the daughters of Judah rejoiced because of thy judgments, O Lord.

9. For thou, Lord, art high above all the earth: thou art exalted far above all gods.

10. Ye that love the Lord, hate evil: he preserveth the souls of his saints; he delivereth them out of the hand of the wicked.

11. Light is sown for the righteous, and gladness for the upright in heart.

12. Rejoice in the LORD, ye righteous; and give thanks at the remembrance of his holiness.

PSALM 100

1. Make a joyful noise unto the LORD, all ye lands.

2. Serve the LORD with gladness: come before his presence with singing.

3. Know ye that the LORD he is God: it is he that hath made us, and not we ourselves; we are his people, and the sheep of his pasture.

4. Enter into his gates with thanksgiving, and into his courts with praise: be thankful unto him, and bless his name.

5. For the LORD is good; his mercy is everlasting; and his truth endureth to all generations.

PSALM 103

1. Bless the LORD, O my soul: and all that is within me, bless his holy name.

2. Bless the LORD, O my soul, and forget not all his benefits:

3. Who forgiveth all thine iniquities; who healeth all thy diseases;

4. Who redeemeth thy life from destruction; who crowneth thee with lovingkindness and tender mercies;

5. Who satisfieth thy mouth with good things; so that thy youth is renewed like the eagle's.

6. The LORD executeth righteousness and judgment for all that are oppressed.

7. He made known his ways unto Moses, his acts unto the children of Israel.

8. The LORD is merciful and gracious, slow to anger, and plenteous in mercy.

9. He will not always chide: neither will he keep his anger for ever.

10. He hath not dealt with us after our sins; nor rewarded us according to our iniquities.

11. For as the heaven is high above the earth, so great is his mercy toward them that fear him.

12. As far as the east is from the west, so far hath he removed our transgressions from us.

13. Like as a father pitieth his children, so the LORD pitieth them that fear him.

14. For he knoweth our frame; he remembereth that we are dust.

15. As for man, his days are as grass: as a flower of the field, so he flourisheth.

16. For the wind passeth over it, and it is gone; and the place thereof shall know it no more.

17. But the mercy of the LORD is from everlasting to everlasting upon them that fear him, and his righteousness unto children's children;

18. To such as keep his covenant, and to those that remember his commandments to do them.

19. The LORD hath prepared his throne in the heavens; and his kingdom ruleth over all.

20. Bless the LORD, ye his angels, that excel in strength, that do his commandments, hearkening unto the voice of his word.

21. Bless ye the LORD, all ye his hosts; ye ministers of his, that do his pleasure.

22. Bless the LORD, all his works in all places of his dominion: bless the LORD, O my soul.

PSALM 119

ALEPH

1. Blessed are the undefiled in the way, who walk in the law of the LORD.

2. Blessed are they that keep his testimonies, and that seek him with the whole heart.

3. They also do no iniquity: they walk in his ways.

4. Thou hast commanded us to keep thy precepts diligently.

5. O that my ways were directed to keep thy statutes!

6. Then shall I not be ashamed, when I have respect unto all thy commandments.

7. I will praise thee with uprightness of heart, when I shall have learned thy righteous judgments.

8. I will keep thy statutes: O forsake me not utterly.

BETH

9. Wherewithal shall a young man cleanse his way? by taking heed thereto according to thy word.

10. With my whole heart have I sought thee: O let me not wander from thy commandments.

11. Thy word have I hid in mine heart, that I might not sin against thee.

12. Blessed art thou, O LORD: teach me thy statutes.

13. With my lips have I declared all the judgments of thy mouth.

14. I have rejoiced in the way of thy testimonies, as much as in all riches.

15. I will meditate in thy precepts, and have respect unto thy ways.

16. I will delight myself in thy statutes: I will not forget thy word.

GIMEL

17. Deal bountifully with thy servant, that I may live, and keep thy word.

18. Open thou mine eyes, that I may behold wondrous things out of thy law.

19. I am a stranger in the earth: hide not thy commandments from me.

20. My soul breaketh for the longing that it hath unto thy judgments at all times.

21. Thou hast rebuked the proud that are cursed, which do err from thy commandments.

22. Remove from me reproach and contempt; for I have kept thy testimonies.

23. Princes also did sit and speak against me: but thy servant did meditate in thy statutes.

24. Thy testimonies also are my delight and my counsellors.

DALETH

25. My soul cleaveth unto the dust: quicken thou me according to thy word.

26. I have declared my ways, and thou heardest me: teach me thy statutes.

27. Make me to understand the way of thy precepts: so shall I talk of thy wondrous works.

28. My soul melteth for heaviness: strengthen thou me according unto thy word.

29. Remove from me the way of lying: and grant me thy law graciously.

30. I have chosen the way of truth: thy judgments have I laid before me.

31. I have stuck unto thy testimonies: O LORD, put me not to shame.

32. I will run the way of thy commandments, when thou shalt enlarge my heart.

HE

33. Teach me, O LORD, the way of thy statutes; and I shall keep it unto the end.

34. Give me understanding, and I shall keep thy law; yea, I shall observe it with my whole heart.

35. Make me to go in the path of thy commandments; for therein do I delight.

36. Incline my heart unto thy testimonies, and not to covetousness.

37. Turn away mine eyes from beholding vanity; and quicken thou me in thy way.

38. Stablish thy word unto thy servant, who is devoted to thy fear.

39. Turn away my reproach which I fear: for thy judgments are good.

40. Behold, I have longed after thy precepts: quicken me in thy righteousness.

VAU

41. Let thy mercies come also unto me, O Lord, even thy salvation, according to thy word.

42. So shall I have wherewith to answer him that reproacheth me: for I trust in thy word.

43. And take not the word of truth utterly out of my mouth; for I have hoped in thy judgments.

44. So shall I keep thy law continually for ever and ever.

45. And I will walk at liberty: for I seek thy precepts.

46. I will speak of thy testimonies also before kings, and will not be ashamed.

47. And I will delight myself in thy commandments, which I have loved.

48. My hands also will I lift up unto thy commandments, which I have loved; and I will meditate in thy statutes.

ZAIN

49. Remember the word unto thy servant, upon which thou hast caused me to hope.

50. This is my comfort in my affliction: for thy word hath quickened me.

51. The proud have had me greatly in derision: yet have I not declined from thy law.

52. I remembered thy judgments of old, O Lord; and have comforted myself.

53. Horror hath taken hold upon me because of the wicked that forsake thy law.

54. Thy statutes have been my songs in the house of my pilgrimage.

55. I have remembered thy name, O Lord, in the night, and have kept thy law.

56. This I had, because I kept thy precepts.

CHETH

57. Thou art my portion, O Lord: I have said that I would keep thy words.

58. I intreated thy favour with my whole heart: be merciful unto me according to thy word.

59. I thought on my ways, and turned my feet unto thy testimonies.

60. I made haste, and delayed not to keep thy commandments.

61. The bands of the wicked have robbed me: but I have not forgotten thy law.

62. At midnight I will rise to give thanks unto thee because of thy righteous judgments.

63. I am a companion of all them that fear thee, and of them that keep thy precepts.

64. The earth, O Lord, is full of thy mercy: teach me thy statutes.

TETH

65. Thou hast dealt well with thy servant, O Lord, according unto thy word.

66. Teach me good judgment and knowledge: for I have believed thy commandments.

67. Before I was afflicted I went astray: but now have I kept thy word.

68. Thou art good, and doest good; teach me thy statutes.

69. The proud have forged a lie against me: but I will keep thy precepts with my whole heart.

70. Their heart is as fat as grease; but I delight in thy law.

71. It is good for me that I have been afflicted; that I might learn thy statutes.

72. The law of thy mouth is better unto me than thousands of gold and silver.

JOD

73. Thy hands have made me and fashioned me: give me understanding, that I may learn thy commandments.

74. They that fear thee will be glad when they see me; because I have hoped in thy word.

75. I know, O Lord, that thy judgments are right, and that thou in faithfulness hast afflicted me.

76. Let, I pray thee, thy merciful kindness be for my comfort, according to thy word unto thy servant.

77. Let thy tender mercies come unto me, that I may live: for thy law is my delight.

78. Let the proud be ashamed; for they dealt perversely with me without a cause: but I will meditate in thy precepts.

79. Let those that fear thee turn unto me, and those that have known thy testimonies.

80. Let my heart be sound in thy statutes; that I be not ashamed.

CAPH

81. My soul fainteth for thy salvation: but I hope in thy word.

82. Mine eyes fail for thy word, saying, When wilt thou comfort me?

83. For I am become like a bottle in the smoke; yet do I not forget thy statutes.

84. How many are the days of thy servant? when wilt thou execute judgment on them that persecute me?

85. The proud have digged pits for me, which are not after thy law.

86. All thy commandments are faithful: they persecute me wrongfully; help thou me.

87. They had almost consumed me upon earth; but I forsook not thy precepts.

88. Quicken me after thy lovingkindness; so shall I keep the testimony of thy mouth.

LAMED

89. For ever, O LORD, thy word is settled in heaven.

90. Thy faithfulness is unto all generations: thou hast established the earth, and it abideth.

91. They continue this day according to thine ordinances: for all are thy servants.

92. Unless thy law had been my delights, I should then have perished in mine affliction.

93. I will never forget thy precepts: for with them thou hast quickened me.

94. I am thine, save me; for I have sought thy precepts.

95. The wicked have waited for me to destroy me: but I will consider thy testimonies.

96. I have seen an end of all perfection: but thy commandment is exceeding broad.

MEM

97. O how love I thy law! it is my meditation all the day.

98. Thou through thy commandments hast made me wiser than mine enemies: for they are ever with me.

99. I have more understanding than all my teachers: for thy testimonies are my meditation.

100. I understand more than the ancients, because I keep thy precepts.

101. I have refrained my feet from every evil way, that I might keep thy word.

102. I have not departed from thy judgments: for thou hast taught me.

103. How sweet are thy words unto my taste! yea, sweeter than honey to my mouth!

104. Through thy precepts I get understanding: therefore I hate every false way.

NUN

105. Thy word is a lamp unto my feet, and a light unto my path.

106. I have sworn, and I will perform it, that I will keep thy righteous judgments.

107. I am afflicted very much: quicken me, O LORD, according unto thy word.

108. Accept, I beseech thee, the free-will offerings of my mouth, O LORD, and teach me thy judgments.

109. My soul is continually in my hand: yet do I not forget thy law.

110. The wicked have laid a snare for me: yet I erred not from thy precepts.

111. Thy testimonies have I taken

as an heritage for ever: for they are the rejoicing of my heart.

112. I have inclined mine heart to perform thy statutes alway, even unto the end.

SAMECH

113. I hate vain thoughts: but thy law do I love.

114. Thou art my hiding place and my shield: I hope in thy word.

115. Depart from me, ye evildoers: for I will keep the commandments of my God.

116. Uphold me according unto thy word, that I may live: and let me not be ashamed of my hope.

117. Hold thou me up and I shall be safe: and I will have respect unto thy statutes continually.

118. Thou hast trodden down all them that err from thy statutes: for their deceit is falsehood.

119. Thou puttest away all the wicked of the earth like dross: therefore I love thy testimonies.

120. My flesh trembleth for fear of thee; and I am afraid of thy judgments.

AIN

121. I have done judgment and justice: leave me not to mine oppressors.

122. Be surety for thy servant for good: let not the proud oppress me.

123. Mine eyes fail for thy salvation, and for the word of thy righteousness.

124. Deal with thy servant according unto thy mercy, and teach me thy statutes.

125. I am thy servant; give me understanding, that I may know thy testimonies.

126. It is time for thee, LORD, to work: for they have made void thy law.

127. Therefore I love thy commandments above gold; yea, above fine gold.

128. Therefore I esteem all thy precepts concerning all things to be right; and I hate every false way.

PE

129. Thy testimonies are wonderful: therefore doth my soul keep them.

130. The entrance of thy words giveth light; it giveth understanding unto the simple.

131. I opened my mouth, and panted: for I longed for thy commandments.

132. Look thou upon me, and be merciful unto me, as thou usest to do unto those that love thy name.

133. Order my steps in thy word: and let not any iniquity have dominion over me.

134. Deliver me from the oppression of man: so will I keep thy precepts.

135. Make thy face to shine upon thy servant; and teach me thy statutes.

136. Rivers of waters run down mine eyes, because they keep not thy law.

TZADDI

137. Righteous art thou, O LORD, and upright are thy judgments.

138. Thy testimonies that thou hast commanded are righteous and very faithful.

139. My zeal hath consumed me, because mine enemies have forgotten thy words.

140. Thy word is very pure: therefore thy servant loveth it.

141. I am small and despised: yet do not I forget thy precepts.

142. Thy righteousness is an everlasting righteousness, and thy law is the truth.

143. Trouble and anguish have taken hold on me: yet thy commandments are my delights.

144. The righteousness of thy testimonies is everlasting: give me understanding, and I shall live.

KOPH

145. I cried with my whole heart; hear me, O LORD: I will keep thy statutes.

146. I cried unto thee; save me, and I shall keep thy testimonies.

147. I prevented the dawning of the morning, and cried: I hoped in thy word.

148. Mine eyes prevent the night watches, that I might meditate in thy word.

149. Hear my voice according unto thy lovingkindness: O LORD, quicken me according to thy judgment.

150. They draw nigh that follow after mischief: they are far from thy law.

151. Thou art near, O LORD; and all thy commandments are truth.

152. Concerning thy testimonies, I have known of old that thou hast founded them for ever.

RESH

153. Consider mine affliction, and deliver me: for I do not forget thy law.

154. Plead my cause, and deliver me: quicken me according to thy word.

155. Salvation is far from the wicked: for they seek not thy statutes.

156. Great are thy tender mercies, O LORD: quicken me according to thy judgments.

157. Many are my persecutors and mine enemies; yet do I not decline from thy testimonies.

158. I beheld the transgressors, and was grieved; because they kept not thy word.

159. Consider how I love thy precepts: quicken me, O LORD, according to thy lovingkindness.

160. Thy word is true from the beginning: and every one of thy righteous judgments endureth for ever.

SCHIN

161. Princes have persecuted me without a cause: but my heart standeth in awe of thy word.

162. I rejoice at thy word, as one that findeth great spoil.

163. I hate and abhor lying: but thy law do I love.

164. Seven times a day do I praise thee because of thy righteous judgments.

165. Great peace have they which love thy law: and nothing shall offend them.

166. LORD, I have hoped for thy salvation, and done thy commandments.

167. My soul hath kept thy testimonies; and I love them exceedingly.

168. I have kept thy precepts and thy testimonies: for all my ways are before thee.

TAU

169. Let my cry come near before thee, O LORD: give me understanding according to thy word.

170. Let my supplication come before thee: deliver me according to thy word.

171. My lips shall utter praise, when thou hast taught me thy statutes.

172. My tongue shall speak of thy word: for all thy commandments are righteousness.

173. Let thine hand help me; for I have chosen thy precepts.

174. I have longed for thy salvation, O LORD; and thy law is my delight.

175. Let my soul live, and it shall praise thee; and let thy judgments help me.

176. I have gone astray like a lost sheep; seek thy servant; for I do not forget thy commandments.

PSALM 122

1. I was glad when they said unto me, Let us go into the house of the LORD.

2. Our feet shall stand within thy gates, O Jerusalem.

3. Jerusalem is builded as a city that is compact together:

4. Whither the tribes go up, the tribes of the LORD, unto the testimony of Israel, to give thanks unto the name of the LORD.

5. For there are set thrones of judgment, the thrones of the house of David.

6. Pray for the peace of Jerusalem: they shall prosper that love thee.

7. Peace be within thy walls, and prosperity within thy palaces.

8. For my brethren and companions' sakes, I will now say, Peace be within thee.

9. Because of the house of the LORD our God I will seek thy good.

PSALM 126

1. When the LORD turned again the captivity of Zion, we were like them that dream.

2. Then was our mouth filled with laughter, and our tongue with singing: then said they among the heathen, The LORD hath done great things for them.

3. The LORD hath done great things for us; whereof we are glad.

4. Turn again our captivity, O LORD, as the streams in the south.

5. They that sow in tears shall reap in joy.

6. He that goeth forth and weepeth, bearing precious seed, shall doubtless come again with rejoicing, bringing his sheaves with him.

PSALM 128

1. Blessed is every one that feareth the LORD; that walketh in his ways.

2. For thou shalt eat the labour of thine hands: happy shalt thou be, and it shall be well with thee.

3. Thy wife shall be as a fruitful vine by the sides of thine house: thy children like olive plants round about thy table.

4. Behold, that thus shall the man be blessed that feareth the LORD.

5. The LORD shall bless thee out of Zion: and thou shalt see the good of Jerusalem all the days of thy life.

6. Yea, thou shalt see thy children's children, and peace upon Israel.

PSALM 130

1. Out of the depths have I cried unto thee, O LORD.

2. Lord, hear my voice: let thine ears be attentive to the voice of my supplications.

3. If thou, LORD, shouldest mark iniquities, O Lord, who shall stand?

4. But there is forgiveness with thee, that thou mayest be feared.

5. I wait for the LORD, my soul doth wait, and in his word do I hope.

6. My soul waiteth for the Lord more than they that watch for the morning: I say, more than they that watch for the morning.

7. Let Israel hope in the LORD: for with the LORD there is mercy, and with him is plenteous redemption.

8. And he shall redeem Israel from all his iniquities.

PSALM 133

1. Behold, how good and how pleasant it is for brethren to dwell together in unity!

2. It is like the precious ointment upon the head, that ran down upon the beard, even Aaron's beard: that went down to the skirts of his garments;

3. As the dew of Hermon, and as the dew that descended upon the mountains of Zion: for there the LORD commanded the blessing, even life for evermore.

PSALM 138

1. I will praise thee with my whole heart: before the gods will I sing praise unto thee.

2. I will worship toward thy holy

temple, and praise thy name for thy lovingkindness and for thy truth: for thou hast magnified thy word above all thy name.

3. In the day when I cried thou answeredst me, and strengthenedst me with strength in my soul.

4. All the kings of the earth shall praise thee, O LORD, when they hear the words of thy mouth.

5. Yea, they shall sing in the ways of the LORD: for great is the glory of the LORD.

6. Though the LORD be high, yet hath he respect unto the lowly; but the proud he knoweth afar off.

7. Though I walk in the midst of trouble, thou wilt revive me: thou shalt stretch forth thine hand against the wrath of mine enemies, and thy right hand shall save me.

8. The LORD will perfect that which concerneth me: thy mercy, O LORD, endureth for ever: forsake not the works of thine own hands.

PSALM 139

1. O LORD, thou hast searched me, and known me.

2. Thou knowest my downsitting and mine uprising, thou understandest my thought afar off.

3. Thou compassest my path and my lying down, and art acquainted with all my ways.

4. For there is not a word in my tongue, but, lo, O LORD, thou knowest it altogether.

5. Thou hast beset me behind and before, and laid thine hand upon me.

6. Such knowledge is too wonderful for me; it is high, I cannot attain unto it.

7. Whither shall I go from thy spirit? or whither shall I flee from thy presence?

8. If I ascend up into heaven, thou art there: if I make my bed in hell, behold, thou art there.

9. If I take the wings of the morning, and dwell in the uttermost parts of the sea;

10. Even there shall thy hand lead me, and thy right hand shall hold me.

11. If I say, Surely the darkness shall cover me; even the night shall be light about me.

12. Yea, the darkness hideth not from thee; but the night shineth as the day: the darkness and the light are both alike to thee.

13. For thou hast possessed my reins: thou hast covered me in my mother's womb.

14. I will praise thee; for I am fearfully and wonderfully made: marvellous are thy works; and that my soul knoweth right well.

15. My substance was not hid from thee, when I was made in secret, and curiously wrought in the lowest parts of the earth.

16. Thine eyes did see my substance, yet being unperfect; and in thy book all my members were written, which in continuance were fashioned, when as yet there was none of them.

17. How precious also are thy thoughts unto me, O God! how great is the sum of them!

18. If I should count them, they are more in number than the sand: when I awake, I am still with thee.

19. Surely thou wilt slay the wicked, O God: depart from me therefore, ye bloody men.

20. For they speak against thee wickedly, and thine enemies take thy name in vain.

21. Do not I hate them, O LORD, that hate thee? and am not I grieved with those that rise up against thee?

22. I hate them with perfect hatred: I count them mine enemies.

23. Search me, O God, and know my heart: try me, and know my thoughts:

24. And see if there be any wicked way in me, and lead me in the way everlasting.

Psalm 143

1. Hear my prayer, O Lord, give ear to my supplications: in thy faithfulness answer me, and in thy righteousness.

2. And enter not into judgment with thy servant: for in thy sight shall no man living be justified.

3. For the enemy hath persecuted my soul; he hath smitten my life down to the ground; he hath made me to dwell in darkness, as those that have been long dead.

4. Therefore is my spirit overwhelmed within me; my heart within me is desolate.

5. I remember the days of old; I meditate on all thy works; I muse on the work of thy hands.

6. I stretch forth my hands unto thee: my soul thirsteth after thee, as a thirsty land. Selah.

7. Hear me speedily, O Lord: my spirit faileth: hide not thy face from me, lest I be like unto them that go down into the pit.

8. Cause me to hear thy lovingkindness in the morning; for in thee do I trust: cause me to know the way wherein I should walk; for I lift up my soul unto thee.

9. Deliver me, O Lord, from mine enemies: I flee unto thee to hide me.

10. Teach me to do thy will; for thou art my God: thy spirit is good; lead me into the land of uprightness.

11. Quicken me, O Lord, for thy name's sake: for thy righteousness' sake bring my soul out of trouble.

12. And of thy mercy cut off mine enemies, and destroy all them that afflict my soul: for I am thy servant.

Psalm 145

1. I will extol thee, my God, O king; and I will bless thy name for ever and ever.

2. Every day will I bless thee; and I will praise thy name for ever and ever.

3. Great is the Lord, and greatly to be praised; and his greatness is unsearchable.

4. One generation shall praise thy works to another, and shall declare thy mighty acts.

5. I will speak of the glorious honour of thy majesty, and of thy wondrous works.

6. And men shall speak of the might of thy terrible acts: and I will declare thy greatness.

7. They shall abundantly utter the memory of thy great goodness, and shall sing of thy righteousness.

8. The Lord is gracious, and full of compassion; slow to anger, and of great mercy.

9. The Lord is good to all: and his tender mercies are over all his works.

10. All thy works shall praise thee, O Lord; and thy saints shall bless thee.

11. They shall speak of the glory of thy kingdom, and talk of thy power;

12. To make known to the sons of men his mighty acts, and the glorious majesty of his kingdom.

13. Thy kingdom is an everlasting kingdom, and thy dominion endureth throughout all generations.

14. The Lord upholdeth all that fall, and raiseth up all those that be bowed down.

15. The eyes of all wait upon thee; and thou givest them their meat in due season.

16. Thou openest thine hand, and satisfiest the desire of every living thing.

17. The Lord is righteous in all his ways, and holy in all his works.

18. The Lord is nigh unto all them that call upon him, to all that call upon him in truth.

19. He will fulfil the desire of them that fear him: he also will hear their cry, and will save them.

20. The Lord preserveth all them that love him: but all the wicked will he destroy.

21. My mouth shall speak the praise of the Lord: and let all flesh bless his holy name for ever and ever.

Psalm 146

1. Praise ye the Lord. Praise the Lord, O my soul.

2. While I live will I praise the Lord: I will sing praises unto my God while I have any being.

3. Put not your trust in princes, nor in the son of man, in whom there is no help.

4. His breath goeth forth, he returneth to his earth; in that very day his thoughts perish.

5. Happy is he that hath the God of Jacob for his help, whose hope is in the Lord his God:

6. Which made heaven, and earth, the sea, and all that therein is: which keepeth truth for ever:

7. Which executeth judgment for the oppressed: which giveth food to the hungry. The Lord looseth the prisoners:

8. The Lord openeth the eyes of the blind: the Lord raiseth them that are bowed down: the Lord loveth the righteous.

9. The Lord preserveth the strangers; he relieveth the fatherless and widow: but the way of the wicked he turneth upside down.

10. The Lord shall reign for ever, even thy God, O Zion, unto all generations. Praise ye the Lord.

Psalm 147

1. Praise ye the Lord: for it is good to sing praises unto our God; for it is pleasant; and praise is comely.

2. The Lord doth build up Jerusalem: he gathereth together the outcasts of Israel.

3. He healeth the broken in heart, and bindeth up their wounds.

4. He telleth the number of the stars; he calleth them all by their names.

5. Great is our Lord, and of great power: his understanding is infinite.

6. The Lord lifteth up the meek: he casteth the wicked down to the ground.

7. Sing unto the Lord with thanksgiving; sing praise upon the harp unto our God:

8. Who covereth the heaven with clouds, who prepareth rain for the earth, who maketh grass to grow upon the mountains.

9. He giveth to the beast his food, and to the young ravens which cry.

10. He delighteth not in the strength of the horse: he taketh not pleasure in the legs of a man.

11. The Lord taketh pleasure in them that fear him, in those that hope in his mercy.

12. Praise the Lord, O Jerusalem; praise thy God, O Zion.

13. For he hath strengthened the bars of thy gates; he hath blessed thy children within thee.

14. He maketh peace in thy borders, and filleth thee with the finest of the wheat.

15. He sendeth forth his commandment upon earth: his word runneth very swiftly.

16. He giveth snow like wool: he scattereth the hoarfrost like ashes.

17. He casteth forth his ice like morsels: who can stand before his cold?

18. He sendeth out his word, and melteth them: he causeth his wind to blow, and the waters flow.

19. He sheweth his word unto Jacob, his statutes and his judgments unto Israel.

20. He hath not dealt so with any nation: and as for his judgments, they have not known them. Praise ye the Lord.

Proverbs

The Hebrew title of this book is
Mishle *meaning "proverbs" or "like-
nesses." It is used often to designate
short maxims or sentences, frequently
making comparisons. It is sometimes
used to designate didactic poems. This
book of Hebrew wisdom was possibly
compiled between the reign of King
Solomon and the Exile of 587 B.C.
Most of the verses are attributed to
King Solomon who was traditionally
held to be the wisest man who ever
lived. Many of the verses, however,
are from unknown authors, possibly
adages that grew up gradually in the
folk lore of the Hebrews and were
attributed to men known to be ex-
tremely sage. Some of the verses are
attributed to wise women.*

CHAPTER 3

1. My son, forget not my law; but
let thine heart keep my commandments:

2. For length of days, and long life,
and peace, shall they add to thee.

3. Let not mercy and truth forsake
thee: bind them about thy neck;
write them upon the table of thine
heart:

4. So shalt thou find favour and
good understanding in the sight of
God and man.

5. Trust in the LORD with all thine
heart; and lean not unto thine own
understanding.

6. In all thy ways acknowledge
him, and he shall direct thy paths.

7. Be not wise in thine own eyes:
fear the LORD, and depart from evil.

8. It shall be health to thy navel,
and marrow to thy bones.

9. Honour the LORD with thy substance, and with the firstfruits of all
thine increase:

10. So shall thy barns be filled with
plenty, and thy presses shall burst
out with new wine.

CHAPTER 4

14. Enter not into the path of the
wicked, and go not in the way of evil
men.

15. Avoid it, pass not by it, turn
from it, and pass away.

16. For they sleep not, except they
have done mischief; and their sleep
is taken away, unless they cause some
to fall.

17. For they eat the bread of
wickedness, and drink the wine of violence.

18. But the path of the just is as
the shining light, that shineth more
and more unto the perfect day.

19. The way of the wicked is as
darkness: they know not at what they
stumble.

CHAPTER 10

1. The proverbs of Solomon. A wise
son maketh a glad father: but a foolish son is the heaviness of his mother.

2. Treasures of wickedness profit
nothing: but righteousness delivereth
from death.

3. The LORD will not suffer the soul
of the righteous to famish: but he
casteth away the substance of the
wicked.

4. He becometh poor that dealeth
with a slack hand: but the hand of
the diligent maketh rich.

5. He that gathereth in summer is a
wise son: but he that sleepeth in harvest is a son that causeth shame.

6. Blessings are upon the head of
the just: but violence covereth the
mouth of the wicked.

7. The memory of the just is
blessed: but the name of the wicked
shall rot.

8. The wise in heart will receive
commandments: but a prating fool
shall fall.

9. He that walketh uprightly walketh surely: but he that perverteth his
ways shall be known.

10. He that winketh with the eye

causeth sorrow: but a prating fool shall fall.

11. The mouth of a righteous man is a well of life: but violence covereth the mouth of the wicked.

12. Hatred stirreth up strifes: but love covereth all sins.

13. In the lips of him that hath understanding wisdom is found: but a rod is for the back of him that is void of understanding.

14. Wise men lay up knowledge: but the mouth of the foolish is near destruction.

15. The rich man's wealth is his strong city: the destruction of the poor is their poverty.

16. The labour of the righteous tendeth to life: the fruit of the wicked to sin.

CHAPTER 12

1. Whoso loveth instruction loveth knowledge: but he that hateth reproof is brutish.

2. A good man obtaineth favour of the LORD: but a man of wicked devices will he condemn.

3. A man shall not be established by wickedness: but the root of the righteous shall not be moved.

4. A virtuous woman is a crown to her husband: but she that maketh ashamed is as rottenness in his bones.

5. The thoughts of the righteous are right: but the counsels of the wicked are deceit.

6. The words of the wicked are to lie in wait for blood: but the mouth of the upright shall deliver them.

7. The wicked are overthrown, and are not: but the house of the righteous shall stand.

8. A man shall be commended according to his wisdom: but he that is of a perverse heart shall be despised.

9. He that is despised, and hath a servant, is better than he that honoureth himself, and lacketh bread.

10. A righteous man regardeth the life of his beast: but the tender mercies of the wicked are cruel.

11. He that tilleth his land shall be satisfied with bread: but he that followeth vain persons is void of understanding.

12. The wicked desireth the net of evil men: but the root of the righteous yieldeth fruit.

13. The wicked is snared by the transgression of his lips: but the just shall come out of trouble.

14. A man shall be satisfied with good by the fruit of his mouth: and the recompense of a man's hands shall be rendered unto him.

15. The way of a fool is right in his own eyes: but he that hearkeneth unto counsel is wise.

16. A fool's wrath is presently known: but a prudent man covereth shame.

17. He that speaketh truth sheweth forth righteousness: but a false witness deceit.

18. There is that speaketh like the piercings of a sword: but the tongue of the wise is health.

19. The lip of truth shall be established for ever: but a lying tongue is but for a moment.

20. Deceit is in the heart of them that imagine evil: but to the counsellors of peace is joy.

21. There shall no evil happen to the just: but the wicked shall be filled with mischief.

22. Lying lips are abomination to the LORD: but they that deal truly are his delight.

23. A prudent man concealeth knowledge: but the heart of fools proclaimeth foolishness.

24. The hand of the diligent shall bear rule: but the slothful shall be under tribute.

25. Heaviness in the heart of man maketh it stoop: but a good word maketh it glad.

26. The righteous is more excellent

than his neighbour: but the way of the wicked seduceth them.

27. The slothful man roasteth not that which he took in hunting: but the substance of a diligent man is precious.

28. In the way of righteousness is life; and in the pathway thereof there is no death.

CHAPTER 14

21. He that despiseth his neighbour sinneth: but he that hath mercy on the poor, happy is he.

22. Do they not err that devise evil? but mercy and truth shall be to them that devise good.

23. In all labour there is profit: but the talk of the lips tendeth only to penury.

24. The crown of the wise is their riches: but the foolishness of fools is folly.

25. A true witness delivereth souls: but a deceitful witness speaketh lies.

26. In the fear of the LORD is strong confidence: and his children shall have a place of refuge.

27. The fear of the LORD is a fountain of life, to depart from the snares of death.

28. In the multitude of people is the king's honour: but in the want of people is the destruction of the prince.

29. He that is slow to wrath is of great understanding: but he that is hasty of spirit exalteth folly.

30. A sound heart is the life of the flesh: but envy the rottenness of the bones.

31. He that oppresseth the poor reproacheth his Maker: but he that honoureth him hath mercy on the poor.

32. The wicked is driven away in his wickedness: but the righteous hath hope in his death.

33. Wisdom resteth in the heart of him that hath understanding: but that which is in the midst of fools is made known.

34. Righteousness exalteth a nation: but sin is a reproach to any people.

CHAPTER 15

1. A soft answer turneth away wrath: but grievous words stir up anger.

2. The tongue of the wise useth knowledge aright: but the mouth of fools poureth out foolishness.

3. The eyes of the LORD are in every place, beholding the evil and the good.

4. A wholesome tongue is a tree of life: but perverseness therein is a breach in the spirit.

5. A fool despiseth his father's instruction: but he that regardeth reproof is prudent.

6. In the house of the righteous is much treasure: but in the revenues of the wicked is trouble.

7. The lips of the wise disperse knowledge: but the heart of the foolish doeth not so.

8. The sacrifice of the wicked is an abomination to the LORD: but the prayer of the upright is his delight.

9. The way of the wicked is an abomination unto the LORD: but he loveth him that followeth after righteousness.

10. Correction is grievous unto him that forsaketh the way: and he that hateth reproof shall die.

11. Hell and destruction are before the LORD: how much more then the hearts of the children of men?

12. A scorner loveth not one that reproveth him: neither will he go unto the wise.

13. A merry heart maketh a cheerful countenance: but by sorrow of the heart the spirit is broken.

14. The heart of him that hath understanding seeketh knowledge:

but the mouth of fools feedeth on foolishness.

15. All the days of the afflicted are evil: but he that is of a merry heart hath a continual feast.

16. Better is little with the fear of the LORD than great treasure and trouble therewith.

17. Better is a dinner of herbs where love is, than a stalled ox and hatred therewith.

18. A wrathful man stirreth up strife: but he that is slow to anger appeaseth strife.

19. The way of the slothful man is as an hedge of thorns: but the way of the righteous is made plain.

20. A wise son maketh a glad father: but a foolish man despiseth his mother.

21. Folly is joy to him that is destitute of wisdom: but a man of understanding walketh uprightly.

22. Without counsel purposes are disappointed: but in the multitude of counsellors they are established.

23. A man hath joy by the answer of his mouth: and a word spoken in due season, how good is it!

24. The way of life is above to the wise, that he may depart from hell beneath.

25. The LORD will destroy the house of the proud: but he will establish the border of the widow.

26. The thoughts of the wicked are an abomination to the LORD: but the words of the pure are pleasant words.

27. He that is greedy of gain troubleth his own house; but he that hateth gifts shall live.

28. The heart of the righteous studieth to answer: but the mouth of the wicked poureth out evil things.

29. The LORD is far from the wicked: but he heareth the prayer of the righteous.

30. The light of the eyes rejoiceth the heart: and a good report maketh the bones fat.

31. The ear that heareth the reproof of life abideth among the wise.

32. He that refuseth instruction despiseth his own soul: but he that heareth reproof getteth understanding.

33. The fear of the LORD is the instruction of wisdom; and before honour is humility.

CHAPTER 16

1. The preparations of the heart in man, and the answer of the tongue, is from the LORD.

2. All the ways of a man are clean in his own eyes; but the LORD weigheth the spirits.

3. Commit thy works unto the LORD, and thy thoughts shall be established.

4. The LORD hath made all things for himself: yea, even the wicked for the day of evil.

5. Every one that is proud in heart is an abomination to the LORD: though hand join in hand, he shall not be unpunished.

6. By mercy and truth iniquity is purged: and by the fear of the LORD men depart from evil.

7. When a man's ways please the LORD, he maketh even his enemies to be at peace with him.

8. Better is a little with righteousness than great revenues without right.

18. Pride goeth before destruction, and an haughty spirit before a fall.

19. Better it is to be of an humble spirit with the lowly, than to divide the spoil with the proud.

20. He that handleth a matter wisely shall find good: and whoso trusteth in the LORD, happy is he.

21. The wise in heart shall be called prudent: and the sweetness of the lips increaseth learning.

22. Understanding is a wellspring of life unto him that hath it: but the instruction of fools is folly.

23. The heart of the wise teacheth

his mouth, and addeth learning to his lips.

24. Pleasant words are as an honeycomb, sweet to the soul, and health to the bones.

25. There is a way that seemeth right unto a man, but the end thereof are the ways of death.

26. He that laboureth laboureth for himself; for his mouth craveth it of him.

27. An ungodly man diggeth up evil: and in his lips there is as a burning fire.

28. A froward man soweth strife: and a whisperer separateth chief friends.

29. A violent man enticeth his neighbour, and leadeth him into the way that is not good.

30. He shutteth his eyes to devise froward things: moving his lips he bringeth evil to pass.

31. The hoary head is a crown of glory, if it be found in the way of righteousness.

32. He that is slow to anger is better than the mighty; and he that ruleth his spirit than he that taketh a city.

33. The lot is cast into the lap; but the whole disposing thereof is of the LORD.

CHAPTER 17

9. He that covereth a transgression seeketh love; but he that repeateth a matter separateth very friends.

10. A reproof entereth more into a wise man than an hundred stripes into a fool.

11. An evil man seeketh only rebellion: therefore a cruel messenger shall be sent against him.

12. Let a bear robbed of her whelps meet a man, rather than a fool in his folly.

13. Whoso rewardeth evil for good, evil shall not depart from his house.

14. The beginning of strife is as when one letteth out water: therefore leave off contention, before it be meddled with.

15. He that justifieth the wicked, and he that condemneth the just, even they both are abomination to the LORD.

16. Wherefore is there a price in the hand of a fool to get wisdom, seeing he hath no heart to it?

17. A friend loveth at all times, and a brother is born for adversity.

18. A man void of understanding striketh hands, and becometh surety in the presence of his friend.

19. He loveth transgression that loveth strife: and he that exalteth his gate seeketh destruction.

20. He that hath a froward heart findeth no good: and he that hath a perverse tongue falleth into mischief.

21. He that begetteth a fool doeth it to his sorrow: and the father of a fool hath no joy.

22. A merry heart doeth good like a medicine: but a broken spirit drieth the bones.

CHAPTER 20

1. Wine is a mocker, strong drink is raging: and whosoever is deceived thereby is not wise.

2. The fear of a king is as the roaring of a lion: whoso provoketh him to anger sinneth against his own soul.

3. It is an honour for a man to cease from strife: but every fool will be meddling.

4. The sluggard will not plow by reason of the cold; therefore shall he beg in harvest, and have nothing.

5. Counsel in the heart of man is like deep water; but a man of understanding will draw it out.

6. Most men will proclaim every one his own goodness: but a faithful man who can find?

7. The just man walketh in his integrity: his children are blessed after him.

8. A king that sitteth in the throne

of judgment scattereth away all evil with his eyes.

9. Who can say, I have made my heart clean, I am pure from my sin?

10. Divers weights, and divers measures, both of them are alike abomination to the LORD.

11. Even a child is known by his doings, whether his work be pure, and whether it be right.

CHAPTER 22

1. A good name is rather to be chosen than great riches, and loving favour rather than silver and gold.

2. The rich and poor meet together: the LORD is the maker of them all.

3. A prudent man foreseeth the evil, and hideth himself: but the simple pass on, and are punished.

4. By humility and the fear of the LORD are riches, and honour, and life.

5. Thorns and snares are in the way of the froward: he that doth keep his soul shall be far from them.

6. Train up a child in the way he should go: and when he is old, he will not depart from it.

7. The rich ruleth over the poor, and the borrower is servant to the lender.

8. He that soweth iniquity shall reap vanity: and the rod of his anger shall fail.

9. He that hath a bountiful eye shall be blessed; for he giveth of his bread to the poor.

CHAPTER 23

1. When thou sittest to eat with a ruler, consider diligently what is before thee:

2. And put a knife to thy throat, if thou be a man given to appetite.

3. Be not desirous of his dainties: for they are deceitful meat.

4. Labour not to be rich: cease from thine own wisdom.

5. Wilt thou set thine eyes upon that which is not? for riches certainly make themselves wings; they fly away as an eagle toward heaven.

6. Eat thou not the bread of him that hath an evil eye, neither desire thou his dainty meats:

7. For as he thinketh in his heart, so is he: Eat and drink, saith he to thee; but his heart is not with thee.

8. The morsel which thou hast eaten shalt thou vomit up, and lose thy sweet words.

9. Speak not in the ears of a fool: for he will despise the wisdom of thy words.

10. Remove not the old landmark; and enter not into the fields of the fatherless:

11. For their redeemer is mighty; he shall plead their cause with thee.

12. Apply thine heart unto instruction, and thine ears to the words of knowledge.

13. Withhold not correction from the child: for if thou beatest him with the rod, he shall not die.

14. Thou shalt beat him with the rod, and shalt deliver his soul from hell.

15. My son, if thine heart be wise, my heart shall rejoice, even mine.

16. Yea, my reins shall rejoice, when thy lips speak right things.

17. Let not thine heart envy sinners: but be thou in the fear of the LORD all the day long.

18. For surely there is an end; and thine expectation shall not be cut off.

19. Hear thou, my son, and be wise, and guide thine heart in the way.

20. Be not among winebibbers; among riotous eaters of flesh:

21. For the drunkard and the glutton shall come to poverty: and drowsiness shall clothe a man with rags.

CHAPTER 28

1. The wicked flee when no man pursueth: but the righteous are bold as a lion.

2. For the transgression of a land many are the princes thereof: but by a man of understanding and knowledge the state thereof shall be prolonged.

3. A poor man that oppresseth the poor is like a sweeping rain which leaveth no food.

4. They that forsake the law praise the wicked: but such as keep the law contend with them.

5. Evil men understand not judgment: but they that seek the LORD understand all things.

6. Better is the poor that walketh in his uprightness, than he that is perverse in his ways, though he be rich.

7. Whoso keepeth the law is a wise son: but he that is a companion of riotous men shameth his father.

8. He that by usury and unjust gain increaseth his substance, he shall gather it for him that will pity the poor.

9. He that turneth away his ear from hearing the law, even his prayer shall be abomination.

10. Whoso causeth the righteous to go astray in an evil way, he shall fall himself into his own pit: but the upright shall have good things in possession.

11. The rich man is wise in his own conceit; but the poor that hath understanding searcheth him out.

12. When righteous men do rejoice, there is great glory: but when the wicked rise, a man is hidden.

13. He that covereth his sins shall not prosper: but whoso confesseth and forsaketh them shall have mercy.

14. Happy is the man that feareth alway: but he that hardeneth his heart shall fall into mischief.

15. As a roaring lion, and a ranging bear; so is a wicked ruler over the poor people.

16. The prince that wanteth understanding is also a great oppressor: but he that hateth covetousness shall prolong his days.

17. A man that doeth violence to the blood of any person shall flee to the pit; let no man stay him.

18. Whoso walketh uprightly shall be saved: but he that is perverse in his ways shall fall at once.

19. He that tilleth his land shall have plenty of bread: but he that followeth after vain persons shall have poverty enough.

20. A faithful man shall abound with blessings: but he that maketh haste to be rich shall not be innocent.

Ecclesiastes

This book is one of the documents usually included in the "Wisdom Literature" of the Hebrews. It is a soliloquy on the vanity of the human race and all its hopes and dreams. The author attributes it to King Solomon so that for many generations it was believed to have been written by that famous king. In the book the king who speaks is called Koheleth, but in the Septuagint he is called Ecclesiastes and in the English versions either the Preacher or the Great Orator. The book concludes that man will find everything "vanity" unless he "fears God and keeps his commandments."

CHAPTER 5

1. Keep thy foot when thou goest to the house of God, and be more ready to hear, than to give the sacrifice of fools: for they consider not that they do evil.

2. Be not rash with thy mouth, and let not thine heart be hasty to utter any thing before God: for God is in heaven, and thou upon earth: therefore let thy words be few.

3. For a dream cometh through the multitude of business; and a fool's voice is known by multitude of words.

4. When thou vowest a vow unto God, defer not to pay it; for he hath no pleasure in fools: pay that which thou hast vowed.

5. Better is it that thou shouldest not vow, than that thou shouldest vow and not pay.

6. Suffer not thy mouth to cause thy flesh to sin; neither say thou before the angel, that it was an error: wherefore should God be angry at thy voice, and destroy the work of thine hands?

7. For in the multitude of dreams and many words there are also divers vanities: but fear thou God.

8. If thou seest the oppression of the poor, and violent perverting of judgment and justice in a province, marvel not at the matter: for he that is higher than the highest regardeth; and there be higher than they.

9. Moreover the profit of the earth is for all: the king himself is served by the field.

10. He that loveth silver shall not be satisfied with silver; nor he that loveth abundance with increase: this is also vanity.

11. When goods increase, they are increased that eat them: and what good is there to the owners thereof, saving the beholding of them with their eyes?

12. The sleep of a labouring man is sweet, whether he eat little or much: but the abundance of the rich will not suffer him to sleep.

13. There is a sore evil which I have seen under the sun, namely, riches kept for the owners thereof to their hurt.

14. But those riches perish by evil travail: and he begetteth a son, and there is nothing in his hand.

15. As he came forth of his mother's womb, naked shall he return to go as he came, and shall take nothing of his labour, which he may carry away in his hand.

16. And this also is a sore evil, that in all points as he came, so shall he go: and what profit hath he that hath laboured for the wind?

17. All his days also he eateth in darkness, and he hath much sorrow and wrath with his sickness.

18. Behold that which I have seen: it is good and comely for one to eat and to drink, and to enjoy the good of all his labour that he taketh under the sun all the days of his life, which God giveth him: for it is his portion.

19. Every man also to whom God hath given riches and wealth, and hath given him power to eat thereof, and to take his portion, and to rejoice in his labour; this is the gift of God.

20. For he shall not much remember the days of his life; because God answereth him in the joy of his heart.

CHAPTER 7

1. A good name is better than precious ointment; and the day of death than the day of one's birth.

2. It is better to go to the house of mourning, than to go to the house of feasting: for that is the end of all men; and the living will lay it to his heart.

3. Sorrow is better than laughter: for by the sadness of the countenance the heart is made better.

4. The heart of the wise is in the house of mourning; but the heart of fools is in the house of mirth.

5. It is better to hear the rebuke of the wise, than for a man to hear the song of fools.

6. For as the crackling of thorns under a pot, so is the laughter of the fool: this also is vanity.

7. Surely oppression maketh a wise man mad; and a gift destroyeth the heart.

8. Better is the end of a thing than the beginning thereof: and the patient in spirit is better than the proud in spirit.

9. Be not hasty in thy spirit to be angry: for anger resteth in the bosom of fools.

10. Say not thou, What is the cause

that the former days were better than these? for thou dost not enquire wisely concerning this.

11. Wisdom is good with an inheritance: and by it there is profit to them that see the sun.

12. For wisdom is a defence, and money is a defence: but the excellency of knowledge is, that wisdom giveth life to them that have it.

13. Consider the work of God: for who can make that straight, which he hath made crooked?

14. In the day of prosperity be joyful, but in the day of adversity consider: God also hath set the one over against the other, to the end that man should find nothing after him.

15. All things have I seen in the days of my vanity: there is a just man that perisheth in his righteousness, and there is a wicked man that prolongeth his life in his wickedness.

16. Be not righteous over much; neither make thyself over wise: why shouldest thou destroy thyself?

17. Be not over much wicked, neither be thou foolish: why shouldest thou die before thy time?

18. It is good that thou shouldest take hold of this; yea, also from this withdraw not thine hand: for he that feareth God shall come forth of them all.

19. Wisdom strengtheneth the wise more than ten mighty men which are in the city.

20. For there is not a just man upon earth, that doeth good, and sinneth not.

21. Also take no heed unto all words that are spoken; lest thou hear thy servant curse thee:

22. For oftentimes also thine own heart knoweth that thou thyself likewise hast cursed others.

23. All this have I proved by wisdom: I said, I will be wise; but it was far from me.

24. That which is far off, and exceeding deep, who can find it out?

25. I applied mine heart to know, and to search, and to seek out wisdom, and the reason of things, and to know the wickedness of folly, even of foolishness and madness:

26. And I find more bitter than death the woman, whose heart is snares and nets, and her hands as bands: whoso pleaseth God shall escape from her; but the sinner shall be taken by her.

27. Behold, this have I found, saith the preacher, counting one by one, to find out the account:

28. Which yet my soul seeketh, but I find not: one man among a thousand have I found; but a woman among all those have I not found.

29. Lo, this only have I found, that God hath made man upright; but they have sought out many inventions.

CHAPTER 9

1. For all this I considered in my heart even to declare all this, that the righteous, and the wise, and their works, are in the hand of God: no man knoweth either love or hatred by all that is before them.

2. All things come alike to all: there is one event to the righteous, and to the wicked; to the good and to the clean, and to the unclean; to him that sacrificeth, and to him that sacrificeth not: as is the good, so is the sinner; and he that sweareth, as he that feareth an oath.

3. This is an evil among all things that are done under the sun, that there is one event unto all: yea, also the heart of the sons of men is full of evil, and madness is in their heart while they live, and after that they go to the dead.

4. For to him that is joined to all the living there is hope: for a living dog is better than a dead lion.

5. For the living know that they shall die: but the dead know not any thing, neither have they any more a

reward; for the memory of them is forgotten.

6. Also their love, and their hatred, and their envy, is now perished; neither have they any more a portion for ever in any thing that is done under the sun.

7. Go thy way, eat thy bread with joy, and drink thy wine with a merry heart; for God now accepteth thy works.

8. Let thy garments be always white, and let thy head lack no ointment.

9. Live joyfully with the wife whom thou lovest all the days of the life of thy vanity, which he hath given thee under the sun, all the days of thy vanity: for that is thy portion in this life, and in thy labour which thou takest under the sun.

10. Whatsoever thy hand findeth to do, do it with thy might; for there is no work, nor device, nor knowledge, nor wisdom, in the grave, whither thou goest.

11. I returned, and saw under the sun, that the race is not to the swift, nor the battle to the strong, neither yet bread to the wise, nor yet riches to men of understanding, nor yet favour to men of skill; but time and chance happeneth to them all.

12. For man also knoweth not his time: as the fishes that are taken in an evil net, and as the birds that are caught in the snare; so are the sons of men snared in an evil time, when it falleth suddenly upon them.

13. This wisdom have I seen also under the sun, and it seemed great unto me:

14. There was a little city, and few men within it; and there came a great king against it, and besieged it, and built great bulwarks against it:

15. Now there was found in it a poor wise man, and he by his wisdom delivered the city; yet no man remembered that same poor man.

16. Then said I, Wisdom is better

than strength: nevertheless the poor man's wisdom is despised, and his words are not heard.

17. The words of wise men are heard in quiet more than the cry of him that ruleth among fools.

18. Wisdom is better than weapons of war: but one sinner destroyeth much good.

Chapter 12

1. Remember now thy Creator in the days of thy youth, while the evil days come not, nor the years draw nigh, when thou shalt say, I have no pleasure in them;

2. While the sun, or the light, or the moon, or the stars, be not darkened, nor the clouds return after the rain:

3. In the day when the keepers of the house shall tremble, and the strong men shall bow themselves, and the grinders cease because they are few, and those that look out of the windows be darkened,

4. And the doors shall be shut in the streets, when the sound of the grinding is low, and he shall rise up at the voice of the bird, and all the daughters of musick shall be brought low;

5. Also when they shall be afraid of that which is high, and fears shall be in the way, and the almond tree shall flourish, and the grasshopper shall be a burden, and desire shall fail: because man goeth to his long home, and the mourners go about the streets:

6. Or ever the silver cord be loosed, or the golden bowl be broken, or the pitcher be broken at the fountain, or the wheel broken at the cistern.

7. Then shall the dust return to the earth as it was: and the spirit shall return unto God who gave it.

8. Vanity of vanities, saith the preacher; all is vanity.

9. And moreover, because the

preacher was wise, he still taught the people knowledge; yea, he gave good heed, and sought out, and set in order many proverbs.

10. The preacher sought to find out acceptable words: and that which was written was upright, even words of truth.

11. The words of the wise are as goads, and as nails fastened by the masters of assemblies, which are given from one shepherd.

12. And further, by these, my son, be admonished: of making many books there is no end; and much study is a weariness of the flesh.

13. Let us hear the conclusion of the whole matter: Fear God, and keep his commandments: for this is the whole duty of man.

14. For God shall bring every work into judgment, with every secret thing, whether it be good, or whether it be evil.

Isaiah

This book is actually two books put together without any attempt to disguise the fact. The first book, which covers chapters 1 to 39, was probably written by the prophet Isaiah and deals with his prophetic career during the reigns of Jotham, Ahaz, and Hezekiah. The second, chapters 40 to 66, was written by some unknown author and is a continuous prophecy dealing with the restoration of Israel from the Babylonian Captivity.

CHAPTER 1

10. Hear the word of the LORD, ye rulers of Sodom; give ear unto the law of our God, ye people of Gomorrah.

11. To what purpose is the multitude of your sacrifices unto me? saith the LORD: I am full of the burnt offerings of rams, and the fat of fed beasts; and I delight not in the blood of bullocks, or of lambs, or of he goats.

12. When ye come to appear before me, who hath required this at your hand, to tread my courts?

13. Bring no more vain oblations; incense is an abomination unto me; the new moons and sabbaths, the calling of assemblies, I cannot away with; it is iniquity, even the solemn meeting.

14. Your new moons and your appointed feasts my soul hateth: they are a trouble unto me; I am weary to bear them.

15. And when ye spread forth your hands, I will hide mine eyes from you: yea, when ye make many prayers, I will not hear: your hands are full of blood.

16. Wash you, make you clean; put away the evil of your doings from before mine eyes; cease to do evil;

17. Learn to do well; seek judgment, relieve the oppressed, judge the fatherless, plead for the widow.

18. Come now, and let us reason together, saith the LORD: though your sins be as scarlet, they shall be as white as snow; though they be red like crimson, they shall be as wool.

19. If ye be willing and obedient, ye shall eat the good of the land:

20. But if ye refuse and rebel, ye shall be devoured with the sword: for the mouth of the LORD hath spoken it.

CHAPTER 25

1. O LORD, thou art my God; I will exalt thee, I will praise thy name; for thou hast done wonderful things; thy counsels of old are faithfulness and truth.

2. For thou hast made of a city an heap; of a defenced city a ruin: a palace of strangers to be no city; it shall never be built.

3. Therefore shall the strong people glorify thee, the city of the terrible nations shall fear thee.

4. For thou hast been a strength to

the poor, a strength to the needy in his distress, a refuge from the storm, a shadow from the heat, when the blast of the terrible ones is as a storm against the wall.

5. Thou shalt bring down the noise of strangers, as the heat in a dry place; even the heat with the shadow of a cloud: the branch of the terrible ones shall be brought low.

6. And in this mountain shall the LORD of hosts make unto all people a feast of fat things, a feast of wines on the lees, of fat things full of marrow, of wines on the lees well refined.

7. And he will destroy in this mountain the face of the covering cast over all people, and the veil that is spread over all nations.

8. He will swallow up death in victory; and the Lord GOD will wipe away tears from off all faces; and the rebuke of his people shall he take away from off all the earth: for the LORD hath spoken it.

9. And it shall be said in that day, Lo, this is our God; we have waited for him, and he will save us: this is the LORD; we have waited for him, we will be glad and rejoice in his salvation.

10. For in this mountain shall the hand of the LORD rest, and Moab shall be trodden down under him, even as straw is trodden down for the dunghill.

11. And he shall spread forth his hands in the midst of them, as he that swimmeth spreadeth forth his hands to swim: and he shall bring down their pride together with the spoils of their hands.

12. And the fortress of the high fort of thy walls shall he bring down, lay low, and bring to the ground, even to the dust.

CHAPTER 26

1. In that day shall this song be sung in the land of Judah; We have

a strong city; salvation will God appoint for walls and bulwarks.

2. Open ye the gates, that the righteous nation which keepeth the truth may enter in.

3. Thou wilt keep him in perfect peace, whose mind is stayed on thee: because he trusteth in thee.

4. Trust ye in the LORD for ever: for in the LORD JEHOVAH is everlasting strength:

5. For he bringeth down them that dwell on high; the lofty city, he layeth it low; he layeth it low, even to the ground; he bringeth it even to the dust.

6. The foot shall tread it down, even the feet of the poor, and the steps of the needy.

7. The way of the just is uprightness: thou, most upright, dost weigh the path of the just.

8. Yea, in the way of thy judgments, O LORD, have we waited for thee; the desire of our soul is to thy name, and to the remembrance of thee.

9. With my soul have I desired thee in the night; yea, with my spirit within me will I seek thee early: for when thy judgments are in the earth, the inhabitants of the world will learn righteousness.

10. Let favour be shewed to the wicked, yet will he not learn righteousness; in the land of uprightness will he deal unjustly, and will not behold the majesty of the LORD.

11. LORD, when thy hand is lifted up, they will not see: but they shall see, and be ashamed for their envy at the people; yea, the fire of thine enemies shall devour them.

12. LORD, thou wilt ordain peace for us: for thou also hast wrought all our works in us.

13. O LORD our God, other lords beside thee have had dominion over us: but by thee only will we make mention of thy name.

14. They are dead, they shall not

live; they are deceased, they shall not rise: therefore hast thou visited and destroyed them, and made all their memory to perish.

15. Thou hast increased the nation, O Lord, thou hast increased the nation: thou art glorified: thou hadst removed it far unto all the ends of the earth.

16. Lord, in trouble have they visited thee, they poured out a prayer when thy chastening was upon them.

17. Like as a woman with child, that draweth near the time of her delivery, is in pain, and crieth out in her pangs; so have we been in thy sight, O Lord.

18. We have been with child, we have been in pain, we have as it were brought forth wind; we have not wrought any deliverance in the earth; neither have the inhabitants of the world fallen.

19. Thy dead men shall live, together with my dead body shall they arise. Awake and sing, ye that dwell in dust: for thy dew is as the dew of herbs, and the earth shall cast out the dead.

Chapter 41

1. Keep silence before me, O islands; and let the people renew their strength: let them come near; then let them speak: let us come near together to judgment.

2. Who raised up the righteous man from the east, called him to his foot, gave the nations before him, and made him rule over kings? he gave them as the dust to his sword, and as driven stubble to his bow.

3. He pursued them, and passed safely; even by the way that he had not gone with his feet.

4. Who hath wrought and done it, calling the generations from the beginning? I the Lord, the first, and with the last; I am he.

5. The isles saw it, and feared; the ends of the earth were afraid, drew near, and came.

6. They helped every one his neighbour; and every one said to his brother, Be of good courage.

7. So the carpenter encouraged the goldsmith, and he that smootheth with the hammer him that smote the anvil, saying, It is ready for the sodering: and he fastened it with nails, that it should not be moved.

8. But thou, Israel, art my servant, Jacob whom I have chosen, the seed of Abraham my friend.

9. Thou whom I have taken from the ends of the earth, and called thee from the chief men thereof, and said unto thee, Thou art my servant; I have chosen thee, and not cast thee away.

10. Fear thou not; for I am with thee: be not dismayed; for I am thy God: I will strengthen thee; yea, I will help thee; yea, I will uphold thee with the right hand of my righteousness.

11. Behold, all they that were incensed against thee shall be ashamed and confounded: they shall be as nothing; and they that strive with thee shall perish.

12. Thou shalt seek them, and shalt not find them, even them that contended with thee: they that war against thee shall be as nothing, and as a thing of nought.

13. For I the Lord thy God will hold thy right hand, saying unto thee, Fear not; I will help thee.

14. Fear not, thou worm Jacob, and ye men of Israel; I will help thee, saith the Lord, and thy redeemer, the Holy One of Israel.

15. Behold, I will make thee a new sharp threshing instrument having teeth: thou shalt thresh the mountains, and beat them small, and shalt make the hills as chaff.

16. Thou shalt fan them, and the wind shall carry them away, and the whirlwind shall scatter them: and

thou shalt rejoice in the LORD, and shalt glory in the Holy One of Israel.

17. When the poor and needy seek water, and there is none, and their tongue faileth for thirst, I the LORD will hear them, I the God of Israel will not forsake them.

18. I will open rivers in high places, and fountains in the midst of the valleys: I will make the wilderness a pool of water, and the dry land springs of water.

19. I will plant in the wilderness the cedar, the shittah tree, and the myrtle, and the oil tree; I will set in the desert the fir tree, and the pine, and the box tree together:

20. That they may see, and know, and consider, and understand together, that the hand of the LORD hath done this, and the Holy One of Israel hath created it.

CHAPTER 42

1. Behold my servant, whom I uphold; mine elect, in whom my soul delighteth; I have put my spirit upon him: he shall bring forth judgment to the Gentiles.

2. He shall not cry, nor lift up, nor cause his voice to be heard in the street.

3. A bruised reed shall he not break, and the smoking flax shall he not quench: he shall bring forth judgment unto truth.

4. He shall not fail nor be discouraged, till he have set judgment in the earth: and the isles shall wait for his law.

CHAPTER 45

1. Thus saith the LORD to his anointed, to Cyrus, whose right hand I have holden, to subdue nations before him; and I will loose the loins of kings, to open before him the two leaved gates; and the gates shall not be shut;

2. I will go before thee, and make the crooked places straight: I will break in pieces the gates of brass, and cut in sunder the bars of iron:

3. And I will give thee the treasures of darkness, and hidden riches of secret places, that thou mayest know that I, the LORD, which call thee by thy name, am the God of Israel.

4. For Jacob my servant's sake, and Israel mine elect, I have even called thee by thy name: I have surnamed thee, though thou hast not known me.

5. I am the LORD, and there is none else, there is no God beside me: I girded thee, though thou hast not known me:

6. That they may know from the rising of the sun, and from the west, that there is none beside me. I am the LORD, and there is none else.

7. I form the light, and create darkness: I make peace, and create evil: I the LORD do all these things.

8. Drop down, ye heavens, from above, and let the skies pour down righteousness: let the earth open, and let them bring forth salvation, and let righteousness spring up together; I the LORD have created it.

9. Woe unto him that striveth with his Maker! Let the potsherd strive with the potsherds of the earth. Shall the clay say to him that fashioneth it, What makest thou? or thy work, He hath no hands?

10. Woe unto him that saith unto his father, What begettest thou? or to the woman, What hast thou brought forth?

11. Thus saith the LORD, the Holy One of Israel, and his Maker, Ask me of things to come concerning my sons, and concerning the work of my hands command ye me.

12. I have made the earth, and created man upon it: I, even my hands, have stretched out the heavens, and all their host have I commanded.

13. I have raised him up in righteousness, and I will direct all his

ways: he shall build my city, and he shall let go my captives, not for price nor reward, saith the LORD of hosts.

14. Thus saith the LORD, The labour of Egypt, and merchandise of Ethiopia and of the Sabeans, men of stature, shall come over unto thee, and they shall be thine: they shall come after thee; in chains they shall come over, and they shall fall down unto thee, they shall make supplication unto thee, saying, Surely God is in thee; and there is none else, there is no God.

15. Verily thou art a God that hidest thyself, O God of Israel, the Saviour.

16. They shall be ashamed, and also confounded, all of them: they shall go to confusion together that are makers of idols.

17. But Israel shall be saved in the LORD with an everlasting salvation: ye shall not be ashamed nor confounded world without end.

18. For thus saith the LORD that created the heavens; God himself that formed the earth and made it; he hath established it, he created it not in vain, he formed it to be inhabited: I am the LORD; and there is none else.

19. I have not spoken in secret, in a dark place of the earth: I said not unto the seed of Jacob, Seek ye me in vain: I the LORD speak righteousness, I declare things that are right.

20. Assemble yourselves and come; draw near together, ye that are escaped of the nations: they have no knowledge that set up the wood of their graven image, and pray unto a god that cannot save.

21. Tell ye, and bring them near; yea, let them take counsel together: who hath declared this from ancient time? who hath told it from that time? have not I the LORD? and there is no God else beside me; a just God

and a Saviour; there is none beside me.

22. Look unto me, and be ye saved, all the ends of the earth: for I am God, and there is none else.

23. I have sworn by myself, the word is gone out of my mouth in righteousness, and shall not return, That unto me every knee shall bow, every tongue shall swear.

24. Surely, shall one say, in the LORD have I righteousness and strength: even to him shall men come; and all that are incensed against him shall be ashamed.

25. In the LORD shall all the seed of Israel be justified, and shall glory.

Lamentations

Most scholars regard the author of this book as unknown, even though we find the work attributed to Jeremiah in the Septuagint, the Targum, (Aramaic translation) and the Talmud. This is due to the fact that although the poem which constitutes this part of the Bible resembles Jeremiah's prophecies greatly, the general structure of the book raises many serious doubts. It consists of five separate poems dealing with the destructi n of Jerusalem by Nebuchadnezzar and the troubles that followed. The Hebrew version has an interesting alphabetical arrangement. Chapters 1, 2, and 4 each consist of 22 verses and the first letter of each verse is the corresponding letter of the Hebrew alphabet. The third chapter consists of 66 verses. Here each third verse begins with the corresponding letter of the alphabet. The fifth chapter has 22 verses but these are not arranged in alphabetical order.

CHAPTER 3

1. I am the man that hath seen affliction by the rod of his wrath.

2. He hath led me, and brought me into darkness, but not into light.

3. Surely against me is he turned; he turneth his hand against me all the day.

4. My flesh and my skin hath he made old; he hath broken my bones.

5. He hath builded against me, and compassed me with gall and travail.

6. He hath set me in dark places, as they that be dead of old.

7. He hath hedged me about, that I cannot get out: he hath made my chain heavy.

8. Also when I cry and shout, he shutteth out my prayer.

9. He hath inclosed my ways with hewn stone, he hath made my paths crooked.

10. He was unto me as a bear lying in wait, and as a lion in secret places.

11. He hath turned aside my ways, and pulled me in pieces: he hath made me desolate.

12. He hath bent his bow, and set me as a mark for the arrow.

13. He hath caused the arrows of his quiver to enter into my reins.

14. I was a derision to all my people; and their song all the day.

15. He hath filled me with bitterness, he hath made me drunken with wormwood.

16. He hath also broken my teeth with gravel stones, he hath covered me with ashes.

17. And thou hast removed my soul far off from peace: I forgat prosperity.

18. And I said, My strength and my hope is perished from the LORD:

19. Remembering mine affliction and my misery, the wormwood and the gall.

20. My soul hath them still in remembrance, and is humbled in me.

21. This I recall to my mind, therefore have I hope.

22. It is of the LORD's mercies that we are not consumed, because his compassions fail not.

23. They are new every morning: great is thy faithfulness.

24. The LORD is my portion, saith my soul; therefore will I hope in him.

25. The LORD is good unto them that wait for him, to the soul that seeketh him.

26. It is good that a man should both hope and quietly wait for the salvation of the LORD.

27. It is good for a man that he bear the yoke in his youth.

28. He sitteth alone and keepeth silence, because he hath borne it upon him.

29. He putteth his mouth in the dust; if so be there may be hope.

30. He giveth his cheek to him that smiteth him: he is filled full with reproach.

31. For the Lord will not cast off for ever:

32. But though he cause grief, yet will he have compassion according to the multitude of his mercies.

33. For he doth not afflict willingly nor grieve the children of men.

34. To crush under his feet all the prisoners of the earth,

35. To turn aside the right of a man before the face of the most High,

36. To subvert a man in his cause, the Lord approveth not.

37. Who is he that saith, and it cometh to pass, when the Lord commandeth it not?

38. Out of the mouth of the most High proceedeth not evil and good?

39. Wherefore doth a living man complain, a man for the punishment of his sins?

40. Let us search and try our ways, and turn again to the LORD.

41. Let us lift up our heart with our hands unto God in the heavens.

42. We have transgressed and have rebelled: thou hast not pardoned.

43. Thou hast covered with anger, and persecuted us: thou hast slain, thou hast not pitied.

44. Thou hast covered thyself with

a cloud, that our prayer should not pass through.

45. Thou hast made us as the off-scouring and refuse in the midst of the people.

46. All our enemies have opened their mouths against us.

47. Fear and a snare is come upon us, desolation and destruction.

48. Mine eye runneth down with rivers of water for the destruction of the daughter of my people.

49. Mine eye trickleth down, and ceaseth not, without any intermission,

50. Till the LORD look down, and behold from heaven.

51. Mine eye affecteth mine heart because of all the daughters of my city.

52. Mine enemies chased me sore, like a bird, without cause.

53. They have cut off my life in the dungeon, and cast a stone upon me.

54. Waters flowed over mine head; then I said, I am cut off.

Ezekiel

Ezekiel, the prophet of the Baby-lonian exile, is the author of this book. He was an aristocratic priest who was sent into exile by King Jehoiachin in 597 B.C. and lived there for many years. What eventually happened to him is unknown although there is a tradition that he was killed by his fel-low exiles because they did not like the tone of his prophecies. The book tells of Israel's downfall because of her sins, heaps curses upon those na-tions who rejoice at this downfall, and predicts the eventual restoration of the nation. The chapters 40 to 48 are allegorical, describing a new Jerusa-lem, an ideal city in which Jehovah will dwell with his people.

CHAPTER 18

5. But if a man be just, and do that which is lawful and right,

6. And hath not eaten upon the mountains, neither hath lifted up his eyes to the idols of the house of Israel, neither hath defiled his neighbour's wife, neither hath come near to a menstruous woman,

7. And hath not oppressed any, but hath restored to the debtor his pledge, hath spoiled none by violence, hath given his bread to the hungry, and hath covered the naked with a gar-ment;

8. He that hath not given forth upon usury, neither hath taken any in-crease, that hath withdrawn his hand from iniquity, hath executed true judgment between man and man,

9. Hath walked in my statutes, and hath kept my judgments, to deal truly; he is just, he shall surely live, saith the Lord GOD.

10. If he beget a son that is a rob-ber, a shedder of blood, and that doeth the like to any one of these things,

11. And that doeth not any of those duties, but even hath eaten upon the mountains, and defiled his neighbour's wife,

12. Hath oppressed the poor and needy, hath spoiled by violence, hath not restored the pledge, and hath lifted up his eyes to the idols, hath committed abomination,

13. Hath given forth upon usury, and hath taken increase: shall he then live? he shall not live: he hath done all these abominations; he shall surely die; his blood shall be upon him.

14. Now, lo, if he beget a son, that seeth all his father's sins which he hath done, and considereth, and doeth not such like,

15. That hath not eaten upon the mountains, neither hath lifted up his eyes to the idols of the house of Israel, hath not defiled his neighbour's wife,

16. Neither hath oppressed any, hath not withholden the pledge, neither hath spoiled by violence, but

hath given his bread to the hungry, and hath covered the naked with a garment,

17. That hath taken off his hand from the poor, that hath not received usury nor increase, hath executed my judgments, hath walked in my statutes; he shall not die for the iniquity of his father, he shall surely live.

18. As for his father, because he cruelly oppressed, spoiled his brother by violence, and did that which is not good among his people, lo, even he shall die in his iniquity.

19. Yet say ye, Why? doth not the son bear the iniquity of the father? When the son hath done that which is lawful and right, and hath kept all my statutes, and hath done them, he shall surely live.

20. The soul that sinneth, it shall die. The son shall not bear the iniquity of the father, neither shall the father bear the iniquity of the son: the righteousness of the righteous shall be upon him, and the wickedness of the wicked shall be upon him.

21. But if the wicked will turn from all his sins that he hath committed, and keep all my statutes, and do that which is lawful and right, he shall surely live, he shall not die.

22. All his transgressions that he hath committed, they shall not be mentioned unto him: in his righteousness that he hath done he shall live.

23. Have I any pleasure at all that the wicked should die? saith the Lord GOD: and not that he should return from his ways, and live?

24. But when the righteous turneth away from his righteousness, and committeth iniquity, and doeth according to all the abominations that the wicked man doeth, shall he live? All his righteousness that he hath done shall not be mentioned: in his trespass that he hath trespassed, and in his sin that he hath sinned, in them shall he die.

THE APOCRYPHA

THERE are two collections of writings which are referred to by the term *Apocrypha* or "writings with hidden or concealed meanings". These are the Old Testament Apocrypha and the New Testament Apocrypha.

The Old Testament Apocrypha is a group of books that appear in early Greek and Latin versions of the Bible, usually at the end of the Old Testament, but which are excluded from the Hebrew canon. The Roman Catholic Church includes these books in the canon. The Church of England excludes them from the canon but accepts them as valuable "for example of life and instruction of manners" although not to "establish doctrine". These books consist of independent works and additions to the canonical works in the form of extra chapters.

The Old Testament Apocrypha includes the following writings: *I Esdras, II Esdras, The Book of Tobit, The Book of Judith, Additions to the Book of Esther, The Wisdom of Solomon, The Wisdom of Jesus the Son of Sirach, The Book of Baruch with the Epistle of Jeremiah, The Song of the Three Holy Children, The History of Susanna, The History of the Destruction of Bel and the Dragon, The Prayer of Manasses,* and the *Four Books of the Maccabees.*

Eight other apocryphal writings of the Old Testament which are sometimes called Pseudepigrapha, are: *The Book of Jubilees* or The Little Genesis, *The Book of Enoch, The Assumption of Moses, The Ascension of Isaiah, The Apocalypse of Baruch, The Sibylline Oracles, The Psalter of Solomon,* and *The Testament of the Twelve Patriarchs.* None of these eight have been given canonical recognition.

The apocryphal books are part of the sacred literature of the Alexandrian Jews and are products of the years subsequent to the Captivity or during the last three centuries before the Christian era.

Tobit

This writing is to be found in a number of early versions in Hebrew, Greek, Latin, and Aramaic. Although scholars are not certain as to its date, they usually attribute it to the first century before Christ.

CHAPTER 4

5. My son, be mindful of the Lord our God all thy days, and let not thy will be set to sin, or to transgress his commandments: do uprightly all thy life long, and follow not the ways of unrighteousness.

6. For if thou deal truly, thy doings shall prosperously succeed to thee, and to all them that live justly.

7. Give alms of thy substance; and when thou givest alms, let not thine eye be envious, neither turn thy face from any poor, and the face of God shall not be turned away from thee.

8. If thou hast abundance, give

alms accordingly: if thou have but a little, be not afraid to give according to that little:

9. For thou layest up a good treasure for thyself against the day of necessity.

10. Because that alms do deliver from death, and suffereth not to come into darkness.

11. For alms is a good gift unto all that give it in the sight of the most High.

12. Beware of all whoredom, my son, and chiefly take a wife of the seed of thy fathers, and take not a strange woman to wife, which is not of thy father's tribe: for we are the children of the prophets, Noe, Abraham, Isaac, and Jacob: remember, my son, that our fathers from the beginning, even that they all married wives of their own kindred, and were blessed in their children, and their seed shall inherit the land.

13. Now therefore, my son, love thy brethren, and despise not in thy heart thy brethren, the sons and daughters of thy people, in not taking a wife of them: for in pride is destruction and much trouble, and in lewdness is decay and great want: for lewdness is the mother of famine.

14. Let not the wages of any man, which hath wrought for thee, tarry with thee, but give him it out of hand: for if thou serve God, he will also repay thee: be circumspect, my son, in all things thou doest, and be wise in all thy conversation.

15. Do that to no man which thou hatest: drink not wine to make thee drunken: neither let drunkenness go with thee in thy journey.

16. Give of thy bread to the hungry, and of thy garments to them that are naked; and according to thine abundance give alms; and let not thine eye be envious, when thou givest alms.

17. Pour out thy bread on the burial of the just, but give nothing to the wicked.

18. Ask counsel of all that are wise, and despise not any counsel that is profitable.

19. Bless the Lord thy God alway, and desire of him that thy ways may be directed, and that all thy paths and counsels may prosper: for every nation hath not counsel; but the Lord himself giveth all good things, and he humbleth whom he will, as he will; now therefore, my son, remember my commandments, neither let them be put out of thy mind.

20. And now I signify this to thee, that I committed ten talents to Gabael the son of Gabrias at Rages in Media.

21. And fear not, my son, that we are made poor: for thou hast much wealth, if thou fear God, and depart from all sin, and do that which is pleasing in his sight.

CHAPTER 13

1. Then Tobit wrote a prayer of rejoicing, and said, Blessed be God that liveth for ever, and blessed be his kingdom.

2. For he doth scourge, and hath mercy: he leadeth down to hell, and bringeth up again: neither is there any that can avoid his hand.

3. Confess him before the Gentiles, ye children of Israel: for he hath scattered us among them.

4. There declare his greatness, and extol him before all the living: for he is our Lord, and he is the God our Father for ever.

5. And he will scourge us for our iniquities, and will have mercy again, and will gather us out of all nations, among whom he hath scattered us.

6. If ye turn to him with your whole heart, and with your whole mind, and deal uprightly before him, then will he turn unto you, and will not hide his face from you. Therefore see what he will do with you, and

confess him with your whole mouth, and praise the Lord of might, and extol the everlasting King. In the land of my captivity do I praise him, and declare his might and majesty to a sinful nation. O ye sinners, turn and do justice before him: who can tell if he will accept you, and have mercy on you?

7. I will extol my God, and my soul shall praise the King of heaven, and shall rejoice in his greatness.

8. Let all men speak, and let all praise him for his righteousness.

9. O Jerusalem, the holy city, he will scourge thee for thy children's works, and will have mercy again on the sons of the righteous.

10. Give praise to the Lord, for he is good: and praise the everlasting King, that his tabernacle may be builded in thee again with joy, and let him make joyful there in thee those that are captives, and love in thee for ever those that are miserable.

11. Many nations shall come from far to the name of the Lord God with gifts in their hands, even gifts to the King of heaven; all generations shall praise thee with great joy.

12. Cursed are all they which hate thee, and blessed shall all be which love thee for ever.

13. Rejoice and be glad for the children of the just: for they shall be gathered together, and shall bless the Lord of the just.

14. O blessed are they which love thee, for they shall rejoice in thy peace: blessed are they which have been sorrowful for all thy scourges; for they shall rejoice for thee, when they have seen all thy glory, and shall be glad for ever.

15. Let my soul bless God the great King.

16. For Jerusalem shall be built up with sapphires, and emeralds, and precious stone: thy walls and towers and battlements with pure gold.

17. And the streets of Jerusalem shall be paved with beryl and carbuncle and stones of Ophir.

18. And all her streets shall say, Alleluia; and they shall praise him, saying, Blessed be God, which hath extolled it for ever.

Wisdom of Solomon

Another title often given this book is The Book of Wisdom. *It is attributed to Solomon simply because of his reputation for learning and not because he was its author who is, in fact, unknown. It was probably composed between 150 and 50* B.C.

CHAPTER 5

1. Then shall the righteous man stand in great boldness before the face of such as have afflicted him, and made no account of his labours.

2. When they see it, they shall be troubled with terrible fear, and shall be amazed at the strangeness of his salvation, so far beyond all that they looked for.

3. And they repenting and groaning for anguish of spirit shall say within themselves, This was he, whom we had sometimes in derision, and a proverb of reproach:

4. We fools accounted his life madness, and his end to be without honour:

5. How is he numbered among the children of God, and his lot is among the saints!

6. Therefore have we erred from the way of truth, and the light of righteousness hath not shined unto us, and the sun of righteousness rose not upon us.

7. We wearied ourselves in the way of wickedness and destruction: yea, we have gone through deserts, where there lay no way: but as for the way of the Lord, we have not known it.

8. What hath pride profited us? or

what good hath riches with our vaunting brought us?

9. All those things are passed away like a shadow, and as a post that hasted by;

10. And as a ship that passeth over the waves of the water, which when it is gone by, the trace thereof cannot be found, neither the pathway of the keel in the waves;

11. Or as when a bird hath flown through the air, there is no token of her way to be found, but the light air being beaten with the stroke of her wings, and parted with the violent noise and motion of them, is passed through, and therein afterwards no sign where she went is to be found;

12. Or like as when an arrow is shot at a mark, it parteth the air, which immediately cometh together again, so that a man cannot know where it went through:

13. Even so we in like manner, as soon as we were born, began to draw to our end, and had no sign of virtue to shew; but were consumed in our own wickedness.

14. For the hope of the ungodly is like dust that is blown away with the wind; like a thin froth that is driven away with the storm; like as the smoke which is dispersed here and there with a tempest, and passeth away as the remembrance of a guest that tarrieth but a day.

15. But the righteous live for evermore; their reward also is with the Lord, and the care of them is with the most High.

Chapter 8

1. Wisdom reacheth from one end to another mightily: and sweetly doth she order all things.

2. I loved her, and sought her out from my youth, I desired to make her my spouse, and I was a lover of her beauty.

3. In that she is conversant with God, she magnifieth her nobility: yea, the Lord of all things himself loved her.

4. For she is privy to the mysteries of the knowledge of God, and a lover of his works.

5. If riches be a possession to be desired in this life; what is richer than wisdom, that worketh all things?

6. And if prudence work; who of all that are is a more cunning workman than she?

7. And if a man love righteousness, her labours are virtues: for she teacheth temperance and prudence, justice and fortitude: which are such things, as men can have nothing more profitable in their life.

8. If a man desire much experience, she knoweth things of old, and conjectureth aright what is to come: she knoweth the subtilties of speeches, and can expound dark sentences: she foreseeth signs and wonders, and the events of seasons and times.

9. Therefore I purposed to take her to me to live with me, knowing that she would be a counsellor of good things, and a comfort in cares and grief.

10. For her sake I shall have estimation among the multitude, and honour with the elders, though I be young.

11. I shall be found of a quick conceit in judgment, and shall be admired in the sight of great men.

12. When I hold my tongue, they shall bide my leisure, and when I speak, they shall give good ear unto me: if I talk much, they shall lay their hands upon their mouth.

13. Moreover by the means of her I shall obtain immortality, and leave behind me an everlasting memorial to them that come after me.

14. I shall set the people in order, and the nations shall be subject unto me.

15. Horrible tyrants shall be afraid, when they do but hear of me; I shall

be found good among the multitude, and valiant in war.

16. After I am come into mine house, I will repose myself with her: for her conversation hath no bitterness; and to live with her hath no sorrow, but mirth and joy.

17. Now when I considered these things in myself, and pondered them in my heart, how that to be allied unto wisdom is immortality;

18. And great pleasure it is to have her friendship; and in the works of her hands are infinite riches; and in the exercise of conference with her, prudence; and in talking with her, a good report; I went about seeking how to take her to me.

19. For I was a witty child, and had a good spirit.

20. Yea rather, being good, I came into a body undefiled.

21. Nevertheless, when I perceived that I could not otherwise obtain her, except God gave her me; and that was a point of wisdom also to know whose gift she was; I prayed unto the Lord, and besought him, and with my whole heart I said,

CHAPTER 9

1. O God of my fathers, and Lord of mercy, who hast made all things with thy word,

2. And ordained man through thy wisdom, that he should have dominion over the creatures which thou hast made,

3. And order the world according to equity and righteousness, and execute judgment with an upright heart:

4. Give me wisdom, that sitteth by thy throne; and reject me not from among thy children:

5. For I thy servant and son of thine handmaid am a feeble person, and of a short time, and too young for the understanding of judgment and laws.

6. For though a man be never so perfect among the children of men, yet if thy wisdom be not with him, he shall be nothing regarded.

7. Thou hast chosen me to be a king of thy people, and a judge of thy sons and daughters:

8. Thou hast commanded me to build a temple upon thy holy mount, and an altar in the city wherein thou dwellest, a resemblance of the holy tabernacle, which thou hast prepared from the beginning.

9. And wisdom was with thee: which knoweth thy works, and was present when thou madest the world, and knew what was acceptable in thy sight, and right in thy commandments.

10. O send her out of thy holy heavens, and from the throne of thy glory, that being present she may labour with me, that I may know what is pleasing unto thee.

11. For she knoweth and understandeth all things, and she shall lead me soberly in my doings, and preserve me in her power.

The Song of the Three Holy Children

This writing is an attempt on the part of an unknown author to add to the Book of Daniel *in the Old Testament by inserting after verse 23 of chapter 3 the verses of this book. This is a song of praise and thanksgiving which the author imagined was spoken by Shadrach, Meshach, and Abednego as they stood in the fiery furnace into which Nebuchadnezzar had thrown them for not bowing down to his image. The song of the three is preceded by a prayer by Azariah. This document was probably written in Hebrew or Aramaic.*

1. And they walked in the midst of the fire, praising God, and blessing the Lord.

2. Then Azarias stood up, and prayed on this manner; and opening

his mouth in the midst of the fire said,

3. Blessed art thou, O Lord God of our fathers: thy name is worthy to be praised and glorified for evermore:

4. For thou art righteous in all the things that thou hast done to us: yea, true are all thy works, thy ways are right, and all thy judgments truth.

5. In all the things that thou hast brought upon us, and upon the holy city of our fathers, even Jerusalem, thou hast executed true judgment: for according to truth and judgment didst thou bring all these things upon us because of our sins.

6. For we have sinned and committed iniquity, departing from thee.

7. In all things have we trespassed, and not obeyed thy commandments, nor kept them, neither done as thou hast commanded us, that it might go well with us.

8. Wherefore all that thou hast brought upon us, and every thing that thou hast done to us, thou hast done in true judgment.

9. And thou didst deliver us into the hands of lawless enemies, most hateful forsakers of God, and to an unjust king, and the most wicked in all the world.

10. And now we cannot open our mouths, we are become a shame and reproach to thy servants, and to them that worship thee.

11. Yet deliver us not up wholly, for thy name's sake, neither disannul thou thy covenant:

12. And cause not thy mercy to depart from us, for thy beloved Abraham's sake, for thy servant Isaac's sake, and for thy holy Israel's sake;

13. To whom thou hast spoken and promised, that thou wouldest multiply their seed as the stars of heaven, and as the sand that lieth upon the seashore.

14. For we, O Lord, are become less than any nation, and be kept under this day in all the world because of our sins.

15. Neither is there at this time prince, or prophet, or leader, or burnt offering, or sacrifice, or oblation, or incense, or place to sacrifice before thee, and to find mercy.

16. Nevertheless in a contrite heart and an humble spirit let us be accepted.

17. Like as in the burnt offerings of rams and bullocks, and like as in ten thousands of fat lambs: so let our sacrifice be in thy sight this day, and grant that we may wholly go after thee: for they shall not be confounded that put their trust in thee.

18. And now we follow thee with all our heart, we fear thee, and seek thy face.

19. Put us not to shame: but deal with us after thy lovingkindness, and according to the multitude of thy mercies.

20. Deliver us also according to thy marvellous works, and give glory to thy name, O Lord: and let all them that do thy servants hurt be ashamed;

21. And let them be confounded in all their power and might, and let their strength be broken;

22. And let them know that thou art Lord, the only God, and glorious over the whole world.

23. And the king's servants, that put them in, ceased not to make the oven hot with rosin, pitch, tow, and small wood;

24. So that the flame streamed forth above the furnace forty and nine cubits.

25. And it passed through, and burned those Chaldeans it found about the furnace.

26. But the angel of the Lord came down into the oven together with Azarias and his fellows, and smote the flame of the fire out of the oven;

27. And made the midst of the furnace as it had been a moist whistling wind, so that the fire touched them not

at all, neither hurt nor troubled them.

28. Then the three, as out of one mouth, praised, glorified, and blessed, God in the furnace, saying,

29. Blessed art thou, O Lord God of our fathers: and to be praised and exalted above all for ever.

30. And blessed is thy glorious and holy name: and to be praised and exalted above all for ever.

31. Blessed art thou in the temple of thine holy glory: and to be praised and glorified above all for ever.

32. Blessed art thou that beholdest the depths, and sittest upon the cherubims: and to be praised and exalted above all for ever.

33. Blessed art thou on the glorious throne of thy kingdom: and to be praised and glorified above all for ever.

34. Blessed art thou in the firmament of heaven: and above all to be praised and glorified for ever.

35. O all ye works of the Lord, bless ye the Lord: praise and exalt him above all for ever.

36. O ye heavens, bless ye the Lord: praise and exalt him above all for ever.

37. O ye angels of the Lord, bless ye the Lord: praise and exalt him above all for ever.

38. O all ye waters that be above the heaven, bless ye the Lord: praise and exalt him above all for ever.

39. O all ye powers of the Lord, bless ye the Lord: praise and exalt him above all for ever.

40. O ye sun and moon, bless ye the Lord: praise and exalt him above all for ever.

41. O ye stars of heaven, bless ye the Lord: praise and exalt him above all for ever.

42. O every shower and dew, bless ye the Lord: praise and exalt him above all for ever.

43. O all ye winds, bless ye the Lord: praise and exalt him above all for ever.

44. O ye fire and heat, bless ye the Lord: praise and exalt him above all for ever.

45. O ye winter and summer, bless ye the Lord: praise and exalt him above all for ever.

46. O ye dews and storms of snow, bless ye the Lord: praise and exalt him above all for ever.

47. O ye nights and days, bless ye the Lord: praise and exalt him above all for ever.

48. O ye light and darkness, bless ye the Lord: praise and exalt him above all for ever.

49. O ye ice and cold, bless ye the Lord: praise and exalt him above all for ever.

50. O ye frost and snow, bless ye the Lord: praise and exalt him above all for ever.

51. O ye lightnings and clouds, bless ye the Lord: praise and exalt him above all for ever.

52. O let the earth bless the Lord: praise and exalt him above all for ever.

53. O ye mountains and little hills, bless ye the Lord: praise and exalt him above all for ever.

54. O all ye things that grow on the earth, bless ye the Lord: praise and exalt him above all for ever.

55. O ye fountains, bless ye the Lord: praise and exalt him above all for ever.

56. O ye seas and rivers, bless ye the Lord: praise and exalt him above all for ever.

57. O ye whales, and all that move in the waters, bless ye the Lord: praise and exalt him above all for ever.

58. O all ye fowls of the air, bless ye the Lord: praise and exalt him above all for ever.

59. O all ye beasts and cattle, bless ye the Lord: praise and exalt him above all for ever.

60. O ye children of men, bless ye the Lord: praise and exalt him above all for ever.

61. O Israel, bless ye the Lord: praise and exalt him above all for ever.

62. O ye priests of the Lord, bless ye the Lord: praise and exalt him above all for ever.

63. O ye servants of the Lord, bless ye the Lord: praise and exalt him above all for ever.

64. O ye spirits and souls of the righteous, bless ye the Lord: praise and exalt him above all for ever.

65. O ye holy and humble men of heart, bless ye the Lord: praise and exalt him above all for ever.

66. O Ananias, Azarias, and Misael, bless ye the Lord: praise and exalt him above all for ever: for he hath delivered us from hell, and saved us from the hand of death, and delivered us out of the midst of the furnace and burning flame: even out of the midst of the fire hath he delivered us.

67. O give thanks unto the Lord, because he is gracious: for his mercy endureth for ever.

68. O all ye that worship the Lord, bless the God of gods, praise him, and give him thanks: for his mercy endureth for ever.

Prayer of Manasses

This is a short prayer supposed to have been uttered by Manasses, King of Judah, while he was a captive in Babylon. It is found in only a few of the early manuscripts of the Septuagint.

O Lord, Almighty God of our fathers, Abraham, Isaac, and Jacob, and of their righteous seed; who hast made heaven and earth, with all the ornament thereof; who hast bound the sea by the word of thy commandment; who hast shut up the deep, and sealed it by thy terrible and glorious name; whom all men fear, and tremble before thy power; for the majesty of thy glory cannot be borne, and thine angry threatening toward sinners is importa-

ble: but thy merciful promise is unmeasurable and unsearchable; for thou art the most high Lord, of great compassion, long-suffering, very merciful, and repentest of the evils of men. Thou, O Lord, according to thy great goodness hast promised repentance and forgiveness to them that have sinned against thee: and of thine infinite mercies hast appointed repentance unto sinners, that they may be saved. Thou therefore, O Lord, that art the God of the just, hast not appointed repentance to the just, as to Abraham, and Isaac, and Jacob, which have not sinned against thee; but thou hast appointed repentance unto me that am a sinner: for I have sinned above the number of the sands of the sea. My transgressions, O Lord, are multiplied: my transgressions are multiplied, and I am not worthy to behold and see the height of heaven for the multitude of mine iniquities. I am bowed down with many iron bands, that I cannot lift up mine head, neither have any release: for I have provoked thy wrath, and done evil before thee: I did not thy will, neither kept I thy commandments: I have set up abominations, and have multiplied offences. Now therefore I bow the knee of mine heart, beseeching thee of grace. I have sinned, O Lord, I have sinned, and I acknowledge mine iniquities: wherefore, I humbly beseech thee, forgive me, O Lord, forgive me, and destroy me not with mine iniquities. Be not angry with me for ever, by reserving evil for me; neither condemn me into the lower parts of the earth. For thou art the God, even the God of them that repent; and in me thou wilt shew all thy goodness: for thou wilt save me, that am unworthy, according to thy great mercy. Therefore I will praise thee for ever all the days of my life: for all the powers of the heavens do praise thee, and thine is the glory for ever and ever. Amen.

VIII

CHRISTIANITY

CHRISTIANITY grew out of Judaism and the Christians claim many of
the Jewish sacred writings as their own. The Christian Bible contains
both the Old Testament and the New Testament while many editions
of the Bible include also the books of the Apocrypha.

The Christian Messiah, Jesus of Nazareth, was a Jew, steeped in
Jewish tradition and culture. He was reared according to the customs
of the Jewish community of the first century and knew, as well as did
any Jewish youth of his day, the law and the prophets. He was proud
of this, and assured his followers that his mission was not to destroy
this law, but to fulfil it. He thought of himself as standing in the line
of the prophets, of giving a true interpretation of that which they had
sought to put into words and deeds. For him, his teaching was merely
the next step in a growing tradition that had begun with Abraham
and had continued down to his day.

This next step for Jesus and his followers was to break away from
the narrow nationalism of the Judaism of the past and to carry the
high ethical idealism of the greatest of the prophets to all people,
whether Jew or non-Jew. Jesus taught first among the Jews, but later
turned to the Gentiles. His was a gospel for all men. "If I be lifted
up," he said, "I shall draw *all* men unto me".

The first four books of the New Testament—Matthew, Mark, Luke,
and John—are four efforts to interpret his life historically. They recount, in so far as that was possible in those days, the life of Jesus.
The fifth book is the story of the followers of Jesus after his death. It
tells of the founding of the Christian church by a small body of
his followers.

The remainder of the books of the New Testament, except the last,
are letters written by early Christians. Most of these were written by
Saint Paul, the first Christian missionary, to churches which he
founded or to friends in these churches. As such, they are important
statements of what this new faith, Christianity, meant to Paul. Some
of these letters are written by authors whose names have been lost.

Revelation, the last book of the New Testament, is an example of the mass of Apocalyptic literature which was circulated among the early churches. It is an account of a vision experienced by one John and is written in symbolic language to which many interpretations can be given.

These books, along with many others, were circulated among the early Christian churches and treasured by them. Often churches exchanged books and they were read to the members. As time went on a need was felt for some authoritative collection of this literature. Thus early scholars attempted to pick out of this great mass of literature those documents which they believed to be authentic products of the earliest years of the church. After many such attempts, leaders of the early church decided upon a canon or authentic group of books that would officially constitute the New Testament. These are the books to be found in any standard version of the New Testament.

However, there are many other books stemming from this early Christian period, which are studied by scholars as throwing some light upon the early church and the doctrines of Christianity. These are published separately from the Bible and are usually available only to scholars. Among these are the *New Testament Apocrypha,* the *Sayings of Jesus,* the writings to which were attached the names of Jesus' disciples to give them an appearance of having been written by these men, and numerous other documents. None of these writings are considered authentic enough to become part of the New Testament canon and are thus not among the sacred writings of the Christians.

Christianity, growing out of the teachings of Jesus of Nazareth, and developing into a religious movement in the Roman Empire, was first persecuted vigorously by Roman authorities. But its strength was such that it eventually conquered the Empire and became the only religion permitted by the Emperor Constantine. With the fall of the Roman Empire, Roman Christianity came to dominate Europe and, from there, to spread throughout the world. Its missionary activities have carried it to all parts of the globe, civilized and uncivilized. The Bible has been translated into more than 1,000 languages and today it is estimated that over 585,000,000 persons in the world belong to the various branches of the Christian church. This forms the largest religious group in the world.

THE NEW TESTAMENT

THE New Testament is the sacred book of the Christians. Although it is referred to as a "book", it is actually a collection of twenty-seven books or writings. These writings were chosen from a mass of documents which circulated among the early Christian churches and became the canon of the Christians.

All of these writings first appeared in the Greek language but have been translated into almost every known language of the world. Numerous versions are available in English today. The most widely known English version is that translated early in the seventeenth century by order of King James of England, which is referred to as the King James Bible or the Authorized Version of the Bible.

Of course, the original manuscripts of these books have been lost and the manuscripts now in existence are copies of copies. A few New Testament manuscripts date back to the fourth and the fifth centuries while most of the manuscripts now known date from the fifth to the tenth centuries. There are more than 1,700 such manuscripts now in existence in museums and in private collections. The oldest complete manuscript of the New Testament is the Aleph or Sinaitic Codex which dates from the middle of the fourth century after Christ. It was discovered at Mount Sinai by Tischendorf in 1859 and now rests in the Imperial Library at Moscow, Russia.

The Gospel According to St. Matthew

This first book of the New Testament was probably written in Palestine between 60 and 70 A.D. by one named Levi who was often called Matthew. It was written for Jewish Christians who wanted to know of the events in the life of Jesus. The author does not follow strict chronological order, but groups events according to their similarity. Most of the book is in narrative form.

CHAPTER 5

1. And seeing the multitudes, he went up into a mountain: and when he was set, his disciples came unto him:

2. And he opened his mouth, and taught them, saying,

3. Blessed are the poor in spirit: for theirs is the kingdom of heaven.

4. Blessed are they that mourn: for they shall be comforted.

5. Blessed are the meek: for they shall inherit the earth.

6. Blessed are they which do hunger and thirst after righteousness: for they shall be filled.

7. Blessed are the merciful: for they shall obtain mercy.

8. Blessed are the pure in heart: for they shall see God.

9. Blessed are the peacemakers: for

they shall be called the children of God.

10. Blessed are they which are persecuted for righteousness' sake: for theirs is the kingdom of heaven.

11. Blessed are ye, when men shall revile you, and persecute you, and shall say all manner of evil against you falsely, for my sake.

12. Rejoice, and be exceeding glad: for great is your reward in heaven: for so persecuted they the prophets which were before you.

13. Ye are the salt of the earth: but if the salt have lost his savour, wherewith shall it be salted? it is thenceforth good for nothing, but to be cast out, and to be trodden under foot of men.

14. Ye are the light of the world. A city that is set on an hill cannot be hid.

15. Neither do men light a candle, and put it under a bushel, but on a candlestick; and it giveth light unto all that are in the house.

16. Let your light so shine before men, that they may see your good works, and glorify your Father which is in heaven.

17. Think not that I am come to destroy the law, or the prophets: I am not come to destroy, but to fulfil.

18. For verily I say unto you, Till heaven and earth pass, one jot or one tittle shall in no wise pass from the law, till all be fulfilled.

19. Whosoever therefore shall break one of these least commandments, and shall teach men so, he shall be called the least in the kingdom of heaven: but whosoever shall do and teach them, the same shall be called great in the kingdom of heaven.

20. For I say unto you, That except your righteousness shall exceed the righteousness of the scribes and Pharisees, ye shall in no case enter into the kingdom of heaven.

21. Ye have heard that it was said by them of old time, Thou shalt not kill; and whosoever shall kill shall be in danger of the judgment:

22. But I say unto you, That whosoever is angry with his brother without a cause shall be in danger of the judgment: and whosoever shall say to his brother, Raca, shall be in danger of the council: but whosoever shall say, Thou fool, shall be in danger of hell fire.

23. Therefore if thou bring thy gift to the altar, and there rememberest that thy brother hath ought against thee;

24. Leave there thy gift before the altar, and go thy way; first be reconciled to thy brother, and then come and offer thy gift.

25. Agree with thine adversary quickly, whiles thou art in the way with him; lest at any time the adversary deliver thee to the judge, and the judge deliver thee to the officer, and thou be cast into prison.

26. Verily I say unto thee, Thou shalt by no means come out thence, till thou hast paid the uttermost farthing.

27. Ye have heard that it was said by them of old time, Thou shalt not commit adultery:

28. But I say unto you, That whosoever looketh on a woman to lust after her hath committed adultery with her already in his heart.

29. And if thy right eye offend thee, pluck it out, and cast it from thee: for it is profitable for thee that one of thy members should perish, and not that thy whole body should be cast into hell.

30. And if thy right hand offend thee, cut it off, and cast it from thee: for it is profitable for thee that one of thy members should perish, and not that thy whole body should be cast into hell.

31. It hath been said, Whosoever shall put away his wife, let him give her a writing of divorcement:

32. But I say unto you, That who-

soever shall put away his wife, saving for the cause of fornication, causeth her to commit adultery: and whosoever shall marry her that is divorced committeth adultery.

33. Again, ye have heard that it hath been said by them of old time, Thou shalt not forswear thyself, but shalt perform unto the Lord thine oaths:

34. But I say unto you, Swear not at all; neither by heaven; for it is God's throne:

35. Nor by the earth; for it is his footstool: neither by Jerusalem; for it is the city of the great King.

36. Neither shalt thou swear by thy head, because thou canst not make one hair white or black.

37. But let your communication be, Yea, yea; Nay, nay: for whatsoever is more than these cometh of evil.

38. Ye have heard that it hath been said, An eye for an eye, and a tooth for a tooth:

39. But I say unto you, That ye resist not evil: but whosoever shall smite thee on thy right cheek, turn to him the other also.

40. And if any man will sue thee at the law, and take away thy coat, let him have thy cloke also.

41. And whosoever shall compel thee to go a mile, go with him twain.

42. Give to him that asketh thee, and from him that would borrow of thee turn not thou away.

43. Ye have heard that it hath been said, Thou shalt love thy neighbour, and hate thine enemy.

44. But I say unto you, Love your enemies, bless them that curse you, do good to them that hate you, and pray for them which despitefully use you, and persecute you;

45. That ye may be the children of your Father which is in heaven: for he maketh his sun to rise on the evil and on the good, and sendeth rain on the just and on the unjust.

46. For if ye love them which love you, what reward have ye? do not even the publicans the same?

47. And if ye salute your brethren only, what do ye more than others? do not even the publicans so?

48. Be ye therefore perfect, even as your Father which is in heaven is perfect.

CHAPTER 6

1. Take heed that ye do not your alms before men, to be seen of them: otherwise ye have no reward of your Father which is in heaven.

2. Therefore when thou doest thine alms, do not sound a trumpet before thee, as the hypocrites do in the synagogues and in the streets, that they may have glory of men. Verily I say unto you, They have their reward.

3. But when thou doest alms, let not thy left hand know what thy right hand doeth:

4. That thine alms may be in secret: and thy Father which seeth in secret himself shall reward thee openly.

5. And when thou prayest, thou shalt not be as the hypocrites are: for they love to pray standing in the synagogues and in the corners of the streets, that they may be seen of men. Verily I say unto you, They have their reward.

6. But thou, when thou prayest, enter into thy closet, and when thou hast shut thy door, pray to thy Father which is in secret; and thy Father which seeth in secret shall reward thee openly.

7. But when ye pray, use not vain repetitions, as the heathen do: for they think that they shall be heard for their much speaking.

8. Be not ye therefore like unto them: for your Father knoweth what things ye have need of, before ye ask him.

9. After this manner therefore pray ye: Our Father which art in heaven, Hallowed be thy name.

10. Thy kingdom come. Thy will be done in earth, as it is in heaven.

11. Give us this day our daily bread.

12. And forgive us our debts, as we forgive our debtors.

13. And lead us not into temptation, but deliver us from evil: For thine is the kingdom, and the power, and the glory, for ever. Amen.

14. For if ye forgive men their trespasses, your heavenly Father will also forgive you:

15. But if ye forgive not men their trespasses, neither will your Father forgive your trespasses.

16. Moreover when ye fast, be not, as the hypocrites, of a sad countenance: for they disfigure their faces, that they may appear unto men to fast. Verily I say unto you, They have their reward.

17. But thou, when thou fastest, anoint thine head, and wash thy face;

18. That thou appear not unto men to fast, but unto thy Father which is in secret: and thy Father, which seeth in secret, shall reward thee openly.

19. Lay not up for yourselves treasures upon earth, where moth and rust doth corrupt, and where thieves break through and steal:

20. But lay up for yourselves treasures in heaven, where neither moth nor rust doth corrupt, and where thieves do not break through nor steal:

21. For where your treasure is, there will your heart be also.

22. The light of the body is the eye: if therefore thine eye be single, thy whole body shall be full of light.

23. But if thine eye be evil, thy whole body shall be full of darkness. If therefore the light that is in thee be darkness, how great is that darkness!

24. No man can serve two masters: for either he will hate the one, and love the other; or else he will hold to the one, and despise the other. Ye cannot serve God and mammon.

25. Therefore I say unto you, Take no thought for your life, what ye shall eat, or what ye shall drink; nor yet for your body, what ye shall put on. Is not the life more than meat, and the body than raiment?

26. Behold the fowls of the air: for they sow not, neither do they reap, nor gather into barns; yet your heavenly Father feedeth them. Are ye not much better than they?

27. Which of you by taking thought can add one cubit unto his stature?

28. And why take ye thought for raiment? Consider the lilies of the field, how they grow; they toil not, neither do they spin:

29. And yet I say unto you, That even Solomon in all his glory was not arrayed like one of these.

30. Wherefore, if God so clothe the grass of the field, which to day is, and to morrow is cast into the oven, shall he not much more clothe you, O ye of little faith?

31. Therefore take no thought, saying, What shall we eat? or, What shall we drink? or, Wherewithal shall we be clothed?

32. (For after all these things do the Gentiles seek:) for your heavenly Father knoweth that ye have need of all these things.

33. But seek ye first the kingdom of God, and his righteousness; and all these things shall be added unto you.

34. Take therefore no thought for the morrow: for the morrow shall take thought for the things of itself. Sufficient unto the day is the evil thereof.

Chapter 7

1. Judge not, that ye be not judged.

2. For with what judgment ye judge, ye shall be judged: and with what measure ye mete, it shall be measured to you again.

3. And why beholdest thou the mote that is in thy brother's eye, but consid-

erest not the beam that is in thine own eye?

4. Or how wilt thou say to thy brother, Let me pull out the mote out of thine eye; and, behold, a beam is in thine own eye?

5. Thou hypocrite, first cast out the beam out of thine own eye; and then shalt thou see clearly to cast out the mote out of thy brother's eye.

6. Give not that which is holy unto the dogs, neither cast ye your pearls before swine, lest they trample them under their feet, and turn again and rend you.

7. Ask, and it shall be given you; seek, and ye shall find; knock, and it shall be opened unto you:

8. For every one that asketh receiveth; and he that seeketh findeth; and to him that knocketh it shall be opened.

9. Or what man is there of you, whom if his son ask bread, will he give him a stone?

10. Or if he ask a fish, will he give him a serpent?

11. If ye then, being evil, know how to give good gifts unto your children, how much more shall your Father which is in heaven give good things to them that ask him?

12. Therefore all things whatsoever ye would that men should do to you, do ye even so to them: for this is the law and the prophets.

13. Enter ye in at the strait gate: for wide is the gate, and broad is the way, that leadeth to destruction, and many there be which go in thereat:

14. Because strait is the gate, and narrow is the way, which leadeth unto life, and few there be that find it.

15. Beware of false prophets, which come to you in sheep's clothing, but inwardly they are ravening wolves.

16. Ye shall know them by their fruits. Do men gather grapes of thorns, or figs of thistles?

17. Even so every good tree bring-

eth forth good fruit; but a corrupt tree bringeth forth evil fruit.

18. A good tree cannot bring forth evil fruit, neither can a corrupt tree bring forth good fruit.

19. Every tree that bringeth not forth good fruit is hewn down, and cast into the fire.

20. Wherefore by their fruits ye shall know them.

21. Not every one that saith unto me, Lord, Lord, shall enter into the kingdom of heaven; but he that doeth the will of my Father which is in heaven.

22. Many will say to me in that day, Lord, Lord, have we not prophesied in thy name? and in thy name have cast out devils? and in thy name done many wonderful works?

23. And then will I profess unto them, I never knew you: depart from me, ye that work iniquity.

24. Therefore whosoever heareth these sayings of mine, and doeth them, I will liken him unto a wise man, which built his house upon a rock:

25. And the rain descended, and the floods came, and the winds blew, and beat upon that house; and it fell not: for it was founded upon a rock.

26. And every one that heareth these sayings of mine, and doeth them not, shall be likened unto a foolish man, which built his house upon the sand:

27. And the rain descended, and the floods came, and the winds blew, and beat upon that house; and it fell: and great was the fall of it.

28. And it came to pass, when Jesus had ended these sayings, the people were astonished at his doctrine:

29. For he taught them as one having authority, and not as the scribes.

Chapter 9

20. And, behold, a woman, which was diseased with an issue of blood

twelve years, came behind him, and touched the hem of his garment:

21. For she said within herself, If I may but touch his garment, I shall be whole.

22. But Jesus turned him about, and when he saw her, he said, Daughter, be of good comfort; thy faith hath made thee whole. And the woman was made whole from that hour.

23. And when Jesus came into the ruler's house, and saw the minstrels and the people making a noise,

24. He said unto them, Give place: for the maid is not dead, but sleepeth. And they laughed him to scorn.

25. But when the people were put forth, he went in, and took her by the hand, and the maid arose.

26. And the fame hereof went abroad into all that land.

27. And when Jesus departed thence, two blind men followed him, crying, and saying, Thou son of David, have mercy on us.

28. And when he was come into the house, the blind men came to him: and Jesus saith unto them, Believe ye that I am able to do this? They said unto him, Yea, Lord.

29. Then touched he their eyes, saying, According to your faith be it unto you.

30. And their eyes were opened; and Jesus straitly charged them, saying, See that no man know it.

31. But they, when they were departed, spread abroad his fame in all that country.

32. As they went out, behold, they brought to him a dumb man possessed with a devil.

33. And when the devil was cast out, the dumb spake: and the multitudes marvelled, saying, It was never so seen in Israel.

34. But the Pharisees said, He casteth out devils through the prince of the devils.

CHAPTER 10

16. Behold, I send you forth as sheep in the midst of wolves: be ye therefore wise as serpents, and harmless as doves.

17. But beware of men: for they will deliver you up to the councils, and they will scourge you in their synagogues;

18. And ye shall be brought before governors and kings for my sake, for a testimony against them and the Gentiles.

19. But when they deliver you up, take no thought how or what ye shall speak: for it shall be given you in that same hour what ye shall speak.

20. For it is not ye that speak, but the Spirit of your Father which speaketh in you.

21. And the brother shall deliver up the brother to death, and the father the child: and the children shall rise up against their parents, and cause them to be put to death.

22. And ye shall be hated of all men for my name's sake: but he that endureth to the end shall be saved.

23. But when they persecute you in this city, flee ye into another: for verily I say unto you, Ye shall not have gone over the cities of Israel, till the Son of man be come.

24. The disciple is not above his master, nor the servant above his lord.

25. It is enough for the disciple that he be as his master, and the servant as his lord. If they have called the master of the house Beelzebub, how much more shall they call them of his household?

26. Fear them not therefore: for there is nothing covered, that shall not be revealed; and hid, that shall not be known.

27. What I tell you in darkness, that speak ye in light: and what ye hear in the ear, that preach ye upon the house tops.

28. And fear not them which kill

the body, but are not able to kill the soul: but rather fear him which is able to destroy both soul and body in hell.

29. Are not two sparrows sold for a farthing? and one of them shall not fall on the ground without your Father.

30. But the very hairs of your head are all numbered.

31. Fear ye not therefore, ye are of more value than many sparrows.

32. Whosoever therefore shall confess me before men, him will I confess also before my Father which is in heaven.

33. But whosoever shall deny me before men, him will I also deny before my Father which is in heaven.

34. Think not that I am come to send peace on earth: I came not to send peace, but a sword.

35. For I am come to set a man at variance against his father, and the daughter against her mother, and the daughter in law against her mother in law.

36. And a man's foes shall be they of his own household.

37. He that loveth father or mother more than me is not worthy of me: and he that loveth son or daughter more than me is not worthy of me.

38. And he that taketh not his cross, and followeth after me, is not worthy of me.

39. He that findeth his life shall lose it: and he that loseth his life for my sake shall find it.

40. He that receiveth you receiveth me, and he that receiveth me receiveth him that sent me.

41. He that receiveth a prophet in the name of a prophet shall receive a prophet's reward; and he that receiveth a righteous man in the name of a righteous man shall receive a righteous man's reward.

42. And whosoever shall give to drink unto one of these little ones a cup of cold water only in the name of a disciple, verily I say unto you, he shall in no wise lose his reward.

CHAPTER 11

25. At that time Jesus answered and said, I thank thee, O Father, Lord of heaven and earth, because thou hast hid these things from the wise and prudent, and hast revealed them unto babes.

26. Even so, Father: for so it seemed good in thy sight.

27. All things are delivered unto me of my Father: and no man knoweth the Son, but the Father; neither knoweth any man the Father, save the Son, and he to whomsoever the Son will reveal him.

28. Come unto me, all ye that labour and are heavy laden, and I will give you rest.

29. Take my yoke upon you, and learn of me; for I am meek and lowly in heart: and ye shall find rest unto your souls.

30. For my yoke is easy, and my burden is light.

CHAPTER 12

31. Wherefore I say unto you, All manner of sin and blasphemy shall be forgiven unto men: but the blasphemy against the Holy Ghost shall not be forgiven unto men.

32. And whosoever speaketh a word against the Son of man, it shall be forgiven him: but whosoever speaketh against the Holy Ghost, it shall not be forgiven him, neither in this world, neither in the world to come.

33. Either make the tree good, and his fruit good; or else make the tree corrupt, and his fruit corrupt: for the tree is known by his fruit.

34. O generation of vipers, how can ye, being evil, speak good things? for out of the abundance of the heart the mouth speaketh.

35. A good man out of the good

treasure of the heart bringeth forth good things: and an evil man out of the evil treasure bringeth forth evil things.

36. But I say unto you, That every idle word that men shall speak, they shall give account thereof in the day of judgment.

37. For by thy words thou shalt be justified, and by thy words thou shalt be condemned.

38. Then certain of the scribes and of the Pharisees answered, saying, Master, we would see a sign from thee.

39. But he answered and said unto them, An evil and adulterous generation seeketh after a sign; and there shall no sign be given to it, but the sign of the prophet Jonas:

40. For as Jonas was three days and three nights in the whale's belly; so shall the Son of man be three days and three nights in the heart of the earth.

41. The men of Nineveh shall rise in judgment with this generation, and shall condemn it: because they repented at the preaching of Jonas; and, behold, a greater than Jonas is here.

42. The queen of the south shall rise up in the judgment with this generation, and shall condemn it: for she came from the uttermost parts of the earth to hear the wisdom of Solomon; and, behold, a greater than Solomon is here.

43. When the unclean spirit is gone out of a man, he walketh through dry places, seeking rest, and findeth none.

44. Then he saith, I will return into my house from whence I came out; and when he is come, he findeth it empty, swept, and garnished.

45. Then goeth he, and taketh with himself seven other spirits more wicked than himself, and they enter in and dwell there: and the last state of that man is worse than the first.

Even so shall it be also unto this wicked generation.

CHAPTER 13

1. The same day went Jesus out of the house, and sat by the sea side.

2. And great multitudes were gathered together unto him, so that he went into a ship, and sat; and the whole multitude stood on the shore.

3. And he spake many things unto them in parables, saying, Behold, a sower went forth to sow;

4. And when he sowed, some seeds fell by the way side, and the fowls came and devoured them up:

5. Some fell upon stony places, where they had not much earth: and forthwith they sprung up, because they had no deepness of earth:

6. And when the sun was up, they were scorched; and because they had no root, they withered away.

7. And some fell among thorns; and the thorns sprung up, and choked them:

8. But other fell into good ground, and brought forth fruit, some an hundredfold, some sixtyfold, some thirtyfold.

9. Who hath ears to hear, let him hear.

10. And the disciples came, and said unto him, Why speakest thou unto them in parables?

11. He answered and said unto them, Because it is given unto you to know the mysteries of the kingdom of heaven, but to them it is not given.

12. For whosoever hath, to him shall be given, and he shall have more abundance: but whosoever hath not, from him shall be taken away even that he hath.

13. Therefore speak I to them in parables: because they seeing see not; and hearing they hear not, neither do they understand.

14. And in them is fulfilled the prophecy of Esaias, which saith, By

hearing ye shall hear, and shall not understand; and seeing ye shall see, and shall not perceive:

15. For this people's heart is waxed gross, and their ears are dull of hearing, and their eyes they have closed; lest at any time they should see with their eyes, and hear with their ears, and should understand with their heart, and should be converted, and I should heal them.

16. But blessed are your eyes, for they see: and your ears, for they hear.

17. For verily I say unto you, That many prophets and righteous men have desired to see those things which ye see, and have not seen them; and to hear those things which ye hear, and have not heard them.

18. Hear ye therefore the parable of the sower.

19. When any one heareth the word of the kingdom, and understandeth it not, then cometh the wicked one, and catcheth away that which was sown in his heart. This is he which received seed by the way side.

20. But he that received the seed into stony places, the same is he that heareth the word, and anon with joy receiveth it;

21. Yet hath he not root in himself, but dureth for a while: for when tribulation or persecution ariseth because of the word, by and by he is offended.

22. He also that received seed among the thorns is he that heareth the word; and the care of this world, and the deceitfulness of riches, choke the word, and he becometh unfruitful.

23. But he that received seed into the good ground is he that heareth the word, and understandeth it; which also beareth fruit, and bringeth forth, some an hundredfold, some sixty, some thirty.

24. Another parable put he forth unto them, saying, The kingdom of heaven is likened unto a man which sowed good seed in his field:

25. But while men slept, his enemy came and sowed tares among the wheat, and went his way.

26. But when the blade was sprung up, and brought forth fruit, then appeared the tares also.

27. So the servants of the householder came and said unto him, Sir, didst not thou sow good seed in thy field? from whence then hath it tares?

28. He said unto them, An enemy hath done this. The servants said unto him, Wilt thou then that we go and gather them up?

29. But he said, Nay; lest while ye gather up the tares, ye root up also the wheat with them.

30. Let both grow together until the harvest: and in the time of harvest I will say to the reapers, Gather ye together first the tares, and bind them in bundles to burn them: but gather the wheat into my barn.

31. Another parable put he forth unto them, saying, The kingdom of heaven is like to a grain of mustard seed, which a man took, and sowed in his field:

32. Which indeed is the least of all seeds: but when it is grown, it is the greatest among herbs, and becometh a tree, so that the birds of the air come and lodge in the branches thereof.

33. Another parable spake he unto them; The kingdom of heaven is like unto leaven, which a woman took, and hid in three measures of meal, till the whole was leavened.

34. All these things spake Jesus unto the multitude in parables; and without a parable spake he not unto them:

35. That it might be fulfilled which was spoken by the prophet, saying, I will open my mouth in parables; I will utter things which have been kept secret from the foundation of the world.

36. Then Jesus sent the multitude away, and went into the house: and

his disciples came unto him, saying, Declare unto us the parable of the tares of the field.

37. He answered and said unto them, He that soweth the good seed is the Son of man;

38. The field is the world; the good seed are the children of the kingdom; but the tares are the children of the wicked one;

39. The enemy that sowed them is the devil; the harvest is the end of the world; and the reapers are the angels.

40. As therefore the tares are gathered and burned in the fire; so shall it be in the end of this world.

41. The Son of man shall send forth his angels, and they shall gather out of his kingdom all things that offend, and them which do iniquity;

42. And shall cast them into a furnace of fire: there shal¯ be wailing and gnashing of teeth.

43. Then shall the righteous shine forth as the sun in the kingdom of their Father. Who hath ears to hear, let him hear.

44. Again, the kingdom of heaven is like unto treasure hid in a field; the which when a man hath found, he hideth, and for joy thereof goeth and selleth all that he hath, and buyeth that field.

45. Again, the kingdom of heaven is like unto a merchant man, seeking goodly pearls:

46. Who, when he had found one pearl of great price, went and sold all that he had, and bought it.

47. Again, the kingdom of heaven is like unto a net, that was cast into the sea, and gathered of every kind:

48. Which, when it was full, they drew to shore, and sat down, and gathered the good into vessels, but cast the bad away.

49. So shall it be at the end of the world: the angels shall come forth, and sever the wicked from among the just,

50. And shall cast them into the furnace of fire: there shall be wailing and gnashing of teeth.

51. Jesus saith unto them, Have ye understood all these things? They say unto him, Yea, Lord.

52. Then said he unto them, Therefore every scribe which is instructed unto the kingdom of heaven is like unto a man that is an householder, which bringeth forth out of his treasure things new and old.

CHAPTER 15

10. And he called the multitude, and said unto them, Hear, and understand:

11. Not that which goeth into the mouth defileth a man; but that which cometh out of the mouth, this defileth a man.

12. Then came his disciples, and said unto him, Knowest thou that the Pharisees were offended, after they heard this saying?

13. But he answered and said, Every plant, which my heavenly Father hath not planted, shall be rooted up.

14. Let them alone: they be blind leaders of the blind. And if the blind lead the blind, both shall fall into the ditch.

15. Then answered Peter and said unto him, Declare unto us this parable.

16. And Jesus said, Are ye also yet without understanding?

17. Do not ye yet understand, that whatsoever entereth in at the mouth goeth into the belly, and is cast out into the draught?

18. But those things which proceed out of the mouth come forth from the heart; and they defile the man.

19. For out of the heart proceed evil thoughts, murders, adulteries, forni⸗ cations, thefts, false witness, blasphe⸗ mies:

20. These are the things which de⸗ file a man: but to eat with unwashen hands defileth not a man.

CHAPTER 16

13. When Jesus came into the coasts of Cæsarea Philippi, he asked his disciples, saying, Whom do men say that I the Son of man am?

14. And they said, Some say that thou art John the Baptist: some, Elias; and others, Jeremias, or one of the prophets.

15. He saith unto them, But whom say ye that I am?

16. And Simon Peter answered and said, Thou art the Christ, the Son of the living God.

17. And Jesus answered and said unto him, Blessed art thou, Simon Barjona: for flesh and blood hath not revealed it unto thee, but my Father which is in heaven.

18. And I say also unto thee, That thou art Peter, and upon this rock I will build my church; and the gates of hell shall not prevail against it.

19. And I will give unto thee the keys of the kingdom of heaven: and whatsoever thou shalt bind on earth shall be bound in heaven: and whatsoever thou shalt loose on earth shall be loosed in heaven.

20. Then charged he his disciples that they should tell no man that he was Jesus the Christ.

21. From that time forth began Jesus to shew unto his disciples, how that he must go unto Jerusalem, and suffer many things of the elders and chief priests and scribes, and be killed, and be raised again the third day.

22. Then Peter took him, and began to rebuke him, saying, Be it far from thee, Lord: this shall not be unto thee.

23. But he turned, and said unto Peter, Get thee behind me, Satan: thou art an offence unto me: for thou savourest not the things that be of God, but those that be of men.

24. Then said Jesus unto his disciples, If any man will come after me,

let him deny himself, and take up his cross, and follow me.

25. For whosoever will save his life shall lose it: and whosoever will lose his life for my sake shall find it.

26. For what is a man profited, if he shall gain the whole world, and lose his own soul? or what shall a man give in exchange for his soul?

27. For the Son of man shall come in the glory of his Father with his angels; and then he shall reward every man according to his works.

28. Verily I say unto you, There be some standing here, which shall not taste of death, till they see the Son of man coming in his kingdom.

CHAPTER 18

1. At the same time came the disciples unto Jesus, saying, Who is the greatest in the kingdom of heaven?

2. And Jesus called a little child unto him, and set him in the midst of them,

3. And said, Verily I say unto you, Except ye be converted, and become as little children, ye shall not enter into the kingdom of heaven.

4. Whosoever therefore shall humble himself as this little child, the same is greatest in the kingdom of heaven.

5. And whoso shall receive one such little child in my name receiveth me.

6. But whoso shall offend one of these little ones which believe in me, it were better for him that a millstone were hanged about his neck, and that he were drowned in the depth of the sea.

7. Woe unto the world because of offences! for it must needs be that offences come; but woe to that man by whom the offence cometh!

8. Wherefore if thy hand or thy foot offend thee, cut them off, and cast them from thee: it is better for thee to enter into life halt or maimed,

rather than having two hands or two feet to be cast into everlasting fire.

9. And if thine eye offend thee, pluck it out, and cast it from thee: it is better for thee to enter into life with one eye, rather than having two eyes to be cast into hell fire.

10. Take heed that ye despise not one of these little ones; for I say unto you, That in heaven their angels do always behold the face of my Father which is in heaven.

11. For the Son of man is come to save that which was lost.

12. How think ye? if a man have an hundred sheep, and one of them be gone astray, doth he not leave the ninety and nine, and goeth into the mountains, and seeketh that which is gone astray?

13. And if so be that he find it, verily I say unto you, he rejoiceth more of that sheep, than of the ninety and nine which went not astray.

14. Even so it is not the will of your Father which is in heaven, that one of these little ones should perish.

15. Moreover if thy brother shall trespass against thee, go and tell him his fault between thee and him alone: if he shall hear thee, thou hast gained thy brother.

16. But if he will not hear thee, then take with thee one or two more, that in the mouth of two or three witnesses every word may be established.

17. And if he shall neglect to hear them, tell it unto the church: but if he neglect to hear the church, let him be unto thee as an heathen man and a publican.

18. Verily I say unto you, Whatsoever ye shall bind on earth shall be bound in heaven: and whatsoever ye shall loose on earth shall be loosed in heaven.

19. Again I say unto you, That if two of you shall agree on earth as touching any thing that they shall ask, it shall be done for them of my Father which is in heaven.

20. For where two or three are gathered together in my name, there am I in the midst of them.

21. Then came Peter to him, and said, Lord, how oft shall my brother sin against me, and I forgive him? till seven times?

22. Jesus saith unto him, I say not unto thee, Until seven times: but, Until seventy times seven.

CHAPTER 19

3. The Pharisees also came unto him, tempting him, and saying unto him, Is it lawful for a man to put away his wife for every cause?

4. And he answered and said unto them, Have ye not read, that he which made them at the beginning made them male and female,

5. And said, For this cause shall a man leave father and mother, and shall cleave to his wife: and they twain shall be one flesh?

6. Wherefore they are no more twain, but one flesh. What therefore God hath joined together, let not man put asunder.

7. They say unto him, Why did Moses then command to give a writing of divorcement, and to put her away?

8. He saith unto them, Moses because of the hardness of your hearts suffered you to put away your wives: but from the beginning it was not so.

9. And I say unto you, Whosoever shall put away his wife, except it be for fornication, and shall marry another, committeth adultery: and whoso marrieth her which is put away doth commit adultery.

13. Then were there brought unto him little children, that he should put his hands on them, and pray: and the disciples rebuked them.

14. But Jesus said, Suffer little children, and forbid them not, to come

unto me: for of such is the kingdom of heaven.

15. And he laid his hands on them, and departed thence.

16. And, behold, one came and said unto him, Good Master, what good thing shall I do, that I may have eternal life?

17. And he said unto him, Why callest thou me good? there is none good but one, that is, God: but if thou wilt enter into life, keep the commandments.

18. He saith unto him, Which? Jesus said, Thou shalt do no murder, Thou shalt not commit adultery, Thou shalt not steal, Thou shalt not bear false witness,

19. Honour thy father and thy mother: and, Thou shalt love thy neighbour as thyself.

20. The young man saith unto him, All these things have I kept from my youth up: what lack I yet?

21. Jesus said unto him, If thou wilt be perfect, go and sell that thou hast, and give to the poor, and thou shalt have treasure in heaven: and come and follow me.

22. But when the young man heard that saying, he went away sorrowful: for he had great possessions.

23. Then said Jesus unto his disciples, Verily I say unto you, That a rich man shall hardly enter into the kingdom of heaven.

24. And again I say unto you, It is easier for a camel to go through the eye of a needle, than for a rich man to enter into the kingdom of God.

25. When his disciples heard it, they were exceedingly amazed, saying, Who then can be saved?

26. But Jesus beheld them, and said unto them, With men this is impossible; but with God all things are possible.

CHAPTER 22

34. But when the Pharisees had heard that he had put the Sadducees to silence, they were gathered together.

35. Then one of them, which was a lawyer, asked him a question, tempting him, and saying,

36. Master, which is the great commandment in the law?

37. Jesus said unto him, Thou shalt love the Lord thy God with all thy heart, and with all thy soul, and with all thy mind.

38. This is the first and great commandment.

39. And the second is like unto it, Thou shalt love thy neighbor as thyself.

40. On these two commandments hang all the law and the prophets.

CHAPTER 23

1. Then spake Jesus to the multitude, and to his disciples,

2. Saying, The scribes and the Pharisees sit in Moses' seat:

3. All therefore whatsoever they bid you observe, that observe and do; but do not ye after their works: for they say, and do not.

4. For they bind heavy burdens and grievous to be borne, and lay them on men's shoulders; but they themselves will not move them with one of their fingers.

5. But all their works they do for to be seen of men: they make broad their phylacteries, and enlarge the borders of their garments,

6. And love the uppermost rooms at feasts, and the chief seats in the synagogues,

7. And greetings in the markets, and to be called of men, Rabbi, Rabbi.

8. But be not ye called Rabbi: for one is your Master, even Christ; and all ye are brethren.

9. And call no man your father upon the earth: for one is your Father, which is in heaven.

10. Neither be ye called masters:

for one is your Master, even Christ.

11. But he that is greatest among you shall be your servant.

12. And whosoever shall exalt himself shall be abased; and he that shall humble himself shall be exalted.

Chapter 25

14. For the kingdom of heaven is as a man travelling into a far country, who called his own servants, and delivered unto them his goods.

15. And unto one he gave five talents, to another two, and to another one; to every man according to his several ability; and straightway took his journey.

16. Then he that had received the five talents went and traded with the same, and made them other five talents.

17. And likewise he that had received two, he also gained other two.

18. But he that had received one went and digged in the earth, and hid his lord's money.

19. After a long time the lord of those servants cometh, and reckoneth with them.

20. And so he that had received five talents came and brought other five talents, saying, Lord, thou deliveredst unto me five talents: behold, I have gained beside them five talents more.

21. His lord said unto him, Well done, thou good and faithful servant: thou hast been faithful over a few things, I will make thee ruler over many things: enter thou into the joy of thy lord.

22. He also that had received two talents came and said, Lord, thou deliveredst unto me two talents: behold, I have gained two other talents beside them.

23. His lord said unto him, Well done, good and faithful servant; thou hast been faithful over a few things, I will make thee ruler over many

things: enter thou into the joy of thy lord.

24. Then he which had received the one talent came and said, Lord, I knew thee that thou art an hard man, reaping where thou hast not sown, and gathering where thou hast not strawed:

25. And I was afraid, and went and hid thy talent in the earth: lo, there thou hast that is thine.

26. His lord answered and said unto him, Thou wicked and slothful servant, thou knewest that I reap where I sowed not, and gather where I have not strawed:

27. Thou oughtest therefore to have put my money to the exchangers, and then at my coming I should have received mine own with usury.

28. Take therefore the talent from him, and give it unto him which hath ten talents.

29. For unto every one that hath shall be given, and he shall have abundance: but from him that hath not shall be taken away even that which he hath.

30. And cast ye the unprofitable servant into outer darkness: there shall be weeping and gnashing of teeth.

31. When the Son of man shall come in his glory, and all the holy angels with him, then shall he sit upon the throne of his glory:

32. And before him shall be gathered all nations; and he shall separate them one from another, as a shepherd divideth his sheep from the goats:

33. And he shall set the sheep on his right hand, but the goats on the left.

34. Then shall the King say unto them on his right hand, Come, ye blessed of my Father, inherit the kingdom prepared for you from the foundation of the world:

35. For I was an hungred, and ye gave me meat: I was thirsty, and ye

gave me drink: I was a stranger, and ye took me in:

36. Naked, and ye clothed me: I was sick, and ye visited me: I was in prison, and ye came unto me.

37. Then shall the righteous answer him, saying, Lord, when saw we thee an hungred, and fed thee? or thirsty, and gave thee drink?

38. When saw we thee a stranger, and took thee in? or naked, and clothed thee?

39. Or when saw we thee sick, or in prison, and came unto thee?

40. And the King shall answer and say unto them, Verily I say unto you, Inasmuch as ye have done it unto one of the least of these my brethren, ye have done it unto me.

41. Then shall he say also unto them on the left hand, Depart from me, ye cursed, into everlasting fire, prepared for the devil and his angels:

42. For I was an hungred, and ye gave me no meat: I was thirsty, and ye gave me no drink:

43. I was a stranger, and ye took me not in: naked, and ye clothed me not: sick, and in prison, and ye visited me not.

44. Then shall they also answer him, saying, Lord, when saw we thee an hungred, or athirst, or a stranger, or naked, or sick, or in prison, and did not minister unto thee?

45. Then shall he answer them, saying, Verily I say unto you, Inasmuch as ye did it not to one of the least of these, ye did it not to me.

46. And these shall go away into everlasting punishment: but the righteous into life eternal.

CHAPTER 26

6. Now when Jesus was in Bethany, in the house of Simon the leper,

7. There came unto him a woman having an alabaster box of very precious ointment, and poured it on his head, as he sat at meat.

8. But when his disciples saw it, they had indignation, saying, To what purpose is this waste?

9. For this ointment might have been sold for much, and given to the poor.

10. When Jesus understood it, he said unto them, Why trouble ye the woman? for she hath wrought a good work upon me.

11. For ye have the poor always with you; but me ye have not always.

12. For in that she hath poured this ointment on my body, she did it for my burial.

13. Verily I say unto you, Wheresoever this gospel shall be preached in the whole world, there shall also this, that this woman hath done, be told for a memorial of her.

The Gospel According to St. Mark

This gospel was written by John Mark between 67 and 70 A.D. He was a close friend of St. Peter and seems to have gotten most of his material for this book from Peter. It is believed that Peter converted John Mark and was so close to him that he referred to him as "son". Although written earlier, the book was not released until after Peter's martyrdom in Rome. The gospel was written, it is believed, in Rome and for the Gentile Christians of that city, telling them of the life of Jesus.

CHAPTER 5

21. And when Jesus was passed over again by ship unto the other side, much people gathered unto him: and he was nigh unto the sea.

22. And, behold, there cometh one of the rulers of the synagogue, Jairus by name; and when he saw him, he fell at his feet,

23. And besought him greatly, saying, My little daughter lieth at the point of death: I pray thee, come and

lay thy hands on her, that she may be healed; and she shall live.

24. And Jesus went with him; and much people followed him, and thronged him.

25. And a certain woman, which had an issue of blood twelve years,

26. And had suffered many things of many physicians, and had spent all that she had, and was nothing bettered, but rather grew worse,

27. When she had heard of Jesus, came in the press behind, and touched his garment.

28. For she said, If I may touch but his clothes, I shall be whole.

29. And straightway the fountain of her blood was dried up; and she felt in her body that she was healed of that plague.

30. And Jesus, immediately knowing in himself that virtue had gone out of him, turned him about in the press, and said, Who touched my clothes?

31. And his disciples said unto him, Thou seest the multitude thronging thee, and sayest thou, Who touched me?

32. And he looked round about to see her that had done this thing.

33. But the woman fearing and trembling, knowing what was done in her, came and fell down before him, and told him all the truth.

34. And he said unto her, Daughter, thy faith hath made thee whole; go in peace, and be whole of thy plague.

35. While he yet spake, there came from the ruler of the synagogue's house certain which said, Thy daughter is dead: why troublest thou the Master any further?

36. As soon as Jesus heard the word that was spoken, he saith unto the ruler of the synagogue, Be not afraid, only believe.

37. And he suffered no man to follow him, save Peter, and James, and John the brother of James.

38. And he cometh to the house of the ruler of the synagogue, and seeth the tumult, and them that wept and wailed greatly.

39. And when he was come in, he saith unto them, Why make ye this ado, and weep? the damsel is not dead, but sleepeth.

40. And they laughed him to scorn. But when he had put them all out, he taketh the father and the mother of the damsel, and them that were with him, and entereth in where the damsel was lying.

41. And he took the damsel by the hand, and said unto her, Talitha cumi; which is, being interpreted, Damsel, I say unto thee, arise.

42. And straightway the damsel arose, and walked; for she was of the age of twelve years. And they were astonished with a great astonishment.

43. And he charged them straitly that no man should know it; and commanded that something should be given her to eat.

CHAPTER 9

14. And when he came to his disciples, he saw a great multitude about them, and the scribes questioning with them.

15. And straightway all the people, when they beheld him, were greatly amazed, and running to him saluted him.

16. And he asked the scribes, What question ye with them?

17. And one of the multitude answered and said, Master, I have brought unto thee my son, which hath a dumb spirit;

18. And wheresoever he taketh him, he teareth him: and he foameth, and gnasheth with his teeth, and pineth away: and I spake to thy disciples that they should cast him out; and they could not.

19. He answereth him, and saith, O faithless generation, how long shall I

be with you? how long shall I suffer you? bring him unto me.

20. And they brought him unto him: and when he saw him, straightway the spirit tare him; and he fell on the ground, and wallowed foaming.

21. And he asked his father, How long is it ago since this came unto him? And he said, Of a child.

22. And ofttimes it hath cast him into the fire, and into the waters, to destroy him: but if thou canst do any thing, have compassion on us, and help us.

23. Jesus said unto him, If thou canst believe, all things are possible to him that believeth.

24. And straightway the father of the child cried out, and said with tears, Lord, I believe; help thou mine unbelief.

25. When Jesus saw that the people came running together, he rebuked the foul spirit, saying unto him, Thou dumb and deaf spirit, I charge thee, come out of him, and enter no more into him.

26. And the spirit cried, and rent him sore, and came out of him: and he was as one dead; insomuch that many said, He is dead.

27. But Jesus took him by the hand, and lifted him up; and he arose.

28. And when he was come into the house, his disciples asked him privately, Why could not we cast him out?

29. And he said unto them, This kind can come forth by nothing, but by prayer and fasting.

CHAPTER 10

2. And the Pharisees came to him, and asked him, Is it lawful for a man to put away his wife? tempting him.

3. And he answered and said unto them, What did Moses command you?

4. And they said, Moses suffered to write a bill of divorcement, and to put her away.

5. And Jesus answered and said unto them, For the hardness of your heart he wrote you this precept.

6. But from the beginning of the creation God made them male and female.

7. For this cause shall a man leave his father and mother, and cleave to his wife.

8. And they twain shall be one flesh: so then they are no more twain, but one flesh.

9. What therefore God hath joined together, let not man put asunder.

10. And in the house his disciples asked him again of the same matter.

11. And he saith unto them, Whosoever shall put away his wife, and marry another, committeth adultery against her.

12. And if a woman shall put away her husband, and be married to another, she committeth adultery.

13. And they brought young children to him, that he should touch them: and his disciples rebuked those that brought them.

14. But when Jesus saw it, he was much displeased, and said unto them, Suffer the little children to come unto me, and forbid them not: for of such is the kingdom of God.

15. Verily I say unto you, Whosoever shall not receive the kingdom of God as a little child, he shall not enter therein.

16. And he took them up in his arms, put his hands upon them, and blessed them.

17. And when he was gone forth into the way, there came one running, and kneeled to him, and asked him, Good Master, what shall I do that I may inherit eternal life?

18. And Jesus said unto him, Why callest thou me good? there is none good but one, that is, God.

19. Thou knowest the commandments, Do not commit adultery, Do not kill, Do not steal, Do not bear

false witness, Defraud not, Honour thy father and mother.

20. And he answered and said unto him, Master, all these have I observed from my youth.

21. Then Jesus beholding him loved him, and said unto him, One thing thou lackest: go thy way, sell whatsoever thou hast, and give to the poor, and thou shalt have treasure in heaven: and come, take up the cross, and follow me.

22. And he was sad at that saying, and went away grieved: for he had great possessions.

23. And Jesus looked round about, and saith unto his disciples, How hardly shall they that have riches enter into the kingdom of God!

24. And the disciples were astonished at his words. But Jesus answereth again, and saith unto them, Children, how hard is it for them that trust in riches to enter into the kingdom of God!

25. It is easier for a camel to go through the eye of a needle, than for a rich man to enter into the kingdom of God.

26. And they were astonished out of measure, saying among themselves, Who then can be saved?

27. And Jesus looking upon them saith, With men it is impossible, but not with God: for with God all things are possible.

Chapter 11

22. And Jesus answering saith unto them, Have faith in God.

23. For verily I say unto you, That whosoever shall say unto this mountain, Be thou removed, and be thou cast into the sea; and shall not doubt in his heart, but shall believe that those things which he saith shall come to pass; he shall have whatsoever he saith.

24. Therefore I say unto you, What things soever ye desire, when ye pray,

believe that ye receive them, and ye shall have them.

25. And when ye stand praying, forgive, if ye have ought against any: that your Father also which is in heaven may forgive you your trespasses.

26. But if ye do not forgive, neither will your Father which is in heaven forgive your trespasses.

Chapter 12

28. And one of the scribes came, and having heard them reasoning together, and perceiving that he had answered them well, asked him, Which is the first commandment of all?

29. And Jesus answered him, The first of all the commandments is, Hear, O Israel; the Lord our God is one Lord:

30. And thou shalt love the Lord thy God with all thy heart, and with all thy soul, and with all thy mind, and with all thy strength: this is the first commandment.

31. And the second is like, namely this, Thou shalt love thy neighbour as thyself. There is none other commandment greater than these.

32. And the scribe said unto him, Well, Master, thou hast said the truth: for there is one God; and there is none other but he:

33. And to love him with all the heart, and with all the understanding, and with all the soul, and with all the strength, and to love his neighbour as himself, is more than all whole burnt offerings and sacrifices.

34. And when Jesus saw that he answered discreetly, he said unto him, Thou art not far from the kingdom of God. And no man after that durst ask him any question.

35. And Jesus answered and said, while he taught in the temple, How say the scribes that Christ is the son of David?

36. For David himself said by the

Holy Ghost, The LORD said to my Lord, Sit thou on my right hand, till I make thine enemies thy footstool.

37. David therefore himself calleth him Lord; and whence is he then his son? And the common people heard him gladly.

38. And he said unto them in his doctrine, Beware of the scribes, which love to go in long clothing, and love salutations in the marketplaces,

39. And the chief seats in the synagogues, and the uppermost rooms at feasts:

40. Which devour widows' houses, and for a pretence make long prayers: these shall receive greater damnation.

41. And Jesus sat over against the treasury, and beheld how the people cast money into the treasury: and many that were rich cast in much.

42. And there came a certain poor widow, and she threw in two mites, which make a farthing.

43. And he called unto him his disciples, and saith unto them, Verily I say unto you, That this poor widow hath cast more in, than all they which have cast into the treasury:

44. For all they did cast in of their abundance; but she of her want did cast in all that she had, even all her living.

CHAPTER 14

17. And in the evening he cometh with the twelve.

18. And as they sat and did eat, Jesus said, Verily I say unto you, One of you which eateth with me shall betray me.

19. And they began to be sorrowful, and to say unto him one by one, Is it I? and another said, Is it I?

20. And he answered and said unto them, It is one of the twelve, that dippeth with me in the dish.

21. The Son of man indeed goeth, as it is written of him: but woe to that man by whom the Son of man is betrayed! good were it for that man if he had never been born.

22. And as they did eat, Jesus took bread, and blessed, and brake it, and gave to them, and said, Take, eat: this is my body.

23. And he took the cup, and when he had given thanks, he gave it to them: and they all drank of it.

24. And he said unto them, This is my blood of the new testament, which is shed for many.

25. Verily I say unto you, I will drink no more of the fruit of the vine, until that day that I drink it new in the kingdom of God.

26. And when they had sung an hymn, they went out into the mount of Olives.

32. And they came to a place which was named Gethsemane: and he saith to his disciples, Sit ye here, while I shall pray.

33. And he taketh with him Peter and James and John, and began to be sore amazed, and to be very heavy;

34. And saith unto them, My soul is exceeding sorrowful unto death: tarry ye here, and watch.

35. And he went forward a little, and fell on the ground, and prayed that, if it were possible, the hour might pass from him.

36. And he said, Abba, Father, all things are possible unto thee; take away this cup from me: nevertheless not what I will, but what thou wilt.

37. And he cometh, and findeth them sleeping, and saith unto Peter, Simon, sleepest thou? couldest not thou watch one hour?

38. Watch ye and pray, lest ye enter into temptation. The spirit truly is ready, but the flesh is weak.

39. And again he went away, and prayed, and spake the same words.

40. And when he returned, he found them asleep again, (for their eyes were heavy,) neither wist they what to answer him.

41. And he cometh the third time,

and saith unto them, Sleep on now, and take your rest: it is enough, the hour is come; behold, the Son of man is betrayed into the hands of sinners.

42. Rise up, let us go; lo, he that betrayeth me is at hand.

The Gospel According to St. Luke

The author of this gospel was named Lucanus. The name "Luke" is an abbreviation. He was a Gentile and a physician, probably a Syrian of Antioch. He was very close to St. Paul, being with him in both his Roman imprisonments. Scholars are convinced that the gospel was written between 60 and 70 A.D. The gospel was written for the whole world, both Jew and Gentile. Throughout it seeks to show Jesus as the Saviour of all mankind and his life as part of the history of the Roman Empire. This is the most complete of the four gospels, the author making use of all the material he could find about Jesus and his teachings.

CHAPTER 4

16. And he came to Nazareth, where he had been brought up: and, as his custom was, he went into the synagogue on the sabbath day, and stood up for to read.

17. And there was delivered unto him the book of the prophet Esaias. And when he had opened the book, he found the place where it was written,

18. The Spirit of the Lord is upon me, because he hath anointed me to preach the gospel to the poor; he hath sent me to heal the brokenhearted, to preach deliverance to the captives, and recovering of sight to the blind, to set at liberty them that are bruised.

19. To preach the acceptable year of the Lord.

20. And he closed the book, and he gave it again to the minister, and sat down. And the eyes of all them that were in the synagogue were fastened on him.

21. And he began to say unto them, This day is this scripture fulfilled in your ears.

22. And all bare him witness, and wondered at the gracious words which proceeded out of his mouth. And they said, Is not this Joseph's son?

23. And he said unto them, Ye will surely say unto me this proverb, Physician, heal thyself: whatsoever we have heard done in Capernaum, do also here in thy country.

24. And he said, Verily I say unto you, No prophet is accepted in his own country.

25. But I tell you of a truth, many widows were in Israel in the days of Elias, when the heaven was shut up three years and six months, when great famine was throughout all the land;

26. But unto none of them was Elias sent, save unto Sarepta, a city of Sidon, unto a woman that was a widow.

27. And many lepers were in Israel in the time of Eliseus the prophet; and none of them was cleansed, saving Naaman the Syrian.

28. And all they in the synagogue, when they heard these things, were filled with wrath,

29. And rose up, and thrust him out of the city, and led him unto the brow of the hill whereon their city was built, that they might cast him down headlong.

30. But he passing through the midst of them went his way,

31. And came down to Capernaum, a city of Galilee, and taught them on the sabbath days.

32. And they were astonished at his doctrine: for his word was with power.

CHAPTER 6

27. But I say unto you which hear, Love your enemies, do good to them which hate you,

28. Bless them that curse you, and pray for them which despitefully use you.

29. And unto him that smiteth thee on the one cheek offer also the other; and him that taketh away thy cloke forbid not to take thy coat also.

30. Give to every man that asketh of thee; and of him that taketh away thy goods ask them not again.

31. And as ye would that men should do to you, do ye also to them likewise.

32. For if ye love them which love you, what thank have ye? for sinners also love those that love them.

33. And if ye do good to them which do good to you, what thank have ye? for sinners also do even the same.

34. And if ye lend to them of whom ye hope to receive, what thank have ye? for sinners also lend to sinners, to receive as much again.

35. But love ye your enemies, and do good, and lend, hoping for nothing again; and your reward shall be great, and ye shall be the children of the Highest: for he is kind unto the unthankful and to the evil.

36. Be ye therefore merciful, as your Father also is merciful.

37. Judge not, and ye shall not be judged: condemn not, and ye shall not be condemned: forgive, and ye shall be forgiven:

38. Give, and it shall be given unto you; good measure, pressed down, and shaken together, and running over, shall men give into your bosom. For with the same measure that ye mete withal it shall be measured to you again.

39. And he spake a parable unto them, Can the blind lead the blind? shall they not both fall into the ditch?

40. The disciple is not above his master: but every one that is perfect shall be as his master.

41. And why beholdest thou the mote that is in thy brother's eye, but perceivest not the beam that is in thine own eye?

42. Either how canst thou say to thy brother, Brother, let me pull out the mote that is in thine eye, when thou thyself beholdest not the beam that is in thine own eye? Thou hypocrite, cast out first the beam out of thine own eye, and then shalt thou see clearly to pull out the mote that is in thy brother's eye.

43. For a good tree bringeth not forth corrupt fruit; neither doth a corrupt tree bring forth good fruit.

44. For every tree is known by his own fruit. For of thorns men do not gather figs, nor of a bramble bush gather they grapes.

45. A good man out of the good treasure of his heart bringeth forth that which is good; and an evil man out of the evil treasure of his heart bringeth forth that which is evil: for of the abundance of the heart his mouth speaketh.

46. And why call ye me, Lord, Lord, and do not the things which I say?

47. Whosoever cometh to me, and heareth my sayings, and doeth them, I will shew you to whom he is like:

48. He is like a man which built an house, and digged deep, and laid the foundation on a rock: and when the flood arose, the stream beat vehemently upon that house, and could not shake it: for it was founded upon a rock.

49. But he that heareth, and doeth not, is like a man that without a foundation built an house upon the earth; against which the stream did beat vehemently, and immediately it fell; and the ruin of that house was great.

Chapter 11

1. And it came to pass, that, as he was praying in a certain place, when he ceased, one of his disciples said unto him, Lord, teach us to pray, as John also taught his disciples.

2. And he said unto them, When ye pray, say, Our Father which art in heaven, Hallowed be thy name. Thy kingdom come. Thy will be done, as in heaven, so in earth.

3. Give us day by day our daily bread.

4. And forgive us our sins; for we also forgive every one that is indebted to us. And lead us not into temptation; but deliver us from evil.

5. And he said unto them, Which of you shall have a friend, and shall go unto him at midnight, and say unto him, Friend, lend me three loaves;

6. For a friend of mine in his journey is come to me, and I have nothing to set before him?

7. And he from within shall answer and say, Trouble me not: the door is now shut, and my children are with me in bed; I cannot rise and give thee.

8. I say unto you, Though he will not rise and give him, because he is his friend, yet because of his importunity he will rise and give him as many as he needeth.

9. And I say unto you, Ask, and it shall be given you; seek, and ye shall find; knock, and it shall be opened unto you.

10. For every one that asketh receiveth; and he that seeketh findeth; and to him that knocketh it shall be opened.

11. If a son shall ask bread of any of you that is a father, will he give him a stone? or if he ask a fish, will he for a fish give him a serpent?

12. Or if he shall ask an egg, will he offer him a scorpion?

13. If ye then, being evil, know how to give good gifts unto your children: how much more shall your heavenly Father give the Holy Spirit to them that ask him?

Chapter 12

1. In the mean time, when there were gathered together an innumerable multitude of people, insomuch that they trode one upon another, he began to say unto his disciples first of all, Beware ye of the leaven of the Pharisees, which is hypocrisy.

2. For there is nothing covered, that shall not be revealed; neither hid, that shall not be known.

3. Therefore whatsoever ye have spoken in darkness shall be heard in the light; and that which ye have spoken in the ear in closets shall be proclaimed upon the house tops.

4. And I say unto you my friends, Be not afraid of them that kill the body, and after that have no more that they can do.

5. But I will forewarn you whom ye shall fear: Fear him, which after he hath killed hath power to cast into hell; yea, I say unto you, Fear him.

6. Are not five sparrows sold for two farthings, and not one of them is forgotten before God?

7. But even the very hairs of your head are all numbered. Fear not therefore: ye are of more value than many sparrows.

8. Also I say unto you, Whosoever shall confess me before men, him shall the Son of man also confess before the angels of God:

9. But he that denieth me before men shall be denied before the angels of God.

10. And whosoever shall speak a word against the Son of man, it shall be forgiven him: but unto him that blasphemeth against the Holy Ghost it shall not be forgiven.

11. And when they bring you unto the synagogues, and unto magistrates,

and powers, take ye no thought how or what thing ye shall answer, or what ye shall say:

12. For the Holy Ghost shall teach you in the same hour what ye ought to say.

13. And one of the company said unto him, Master, speak to my brother, that he divide the inheritance with me.

14. And he said unto him, Man, who made me a judge or a divider over you?

15. And he said unto them, Take heed, and beware of covetousness: for a man's life consisteth not in the abundance of the things which he possesseth.

16. And he spake a parable unto them, saying, The ground of a certain rich man brought forth plentifully:

17. And he thought within himself, saying, What shall I do, because I have no room where to bestow my fruits?

18. And he said, This will I do: I will pull down my barns, and build greater; and there will I bestow all my fruits and my goods.

19. And I will say to my soul, Soul, thou hast much goods laid up for many years; take thine ease, eat, drink, and be merry.

20. But God said unto him, Thou fool, this night thy soul shall be required of thee: then whose shall those things be, which thou hast provided?

21. So is he that layeth up treasure for himself, and is not rich toward God.

22. And he said unto his disciples, Therefore I say unto you, Take no thought for your life, what ye shall eat; neither for the body, what ye shall put on.

23. The life is more than meat, and the body is more than raiment.

24. Consider the ravens: for they neither sow nor reap; which neither have storehouse nor barn; and God feedeth them: how much more are ye better than the fowls?

25. And which of you with taking thought can add to his stature one cubit?

26. If ye then be not able to do that thing which is least, why take ye thought for the rest?

27. Consider the lilies how they grow: they toil not, they spin not; and yet I say unto you, that Solomon in all his glory was not arrayed like one of these.

28. If then God so clothe the grass, which is to day in the field, and to morrow is cast into the oven; how much more will he clothe you, O ye of little faith?

29. And seek not ye what ye shall eat, or what ye shall drink, neither be ye of doubtful mind.

30. For all these things do the nations of the world seek after: and your Father knoweth that ye have need of these things.

31. But rather seek ye the kingdom of God; and all these things shall be added unto you.

32. Fear not, little flock; for it is your Father's good pleasure to give you the kingdom.

33. Sell that ye have, and give alms; provide yourselves bags which wax not old, a treasure in the heavens that faileth not, where no thief approacheth, neither moth corrupteth.

34. For where your treasure is, there will your heart be also.

35. Let your loins be girded about, and your lights burning;

36. And ye yourselves like unto men that wait for their lord, when he will return from the wedding; that when he cometh and knocketh, they may open unto him immediately.

37. Blessed are those servants, whom the lord when he cometh shall find watching: verily I say unto you, that he shall gird himself, and make them to sit down to meat, and will come forth and serve them.

38. And if he shall come in the second watch, or come in the third watch, and find them so, blessed are those servants.

39. And this know, that if the goodman of the house had known what hour the thief would come, he would have watched, and not have suffered his house to be broken through.

40. Be ye therefore ready also: for the Son of man cometh at an hour when ye think not.

CHAPTER 13

18. Then said he, Unto what is the kingdom of God like? and whereunto shall I resemble it?

19. It is like a grain of mustard seed, which a man took, and cast into his garden; and it grew, and waxed a great tree; and the fowls of the air lodged in the branches of it.

20. And again he said, Whereunto shall I liken the kingdom of God?

21. It is like leaven, which a woman took and hid in three measures of meal, till the whole was leavened.

22. And he went through the cities and villages, teaching, and journeying toward Jerusalem.

23. Then said one unto him, Lord, are there few that be saved? And he said unto them,

24. Strive to enter in at the strait gate: for many, I say unto you, will seek to enter in, and shall not be able.

25. When once the master of the house is risen up, and hath shut to the door, and ye begin to stand without, and to knock at the door saying, Lord, Lord, open unto us; and he shall answer and say unto you, I know you not whence ye are:

26. Then shall ye begin to say, We have eaten and drunk in thy presence, and thou hast taught in our streets.

27. But he shall say, I tell you, I know you not whence ye are; depart from me, all ye workers of iniquity.

28. There shall be weeping and gnashing of teeth, when ye shall see Abraham, and Isaac, and Jacob, and all the prophets, in the kingdom of God, and you yourselves thrust out.

29. And they shall come from the east, and from the west, and from the north, and from the south, and shall sit down in the kingdom of God.

30. And, behold, there are last which shall be first, and there are first which shall be last.

31. The same day there came certain of the Pharisees, saying unto him, Get thee out, and depart hence: for Herod will kill thee.

32. And he said unto them, Go ye, and tell that fox, Behold, I cast out devils, and I do cures to day and to morrow, and the third day I shall be perfected.

33. Nevertheless I must walk to day, and to morrow, and the day following: for it cannot be that a prophet perish out of Jerusalem.

34. O Jerusalem, Jerusalem, which killest the prophets, and stonest them that are sent unto thee; how often would I have gathered thy children together, as a hen doth gather her brood under her wings, and ye would not!

35. Behold, your house is left unto you desolate: and verily I say unto you, Ye shall not see me, until the time come when ye shall say, Blessed is he that cometh in the name of the Lord.

CHAPTER 14

3. And Jesus answering spake unto the lawyers and Pharisees, saying, Is it lawful to heal on the sabbath day?

4. And they held their peace. And he took him, and healed him, and let him go;

5. And answered them, saying, Which of you shall have an ass or an

ox fallen into a pit, and will not straightway pull him out on the sabbath day?

6. And they could not answer him again to these things.

7. And he put forth a parable to those which were bidden, when he marked how they chose out the chief rooms; saying unto them,

8. When thou art bidden of any man to a wedding, sit not down in the highest room; lest a more honourable man than thou be bidden of him;

9. And he that bade thee and him come and say to thee, Give this man place; and thou begin with shame to take the lowest room.

10. But when thou art bidden, go and sit down in the lowest room; that when he that bade thee cometh, he may say unto thee, Friend, go up higher: then shalt thou have worship in the presence of them that sit at meat with thee.

11. For whosoever exalteth himself shall be abased; and he that humbleth himself shall be exalted.

12. Then said he also to him that bade him, When thou makest a dinner or a supper, call not thy friends, nor thy brethren, neither thy kinsmen, nor thy rich neighbours; lest they also bid thee again, and a recompence be made thee.

13. But when thou makest a feast, call the poor, the maimed, the lame, the blind:

14. And thou shalt be blessed; for they cannot recompense thee: for thou shalt be recompensed at the resurrection of the just.

Chapter 15

3. And he spake this parable unto them, saying,

4. What man of you, having an hundred sheep, if he lose one of them, doth not leave the ninety and nine in the wilderness, and go after that which is lost, until he find it?

5. And when he hath found it, he layeth it on his shoulders, rejoicing.

6. And when he cometh home, he calleth together his friends and neighbours, saying unto them, Rejoice with me; for I have found my sheep which was lost.

7. I say unto you, that likewise joy shall be in heaven over one sinner that repenteth, more than over ninety and nine just persons, which need no repentance.

Chapter 17

3. Take heed to yourselves: If thy brother trespass against thee, rebuke him; and if he repent, forgive him.

4. And if he trespass against thee seven times in a day, and seven times in a day turn again to thee, saying, I repent; thou shalt forgive him.

5. And the apostles said unto the Lord, Increase our faith.

6. And the Lord said, If ye had faith as a grain of mustard seed, ye might say unto this sycamine tree, Be thou plucked up by the root, and be thou planted in the sea; and it should obey you.

7. But which of you, having a servant plowing or feeding cattle, will say unto him by and by, when he is come from the field, Go and sit down to meat?

8. And will not rather say unto him, Make ready wherewith I may sup, and gird thyself, and serve me, till I have eaten and drunken; and afterward thou shalt eat and drink?

9. Doth he thank that servant because he did the things that were commanded him? I trow not.

10. So likewise ye, when ye shall have done all those things which are commanded you, say, We are unprofitable servants: we have done that which was our duty to do.

11. And it came to pass, as he went to Jerusalem, that he passed through the midst of Samaria and Galilee.

12. And as he entered into a certain village, there met him ten men that were lepers, which stood afar off:

13. And they lifted up their voices, and said, Jesus, Master, have mercy on us.

14. And when he saw them, he said unto them, Go shew yourselves unto the priests. And it came to pass, that, as they went, they were cleansed.

15. And one of them, when he saw that he was healed, turned back, and with a loud voice glorified God,

16. And fell down on his face at his feet, giving him thanks: and he was a Samaritan.

17. And Jesus answering said, Were there not ten cleansed? But where are the nine?

18. There are not found that returned to give glory to God, save this stranger.

19. And he said unto him, Arise, go thy way: thy faith hath made thee whole.

20. And when he was demanded of the Pharisees, when the kingdom of God should come, he answered them and said, The kingdom of God cometh not with observation:

21. Neither shall they say, Lo here! or, lo there! for, behold, the kingdom of God is within you.

Chapter 18

9. And he spake this parable unto certain which trusted in themselves that they were righteous, and despised others:

10. Two men went up into the temple to pray; the one a Pharisee, and the other a publican.

11. The Pharisee stood and prayed thus with himself, God, I thank thee, that I am not as other men are, extortioners, unjust, adulterers, or even as this publican.

12. I fast twice in the week, I give tithes of all that I possess.

13. And the publican, standing afar off, would not lift up so much as his eyes unto heaven, but smote upon his breast, saying, God be merciful to me a sinner.

14. I tell you, this man went down to his house justified rather than the other: for every one that exalteth himself shall be abased; and he that humbleth himself shall be exalted.

15. And they brought unto him also infants, that he would touch them: but when his disciples saw it, they rebuked them.

16. But Jesus called them unto him, and said, Suffer little children to come unto me, and forbid them not: for of such is the kingdom of God.

17. Verily I say unto you, Whosoever shall not receive the kingdom of God as a little child shall in no wise enter therein.

18. And a certain ruler asked him, saying, Good Master, what shall I do to inherit eternal life?

19. And Jesus said unto him, Why callest thou me good? none is good, save one, that is, God.

20. Thou knowest the commandments, Do not commit adultery, Do not kill, Do not steal, Do not bear false witness, Honour thy father and thy mother.

21. And he said, All these have I kept from my youth up.

22. Now when Jesus heard these things, he said unto him, Yet lackest thou one thing: sell all that thou hast, and distribute unto the poor, and thou shalt have treasure in heaven: and come, follow me.

23. And when he heard this, he was very sorrowful: for he was very rich.

24. And when Jesus saw that he was very sorrowful, he said, How hardly shall they that have riches enter into the kingdom of God!

25. For it is easier for a camel to go through a needle's eye, than for a rich man to enter into the kingdom of God.

26. And they that heard it said, Who then can be saved?

27. And he said, The things which are impossible with men are possible with God.

28. Then Peter said, Lo, we have left all, and followed thee.

29. And he said unto them, Verily I say unto you, There is no man that hath left house, or parents, or brethren, or wife, or children, for the kingdom of God's sake,

30. Who shall not receive manifold more in this present time, and in the world to come life everlasting.

The Gospel According to St. John

This gospel has been called "the most influential book in all literature." Scholars are agreed that it was written by St. John, the apostle of Jesus. Its date cannot be set accurately, but is probably between 80 and 95 A.D., and is said to have been written at the request of John's fellow disciples and the elders at Ephesus.

John was interested in writing for adult Christians to confirm their faith that "Jesus is the Christ, the Son of God." Being a philosopher, the author associates Jesus with Greek philosophy through the doctrine of the "Logos." Thus he omits much that is found in the other gospels, but adds many discourses of Jesus and discussions of philosophic points. Further, the Jesus of this gospel is a mystical individual of deep spiritual understanding.

This is the most original of the gospels, John speaking of things which he had seen and known, adding incidents with which other writers were not familiar.

CHAPTER 5

17. But Jesus answered them, My Father worketh hitherto, and I work.

18. Therefore the Jews sought the more to kill him, because he not only had broken the sabbath, but said also that God was his Father, making himself equal with God.

19. Then answered Jesus and said unto them, Verily, verily, I say unto you, The Son can do nothing of himself, but what he seeth the Father do: for what things soever he doeth, these also doeth the Son likewise.

20. For the Father loveth the Son, and sheweth him all things that himself doeth: and he will shew him greater works than these, that ye may marvel.

21. For as the Father raiseth up the dead, and quickeneth them; even so the Son quickeneth whom he will.

22. For the Father judgeth no man, but hath committed all judgment unto the Son:

23. That all men should honour the Son, even as they honour the Father. He that honoureth not the Son honoureth not the Father which hath sent him.

24. Verily, verily, I say unto you, He that heareth my word, and believeth on him that sent me, hath everlasting life, and shall not come into condemnation; but is passed from death unto life.

25. Verily, verily, I say unto you, The hour is coming, and now is, when the dead shall hear the voice of the Son of God: and they that hear shall live.

26. For as the Father hath life in himself; so hath he given to the Son to have life in himself;

27. And hath given him authority to execute judgment also, because he is the Son of man.

28. Marvel not at this: for the hour is coming, in the which all that are in the graves shall hear his voice,

29. And shall come forth; they that have done good, unto the resurrection of life; and they that have done evil, unto the resurrection of damnation.

30. I can of mine own self do noth-

ing: as I hear, I judge: and my judgment is just; because I seek not mine own will, but the will of the Father which hath sent me.

31. If I bear witness of myself, my witness is not true.

32. There is another that beareth witness of me; and I know that the witness which he witnesseth of me is true.

33. Ye sent unto John, and he bare witness unto the truth.

34. But I receive not testimony from man: but these things I say, that ye might be saved.

35. He was a burning and a shining light: and ye were willing for a season to rejoice in his light.

36. But I have greater witness than that of John: for the works which the Father hath given me to finish, the same works that I do, bear witness of me, that the Father hath sent me.

37. And the Father himself, which hath sent me, hath borne witness of me. Ye have neither heard his voice at any time, nor seen his shape.

38. And ye have not his word abiding in you: for whom he hath sent, him ye believe not.

39. Search the scriptures; for in them ye think ye have eternal life: and they are they which testify of me.

40. And ye will not come to me, that ye might have life.

41. I receive not honour from men.

42. But I know you, that ye have not the love of God in you.

43. I am come in my Father's name, and ye receive me not: if another shall come in his own name, him ye will receive.

44. How can ye believe, which receive honour one of another, and seek not the honour that cometh from God only?

45. Do not think that I will accuse you to the Father: there is one that accuseth you, even Moses, in whom ye trust.

46. For had ye believed Moses, ye would have believed me: for he wrote of me.

47. But if ye believe not his writings, how shall ye believe my words?

Chapter 7

14. Now about the midst of the feast Jesus went up into the temple, and taught.

15. And the Jews marvelled, saying, How knoweth this man letters, having never learned?

16. Jesus answered them, and said, My doctrine is not mine, but his that sent me.

17. If any man will do his will, he shall know of the doctrine, whether it be of God, or whether I speak of myself.

18. He that speaketh of himself seeketh his own glory: but he that seeketh his glory that sent him, the same is true, and no unrighteousness is in him.

19. Did not Moses give you the law, and yet none of you keepeth the law? Why go ye about to kill me?

20. The people answered and said, Thou hast a devil: who goeth about to kill thee?

21. Jesus answered and said unto them, I have done one work, and ye all marvel.

22. Moses therefore gave unto you circumcision; (not because it is of Moses, but of the fathers;) and ye on the sabbath day circumcise a man.

23. If a man on the sabbath day receive circumcision, that the law of Moses should not be broken; are ye angry at me, because I have made a man every whit whole on the sabbath day?

24. Judge not according to the appearance, but judge righteous judgment.

25. Then said some of them of Jerusalem, Is not this he, whom they seek to kill?

26. But, lo, he speaketh boldly, and

they say nothing unto him. Do the rulers know indeed that this is the very Christ?

27. Howbeit we know this man whence he is: but when Christ cometh, no man knoweth whence he is.

28. Then cried Jesus in the temple as he taught, saying, Ye both know me, and ye know whence I am: and I am not come of myself, but he that sent me is true, whom ye know not.

29. But I know him: for I am from him, and he hath sent me.

30. Then they sought to take him: but no man laid hands on him, because his hour was not yet come.

31. And many of the people believed on him, and said, When Christ cometh, will he do more miracles than these which this man hath done?

CHAPTER 14

1. Let not your heart be troubled: ye believe in God, believe also in me.

2. In my Father's house are many mansions: if it were not so, I would have told you. I go to prepare a place for you.

3. And if I go and prepare a place for you, I will come again, and receive you unto myself; that where I am, there ye may be also.

4. And whither I go ye know, and the way ye know.

5. Thomas saith unto him, Lord, we know not whither thou goest; and how can we know the way?

6. Jesus saith unto him, I am the way, the truth, and the life: no man cometh unto the Father, but by me.

7. If ye had known me, ye should have known my Father also: and from henceforth ye know him, and have seen him.

8. Philip saith unto him, Lord, shew us the Father, and it sufficeth us.

9. Jesus saith unto him, Have I been so long time with you, and yet hast thou not known me, Philip? he that hath seen me hath seen the Father; and how sayest thou then, Shew us the Father?

10. Believest thou not that I am in the Father, and the Father in me? the words that I speak unto you I speak not of myself: but the Father that dwelleth in me, he doeth the works.

11. Believe me that I am in the Father, and the Father in me: or else believe me for the very works' sake.

12. Verily, verily, I say unto you, He that believeth on me, the works that I do shall he do also; and greater works than these shall he do; because I go unto my Father.

13. And whatsoever ye shall ask in my name, that will I do, that the Father may be glorified in the Son.

14. If ye shall ask any thing in my name, I will do it.

15. If ye love me, keep my commandments.

16. And I will pray the Father, and he shall give you another Comforter, that he may abide with you for ever;

17. Even the Spirit of truth; whom the world cannot receive, because it seeth him not, neither knoweth him: but ye know him; for he dwelleth with you, and shall be in you.

18. I will not leave you comfortless: I will come to you.

19. Yet a little while, and the world seeth me no more; but ye see me: because I live, ye shall live also.

20. At that day ye shall know that I am in my Father, and ye in me, and I in you.

21. He that hath my commandments, and keepeth them, he it is that loveth me: and he that loveth me shall be loved of my Father, and I will love him, and will manifest myself to him.

22. Judas saith unto him, not Iscariot, Lord, how is it that thou wilt manifest thyself unto us, and not unto the world?

23. Jesus answered and said unto him, If a man love me, he will keep

my words: and my Father will love him, and we will come unto him, and make our abode with him.

24. He that loveth me not keepeth not my sayings: and the word which ye hear is not mine, but the Father's which sent me.

25. These things have I spoken unto you, being yet present with you.

26. But the Comforter, which is the Holy Ghost, whom the Father will send in my name, he shall teach you all things, and bring all things to your remembrance, whatsoever I have said unto you.

27. Peace I leave with you, my peace I give unto you: not as the world giveth, give I unto you. Let not your heart be troubled, neither let it be afraid.

28. Ye have heard how I said unto you, I go away, and come again unto you. If ye loved me, ye would rejoice, because I said, I go unto the Father: for my Father is greater than I.

29. And now I have told you before it come to pass, that, when it is come to pass, ye might believe.

30. Hereafter I will not talk much with you: for the prince of this world cometh, and hath nothing in me.

31. But that the world may know that I love the Father; and as the Father gave me commandment, even so I do. Arise, let us go hence.

Chapter 15

1. I am the true vine, and my Father is the husbandman.

2. Every branch in me that beareth not fruit he taketh away: and every branch that beareth fruit, he purgeth it, that it may bring forth more fruit.

3. Now ye are clean through the word which I have spoken unto you.

4. Abide in me, and I in you. As the branch cannot bear fruit of itself, except it abide in the vine; no more can ye, except ye abide in me.

5. I am the vine, ye are the branches: He that abideth in me, and I in him, the same bringeth forth much fruit: for without me ye can do nothing.

6. If a man abide not in me, he is cast forth as a branch, and is withered; and men gather them, and cast them into the fire, and they are burned.

7. If ye abide in me, and my words abide in you, ye shall ask what ye will, and it shall be done unto you.

8. Herein is my Father glorified, that ye bear much fruit; so shall ye be my disciples.

9. As the Father hath loved me, so have I loved you: continue ye in my love.

10. If ye keep my commandments, ye shall abide in my love; even as I have kept my Father's commandments, and abide in his love.

11. These things have I spoken unto you, that my joy might remain in you, and that your joy might be full.

12. This is my commandment, That ye love one another, as I have loved you.

13. Greater love hath no man than this, that a man lay down his life for his friends.

14. Ye are my friends, if ye do whatsoever I command you.

15. Henceforth I call you not servants; for the servant knoweth not what his lord doeth: but I have called you friends; for all things that I have heard of my Father I have made known unto you.

16. Ye have not chosen me, but I have chosen you, and ordained you, that ye should go and bring forth fruit, and that your fruit should remain: that whatsoever ye shall ask of the Father in my name, he may give it you.

17. These things I command you, that ye love one another.

18. If the world hate you, ye know that it hated me before it hated you.

19. If ye were of the world, the world would love his own: but be-

cause ye are not of the world, but I have chosen you out of the world, therefore the world hateth you.

20. Remember the word that I said unto you, The servant is not greater than his lord. If they have persecuted me, they will also persecute you; if they have kept my saying, they will keep yours also.

21. But all these things will they do unto you for my name's sake, because they know not him that sent me.

22. If I had not come and spoken unto them, they had not had sin: but now they have no cloke for their sin.

23. He that hateth me hateth my Father also.

24. If I had not done among them the works which none other man did, they had not had sin: but now have they both seen and hated both me and my Father.

25. But this cometh to pass, that the word might be fulfilled that is written in their law, They hated me without a cause.

26. But when the Comforter is come, whom I will send unto you from the Father, even the Spirit of truth, which proceedeth from the Father, he shall testify of me:

27. And ye also shall bear witness, because ye have been with me from the beginning.

The Acts of the Apostles

This book, usually referred to as "Acts," was written by Lucanus or "Luke," the author of the third gospel, sometime between 62 and 70 A.D. The material in the first part of the book is based on research made by Luke as he talked with others. However, the latter parts of the book are written from first-hand experiences since he was a close friend and companion of St. Paul, the chief actor in these passages. Since Luke considered this book as a continuation of his other book, the Gospel, he gave it no title.

The one that it usually carries was given it much later because it tells of the activities of the followers of Jesus after his death and of the early growth of the Christian church.

Chapter 2

14. But Peter, standing up with the eleven, lifted up his voice, and said unto them, Ye men of Judæa, and all ye that dwell at Jerusalem, be this known unto you, and hearken to my words:

15. For these are not drunken, as ye suppose, seeing it is but the third hour of the day.

16. But this is that which was spoken by the prophet Joel;

17. And it shall come to pass in the last days, saith God, I will pour out of my Spirit upon all flesh: and your sons and your daughters shall prophesy, and your young men shall see visions, and your old men shall dream dreams:

18. And on my servants and on my handmaidens I will pour out in those days of my Spirit; and they shall prophesy:

19. And I will shew wonders in heaven above, and signs in the earth beneath; blood, and fire, and vapour of smoke:

20. The sun shall be turned into darkness, and the moon into blood, before that great and notable day of the Lord come:

21. And it shall come to pass, that whosoever shall call on the name of the Lord shall be saved.

22. Ye men of Israel, hear these words; Jesus of Nazareth, a man approved of God among you by miracles and wonders and signs, which God did by him in the midst of you, as ye yourselves also know:

23. Him, being delivered by the determinate counsel and foreknowledge of God, ye have taken, and by wicked hands have crucified and slain:

24. Whom God hath raised up, having loosed the pains of death: because it was not possible that he should be holden of it.

25. For David speaketh concerning him, I foresaw the LORD always before my face, for he is on my right hand, that I should not be moved:

26. Therefore did my heart rejoice, and my tongue was glad; moreover also my flesh shall rest in hope:

27. Because thou wilt not leave my soul in hell, neither wilt thou suffer thine Holy One to see corruption.

28. Thou hast made known to me the ways of life; thou shalt make me full of joy with thy countenance.

29. Men and brethren, let me freely speak unto you of the patriarch David, that he is both dead and buried, and his sepulchre is with us unto this day.

30. Therefore being a prophet, and knowing that God had sworn with an oath to him, that of the fruit of his loins, according to the flesh, he would raise up Christ to sit on his throne;

31. He seeing this before spake of the resurrection of Christ, that his soul was not left in hell, neither his flesh did see corruption.

32. This Jesus hath God raised up, whereof we all are witnesses.

33. Therefore being by the right hand of God exalted, and having received of the Father the promise of the Holy Ghost, he hath shed forth this, which ye now see and hear.

34. For David is not ascended into the heavens: but he saith himself, The LORD said unto my Lord, Sit thou on my right hand,

35. Until I make thy foes thy footstool.

36. Therefore let all the house of Israel know assuredly, that God hath made that same Jesus, whom ye have crucified, both Lord and Christ.

37. Now when they heard this, they were pricked in their heart, and said unto Peter and to the rest of the apostles, Men and brethren, what shall we do?

38. Then Peter said unto them, Repent, and be baptized every one of you in the name of Jesus Christ for the remission of sins, and ye shall receive the gift of the Holy Ghost.

39. For the promise is unto you, and to your children, and to all that are afar off, even as many as the Lord our God shall call.

40. And with many other words did he testify and exhort, saying, Save yourselves from this untoward generation.

CHAPTER 4

23. And being let go, they went to their own company, and reported all that the chief priests and elders had said unto them.

24. And when they heard that, they lifted up their voice to God with one accord, and said, Lord, thou art God, which hast made heaven, and earth, and the sea, and all that in them is:

25. Who by the mouth of thy servant David hast said, Why did the heathen rage, and the people imagine vain things?

26. The kings of the earth stood up, and the rulers were gathered together against the Lord, and against his Christ.

27. For of a truth against thy holy child Jesus, whom thou hast anointed, both Herod, and Pontius Pilate, with the Gentiles, and the people of Israel, were gathered together,

28. For to do whatsoever thy hand and thy counsel determined before to be done.

29. And now, Lord, behold their threatenings: and grant unto thy servants, that with all boldness they may speak thy word,

30. By stretching forth thine hand to heal; and that signs and wonders may be done by the name of thy holy child Jesus.

CHAPTER 5

29. Then Peter and the other apostles answered and said, We ought to obey God rather than men.

30. The God of our fathers raised up Jesus, whom ye slew and hanged on a tree.

31. Him hath God exalted with his right hand to be a Prince and a Saviour, for to give repentance to Israel, and forgiveness of sins.

32. And we are his witnesses of these things; and so is also the Holy Ghost, whom God hath given to them that obey him.

CHAPTER 8

20. But Peter said unto him, Thy money perish with thee, because thou hast thought that the gift of God may be purchased with money.

21. Thou hast neither part nor lot in this matter: for thy heart is not right in the sight of God.

22. Repent therefore of this thy wickedness, and pray God, if perhaps the thought of thine heart may be forgiven thee.

CHAPTER 10

25. And as Peter was coming in, Cornelius met him, and fell down at his feet, and worshipped him.

26. But Peter took him up, saying, Stand up; I myself also am a man.

27. And as he talked with him, he went in, and found many that were come together.

28. And he said unto them, Ye know how that it is an unlawful thing for a man that is a Jew to keep company, or come unto one of another nation; but God hath shewed me that I should not call any man common or unclean.

29. Therefore came I unto you without gainsaying, as soon as I was sent for: I ask therefore for what intent ye have sent for me?

30. And Cornelius said, Four days ago I was fasting until this hour; and at the ninth hour I prayed in my house, and, behold, a man stood before me in bright clothing,

31. And said, Cornelius, thy prayer is heard, and thine alms are had in remembrance in the sight of God.

32. Send therefore to Joppa, and call hither Simon, whose surname is Peter; he is lodged in the house of one Simon a tanner by the sea side: who, when he cometh, shall speak unto thee.

33. Immediately therefore I sent to thee; and thou hast well done that thou art come. Now therefore are we all here present before God, to hear all things that are commanded thee of God.

34. Then Peter opened his mouth, and said, Of a truth I perceive that God is no respecter of persons:

35. But in every nation he that feareth him, and worketh righteousness, is accepted with him.

36. The word which God sent unto the children of Israel, preaching peace by Jesus Christ: (he is Lord of all:)

37. That word, I say, ye know, which was published throughout all Judæa, and began from Galilee, after the baptism which John preached;

38. How God anointed Jesus of Nazareth with the Holy Ghost and with power: who went about doing good, and healing all that were oppressed of the devil; for God was with him.

39. And we are witnesses of all things which he did both in the land of the Jews, and in Jerusalem; whom they slew and hanged on a tree:

40. Him God raised up the third day, and shewed him openly;

41. Not to all the people, but unto witnesses chosen before of God, even to us, who did eat and drink with him after he rose from the dead.

42. And he commanded us to preach unto the people, and to testify

that it is he which was ordained of God to be the Judge of quick and dead.

43. To him give all the prophets witness, that through his name whosoever believeth in him shall receive remission of sins.

CHAPTER 17

22. Then Paul stood in the midst of Mars' hill, and said, Ye men of Athens, I perceive that in all things ye are too superstitious.

23. For as I passed by, and beheld your devotions, I found an altar with this inscription, TO THE UNKNOWN GOD. Whom therefore ye ignorantly worship, him declare I unto you.

24. God that made the world and all things therein, seeing that he is Lord of heaven and earth, dwelleth not in temples made with hands;

25. Neither is worshipped with men's hands, as though he needed any thing, seeing he giveth to all life, and breath, and all things;

26. And hath made of one blood all nations of men for to dwell on all the face of the earth, and hath determined the times before appointed, and the bounds of their habitation;

27. That they should seek the Lord, if haply they might feel after him, and find him, though he be not far from every one of us:

28. For in him we live, and move, and have our being; as certain also of your own poets have said, For we are also his offspring.

29. Forasmuch then as we are the offspring of God, we ought not to think that the Godhead is like unto gold, or silver, or stone, graven by art and man's device.

30. And the times of this ignorance God winked at; but now commandeth all men every where to repent:

31. Because he hath appointed a day, in the which he will judge the world in righteousness by that man

whom he hath ordained; whereof he hath given assurance unto all men, in that he hath raised him from the dead.

The Epistle to the Romans

This book is a letter that St. Paul wrote to the Greek-speaking Roman church, which was made up of both Jews and Gentiles, many of whom had migrated to Rome while others were natives of that city. It was written in Corinth, in the Greek language, during the spring of 58 A.D. Paul recognized the importance of the church in Rome, the capital of a great empire, and devoted much thought to this letter in order to impress upon the members their responsibility for the spread of Christianity. He was anxious that this church become the source of missionaries who would spread the gospel.

CHAPTER 1

13. Now I would not have you ignorant, brethren, that oftentimes I purposed to come unto you, (but was let hitherto,) that I might have some fruit among you also, even as among other Gentiles.

14. I am debtor both to the Greeks, and to the Barbarians; both to the wise, and to the unwise.

15. So, as much as in me is, I am ready to preach the gospel to you that are at Rome also.

16. For I am not ashamed of the gospel of Christ: for it is the power of God unto salvation to every one that believeth; to the Jew first, and also to the Greek.

17. For therein is the righteousness of God revealed from faith to faith: as it is written, The just shall live by faith.

18. For the wrath of God is revealed from heaven against all ungodliness and unrighteousness of men,

who hold the truth in unrighteousness;

19. Because that which may be known of God is manifest in them; for God hath shewed it unto them.

20. For the invisible things of him from the creation of the world are clearly seen, being understood by the things that are made, even his eternal power and Godhead; so that they are without excuse:

21. Because that, when they knew God, they glorified him not as God, neither were thankful; but became vain in their imaginations, and their foolish heart was darkened.

22. Professing themselves to be wise, they became fools,

23. And changed the glory of the uncorruptible God into an image made like to corruptible man, and to birds, and fourfooted beasts, and creeping things.

CHAPTER 2

1. Therefore thou art inexcusable, O man, whosoever thou art that judgest: for wherein thou judgest another, thou condemnest thyself; for thou that judgest doest the same things.

2. But we are sure that the judgment of God is according to truth against them which commit such things.

3. And thinkest thou this, O man, that judgest them which do such things, and doest the same, that thou shalt escape the judgment of God?

4. Or despisest thou the riches of his goodness and forbearance and longsuffering; not knowing that the goodness of God leadeth thee to repentance?

5. But after thy hardness and impenitent heart treasurest up unto thyself wrath against the day of wrath and revelation of the righteous judgment of God;

6. Who will render to every man according to his deeds:

7. To them who by patient continuance in well doing seek for glory and honour and immortality, eternal life:

8. But unto them that are contentious, and do not obey the truth, but obey unrighteousness, indignation and wrath,

9. Tribulation and anguish, upon every soul of man that doeth evil, of the Jew first, and also of the Gentile;

10. But glory, honour, and peace, to every man that worketh good, to the Jew first, and also to the Gentile:

11. For there is no respect of persons with God.

12. For as many as have sinned without law shall also perish without law: and as many as have sinned in the law shall be judged by the law;

13. (For not the hearers of the law are just before God, but the doers of the law shall be justified.

14. For when the Gentiles, which have not the law, do by nature the things contained in the law, these, having not the law, are a law unto themselves:

15. Which shew the work of the law written in their hearts, their conscience also bearing witness, and their thoughts the mean while accusing or else excusing one another;)

16. In the day when God shall judge the secrets of men by Jesus Christ according to my gospel.

CHAPTER 5

1. Therefore being justified by faith, we have peace with God through our Lord Jesus Christ:

2. By whom also we have access by faith into this grace wherein we stand, and rejoice in hope of the glory of God.

3. And not only so, but we glory in tribulations also: knowing that tribulation worketh patience;

4. And patience, experience; and experience, hope:

5. And hope maketh not ashamed;

because the love of God is shed abroad in our hearts by the Holy Ghost which is given unto us.

6. For when we were yet without strength, in due time Christ died for the ungodly.

Chapter 6

12. Let not sin therefore reign in your mortal body, that ye should obey it in the lusts thereof.

13. Neither yield ye your members as instruments of unrighteousness unto sin: but yield yourselves unto God, as those that are alive from the dead, and your members as instruments of righteousness unto God.

14. For sin shall not have dominion over you: for ye are not under the law, but under grace.

15. What then? shall we sin, because we are not under the law, but under grace? God forbid.

16. Know ye not, that to whom ye yield yourselves servants to obey, his servants ye are to whom ye obey; whether of sin unto death, or of obedience unto righteousness?

17. But God be thanked, that ye were the servants of sin, but ye have obeyed from the heart that form of doctrine which was delivered you.

18. Being then made free from sin, ye became the servants of righteousness.

19. I speak after the manner of men because of the infirmity of your flesh: for as ye have yielded your members servants to uncleanness and to iniquity unto iniquity; even so now yield your members servants to righteousness unto holiness.

20. For when ye were the servants of sin, ye were free from righteousness.

21. What fruit had ye then in those things whereof ye are now ashamed? for the end of those things is death.

22. But now being made free from sin, and become servants to God, ye

have your fruit unto holiness, and the end everlasting life.

23. For the wages of sin is death; but the gift of God is eternal life through Jesus Christ our Lord.

Chapter 8

1. There is therefore now no condemnation to them which are in Christ Jesus, who walk not after the flesh, but after the Spirit.

2. For the law of the Spirit of life in Christ Jesus hath made me free from the law of sin and death.

3. For what the law could not do, in that it was weak through the flesh, God sending his own Son in the likeness of sinful flesh, and for sin, condemned sin in the flesh:

4. That the righteousness of the law might be fulfilled in us, who walk not after the flesh, but after the Spirit.

5. For they that are after the flesh do mind the things of the flesh; but they that are after the Spirit the things of the Spirit.

6. For to be carnally minded is death; but to be spiritually minded is life and peace.

7. Because the carnal mind is enmity against God: for it is not subject to the law of God, neither indeed can be.

8. So then they that are in the flesh cannot please God.

9. But ye are not in the flesh, but in the Spirit, if so be that the Spirit of God dwell in you. Now if any man have not the Spirit of Christ, he is none of his.

10. And if Christ be in you, the body is dead because of sin; but the Spirit is life because of righteousness.

11. But if the Spirit of him that raised up Jesus from the dead dwell in you, he that raised up Christ from the dead shall also quicken your mortal bodies by his Spirit that dwelleth in you.

12. Therefore, brethren, we are

debtors, not to the flesh, to live after the flesh.

13. For if ye live after the flesh, ye shall die: but if ye through the Spirit do mortify the deeds of the body, ye shall live.

14. For as many as are led by the Spirit of God, they are the sons of God.

15. For ye have not received the spirit of bondage again to fear; but ye have received the Spirit of adoption, whereby we cry, Abba, Father.

16. The Spirit itself beareth witness with our spirit, that we are the children of God:

17. And if children, then heirs; heirs of God, and joint-heirs with Christ; if so be that we suffer with him, that we may be also glorified together.

18. For I reckon that the sufferings of this present time are not worthy to be compared with the glory which shall be revealed in us.

19. For the earnest expectation of the creature waiteth for the manifestation of the sons of God.

20. For the creature was made subject to vanity, not willingly, but by reason of him who hath subjected the same in hope,

21. Because the creature itself also shall be delivered from the bondage of corruption into the glorious liberty of the children of God.

22. For we know that the whole creation groaneth and travaileth in pain together until now.

23. And not only they, but ourselves also, which have the firstfruits of the Spirit, even we ourselves groan within ourselves, waiting for the adoption, to wit, the redemption of our body.

24. For we are saved by hope: but hope that is seen is not hope: for what a man seeth, why doth he yet hope for?

25. But if we hope for that we see not, then do we with patience wait for it.

26. Likewise the Spirit also helpeth our infirmities: for we know not what we should pray for as we ought: but the Spirit itself maketh intercession for us with groanings which cannot be uttered.

27. And he that searcheth the hearts knoweth what is the mind of the Spirit, because he maketh intercession for the saints according to the will of God.

28. And we know that all things work together for good to them that love God, to them who are the called according to his purpose.

29. For whom he did foreknow, he also did predestinate to be conformed to the image of his Son, that he might be the firstborn among many brethren.

30. Moreover whom he did predestinate, them he also called: and whom he called, them he also justified: and whom he justified, them he also glorified.

31. What shall we then say to these things? If God be for us, who can be against us?

32. He that spared not his own Son, but delivered him up for us all, how shall he not with him also freely give us all things?

33. Who shall lay any thing to the charge of God's elect? It is God that justifieth.

34. Who is he that condemneth? It is Christ that died, yea rather, that is risen again, who is even at the right hand of God, who also maketh intercession for us.

35. Who shall separate us from the love of Christ? shall tribulation, or distress, or persecution, or famine, or nakedness, or peril, or sword?

36. As it is written, For thy sake we are killed all the day long; we are accounted as sheep for the slaughter.

37. Nay, in all these things we are more than conquerors through him that loved us.

38. For I am persuaded, that neither death, nor life, nor angels, nor principalities, nor powers, nor things present, nor things to come,

39. Nor height, nor depth, nor any other creature, shall be able to separate us from the love of God, which is in Christ Jesus our Lord.

CHAPTER 10

10. For with the heart man believeth unto righteousness; and with the mouth confession is made unto salvation.

11. For the scripture saith, Whosoever believeth on him shall not be ashamed.

12. For there is no difference between the Jew and the Greek: for the same Lord over all is rich unto all that call upon him.

13. For whosoever shall call upon the name of the Lord shall be saved.

14. How then shall they call on him in whom they have not believed? and how shall they believe in him of whom they have not heard? and how shall they hear without a preacher?

15. And how shall they preach, except they be sent? as it is written, How beautiful are the feet of them that preach the gospel of peace, and bring glad tidings of good things!

CHAPTER 12

1. I beseech you therefore, brethren, by the mercies of God, that ye present your bodies a living sacrifice, holy, acceptable unto God, which is your reasonable service.

2. And be not conformed to this world: but be ye transformed by the renewing of your mind, that ye may prove what is that good, and acceptable, and perfect, will of God.

3. For I say, through the grace given unto you, to every man that is among you, not to think of himself more highly than he ought to think;

but to think soberly, according as God hath dealt to every man the measure of faith.

4. For as we have many members in one body, and all members have not the same office:

5. So we, being many, are one body in Christ, and every one members one of another.

6. Having then gifts differing according to the grace that is given to us, whether prophecy, let us prophesy according to the proportion of faith;

7. Or ministry, let us wait on our ministering: or he that teacheth, on teaching;

8. Or he that exhorteth, on exhortation: he that giveth, let him do it with simplicity; he that ruleth, with diligence; he that sheweth mercy, with cheerfulness.

9. Let love be without dissimulation. Abhor that which is evil; cleave to that which is good.

10. Be kindly affectioned one to another with brotherly love; in honour preferring one another;

11. Not slothful in business; fervent in spirit; serving the Lord;

12. Rejoicing in hope; patient in tribulation; continuing instant in prayer;

13. Distributing to the necessity of saints; given to hospitality.

14. Bless them which persecute you: bless, and curse not.

15. Rejoice with them that do rejoice, and weep with them that weep.

16. Be of the same mind one toward another. Mind not high things, but condescend to men of low estate. Be not wise in your own conceits.

17. Recompense to no man evil for evil. Provide things honest in the sight of all men.

18. If it be possible, as much as lieth in you, live peaceably with all men.

19. Dearly beloved, avenge not yourselves, but rather give place unto wrath: for it is written, Vengeance

is mine; I will repay, saith the Lord.

20. Therefore if thine enemy hunger, feed him; if he thirst, give him drink: for in so doing thou shalt heap coals of fire on his head.

21. Be not overcome of evil, but overcome evil with good.

Chapter 13

7. Render therefore to all their dues: tribute to whom tribute is due; custom to whom custom; fear to whom fear; honour to whom honour.

8. Owe no man any thing, but to love one another: for he that loveth another hath fulfilled the law.

9. For this, Thou shalt not commit adultery, Thou shalt not kill, Thou shalt not steal, Thou shalt not bear false witness, Thou shalt not covet; and if there be any other commandment, it is briefly comprehended in this saying, namely, Thou shalt love thy neighbour as thyself.

10. Love worketh no ill to his neighbour: therefore love is the fulfilling of the law.

Chapter 14

1. Him that is weak in the faith receive ye, but not to doubtful disputations.

2. For one believeth that he may eat all things: another, who is weak, eateth herbs.

3. Let not him that eateth despise him that eateth not; and let not him which eateth not judge him that eateth: for God hath received him.

4. Who art thou that judgest another man's servant? to his own master he standeth or falleth. Yea, he shall be holden up: for God is able to make him stand.

5. One man esteemeth one day above another: another esteemeth every day alike. Let every man be fully persuaded in his own mind.

6. He that regardeth the day, regardeth it unto the Lord; and he that regardeth not the day, to the Lord he doth not regard it. He that eateth, eateth to the Lord, for he giveth God thanks; and he that eateth not, to the Lord he eateth not, and giveth God thanks.

7. For none of us liveth to himself, and no man dieth to himself.

8. For whether we live, we live unto the Lord; and whether we die, we die unto the Lord: whether we live therefore, or die, we are the Lord's.

9. For to this end Christ both died, and rose, and revived, that he might be Lord both of the dead and living.

10. But why dost thou judge thy brother? or why dost thou set at nought thy brother? for we shall all stand before the judgment seat of Christ.

11. For it is written, As I live, saith the Lord, every knee shall bow to me, and every tongue shall confess to God.

12. So then every one of us shall give account of himself to God.

13. Let us not therefore judge one another any more: but judge this rather, that no man put a stumblingblock or an occasion to fall in his brother's way.

14. I know, and am persuaded by the Lord Jesus, that there is nothing unclean of itself: but to him that esteemeth any thing to be unclean, to him it is unclean.

15. But if thy brother be grieved with thy meat, now walkest thou not charitably. Destroy not him with thy meat, for whom Christ died.

16. Let not then your good be evil spoken of:

17. For the kingdom of God is not meat and drink; but righteousness, and peace, and joy in the Holy Ghost.

18. For he that in these things serveth Christ is acceptable to God, and approved of men.

19. Let us therefore follow after the things which make for peace, and things wherewith one may edify another.

20. For meat destroy not the work of God. All things indeed are pure; but it is evil for that man who eateth with offence.

21. It is good neither to eat flesh, nor to drink wine, nor any thing whereby thy brother stumbleth, or is offended, or is made weak.

22. Hast thou faith? have it to thyself before God. Happy is he that condemneth not himself in that thing which he alloweth.

23. And he that doubteth is damned if he eat, because he eateth not of faith: for whatsoever is not of faith is sin.

CHAPTER 15

1. We then that are strong ought to bear the infirmities of the weak, and not to please ourselves.

2. Let every one of us please his neighbour for his good to edification.

3. For even Christ pleased not himself; but, as it is written, The reproaches of them that reproached thee fell on me.

4. For whatsoever things were written aforetime were written for our learning, that we through patience and comfort of the scriptures might have hope.

5. Now the God of patience and consolation grant you to be likeminded one toward another according to Christ Jesus:

6. That ye may with one mind and one mouth glorify God, even the Father of our Lord Jesus Christ.

7. Wherefore receive ye one another, as Christ also received us to the glory of God.

8. Now I say that Jesus Christ was a minister of the circumcision for the truth of God, to confirm the promises made unto the fathers:

9. And that the Gentiles might glorify God for his mercy; as it is written, For this cause I will confess to thee among the Gentiles, and sing unto thy name.

10. And again he saith, Rejoice, ye Gentiles, with his people.

11. And again, Praise the Lord, all ye Gentiles; and laud him, all ye people.

12. And again, Esaias saith, There shall be a root of Jesse, and he that shall rise to reign over the Gentiles; in him shall the Gentiles trust.

13. Now the God of hope fill you with all joy and peace in believing, that ye may abound in hope, through the power of the Holy Ghost.

The First Epistle to the Corinthians

This letter was written to the church at Corinth by St. Paul just before Pentecost in 57 A.D. At this time Paul was in Ephesus, stopping there on his third great missionary journey. This church was located in the center of a city that had become the commercial and political capital of Greece. As such, the city was rank with licentiousness. This had been creeping into the church, and Paul wrote seeking to admonish the members for their sin and divisions and to restore them to the purity of the Christian life.

CHAPTER 1

26. For ye see your calling, brethren, how that not many wise men after the flesh, not many mighty, not many noble, are called:

27. But God hath chosen the foolish things of the world to confound the wise; and God hath chosen the weak things of the world to confound the things which are mighty;

28. And base things of the world, and things which are despised, hath God chosen, yea, and things which are not, to bring to nought things that are:

29. That no flesh should glory in his presence.

30. But of him are ye in Christ Jesus, who of God is made unto us wisdom, and righteousness, and sanctification, and redemption:

31. That, according as it is written, He that glorieth, let him glory in the Lord.

CHAPTER 2

9. But as it is written, Eye hath not seen, nor ear heard, neither have entered into the heart of man, the things which God hath prepared for them that love him.

10. But God hath revealed them unto us by his Spirit: for the Spirit searcheth all things, yea, the deep things of God.

11. For what man knoweth the things of a man, save the spirit of man which is in him? even so the things of God knoweth no man, but the Spirit of God.

12. Now we have received, not the spirit of the world, but the spirit which is of God; that we might know the things that are freely given to us of God.

13. Which things also we speak, not in the words which man's wisdom teacheth, but which the Holy Ghost teacheth; comparing spiritual things with spiritual.

14. But the natural man receiveth not the things of the Spirit of God: for they are foolishness unto him: neither can he know them, because they are spiritually discerned.

15. But he that is spiritual judgeth all things, yet he himself is judged of no man.

16. For who hath known the mind of the Lord, that he may instruct him? But we have the mind of Christ.

CHAPTER 3

9. For we are labourers together with God: ye are God's husbandry, ye are God's building.

10. According to the grace of God which is given unto me, as a wise masterbuilder, I have laid the foundation, and another buildeth thereon. But let every man take heed how he buildeth thereupon.

11. For other foundation can no man lay than that is laid, which is Jesus Christ.

12. Now if any man build upon this foundation gold, silver, precious stones, wood, hay, stubble;

13. Every man's work shall be made manifest: for the day shall declare it, because it shall be revealed by fire; and the fire shall try every man's work of what sort it is.

14. If any man's work abide which he hath built thereupon, he shall receive a reward.

15. If any man's work shall be burned, he shall suffer loss: but he himself shall be saved; yet so as by fire.

16. Know ye not that ye are the temple of God, and that the Spirit of God dwelleth in you?

17. If any man defile the temple of God, him shall God destroy; for the temple of God is holy, which temple ye are.

18. Let no man deceive himself. If any man among you seemeth to be wise in this world, let him become a fool, that he may be wise.

19. For the wisdom of this world is foolishness with God. For it is written, He taketh the wise in their own craftiness.

20. And again, The Lord knoweth the thoughts of the wise, that they are vain.

21. Therefore let no man glory in men. For all things are yours;

22. Whether Paul, or Apollos, or Cephas, or the world, or life, or death, or things present, or things to come; all are yours;

23. And ye are Christ's; and Christ is God's.

CHAPTER 6

9. Know ye not that the unrighteous shall not inherit the kingdom of God? Be not deceived: neither fornicators, nor idolaters, nor adulterers, nor effeminate, nor abusers of themselves with mankind,

10. Nor thieves, nor covetous, nor drunkards, nor revilers, nor extortioners, shall inherit the kingdom of God.

11. And such were some of you: but ye are washed, but ye are sanctified, but ye are justified in the name of the Lord Jesus, and by the Spirit of our God.

12. All things are lawful unto me, but all things are not expedient: all things are lawful for me, but I will not be brought under the power of any.

13. Meats for the belly, and the belly for meats: but God shall destroy both it and them. Now the body is not for fornication, but for the Lord; and the Lord for the body.

14. And God hath both raised up the Lord, and will also raise up us by his own power.

15. Know ye not that your bodies are the members of Christ? shall I then take the members of Christ, and make them the members of an harlot? God forbid.

16. What? know ye not that he which is joined to an harlot is one body? for two, saith he, shall be one flesh.

17. But he that is joined unto the Lord is one spirit.

18. Flee fornication. Every sin that a man doeth is without the body; but he that committeth fornication sinneth against his own body.

19. What? know ye not that your body is the temple of the Holy Ghost which is in you, which ye have of God, and ye are not your own?

20. For ye are bought with a price: therefore glorify God in your body, and in your spirit, which are God's.

CHAPTER 8

1. Now as touching things offered unto idols, we know that we all have knowledge. Knowledge puffeth up, but charity edifieth.

2. And if any man think that he knoweth any thing, he knoweth nothing yet as he ought to know.

3. But if any man love God, the same is known of him.

4. As concerning therefore the eating of those things that are offered in sacrifice unto idols, we know that an idol is nothing in the world, and that there is none other God but one.

5. For though there be that are called gods, whether in heaven or in earth, (as there be gods many, and lords many,)

6. But to us there is but one God, the Father, of whom are all things, and we in him; and one Lord Jesus Christ, by whom are all things, and we by him.

7. Howbeit there is not in every man that knowledge: for some with conscience of the idol unto this hour eat it as a thing offered unto an idol; and their conscience being weak is defiled.

8. But meat commendeth us not to God: for neither, if we eat, are we the better; neither, if we eat not, are we the worse.

9. But take heed lest by any means this liberty of yours become a stumblingblock to them that are weak.

10. For if any man see thee which hast knowledge sit at meat in the idol's temple, shall not the conscience of him which is weak be emboldened to eat those things which are offered to idols;

11. And through thy knowledge shall the weak brother perish, for whom Christ died?

12. But when ye sin so against the

brethren, and wound their weak conscience, ye sin against Christ.

13. Wherefore, if meat make my brother to offend, I will eat no flesh while the world standeth, lest I make my brother to offend.

Chapter 9

19. For though I be free from all men, yet have I made myself servant unto all, that I might gain the more.

20. And unto the Jews I became as a Jew, that I might gain the Jews; to them that are under the law, as under the law, that I might gain them that are under the law;

21. To them that are without law, as without law, (being not without law to God, but under the law to Christ,) that I might gain them that are without law;

22. To the weak became I as weak, that I might gain the weak: I am made all things to all men, that I might by all means save some.

23. And this I do for the gospel's sake, that I might be partaker thereof with you.

24. Know ye not that they which run in a race run all, but one receiveth the prize? So run, that ye may obtain.

25. And every man that striveth for the mastery is temperate in all things. Now they do it to obtain a corruptible crown; but we an incorruptible.

26. I therefore so run, not as uncertainly; so fight I, not as one that beateth the air:

27. But I keep under my body, and bring it into subjection: lest that by any means, when I have preached to others, I myself should be a castaway.

Chapter 10

12. Wherefore let him that thinketh he standeth take heed lest he fall.

13. There hath no temptation taken you but such as is common to man: but God is faithful, who will not suffer you to be tempted above that ye are able; but will with the temptation also make a way to escape, that ye may be able to bear it,

14. Wherefore, my dearly beloved, flee from idolatry.

15. I speak as to wise men; judge ye what I say.

16. The cup of blessing which we bless, is it not the communion of the blood of Christ? The bread which we break, is it not the communion of the body of Christ?

17. For we being many are one bread, and one body: for we are all partakers of that one bread.

18. Behold Israel after the flesh: are not they which eat of the sacrifices partakers of the altar?

19. What say I then? that the idol is any thing, or that which is offered in sacrifice to idols is any thing?

20. But I say, that the things which the Gentiles sacrifice, they sacrifice to devils, and not to God: and I would not that ye should have fellowship with devils.

21. Ye cannot drink the cup of the Lord, and the cup of devils: ye cannot be partakers of the Lord's table, and of the table of devils.

22. Do we provoke the Lord to jealousy? are we stronger than he?

23. All things are lawful for me, but all things are not expedient: all things are lawful for me, but all things edify not.

24. Let no man seek his own, but every man another's wealth.

25. Whatsoever is sold in the shambles, that eat, asking no question for conscience sake:

26. For the earth is the Lord's, and the fulness thereof.

27. If any of them that believe not bid you to a feast, and ye be disposed to go; whatsoever is set before you, eat, asking no question for conscience sake.

28. But if any man say unto you, This is offered in sacrifice unto idols, eat not for his sake that shewed it, and for conscience sake: for the earth is the Lord's, and the fulness thereof:

29. Conscience, I say, not thine own, but of the other; for why is my liberty judged of another man's conscience?

30. For if I by grace be a partaker, why am I evil spoken of for that for which I give thanks?

31. Whether therefore ye eat, or drink, or whatsoever ye do, do all to the glory of God.

32. Give none offence, neither to the Jews, nor to the Gentiles, nor to the church of God:

33. Even as I please all men in all things, not seeking mine own profit, but the profit of many, that they may be saved.

Chapter 12

1. Now concerning spiritual gifts, brethren, I would not have you ignorant.

2. Ye know that ye were Gentiles, carried away unto these dumb idols, even as ye were led.

3. Wherefore I give you to understand, that no man speaking by the Spirit of God calleth Jesus accursed: and that no man can say that Jesus is the Lord, but by the Holy Ghost.

4. Now there are diversities of gifts, but the same Spirit.

5. And there are differences of administrations, but the same Lord.

6. And there are diversities of operations, but it is the same God which worketh all in all.

7. But the manifestation of the Spirit is given to every man to profit withal.

8. For to one is given by the Spirit the word of wisdom; to another the word of knowledge by the same Spirit;

9. To another faith by the same Spirit; to another the gifts of healing by the same Spirit;

10. To another the working of miracles; to another prophecy; to another discerning of spirits; to another divers kinds of tongues; to another the interpretation of tongues:

11. But all these worketh that one and the selfsame Spirit, dividing to every man severally as he will.

12. For as the body is one, and hath many members, and all the members of that one body, being many, are one body: so also is Christ.

Chapter 13

1. Though I speak with the tongues of men and of angels, and have not charity, I am become as sounding brass, or a tinkling cymbal.

2. And though I have the gift of prophecy, and understand all mysteries, and all knowledge; and though I have all faith, so that I could remove mountains, and have not charity, I am nothing.

3. And though I bestow all my goods to feed the poor, and though I give my body to be burned, and have not charity, it profiteth me nothing.

4. Charity suffereth long, and is kind; charity envieth not; charity vaunteth not itself, is not puffed up,

5. Doth not behave itself unseemly, seeketh not her own, is not easily provoked, thinketh no evil;

6. Rejoiceth not in iniquity, but rejoiceth in the truth;

7. Beareth all things, believeth all things, hopeth all things, endureth all things.

8. Charity never faileth: but whether there be prophecies, they shall fail; whether there be tongues, they shall cease; whether there be knowledge, it shall vanish away.

9. For we know in part, and we prophesy in part.

10. But when that which is perfect is come, then that which is in part shall be done away.

11. When I was a child, I spake as

a child, I understood as a child, I thought as a child: but when I became a man, I put away childish things.

12. For now we see through a glass, darkly; but then face to face: now I know in part; but then shall I know even as also I am known.

13. And now abideth faith, hope, charity, these three; but the greatest of these is charity.

CHAPTER 15

33. Be not deceived: evil communications corrupt good manners.

34. Awake to righteousness, and sin not; for some have not the knowledge of God: I speak this to your shame.

35. But some man will say, How are the dead raised up? and with what body do they come?

36. Thou fool, that which thou sowest is not quickened, except it die:

37. And that which thou sowest, thou sowest not that body that shall be, but bare grain, it may chance of wheat, or of some other grain:

38. But God giveth it a body as it hath pleased him, and to every seed his own body.

39. All flesh is not the same flesh: but there is one kind of flesh of men, another flesh of beasts, another of fishes, and another of birds.

40. There are also celestial bodies, and bodies terrestrial: but the glory of the celestial is one, and the glory of the terrestrial is another.

41. There is one glory of the sun, and another glory of the moon, and another glory of the stars: for one star differeth from another star in glory.

42. So also is the resurrection of the dead. It is sown in corruption; it is raised in incorruption:

43. It is sown in dishonour; it is raised in glory: it is sown in weakness; it is raised in power:

44. It is sown a natural body; it is raised a spiritual body. There is a natural body, and there is a spiritual body.

45. And so it is written, The first man Adam was made a living soul; the last Adam was made a quickening spirit.

46. Howbeit that was not first which is spiritual, but that which is natural; and afterward that which is spiritual.

47. The first man is of the earth, earthy: the second man is the Lord from heaven.

48. As is the earthy, such are they also that are earthy: and as is the heavenly, such are they also that are heavenly.

49. And as we have borne the image of the earthy, we shall also bear the image of the heavenly.

50. Now this I say, brethren, that flesh and blood cannot inherit the kingdom of God; neither doth corruption inherit incorruption.

51. Behold, I shew you a mystery; We shall not all sleep, but we shall all be changed,

52. In a moment, in the twinkling of an eye, at the last trump: for the trumpet shall sound, and the dead shall be raised incorruptible, and we shall be changed.

53. For this corruptible must put on incorruption, and this mortal must put on immortality.

54. So when this corruptible shall have put on incorruption, and this mortal shall have put on immortality, then shall be brought to pass the saying that is written, Death is swallowed up in victory.

55. O death, where is thy sting? O grave, where is thy victory?

56. The sting of death is sin; and the strength of sin is the law.

57. But thanks be to God, which giveth us the victory through our Lord Jesus Christ.

58. Therefore, my beloved brethren, be ye stedfast, unmoveable, always

abounding in the work of the Lord, forasmuch as ye know that your labour is not in vain in the Lord.

The Second Epistle to the Corinthians

St. Paul's first letter to the church at Corinth was not well received. The Judaizing party was working against the authority of Paul and used every means possible to dispute his teachings and break up the Corinthian church. So in the autumn of 57 A.D., Paul wrote another letter to the church in which he sought to justify himself and his work. For this reason, the letter is largely autobiographical, telling not only of the life of the author but also of his personal feelings and beliefs. The letter is largely a defense of Paul's acts and an exposition of his faith.

CHAPTER 1

3. Blessed be God, even the Father of our Lord Jesus Christ, the Father of mercies, and the God of all comfort;

4. Who comforteth us in all our tribulation, that we may be able to comfort them which are in any trouble, by the comfort wherewith we ourselves are comforted of God.

5. For as the sufferings of Christ abound in us, so our consolation also aboundeth by Christ.

6. And whether we be afflicted, it is for your consolation and salvation, which is effectual in the enduring of the same sufferings which we also suffer: or whether we be comforted, it is for your consolation and salvation.

7. And our hope of you is stedfast, knowing, that as ye are partakers of the sufferings, so shall ye be also of the consolation.

8. For we would not, brethren, have you ignorant of our trouble which came to us in Asia, that we were pressed out of measure, above

strength, insomuch that we despaired even of life:

9. But we had the sentence of death in ourselves, that we should not trust in ourselves, but in God which raiseth the dead:

10. Who delivered us from so great a death, and doth deliver: in whom we trust that he will yet deliver us;

11. Ye also helping together by prayer for us, that for the gift bestowed upon us by the means of many persons thanks may be given by many on our behalf.

12. For our rejoicing is this, the testimony of our conscience, that in simplicity and godly sincerity, not with fleshly wisdom, but by the grace of God, we have had our conversation in the world, and more abundantly to you-ward.

13. For we write none other things unto you, than what ye read or acknowledge; and I trust ye shall acknowledge even to the end;

14. As also ye have acknowledged us in part, that we are your rejoicing, even as ye also are ours in the day of the Lord Jesus.

15. And in this confidence I was minded to come unto you before, that ye might have a second benefit;

16. And to pass by you into Macedonia, and to come again out of Macedonia unto you, and of you to be brought on my way toward Judæa.

17. When I therefore was thus minded, did I use lightness? or the things that I purpose, do I purpose according to the flesh, that with me there should be yea yea, and nay nay?

18. But as God is true, our word toward you was not yea and nay.

19. For the Son of God, Jesus Christ, who was preached among you by us, even by me and Silvanus and Timotheus, was not yea and nay, but in him was yea.

20. For all the promises of God in him are yea, and in him Amen, unto the glory of God by us.

21. Now he which stablisheth us with you in Christ, and hath anointed us, is God;

22. Who hath also sealed us, and given the earnest of the Spirit in our hearts.

23. Moreover I call God for a record upon my soul, that to spare you I came not as yet unto Corinth.

24. Not for that we have dominion over your faith, but are helpers of your joy: for by faith ye stand.

CHAPTER 9

6. But this I say, He which soweth sparingly shall reap also sparingly; and he which soweth bountifully shall reap also bountifully.

7. Every man according as he purposeth in his heart, so let him give; not grudgingly, or of necessity: for God loveth a cheerful giver.

8. And God is able to make all grace abound toward you; that ye, always having all sufficiency in all things, may abound to every good work:

9. (As it is written, He hath dispersed abroad; he hath given to the poor: his righteousness remaineth for ever.

10. Now he that ministereth seed to the sower both minister bread for your food, and multiply your seed sown, and increase the fruits of your righteousness;)

11. Being enriched in every thing to all bountifulness, which causeth through us thanksgiving to God.

12. For the administration of this service not only supplieth the want of the saints, but is abundant also by many thanksgivings unto God;

13. Whiles by the experiment of this ministration they glorify God for your professed subjection unto the gospel of Christ, and for your liberal distribution unto them, and unto all men;

14. And by their prayer for you, which long after you for the exceeding grace of God in you.

15. Thanks be unto God for his unspeakable gift.

CHAPTER 13

8. For we can do nothing against the truth, but for the truth.

9. For we are glad, when we are weak, and ye are strong: and this also we wish, even your perfection.

10. Therefore I write these things being absent, lest being present I should use sharpness, according to the power which the Lord hath given me to edification, and not to destruction.

11. Finally, brethren, farewell. Be perfect, be of good comfort, be of one mind, live in peace; and the God of love and peace shall be with you.

12. Greet one another with an holy kiss.

The Epistle to the Galatians

This epistle was probably written by St. Paul late in 57 A.D. It is not certain whether he wrote only to the churches in Galatia proper or to those in the whole Roman province of Galatia, a much larger territory. But, in either case, the Galatian churches were highly fickle. While Paul was with them, they had accepted his preaching with enthusiasm. But later the arguments of the Judaizers that they had to obey the Jewish laws in order to be good Christians nearly convinced them. In order to counter this teaching, Paul wrote this letter. In it he argues for his authority and seeks to show that Jesus had freed men from bondage to the ancient Mosaic laws. The letter is written hastily and with great emotion.

CHAPTER 3

7. Know ye therefore that they which are of faith, the same are the children of Abraham.

8. And the scripture, foreseeing that God would justify the heathen through faith, preached before the gospel unto Abraham, saying, In thee shall all nations be blessed.

9. So then they which be of faith are blessed with faithful Abraham.

10. For as many as are of the works of the law are under the curse: for it is written, Cursed is every one that continueth not in all things which are written in the book of the law to do them.

11. But that no man is justified by the law in the sight of God, it is evident: for, The just shall live by faith.

12. And the law is not of faith: but, The man that doeth them shall live in them.

13. Christ hath redeemed us from the curse of the law, being made a curse for us: for it is written, Cursed is every one that hangeth on a tree.

Chapter 5

13. For, brethren, ye have been called unto liberty; only use not liberty for an occasion to the flesh, but by love serve one another.

14. For all the law is fulfilled in one word, even in this; Thou shalt love thy neighbour as thyself.

15. But if ye bite and devour one another, take heed that ye be not consumed one of another.

16. This I say then, Walk in the Spirit, and ye shall not fulfil the lust of the flesh.

17. For the flesh lusteth against the Spirit, and the Spirit against the flesh: and these are contrary the one to the other: so that ye cannot do the things that ye would.

18. But if ye be led of the Spirit, ye are not under the law.

19. Now the works of the flesh are manifest, which are these; Adultery, fornication, uncleanness, lasciviousness,

20. Idolatry, witchcraft, hatred, variance, emulations, wrath, strife, seditions, heresies,

21. Envyings, murders, drunkenness, revellings, and such like: of the which I tell you before, as I have also told you in time past, that they which do such things shall not inherit the kingdom of God.

22. But the fruit of the Spirit is love, joy, peace, longsuffering, gentleness, goodness, faith,

23. Meekness, temperance: against such there is no law.

24. And they that are Christ's have crucified the flesh with the affections and lusts.

25. If we live in the Spirit, let us also walk in the Spirit.

26. Let us not be desirous of vain glory, provoking one another, envying one another.

Chapter 6

1. Brethren, if a man be overtaken in a fault, ye which are spiritual, restore such an one in the spirit of meekness; considering thyself, lest thou also be tempted.

2. Bear ye one another's burdens, and so fulfil the law of Christ.

3. For if a man think himself to be something, when he is nothing, he deceiveth himself.

4. But let every man prove his own work, and then shall he have rejoicing in himself alone, and not in another.

5. For every man shall bear his own burden.

6. Let him that is taught in the word communicate unto him that teacheth in all good things.

7. Be not deceived; God is not mocked: for whatsoever a man soweth, that shall he also reap.

8. For he that soweth to his flesh shall of the flesh reap corruption; but he that soweth to the Spirit shall of the Spirit reap life everlasting.

9. And let us not be weary in well

doing: for in due season we shall reap, if we faint not.

10. As we have therefore opportunity, let us do good unto all men, especially unto them who are of the household of faith.

The Epistle to the Ephesians

This was a circular letter which St. Paul sent to many of the churches. It was written while he was a prisoner in Rome, about the year 63 A.D. Here the emphasis is upon the catholicity of the church as the continuation of the spirit and energy of Jesus. This copy went to Ephesus, while other copies were sent to each of the churches in Asia.

CHAPTER 2

8. For by grace are ye saved through faith; and that not of yourselves: it is the gift of God:

9. Not of works, lest any man should boast.

10. For we are his workmanship, created in Christ Jesus unto good works, which God hath before ordained that we should walk in them.

11. Wherefore remember, that ye being in time past Gentiles in the flesh, who are called Uncircumcision by that which is called the Circumcision in the flesh made by hands;

12. That at that time ye were without Christ, being aliens from the commonwealth of Israel, and strangers from the covenants of promise, having no hope, and without God in the world:

13. But now in Christ Jesus ye who sometimes were far off are made nigh by the blood of Christ.

14. For he is our peace, who hath made both one, and hath broken down the middle wall of partition between us;

15. Having abolished in his flesh the enmity, even the law of commandments contained in ordinances; for to make in himself of twain one new man, so making peace;

16. And that he might reconcile both unto God in one body by the cross, having slain the enmity thereby:

17. And came and preached peace to you which were afar off, and to them that were nigh.

18. For through him we both have access by one Spirit unto the Father.

19. Now therefore ye are no more strangers and foreigners, but fellow-citizens with the saints, and of the household of God;

20. And are built upon the foundation of the apostles and prophets, Jesus Christ himself being the chief corner stone;

21. In whom all the building fitly framed together groweth unto an holy temple in the Lord:

22. In whom ye also are builded together for an habitation of God through the Spirit.

CHAPTER 4

1. I therefore, the prisoner of the Lord, beseech you that ye walk worthy of the vocation wherewith ye are called,

2. With all lowliness and meekness, with longsuffering, forbearing one another in love;

3. Endeavouring to keep the unity of the Spirit in the bond of peace.

4. There is one body, and one Spirit, even as ye are called in one hope of your calling;

5. One Lord, one faith, one baptism,

6. One God and Father of all, who is above all, and through all, and in you all.

7. But unto every one of us is given grace according to the measure of the gift of Christ.

8. Wherefore he saith, When he ascended up on high, he led captivity captive, and gave gifts unto men.

9. (Now that he ascended, what is

it but that he also descended first into the lower parts of the earth?

10. He that descended is the same also that ascended up far above all heavens, that he might fill all things.)

11. And he gave some, apostles; and some, prophets; and some, evangelists; and some, pastors and teachers;

12. For the perfecting of the saints, for the work of the ministry, for the edifying of the body of Christ:

13. Till we all come in the unity of the faith, and of the knowledge of the Son of God, unto a perfect man, unto the measure of the stature of the fulness of Christ:

14. That we henceforth be no more children, tossed to and fro, and carried about with every wind of doctrine, by the sleight of men, and cunning craftiness, whereby they lie in wait to deceive;

15. But speaking the truth in love, may grow up into him in all things, which is the head, even Christ:

16. From whom the whole body fitly joined together and compacted by that which every joint supplieth, according to the effectual working in the measure of every part, maketh increase of the body unto the edifying of itself in love.

17. This I say therefore, and testify in the Lord, that ye henceforth walk not as other Gentiles walk, in the vanity of their mind,

18. Having the understanding darkened, being alienated from the life of God through the ignorance that is in them, because of the blindness of their heart:

19. Who being past feeling have given themselves over unto lasciviousness, to work all uncleanness with greediness.

20. But ye have not so learned Christ;

21. If so be that ye have heard him, and have been taught by him, as the truth is in Jesus:

22. That ye put off concerning the former conversation the old man, which is corrupt according to the deceitful lusts;

23. And be renewed in the spirit of your mind;

24. And that ye put on the new man, which after God is created in righteousness and true holiness.

25. Wherefore putting away lying, speak every man truth with his neighbour: for we are members one of another.

26. Be ye angry, and sin not: let not the sun go down upon your wrath:

27. Neither give place to the devil.

28. Let him that stole steal no more: but rather let him labour, working with his hands the thing which is good, that he may have to give to him that needeth.

29. Let no corrupt communication proceed out of your mouth, but that which is good to the use of edifying, that it may minister grace unto the hearers.

30. And grieve not the holy Spirit of God, whereby ye are sealed unto the day of redemption.

31. Let all bitterness, and wrath, and anger, and clamour, and evil speaking, be put away from you, with all malice:

32. And be ye kind one to another, tenderhearted, forgiving one another, even as God for Christ's sake hath forgiven you.

CHAPTER 5

6. Let no man deceive you with vain words: for because of these things cometh the wrath of God upon the children of disobedience.

7. Be not ye therefore partakers with them.

8. For ye were sometimes darkness, but now are ye light in the Lord: walk as children of light:

9. (For the fruit of the Spirit is in

all goodness and righteousness and truth;)

10. Proving what is acceptable unto the Lord.

11. And have no fellowship with the unfruitful works of darkness, but rather reprove them.

12. For it is a shame even to speak of those things which are done of them in secret.

13. But all things that are reproved are made manifest by the light: for whatsoever doth make manifest is light.

14. Wherefore he saith, Awake thou that sleepest, and arise from the dead, and Christ shall give thee light.

15. See then that ye walk circumspectly, not as fools, but as wise,

16. Redeeming the time, because the days are evil.

17. Wherefore be ye not unwise, but understanding what the will of the Lord is.

18. And be not drunk with wine, wherein is excess; but be filled with the Spirit.

CHAPTER 6

1. Children, obey your parents in the Lord: for this is right.

2. Honour thy father and mother; which is the first commandment with promise;

3. That it may be well with thee, and thou mayest live long on the earth.

4. And, ye fathers, provoke not your children to wrath: but bring them up in the nurture and admonition of the Lord.

5. Servants, be obedient to them that are your masters according to the flesh, with fear and trembling, in singleness of your heart, as unto Christ;

6. Not with eyeservice, as menpleasers; but as the servants of Christ, doing the will of God from the heart;

7. With good will doing service, as to the Lord, and not to men:

8. Knowing that whatsoever good thing any man doeth, the same shall he receive of the Lord, whether he be bond or free.

9. And, ye masters, do the same things unto them, forbearing threatening: knowing that your Master also is in heaven; neither is there respect of persons with him.

10. Finally, my brethren, be strong in the Lord, and in the power of his might.

11. Put on the whole armour of God, that ye may be able to stand against the wiles of the devil.

12. For we wrestle not against flesh and blood, but against principalities, against powers, against the rulers of the darkness of this world, against spiritual wickedness in high places.

13. Wherefore take unto you the whole armour of God, that ye may be able to withstand in the evil day, and having done all, to stand.

14. Stand therefore, having your loins girt about with truth, and having on the breastplate of righteousness;

15. And your feet shod with the preparation of the gospel of peace;

16. Above all, taking the shield of faith, wherewith ye shall be able to quench all the fiery darts of the wicked.

17. And take the helmet of salvation, and the sword of the Spirit, which is the word of God:

18. Praying always with all prayer and supplication in the Spirit, and watching thereunto with all perseverance and supplication for all saints.

Philippians

The church in Philippi was the one closest to the heart of St. Paul. He had visited it several times and had received pecuniary help from it on more than one occasion. Among its members were many of his closest friends. Hence this letter is a sponta-

neous outflowing of his affection and regard for the church and his many close friends there. These friends were especially remembered at this time because they had sent him some help as he waited in a Roman prison in about 63 A.D. This is the only letter of Paul's in which there is no expression of rebuke or disappointment. Its constant theme is cheerful.

CHAPTER 1

3. I thank my God upon every remembrance of you,

4. Always in every prayer of mine for you all making request with joy,

5. For your fellowship in the gospel from the first day until now;

6. Being confident of this very thing, that he which hath begun a good work in you will perform it until the day of Jesus Christ:

7. Even as it is meet for me to think this of you all, because I have you in my heart; inasmuch as both in my bonds, and in the defence and confirmation of the gospel, ye all are partakers of my grace.

8. For God is my record, how greatly I long after you all in the bowels of Jesus Christ.

9. And this I pray, that your love may abound yet more and more in knowledge and in all judgment;

10. That ye may approve things that are excellent; that ye may be sincere and without offence till the day of Christ;

11. Being filled with the fruits of righteousness, which are by Jesus Christ, unto the glory and praise of God.

12. But I would ye should understand, brethren, that the things which happened unto me have fallen out rather unto the furtherance of the gospel;

13. So that my bonds in Christ are manifest in all the palace, and in all other places;

14. And many of the brethren in the Lord, waxing confident by my bonds, are much more bold to speak the word without fear.

15. Some indeed preach Christ even of envy and strife; and some also of good will:

16. The one preach Christ of contention, not sincerely, supposing to add affliction to my bonds:

17. But the other of love, knowing that I am set for the defence of the gospel.

18. What then? notwithstanding, every way, whether in pretence, or in truth, Christ is preached; and I therein do rejoice, yea, and will rejoice.

19. For I know that this shall turn to my salvation through your prayer, and the supply of the Spirit of Jesus Christ,

20. According to my earnest expectation and my hope, that in nothing I shall be ashamed, but that with all boldness, as always, so now also Christ shall be magnified in my body, whether it be by life, or by death.

21. For to me to live is Christ, and to die is gain.

22. But if I live in the flesh, this is the fruit of my labour: yet what I shall choose I wot not.

23. For I am in a strait betwixt two, having a desire to depart, and to be with Christ; which is far better:

24. Nevertheless to abide in the flesh is more needful for you.

25. And having this confidence, I know that I shall abide and continue with you all for your furtherance and joy of faith;

26. That your rejoicing may be more abundant in Jesus Christ for me by my coming to you again.

27. Only let your conversation be as it becometh the gospel of Christ: that whether I come and see you, or else be absent, I may hear of your affairs, that ye stand fast in one spirit,

with one mind striving together for the faith of the gospel;

28. And in nothing terrified by your adversaries: which is to them an evident token of perdition, but to you of salvation, and that of God.

29. For unto you it is given in the behalf of Christ, not only to believe on him, but also to suffer for his sake.

CHAPTER 2

2. Fulfil ye my joy, that ye be likeminded, having the same love, being of one accord, of one mind.

3. Let nothing be done through strife or vainglory; but in lowliness of mind let each esteem other better than themselves.

4. Look not every man on his own things, but every man also on the things of others.

5. Let this mind be in you, which was also in Christ Jesus:

6. Who, being in the form of God, thought it not robbery to be equal with God:

7. But made himself of no reputation, and took upon him the form of a servant, and was made in the likeness of men:

8. And being found in fashion as a man, he humbled himself, and became obedient unto death, even the death of the cross.

9. Wherefore God also hath highly exalted him, and given him a name which is above every name:

10. That at the name of Jesus every knee should bow, of things in heaven, and things in earth, and things under the earth;

11. And that every tongue should confess that Jesus Christ is Lord, to the glory of God the Father.

12. Wherefore, my beloved, as ye have always obeyed, not as in my presence only, but now much more in my absence, work out your own salvation with fear and trembling.

13. For it is God which worketh in you both to will and to do of his good pleasure.

CHAPTER 3

13. Brethren, I count not myself to have apprehended: but this one thing I do, forgetting those things which are behind, and reaching forth unto those things which are before,

14. I press toward the mark for the prize of the high calling of God in Christ Jesus.

The Epistle to the Colossians

This letter was written in 63 A.D., shortly before St. Paul was released from his first Roman imprisonment. It was written to a very insignificant church in Colossae which Paul had never visited. But he had heard of "their faith" and wished to commend them. The theme of the letter is expressed in the phrase, "Christ is all and in all".

CHAPTER 1

12. Giving thanks unto the Father, which hath made us meet to be partakers of the inheritance of the saints in light:

13. Who hath delivered us from the power of darkness, and hath translated us into the kingdom of his dear Son:

14. In whom we have redemption through his blood, even the forgiveness of sins:

15. Who is the image of the invisible God, the firstborn of every creature:

16. For by him were all things created, that are in heaven, and that are in earth, visible and invisible, whether they be thrones, or dominions, or principalities, or powers: all things were created by him, and for him:

17. And he is before all things, and by him all things consist.

18. And he is the head of the body,

the church: who is the beginning, the firstborn from the dead; that in all things he might have the pre-eminence.

19. For it pleased the Father that in him should all fulness dwell;

20. And, having made peace through the blood of his cross, by him to reconcile all things unto himself; by him, I say, whether they be things in earth, or things in heaven.

21. And you, that were sometime alienated and enemies in your mind by wicked works, yet now hath he reconciled

22. In the body of his flesh through death, to present you holy and unblameable and unreproveable in his sight:

23. If ye continue in the faith grounded and settled, and be not moved away from the hope of the gospel, which ye have heard, and which was preached to every creature which is under heaven; whereof I Paul am made a minister;

24. Who now rejoice in my sufferings for you, and fill up that which is behind of the afflictions of Christ in my flesh for his body's sake, which is the church:

25. Whereof I am made a minister, according to the dispensation of God which is given to me for you, to fulfil the word of God;

26. Even the mystery which hath been hid from ages and from generations, but now is made manifest to his saints:

27. To whom God would make known what is the riches of the glory of this mystery among the Gentiles; which is Christ in you, the hope of glory:

28. Whom we preach, warning every man, and teaching every man in all wisdom; that we may present every man perfect in Christ Jesus:

29. Whereunto I also labour, striving according to his working, which worketh in me mightily.

Chapter 3

1. If ye then be risen with Christ, seek those things which are above, where Christ sitteth on the right hand of God.

2. Set your affection on things above, not on things on the earth.

3. For ye are dead, and your life is hid with Christ in God.

4. When Christ, who is our life, shall appear, then shall ye also appear with him in glory.

5. Mortify therefore your members which are upon the earth; fornication, uncleanness, inordinate affection, evil concupiscence, and covetousness, which is idolatry:

6. For which things' sake the wrath of God cometh on the children of disobedience:

7. In the which ye also walked some time, when ye lived in them.

8. But now ye also put off all these; anger, wrath, malice, blasphemy, filthy communication out of your mouth.

9. Lie not one to another, seeing that ye have put off the old man with his deeds;

10. And have put on the new man, which is renewed in knowledge after the image of him that created him:

11. Where there is neither Greek nor Jew, circumcision nor uncircumcision, Barbarian, Scythian, bond nor free: but Christ is all, and in all.

12. Put on therefore, as the elect of God, holy and beloved, bowels of mercies, kindness, humbleness of mind, meekness, longsuffering;

13. Forbearing one another, and forgiving one another, if any man have a quarrel against any: even as Christ forgave you, so also do ye.

14. And above all these things put on charity, which is the bond of perfectness.

15. And let the peace of God rule in your hearts, to the which also ye are called in one body; and be ye thankful.

CHAPTER 4

1. Masters, give unto your servants that which is just and equal; knowing that ye also have a Master in heaven.

2. Continue in prayer, and watch in the same with thanksgiving;

3. Withal praying also for us, that God would open unto us a door of utterance, to speak the mystery of Christ, for which I am also in bonds:

4. That I may make it manifest, as I ought to speak.

5. Walk in wisdom toward them that are without, redeeming the time.

6. Let your speech be alway with grace, seasoned with salt, that ye may know how ye ought to answer every man.

The First Epistle to the Thessalonians

This is probably the first of the letters of St. Paul, written late in 52 or early in 53 A.D. from Corinth. As such, it is believed to be the earliest Christian document now in existence. The church at Thessalonica was founded by Paul in 52 A.D. among the Jews who had moved to that city for its commercial advantages. But persecution was so severe that Paul had to flee the city. After he left, the church became concerned about the end of the world so that many were idle and prone to heathen vices. Paul wrote to answer their questions and to admonish them for their sins.

CHAPTER 4

9. But as touching brotherly love ye need not that I write unto you: for ye yourselves are taught of God to love one another.

10. And indeed ye do it toward all the brethren which are in all Macedonia: but we beseech you, brethren, that ye increase more and more;

11. And that ye study to be quiet, and to do your own business, and to work with your own hands, as we commanded you;

12. That ye may walk honestly toward them that are without, and that ye may have lack of nothing.

13. But I would not have you to be ignorant, brethren, concerning them which are asleep, that ye sorrow not, even as others which have no hope.

14. For if we believe that Jesus died and rose again, even so them also which sleep in Jesus will God bring with him.

15. For this we say unto you by the word of the Lord, that we which are alive and remain unto the coming of the Lord shall not prevent them which are asleep.

16. For the Lord himself shall descend from heaven with a shout, with the voice of the archangel, and with the trump of God: and the dead in Christ shall rise first:

17. Then we which are alive and remain shall be caught up together with them in the clouds, to meet the Lord in the air: and so shall we ever be with the Lord.

18. Wherefore comfort one another with these words.

CHAPTER 5

2. For yourselves know perfectly that the day of the Lord so cometh as a thief in the night.

3. For when they shall say, Peace and safety; then sudden destruction cometh upon them, as travail upon a woman with child; and they shall not escape.

4. But ye, brethren, are not in darkness, that that day should overtake you as a thief.

5. Ye are all the children of light, and the children of the day: we are not of the night, nor of darkness.

6. Therefore let us not sleep, as do others; but let us watch and be sober.

7. For they that sleep sleep in the

night; and they that be drunken are drunken in the night.

8. But let us, who are of the day, be sober, putting on the breastplate of faith and love; and for an helmet, the hope of salvation.

9. For God hath not appointed us to wrath, but to obtain salvation by our Lord Jesus Christ,

10. Who died for us, that, whether we wake or sleep, we should live together with him.

11. Wherefore comfort yourselves together, and edify one another, even as also ye do.

12. And we beseech you, brethren, to know them which labour among you, and are over you in the Lord, and admonish you;

13. And to esteem them very highly in love for their work's sake. And be at peace among yourselves.

14. Now we exhort you, brethren, warn them that are unruly, comfort the feebleminded, support the weak, be patient toward all men.

15. See that none render evil for evil unto any man; but ever follow that which is good, both among yourselves, and to all men.

16. Rejoice evermore.

17. Pray without ceasing.

18. In every thing give thanks: for this is the will of God in Christ Jesus concerning you.

19. Quench not the Spirit.

20. Despise not prophesyings.

21. Prove all things; hold fast that which is good.

22. Abstain from all appearance of evil.

23. And the very God of peace sanctify you wholly; and I pray God your whole spirit and soul and body be preserved blameless unto the coming of our Lord Jesus Christ.

24. Faithful is he that calleth you, who also will do it.

25. Brethren, pray for us.

26. Greet all the brethren with an holy kiss.

27. I charge you by the Lord that this epistle be read unto all the holy brethren.

28. The grace of our Lord Jesus Christ be with you. Amen.

The Second Epistle to the Thessalonians

This epistle was written by St. Paul sometime after the early part of 53 and before 58 A.D., possibly while he was still at Corinth from which he wrote the first epistle to the Thessalonians. In it Paul seeks to explain that the end of the world is not to be expected immediately and people should not become idle waiting for it. He urges that the members of the church continue to work and pray as this is the best preparation for any end that may come.

Chapter 3

1. Finally, brethren, pray for us, that the word of the Lord may have free course, and be glorified, even as it is with you:

2. And that we may be delivered from unreasonable and wicked men: for all men have not faith.

3. But the Lord is faithful, who shall stablish you, and keep you from evil.

4. And we have confidence in the Lord touching you, that ye both do and will do the things which we command you.

5. And the Lord direct your hearts into the love of God, and into the patient waiting for Christ.

6. Now we command you, brethren, in the name of our Lord Jesus Christ, that ye withdraw yourselves from every brother that walketh disorderly, and not after the tradition which he received of us.

7. For yourselves know how ye

ought to follow us: for we behaved not ourselves disorderly among you;

8. Neither did we eat any man's bread for nought; but wrought with labour and travail night and day, that we might not be chargeable to any of you:

9. Not because we have not power, but to make ourselves an ensample unto you to follow us.

10. For even when we were with you, this we commanded you, that if any would not work, neither should he eat.

11. For we hear that there are some which walk among you disorderly, working not at all, but are busybodies.

12. Now them that are such we command and exhort by our Lord Jesus Christ, that with quietness they work, and eat their own bread.

13. But ye, brethren, be not weary in well doing.

14. And if any man obey not our word by this epistle, note that man, and have no company with him, that he may be ashamed.

15. Yet count him not as an enemy, but admonish him as a brother.

16. Now the Lord of peace himself give you peace always by all means. The Lord be with you all.

17. The salutation of Paul with mine own hand, which is the token in every epistle: so I write.

18. The grace of our Lord Jesus Christ be with you all. Amen.

The First Epistle to Timothy

Paul had left his convert, Timothy, in Ephesus to check erroneous doctrine which was being spread. Since he was detained in Macedonia, he wrote this epistle to instruct his young aide. The date was probably near 65 A.D. Timothy was possibly 35 years old at this time and Paul was nearing 70. The letter gives specific instructions along several lines.

CHAPTER 1

5. Now the end of the commandment is charity out of a pure heart, and of a good conscience, and of faith unfeigned:

6. From which some having swerved have turned aside unto vain jangling;

7. Desiring to be teachers of the law; understanding neither what they say, nor whereof they affirm.

8. But we know that the law is good, if a man use it lawfully;

9. Knowing this, that the law is not made for a righteous man, but for the lawless and disobedient, for the ungodly and for sinners, for unholy and profane, for murderers of fathers and murderers of mothers, for manslayers,

10. For whoremongers, for them that defile themselves with mankind, for menstealers, for liars, for perjured persons, and if there be any other thing that is contrary to sound doctrine;

11. According to the glorious gospel of the blessed God, which was committed to my trust.

12. And I thank Christ Jesus our Lord, who hath enabled me, for that he counted me faithful, putting me into the ministry;

13. Who was before a blasphemer, and a persecutor, and injurious: but I obtained mercy, because I did it ignorantly in unbelief.

14. And the grace of our Lord was exceeding abundant with faith and love which is in Christ Jesus.

15. This is a faithful saying, and worthy of all acceptation, that Christ Jesus came into the world to save sinners; of whom I am chief.

16. Howbeit for this cause I obtained mercy, that in me first Jesus Christ might shew forth all longsuffering, for a pattern to them which should hereafter believe on him to life everlasting.

17. Now unto the King eternal,

immortal, invisible, the only wise God, be honour and glory for ever and ever. Amen.

Chapter 2

1. I exhort therefore, that, first of all, supplications, prayers, intercessions, and giving of thanks, be made for all men;

2. For kings, and for all that are in authority; that we may lead a quiet and peaceable life in all godliness and honesty.

3. For this is good and acceptable in the sight of God our Saviour;

4. Who will have all men to be saved, and to come unto the knowledge of the truth.

5. For there is one God, and one mediator between God and men, the man Christ Jesus;

6. Who gave himself a ransom for all, to be testified in due time.

Chapter 4

4. For every creature of God is good, and nothing to be refused, if it be received with thanksgiving:

5. For it is sanctified by the word of God and prayer.

6. If thou put the brethren in remembrance of these things, thou shalt be a good minister of Jesus Christ, nourished up in the words of faith and of good doctrine, whereunto thou hast attained.

7. But refuse profane and old wives' fables, and exercise thyself rather unto godliness.

8. For bodily exercise profiteth little: but godliness is profitable unto all things, having promise of the life that now is, and of that which is to come.

9. This is a faithful saying and worthy of all acceptation.

10. For therefore we both labour and suffer reproach, because we trust in the living God, who is the Saviour of all men, specially of those that believe.

11. These things command and teach.

12. Let no man despise thy youth; but be thou an example of the believers, in word, in conversation, in charity, in spirit, in faith, in purity.

13. Till I come, give attendance to reading, to exhortation, to doctrine.

14. Neglect not the gift that is in thee, which was given thee by prophecy, with the laying on of the hands of the presbytery.

15. Meditate upon these things; give thyself wholly to them; that thy profiting may appear to all.

16. Take heed unto thyself, and unto the doctrine; continue in them: for in doing this thou shalt both save thyself, and them that hear thee.

Chapter 6

9. But they that will be rich fall into temptation and a snare, and into many foolish and hurtful lusts, which drown men in destruction and perdition.

10. For the love of money is the root of all evil: which while some coveted after, they have erred from the faith, and pierced themselves through with many sorrows.

11. But thou, O man of God, flee these things; and follow after righteousness, godliness, faith, love, patience, meekness.

12. Fight the good fight of faith, lay hold on eternal life, whereunto thou art also called, and hast professed a good profession before many witnesses.

13. I give thee charge in the sight of God, who quickeneth all things, and before Christ Jesus, who before Pontius Pilate witnessed a good confession;

14. That thou keep this commandment without spot, unrebukeable, until the appearing of our Lord Jesus Christ:

15. Which in his times he shall shew, who is the blessed and only Potentate, the King of kings, and Lord of lords;

16. Who only hath immortality, dwelling in the light which no man can approach unto; whom no man hath seen, nor can see: to whom be honour and power everlasting. Amen.

17. Charge them that are rich in this world, that they be not high-minded, nor trust in uncertain riches, but in the living God, who giveth us richly all things to enjoy;

18. That they do good, that they be rich in good works, ready to distribute, willing to communicate;

19. Laying up in store for themselves a good foundation against the time to come, that they may lay hold on eternal life.

The Second Epistle to Timothy

St. Paul wrote this letter to Timothy from his prison in Rome in either 67 or 68 A.D. When he wrote it, he was certain that death was near and he wanted very much to see his dear friend and aide. The letter is full of instructions to Timothy regarding the Christian life and work in the church. As such it has served as a manual of instructions to all ministers of the church.

CHAPTER 1

7. For God hath not given us the spirit of fear; but of power, and of love, and of a sound mind.

8. Be not thou therefore ashamed of the testimony of our Lord, nor of me his prisoner: but be thou partaker of the afflictions of the gospel according to the power of God;

9. Who hath saved us, and called us with an holy calling, not according to our works, but according to his own purpose and grace, which was given us in Christ Jesus before the world began.

CHAPTER 2

15. Study to shew thyself approved unto God, a workman that needeth not to be ashamed, rightly dividing the word of truth.

16. But shun profane and vain babblings: for they will increase unto more ungodliness.

17. And their word will eat as doth a canker: of whom is Hymenæus and Philetus;

18. Who concerning the truth have erred, saying that the resurrection is past already; and overthrow the faith of some.

19. Nevertheless the foundation of God standeth sure, having this seal, The Lord knoweth them that are his. And, Let every one that nameth the name of Christ depart from iniquity.

20. But in a great house there are not only vessels of gold and of silver, but also of wood and of earth; and some to honour, and some to dishonour.

21. If a man therefore purge himself from these, he shall be a vessel unto honour, sanctified, and meet for the master's use, and prepared unto every good work.

22. Flee also youthful lusts: but follow righteousness, faith, charity, peace, with them that call on the Lord out of a pure heart.

23. But foolish and unlearned questions avoid, knowing that they do gender strifes.

24. And the servant of the Lord must not strive; but be gentle unto all men, apt to teach, patient,

25. In meekness instructing those that oppose themselves; if God peradventure will give them repentance to the acknowledging of the truth;

26. And that they may recover themselves out of the snare of the devil, who are taken captive by him at his will.

CHAPTER 3

16. All scripture is given by inspiration of God, and is profitable for doctrine, for reproof, for correction, for instruction in righteousness:

17. That the man of God may be perfect, throughly furnished unto all good works.

The Epistle to Titus

This epistle was written by St. Paul to Titus, one of his most trusted apostles. Titus was an occasional companion of Paul, who seems to have worked more or less independently, but to have been strong and stable in the faith. Paul is writing to him in about 65 A.D. to give him instructions for carrying on in Crete the work that he had left incomplete. Thus, the letter has many direct and particular suggestions and directions for organizing a regular ministry by appointing elders, and for combating false doctrines.

CHAPTER 1

7. For a bishop must be blameless, as the steward of God; not selfwilled, not soon angry, not given to wine, no striker, not given to filthy lucre;

8. But a lover of hospitality, a lover of good men, sober, just, holy, temperate;

9. Holding fast the faithful word as he hath been taught, that he may be able by sound doctrine both to exhort and to convince the gainsayers.

10. For there are many unruly and vain talkers and deceivers, specially they of the circumcision:

11. Whose mouths must be stopped, who subvert whole houses, teaching things which they ought not, for filthy lucre's sake.

12. One of themselves, even a prophet of their own, said, The Cretians are alway liars, evil beasts, slow bellies.

13. This witness is true. Wherefore rebuke them sharply, that they may be sound in the faith;

14. Not giving heed to Jewish fables, and commandments of men, that turn from the truth.

15. Unto the pure all things are pure: but unto them that are defiled and unbelieving is nothing pure; but even their mind and conscience is defiled.

16. They profess that they know God; but in works they deny him, being abominable, and disobedient, and unto every good work reprobate.

CHAPTER 2

1. But speak thou the things which become sound doctrine:

2. That the aged men be sober, grave, temperate, sound in faith, in charity, in patience.

3. The aged women likewise, that they be in behaviour as becometh holiness, not false accusers, not given to much wine, teachers of good things;

4. That they may teach the young women to be sober, to love their husbands, to love their children,

5. To be discreet, chaste, keepers at home, good, obedient to their own husbands, that the word of God be not blasphemed.

6. Young men likewise exhort to be sober minded.

7. In all things shewing thyself a pattern of good works: in doctrine shewing uncorruptness, gravity, sincerity,

8. Sound speech, that cannot be condemned; that he that is of the contrary part may be ashamed, having no evil thing to say of you.

9. Exhort servants to be obedient unto their own masters, and to please them well in all things; not answering again;

10. Not purloining, but shewing all good fidelity; that they may adorn the

doctrine of God our Saviour in all things.

11. For the grace of God that bringeth salvation hath appeared to all men,

12. Teaching us that, denying ungodliness and worldly lusts, we should live soberly, righteously, and godly, in this present world;

13. Looking for that blessed hope, and the glorious appearing of the great God and our Saviour Jesus Christ;

14. Who gave himself for us, that he might redeem us from all iniquity, and purify unto himself a peculiar people, zealous of good works.

15. These things speak, and exhort, and rebuke with all authority. Let no man despise thee.

CHAPTER 3

5. Not by works of righteousness which we have done, but according to his mercy he saved us, by the washing of regeneration, and renewing of the Holy Ghost;

6. Which he shed on us abundantly through Jesus Christ our Saviour;

7. That being justified by his grace, we should be made heirs according to the hope of eternal life.

The Epistle to the Hebrews

The author of this epistle is unknown. Scholars are agreed that he was a Christian Jew, a Hellenist who knew the Hebrew scriptures well. He was a companion of St. Paul and shows that Paul influenced him much. The epistle was written to a group of Jewish Christians, possibly those in Jerusalem, for the purpose of combating a strong tendency to return to Judaism. Its date is probably a little before 62 A.D. Though there are many uncertainties about the authorship and purpose of this epistle, it has exerted a great influence in the Christian church.

CHAPTER 2

3. How shall we escape, if we neglect so great salvation; which at the first began to be spoken by the Lord, and was confirmed unto us by them that heard him;

4. God also bearing them witness, both with signs and wonders, and with divers miracles, and gifts of the Holy Ghost, according to his own will?

5. For unto the angels hath he not put in subjection the world to come, whereof we speak.

6. But one in a certain place testified, saying, What is man, that thou art mindful of him? or the son of man, that thou visitest him?

7. Thou madest him a little lower than the angels; thou crownedst him with glory and honour, and didst set him over the works of thy hands:

8. Thou hast put all things in subjection under his feet. For in that he put all in subjection under him, he left nothing that is not put under him. But now we see not yet all things put under him.

CHAPTER 6

1. Therefore leaving the principles of the doctrine of Christ, let us go on unto perfection; not laying again the foundation of repentance from dead works, and of faith toward God,

2. Of the doctrine of baptisms, and of laying on of hands, and of resurrection of the dead, and of eternal judgment.

3. And this will we do, if God permit.

4. For it is impossible for those who were once enlightened, and have tasted of the heavenly gift, and were made partakers of the Holy Ghost,

5. And have tasted the good word of God, and the powers of the world to come,

6. If they shall fall away, to renew them again unto repentance; seeing

they crucify to themselves the Son of God afresh, and put him to an open shame.

7. For the earth which drinketh in the rain that cometh oft upon it, and bringeth forth herbs meet for them by whom it is dressed, receiveth blessing from God:

8. But that which beareth thorns and briers is rejected, and is nigh unto cursing; whose end is to be burned.

9. But, beloved, we are persuaded better things of you, and things that accompany salvation, though we thus speak.

10. For God is not unrighteous to forget your work and labour of love, which ye have shewed toward his name, in that ye have ministered to the saints, and do minister.

11. And we desire that every one of you do shew the same diligence to the full assurance of hope unto the end:

12. That ye be not slothful, but followers of them who through faith and patience inherit the promises.

13. For when God made promise to Abraham, because he could swear by no greater, he sware by himself,

14. Saying, Surely blessing I will bless thee, and multiplying I will multiply thee.

15. And so, after he had patiently endured, he obtained the promise.

16. For men verily swear by the greater: and an oath for confirmation is to them an end of all strife.

17. Wherein God, willing more abundantly to shew unto the heirs of promise the immutability of his counsel, confirmed it by an oath:

18. That by two immutable things, in which it was impossible for God to lie, we might have a strong consolation, who have fled for refuge to lay hold upon the hope set before us:

19. Which hope we have as an anchor of the soul, both sure and stedfast, and which entereth into that within the veil.

Chapter 10

18. Now where remission of these is, there is no more offering for sin.

19. Having therefore, brethren, boldness to enter into the holiest by the blood of Jesus,

20. By a new and living way, which he hath consecrated for us, through the veil, that is to say, his flesh;

21. And having an high priest over the house of God;

22. Let us draw near with a true heart in full assurance of faith, having our hearts sprinkled from an evil conscience, and our bodies washed with pure water.

23. Let us hold fast the profession of our faith without wavering; (for he is faithful that promised;)

24. And let us consider one another to provoke unto love and to good works:

25. Not forsaking the assembling of ourselves together, as the manner of some is; but exhorting one another: and so much the more, as ye see the day approaching.

26. For if we sin wilfully after that we have received the knowledge of the truth, there remaineth no more sacrifice for sins,

27. But a certain fearful looking for of judgment and fiery indignation, which shall devour the adversaries.

28. He that despised Moses' law died without mercy under two or three witnesses:

29. Of how much sorer punishment, suppose ye, shall he be thought worthy, who hath trodden under foot the Son of God, and hath counted the blood of the covenant, wherewith he was sanctified, an unholy thing, and hath done despite unto the Spirit of grace?

30. For we know him that hath said, Vengeance belongeth unto me, I will recompense, saith the Lord. And again, The Lord shall judge his people.

31. It is a fearful thing to fall into the hands of the living God.

32. But call to remembrance the former days, in which, after ye were illuminated, ye endured a great fight of afflictions;

33. Partly, whilst ye were made a gazingstock both by reproaches and afflictions; and partly, whilst ye became companions of them that were so used.

34. For ye had compassion of me in my bonds, and took joyfully the spoiling of your goods, knowing in yourselves that ye have in heaven a better and an enduring substance.

35. Cast not away therefore your confidence, which hath great recompence of reward.

36. For ye have need of patience, that, after ye have done the will of God, ye might receive the promise.

37. For yet a little while, and he that shall come will come, and will not tarry.

38. Now the just shall live by faith: but if any man draw back, my soul shall have no pleasure in him.

39. But we are not of them who draw back unto perdition; but of them that believe to the saving of the soul.

Chapter 11

1. Now faith is the substance of things hoped for, the evidence of things not seen.

2. For by it the elders obtained a good report.

3. Through faith we understand that the worlds were framed by the word of God, so that things which are seen were not made of things which do appear.

4. By faith Abel offered unto God a more excellent sacrifice than Cain, by which he obtained witness that he was righteous, God testifying of his gifts: and by it he being dead yet speaketh.

5. By faith Enoch was translated that he should not see death; and was not found, because God had translated him: for before his translation he had this testimony, that he pleased God.

6. But without faith it is impossible to please him: for he that cometh to God must believe that he is, and that he is a rewarder of them that diligently seek him.

Chapter 12

1. Wherefore seeing we also are compassed about with so great a cloud of witnesses, let us lay aside every weight, and the sin which doth so easily beset us, and let us run with patience the race that is set before us,

2. Looking unto Jesus the author and finisher of our faith; who for the joy that was set before him endured the cross, despising the shame, and is set down at the right hand of the throne of God.

3. For consider him that endured such contradiction of sinners against himself, lest ye be wearied and faint in your minds.

4. Ye have not yet resisted unto blood, striving against sin.

5. And ye have forgotten the exhortation which speaketh unto you as unto children, My son, despise not thou the chastening of the Lord, nor faint when thou art rebuked of him:

6. For whom the Lord loveth he chasteneth, and scourgeth every son whom he receiveth.

7. If ye endure chastening, God dealeth with you as with sons; for what son is he whom the father chasteneth not?

8. But if ye be without chastisement, whereof all are partakers, then are ye bastards, and not sons.

9. Furthermore we have had fathers of our flesh which corrected us, and we gave them reverence: shall we not much rather be in subjection unto the Father of spirits, and live?

10. For they verily for a few days chastened us after their own pleasure;

but he for our profit, that we might be partakers of his holiness.

11. Now no chastening for the present seemeth to be joyous, but grievous: nevertheless afterward it yieldeth the peaceable fruit of righteousness unto them which are exercised thereby.

CHAPTER 13

1. Let brotherly love continue.

2. Be not forgetful to entertain strangers: for thereby some have entertained angels unawares.

3. Remember them that are in bonds, as bound with them; and them which suffer adversity, as being yourselves also in the body.

4. Marriage is honourable in all, and the bed undefiled: but whoremongers and adulterers God will judge.

5. Let your conversation be without covetousness; and be content with such things as ye have: for he hath said, I will never leave thee, nor forsake thee.

6. So that we may boldly say, The Lord is my helper, and I will not fear what man shall do unto me.

7. Remember them which have the rule over you, who have spoken unto you the word of God: whose faith follow, considering the end of their conversation.

8. Jesus Christ the same yesterday, and to day, and for ever.

9. Be not carried about with divers and strange doctrines. For it is a good thing that the heart be established with grace; not with meats, which have not profited them that have been occupied therein.

10. We have an altar, whereof they have no right to eat which serve the tabernacle.

11. For the bodies of those beasts, whose blood is brought into the sanctuary by the high priest for sin, are burned without the camp.

12. Wherefore Jesus also, that he might sanctify the people with his own blood, suffered without the gate.

13. Let us go forth therefore unto him without the camp, bearing his reproach.

14. For here have we no continuing city, but we seek one to come.

15. By him therefore let us offer the sacrifice of praise to God continually, that is, the fruit of our lips giving thanks to his name.

16. But to do good and to communicate forget not: for with such sacrifices God is well pleased.

17. Obey them that have the rule over you, and submit yourselves: for they watch for your souls, as they that must give account, that they may do it with joy, and not with grief: for that is unprofitable for you.

18. Pray for us: for we trust we have a good conscienc , in all things willing to live honestly.

19. But I beseech you the rather to do this, that I may be restored to you the sooner.

20. Now the God of peace, that brought again from the dead our Lord Jesus, that great shepherd of the sheep, through the blood of the everlasting covenant,

21. Make you perfect in every good work to do his will, working in you that which is wellpleasing in his sight, through Jesus Christ; to whom be glory for ever and ever. Amen.

The Epistle of James

This epistle was probably written sometime before 62 or 63 A.D. by James the Just, the brother of Jesus. Thus it contains many reminiscences of Jesus not found in the Gospels. It was addressed to Jewish Christian communities outside of Palestine, which are warned against substituting words for deeds.

CHAPTER 1

1. James, a servant of God and of the Lord Jesus Christ, to the twelve tribes which are scattered abroad, greeting.

2. My brethren, count it all joy when ye fall into divers temptations;

3. Knowing this, that the trying of your faith worketh patience.

4. But let patience have her perfect work, that ye may be perfect and entire, wanting nothing.

5. If any of you lack wisdom, let him ask of God, that giveth to all men liberally, and upbraideth not; and it shall be given him.

6. But let him ask in faith, nothing wavering. For he that wavereth is like a wave of the sea driven with the wind and tossed.

7. For let not that man think that he shall receive any thing of the Lord.

8. A double minded man is unstable in all his ways.

9. Let the brother of low degree rejoice in that he is exalted:

10. But the rich, in that he is made low: because as the flower of the grass he shall pass away.

11. For the sun is no sooner risen with a burning heat, but it withereth the grass, and the flower thereof falleth, and the grace of the fashion of it perisheth: so also shall the rich man fade away in his ways.

12. Blessed is the man that endureth temptation: for when he is tried, he shall receive the crown of life, which the Lord hath promised to them that love him.

13. Let no man say when he is tempted, I am tempted of God: for God cannot be tempted with evil, neither tempteth he any man:

14. But every man is tempted, when he is drawn away of his own lust, and enticed.

15. Then when lust hath conceived, it bringeth forth sin: and sin, when it is finished, bringeth forth death.

16. Do not err, my beloved brethren.

17. Every good gift and every perfect gift is from above, and cometh down from the Father of lights, with whom is no variableness, neither shadow of turning.

18. Of his own will begat he us with the word of truth, that we should be a kind of firstfruits of his creatures.

19. Wherefore, my beloved brethren, let every man be swift to hear, slow to speak, slow to wrath:

20. For the wrath of man worketh not the righteousness of God.

21. Wherefore lay apart all filthiness and superfluity of naughtiness, and receive with meekness the engrafted word, which is able to save your souls.

22. But be ye doers of the word, and not hearers only, deceiving your own selves.

23. For if any be a hearer of the word, and not a doer, he is like unto a man beholding his natural face in a glass:

24. For he beholdeth himself, and goeth his way, and straightway forgetteth what manner of man he was.

25. But whoso looketh into the perfect law of liberty, and continueth therein, he being not a forgetful hearer, but a doer of the work, this man shall be blessed in his deed.

26. If any man among you seem to be religious, and bridleth not his tongue, but deceiveth his own heart, this man's religion is vain.

27. Pure religion and undefiled before God and the Father is this, To visit the fatherless and widows in their affliction, and to keep himself unspotted from the world.

CHAPTER 2

5. Hearken, my beloved brethren, Hath not God chosen the poor of this world rich in faith, and heirs of the

kingdom which he hath promised to them that love him?

6. But ye have despised the poor. Do not rich men oppress you, and draw you before the judgment seats?

7. Do not they blaspheme that worthy name by the which ye are called?

8. If ye fulfil the royal law according to the scripture, Thou shalt love thy neighbour as thyself, ye do well:

9. But if ye have respect to persons, ye commit sin, and are convinced of the law as transgressors.

10. For whosoever shall keep the whole law, and yet offend in one point, he is guilty of all.

11. For he that said, Do not commit adultery, said also, Do not kill. Now if thou commit no adultery, yet if thou kill, thou art become a transgressor of the law.

12. So speak ye, and so do, as they that shall be judged by the law of liberty.

13. For he shall have judgment without mercy, that hath shewed no mercy; and mercy rejoiceth against judgment.

14. What doth it profit, my brethren, though a man say he hath faith, and have not works? can faith save him?

15. If a brother or sister be naked, and destitute of daily food,

16. And one of you say unto them, Depart in peace, be ye warmed and filled; notwithstanding ye give them not those things which are needful to the body; what doth it profit?

Chapter 3

1. My brethren, be not many masters, knowing that we shall receive the greater condemnation.

2. For in many things we offend all. If any man offend not in word, the same is a perfect man, and able also to bridle the whole body.

3. Behold, we put bits in the horses'

mouths, that they may obey us; and we turn about their whole body.

4. Behold also the ships, which though they be so great, and are driven of fierce winds, yet are they turned about with a very small helm, whithersoever the governor listeth.

5. Even so the tongue is a little member, and boasteth great things. Behold, how great a matter a little fire kindleth!

6. And the tongue is a fire, a world of iniquity: so is the tongue among our members, that it defileth the whole body, and setteth on fire the course of nature; and it is set on fire of hell.

7. For every kind of beasts, and of birds, and of serpents, and of things in the sea, is tamed, and hath been tamed of mankind:

8. But the tongue can no man tame; it is an unruly evil, full of deadly poison.

9. Therewith bless we God, even the Father; and therewith curse we men, which are made after the similitude of God.

10. Out of the same mouth proceedeth blessing and cursing. My brethren, these things ought not so to be.

11. Doth a fountain send forth at the same place sweet water and bitter?

12. Can the fig tree, my brethren, bear olive berries? either a vine, figs? so can no fountain both yield salt water and fresh.

13. Who is a wise man and endued with knowledge among you? let him shew out of a good conversation his works with meekness of wisdom.

14. But if ye have bitter envying and strife in your hearts, glory not, and lie not against the truth.

15. This wisdom descendeth not from above, but is earthly, sensual, devilish.

16. For where envying and strife is, there is confusion and every evil work.

17. But the wisdom that is from

above is first pure, then peaceable, gentle, and easy to be intreated, full of mercy and good fruits, without partiality, and without hypocrisy.

18. And the fruit of righteousness is sown in peace of them that make peace.

CHAPTER 4

1. From whence come wars and fightings among you? come they not hence, even of your lusts that war in your members?

2. Ye lust, and have not: ye kill, and desire to have, and cannot obtain: ye fight and war, yet ye have not, because ye ask not.

3. We ask, and receive not, because ye ask amiss, that ye may consume it upon your lusts.

4. Ye adulterers and adulteresses, know ye not that the friendship of the world is enmity with God? whosoever therefore will be a friend of the world is the enemy of God.

5. Do ye think that the scripture saith in vain, The spirit that dwelleth in us lusteth to envy?

6. But he giveth more grace. Wherefore he saith, God resisteth the proud, but giveth grace unto the humble.

7. Submit yourselves therefore to God. Resist the devil, and he will flee from you.

8. Draw nigh to God, and he will draw nigh to you. Cleanse your hands, ye sinners; and purify your hearts, ye double minded.

9. Be afflicted, and mourn, and weep: let your laughter be turned to mourning, and your joy to heaviness.

10. Humble yourselves in the sight of the Lord, and he shall lift you up.

11. Speak not evil one of another, brethren. He that speaketh evil of his brother, and judgeth his brother, speaketh evil of the law, and judgeth the law: but if thou judge the law, thou art not a doer of the law, but a judge.

12. There is one lawgiver, who is able to save and to destroy: who art thou that judgest another?

13. Go to now, ye that say, To day or to morrow we will go into such a city, and continue there a year, and buy and sell, and get gain:

14. Whereas ye know not what shall be on the morrow. For what is your life? It is even a vapour, that appeareth for a little time, and then vanisheth away.

15. For that ye ought to say, If the Lord will, we shall live, and do this, or that.

16. But now ye rejoice in your boastings: all such rejoicing is evil.

17. Therefore to him that knoweth to do good, and doeth it not, to him it is sin.

CHAPTER 5

4. Behold, the hire of the labourers who have reaped down your fields, which is of you kept back by fraud, crieth: and the cries of them which have reaped are entered into the ears of the Lord of sabaoth.

5. Ye have lived in pleasure on the earth, and been wanton; ye have nourished your hearts, as in a day of slaughter.

6. Ye have condemned and killed the just; and he doth not resist you.

7. Be patient therefore, brethren, unto the coming of the Lord. Behold, the husbandman waiteth for the precious fruit of the earth, and hath long patience for it, until he receive the early and latter rain.

8. Be ye also patient; stablish your hearts: for the coming of the Lord draweth nigh.

9. Grudge not one against another, brethren, lest ye be condemned: behold, the judge standeth before the door.

10. Take, my brethren, the prophets, who have spoken in the name of the Lord, for an example of suffering affliction, and of patience.

11. Behold, we count them happy

which endure. Ye have heard of the patience of Job, and have seen the end of the Lord; that the Lord is very pitiful, and of tender mercy.

12. But above all things, my brethren, swear not, neither by heaven, neither by the earth, neither by any other oath: but let your yea be yea; and your nay, nay; lest ye fall into condemnation.

13. Is any among you afflicted? let him pray. Is any merry? let him sing psalms.

14. Is any sick among you? let him call for the elders of the church; and let them pray over him, anointing him with oil in the name of the Lord:

15. And the prayer of faith shall save the sick, and the Lord shall raise him up; and if he have committed sins, they shall be forgiven him.

16. Confess your faults one to another, and pray one for another, that ye may be healed. The effectual fervent prayer of a righteous man availeth much.

The First Epistle of Peter

St. Peter is the author of this epistle. He wrote it from Rome during or soon after 64 A.D. to the many Christians who had fled from Nero's persecution of the church and had found a haven in Asia Minor. His purpose is to inspire patience and hope in these refugees.

CHAPTER 1

3. Blessed be the God and Father of our Lord Jesus Christ, which according to his abundant mercy hath begotten us again unto a lively hope by the resurrection of Jesus Christ from the dead,

4. To an inheritance incorruptible, and undefiled, and that fadeth not away, reserved in heaven for you,

5. Who are kept by the power of God through faith unto salvation ready to be revealed in the last time.

6. Wherein ye greatly rejoice, though now for a season, if need be, ye are in heaviness through manifold temptations:

7. That the trial of your faith, being much more precious than of gold that perisheth, though it be tried with fire, might be found unto praise and honour and glory at the appearing of Jesus Christ:

8. Whom having not seen, ye love; in whom, though now ye see him not, yet believing, ye rejoice with joy unspeakable and full of glory:

9. Receiving the end of your faith, even the salvation of your souls.

10. Of which salvation the prophets have enquired and searched diligently, who prophesied of the grace that should come unto you:

11. Searching what, or what manner of time the Spirit of Christ which was in them did signify, when it testified beforehand the sufferings of Christ, and the glory that should follow.

12. Unto whom it was revealed, that not unto themselves, but unto us they did minister the things, which are now reported unto you by them that have preached the gospel unto you with the Holy Ghost sent down from heaven; which things the angels desire to look into.

13. Wherefore gird up the loins of your mind, be sober, and hope to the end for the grace that is to be brought unto you at the revelation of Jesus Christ;

14. As obedient children, not fashioning yourselves according to the former lusts in your ignorance:

15. But as he which hath called you is holy, so be ye holy in all manner of conversation;

16. Because it is written, Be ye holy; for I am holy.

17. And if ye call on the Father, who without respect of persons judgeth according to every man's work, pass the time of your sojourning here in fear:

18. Forasmuch as ye know that ye were not redeemed with corruptible things, as silver and gold, from your vain conversation received by tradition from your fathers;

19. But with the precious blood of Christ, as of a lamb without blemish and without spot:

20. Who verily was foreordained before the foundation of the world, but was manifest in these last times for you,

21. Who by him do believe in God, that raised him up from the dead, and gave him glory; that your faith and hope might be in God.

22. Seeing ye have purified your souls in obeying the truth through the Spirit unto unfeigned love of the brethren, see that ye love one another with a pure heart fervently:

23. Being born again, not of corruptible seed, but of incorruptible, by the word of God, which liveth and abideth for ever.

24. For all flesh is as grass, and all the glory of man as the flower of grass. The grass withereth, and the flower thereof falleth away:

25. But the word of the Lord endureth for ever. And this is the word which by the gospel is preached unto you.

Chapter 2

1. Wherefore laying aside all malice, and all guile, and hypocrisies, and envies, and all evil speakings,

2. As newborn babes, desire the sincere milk of the word, that ye may grow thereby:

3. If so be ye have tasted that the Lord is gracious.

4. To whom coming, as unto a living stone, disallowed indeed of men, but chosen of God, and precious,

5. Ye also, as lively stones, are built up a spiritual house, an holy priesthood, to offer up spiritual sacrifices, acceptable to God by Jesus Christ.

6. Wherefore also it is contained in the scripture, Behold, I lay in Sion a chief corner stone, elect, precious: and he that believeth on him shall not be confounded.

7. Unto you therefore which believe he is precious: but unto them which be disobedient, the stone which the builders disallowed, the same is made the head of the corner,

8. And a stone of stumbling, and a rock of offence, even to them which stumble at the word, being disobedient: whereunto also they were appointed.

9. But ye are a chosen generation, a royal priesthood, an holy nation, a peculiar people; that ye should shew forth the praises of him who hath called you out of darkness into his marvellous light:

10. Which in time past were not a people, but are now the people of God: which had not obtained mercy, but now have obtained mercy.

11. Dearly beloved, I beseech you as strangers and pilgrims, abstain from fleshly lusts, which war against the soul;

12. Having your conversation honest among the Gentiles: that, whereas they speak against you as evildoers, they may by your good works, which they shall behold, glorify God in the day of visitation.

13. Submit yourselves to every ordinance of man for the Lord's sake: whether it be to the king, as supreme;

14. Or unto governors, as unto them that are sent by him for the punishment of evildoers, and for the praise of them that do well.

15. For so is the will of God, that with well doing ye may put to silence the ignorance of foolish men:

16. As free, and not using your liberty for a cloke of maliciousness, but as the servants of God.

17. Honour all men. Love the brotherhood. Fear God. Honour the king.

18. Servants, be subject to your

masters with all fear; not only to the good and gentle, but also to the froward.

19. For this is thankworthy, if a man for conscience toward God endure grief, suffering wrongfully.

20. For what glory is it, if, when ye be buffeted for your faults, ye shall take it patiently? but if, when ye do well, and suffer for it, ye take it patiently, this is acceptable with God.

21. For even hereunto were ye called: because Christ also suffered for us, leaving us an example, that ye should follow his steps:

22. Who did no sin, neither was guile found in his mouth:

23. Who, when he was reviled, reviled not again; when he suffered, he threatened not; but committed himself to him that judgeth righteously:

24. Who his own self bare our sins in his own body on the tree, that we, being dead to sins, should live unto righteousness: by whose stripes ye were healed.

25. For ye were as sheep going astray; but are now returned unto the Shepherd and Bishop of your souls.

CHAPTER 3

8. Finally, be ye all of one mind, having compassion one of another, love as brethren, be pitiful, be courteous:

9. Not rendering evil for evil or railing for railing: but contrariwise blessing; knowing that ye are thereunto called, that ye should inherit a blessing.

10. For he that will love life, and see good days, let him refrain his tongue from evil, and his lips that they speak no guile:

11. Let him eschew evil, and do good; let him seek peace, and ensue it.

12. For the eyes of the Lord are over the righteous, and his ears are open unto their prayers: but the face of the Lord is against them that do evil.

13. And who is he that will harm you, if ye be followers of that which is good?

14. But and if ye suffer for righteousness' sake, happy are ye: and be not afraid of their terror, neither be troubled;

15. But sanctify the Lord God in your hearts: and be ready always to give an answer to every man that asketh you a reason of the hope that is in you with meekness and fear:

16. Having a good conscience; that, whereas they speak evil of you, as of evildoers, they may be ashamed that falsely accuse your good conversation in Christ.

17. For it is better, if the will of God be so, that ye suffer for well doing, than for evil doing.

18. For Christ also hath once suffered for sins, the just for the unjust, that he might bring us to God, being put to death in the flesh, but quickened by the Spirit:

19. By which also he went and preached unto the spirits in prison;

20. Which sometime were disobedient, when once the longsuffering of God waited in the days of Noah, while the ark was a preparing, wherein few, that is, eight souls were saved by water.

CHAPTER 4

9. Use hospitality one to another without grudging.

10. As every man hath received the gift, even so minister the same one to another, as good stewards of the manifold grace of God.

11. If any man speak, let him speak as the oracles of God; if any man minister, let him do it as of the ability which God giveth: that God in all things may be glorified through Jesus Christ, to whom be praise and dominion for ever and ever. Amen.

12. Beloved, think it not strange concerning the fiery trial which is to

try you, as though some strange thing happened unto you:

13. But rejoice, inasmuch as ye are partakers of Christ's sufferings; that, when his glory shall be revealed, ye may be glad also with exceeding joy.

14. If ye be reproached for the name of Christ, happy are ye; for the spirit of glory and of God resteth upon you: on their part he is evil spoken of, but on your part he is glorified.

15. But let none of you suffer as a murderer, or as a thief, or as an evildoer, or as a busybody in other men's matters.

16. Yet if any man suffer as a Christian, let him not be ashamed; but let him glorify God on this behalf.

17. For the time is come that judgment must begin at the house of God: and if it first begin at us, what shall the end be of them that obey not the gospel of God?

18. And if the righteous scarcely be saved, where shall the ungodly and the sinner appear?

19. Wherefore let them that suffer according to the will of God commit the keeping of their souls to him in well doing, as unto a faithful Creator.

CHAPTER 5

5. Likewise, ye younger, submit yourselves unto the elder. Yea, all of you be subject one to another, and be clothed with humility: for God resisteth the proud, and giveth grace to the humble.

6. Humble yourselves therefore under the mighty hand of God, that he may exalt you in due time:

7. Casting all your care upon him; for he careth for you.

8. Be sober, be vigilant; because your adversary the devil, as a roaring lion, walketh about, seeking whom he may devour:

9. Whom resist stedfast in the faith, knowing that the same afflictions are accomplished in your brethren that are in the world.

10. But the God of all grace, who hath called us unto his eternal glory by Christ Jesus, after that ye have suffered a while, make you perfect, stablish, strengthen, settle you.

The Second Epistle of Peter

Scholars are not agreed as to who wrote this epistle. Many hold that it was the chief apostle of Jesus, Peter, while others are just as sure that it was someone else who merely used the name of this famous figure. While it seems to have been written from Rome shortly before Peter's death, the evidence is so confusing that it seems best to accept the letter for its value and leave questions as to its authorship and time to others.

CHAPTER 1

3. According as his divine power hath given unto us all things that pertain unto life and godliness, through the knowledge of him that hath called us to glory and virtue:

4. Whereby are given unto us exceeding great and precious promises: that by these ye might be partakers of the divine nature, having escaped the corruption that is in the world through lust.

5. And beside this, giving all diligence, add to your faith virtue; and to virtue knowledge;

6. And to knowledge temperance; and to temperance patience; and to patience godliness;

7. And to godliness brotherly kindness; and to brotherly kindness charity.

The First Epistle of John

This epistle was written by the author of the fourth Gospel, St. John. He was at Ephesus at the time, a city where John spent a good part of his life. The date of this letter is some time between 85 and 95 A.D. It is called "catholic" since it is addressed to the entire church rather than to any one group of Christians. Indeed, it is hardly a letter at all, but a sermon in which the author gives much moral and practical advice.

Chapter 1

5. This then is the message which we have heard of him, and declare unto you, that God is light, and in him is no darkness at all.

6. If we say that we have fellowship with him, and walk in darkness, we lie, and do not the truth:

7. But if we walk in the light, as he is in the light, we have fellowship one with another, and the blood of Jesus Christ his Son cleanseth us from all sin.

8. If we say that we have no sin, we deceive ourselves, and the truth is not in us.

9. If we confess our sins, he is faithful and just to forgive us our sins, and to cleanse us from all unrighteousness.

10. If we say that we have not sinned, we make him a liar, and his word is not in us.

Chapter 2

3. And hereby we do know that we know him, if we keep his commandments.

4. He that saith, I know him, and keepeth not his commandments, is a liar, and the truth is not in him.

5. But whoso keepeth his word, in him verily is the love of God perfected: hereby know we that we are in him.

6. He that saith he abideth in him ought himself also so to walk, even as he walked.

7. Brethren, I write no new commandment unto you, but an old commandment which ye had from the beginning. The old commandment is the word which ye have heard from the beginning.

8. Again, a new commandment I write unto you, which thing is true in him and in you: because the darkness is past, and the true light now shineth.

9. He that saith he is in the light, and hateth his brother, is in darkness even until now.

10. He that loveth his brother abideth in the light, and there is none occasion of stumbling in him.

11. But he that hateth his brother is in darkness, and walketh in darkness, and knoweth not whither he goeth, because that darkness hath blinded his eyes.

12. I write unto you, little children, because your sins are forgiven you for his name's sake.

13. I write unto you, fathers, because ye have known him that is from the beginning. I write unto you, young men, because ye have overcome the wicked one. I write unto you, little children, because ye have known the Father.

14. I have written unto you, fathers, because ye have known him that is from the beginning. I have written unto you, young men, because ye are strong, and the word of God abideth in you, and ye have overcome the wicked one.

15. Love not the world, neither the things that are in the world. If any man love the world, the love of the Father is not in him.

16. For all that is in the world, the lust of the flesh, and the lust of the eyes, and the pride of life, is not of the Father, but is of the world.

17. And the world passeth away, and the lust thereof: but he that doeth the will of God abideth for ever.

Chapter 3

1. Behold, what manner of love the Father hath bestowed upon us, that we

should be called the sons of God: therefore the world knoweth us not, because it knew him not.

2. Beloved, now are we the sons of God, and it doth not yet appear what we shall be: but we know that, when he shall appear, we shall be like him; for we shall see him as he is.

3. And every man that hath this hope in him purifieth himself, even as he is pure.

4. Whosoever committeth sin transgresseth also the law: for sin is the transgression of the law.

5. And ye know that he was manifested to take away our sins; and in him is no sin.

6. Whosoever abideth in him sinneth not: whosoever sinneth hath not seen him, neither known him.

7. Little children, let no man deceive you: he that doeth righteousness is righteous, even as he is righteous.

8. He that committeth sin is of the devil; for the devil sinneth from the beginning. For this purpose the Son of God was manifested, that he might destroy the works of the devil.

9. Whosoever is born of God doth not commit sin; for his seed remaineth in him: and he cannot sin, because he is born of God.

10. In this the children of God are manifest, and the children of the devil: whosoever doeth not righteousness is not of God, neither he that loveth not his brother.

11. For this is the message that ye heard from the beginning, that we should love one another.

12. Not as Cain, who was of that wicked one, and slew his brother. And wherefore slew he him? Because his own works were evil, and his brother's righteous.

13. Marvel not, my brethren, if the world hate you.

14. We know that we have passed from death unto life, because we love the brethren. He that loveth not his brother abideth in death.

15. Whosoever hateth his brother is a murderer: and ye know that no murderer hath eternal life abiding in him.

16. Hereby perceive we the love of God, because he laid down his life for us: and we ought to lay down our lives for the brethren.

17. But whoso hath this world's good, and seeth his brother have need, and shutteth up his bowels of compassion from him, how dwelleth the love of God in him?

18. My little children, let us not love in word, neither in tongue; but in deed and in truth.

19. And hereby we know that we are of the truth, and shall assure our hearts before him.

20. For if our heart condemn us, God is greater than our heart, and knoweth all things.

21. Beloved, if our heart condemn us not, then have we confidence toward God.

22. And whatsoever we ask, we receive of him, because we keep his commandments, and do those things that are pleasing in his sight.

23. And this is his commandment, That we should believe on the name of his Son Jesus Christ, and love one another, as he gave us commandment.

24. And he that keepeth his commandments dwelleth in him, and he in him. And hereby we know that he abideth in us, by the Spirit which he hath given us.

CHAPTER 4

7. Beloved, let us love one another: for love is of God; and every one that loveth is born of God, and knoweth God.

8. He that loveth not knoweth not God; for God is love.

9. In this was manifested the love of God toward us, because that God sent his only begotten Son into the world, that we might live through him.

10. Herein is love, not that we loved God, but that he loved us, and sent his Son to be the propitiation for our sins.

11. Beloved, if God so loved us, we ought also to love one another.

12. No man hath seen God at any time. If we love one another, God dwelleth in us, and his love is perfected in us.

13. Hereby know we that we dwell in him, and he in us, because he hath given us of his Spirit.

14. And we have seen and do testify that the Father sent the Son to be the Saviour of the world.

15. Whosoever shall confess that Jesus is the Son of God, God dwelleth in him, and he in God.

16. And we have known and believed the love that God hath to us. God is love; and he that dwelleth in love dwelleth in God, and God in him.

17. Herein is our love made perfect, that we may have boldness in the day of judgment: because as he is, so are we in this world.

18. There is no fear in love; but perfect love casteth out fear: because fear hath torment. He that feareth is not made perfect in love.

19. We love him, because he first loved us.

20. If a man say, I love God, and hateth his brother, he is a liar: for he that loveth not his brother whom he hath seen, how can he love God whom he hath not seen?

21. And this commandment have we from him, That he who loveth God love his brother also.

Chapter 5

1. Whosoever believeth that Jesus is the Christ is born of God: and every one that loveth him that begat loveth him also that is begotten of him.

2. By this we know that we love the children of God, when we love God, and keep his commandments.

3. For this is the love of God, that we keep his commandments: and his commandments are not grievous.

4. For whatsoever is born of God overcometh the world: and this is the victory that overcometh the world, even our faith.

5. Who is he that overcometh the world, but he that believeth that Jesus is the Son of God?

6. This is he that came by water and blood, even Jesus Christ; not by water only, but by water and blood. And it is the Spirit that beareth witness, because the Spirit is truth.

7. For there are three that bear record in heaven, the Father, the Word, and the Holy Ghost: and these three are one.

8. And there are three that bear witness in earth, the spirit, and the water, and the blood: and these three agree in one.

9. If we receive the witness of men, the witness of God is greater: for this is the witness of God which he hath testified of his Son.

10. He that believeth on the Son of God hath the witness in himself: he that believeth not God hath made him a liar; because he believeth not the record that God gave of his Son.

11. And this is the record, that God hath given to us eternal life, and this life is in his Son.

12. He that hath the Son hath life; and he that hath not the Son of God hath not life.

13. These things have I written unto you that believe on the name of the Son of God; that ye may know that ye have eternal life, and that ye may believe on the name of the Son of God.

14. And this is the confidence that we have in him, that, if we ask any thing according to his will, he heareth us:

15. And if we know that he hear us, whatsoever we ask, we know that we

have the petitions that we desired of him.

The Revelation of St. John the Divine

Although there are many who disagree, the weight of evidence seems to indicate that this book was written by the apostle John either in 68 A.D. or 95 A.D. Both dates seem equally attested by evidence. The book is one of prophecy. It is written in figurative language and is, therefore, open to many interpretations.

CHAPTER 2

10. Fear none of those things which thou shalt suffer: behold, the devil shall cast some of you into prison, that ye may be tried; and ye shall have tribulation ten days: be thou faithful unto death, and I will give thee a crown of life.

11. He that hath an ear, let him hear what the Spirit saith unto the churches; He that overcometh shall not be hurt of the second death.

CHAPTER 4

1. After this I looked, and, behold, a door was opened in heaven: and the first voice which I heard was as it were of a trumpet talking with me; which said, Come up hither, and I will shew thee things which must be hereafter.

2. And immediately I was in the spirit: and, behold, a throne was set in heaven, and one sat on the throne.

3. And he that sat was to look upon like a jasper and a sardine stone: and there was a rainbow round about the throne, in sight like unto an emerald.

4. And round about the throne were four and twenty seats: and upon the seats I saw four and twenty elders sitting, clothed in white raiment; and they had on their heads crowns of gold.

5. And out of the throne proceeded lightnings and thunderings and voices: and there were seven lamps of fire burning before the throne, which are the seven Spirits of God.

6. And before the throne there was a sea of glass like unto crystal: and in the midst of the throne, and round about the throne, were four beasts full of eyes before and behind.

7. And the first beast was like a lion, and the second beast like a calf, and the third beast had a face as a man, and the fourth beast was like a flying eagle.

8. And the four beasts had each of them six wings about him; and they were full of eyes within: and they rest not day and night, saying, Holy, holy, holy, Lord God Almighty, which was, and is, and is to come.

9. And when those beasts give glory and honour and thanks to him that sat on the throne, who liveth for ever and ever,

10. The four and twenty elders fall down before him that sat on the throne, and worship him that liveth for ever and ever, and cast their crowns before the throne, saying,

11. Thou art worthy, O Lord, to receive glory and honour and power: for thou hast created all things, and for thy pleasure they are and were created.

CHAPTER 15

1. And I saw another sign in heaven, great and marvellous, seven angels having the seven last plagues; for in them is filled up the wrath of God.

2. And I saw as it were a sea of glass mingled with fire: and them that had gotten the victory over the beast, and over his image, and over his mark, and over the number of his

name, stand on the sea of glass, having the harps of God.

3. And they sing the song of Moses the servant of God, and the song of the Lamb, saying, Great and marvellous are thy works, Lord God Almighty; just and true are thy ways, thou King of saints.

4. Who shall not fear thee, O Lord, and glorify thy name? for thou only art holy: for all nations shall come and worship before thee; for thy judgments are made manifest.

5. And after that I looked, and, behold, the temple of the tabernacle of the testimony in heaven was opened:

6. And the seven angels came out of the temple, having the seven plagues, clothed in pure and white linen, and having their breasts girded with golden girdles.

7. And one of the four beasts gave unto the seven angels seven golden vials full of the wrath of God, who liveth for ever and ever.

8. And the temple was filled with smoke from the glory of God, and from his power; and no man was able to enter into the temple, till the seven plagues of the seven angels were fulfilled.

Chapter 19

1. And after these things I heard a great voice of much people in heaven, saying, Alleluia; Salvation, and glory, and honour, and power, unto the Lord our God:

2. For true and righteous are his judgments: for he hath judged the great whore, which did corrupt the earth with her fornication, and hath avenged the blood of his servants at her hand.

3. And again they said, Alleluia. And her smoke rose up for ever and ever.

4. And the four and twenty elders and the four beasts fell down and worshipped God that sat on the throne, saying, Amen; Alleluia.

5. And a voice came out of the throne, saying, Praise our God, all ye his servants, and ye that fear him, both small and great.

6. And I heard as it were the voice of a great multitude, and as the voice of many waters, and as the voice of mighty thunderings, saying, Alleluia: for the Lord God omnipotent reigneth.

7. Let us be glad and rejoice, and give honour to him: for the marriage of the Lamb is come, and his wife hath made herself ready.

8. And to her was granted that she should be arrayed in fine linen, clean and white: for the fine linen is the righteousness of saints.

X

MOHAMMEDANISM

MOHAMMEDANISM, or Islam, is one of the world's most widespread religions. In India alone there are more than 68,000,000 Mohammedans, while the entire number of believers has been estimated as above 221,000,000. With the exception of Sikhism, it is the newest of the world's great religions, dating from the Hegira, or flight of the prophet from Mecca, 622 A.D.

Mohammed, the founder, was born in 570 A.D. at Mecca, the chief city of Arabia, and followed his tribal business of shepherding and trading for many years. As a trader, he traveled much and came into contact with many peoples of varied religious beliefs. The general moral and social degradation which he found everywhere inspired him to devote himself to reform. This led to a conviction that God had given him a special appointment to preach a new religion. Then came "visions" and long "talks" with Allah whose prophet he believed himself to be.

At the age of 52, Mohammed went to Medina where he set himself up as the dictator and special envoy of Allah. His following increased rapidly. When he felt himself strong enough, he returned to Mecca, from which he had fled in 622, and from there ruled all Arabia. Mecca became the hub of a great wheel of Mohammedan faith from which spokes radiated in every direction and from which representatives went to many nations demanding that they accept his faith.

Mohammed died of a fever in 632 A.D., at the age of 62, believing that he would be translated immediately to "the blessed companionship on high".

His death left the powerful movement which he had founded without a successor or leader. For 28 years his devoted followers carried on the work and the leadership of the movement was held successively by Abu Bekr, Omar, Othman, and Ali, each one known as a caliph. After the death of Ali by assassination, the movement broke up into sects or different caliphates, each fighting against the others. At present there are approximately 72 distinct sects or denominations with beliefs and doctrines often far apart. Indeed, Mohammedanism has tended to take on something of the color of the culture into which it has migrated.

Although Mohammed is found in some places in the Koran to bemean himself as a common man and "the illiterate prophet", in other places he is so closely associated with Allah as to give ground for the belief that he was superhuman. Thus, after his death his followers came more and more to worship him as a prophet second only to Allah. Numerous miracle stories grew up about his life and he was venerated with absolute devotion.

Chief among the doctrines of Mohammedanism is the conception of Allah as the one and supreme being. This was "monotheism", belief in one and only one God. Allah is claimed to be "absolutely unitary", "all-seeing", "all-hearing", "all-speaking", "all-knowing", "all-willing", and "all-powerful". Other beliefs prominent in Mohammedanism are: belief in angels, belief in the Koran as a book coming directly from Allah, belief in Mohammed as the prophet of Allah, belief in judgment, paradise, and hell, and belief in the divine law of Allah which predestines everything for man and the world.

Mohammedanism holds that man has five supreme duties which he neglects at his soul's peril. These are: repetition of the creed, prayer, almsgiving, fasting, and pilgrimage to Mecca. Every Mohammedan must, once in his life, travel to Mecca, walk around the sacred Mosque, and kiss the Black Stone of the *Kaaba,* or shrine, seven times. If this trip is entirely impossible, he may send a substitute, but this is allowed only as a last resort.

THE KORAN

THE *Koran,* sacred book of the Mohammedans, is avowed to be a direct revelation of God to the prophet Mohammed. Throughout Allah speaks, sometimes directly to Mohammed and at others through the mouth of the prophet.

A little more than a year after the death of Mohammed, Abu Bekr, who took over the movement, supervised the collecting and writing of the teachings of the prophet as they were remembered by those who knew him best. But this did not settle the question of what the prophet had actually said. Consequently, some twelve years later Othman, third caliph, commanded that all copies of the original work be destroyed and a new and authentic version be prepared. This accepted volume contains scraps of beliefs from many religious sources, chief of which are Arabic traditions and folk lore, Zoroastrianism, and Jewish and Christian theology.

The present *Koran* consists of 114 *suras* or chapters. The first is a short prayer, the famous *Fatihah.* The remaining 113 chapters are arranged in the order of their length, the first having 286 verses and the last having only three verses.

The *Koran* has been the most influential book in Arabic literature, being quoted by practically every important Arabic writer. At the modern Mohammedan university of Al-Azhar in Cairo it is the chief textbook which every student must know.

Sura I

1. Praise be to God, Lord of the worlds!
2. The compassionate, the merciful!
3. King on the day of reckoning!
4. Thee only do we worship, and to Thee do we cry for help.
5. Guide Thou us on the straight path,
6. The path of those to whom Thou hast been gracious;—with whom thou art not angry, and who go not astray.

Sura II.—The Cow

1. No doubt is there about this Book: It is a guidance to the God-fearing,
2. Who believe in the unseen, who observe prayer, and out of what we have bestowed on them, expend for God;
3. And who believe in what hath been sent down to thee, and in what hath been sent down before thee, and full faith have they in the life to come:
4. These are guided by their Lord; and with these it shall be well.
5. As to the infidels, alike is it to them whether thou warn them or warn them not—they will not believe:
6. Their hearts and their ears hath God sealed up; and over

their eyes is a covering. For them, a severe chastisement!

9. Diseased are their hearts! And that disease hath God increased to them. Theirs a sore chastisement, for that they treated their prophet as a liar!

10. And when it is said to them, "Cause not disorders in the earth": they say, "Nay, rather do we set them right."

11. Is it not that they are themselves the authors of disorder? But they perceive it not!

12. And when it is said to them, "Believe as other men have believed;" they say, "Shall we believe as the fools have believed?" Is it not that they are themselves the fools? But they know it not!

13. And when they meet the faithful they say, "We believe;" but when they are apart with their Satans they say, "Verily we hold with you, and at them we only mock."

14. God shall mock at them, and keep them long in their rebellion, wandering in perplexity.

15. These are they who have purchased error at the price of guidance: but their traffic hath not been gainful, neither are they guided at all.

26. How can ye withhold faith from God? Ye were dead and He gave you life; next He will cause you to die; next He will restore you to life: next shall ye return to Him!

27. He it is who created for you all that is on Earth, then proceeded to the Heaven, and into seven Heavens did He

fashion it: and He knoweth all things.

28. When thy Lord said to the angels, "Verily, I am about to place one in my stead on earth," they said, "Wilt thou place there one who will do ill therein and shed blood, when we celebrate thy praise and extol thy holiness?" God said, "Verily, I know what ye know not."

29. And he taught Adam the names of all things, and then set them before the angels, and said, "Tell me the names of these, if ye are endued with wisdom."

30. They said, "Praise be to Thee! We have no knowledge but what Thou hast given us to know. Thou! Thou art the Knowing, the Wise."

31. He said, "O Adam, inform them of their names." And when he had informed them of their names, He said, "Did I not say to you that I know the hidden things of the Heavens and of the Earth, and that I know what ye bring to light, and what ye hide?"

32. And when we said to the angels, "Bow down and worship Adam," then worshipped they all, save Eblis. He refused and swelled with pride, and became one of the unbelievers.

33. And we said, "O Adam! dwell thou and thy wife in the Garden, and eat ye plentifully therefrom wherever ye list; but to this tree come not nigh, lest ye become of the transgressors."

34. But Satan made them slip from it, and caused their banishment from the place in which they were. And we

said, "Get ye down, the one of you an enemy to the other: and there shall be for you in the earth a dwelling-place, and a provision for a time."

35. And words of prayer learned Adam from his Lord: and God turned to him; for He loveth to turn, the Merciful.

36. We said, "Get ye down from it, all together: and if Guidance shall come to you from me, whoso shall follow my guidance, on them shall come no fear, neither shall they be grieved:

37. But they who shall not believe, and treat our signs as falsehoods, these shall be inmates of the fire; in it shall they remain for ever."

98. O ye who believe! say not to our apostle, "Raina" (Look at us); but say, "Ondhorna" (Regard us). And attend to this; for, the Infidels shall suffer a grievous chastisement.

99. The unbelievers among the people of the Book, and among the idolaters, desire not that any good should be sent down to you from your Lord: but God will shew His special mercy to whom He will, for He is of great bounty.

100. Whatever verses we cancel, or cause thee to forget, we bring a better or its like. Knowest thou not that God hath power over all things?

101. Knowest thou not that the dominion of the Heavens and of the Earth is God's? and that ye have neither patron nor helper, save God?

102. Would ye ask of your apostle what of old was asked of Moses? But he who ex-

changeth faith for unbelief, hath already erred from the even way.

103. Many of the people of the Book desire to bring you back to unbelief after ye have believed, out of selfish envy, even after the truth hath been clearly shewn them. But forgive them, and shun them till God shall come in with His working. Truly God hath power over all things.

104. And observe prayer and pay the legal impost: and whatever good thing ye have sent on before for your soul's sake, ye shall find it with God. Verily God seeth what ye do.

105. And they say, "None but Jews or Christians shall enter Paradise": This is their wish. SAY: Give your proofs if ye speak the truth.

106. But they who set their face with resignation Godward, and do what is right,—their reward is with their Lord; no fear shall come on them, neither shall they be grieved.

107. Moreover, the Jews say, "The Christians lean on nought:" "On nought lean the Jews," say the Christians: Yet both are readers of the Book. So with like words say they who have no knowledge. But on the resurrection day, God shall judge between them as to that in which they differ.

108. And who committeth a greater wrong than he who hindereth God's name from being remembered in his temples, and who hasteth to ruin them? Such men cannot enter them but with fear. Theirs is shame in this

world, and a severe torment in the next.

109. The East and the West is God's: therefore, whichever way ye turn, there is the face of God: Truly God is immense and knoweth all.

110. And they say, "God hath a son:" No! Praise be to Him! But —His, whatever is in the Heavens and the Earth! All obeyeth Him,

111. Sole maker of the Heavens and of the Earth! And when He decreeth a thing, He only saith to it, "Be," and it is.

112. And they who have no knowledge say, "Unless God speak to us, or thou shew us a sign . . . !" So, with like words, said those who were before them: their hearts are alike: Clear signs have we already shewn for those who have firm faith:

113. Verily, with the Truth have we sent thee, a bearer of good tidings and a warner: and of the people of Hell thou shalt not be questioned.

114. But until thou follow their religion, neither Jews nor Christians will be satisfied with thee. SAY: Verily, guidance of God,—that is the guidance! And if, after "the Knowledge" which hath reached thee, thou follow their desires, thou shalt find neither helper nor protector against God.

115. They to whom we have given the Book, and who read it as it ought to be read,— these believe therein: but whoso believeth not therein, shall meet with perdition.

116. O children of Israel! remember my favour wherewith I have favoured you, and that high

above all mankind have I raised you:

117. And dread the day when not in aught shall soul satisfy for soul, nor shall any ransom be taken from it, nor shall any intercession avail, and they shall not be helped.

141. They to whom we have given the Scriptures know him— the apostle—even as they know their own children: but truly a part of them do conceal the truth, though acquainted with it.

142. The truth is from thy Lord. Be not then of those who doubt.

143. All have a quarter of the Heavens to which they turn them; but wherever ye be, hasten emulously after good: God will one day bring you all together; verily, God is all-powerful.

144. And from whatever place thou comest forth, turn thy face toward the sacred Mosque; for this is the truth from thy Lord; and God is not inattentive to your doings.

145. And from whatever place thou comest forth, turn thy face toward the sacred Mosque; and wherever ye be, to that part turn your faces, lest men have cause of dispute against you: but as for the impious among them, fear them not; but fear me, that I may perfect my favours on you, and that ye may be guided aright.

146. And we sent to you an apostle from among yourselves to rehearse our signs unto you, and to purify you, and to instruct you in "the Book," and in the wisdom, and to teach you that which ye knew not:

147. Therefore remember me: I will

remember you; and give me thanks and be not ungrateful.

148. O ye who believe! seek help with patience and with prayer, for God is with the patient.

149. And say not of those who are slain on God's path that they are Dead; nay, they are Living! But ye understand not.

150. With somewhat of fear and hunger, and loss of wealth, and lives, and fruits, will we surely prove you: but bear good tidings to the patient,

151. Who when a mischance chanceth them, say, "Verily we are God's, and to Him shall we return:"

152. On them shall be blessings from their Lord, and mercy: and these!—they are the rightly guided.

153. Verily, Safa and Marwah are among the monuments of God: whoever then maketh a pilgrimage to the temple, or visiteth it, shall not be to blame if he go round about them both. And as for him who of his own accord doeth what is good—God is Grateful, Knowing.

154. They who conceal aught that we have sent down, either of clear proof or of guidance, after what we have so clearly shewn to men in the Book, God shall curse them, and they who curse shall curse them.

155. But as for those who turn to me, and amend and make known the truth, even unto them will I turn me, for I am He who Turneth, the Merciful.

156. Verily, they who are infidels and die infidels,—these! upon them shall be the malison of God and of angels and of all men:

157. Under it shall they remain for ever: their torment shall not be lightened, and God will not even look upon them!

158. Your God is one God: there is no God but He, the Compassionate, the Merciful.

159. Assuredly in the creation of the Heavens and of the Earth; and in the alternation of night and day; and in the ships which pass through the sea with what is useful to man; and in the rain which God sendeth down from Heaven, giving life by it to the earth after its death, and by scattering over it all kinds of cattle; and in the change of the winds, and in the clouds that are made to do service between the Heaven and the Earth;—are signs for those who understand.

160. Yet there are men who take to them idols along with God, and love them with the love of God: But stronger in the faithful is the love of God. Oh! the impious will see, when they see their chastisement, that all power is God's, and that God is severe in chastising.

167. O ye who believe! eat of the good things with which we have supplied you, and give God thanks if ye are His worshippers.

168. But that which dieth of itself, and blood, and swine's flesh, and that over which any other name than that of God hath been invoked, is forbidden you. But he who shall partake of them by constraint, without lust or

wilfulness, no sin shall be upon him. Verily God is Indulgent, Merciful.

169. They truly who hide the Scriptures which God hath sent down, and barter them for a mean price—these shall swallow into their bellies nought but fire. God will not speak to them, or assoil them, on the day of the Resurrection: and theirs shall be a grievous torment.

170. These are they who have bartered guidance for error, and pardon for torment; But how great their endurance in fire!

171. This shall be their doom, because God had sent down "the Book" with the very truth. And verily they who dispute about that Book are in a far-gone severance from it.

172. There is no piety in turning your faces toward the east or the west, but he is pious who believeth in God, and the last day, and the angels, and the Scriptures, and the prophets; who for the love of God disburseth his wealth to his kindred, and to the orphans, and the needy, and the wayfarer, and those who ask, and for ransoming; who observeth prayer, and payeth the legal alms, and who is of those who are faithful to their engagements when they have engaged in them, and patient under ills and hardships, and in time of trouble: these are they who are just, and these are they who fear the Lord.

179. O believers! a Fast is prescribed to you as it was prescribed to those before you, that ye may fear God,

180. For certain days. But he among you who shall be sick, or on a journey, shall fast that same number of other days: and as for those who are able to keep it and yet break it, the expiation of this shall be the maintenance of a poor man. And he who of his own accord performeth a good work, shall derive good from it: and good shall it be for you to fast—if ye knew it.

181. As to the month Ramadhan in which the Koran was sent down to be man's guidance, and an explanation of that guidance, and of that illumination, as soon as any one of you observeth the moon, let him set about the fast; but he who is sick, or upon a journey, shall fast a like number of other days. God wisheth you ease, but wisheth not your discomfort, and that you fulfil the number of days, and that you glorify God for his guidance, and that you be thankful.

182. And when my servants ask thee concerning me, then will I be nigh unto them. I will answer the cry of him that crieth, when he crieth unto me: but let them hearken unto me, and believe in me, that they may proceed aright.

183. You are allowed on the night of the fast to approach your wives: they are your garment and ye are their garment. God knoweth that ye defraud yourselves therein, so He turneth unto you and forgiveth you! Now, there-

fore, go in unto them with full desire for that which God hath ordained for you; and eat and drink until ye can discern a white thread from a black thread by the daybreak: then fast strictly till night, and go not in unto them, but rather pass the time in the Mosques. These are the bounds set up by God: therefore come not near them. Thus God maketh his signs clear to men that they may fear Him.

184. Consume not your wealth among yourselves in vain things, nor present it to judges that ye may consume a part of other men's wealth unjustly, while ye know the sin which ye commit.

191. Give freely for the cause of God, and throw not yourselves with your own hands into ruin; and do good, for God loveth those who do good.

192. Accomplish the Pilgrimage and the Visitation of the holy places in honour of God: and if ye be hemmed in by foes, send whatever offering shall be the easiest: and shave not your heads until the offering reach the place of sacrifice. But whoever among you is sick, or hath an ailment of the head, must satisfy by fasting, or alms, or an offering. And when ye are safe from foes, he who contents himself with the Visitation of the holy places, until the Pilgrimage, shall bring whatever offering shall be the easiest. But he who findeth nothing to offer, shall fast three days in the Pilgrimage itself, and seven days when ye return: they shall be ten days in all. This is binding on him whose family shall not be present at the sacred Mosque. And fear God, and know that God is terrible in punishing.

193. Let the Pilgrimage be made in the months already known: whoever therefore undertaketh the Pilgrimage therein, let him not know a woman, nor transgress, nor wrangle in the Pilgrimage. The good which ye do, God knoweth it. And provide for your journey; but the best provision is the fear of God: fear me, then, O men of understanding!

194. It shall be no crime in you if ye seek an increase from your Lord; and when ye pour swiftly on from Arafat, then remember God near the holy monument; and remember Him, because He hath guided you who before this were of those who went astray:

195. Then pass on quickly where the people quickly pass, and ask pardon of God, for God is Forgiving, Merciful.

196. And when ye have finished your holy rites, remember God as ye remember your own fathers, or with a yet more intense remembrance! Some men there are who say, "O our Lord! give us our portion in this world:" but such shall have no portion in the next life:

197. And some say, "O our Lord! give us good in this world and good in the next, and keep us from the torment of the fire."

198. They shall have the lot which they have merited: and God is swift to reckon.

199. Bear God in mind during the stated days: but if any haste away in two days, it shall be no fault in him: And if any tarry longer, it shall be ~o fault in him, if he fear God, then, and know that to Him shall ye be gathered.

209. Mankind was but one people; and God sent prophets to announce glad tidings and to warn; and He sent down with them the Book of Truth, that it might decide the disputes of men; and none disputed but those to whom the Book had been given, after the clear tokens had reached them,—being full of mutual jealousy. And God guided those who believed to the truth of that about which, by his permission, they had disputed; for God guideth whom he pleaseth into the straight path.

210. Think ye to enter Paradise, when no such things have come upon you, as on those who flourished before you? Ills and troubles tried them; and so tossed were they by trials, that the Apostle and they who shared his faith, said, "When will the help of God come?"—Is not the help of God nigh?

216. They will ask thee concerning wine and games of chance. SAY: In both is great sin, and advantage also, to men; but their sin is greater than their advantage. They will ask thee also what they shall bestow in alms:

217. SAY: What ye can spare. Thus God sheweth you his signs that ye may ponder

218. On this present world, and on the next. They will also ask thee concerning orphans. SAY: Fair dealing with them is best;

219. But if ye mix yourselves up (in their affairs)—they are your brethren: God knoweth the foul dealer from the fair: and, if God pleased, he could indeed afflict you! Verily, God is Mighty, Wise.

220. Marry not idolatresses until they believe; a slave who believeth is better than an idolatress, though she please you more. And wed not your daughters to idolaters until they believe; for a slave who is a believer, is better than an idolater, though he please you.

221. They invite to the Fire; but God inviteth to Paradise, and to pardon, if he so will, and maketh clear his signs to men that they may remember.

222. They will also question thee as to the courses of women. SAY: They are a pollution. Separate yourselves therefore from women and approach them not, until they be cleansed. But when they are cleansed, go in unto them as God hath ordained for you. Verily God loveth those who turn to Him, and loveth those who seek to be clean.

223. Your wives are your field: go in, therefore, to your field as ye will; but do first some act for your souls' good: and fear ye God, and know that ye must meet Him; and bear these good tidings to the faithful.

244. Hast thou not thought on those who quitted their dwellings —and they were thousands —for fear of death? God said to them, "Die:" then He restored them to life, for full of bounty towards man is God. But most men give not thanks!

245. Fight for the cause of God; and know that God is He who Heareth, Knoweth.

246. Who is he that will lend to God a goodly loan? He will double it to him again and again: God is close, but open handed also: and to Him shall ye return.

256. God! There is no God but He; the Living, the Eternal; Nor slumber seizeth Him, nor sleep; His, whatsoever is in the Heavens and whatsoever is in the Earth! Who is he that can intercede with Him but by His own permission? He knoweth what hath been before them and what shall be after them; yet nought of His knowledge shall they grasp, save what He willeth. His Throne reacheth over the Heavens and the Earth, and the upholding of both burdeneth Him not; and He is the High, the Great!

257. Let there be no compulsion in Religion. Now is the right way made distinct from error: Whoever therefore shall deny Thagout and believe in God—he will have taken hold on a strong handle that shall not be broken: and God is He who Heareth, Knoweth.

263. The likeness of those who expend their wealth for the cause of God, is that of a grain of corn which produceth seven ears, and in each ear a hundred grains; and God will multiply to whom He pleaseth: God is Liberal, Knowing!

264. They who expend their wealth for the cause of God, and never follow what they have laid out with reproaches or harm, shall have their reward with their Lord; no fear shall come upon them, neither shall they be put to grief.

265. A kind speech and forgiveness is better than alms followed by injury. God is Rich, Clement.

269. O ye who believe! bestow alms of the good things which ye have acquired, and of that which we have brought forth for you out of the earth, and choose not the bad for almsgiving,

270. Such as ye would accept yourselves only by connivance: and know that God is Rich, Praiseworthy.

271. Satan menaceth you with poverty, and enjoineth base actions: but God promiseth you pardon from himself and abundance: God is All-bounteous, Knowing.

272. He giveth wisdom to whom He will: and he to whom wisdom is given, hath had much good given him; but none will bear it in mind, except the wise of heart.

273. And whatever alms ye shall give, or whatever vow ye shall vow, of a truth God knoweth it: but they who act unjustly shall have no helpers. Give ye your alms openly? it is well. Do ye conceal them and give them to the poor? This, too, will be of advantage to you, and

will do away your sins: and God is cognizant of your actions.

274. Their guidance is not thine affair, O Muhammad; but God guideth whom he pleaseth. And the good that ye shall give in alms shall redound unto yourselves; and ye shall not give but as seeking the face of God; and whatever good thing ye shall have given in alms, shall be repaid you, and ye shall not be wronged. There are among you the poor, who being shut up to fighting for the cause of God, have it not in their power to strike out into the earth for riches. Those who know them not, think them rich because of their modesty. By this their token thou shalt know them—they ask not of men with importunity: and of whatever good thing ye shall give them in alms, of a truth God will take knowledge.

275. They who give away their substance in alms, by night and day, in private and in public, shall have their reward with their Lord: no fear shall come on them, neither shall they be put to grief.

276. They who swallow down usury, shall arise in the resurrection only as he ariseth whom Satan hath infected by his touch. This, for that they say, "Selling is only the like of usury:" and yet God hath allowed selling, and forbidden usury. He then who when this warning shall come to him from his Lord, abstaineth, shall have pardon for the past, and his lot shall be with God. But they who return to usury, shall be given over to the fire; therein shall they abide for ever.

277. God will bring usury to nought, but will increase alms with usury, and God loveth no infidel, or evil person. But they who believe and do the things that are right, and observe the prayers, and pay the legal impost, they shall have their reward with their Lord: no fear shall come on them, neither shall they be put to grief.

278. O believers! fear God and abandon your remaining usury, if ye are indeed believers.

279. But if ye do it not, then hearken for war on the part of God and his apostle: yet if ye repent, ye shall have the principal of your money. Wrong not, and ye shall not be wronged.

280. If any one find difficulty in discharging a debt, then let there be a delay until it be easy for him: but if ye remit it as alms it will be better for you, if ye knew it.

281. Fear the day wherein ye shall return to God: then shall every soul be rewarded according to its desert, and none shall have injustice done to them.

Sura III.—The Family of Imran

4. God! nought that is in Earth or that is in Heaven, is hidden unto Him. He it is who formeth you in your mothers' wombs. There is no god but He; the Mighty, the Wise!

5. He it is who hath sent down to thee "the Book." Some of its signs are of themselves perspicuous;—these are the basis of the Book—and others are figurative. But they whose hearts are given to err, follow its figures, craving discord, craving an interpretation; yet none knoweth its interpretation but God. And the stable in knowledge say, "We believe in it: it is all from our Lord." But none will bear this in mind, save men endued with understanding.

6. O our Lord! suffer not our hearts to go astray after that thou hast once guided us, and give us mercy from before thee; for verily thou art He who giveth.

7. O our Lord! For the day of whose coming there is not a doubt, thou wilt surely gather mankind together. Verily, God will not fail the promise.

8. As for the infidels, their wealth, and their children, shall avail them nothing against God. They shall be fuel for the fire.

9. After the wont of the people of Pharaoh, and of those who went before them, they treated our signs as falsehoods. Therefore God laid hold of them in their sins; and God is severe in punishing!

10. SAY to the infidels: ye shall be worsted, and to Hell shall ye be gathered together; and wretched the couch!

11. Ye have already had a sign in the meeting of the two hosts. The one host fought in the cause of God, and the other was infidel. To their own eyesight, the infidels saw you twice as many as themselves: And God aided with his succour whom He would: And in this truly was a lesson for men endued with discernment.

12. Fair-seeming to men is the love of pleasures from women and children, and the treasured treasures of gold and silver, and horses of mark, and flocks, and cornfields! Such the enjoyment of this world's life. But God! goodly the home with Him.

13. SAY: Shall I tell you of better things than these, prepared for those who fear God, in His presence? Theirs shall be gardens, beneath whose pavilions the rivers flow, and in which shall they abide for aye: and wives of stainless purity, and acceptance with God: for God regardeth his servants—

14. Who say, "O our Lord! we have indeed believed; pardon us our sins, and keep us from the torment of the fire;"—

15. The patient, and the truthful, the lowly, and the charitable, and they who seek pardon at each daybreak.

25. SAY: O God, possessor of all power, thou givest power to whom thou wilt, and from whom thou wilt, thou takest it away! Thou raisest up whom thou wilt, and whom thou wilt thou dost abase! In thy hand is good; for thou art over all things potent.

26. Thou causest the night to pass into the day, and thou causest the day to pass into the night. Thou bringest the living out of the dead, and thou bringest the dead

out of the living; and thou givest sustenance to whom thou wilt, without measure.

27. Let not believers take infidels for their friends rather than believers: whoso shall do this hath nothing to hope from God—unless, indeed, ye fear a fear from them: But God would have you beware of Himself; for to God ye return. SAY: Whether ye hide what is in your breasts, or whether ye publish it abroad, God knoweth it: He knoweth what is in the heavens and what is in the earth; and over all things is God potent.

28. On that day shall every soul find present to it, whatever it hath wrought of good: and as to what it hath wrought of evil, it will wish that wide were the space between itself and it! But God would have you beware of Himself; for God is kind to His servants.

29. SAY: If ye love God, then follow me: God will love you, and forgive your sins, for God is Forgiving, Merciful. SAY: Obey God and the Apostle; but if ye turn away, then verily, God loveth not the unbelievers.

120. Then thou didst say to the faithful, "Is it not enough for you that your Lord aideth you with three thousand angels sent down from on high?"

121. Aye: but if ye be steadfast and fear God, and the foe come upon you in hot haste, your Lord will help you with five thousand angels in their cognizances!

122. This, as pure good tidings for you, did God appoint, that your hearts might be assured—for only from God, the Mighty, the Wise, cometh the Victory—and that He might cut off the uttermost part of those who believed not, or cast them down so that they should be overthrown, defeated without resource.

123. It is none of thy concern whether He be turned unto them in kindness or chastise them: for verily they are wrongful doers.

124. Whatever is in the Heavens and the Earth is God's! He forgiveth whom He will, and whom He will, chastiseth: for God is Forgiving, Merciful.

125. O ye who believe! devour not usury, doubling it again and again! But fear God, that ye may prosper.

126. And fear the fire which is prepared for them that believe not; and obey God and the apostle, that ye may find mercy:

127. And vie in haste for pardon from your Lord, and a Paradise, vast as the Heavens and the Earth, prepared for the God-fearing,

128. Who give alms, alike in prosperity and in success, and who master their anger, and forgive others! God loveth the doers of good.

129. They who, after they have done a base deed or committed a wrong against their own selves, remember God and implore forgiveness of their sins—and who will forgive sins but God only?—and persevere not in what they have wittingly done amiss.

130. As for these! Pardon from their

Lord shall be their recompense, and gardens 'neath which the rivers flow; for ever shall they abide therein: And goodly the reward of those who labour!

140. How many a prophet hath combated those who had with them many myriads! Yet were they not daunted at what befel them on the path of God, nor were they weakened, nor did they basely submit! God loveth those who endure with steadfastness,

141. Nor said they more than this: "O our Lord! forgive us our sins and our mistakes in this our work; and set our feet firm; and help us against the unbelieving people." And God gave them the recompense of this world, and the excellence of the recompense of the next. For God loveth the doers of what is excellent.

142. O ye who have believed! if ye obey the infidels, they will cause you to turn upon your heels, and ye will fall back into perdition:

143. But God is your liege lord, and He is the best of helpers.

144. We will cast a dread into hearts of the infidels because they have joined gods with God without warranty sent down; their abode shall be the fire; and wretched shall be the mansion of the evil doers.

145. Already had God made good to you His promise, when by His permission ye destroyed your foes, until your courage failed you, and ye disputed about the order, and disobeyed, after that the Prophet had brought you within view of that for which ye longed.

146. Some of you were for this world, and some for the next. Then, in order to make trial of you, He turned you to flight from them,—yet hath He now forgiven you; for all-bounteous is God to the faithful—

147. When ye came up the height and took no heed of any one, while the Prophet in your rear was calling you to the fight! God hath rewarded you with trouble upon trouble, that ye might learn not to be chagrined at your loss of booty, or at what befel you! God is acquainted with your actions.

148. Then after the trouble God sent down security upon you. Slumber fell upon a part of you: as to the other part—their own passions stirred them up to think unjustly of God with thoughts of ignorance! They said—What gain we by this affair? SAY: Verily the affair resteth wholly with God. They hid in their minds what they did not speak out to thee, saying, "Were we to have gained aught in this affair, none of us had been slain at this place." SAY: Had ye remained in your homes, they who were decreed to be slain would have gone forth to the places where they lie:—in order that God might make trial of what was in your breasts, and might discover what was in your hearts, for God knoweth the very secrets of the breast.

149. Of a truth it was Satan alone who caused those of you to

fail in duty who turned back on the day when the hosts met, for some of their doings! But now hath God pardoned them; For God is Forgiving, Gracious.

150. O ye who believe! be not like the infidels, who said of their brethren when they had travelled by land or had gone forth to war, "Had they kept with us, they had not died, and had not been slain!" God purposed that this affair should cause them heart sorrow! God maketh alive and killeth; and God beholdeth your actions.

151. And if ye shall be slain or die on the path of God, then pardon from God and mercy is better than all your amassings;

152. For if ye die or be slain, verily unto God shall ye be gathered.

153. Of the mercy of God thou hast spoken to them in gentle terms. Hadst thou been severe and harsh-hearted, they would have broken away from thee. Therefore, forgive and ask for pardon for them, and consult them in the affair of war, and when thou art resolved, then put thou thy trust in God, for God loveth those who trust in Him.

154. If God help you, none shall overcome you; but if He abandon you, who is he that shall help you when He is gone? In God, then, let the faithful trust.

155. It is not the Prophet who will defraud you;—But he who shall defraud, shall come forth with his defraudings on the day of the resurrec-

tion: then shall every soul be paid what it hath merited, and they shall not be treated with injustice.

156. Shall he who hath followed the good pleasure of God be as he who hath brought on himself wrath from God, and whose abode shall be Hell? and wretched the journey thither!

157. There are varying grades with God: and God beholdeth what ye do.

158. Now hath God been gracious to the faithful, when he raised up among them an apostle out of their own people, to rehearse unto them his signs, and to cleanse them, and to give them knowledge of the Book and of Wisdom: for before they were in manifest error.

159. When a reverse hath befallen you, the like of which ye had before inflicted, say ye, "Whence is this?" Say: It is from yourselves. For God hath power over all things.

160. And that which befel you on the day when the armies met, was certainly by the will of God, and that he might know the faithful, and that he might know the hypocrites! And when the word was "Advance, fight on the path of God, or drive back the foe,"—they said, "Had we known how to fight, we would have followed you." Nearer were some of them on that day to unbelief, than to faith:

161. They said with their lips what was not in their hearts! But God knew what they concealed,

162. Who said of their brethren while themselves sat at home,

"Had they obeyed us, they had not been slain." SAY: Keep back death from yourselves if ye speak truth.

163. And repute not those slain on God's path to be dead. Nay, alive with their Lord, are they richly sustained;

164. Rejoicing in what God of his bounty hath vouchsafed them, filled with joy for those who follow after them, but have not yet overtaken them, that on them nor fear shall come, nor grief;

165. Filled with joy at the favours of God, and at his bounty: and that God suffereth not the reward of the faithful to perish.

185. Suppose not that they who rejoice in what they have brought to pass, and love to be praised for what they have not done—suppose not they shall escape the chastisement. An afflictive chastisement doth await them.

186. For the Kingdom of the Heavens and the Earth is God's, and God hath power over all things.

187. Verily, in the creation of the Heavens and of the Earth, and in the succession of the night and of the day, are signs for men of understanding heart;

188. Who standing, and sitting, and reclining, bear God in mind, and muse on the creation of the Heavens and of the Earth. "O our Lord!" say they, "thou hast not created this in vain. No. Glory be to Thee! Keep us, then, from the torment of the fire.

189. O our Lord! surely thou wilt put him to shame whom thou shalt cause to enter into the Fire, and the wrong-doers shall have none to help them

190. O our Lord! we have indeed heard the voice of one that called. He called us to the faith—'Believe ye on your Lord'—and we have believed.

191. O our Lord! forgive us then our sin, and hide away from us our evil deeds, and cause us to die with the righteous.

192. O our Lord! and give us what thou hast promised us by thine apostles, and put us not to shame on the day of the resurrection. Verily, Thou wilt not fail thy promise."

193. And their Lord answereth them, "I will not suffer the work of him among you that worketh, whether of male or female, to be lost. The one of you is the issue of the other.

194. And they who have fled their country and quitted their homes and suffered in my cause, and have fought and fallen, I will blot out their sins from them, and I will bring them into gardens beneath which the streams do flow."

195. A recompense from God! and God! with Him is the perfection of recompense!

196. Let not prosperity in the land on the part of those who believe not, deceive thee. 'Tis but a brief enjoyment! Then shall Hell be their abode; and wretched the bed!

197. But as to those who fear their Lord—for them are the gardens 'neath which the rivers flow: therein shall they abide for aye. Such their reception with God—and that which

is with God is best for the righteous.

198. Among the people of the Book are those who believe in God, and in what He hath sent down to you, and in what He hath sent down to them, humbling themselves before God. They barter not the signs of God for a mean price.

199. These! their recompense awaiteth them with their Lord: aye! God is swift to take account.

200. O ye who believe! be patient, and vie in patience, and be firm, and fear God, that it may be well with you.

Sura IV.—Women

1. O men! fear your Lord, who hath created you of one man (*nafs,* soul), and of him created his wife, and from these twain hath spread abroad so many men and WOMEN. And fear ye God, in whose name ye ask mutual favours,—and reverence the wombs that bare you. Verily is God watching over you!

2. And give to the orphans their property; substitute not worthless things of your own for their valuable ones, and devour not their property after adding it to your own; for this is a great crime.

40. Worship God, and join not aught with Him in worship. Be good to parents, and to kindred, and to orphans, and to the poor, and to a neighbour, whether kinsman or new-comer, and to a fellow traveller, and to the wayfarer, and to the slaves whom your right hands

hold; verily, God loveth not the proud, the vain boaster,

41. Who are niggardly themselves, and bid others be niggards, and hide away what God of his bounty hath given them. We have made ready a shameful chastisement for the unbelievers,

42. And for those who bestow their substance in alms to be seen of men, and believe not in God and in the last day. Whoever hath Satan for his companion, an evil companion hath he!

43. But what blessedness would be theirs, if they should believe in God and in the last day, and bestow alms out of what God hath vouchsafed them; for God taketh knowledge of them!

44. God truly will not wrong any one of the weight of a mote; and if there be any good deed, he will repay it doubly; and from his presence shall be given a great recompense.

45. How! when we shall bring up against them witnesses from all peoples, and when we shall bring thee up as a witness against these? On that day they who were Infidels and rebelled against the prophet, shall wish that the earth were levelled with them! But nothing shall they hide from God.

104. And when ye shall have ended the prayer, make mention of God, standing, and sitting, and reclining: and as soon as ye are secure, observe prayer; for to the faithful, prayer is a prescribed duty, and for stated hours.

105. Slacken not in pursuit of the foe. If ye suffer, assuredly they suffer also as ye suffer; but

ye hope from God for what they cannot hope! And God is Knowing, Wise!

106. Verily, we have sent down the Book to thee with the truth, that thou mayest judge between men according as God hath given thee insight: But with the deceitful ones dispute not: and implore pardon of God. Verily, God is Forgiving, Merciful.

107. And plead not with us for those who are self-deceivers; for God loveth not him who is deceitful, criminal.

108. From men they hide themselves; but they cannot hide themselves from God: and when they hold nightly discourses which please Him not, He is with them. God is round about their doings!

109. Oh! ye are they who plead in their favour in this present life; but who shall plead with God for them on the day of the resurrection? Who will be the guardian over them?

110. Yet he who doth evil, or shall have acted against his own weal, and then shall ask pardon of God, will find God Forgiving, Merciful:

111. And whoever committeth a crime, committeth it to his own hurt. And God is Knowing, Wise!

112. And whoever committeth an involuntary fault or a crime, and then layeth it on the innocent, shall surely bear the guilt of calumny and of a manifest crime.

113. But for the grace and mercy of God upon thee, a party among them had resolved to mislead thee, but they shall only mislead themselves; nor in aught shall they harm thee. God hath caused the Book and the wisdom to descend upon thee: and what thou knowest not He hath caused thee to know: and the grace of God toward thee hath been great.

120. These! their dwelling Hell! no escape shall they find from it!

121. But they who believe and do the things that are right, we will bring them into gardens beneath which the rivers flow; For ever shall they abide therein. Truly it is the promise of God: And whose word is more sure than God's?

122. Not according to your wishes, or the wishes of the people of the Book, shall these things be. He who doth evil shall be recompensed for it. Patron or helper, beside God, shall he find none.

123. But whoso doth the things that are right, whether male or female, and he or she a believer,—these shall enter Paradise, nor shall they be wronged the skin of a date stone.

124. And who hath a better religion than he who resigneth himself to God, who doth what is good, and followeth the faith of Abraham in all sincerity? And God took Abraham for his friend.

125. All that is in the Heavens and all that is on the Earth is God's: and God encompasseth all things!

135. O ye who believe! believe in God and his Apostle, and the Book which he hath sent down to his Apostle, and the Book which he hath sent down aforetime. Whoever believeth not on God and his Angels and his Books

and his Apostles, and in the last day, he verily hath erred with far-gone error.

136. Verily, they who believed, then became unbelievers, then believed, and again became unbelievers, and then increased their unbelief—it is not God who will forgive them or guide them into the way.

137. Announce to the hypocrites that a dolorous torment doth await them.

138. Those who take the unbelievers for friends besides the faithful—do they seek honour at their hands? Verily, all honour belongeth unto God!

139. And already hath He sent this down to you in the Book "WHEN YE SHALL HEAR THE SIGNS OF GOD THEY SHALL NOT BE BELIEVED BUT SHALL BE MOCKED AT." Sit ye not therefore with such, until they engage in other discourse; otherwise, ye will become like them. Verily God will gather the hypocrites and the infidels all together in Hell.

140. They watch you narrowly. Then if God grant you a victory, they say, "Are we not with you?" and if the infidels meet with a success, they say to them, "Were we not superior to you: and did we not defend you from those believers?" God shall judge betwixt ye on the day of the resurrection, and God will by no means make a way for the infidels over the believers.

141. The hypocrites would deceive God, but He will deceive them! When they stand up for prayer, they stand carelessly, to be seen of men,

and they remember God but little:

142. Wavering between the one and the other—belonging neither to these nor those! and by no means shalt thou find a path for him whom God misleadeth.

143. O believers! take not infidels for friends rather than believers. Would ye furnish God with clear right to punish you?

144. Verily the hypocrites shall be in the lowest abyss of the fire: and, by no means shalt thou find a helper for them;

145. Save for those who turn and amend, and lay fast hold on God, and approve the sincerity of their religion to God; these shall be numbered with the faithful, and God will at last bestow on the faithful a great reward.

146. Why should God inflict a chastisement upon you, if ye are grateful, and believe? God is Grateful, Wise!

Sura V.—The Table

1. O Believers! be faithful to your engagements. You are allowed the flesh of cattle other than what is hereinafter recited, except game, which is not allowed you while ye are on pilgrimage. Verily, God ordaineth what he pleaseth.

2. O Believers! violate neither the rites of God, nor the sacred month Muharram, nor the offering, nor its ornaments, nor those who press on to the sacred house seeking favour from their Lord and his good pleasure in them.

3. But when all is over, then take to the chase: and let not ill will at those who would

have kept you from the sacred mosque lead you to transgress, but rather be helpful to one another according to goodness and piety, but be not helpful for evil and malice: and fear ye God. Verily, God is severe in punishing!

8. O Believers! when ye address yourselves to prayer, wash your faces, and your hands up to the elbow, and wipe your heads, and your feet to the ankles.

9. And if ye have become unclean, then purify yourselves. But if ye are sick, or on a journey, or if one of you come from the place of retirement, or if ye have touched women, and ye find no water, then take clean sand and rub your faces and your hands with it. God desireth not to lay a burden upon you, but he desireth to purify you, and He would fill up the measure of His favour upon you, that ye may be grateful.

10. And remember the favour of God upon you, and His covenant which He hath covenanted with you, when ye said, "We have heard and will obey;" and fear God; verily, God knoweth the very secrets of the breast.

11. O Believers! stand up as witnesses for God by righteousness: and let not ill-will at any, induce you not to act uprightly. Act uprightly. Next will this be to the fear of God. And fear ye God: verily, God is apprized of what ye do.

12. God hath promised to those who believe, and do the things that are right, that for them is pardon and a great reward.

13. But they who are Infidels and treat our signs as lies—these shall be mated with Hell fire.

14. O Believers! recollect God's favour upon you, when certain folk were minded to stretch forth their hands against you, but He kept their hands from you. Fear God then: and on God let the faithful trust.

15. Of old did God accept the covenant of the children of Israel, and out of them we raised up twelve leaders, and God said, "Verily, I will be with you. If ye observe prayer and pay the obligatory alms, and believe in my Apostles and help them, and lend God a liberal loan, I will surely put away from you your evil deeds, and I will bring you into gardens 'neath which the rivers flow! But whoso of you after this believeth not, hath gone astray from the even path."

16. But for their breaking their covenant we have cursed them, and have hardened their hearts. They shift the words of Scripture from their places, and have forgotten part of what they were taught. Thou wilt not cease to discover deceit on their part, except in a few of them. But forgive them, and pass it over: verily, God loveth those who act generously!

17. And of those who say, "We are Christians," have we accepted the covenant. But they too have forgotten a part of what they were

taught; wherefore we have stirred up enmity and hatred among them that shall last till the day of the Resurrection; and in the end will God tell them of their doings.

18. O people of the Scriptures! now is our Apostle come to you to clear up to you much that ye concealed of those Scriptures, and to pass over many things. Now hath a light and a clear Book come to you from God, by which God will guide him who shall follow after his good pleasure, to paths of peace, and will bring them out of the darkness to the light, by his will: and to the straight path will he guide them.

19. Infidels now are they who say, "Verily God is the Messiah Ibn Maryam (son of Mary)!" SAY: And who could aught obtain from God, if he chose to destroy the Messiah Ibn Maryam, and his mother, and all who are on the earth together?

20. For with God is the sovereignty of the Heavens and of the Earth, and of all that is between them! He createth what He will; and over all things is God potent.

21. Say the Jews and Christians, "Sons are we of God and his beloved." SAY: Why then doth he chastise you for your sins? Nay! ye are but a part of the men whom he hath created! He will pardon whom he pleaseth, and chastise whom he pleaseth, and with God is the sovereignty of the Heavens and of the Earth, and of all that is between them, and unto Him shall all things return.

22. O people of the Book! now hath our Apostle come to you to clear up to you the cessation of Apostles, lest you should say, "There hath come to us no bearer of good tidings, nor any warner." But now hath a bearer of good tidings and a warner reached you. And God is Almighty.

89. O ye who believe! interdict not the healthful viands which God hath allowed you; go not beyond this limit. God loveth not those who outstep it.

90. And eat of what God hath given you for food, that which is lawful and wholesome: and fear God, in whom ye believe.

91. God will not punish you for a mistaken word in your oaths: but he will punish you in regard to an oath taken seriously. Its expiation shall be to feed ten poor persons with such middling food as ye feed your own families with, or to clothe them; or to set free a captive. But he who cannot find means, shall fast three days. This is the expiation of your oaths when ye shall have sworn. Keep then your oaths. Thus God maketh his signs clear to you, that ye may give thanks.

92. O believers! surely wine and games of chance, and statues, and the divining arrows, are an abomination of Satan's work! Avoid them, that ye may prosper.

93. Only would Satan sow hatred and strife among you, by wine and games of chance, and turn you aside from the remembrance of God, and

from prayer: will ye not, therefore, abstain from them? Obey God and obey the Apostle, and be on your guard: but if ye turn back, know that our Apostle is only bound to deliver a plain announcement.

94. No blame shall attach to those who believe and do good works, in regard to any food they have taken, in case they fear God and believe, and do the things that are right, and shall still fear God and believe, and shall still fear him, and do good; for God loveth those who do good.

95. O ye who believe! God will surely make trial of you with such game as ye may take with your hands, or your lances, that God may know who feareth him in secret: and whoever after this transgresseth, shall suffer a grievous chastisement.

Sura VI.—Cattle

1. Praise be to God, who hath created the Heavens and the Earth, and ordained the darkness and the light! Yet unto their Lord do the infidels give peers!

2. He it is who created you of clay—then decreed the term of your life: and with Him is another prefixed term for the resurrection. Yet have ye doubts thereof!

3. And He is God in the Heavens and on the Earth! He knoweth your secrets and your disclosures! and He knoweth what ye deserve.

4. Never did one single sign from among the signs of their Lord come to them, but they turned away from it;

5. And now, after it hath reached them, have they treated the truth itself as a lie. But in the end, a message as to that which they have mocked, shall reach them.

50. SAY: I say not to you, "In my possession are the treasures of God;" neither say I, "I know things secret;" neither do I say to you, "Verily, I am an angel:" Only what is revealed to me do I follow. SAY: Shall the blind and the seeing be esteemed alike? Will ye not then reflect?

51. And warn those who dread their being gathered to their Lord, that patron or intercessor they shall have none but Him—to the intent that they may fear Him!

52. And thrust not thou away those who cry to their Lord at morn and even, craving to behold his face. It is not for thee in anything to judge of their motives, nor for them in anything to judge of thee. If thou thrust them away thou wilt be of the doers of wrong.

53. Thus have we made proof of some of them by others, that they may say, "Are these they among us to whom God hath been gracious?" Doth not God best know the thankful?

54. And when they who believe in our signs come to thee, SAY: Peace be upon you! Your Lord hath laid down for himself a law of mercy; so that if any one of you commit a fault through ignorance, and afterwards turn and amend, He surely will be Gracious, Merciful.

55. Thus have we distinctly set forth our signs, that the way of

the wicked might be made known.

70. SAY: Shall we, beside God, call upon those who can neither help nor hurt us? Shall we turn upon our heel after that God hath guided us? Like some bewildered man whom the Satans have spellbound in the desert, though his companions call him to the true guidance, with, "Come to us!" SAY: Verily, guidance from God, that is the true guidance; and we are commanded to surrender ourselves to the Lord of the Worlds.

71. And observe ye the times of prayer, and fear ye God: for it is He to whom ye shall be gathered.

72. And it is He who hath created the Heavens and the Earth, in truth, and when He saith to a thing, "Be," it is.

73. His word is the truth: and His the kingdom, on the day when there shall be a blast on the trumpet: He knoweth alike the unseen and the seen: and He is the Wise, the Cognizant.

155. Then gave we the Book to Moses —complete for him who should do right, and a decision for all matters, and a guidance, and a mercy, that they might believe in the meeting with their Lord.

156. Blessed, too, this Book which we have sent down. Wherefore follow it and fear God, that ye may find mercy:

157. Lest ye should say, "The Scriptures were indeed sent down only unto two peoples before us, but we were not able to go deep into their studies:"

158. Or lest ye should say, "If a book had been sent down to us, we had surely followed the guidance better than they." But now hath a clear exposition come to you from your Lord, and a guidance and a mercy. Who then is more wicked than he who treateth the signs of God as lies, and turneth aside from them? We will recompense those who turn aside from our signs with an evil punishment, because they have turned aside.

159. What wait they for, but the coming of the angels to them, or the coming of thy Lord Himself, or that some of the signs of thy Lord should come to pass? On the day when some of thy Lord's signs shall come to pass, its faith shall not profit a soul which believed not before, nor wrought good works in virtue of its faith. SAY: Wait ye. Verily, we will wait also.

160. As to those who split up their religion and become sects, have thou nothing to do with them: their affair is with God only. Hereafter shall he tell them what they have done.

161. He who shall present himself with good works shall receive a tenfold reward; but he who shall present himself with evil works shall receive none other than a like punishment: and they shall not be treated unjustly.

162. SAY: As for me, my Lord hath guided me into a straight path; a true religion, the creed of Abraham, the sound in faith; for he was not of those who join gods with God.

163. SAY: My prayers and my worship and my life and my death are unto God, Lord of the Worlds. He hath no associate. This am I commanded, and I am the first of the Muslims.

164. SAY: Shall I seek any other Lord than God, when He is Lord of all things? No soul shall labour but for itself; and no burdened one shall bear another's burden. At last ye shall return to your Lord, and he will declare that to you about which you differ.

165. And it is He who hath made you the successors of others on the earth, and hath raised some of you above others by various grades, that he may prove you by his gifts. Verily thy Lord is swift to punish. But He is also Gracious, Merciful!

Sura VII.—Al Araf

26. O children of Adam! let not Satan bring you into trouble, as he drove forth your parents from the Garden, by despoiling them of their raiment, that he might cause them to see their nakedness: He truly seeth you, he and his comrades, whence ye see not them. Verily, we have made the Satans tutelars of those who believe not.

27. And when the wicked commit some filthy deed, they say, "We found our fathers practising it, and to us hath God commanded it"—SAY: God enjoineth not filthy deeds. Will ye speak of God ye know not what?

28. SAY: My Lord hath enjoined what is right. Turn your faces therefore towards every place where he is worshipped, and call upon him with sincere religion. As he created you, to him shall ye return: some hath he guided, and some hath he justly left in error, because they have taken the Satans as their tutelars beside God, and have deemed that they were guided aright.

29. O children of Adam! wear your goodly apparel when ye repair to any mosque, and eat ye and drink; but exceed not, for He loveth not those who exceed.

30. SAY: Who hath prohibited God's goodly raiment, and the healthful viands which He hath provided for his servants? SAY: These are for the faithful in this present life, but above all on the day of the resurrection. Thus make we our signs plain for people of knowledge.

31. SAY: Truly my Lord hath forbidden filthy actions whether open or secret, and iniquity, and unjust violence, and to associate with God that for which He hath sent down no warranty, and to speak of God that ye know not.

32. Every nation hath its set time. And when their time is come, they shall not retard it an hour; and they shall not advance it.

33. O children of Adam! there shall come to you Apostles from among yourselves, rehearsing my signs to you; and whoso shall fear God and do good works, no fear shall be upon them, neither shall they be put to grief.

34. But they who charge our signs with falsehood, and turn away from them in their

pride, shall be inmates of the fire: for ever shall they abide therein.

35. And who is worse than he who deviseth a lie of God, or treateth our signs as lies? To them shall a portion here below be assigned in accordance with the Book of our decrees, until the time when our messengers, as they receive their souls, shall say, "Where are they on whom ye called beside God?" They shall say: "Gone from us." And they shall witness against themselves that they were infidels.

36. He shall say, "Enter ye into the Fire with the generations of Djinn and men who have preceded you. So oft as a fresh generation entereth, it shall curse its sister, until when they have all reached it, the last comers shall say to the former, 'O our Lord! these are they who led us astray: assign them therefore a double torment of the fire:'" He will say, "Ye shall all have double." But of this are ye ignorant.

37. And the former of them shall say to the latter, "What advantage have ye over us? Taste ye therefore the torment for that which ye have done."

38. Verily, they who have charged our signs with falsehood and have turned away from them in their pride, Heaven's gates shall not be opened to them, nor shall they enter Paradise, until the camel passeth through the eye of the needle. After this sort will we recompense the transgressors.

39. They shall make their bed in Hell, and above them shall be coverings of fire! After this sort will we recompense the evil doers.

40. But as to those who have believed and done the things which are right, (we will lay on no one a burden beyond his power)—These shall be inmates of Paradise: for ever shall they abide therein;

41. And we will remove whatever rancour was in their bosoms: rivers shall roll at their feet: and they shall say, "Praise be to God who hath guided us hither! We had not been guided had not God guided us! Of a surety the Apostles of our Lord came to us with truth." And a voice shall cry to them, "This is Paradise, of which, as the meed of your works, ye are made heirs."

42. And the inmates of Paradise shall cry to the inmates of the Fire, "Now have we found what our Lord promised us to be true. Have ye too found what your Lord promised you to be true?" And they shall answer, "Yes." And a Herald shall proclaim between them: "The curse of God be upon the evil doers,

43. Who turn men aside from the way of God, and seek to make it crooked, and who believe not in the life to come!"

44. And between them shall be a partition; and on the wall AL ARAF shall be men who will know all, by their tokens, and they shall cry to the inmates of Paradise, "Peace be on you!" but they

shall not yet enter it, although they long to do so.

45. And when their eyes are turned towards the inmates of the Fire, they shall say, "O our Lord! place us not with the offending people."

46. And they who are upon Al Araf shall cry to those whom they shall know by their tokens, "Your amassings and your pride have availed you nothing.

47. Are these they on whom ye sware God would not bestow mercy? Enter ye into Paradise! where no fear shall be upon you, neither shall ye be put to grief."

48. And the inmates of the Fire shall cry to the inmates of Paradise: "Pour upon us some water, or of the refreshments God hath given you?" They shall say, "Truly God hath forbidden both to unbelievers,

49. Who made their religion a sport and pastime, and whom the life of the world hath deceived." This day therefore will we forget them, as they forgot the meeting of this their day, and as they did deny our signs.

50. And now have we brought them the Book: with knowledge have we explained it; a guidance and a mercy to them that believe.

51. What have they to wait for now but its interpretation? When its interpretation shall come, they who aforetime were oblivious of it shall say, "The Prophets of our Lord did indeed bring the truth; shall we have any intercessor to intercede for us? or could we not be sent back? Then would we act otherwise than we have acted." But they have ruined themselves; and the deities of their own devising have fled from them!

52. Your Lord is God, who in six days created the Heavens and the Earth, and then mounted the throne: He throweth the veil of night over the day: it pursueth it swiftly: and he created the sun and the moon and the stars, subjected to laws by His behest: Is not all creation and its empire His? Blessed be God the Lord of the Worlds!

53. Call upon your Lord with lowliness and in secret, for He loveth not transgressors.

54. And commit not disorders on the earth after it hath been well ordered; and call on Him with fear and longing desire: Verily the mercy of God is nigh unto the righteous.

55. And He it is who sendeth forth the winds as the heralds of his compassion, until they bring up the laden clouds, which we drive along to some dead land and send down water thereon, by which we cause an upgrowth of all kinds of fruit. —Thus will we bring forth the dead. Haply ye will reflect.

56. In a rich soil, its plants spring forth abundantly by the will of its Lord, and in that which is bad, they spring forth but scantily. Thus do We diversify our signs for those who are thankful.

Sura VIII.—The Spoils

1. They will question thee about THE SPOILS. Say: The

spoils are God's and the apostle's. Therefore, fear God, and settle this among yourselves; and obey God and his apostle, if you are believers.

2. Believers are they only whose hearts thrill with fear when God is named, and whose faith increaseth at each recital of his signs, and who put their trust in their Lord;

3. Who observe the prayers, and give alms out of that with which we have supplied them;

4. These are the believers their due grade awaiteth them in the presence of their Lord, and forgiveness, and a generous provision.

5. Remember how thy Lord caused thee to go forth from thy home on a mission of truth, and part of the believers were quite averse to it:

6. They disputed with thee about the truth which had been made so clear, as if they were being led forth to death, and saw it before them:

7. And remember when God promised you that one of the two troops should fall to you, and ye desired that they who had no arms should fall to you: but God purposed to prove true the truth of his words, and to cut off the uttermost part of the infidels;

8. That he might prove his truth to be the truth, and bring to nought that which is nought, though the impious were averse to it:

9. When ye sought succour of your Lord, and he answered you, "I will verily aid you with

a thousand angels, rank on rank:"

10. And God made this promise as pure good tidings, and to assure your hearts by it: for succour cometh from God alone! Verily God is Mighty, Wise.

71. O prophet! say to the captives who are in your hands, "If God shall know good to be in your hearts, He will give you good beyond all that hath been taken from you, and will forgive you: for God is Forgiving, Merciful."

72. But if they seek to deal treacherously with you—they have already dealt treacherously with God before! Therefore hath He given you power over them. God is Knowing, Wise.

73. Verily, they who have believed and fled their homes and spent their substance for the cause of God, and they who have taken in the prophet and been helpful to him, shall be near of kin the one to the other. And they who who have believed, but have not fled their homes, shall have no rights of kindred with you at all, until they too fly their country. Yet if they seek aid from you on account of the faith, your part it is to give them aid, except against a people between whom and yourselves there shall be a treaty. And God beholdeth your actions.

74. The infidels lend one another mutual help. Unless ye do the same, there will be discord in the land and great corruption.

75. But as for those who have believed and fled their country, and fought on the path

of God, and given the prophet an asylum, and been helpful to him, these are the faithful; Mercy is their due and a noble provision.

76. And they who have believed and fled their country since, and have fought at your side, these also are of you. Those who are united by ties of blood are the nearest of kin to each other. This is in the Book of God. Verily, God knoweth all things.

Sura X.—Jonah, Peace Be On Him.

50. SAY: I have no power over my own weal or woe, but as God pleaseth. Every people hath its time: when their time is come, they shall neither retard nor advance it an hour.

51. SAY: How think ye? if God's punishment came on you by night or by day, what portion of it would the wicked desire to hasten on?

52. When it falleth on you, will ye believe it then? Yes! ye will believe it then. Yet did ye challenge its speedy coming.

53. Then shall it be said to the transgressors, "Taste ye the punishment of eternity! Shall ye be rewarded but as ye have wrought?"

54. They will desire thee to inform them whether this be true? SAY: Yes! by my Lord it is the truth: and it is not ye who can weaken Him.

55. And every soul that hath sinned, if it possessed all that is on earth, would assuredly ransom itself therewith; and they will proclaim their repentance when they have seen the punishment: and there shall be a rightful decision between them, and they shall not be unjustly dealt with.

56. Is not whatever is in the Heavens and the Earth God's? Is not then the promise of God true? Yet most of them know it not.

57. He maketh alive and He causeth to die, and to Him shall ye return.

58. O men! now hath a warning come to you from your Lord, and a medicine for what is in your breasts, and a guidance and a mercy to believers.

59. SAY: Through the grace of God and his mercy! and in this therefore let them rejoice: better is this than all ye amass.

60. SAY: What think ye? of what God hath sent down to you for food, have ye made unlawful and lawful? SAY: Hath God permitted you? or invent ye on the part of God?

61. But what on the day of Resurrection will be the thought of those who invent a lie on the part of God? Truly God is full of bounties to man; but most of them give not thanks.

62. Thou shalt not be employed in affairs, nor shalt thou read a text out of the Koran, nor shall ye work any work, but we will be witnesses over you when ye are engaged therein: and not the weight of an atom on Earth or in Heaven escapeth thy Lord; nor is there aught that is less than this or greater, but it is in the perspicuous Book.

63. Are not the friends of God, those on whom no fear shall come, nor shall they be put to grief?

64. They who believe and fear God—

65. For them are good tidings in this life, and in the next! There is no change in the words of God! This, the great felicity!

66. And let not their discourse grieve thee: for all might is God's: the Hearer, the Knower, He!

67. Is not whoever is in the Heavens and the Earth subject to God? What then do they follow who, beside God, call upon deities they have joined with Him? They follow but a conceit, and they are but liars!

68. It is He who hath ordained for you the night wherein to rest, and the lightsome day. Verily in this are signs for those who hearken.

Sura XI.—Hound

112. Of old gave we Moses the Book, and they fell to variance about it. If a decree of respite had not gone forth from thy Lord, there had surely been a decision between them. Thy people also are in suspicious doubts about the Koran.

113. And truly thy Lord will repay every one according to their works! for He is well aware of what they do.

114. Go straight on then as thou hast been commanded, and he also who hath turned to God with thee, and let him transgress no more. He beholdeth what ye do.

115. Lean not on the evil doers lest the Fire lay hold on you.

Ye have no protector, save God, and ye shall not be helped against Him.

116. And observe prayer at early morning, at the close of the day, and at the approach of night; for the good deeds drive away the evil deeds. This is a warning for those who reflect:

117. And persevere steadfastly, for verily God will not suffer the reward of the righteous to perish.

118. Were the generations before you, endued with virtue, and who forbad corrupt doings on the earth, more than a few of those whom we delivered? but the evil doers followed their selfish pleasures, and became transgressors.

119. And thy Lord was not one who would destroy those cities unjustly, when its inhabitants were righteous.

120. Had thy Lord pleased he would have made mankind of one religion: but those only to whom thy Lord hath granted his mercy will cease to differ. And unto this hath He created them; for the word of thy Lord shall be fulfilled, "I will wholly fill hell with Djinn and men."

121. And all that we have related to thee of the histories of these Apostles, is to confirm thy heart thereby. By these hath the truth reached thee, and a monition and warning to those who believe.

122. But say to those who believe not, "Act as ye may and can: we will act our part: and wait ye; we verily will wait.

123. To God belong the secret things of the Heavens and of the Earth: all things return to

him: worship him then and put thy trust in Him: thy Lord is not regardless of your doings.

Sura XIII.—Thunder

19. Shall he then who knoweth that what hath been sent down to thee from thy Lord is the truth, act like him who is blind? Men of insight only will bear this in mind,

20. Who fulfil their pledge to God, and break not their compact:

21. And who join together what God hath bidden to be joined, and who fear their Lord, and dread an ill reckoning;

22. And who, from desire to see the face of their Lord, are constant amid trials, and observe prayer and give alms, in secret and openly, out of what we have bestowed upon them, and turn aside evil by good: for these is the recompense of that abode,

23. Gardens of Eden—into which they shall enter together with the just of their fathers, and their wives, and their descendants: and the angels shall go in unto them at every portal:

24. "Peace be with you!" say they, "because ye have endured all things!" Charming the recompense of their abode!

25. But those who, after having contracted it, break their covenant with God, and cut asunder what God hath bidden to be united, and commit misdeeds on the earth, these, a curse awaiteth them, and an ill abode!

26. God is open-handed with supplies to whom he will, or is sparing. They rejoice in the life that now is, but this present life is but a passing good, in respect of the life to come!

27. And they who believe not say, "Unless a sign be sent down to him from his Lord. . . ." SAY: God truly will mislead whom he will; and He will guide to Himself him who turneth to Him,

28. Those who believe, and whose hearts rest securely on the thought of God. What! Shall not men's hearts repose in the thought of God? They who believe and do the things that be right— blessedness awaiteth them, and a goodly home.

29. Thus have we sent thee to a people whom other peoples have preceded, that thou mightest rehearse to them our revelations to thee. Yet they believe not on the God of Mercy. SAY: He is my Lord. There is no God but He. In Him do I put my trust. To Him must I return.

30. If there were a Koran by which the mountains could be set in motion, or the earth cleft, or the dead be made to speak. . . . ! But all sovereignty is in the hands of God. Do then believers doubt that had He pleased God would certainly have guided all men aright?

31. Misfortune shall not cease to light on the unbelievers for what they have done, or to take up its abode hard by their dwellings, until the threat of God come to pass. Verily, God will not fail his plighted word.

32. Before thee indeed have apostles

been mocked at; but though I bore long with the unbelievers, at last I seized upon them;—and how severe was my punishment!

33. Who is it then that is standing over every soul to mark its actions? Yet have they set up associates with God. SAY: Name them. What! Would ye inform God of that which He knoweth not on the Earth? Or are they not a mere empty name? But prepared of old for the infidels was this fraud of theirs; and they are turned aside from the path; and whom God causeth to err, no guide shall there be for him!

34. Chastisement awaiteth them in this present life, and more grievous shall be the chastisement of the next: and none shall screen them from God.

35. A picture of the Paradise which God hath promised to them that fear Him. The rivers flow beneath its bowers: its food and its shades are perpetual. This is the reward of those who fear God; but the reward of the unbelievers is the Fire.

36. They to whom we have given the Book rejoice in what hath been sent down to thee; yet some are banded together who deny a part of it. SAY: I am commanded to worship God, and not to associate any creature with Him. On Him do I call, and to Him shall I return.

37. Thus, then, as a code in the Arabic tongue have we sent down the Koran; and truly, if after the knowledge that hath reached thee thou follow their desires, thou shalt have no guardian nor protector against God.

38. Apostles truly have we already sent before thee, and wives and offspring have we given them. Yet no apostle had come with miracles unless by the leave of God. To each age its Book.

39. What He pleaseth will God abrogate or confirm: for with Him is the source of revelation.

40. Moreover, whether we cause thee to see the fulfilment of part of our menaces, or whether we take thee hence, verily, thy work is preaching only, and ours to take account.

41. See they not that we come into their land and cut short its borders? God pronounceth a doom, and there is none to reverse his doom. And swift is He to take account.

42. Those who lived before them made plots: but all plotting is controlled by God: He knoweth the works of every one, and the infidels shall know whose will be the recompense of the abode.

43. The infidels, moreover, will say; Thou are not sent of God. SAY: God is witness enough betwixt me and you, and, whoever hath knowledge of the Book.

Sura XVI.—The Bee

110. These are they whose hearts and ears and eyes God hath sealed up: these are the careless ones: in the next world shall they perish beyond a doubt.

111. To those also who after their trials fled their country,

then fought and endured with patience, verily, thy Lord will in the end be forgiving, gracious.

112. On a certain day shall every soul come to plead for itself, and every soul shall be repaid according to its deeds; and they shall not be wronged.

113. God proposeth the instance of a city, secure and at ease, to which its supplies came in plenty from every side. But she was thankless for the boons of God; God therefore made her taste the woe of famine and of fear, for what they had done.

114. Moreover, an apostle of their own people came to them, and they treated him as an impostor. So chastisement overtook them because they were evil doers.

115. Of what God hath supplied you eat the lawful and good, and be grateful for the favours of God, if ye are his worshippers.

116. Forbidden to you is that only which dieth of itself, and blood, and swine's flesh, and that which hath been slain in the name of any other than God: but if any be forced, and neither lust for it nor wilfully transgress, then verily God is forgiving, gracious.

117. And say not with a lie upon your tongue, "This is lawful and this is forbidden:" for so will ye invent a lie concerning God: but they who invent a lie of God shall not prosper:

118. Brief their enjoyment, but sore their punishment!

119. To the Jews we have forbidden that of which we before told

thee; we injured them not, but they injured themselves.

120. To those who have done evil in ignorance, then afterwards have repented and amended, verily thy Lord is in the end right gracious, merciful.

121. Verily, Abraham was a leader in religion: obedient to God, sound in faith: he was not of those who join gods with God.

122. Grateful was he for His favours: God chose him and guided him into the straight way;

123. And we bestowed on him good things in this world: and in the world to come he shall be among the just.

124. We have moreover revealed to thee that thou follow the religion of Abraham, the sound in faith. He was not of those who join gods with God.

125. The Sabbath was only ordained for those who differed about it: and of a truth thy Lord will decide between them on the day of resurrection as to the subject of their disputes.

126. Summon thou to the way of thy Lord with wisdom and with kindly warning: dispute with them in the kindest manner: thy Lord best knoweth those who stray from his way, and He best knoweth those who have yielded to his guidance.

127. If ye make reprisals, then make them to the same extent that ye were injured: but if ye can endure patiently, best will it be for the patiently enduring.

128. Endure then with patience. But thy patient endurance must be sought in none but God. And be not grieved about

the infidels, and be not troubled at their devices; for God is with those who fear him and do good deeds.

Sura XXII.—The Pilgrimage

35. And to every people have we appointed rites, that they may commemorate the name of God over the brute beasts which He hath provided for them. And your God is the one God. To Him, therefore, surrender yourselves: and bear thou good tidings to those who humble them,—

36. Whose hearts, when mention is made of God, thrill with awe; and to those who remain stedfast under all that befalleth them, and observe prayer, and give alms of that with which we have supplied them.

37. And the camels have we appointed you for the sacrifice to God: much good have ye in them. Make mention, therefore, of the name of God over them when ye slay them, as they stand in a row; and when they are fallen over on their sides, eat of them, and feed him who is content and asketh not, and him who asketh. Thus have We subjected them to you, to the intent ye should be thankful.

38. By no means can their flesh reach unto God, neither their blood; but piety on your part reacheth Him. Thus hath He subjected them to you, that ye might magnify God for His guidance: moreover, announce to those who do good deeds

39. That God will ward off mischief from believers: for God loveth not the false, the Infidel.

40. A sanction is given to those who, because they have suffered outrages, have taken up arms; and verily, God is well able to succour them:

41. Those who have been driven forth from their homes wrongfully, only because they say "Our Lord is the God." And if God had not repelled some men by others, cloisters, and churches, and oratories, and mosques, wherein the name of God is ever commemorated, would surely have been destroyed. And him who helpeth God will God surely help: for God is right Strong, Mighty:—

42. Those who, if we stablish them in this land, will observe prayer, and pay the alms of obligation, and enjoin what is right, and forbid what is evil. And the final issue of all things is unto God.

43. Moreover, if they charge thee with imposture, then already, before them, the people of Noah, and Ad and Themoud, and the people of Abraham, and the people of Lot, and the dwellers in Madian, have charged their prophets with imposture! Moses, too, was charged with imposture! And I bore long with the unbelievers; then seized on them: and how great was the change I wrought!

44. And how many cities which had been ungodly, and whose roofs are now laid low in ruin, have We destroyed! And wells have been

abandoned and lofty castles!

45. Have they not journeyed through the land? Have they not hearts to understand with, or ears to hear with? It is not that to these sights their eyes are blind, but the hearts in their breasts are blind!

46. And they will bid thee to hasten the chastisement. But God cannot fail His threat. And verily, a day with thy Lord is as a thousand years, as ye reckon them!

Sura XXIII.—The Believers

1. Happy now the BELIEVERS,
2. Who humble them in their prayer,
3. And who keep aloof from vain words,
4. And who are doers of alms deeds,
5. And who restrain their appetites,
6. (Save with their wives, or the slaves whom their right hands possess: for in that case they shall be free from blame:
7. But they whose desires reach further than this are transgressors:)
8. And who tend well their trusts and their covenants,
9. And who keep them strictly to their prayers:
10. These shall be the heritors, Who shall inherit the paradise, to abide therein for ever.

Sura XXVI.—The Poets

69. And recite to them the story of Abraham
70. When he said to his Father and to his people, "What worship ye?"
71. They said, "We worship idols,

and constant is our devotion to them."

72. He said, "Can they hear you when ye cry to them?
73. Or help you or do you harm?"
74. They said, "But we found our Fathers do the like."
75. He said, "How think ye? They whom ye worship,
76. Ye and your fathers of early days,
77. Are my foes: but not so the Lord of the Worlds,
78. Who hath created me, and guideth me,
79. Who giveth me food and drink;
80. And when I am sick, he healeth me,
81. And who will cause me to die and again quicken me,
82. And who, I hope, will forgive me my sins in the day of reckoning.
83. My Lord! bestow on me wisdom and join me to the just,
84. And give me a good name among posterity,
85. And make me one of the heirs of the garden of delight,
86. And forgive my father, for he was one of the erring,
87. And put me not to shame on the day when mankind shall be raised up,
88. The day when neither wealth nor children shall avail,
89. Save to him who shall come to God with a sound heart:
90. When Paradise shall be brought near the pious,
91. And Hell shall lay open for those who have gone astray.

Sura XXVIII.—The Story

68. And thy Lord createth what he will and hath a free choice. But they, the false gods, have no power to choose. Glory be to God! and high let him be exalted above

those whom they associate with him.

69. And thy Lord knoweth what their breasts conceal and what they bring to light.

70. And He is God! There is no god but He! His, all praise in this life and in the next, and His the power supreme, and to Him shall ye be brought back!

71. SAY: What think ye? If God should enshroud you with a long night until the day of resurrection, what god beside God would bring you light? Will ye not then hearken?

72. SAY: What think ye? If God should make it one long day for you until the day of resurrection, what god but God could bring you the night in which to take your rest? Will ye not then see?

73. Of His mercy he hath made for you the night that ye may take your rest in it; and the day that ye may seek what ye need out of his bounteous supplies, and that ye may give thanks.

74. One day God will call to them and say, "Where are my companions as ye supposed them?"

75. And we will bring up a witness out of every nation and say, "Bring your proofs." And they shall know that the truth is with God alone, and the gods of their own devising shall desert them.

76. Now Korah was of the people of Moses: but he behaved haughtily toward them; for we had given him such treasure that its keys would have burdened a company of men of strength. When his people said to him,

"Exult not, for God loveth not those who exult;

77. But seek, by means of what God hath given thee, to attain the future Mansion; and neglect not thy part in this world, but be bounteous to others as God hath been bounteous to thee, and seek not to commit excesses on the earth; for God loveth not those who commit excesses:"

78. He said, "It hath been given me only on account of the knowledge that is in me." Did he not know that God had destroyed before him generations that were mightier than he in strength and had amassed more abundant wealth? But the wicked shall not be asked of their crimes.

79. And Korah went forth to his people in his pomp. Those who were greedy for this present life said, "Oh that we had the like of that which hath been bestowed on Korah! Truly he is possessed of great good fortune."

80. But they to whom knowledge had been given said, "Woe to you! the reward of God is better for him who believeth and worketh righteousness, and none shall win it but those who have patiently endured."

81. And we clave the earth for him and for his palace, and he had no forces, in the place of God, to help him, nor was he among those who are succoured.

82. And in the morning those who the day before had coveted his lot said, "Aha! God enlargeth supplies to whom he pleaseth of his servants,

or is sparing. Had not God been gracious to us, He had caused it to cleave for us. Aha! the ungrateful can never prosper."

83. As to this future mansion, we will bestow it on those who seek not to exalt them in the earth or to do wrong: And there is a happy issue for the God-fearing.

84. Whoso doeth good shall have reward beyond its merits, and whoso doeth evil, they who do evil shall be rewarded only as they shall have wrought.

Sura XXXI.—Lokman

1. Elif. Lam. Mim. These are the verses (signs) of the wise Book,

2. A guidance and a mercy to the righteous,

3. Who observe prayer, and pay the impost, and believe firmly in the life to come:—

4. These rest on guidance from their Lord, and with these it shall be well.

5. But a man there is who buyeth an idle tale, that in his lack of knowledge he may mislead others from the way of God, and turn it to scorn. For such is prepared a shameful punishment!

6. And when our signs are rehearsed to him, he turneth away disdainfully, as though he heard them not,—as though his ears were heavy with deafness. Announce to him therefore tidings of an afflictive punishment!

7. But they who shall have believed and wrought good works, shall enjoy the gardens of delight:

8. For ever shall they dwell therein:

it is God's true promise! and He is the Mighty, the Wise.

9. Without pillars that can be seen hath He created the heavens, and on the earth hath thrown mountains lest it should move with you; and He hath scattered over it animals of every sort: and from the Heaven we send down rain and cause every kind of noble plant to grow up therein.

10. This is the creation of God: Shew me now what others than He have created. Ah! the ungodly are in a manifest delusion.

11. Of old we bestowed wisdom upon LOKMAN, and taught him thus—"Be thankful to God: for whoever is thankful, is thankful to his own behoof; and if any shall be thankless . . . God truly is self-sufficient, worthy of all praise!"

12. And bear in mind when Lokman said to his son by way of warning, "O my son! join not other gods with God, for the joining gods with God is the great impiety."

13. (We have commanded man concerning his parents. His mother carrieth him with weakness upon weakness; nor until after two years is he weaned. Be grateful to me, and to thy parents. Unto me shall all come.

14. But if they importune thee to join that with Me of which thou hast no knowledge, obey them not: comport thyself towards them in this world as is meet and right; but follow the way of him who turneth unto me. Unto me shall ye return at last,

and then will I tell you of your doings;)

15. "O my son! verily God will bring everything to light, though it were but the weight of a grain of mustard-seed, and hidden in a rock or in the heavens or in the earth; for, God is subtile, informed of all.

16. O my son! observe prayer, and enjoin the right and forbid the wrong, and be patient under whatever shall betide thee: for this is a bounden duty.

17. And distort not thy face at men; nor walk thou loftily on the earth; for God loveth no arrogant vain-glorious one.

18. But let thy pace be middling; and lower thy voice: for the least pleasing of voices is surely the voice of asses."

19. See ye not how that God hath put under you all that is in the heavens and all that is on the earth, and hath been bounteous to you of his favours, both for soul and body. But some are there who dispute of God without knowledge, and have no guidance and no illuminating Book:

20. And when it is said to them, Follow ye what God hath sent down, they say, "Nay; that religion in which we found our fathers will we follow." What! though Satan bid them to the torment of the flame?

21. But whoso setteth his face toward God with self-surrender, and is a doer of that which is good, hath laid hold on a sure handle; for unto God is the issue of all things.

22. But let not the unbelief of the unbelieving grieve thee: unto us shall they return: then will we tell them of their doings; for God knoweth the very secrets of the breast.

23. Yet a little while will we provide for them: afterwards will we force them to a stern punishment.

24. If thou ask them who hath created the heavens and the earth, they will certainly reply, "God." SAY: God be praised! But most of them have no knowledge.

25. God's, whatever is in the Heavens and the Earth! for God, He is the Rich, the Praiseworthy.

26. If all the trees that are upon the earth were to become pens, and if God should after that swell the sea into seven seas of ink, His words would not be exhausted: for God is Mighty, Wise.

27. Your creation and your quickening hereafter, are but as those of a single individual. Verily, God Heareth, Seeth!

28. Seest thou not that God causeth the night to come in upon the day, and the day to come in upon the night? and that he hath subjected the sun and the moon to laws by which each speedeth along to an appointed goal? and that God therefore is acquainted with that which ye do?

29. This, for that God is the truth; and that whatever ye call upon beside Him is a vain thing; and that God—He is the High, the Great.

30. Seest thou not how the ships speed on in the sea, through the favour of God, that he may shew you of his signs?

for herein are signs to all patient, grateful ones.

31. When the waves cover them like dark shadows they call upon God as with sincere religion; but when He safely landeth them, some of them there are who halt between two opinions. Yet none reject our signs but all deceitful, ungrateful ones.

32. O men! fear ye your Lord, and dread the day whereon father shall not atone for son, neither shall a son in the least atone for his father.

33. Aye! the promise of God is a truth. Let not this present life then deceive you; neither let the deceiver deceive you concerning God.

34. Aye! God!—with Him is the knowledge of the Hour: and He sendeth down the rain—and He knoweth what is in the wombs—but no soul knoweth what it shall have gotten on the morrow: neither knoweth any soul in what land it shall die. But God is knowing, informed of all.

Sura XL.—The Believer

1. Ha. Mim. The Revelation (sending down) of the Book is from God the Almighty, the All-knowing,

2. Forgiver of sin, and receiver of penitence, — vehement in chastisement,

3. Long-suffering! There is no God but He: to Him shall be the final gathering.

4. None but infidels gainsay the signs of God: but let not their prosperity in the land deceive thee.

5. The people of Noah, and the confederates after them, have brought the charge of imposture before these Meccans: each nation schemed against their apostle to lay violent hold on him, and disputed with vain words to refute the truth. Therefore did I lay violent hold on them; and how great was my chastisement!

6. Thus is it that thy Lord's sentence, that inmates shall they be of the fire, was accomplished upon the infidels.

7. They who bear the throne and they who encircle it, celebrate the praise of their Lord and believe in Him, and implore forgiveness for the believers:—"O our Lord! thou embracest all things in mercy and knowledge; forgive, therefore, those who turn to thee and follow thy path; keep them from the pains of hell:

8. O our Lord! and bring them into the Gardens of Eden which thou hast promised to them, and to the righteous ones of their fathers and their wives and their children; for thou art the Allmighty, the All-wise:

9. And keep them from evil: for on him hast thou mercy whom on that day thou shalt keep from evil;" and this will be the great felicity.

10. But to the infidels shall a voice cry, "Surely the hatred of God is more grievous than your hatred of yourselves, when ye were called to the faith, and remained unbelievers."

Sura XLIX.—The Apartments

1. O Believers! enter not upon any affair ere God and His Apos-

tle permit you; and fear ye God: for God Heareth, Knoweth.

2. O Believers! raise not your voices above the voice of the Prophet, neither speak loud to him as ye speak loud one to another, lest your works come to nought, and ye unaware of it.

3. They who lower their voices in the presence of the Apostle of God, are the persons whose hearts God hath inclined to piety. Forgiveness shall be theirs and a rich reward.

4. They who call out to thee while thou art within thine APARTMENTS, have most of them no right perception of what is due to thee.

5. But if they wait patiently till thou come forth to them, it were far better for them. But God is Indulgent, Merciful.

6. O Believers! if any bad man come to you with news, clear it up at once, lest through ignorance ye harm others, and speedily have to repent of what ye have done.

7. And know that an Apostle of God is among you! should he give way to you in many matters ye would certainly become guilty of a crime. But God hath endeared the faith to you, and hath given it favour in your hearts, and hath made unbelief, and wickedness, and disobedience hateful to you. Such are they who pursue a right course,

8. Through the bounty and grace which is from God: and God is Knowing, Wise.

9. If two bodies of the faithful are at war, then make ye peace between them: and if the one of them wrong the other, fight against that party which doth the wrong, until they come back to the precepts of God: if they come back, make peace between them with fairness, and act impartially; God 'loveth those who act with impartiality.

10. Only the faithful are brethren; wherefore make peace between your brethren; and fear God, that ye may obtain mercy.

11. O Believers! let not men laugh men to scorn who haply may be better than themselves; neither let women laugh women to scorn who may haply be better than themselves! Neither defame one another, nor call one another by nicknames. Bad is it to be called wicked after having professed the faith: and whoso repent not of this are doers of wrong.

12. O Believers! avoid frequent suspicions, for some suspicions are a crime; and pry not: neither let the one of you traduce another in his absence. Would any one of you like to eat the flesh of his dead brother? Surely ye would loathe it. And fear ye God: for God is Ready to turn, Merciful.

13. O men! verily, we have created you of a male and a female; and we have divided you into peoples and tribes that ye might have knowledge one of another. Truly, the most worthy of honour in the sight of God is he who feareth Him most. Verily, God is Knowing, Cognizant.

14. The Arabs of the desert say,

"We believe." SAY thou: Ye believe not; but rather say, "We profess Islam;" for the faith hath not yet found its way into your hearts. But if ye obey God and His Apostle, he will not allow you to lose any of your actions: for God is Indulgent, Merciful.

15. The true believers are those only who believe in God and His Apostle, and afterwards doubt not; and who contend with their substance and their persons on the path of God. These are the sincere.

16. SAY: Will ye teach God about your religion? when God knoweth whatever is in the Heavens and on the Earth: yea, God hath knowledge of all things.

17. They taunt thee with their having embraced Islam. SAY: Taunt me not with your having embraced Islam: God rather taunteth you with His having guided you to the faith: acknowledge this if ye are sincere.

18. Verily, God knoweth the secrets of the Heavens and of the Earth: and God beholdeth what ye do.

X

SHINTO

SHINTO is the national religion of Japan. According to some authorities, it "unquestionably represents the distinctive religious genius of Japan from the very beginning of its history". Others, while recognizing its deep significance for Japanese life, argue that it is in no sense a religion but is rather a patriotic cult. Whether we call it a religion or not, it has unquestionably made a significant contribution to the political theory and national stability of Japan.

According to Shinto, the islands of Japan were the first pieces of land created by the gods and are thus designed to be the center of the world. The first Japanese Emperor was, the scriptures of Shinto teach, the direct descendant of the heavenly Sun Goddess. He is, thereby, chosen to rule the entire world from his islands and to function as the representative and emissary of the divine. All emperors of Japan are believed to be direct descendants of this first Emperor and thus of the Sun Goddess. Consequently, they too have the divine authority to rule the world.

So thoroughly has this belief been fostered in the minds of the Japanese by Shinto that the Constitution of 1889 begins by declaring that the Mikado sits upon "the throne of a lineal succession unbroken for ages eternal" and that he has all the authority which the Sun Goddess gave to the first Emperor.

However, Shinto has for 1440 years coexisted and intermingled with other religions, chief among which are Confucianism, Buddhism, and Taoism, to such an extent that even its name today is Chinese. The Japanese name is *Kami-no Michi,* translated "The Way of the Gods". But this has been translated into Chinese as *Shin-tao,* the *tao* being the same as we find it in Taoism. This form has been shortened to Shinto.

Two writings are fundamental to Shinto and have become the sacred scriptures of the religion. Both make the claim of being purely historical, although they are loaded with myths, legends, and unfounded tales. The earliest of these documents is the *Kojiki* or *Records of Ancient Matters.* This work dates from 712 A.D. and professes to tell the story of the "Age of the Gods", before men were created, and of the early emperors. This book was followed in 720 A.D. by the *Nihongi* or *Chronicles of Japan.* This work tells the stories of the emperors of Japan, recites their genealogies, and claims to quote them on various matters.

One feature of the Kojiki needs mentioning. Christian readers may find some parts of it morally offensive. Indeed, numerous passages are so objectionable to Western minds that the English translator refused to render them into English, but turned to Latin for the translation.

The *Engishiki* or *Institutes of the Period of Engi,* another of the sacred documents of Shinto, tells the story of the rise of the Shinto cult and contains 25 prayers for various ceremonial occasions. This work comes from the tenth century.

Still another portion of Shinto scripture is the *Manyoshu* or *Collection of Ten Thousand Leaves,* an anthology of 4496 poems dating from the fifth to the eighth centuries.

The gods of Shinto are untold in number. They are said in one place to number 80 myriads and in another to number 800 myriads. These gods lived as men and women, subject to all the passions of human beings. One of the most important among these deities was the sun, an indication of the nature worship fundamental to this religion. However, the sun is not thought of as being male, as in other religions where the sun is worshiped. It is female and is the source of the line of Japanese emperors. Because of this, the Mikado is worshiped as divine and is held to be sacred, inviolable, and infallible for all time. So sacred is the Emperor that until 1922 no one was permitted to look down upon him even in a physical sense. Since that time the Mikado has, as Prince, moved among the people to some extent, even passing along the streets of various cities in Japan.

Worship of the Sun Goddess is emblemized in the national flag of Japan, a rising sun. This religious and patriotic symbol means to each Japanese a promise that, as all the world depends for its life upon the sun, so it must depend for its political life upon Japan and each Japanese is divinely commissioned to force the rule of the Sun Goddess upon the rest of the world.

KOJIKI

THE *Kojiki,* or *Records of Ancient Matters,* was completed in 712 A.D. Though its date of completion is late, it records for us the most ancient mythology, legends, and traditional history of Japan. Soon after this work was compiled the old Japanese culture was so infused with Chinese culture as to lose almost all of its originality. But this book gives us the story of ancient Japan in an almost pure form.

The book is a pseudo-historical account of the lives and deeds of Japan's rulers. It begins with the ancient legends of the creation of the deities and the formation of the islands of Japan. As in the early legends of other religions, this story begins with the forces of light and darkness eventually producing the universe and peopling it with many deities. These deities create the land and the people in it. Then follow short descriptions of the lives of the emperors. All of these rulers are declared to be divine, direct descendants of the early deities.

We have selected the accounts of the creation of the universe and particularly of the islands of Japan.

Vol. I.—Preface:

I Yasumaro say:

Now when chaos had begun to condense, but force and form were not yet manifest, and there was nought named, nought done, who could know its shape? Nevertheless Heaven and Earth first parted, and the Three Deities performed the commencement of creation; the Passive and Active Essences then developed, and the Two Spirits became the ancestors of all things. Therefore did he enter obscurity and emerge into light, and the Sun and Moon were revealed by the washing of his eyes; he floated on and plunged into the sea-water, and Heavenly and Earthly Deities appeared through the ablutions of his person. So in the dimness of the great commencement, we, by relying on the original teaching, learn the time of the conception of the earth and of the birth of islands; in the remoteness of the original beginning, we, by trusting the former sages, perceive the era of the genesis of Deities and the establishment of men. . . .

. . . So from the Deity Master-of-the-August-Centre-of-Heaven down to His Augustness Prince-Wave-Limit-Brave - Cormorant - Thatch - Meeting-Incompletely makes the First Volume; from the Heavenly Sovereign Kamu-Yamato-Ihare-Biko down to the august reign of Homuda makes the Second Volume; from the Emperor Oho-Sazaki down to the great palace of Woharida makes the Third Volume. Altogether I have written Three Volumes, which I reverently and respectfully present. I Yasumaro, with true trembling and true fear, bow my head, bow my head.

Vol. I, Section 3:

Hereupon all the Heavenly Deities commanded the two Deities His Augustness the Male-Who-Invites and Her Augustness the Female-Who-

Invites, ordering them to "make, consolidate, and give birth to this drifting land". Granting to them an heavenly jewelled spear, they (thus) deigned to charge them. So the two Deities, standing upon the Floating Bridge of Heaven, pushed down the jewelled spear and stirred with it, whereupon, when they had stirred the brine till it went curdlecurdle, and drew (the spear) up, the brine that dripped down from the end of the spear was piled up and became an island. This is the island of Onogoro.

Vol. I, Section 7:

The total number of islands given birth to jointly by the two Deities the Male-Who-Invites and the Female-Who-Invites was fourteen, and of Deities thirty-five.

Vol. III, Section 133:

Going up and reaching Yamato, he said: "I will halt here to-day and, having purified myself, will go forth tomorrow and worship at the temple of the Deity". So that place is called by the name of Toho-tsu-Asuka. . . .

SELECTED MATERIALS

A GREAT many Shinto documents have been translated by W. G. Aston in his scholarly work entitled *Shinto (The Way of the Gods)*. These reveal some of the religious ideals of the religion and are valuable for an understanding of the beliefs and hopes of many followers of Shinto. We have selected a few of these, in each case the most representative.

God of Fujiyama:

Ye men of mine. Shun desire. If you shun desire you will ascend to a level with the Gods. Every little yielding to anxiety is a step away from the natural heart of man. If one leaves the natural heart of man, he becomes a beast. That men should be made so, is to me intolerable pain and unending sorrow.

Oracle of the God of Kashima:

I am the protector of Japan against foreign violence and break the spear-points of Heavenly demons and Earthly demons. All enjoy my divine power. I derive strength from the multiplication of devout men in the land. Then do the forces of demons melt away like snow in the sun. When devout men are few, my powers dwindle, my heart is distressed and the demon powers gain vigour while the divine power is weakened.

God of a Tajima Shrine:

When the sky is clear, and the wind hums in the fir-trees, 'tis the heart of a God who thus reveals himself.

Oracle of Itsukushima in Aki:

Of old the people of my country knew not my name. Therefore I was born into the visible world and endured a base existence. In highest Heaven I am the Deity of the Sun, in the mid-sky I show my doings. I hide in the great Earth and produce all things: in the midst of the Ocean I am the eight Dragon-kings, and my power pervades the four seas. If the poorest of mankind come here once for worship, show me their faces and declare their wishes, within seven days, fourteen days, twenty-one days, or it may be three years or seven years, according to the person and the importance of his prayer, I will surely grant their heart's desire. But the wicked of heart must not apply to me. Those who do not abandon mercy will not be abandoned by me.

Oracle of the Gods of Kasuga:

Even though men prepare for us a pure abode and offer there the rare things of the land, though they hang up offerings of the seven precious things, and with anxious hearts pray to us for hundreds of days, yet will we refuse to enter the house of the depraved and miserly. But we will surely visit the dwellings even of those in deep mourning without an invitation, if loving-kindness is there always. The reason is that we make loving-kindness our *shintai*.

Hear all men! If you desire to obtain help from the Gods, put away pride. Even a hair of pride shuts you off from the Gods as it were by a great cloud.

Hear all men! The good Kami find their strength and their support in piety. Therefore they love not the

351

offerings of those who practice tedious ceremonies.

Oracle of Tatsuta (the Wind-God):

All ye of high and low degree, rather than pray to Heaven-and-Earth, rather than pray to all the Kami, dutifully serve your parents. For your parents are the Gods of without and within. If that which is within is not bright it is useless to pray only for that which is without.

An Oracle of Hachiman:

I refuse the offerings of the impure heart. Some Gods are great, some small, some good and others bad. My name is *Dai jizai wo bosatsu.*

Oracle of Temman Tenjin:

All ye who come before me hoping to attain the accomplishment of your desires, pray with hearts pure from falsehood, clean within and without, reflecting the truth like a mirror. If those who are falsely accused of crime come to me for help, within seven days their prayer will be granted, or else call me not a God.

Oracle of Atago (the Fire-God):

Leave the things of this world and come to me daily and monthly with pure bodies and pure hearts. You will then enjoy paradise in this world and have all your desires accomplished.

The Deity of Matsunowo:

Any one who makes a single obeisance to one Kami will receive infinite help: much more so any one who makes pure his heart and enters the great way of single-minded uprightness.

Poem Revealed to Mikado Seiwa:

If we keep unperverted the human heart, which is like unto Heaven and received from Earth, that is God. The Gods have their abode in the heart. Amongst the various ordinances none is more excellent than that of religious meditation.

Dream of a Son of a Mikado:

It is the upright heart of all men which is identical with the highest of the high, and therefore the God of Gods. There is no room in Heaven-and-Earth for the false and crooked person.

Oracle of the God of Atsuta:

All ye men who dwell under Heaven. Receive the just commands of the Gods. Regard Heaven as your father, Earth as your mother, and all things as your brothers and sisters. You will then enjoy this divine country which excels all others, free from hate and sorrow. Obey the instructions of the Heaven-shining Deity and honor the Mikado. If any are rebellious, come before me and name their names. I will surely crush the foe and yield you satisfaction.

Prayer to the Sun Goddess:

"By order of the Mikado we declare with deepest reverence in the spacious presence of (with awe be her name pronounced) the Sovran Great Heaven-shining Deity, whose praises are fulfilled in the Great Shrine, whose pillars are broad-based on the northern-most rocks, and whose cross-beams rise aloft to the Plain of High Heaven on the bank of the River Isuzu in Uji, of Watarahi in Ise, as follows:

"Since the past sixth month reports have been received from the Dazaifu that two pirate-ships of Shiraki appeared at Aratsu, in the district of Naka, in the province of Chikuzen, and carried off as plunder the silk of a tribute-ship of the province of Buzen. Moreover, that there having been an omen of a crane which alighted on the arsenal of the Government House, the diviners declared that it presaged war with a neighbouring country. Also that there had been earthquakes with storms and floods in the province of Hizen by which all the houses had been overturned and many of the inhabitants swept away. Even the old men affirmed that no such great calamity had ever been heard of before.

"Meanwhile news was received from the province of Michinoku of an unusually disastrous earthquake, and from other provinces grave calamities were reported.

"The mutual enmity between those men of Shiraki and our Land of Yamato has existed for long ages. Their present invasion of our territory, however, and their plunder of tribute, show that they have no fear of us. When we reflect on this, it seems possible that a germ of war may spring from it. Our government has for a long time had no warlike expeditions, the provision for defence has been wholly forgotten, and we cannot but look forward to war with dread and caution. But our Japan is known as the country of the Gods. If the Gods deign to help and protect it, what foe will dare to approach it? Much more so, seeing that the Great Deity in her capacity (with awe be it spoken) as ancestress of the Mikado bestows light and protection on the Under-Heaven which he governs. How, therefore, shall she not deign to restrain and ward off outrages by strangers from foreign lands as soon as she becomes aware of them?

"Under these circumstances, we . . . present these great offerings by the hands of Komaye, Imbe no Sukune, Vice-Minister of the Bureau of Imbe, who, hanging stout straps on weak shoulders, has purely prepared and brought them hither. Be pleased graciously to hearken to this memorial. But if unfortunately such hostile acts as we have spoken of should be committed let the (with awe be it spoken) Great Deity, placing herself at the head of all the deities of the land, stay and ward off, sweep away and expel the enemy before his first arrow is shot. Should his designs ripen so far that his ships must come hither, let them not enter within our borders, but send them back to drift and founder. Suffer not the solid reasons for our country being feared as the Divine Country to be sodden and destroyed. If, apart from these, there should be danger of rebellion or riot by savages, or of disturbance by brigands at home, or again of drought, floor or storm, of pestilence or famine such as would cause great disaster to the State or deep sorrow to the people, deign to sweep away and destroy it utterly before it takes form. Be pleased to let the Under-Heaven be free from alarms and all the country enjoy peace by thy help and protection. Grant thy gracious favour to the Sovran Grandchild, guarding his august person by day and by night, firm and enduring as Heaven and Earth, as the Sun and the Moon.

"Declared with deep reverence".

Oracle of Temmangu:

"He still hates the wicked, who do not keep the ways of filial piety, and withholds his favours from those who dislike learning. You must therefore attend strictly to the commands of your parents and the instructions of your teachers. You must serve your chief with diligence, be upright of heart, eschew falsehood, and be diligent in study so that you may conform to the wishes of Temmangu. If you fail to do so, you will be cursed by him, and sooner or later incur calamity. For although the Kami cannot be seen by men, they will know whether their conduct is good or bad, and whether their hearts are upright or perverted".

Nihongi:

55. "The Yemishi rebelled. Tamichi was sent to attack them. He was worsted by the Yemishi, and slain at the harbour of Ishimi. Now one of his followers obtained Tamichi's armlet and gave it to his wife, who embraced the armlet and strangled herself. When the men of that time heard of this they shed tears. After this the Yemishi again made an incursion and dug up Tamichi's tomb, upon which a great serpent started up with glaring eyes and came out of the tomb. It bit the Yemishi, who were every one affected by the serpent's poison, so that many of them died, and only one or two escaped. Therefore the men of that time said: 'Although dead Tamichi at last had his revenge. How can it be said that the dead have no knowledge?' "

69–70. "A man of the neighbourhood of the River Fuji, in the East Country, named Ohofube no Ohoshi, urged his fellow-villagers to worship an insect, saying: 'This is the God of the Everlasting World. Those who worship this God will have long life and riches'. At length the wizards (kannagi) and witches (miko) pretending an inspiration of the Gods, said: 'Those who worship the God of the Everlasting World will, if poor, become rich, and, if old, will become young again'. So they more and more persuaded the people to cast out the valuables of their houses, and to set out by the roadside sake, vegetables, and the six domestic animals. They also made them cry out: 'The new riches have come!' Both in the country and in the metropolis people took the insect of the Everlasting World and, placing it in a pure place, with song and dance invoked happiness. They threw away their treasures, but to no purpose whatever. The loss and waste was extreme. Hereupon Kahakatsu, Kadono no Hada no Miyakko, was wroth that the people should be so much deluded, and slew Ohofube no Ohoshi. The wizards and witches were intimidated, and ceased to persuade people to this worship. The men of that time made a song, saying:

"Udzumasa
Has executed
The God of the Everlasting World
Who we were told
Was the very God of Gods.

"This insect is usually bred on orange trees, and sometimes on the hosoki. It is over four inches in length, and about as thick as a thumb. It is of a grass-green colour with black spots, and in appearance very much resembles the silkworm".

XI

SIKHISM

SIKHISM, with its little more than 4,000,000 adherents, is among the most modern of great living religions. Its founder, Nanak, lived between 1469 and 1538 A.D. in the province of Punjab in India. Though small in number, only Zoroastrianism and Jainism being smaller, and though founded within modern times, Sikhism has exerted considerable influence upon the religious life of the East, all the way from the north of India to Ceylon. Nevertheless, Sikhism has remained concentrated largely in the Punjab, approximately 95 per cent of all the Sikhs in the world being found there today.

Travelers to India find themselves drawn to two great masterpieces of architecture: the beautiful Mohammedan monument, the Taj Mahal, at Agra; and the Golden Temple in the Pool of Immortality at Amritsar. The latter is the central shrine of Sikhism, and has been called by some authorities one of the most magnificent sights in all India. Here one finds a great pool of water over which passes a marble causeway to a splendid temple with a gilded dome and many cupolas, "one of those rare sights seen at intervals during life which fix themselves indelibly on the memory".

Sikhism grew out of an attempt to harmonize Mohammedanism and Hinduism, the monotheism of the one and the mystic pantheism of the other. This attempt was made by Nanak, the precocious son of common villagers, born in a little town about 30 miles southwest of Lahore, the capital of Punjab. During his childhood and youth he found no interest in the ways of men and devoted himself wholly to religious thought and practices much to the consternation of his parents and relatives, even though his mother was a highly religious woman.

While still a young man he came to the conclusion that "there is no Hindu and no Musalman", but that both were united under the One True God of all people. He went through the country preaching this gospel, visiting religious shrines, and proclaiming his belief. These efforts were highly successful and many were impressed or converted by him and his faithful disciples.

As with many religious leaders, a host of miracle stories have been told about him. One is that when he was about to die he went and lay down under a withered acacia tree. Immediately the tree became green, produced leaves and blossoms. These stories, written into the sacred scriptures of Sikhism, have served to make of Nanak a being apart from men and one to be worshiped by his followers.

The Sikh scriptures are known as *Granth,* meaning "The Book". The original *Granth,* the *Adi Granth,* was compiled about 1604 by the fifth *Guru,* or "Religious Teacher", from material that was believed to have come from Nanak and other Sikh teachers. This work consists of 29,480 rhymed verses from different authors and written in 31 different meters.

More than a hundred years later another volume, consisting of works of 37 authors, was issued under the title of the *Dasam Granth* or *The Granth of the Tenth Guru.* This work is accepted by most orthodox Sikhs as authoritative and is placed alongside of the *Adi Granth.*

Since Sikhism is an attempt to harmonize diverse religious positions, its scriptures are written in a variety of languages. Among these are Panjabi, Multani, Persian, Prakrit, Hindi, and Marathi, plus several other dialects. Consequently, there are only a few people in the world who can read all these scriptures in their original languages and there are probably no Sikhs who have read the entire works. Only small portions of the *Granths* have been translated into English or made available to English scholars.

The Sikh monarchy, set up soon after the death of Nanak, lasted until some time after the death of the tenth *Guru,* Govind Singh. Then it broke up into several feudal states. These continued until 1849 when the political organization of Sikhism as a militant church state became extinct. At this time Maharaja Dhulip Singh, the last independent Sikh king, surrendered to the British and gave Queen Victoria the world-famous Koh-i-nur diamond. Nine years later Victoria became Empress of India and the deposed king embraced Christianity.

Today most of the Sikhs live in the Punjab as farmers. However, many of them are to be found acting as bodyguards of provincial governors or serving as policemen throughout the Far Eastern possessions of the British Empire.

THE JAPJI

This short document is held by the Sikhs to be the key to their scriptures, the highest and most complete of their doctrinal statements. It must be known by all orthodox Sikhs and repeated early in the morning. If a Sikh cannot read, he must have someone read this book to him until he knows it by heart and can repeat it at the appointed time. It is believed that Guru Nanak wrote this himself sometime near the close of his life.

Preamble: There is but one God whose name is true, the Creator, devoid of fear and enmity, immortal, unborn, self-existent; by the favour of the Guru.

REPEAT HIS NAME

The True One was in the beginning; the True One was in the primal age.

The True One is now also, O Nanak; the True One also shall be.

1. By thinking I cannot obtain a conception of Him, even though I think hundreds of thousands of times.

Even though I be silent and keep my attention firmly fixed on Him, I cannot preserve silence.

The hunger of the hungry for God subsideth not though they obtain the load of the worlds.

If man should have thousands and hundreds of thousands of devices, even one would not assist him in obtaining God.

How shall man become true before God? How shall the veil of falsehood be rent?

By walking, I Nanak, according to the will of the Commander as preordained.

3. Who can sing His power? Who hath power to sing it?

Who can sing His gifts or know His signs?

Who can sing His attributes, His greatness, and His deeds?

Who can sing His knowledge whose study is arduous?

Who can sing Him, who fashioneth the body and again destroyeth it?

Who can sing Him, who taketh away life and again restoreth it?

Who can sing Him, who appeareth to be far, but is known to be near.

Who can sing Him, who is all-seeing and omnipresent?

In describing Him there would never be an end.

Millions of men give millions upon millions of descriptions of Him, but they fail to describe Him.

The Giver giveth; the receiver groweth weary of receiving.

In every age man subsisteth by His bounty.

The Commander by His order hath laid out the way of the world.

Nanak, God the unconcerned is happy.

5. He is not established, nor is He created.

The pure one existeth by Himself.

They who worshipped Him have obtained honour.

Nanak, sing His praises who is the Treasury of excellences.

Sing and hear and put His love into your hearts.

Thus shall your sorrows be removed, and you shall be absorbed in Him who is the abode of happiness.

Under the Guru's instruction God's word is heard; under the Guru's instruction its knowledge is acquired; under the Guru's instruction man

357

learns that God is everywhere contained.

The Guru is Shiv; the Guru is Vishnu and Brahma; the Guru is Parbati, Lakhshmi, and Saraswati.

If I knew Him, should I not describe Him? He cannot be described by words.

My Guru hath explained one thing to me—

That there is but one Bestower on all living beings; may I not forget Him!

13. By obeying Him wisdom and understanding enter the mind;

By obeying Him man knoweth all worlds;

By obeying Him man suffereth not punishment;

By obeying Him man shall not depart with Jam—

So pure is God's name—

Whoever obeyeth God knoweth the pleasure of it in his own heart.

14. By obeying Him man's path is not obstructed;

By obeying Him man departeth with honour and distinction;

By obeying Him man proceedeth in ecstasy on his way;

By obeying Him man formeth an alliance with virtue—

So pure is God's name—

Whoever obeyeth God knoweth the pleasure of it in his own heart.

15. By obeying Him man attaineth the gate of salvation;

By obeying Him man is saved with his family;

By obeying Him the Guru is saved, and saveth his disciples;

By obeying Him, O Nanak, man wandereth not in quest of alms—

So pure is God's name—

Whoever obeyeth God knoweth the pleasure of it in his own heart.

20. When the hands, feet, and other members of the body are covered with filth,

It is removed by washing with water.

When the clothes are polluted,

Apply soap, and the impurity shall be washed away.

So when the mind is defiled by sin,

It is cleansed by the love of the Name.

Men do not become saints or sinners by merely calling themselves so.

The recording angels take with them a record of man's acts.

It is he himself soweth, and he himself eateth.

Nanak, man suffereth transmigration by God's order.

21. Pilgrimage, austerities, mercy, and almsgiving on general and special occasions.

Whosoever performeth, may obtain some little honour;

But he who heareth and obeyeth and loveth God in his heart,

Shall wash off his impurity in the place of pilgrimage within him.

All virtues are Thine, O Lord; none are mine.

There is no devotion without virtue.

From the Self-existent proceeded Maya (athi), whence issued a word which produced Brahma and the rest—

"Thou art true, Thou art beautiful, there is ever pleasure in Thy heart!"

What the time, what the epoch, what the lunar day, and what the week-day,

What the season, and what the month when the world was created,

The Pandits did not discover; had they done so, they would have recorded it in the Purans.

Nor did the Qazis discover it; had they done so, they would have recorded it in the Quran:

Neither the Jogi nor any other mortal knows the lunar day, or the week-day, or the season, or the month.

Only the Creator who fashioned the world knoweth when He did so.

How shall I address Thee, O God? how shall I praise Thee? how shall I describe Thee? and how shall I know Thee?

Saith Nanak, everybody speaketh of Thee, one wiser than another.

Great is the Lord, great is His name; what He doeth cometh to pass.

Nanak, he who is proud shall not be honoured on his arrival in the next world.

27. What is that gate, what is that mansion where Thou, O God, sittest and watchest over all things?

How many various and countless instruments are played! How many musicians,

How many musical measures with their consorts, and how many singers sing Thee!

Wind, water, and fire sing Thee; Dharmraj sings at Thy gate.

The recording angels, who know how to write, and on whose record Dharmraj judgeth sing Thee.

Ishar, Brahma, and Devi, ever beautiful as adorned by Thee, sing Thee.

Indar seated on his throne with the gods at Thy gate sing Thee.

Sikhs in meditation sing Thee; holy men in contemplation sing Thee.

The continent, the true, and the patient sing Thee; unyielding heroes sing Thee.

The pandits and the supreme Rikhis, reading their Veds, sing Thee in every age.

The lovely celestial maids who beguile the heart in the upper, middle, and nether regions sing Thee.

The jewels created by Thee with the sixty-eight places of Hindu pilgrimage sing Thee.

Mighty warriors and divine heroes sing Thee; the four sources of life sing Thee.

The continents, the worlds, and the universe made and supported by Thy hand sing Thee.

The saints who please Thee, and who are imbued with Thy love sing Thee.

The many others who sing Thee I cannot remember; how could Nanak recount them?

That God is ever true, He is the true Lord, and the true Name.

He who made this world is and shall be; He shall neither depart, nor be made to depart.

He who created things of different colours, descriptions, and species,

Beholdeth His handiwork which attesteth His greatness.

He will do what pleaseth Himself; no order may be issued to Him.

He is King, the King of kings, O Nanak; all remain subject to His will.

34. God created nights, seasons, lunar days, and week days,

Wind, water, fire, and the nether regions.

In the midst of these He established the earth as a temple.

In it He placed living beings of different habits and kinds.

Their names are various and endless,

And they are judged according to their acts.

True is God, and true is His court.

There the elect are accepted and honoured.

The Merciful One maketh them according to their acts.

The bad and the good shall there be distinguished.

Nanak, on arrival there, this shall be seen.

35. Such is the practice in the realm of righteousness.

I now describe the condition in the realm of knowledge.

How many winds, waters, and fires! how many Krishnas and Shivs!

How many Brahmas who fashioned worlds! how many forms, colours, and garbs!

How many lands of grace like this! how many mountains! how many Dhrus and instructors such as his.

How many Indars, how many moons and suns, how many regions and countries!

How many Sikhs, Budhs, how many Naths! how many goddesses and representations of them!

How many demigods and demons! how many saints, how many jewels and seas!

How many sources of life! how many languages! and how many lines of kings!

How many possessors of divine knowledge! how many worshippers! Nanak, there is no end of them.

ASA KI WAR

This is a collection of hymns of praise to God. It consists of a number of stanzas, or *pauris*, (literally: "ladders") which were sung or chanted by professional minstrels. The *Asa Ki War* is repeated by orthodox and devout Sikhs each morning of divine service and after the *Japji*. Here the *pauris* are written by Guru Nanak.

Slok III.—

GURU NANAK

Wonderful Thy word, wonderful Thy knowledge;
Wonderful Thy creatures, wonderful their species;
Wonderful their forms, wonderful their colours;
Wonderful the animals which wander naked;
Wonderful Thy wind; wonderful Thy water;
Wonderful Thy fire which sporteth wondrously;
Wonderful the earth, wonderful the sources of production;
Wonderful the pleasures to which mortals are attached;
Wonderful is meeting, wonderful parting from Thee;
Wonderful is hunger, wonderful repletion;
Wonderful Thy praises, wonderful Thy eulogies;
Wonderful the desert, wonderful the road;
Wonderful Thy nearness, wonderful Thy remoteness;
Wonderful to behold Thee present.
Beholding these wonderful things I remain wondering.
Nanak, they who understand them are supremely fortunate.

GURU NANAK

By Thy power we see, by Thy power we hear, by Thy power we fear, or enjoy the highest happiness;
By Thy power were made the nether regions and the heavens; by Thy power all creation;
By Thy power were produced the Veds, the Purans, the Muhammadan books, and by Thy power all compositions;
By Thy power we eat, drink, and clothe ourselves; by Thy power springeth all affection;
By Thy power are the species, genera, and colours of creatures; by Thy power are the animals of the world.
By Thy power are virtues; by Thy power are vices: by Thy power, honour and dishonour;
By Thy power are wind, water, and fire; by Thy power is the earth.
Everything existeth by Thy power; Thou art the omnipotent Creator; Thy name is the holiest of the holy.
Saith Nanak, Thou beholdest and pervadest all things subject to Thy command: Thou art altogether unrivalled.

Slok V.—

O Nanak, the tumblers are innumerable and endless.
In the same way those bound in entanglements are swung round;
Every one danceth according to his own acts—
They who dance and laugh shall weep on their departure;
They cannot fly or obtain supernatural power.
Leaping and dancing are human recreations;

Nanak, they who have the fear of God in their hearts have also love.

Pauri V.—

Thy name is the Formless: by repeating it man goeth not to hell.

The soul and body are all Thine: what Thou giveth man eateth: to say aught else were waste of words.

O man, if thou desire thine advantage, do good acts and be lowly.

Even though thou stave off old age, it shall come to thee in the disguise of death.

None may remain when his measure is full.

Slok VI.—

The Musalmans praise the Sharia, read it, and reflect on it;

But God's servants are they who employ themselves in His service in order to behold Him.

The Hindus praise the Praised One whose appearance and form are incomparable;

They bathe in holy streams, perform idol-worship and adoration, use copious incense of sandal.

The Jogis meditate on God the Creator, whom they call the Unseen,

Whose form is minute, whose name is the Bright One, and who is the image of their bodies.

In the minds of the generous contentment is produced in their desire to give.

Others give, but ask a thousand-fold more, and still want the world to honour them.

Why mention thieves, adulterers, perjurers, evil and sinful men?

Many depart from here after eating what they had amassed in previous births; shall they have any business whatever in the next world?

The animals which live in the water, dry land, the fourteen worlds, and all creation—

What they say Thou alone knowest; for them too Thou carest.

Saith Nanak, the saints hunger to praise Thee; the true Name is their support.

In everlasting joy they abide day and night: may I obtain the dust of the feet of such virtuous men!

Slok VII.—

In pride man cometh, in pride he departeth;

In pride is man born, in pride he dieth;

In pride he giveth, in pride he taketh;

In pride he earneth, in pride he spendeth;

In pride man becomes true or false;

In pride man meditateth evil or good;

In pride he goeth to hell or heaven;

In pride he rejoiceth, in pride he mourneth;

In pride he becometh filthy, in pride he is cleansed;

In pride man loseth his caste and race;

In pride are the ignorant, in pride the clever;

In pride one knoweth not the value of deliverance or salvation;

In pride is mammon and in pride its effect on the heart;

In pride are animals created.

When pride is removed, God's gate is seen.

Without divine knowledge man worrieth himself by talking.

Nanak, the Commander hath thus ordained it;

As man regardeth God, so God regardeth him.

Pauri VII.—

They who have meditated on God as the truest of the true, have done real worship and are contented;

They have refrained from evil, done good deeds, and practiced honesty;

They have lived on a little corn and water, and burst the entanglements of the world.

Thou art the great Bestower; ever Thou givest gifts which increase a quarterfold.

They who have magnified the great God have found Him.

Slok X.—

Man is known as true when truth is in his heart;

When the filth of falsehood departeth, man washeth his body clean.

Man is known as true when he beareth love to the True One;

When the mind is enraptured on hearing the Name, man attaineth the door of salvation.

Man shall be known as true when he knoweth the true way;

Having prepared the field of the body, put into it the seed of the Creator.

Man shall be known as true when he receiveth true instruction;

Let man show mercy to living things and perform some works of charity.

Man shall be known as true, when he dwelleth in the pilgrimage of his heart;

Let man after inquiry from the true Guru rest and abide in his own heart;

Truth is the medicine for all; it removeth and washeth away sin.

Nanak maketh supplication to those who are in possession of truth.

Pauri X.—

Be mine the gift of the dust of the saints' feet: if I obtain it, I shall apply it to my forehead.

Forsake false covetousness; concentrate thy mind and meditate on the Unseen One.

Thou shalt obtain a reward in proportion to what thou hast done.

If it have been so allotted from the beginning, man shall obtain the dust of the saints' feet.

Ruin not thyself with scant service.

Slok XI.—

Greed and sin are ruler and village accountant; falsehood is master of the mint.

Lust, his minister, summoneth and examineth men, and sitteth in judgment on them.

The subjects are blind and without divine knowledge, and satisfy the judge's greed with bribes.

Priests dance, play musical instruments, disguise, and decorate themselves;

They shout aloud, sing of battles, and heroes' praises.

Fools call themselves pandits and with tricks and cavilling love to amass wealth.

Pretended religious men spoil their religious acts, and yet want the door of salvation;

They call themselves continent, and leave their houses and homes, yet they know not the way.

Every one is perfect to himself: no one admitteth himself wanting.

If the weight of honour be put into the scale, then, Nanak, man shall appear properly weighed.

Pauri XVI.—

All are within Thy ken, O Lord; Thou seest all, and Thou movest them beneath Thy glance.

God himself bestoweth greatness; He Himself causeth men to do good works.

He is the greatest of the great; great is His world; He appointeth all men to their respective duties.

If He cast a backward glance, He maketh monarchs as grass;

They may beg from door to door and receive no alms.

Slok XVII.—

If a robber break a house and sacrifice the fruits of that robbery to his ancestors,

The sacrifice shall be known in the next world, and make out the ancestors to be thieves.

The hand of the Brahman go-between shall be cut off; thus will God do justice.

Nanak, it is only the fruit of what man giveth from his earnings and toil that shall be obtained in the next world.

Guru Nanak

As a woman hath her recurring courses, so falsehood dwelleth in the mouth of the false one, and he is ever despised.

He should not be called pure who sitteth and washeth his body;

Rather is he pure, Nanak, in whose heart God dwelleth.

Pauri XXI.—

Ever remember that Lord by worshipping whom thou shalt find happiness.

Why hast thou done such evil deeds as thou shalt suffer for?

Do absolutely nothing evil, look well before thee;

So throw the dice that thou mayst not lose with the Lord.

Nay, that thou mayst gain some profit.

Pauri XXII.—

If the servant who is employed in service act according to his master's wishes,

His honour is all the more, and he receiveth double wages.

If he vie with his master, he will excite his jealousy,

Lose his large salary, and receive show-beating on the mouth.

Thank Him by whose gifts thou livest.

Nanak, commands will not succeed with Him; the Master must be implored.

Pauri XXIV.—

The greatness of the great God cannot be expressed;

He is the Creator, the Omnipotent, the Bounteous; He provideth His creatures with sustenance.

Man must do the work which God destined for him from the beginning.

Nanak, except in the one God alone there is no abiding place.

He doeth what He pleaseth.

THE RAHIRAS

This short document is a collection of hymns written by several *Gurus:* Nanak, Amar Das, Ram Das, and Arjan. In many aspects it resembles closely the sayings of Jesus and other passages in both the Old and New Testaments. The *Rahiras* is recited by devout Sikhs as divine service at sunset.

GURU ARJAN, RAG GUJARI:

O my soul, why proposeth thou exertion when God Himself is engaged in effort for thee?

He even putteth their food before the insects which He created in rocks and stones.

O my God, they who meet the society of the saints are saved.

Through the favour of the Guru they obtain the highest rank; though they be as dry wood, they are made green.

No one can rely on mother, father, friends, children, or wives.

God provideth every one with his daily food; why, O man, art thou afraid?

The *kulang* flieth away hundreds of miles, leaving her young behind her.

Who feedeth them? Who giveth them morsels to peck at? Have you not considered this?

God holdeth in the palm of His hand all treasures and the eighteen supernatural powers.

Nanak is ever a sacrifice unto Thee; O God, Thou hast no end of bounds.

GURU NANAK, RAG ASA:

Man hath obtained a dwelling in that tank whose water God hath made as hot as fire.

Man's feet cannot move in the mire of worldly love; we have seen him drowning therein.

O foolish man, thou hast not thought of the one God in thy heart;

Through forgetfulness of Him thy virtues have melted away.

I am not continent, or true, or learned; I was born a stupid fool.

Nanak representeth, he hath sought the shelter of those who forget Thee not, O God.

GURU ARJAN, RAG ASA:

Since thou hast now obtained a human body O man,

It is time for thee to meet God;

All else that thou doest is of no avail;

Join the company of the saints and only repeat God's name;

Apply thyself to preparation for crossing the terrible ocean.

Thy life is vainly passing in worldly love;

Thou hast not repeated God's name, performed penance, austerities, or other religious works;

Thou hast not served holy men or known God.

Nanak saith, base have been mine acts;

Preserve mine honour who have taken shelter in Thee.

XII

MORMONISM

THE *Book of Mormon,* regarded as sacred scripture by almost a million people, is responsible for the nickname "Mormon" as applied to members of the Church of Jesus Christ of Latter-day Saints. It is, however, only one of four books regarded by them as containing the revealed word of the Lord. The Bible, the *Book of Mormon,* the *Doctrine and Covenants* and the *Pearl of Great Price* constitute the standard works of the Church. They have other writings which they consider inspired, but these four works occupy a unique position as the sacred scripture of the Church.[1]

One of the Articles of Faith of the Church states: "We believe all that God has revealed, all that He does now reveal, and we believe that He will yet reveal many great and important things pertaining to the Kingdom of God." Throughout their history the Latter-day Saints have accepted the Bible as the word of God, but have also maintained that the canon of scripture was not filled with the Bible; that, as is made evident in the *Book of Mormon,* in ancient times God revealed His will to people other than those mentioned in the Bible; that He has revealed His will in modern times, as found in the *Doctrine and Covenants* and the *Pearl of Great Price;* and that He will yet further reveal His will as the need arises.

The *Book of Mormon,* it is believed, is a record of peoples who anciently inhabited the western hemisphere. Like the Bible, it consists of various books, written over a number of centuries. This record, engraved on plates of gold, is held by believers to have been found by Joseph Smith in a stone box on the side of a hill near the village of Manchester, Ontario County, New York, in 1823. The location was

[1]The material for this section on *Mormonism* was prepared with the assistance of the Latter-day Saints Church Publicity and Mission Literature Committee and its use here has the full permission of the Committee and the Church of Jesus Christ of Latter-day Saints.

revealed by an angel—Moroni by name, the last of those who anciently compiled the record—a statue to whom now stands atop the hill. Joseph Smith stated that the book was translated "by the gift and power of God."

The book was to come forth, so the record states, as the testimony of other nations, "that Jesus is the Christ, the Eternal God." The Latter-day Saints hold it to be a new witness for Christ to this genera, tion, and also an added witness to the truths of the Bible.

Since its translation into English in 1830, it has been translated into 23 other languages. It has been published in 19 of these, and also in Braille.

The book consists of 15 writings, or books. Chronologically the first of these is the Book of Ether. This is a record of the Jaredites which was engraved on 24 golden plates by the Prophet Ether. It is believed that the Jaredites left Babylonia in 2200 B.C. and came to America where they founded and developed a great nation. Because of sin, the Jaredites were eventually destroyed.

The First Book of Nephi is a record of the Prophet Lehi and his family who traveled from Jerusalem and founded a new home in the Americas between 600 and 570 B.C.

The Second Book of Nephi continues the story of the first book from 570 to 545 B.C.

The Book of Jacob tells the story of Jacob's preaching and teaching and the story of Sherem. These events took place between 544 and 421 B.C.

The Book of Enos is a record of events from 544 to 421 B.C. written by Enos, the Son of Jacob.

The Book of Omni is a record of events from 361 to 130 B.C. and recounts the migrations of the people, their political history, and a battle with other inhabitants of the lands.

The Words of Mormon is a short work written about 385 A.D. and tells the story of King Benjamin.

The Book of Mosiah contains records of the people from 124 to 91 B.C.

The Book of Alma was written by Alma, the Younger, and records the history of the Nephite Nation from 91 to 51 B.C.

The Book of Helaman carries this history from 52 to 2 B.C.

The Book of Third Nephi is the record of the life of Jesus from 1 to 35 A.D. and is much like the story in the New Testament Gospels. Many of the passages in this book are near quotations from these Gospels.

The Book of Fourth Nephi tells the story of the People of Nephi from 34 to 321 A.D. It is held to have been written by "one of the disciples of Jesus Christ", Nephi.

The Book of Mormon covers the history of the Nephites from 322 to 401 A.D. and is held to have been written by the Prophet Mormon, Commander-in-Chief of the Nephite army. It is a military book.

The Book of Moroni is held to have been composed by Moroni, son of the Prophet Mormon, and to tell the story of Mormon's life and teachings between 401 and 421 A.D.

These writings were first published as the *Book of Mormon,* from a translation made by Joseph Smith, in 1830.

THE BOOK OF MORMON

The Book of Ether:

1. And . . . the brother of Jared did cry unto the Lord according to that which had been spoken by the mouth of Jared. And . . . the Lord did hear the brother of Jared, and had compassion upon him, and said unto him:

"Go to and gather together thy flocks, both male and female of every kind; and also of the seed of the earth of every kind; and thy families; and also Jared, thy brother and his family; and also thy friends and their families, and the friends of Jared and their families.

"And when thou hast done this thou shalt go at the head of them down into the valley which is northward. And there will I meet thee, and I will go before thee into a land which is choice above all the lands of the earth. And there will I bless thee and thy seed, and raise up unto me of thy seed, and of the seed of thy brother, and they who shall go with thee, a great nation, and there shall be none greater than the nation which I will raise up unto me of thy seed, upon all the face of the earth. And thus will I do unto thee because this long time ye have cried unto me".

(Ether 1: 39–43)

3. And when he had said these words, behold, the Lord showed himself unto him and said:

"Because thou knowest these things ye are redeemed from the Fall; there ye are brought back into My presence; therefore, I show Myself unto you.

"Behold, I am He who was prepared from the foundation of the world to redeem My people. Behold, I am Jesus Christ. I am the Father and the Son. In Me shall all mankind have light, and that eternally, even they who shall believe on My name; and they shall become My sons and My daughters.

"And never have I showed Myself unto man whom I have created; for never has man believed in Me as thou hast. Seest thou that ye are created after Mine own image? Yea, even all men were created in the beginning after Mine own image."

(Ether 3:13–15)

4. "And blessed is he that is found faithful unto My name at the last day, for he shall be lifted up to dwell in the kingdom prepared for him from the foundation of the world . . ."

(Ether 4:19)

12. "For if there be no faith among the children of men God can do no miracle among them; wherefore, he showed not Himself until after their faith . . ."

"And again, I remember that Thou hast said that Thou hast loved the world, even unto the laying down of Thy life for the world, that Thou mightest take it again to prepare a place for the children of men.

"And now I know that this love which Thou hast had for the children of men is charity; wherefore, except men shall have charity they cannot inherit that place which Thou hast prepared in the mansions of Thy Father".

(Ether 12:12–34)

The First Book of Nephi:

9. Wherefore, the Lord hath commanded me to make these plates for a wise purpose in Him, which purpose I know not. But the Lord knoweth all things from the beginning; wherefore,

He prepareth a way to accomplish all His works among the children of men; for behold; He hath all power unto the fulfilling of all His words. And thus it is. Amen.

(I Nephi 9:5,6)

3. ". . . I will go and do the things which the Lord hath commanded; for I know that the Lord giveth no commandments unto the children of men, save He shall prepare a way for them that they may accomplish the thing which He commandeth them".

(I Nephi 3:7)

4. ". . . It is better that one man should perish than that a nation should dwindle and perish in unbelief."

(I Nephi 4:13)

10. . . . Having heard all the words of my father, concerning the things which he saw in a vision and also the things which he spake by the power of the Holy Ghost, which power he received by faith on the Son of God —and the Son of God was the Messiah who should come—I, Nephi, was desirous also that I might see and hear and know of these things, by the power of the Holy Ghost, which is the gift of God unto all those who diligently seek Him, as well in times of old as in the time that He should manifest Himself unto the children of men.

For He is the same yesterday, today, and forever
And the way is prepared for all men
From the foundation of the world,
If it so be that they repent and come unto Him.
For he that diligently seeketh shall find;
And the mysteries of God shall be unfolded unto them,
By the power of the Holy Ghost,
As well in these times as in times of old,

And as well in times of old as in times to come;
Wherefore, the course of the Lord is one eternal round.
Therefore remember, O man,
For all thy doings thou shalt be brought
Into judgment.

Wherefore if ye have sought to do wickedly in the days of your probation, then ye are found unclean before the judgment seat of God; and no unclean thing can dwell with God, wherefore ye must be cast off forever.

And the Holy Ghost giveth authority that I should speak these things and deny them not.

(I Nephi 10:17–22)

The Second Book of Nephi:

1. "Awake and arise from the dust,
And hear the words of a trembling parent,
Whose limbs ye must soon lay down in the cold and silent grave,
From whence no traveler can return.
A few more days and I go the way of all the earth.
But behold, the Lord hath redeemed my soul from hell.
I have beheld His glory and I am encircled about eternally
In the arms of His love."

(II Nephi 1:14,15)

2. "And now, my sons, I speak unto you these things, for your profit and learning, for there is a God, and He hath created all things, both the heavens and the earth, and all things that in them are, both things to act and things to be acted upon.

". . . Wherefore, the Lord God gave unto man that he should act for himself. . . .

"But behold, all things have been done in the wisdom of Him who knoweth all things.

"Adam fell that men might be; and

men are that they might have joy . . .

"Wherefore, men are free according to the flesh; and all things are given them which are expedient unto man. And they are free to choose liberty and eternal life, through the great mediation of all men, or to choose captivity and death, according to the captivity and power of the devil; for he seeketh that all men might be miserable like unto himself."

(II Nephi 2:14–27)

9. "But woe unto the rich who are rich as to the things of the world. For because they are rich they despise the poor, and they persecute the meek, and their hearts are upon their treasures; wherefore their treasure is their God. And behold their treasure shall perish with them also.

"Woe unto the deaf that will not hear, for they shall perish.

"Woe unto the blind that will not see, for they shall perish also.

"Woe unto the uncircumcised of heart, for a knowledge of their iniquities shall smite them at the last day.

"Woe unto the liar, for he shall be thrust down to hell.

"Woe unto the murderer who deliberately killeth, for he shall die.

"Woe unto them who commit whoredoms, for they shall be thrust down to hell.

"Yea, woe unto those that worship idols, for the devil of all devils delighteth in them.

"And, in fine, woe unto all those who die in their sins; for they shall return to God, and behold His face, and remain in their sins.

"O, my beloved brethren, remember the awfulness in transgressing against that Holy God, and also the awfulness of yielding to the enticings of that cunning one. Remember, to be carnally minded is death and to be spiritually minded is life eternal."

(II Nephi 9:30–39)

10. "Therefore, cheer up your hearts, and remember that ye are free to act for yourselves—to choose the way of everlasting death or the way of eternal life.

"Wherefore, my beloved brethren, reconcile yourselves to the will of God, and not to the will of the devil and the flesh; and remember, after ye are reconciled unto God, that it is only in and through the grace of God that ye are saved.

"Wherefore, may God raise you from death by the power of the resurrection, and also from everlasting death by the power of the atonement, that ye may be received into the eternal kingdom of God, that ye may praise Him through grace divine. Amen."

(II Nephi 10:23–25)

The Book of Jacob:

2. "But before ye seek for riches, seek ye for the Kingdom of God. And after ye have obtained a hope in Christ ye shall obtain riches, if ye seek them; and ye will seek them for the intent to do good—to clothe the naked and to feed the hungry, and to liberate the captive, and administer relief to the sick and the afflicted."

(Jacob 2:18, 19)

4. Behold, great and marvelous are the works of the Lord! How unsearchable are the depths of the mysteries of Him! And it is impossible that man should find out all His ways. And no man knoweth of His ways save it be revealed unto him; wherefore, brethren, despise not the revelations of God.

For behold, by the power of His word man came upon the face of the earth, which earth was created by the power of His word. Wherefore, if God being able to speak and the world was, and to speak and man was created, O then, why not able to command the earth, or the workmanship of His hands upon the face of it, according to His will and pleasure?

(Jacob 4:8, 9)

The Book of Enos:

And my soul hungered;
And I kneeled down before my Maker,
And I cried unto Him in mighty prayer
And supplication for mine own soul;
And all the day long did I cry unto Him;
Yea, and when the night came,
I did still raise my voice high
That it reached the heavens.

.   .   .   .   .

And while I was thus struggling in the spirit,
Behold, the voice of the Lord
Came into my mind again, saying:
"I will visit thy brethren
According to their diligence
In keeping My commandments.
I have given unto them this land,
And it is a holy land;
And I curse it not
Save it be for the cause of iniquity;
Wherefore, I will visit thy brethren
According as I have said;
And their transgressions will I bring down
With sorrow upon their own heads."

.   .   .   .   .

"I will grant unto thee according to thy desires, because of thy faith. . . ."

And I soon go to the place of my rest,
Which is with my Redeemer;
For I know that in Him I shall rest,
And I rejoice in the day
When my mortal shall put on immortality,
And shall stand before Him.
Then shall I see His face with pleasure,
And He will say unto me:
"Come unto Me, ye blessed,
There is a place prepared for you
In the mansions of my Father." Amen.

(Enos verses 4–27)

The Book of Jarom:

And as many as are not stiffnecked and have faith, have communion with the Holy Spirit, which maketh manifest unto the children of men, according to their faith.

(Jarom verse 4)

The Book of Omni:

. . . for there is nothing which is good save it comes from the Lord; and that which is evil cometh from the devil.

(Omni verse 25)

The Words of Mormon:

. . . And now I do not know all things, but the Lord knoweth all things which are to come, wherefore, He worketh in me to do according to His will.

(Words of Mormon verse 7)

The Book of Mosiah:

2. "And behold, I tell you these things that ye may learn wisdom; that ye may learn that when ye are in the service of your fellow beings, ye are only in the service of your God."

(Mosiah 2:17)

3. " 'For behold He judgeth, and His judgment is just; and the infant perisheth not that dieth in his infancy; but men drink damnation to their own souls except they humble themselves and become as little children, and believe that salvation was, and is, and is to come, in and through the atoning blood of Christ, the Lord Omnipotent.' "

(3:18)

7. "For behold the Lord hath said: 'I will not succor my people in the day of their transgression; but I will hedge up their ways that they prosper

not; and their doings shall be as a stumbling block before them.'

"And again, He saith: 'If my people shall sow filthiness they shall reap the chaff thereof in the whirlwind; and the effect thereof is poison.'

"And again He saith, 'If my people shall sow filthiness, they shall reap the east wind, which bringeth immediate destruction.' "

(7:29, 31)

23. . . . 'Ye shall not esteem one flesh above another, or one man shall not think himself above another'. . . .

Thus did Alma teach his people, that every man should love his neighbor as himself that there should be no contention among them.

(23:7, 15)

26. "Yea, and as often as My people repent will I forgive them their trespasses against Me.

"And ye shall also forgive one another your trespasses; for verily I say unto you, he that forgiveth not his neighbor's trespasses when he says that he repents, the same hath brought himself under condemnation."

(26:30, 31)

The Book of Alma:

11. "Now, there is a death which is called a temporal death; and the death of Christ shall loose the bands of this temporal death, that all shall be raised from this temporal death.

"The spirit and the body shall be reunited again in its perfect form; both limb and joint shall be restored to its proper frame, even as we now are at this time. And we shall be brought to stand before God, knowing even as we know now, and have a bright recollection of all our guilt."

(Alma 11:42, 43)

17. . . . and they had waxed strong in the knowledge of the truth; for they were men of sound understanding and they had searched the scriptures diligently that they might know the word of God.

But this is not all; they had given themselves to much prayer and fasting; therefore they had the spirit of prophecy, and the spirit of revelation, and when they taught, they taught with power and authority of God.

(17:2, 3)

34. "Therefore, if ye do not remember
To be charitable,
Ye are as dross
Which the refiners do cast out,
It being of no worth,
And is trodden under foot of men."

(34:29)

40. "Behold, there is a time appointed that all shall come forth from the dead. Now when this time cometh no one knows; but God knoweth the time which is appointed." . . .

"Now, concerning the state of the soul between death and the resurrection—Behold it has been made known unto me by an angel, that the spirits of all men, as soon as they are departed from this mortal body, yea, the spirits of all men, whether they be good or evil, are taken home to that God who gave them life.

"And then shall it come to pass, that the spirits of those who are righteous are received into a state of happiness, which is called Paradise, a state of rest, a state of peace, where they shall rest from all their troubles and from all care and sorrow." . . .

"The soul shall be restored to the body, and the body to the soul; yea, and every limb and joint shall be restored to its body; yea, even a hair of the head shall not be lost; but all things shall be restored to their proper and perfect frame."

(40:4–23)

The Book of Helaman:

12. They that have done good shall have everlasting life; and they that have done evil shall have everlasting damnation.

(Helaman 12:26)

The Book of Third Nephi:

16. "Verily, verily, I say unto you, thus hath the Father commanded Me—that I should give unto this people this land for their inheritance.

"And then the words of the prophet Isaiah shall be fulfilled which say:

" 'Thy watchmen shall lift up the voice;
With the voice together shall they sing,
For they shall see eye to eye
When the Lord shall bring again Zion.

" 'Break forth into joy, sing together
Ye waste places of Jerusalem;
For the Lord hath comforted His people,
He hath redeemed Jerusalem.

" 'The Lord hath made bare His holy arm

In the eyes of all the nations
And all the ends of the earth
Shall see the salvation of God.' "

(III Nephi 16:16–20)

The Book of Fourth Nephi:

And they had all things common among them; therefore there were not rich and poor, bond and free, but they were all made free, and partakers of the Heavenly Gift.

(IV Nephi verse 3)

The Book of Mormon:

3. "Cry unto this people, 'Repent ye, and come unto Me, and be ye baptized, and build up again My church and ye shall be spared.' "

(Mormon 3:10)

The Book of Moroni:

7. ". . . For all things must fail, but charity is the pure love of Christ; and it endureth forever; and whoso is found possessed of it at the last day, it shall be well with him."

(Moroni 7:46, 47)

DOCTRINE AND COVENANTS

THE *Doctrine and Covenants* is considered the revealed word of God to this generation. It consists in large part of the revelations given through Joseph Smith for the guidance and blessing of those associated with him in the "restoration of the Gospel of Jesus Christ in these, the latter days". It deals with a great variety of things, of both a temporal and a spiritual nature. It consists of 136 sections, analogous to chapters.

O ye that embark in the service of God, see that ye serve him with all your heart, might, mind and strength, that ye may stand blameless before God at the last day. (4:2)

And no one can assist in this work except he shall be humble and full of love, having faith, hope, and charity, being temperate in all things, whatsoever shall be entrusted to his care. (12:8)

Remember the worth of souls is great in the sight of God; for behold, the Lord your Redeemer suffered death in the flesh; wherefore he suffered the pain of all men, that all men might repent and come unto him . . . And how great is his joy in the soul that repenteth. (18:10–13)

For my soul delighteth in the song of the heart; yea, the song of the righteous is a prayer unto me. (25:12)

That which doth not edify is not of God, and is darkness. That which is of God is light; and he that receiveth light, and continueth in God, receiveth more light; and that light groweth brighter and brighter until the perfect day. (50:23, 24)

For behold, it is not meet that I should command in all things; for he that is compelled in all things, the same is a slothful and not a wise servant; wherefore he receiveth no reward. Verily, I say, men should be anxiously engaged in a good cause, and do many things of their own free will, and bring to pass much righteousness. (58:26,27)

Thou shalt thank the Lord thy God in all things . . .

And that thou mayest more fully keep thyself unspotted from the sins of the world, thou shalt go to the house of prayer and offer up thy sacraments upon my holy day;

For verily this is a day appointed unto you to rest from your labors, and to pay thy devotions unto the Most High;

Nevertheless thy vows shall be offered up on righteousness on all days and at all times;

But remember that on this, the Lord's day, thou shalt offer up thine oblations and thy sacraments unto the Most High. (59:7–12)

And in nothing doth man offend God, or against none is his wrath kindled, save those who confess not his hand in all things, and obey not his commandments. (59:21)

Hear, O ye heavens, and give ear, O earth, and rejoice ye inhabitants thereof, for the Lord is God, and beside him there is no Saviour.

Great is his wisdom, marvelous are his ways, and the extent of his doings none can find out.

His purposes fail not, neither are there any who can stay his hand.

From eternity to eternity he is the same, and his years never fail. (76:1–4)

I, the Lord, am bound when ye do

what I say; but when ye do not what I say, ye have no promise. (82:10)

For you shall live by every word that proceedeth out of the mouth of God.

For the word of the Lord is truth, and whatsoever is truth is light, and whatsoever is light is Spirit, even the Spirit of Jesus Christ. (84:44,45)

And I give unto you a commandment that you shall teach one another the doctrine of the kingdom.

Teach ye diligently and my grace shall attend you, that you may be instructed more perfectly in theory, in principle, in doctrine, in the law of the gospel, in all things that pertain unto the kingdom of God, that are expedient for you to understand;

Of things both in heaven and in the earth, and under the earth; things which have been, things which are, things which must shortly come to pass; things which are at home, things which are abroad, the wars and the perplexities of the nations, and the judgments which are on the land; and a knowledge also of countries and of kingdoms. (88:77-79)

As all have not faith, seek ye diligently and teach one another words of wisdom; yea, seek ye out of the best books words of wisdom; seek learning even by study and also by faith. (88:118)

Truth is knowledge of things as they are, and as they were, and as they are to come. (93:24)

The glory of God is intelligence. (93:36)

No power or influence can or ought to be maintained by virtue of the priesthood, only by persuasion, by long-suffering, by gentleness and meekness, and by love unfeigned;

By kindness and by pure knowledge, which shall greatly enlarge the soul without hypocrisy and without guile—

Reproving betimes with sharpness when moved upon by the Holy Ghost; and then showing forth afterwards an increase of love toward him whom thou hast reproved, lest he esteem thee to be his enemy;

That he may know that thy faithfulness is stronger than the cords of death. (121:41-44)

Whatever principle of intelligence we attain unto in this life, it will rise with us in the resurrection. And if a person gains more knowledge and intelligence in this life through his diligence and obedience than another, he will have so much the advantage in the world to come. (130:18, 19)

There is a law, irrevocably decreed in heaven before the foundations of this world, upon which all blessings are predicated—and when we obtain any blessing from God, it is by obedience to that law upon which it is predicated. (130:20, 21)

It is impossible for a man to be saved in ignorance. (131:6)

THE PEARL OF GREAT PRICE

THE *Pearl of Great Price* is a small volume of about 60 pages containing (1) *The Book of Moses,* as revealed to Joseph Smith in June, 1830; (2) *The Book of Abraham,* a translation of some ancient records, "The writings of Abraham while he was in Egypt, written by his own hand, upon papyrus;" (3) The Writings of Joseph Smith; and (4) The Articles of Faith of the Church of Jesus Christ of Latter-day Saints. This little volume makes known God's purpose in creating heaven and earth, the great purpose to which all other purposes and activities are secondary:

> And it came to pass that Moses spake unto the Lord, saying: Be merciful unto thy servant, O God, and tell me concerning this earth, and the inhabitants thereof, and also the heavens, and then thy servant will be content. And the Lord God spake unto Moses, saying: The heavens, they are many, and they cannot be numbered unto man; but they are numbered unto me, for they are mine. And as one earth shall pass away, and the heavens thereof, even so shall another come; and there is no end to my works, neither to my words. For behold, this is my work and my glory— to bring to pass the immortality and eternal life of man. (Moses 1:36–39)

Now the Lord had shown unto me, Abraham, the intelligences that were organized before the world was; and among all these there were many of the noble and great ones;

And God saw these souls that they were good, and he stood in the midst of them, and he said: These I will make my rulers; for he stood among those that were spirits, and he saw that they were good, and he said unto me: Abraham, thou art one of them; thou wast chosen before thou wast born.

And there stood one among them that was like unto God, and he said unto those who were with him: We will go down, for there is space there, and we will take of these materials, and we will make an earth whereon these may dwell;

And we will prove them herewith, to see if they will do all things whatsoever the Lord their God shall command them;

And they who keep their first estate shall be added upon; and they who keep not their first estate shall not have glory in the same kingdom with those who keep their first estate; and they who keep their second estate shall have glory added upon their heads forever and ever. (Abraham 3:22–26)

XIII

CHRISTIAN SCIENCE

THE incident which directly led to the discovery of Christian Science[1] was the healing of its discoverer, Mary Baker Eddy, of the results of an accident, through prayer and the reading of a passage in the Bible.

Mrs. Eddy, a native of New Hampshire and at the time of this experience a resident of Swampscott, Massachusetts, had been especially interested in religion from childhood; and, in her early youth, she became a member of the Congregational Church. She had been deeply impressed by the assurances of Jesus that his followers should do the works that he did—assurances of which her mother often reminded her. At the age of twelve, she succeeded in healing herself of a severe fever through prayer, and occasionally after she was grown, without knowing quite how she did it, she had helped herself and others in a similar manner. For years before her healing at Swampscott, she had been seeking, as she writes (*Retrospection and Introspection,* page 24), "to trace all physical effects to a mental cause".

In February, 1866, she fell on an icy pavement, and was taken up in an apparently desperate condition. The physician who examined her found her partially unconscious. He said she appeared to be suffering from a concussion and also possibly from a spinal dislocation. He gave no hope of her recovery. On the third day afterward, when she was still considered to be hopelessly ill, she called for her Bible, and turned to Matthew 9:2, the beginning of the account of Jesus' healing of the "man sick of the palsy". "As I read," Mrs. Eddy has written (*Miscellaneous Writings,* page 24), "the healing Truth dawned upon my sense; and the result was that I rose, dressed myself, and ever after was in better health than I had before enjoyed." She was able at once to walk into the next room where friends were mourning for her, and assure them of her recovery.

---

[1]The material dealing with Christian Science was prepared with the assistance of the Christian Science Committee on Publications and is released by The Christian Science Board of Directors.

Her great and persistent endeavor after this healing was to see just how it had occurred. For three years she devoted herself almost exclusively to study of the Bible. Gradually Christian Science, which she also has called the Science of Christianity, that is of the teaching and practice of Jesus, unfolded in her thought; and she found presently that she could heal others, and know just how she healed them. Then within a brief time she healed many others. She found also that she could teach Christian Science, so that those who studied with her could do like healing work.

The numbers of those healed, and of her students, grew substantially before she issued any printed work. In 1875, after thorough practical tests of her discovery, she published the Christian Science textbook, first called simply, *Science and Health* and subsequently *Science and Health with Key to the Scriptures,* which now has gone through many hundreds of editions and is studied, in conjunction with the Bible, by Christian Scientists everywhere.

Mrs. Eddy at first hoped that Christian Science would be adopted by the existing Christian churches. When this result seemed unlikely to follow within a reasonable time, she established the Christian Science church, which now consists of The Mother Church—The First Church of Christ, Scientist, in Boston, Massachusetts—with 2,975 branches in 40 countries.[2]

To further the healing and educational work of Christian Science, Mrs. Eddy published several other books, and established five periodicals—the monthly *Christian Science Journal,* the quarterly *Christian Science Bible Lessons,* the monthly and quarterly *Herald of Christian Science,* now published in seven languages and Braille, and the international daily newspaper, *The Christian Science Monitor.* She also established a Board of Lectureship, whose members regularly deliver lectures wherever there are branches of The Mother Church, and the public practice of Christian Science healing, the recognized practitioners of which now number many thousands in many countries. She provided in addition for the free public Reading Rooms, which are maintained by all Christian Science churches.

Among the published works of Mrs. Eddy is the *Church Manual,* containing by-laws under which The Mother Church and its branches are governed. These by-laws provide for, and are administered under the direction of, The Christian Science Board of Directors, whose offices are in Boston, Massachusetts.

[2]These figures include the branches which were functioning in Axis countries just before the beginning of hostilities in 1939.

SCIENCE AND HEALTH

THE BASIC LITERATURE of Christian Science consists of the Bible—the Authorized or King James version—and the writings of Mary Baker Eddy. The latter include, in addition to *Science and Health* and the *Church Manual, Miscellaneous Writings, Retrospection and Introspection* (which includes an autobiographical sketch), *Unity of Good, Pulpit and Press, Rudimental Divine Science, No and Yes, The First Church of Christ, Scientist, and Miscellany,* and other shorter writings. All these are important for the student of Christian Science, but *Science and Health with Key to the Scriptures* is the most important. It is the Christian Science textbook and it presents, as its author states, "the complete Science of Mind-healing." From this book, together with the Bible, the Lesson-Sermons read in the Sunday services of all Christian Science churches, and also the readings used in their mid-week testimonial meetings, are compiled.

The following pages are intended to indicate, by quotation and otherwise, the character of this book and also something of the substance of its teaching.

How did Jesus of Nazareth do his great works? By what understanding and method did he heal the sick and sorrowing, replace lack with abundance, still the tempest, release himself and others from trouble of every sort, including death? He showed plainly that prayer was the means of these achievements and he reminded his followers continually that similar prayer and similar results were possible for them. He said, "ask, and ye shall receive, that your joy may be full," and "Ye shall ask what ye will, and it shall be done unto you." But what is this "asking," this prayer?

The purpose of the Christian Science textbook, *Science and Health with Key to the Scriptures,* by Mary Baker Eddy, is to answer these questions scientifically. For the book accepts the teaching of Jesus not only as religious instruction of the highest order, but as demonstrable Science, applicable to the needs of today no less than of his time. The book grew out of the author's devoted study of the Bible and her resulting experience. Its aim is to set forth the Science of Life and the method of true spiritual healing, so that all may understand and use them; and large and increasing numbers of people in many countries testify that the book has enabled them to do this. The author writes of Jesus (pages 328 and 329): "The purpose of his great life-work extends through time and includes universal humanity. Its Principle is infinite, reaching beyond the pale of a single period or of a limited following."

The answer to all questions concerning the character and means of the Master's work is to be found, Mrs. Eddy shows, in the nature of God and its logical implications for mankind. She acknowledges as basic Science the Scriptural teaching that God is All and that He is wholly good. She further affirms, in accordance with the

Bible, that He is infinite Spirit or Mind, omnipotent Life, Truth, and Love; and that man and the universe, as they really are, express Him perfectly, and are inseparable from Him.

The textbook points out that ordinary material appearances, including disease, lack, strife, and the tendency of practically everything to deteriorate, are not in accord with reality as thus understood, but it also points out that these appearances are evident only to the material senses, which are never accurate. The testimony of these senses, the author reasons, is by no means to be weighed scientifically against the demonstrable fact of the allness and goodness of God. What they perceive and report, she teaches, is but a meager and mistaken sense of reality, of the infinite and imperishable riches of Mind, or God; and she further urges as inescapable logic and truth the fact that evil or error of every sort, by reason of its unlikeness to God, is necessarily unreal, an illusion of the material senses. This she emphasizes as a fact of the largest practical interest and value—the key fact for all true healing and liberation.

She writes *(Science and Health,* page 466): "Truth is immortal; error is mortal. Truth is limitless; error is limited. Truth is intelligent; error is non-intelligent. Moreover, Truth is real, and error is unreal. This last statement contains the point you will most reluctantly admit, although first and last it is the most important to understand." And elsewhere *(Unity of Good,* page 9), she writes: "What is the cardinal point of the difference in my metaphysical system? This: that *by knowing the unreality of disease, sin, and death, you demonstrate* the allness of God."

Regardless, then, of the appearances before the material senses, the Christian Science textbook insists that the real man, the actual identity or self of everyone, expresses God without in-

terruption; is made forever in His perfect likeness; is indeed the kind of man that a God not limited in intelligence, power, or love would naturally make. And the book presents a practical procedure designed for enabling everyone to prove step by step that this is the kind of man he is. Thus the author declares (pages 12 and 13 of *Science and Health*): "In divine Science, where prayers are mental, *all* may avail themselves of God as 'a very present help in trouble.'" And again (page 462): "Some individuals assimilate truth more readily than others, but any student, who adheres to the divine rules of Christian Science and imbibes the spirit of Christ, can demonstrate Christian Science, cast out error, heal the sick, and add continually to his store of spiritual understanding, potency, enlightenment, and success."

What actually occurs in an instance of healing or of improvement in any human condition through Christian Science, the book explains, is the disappearing in some measure of a false sense of being in favor of the true. The individual in some further degree awakens mentally to find himself and the universe as God's likeness, and he is proportionally satisfied, in accordance with the Psalmist's statement (Psalm 17: 15), "I shall be satisfied, when I awake, with thy likeness." Mrs. Eddy writes *(Science and Health,* page 516), "The substance, Life, intelligence, Truth, and Love, which constitute Deity, are reflected by His creation; and when we subordinate the false testimony of the corporeal senses to the facts of Science, we shall see this true likeness and reflection everywhere."

One may put all this in another way. To believe that evil is real is, clearly, to engage in something less than the true, full worship of God. It is a denial in some measure of His allness; and it is proportionally unscientific. On the other hand, to acknowledge His allness, and thereby to reject evil as unreal, is to worship Him aright, and it is at the same time to have proof of His allness. For all there is to evil, in the light of Christian Science, is a false sense of being, which naturally and necessarily disappears in proportion to one's recognition of Truth. "It is our ignorance of God, the divine Principle," Mrs. Eddy writes (*ibid.*, page 390), "which produces apparent discord, and the right understanding of Him restores harmony."

What, then, are the things in human experience that are unlike God? Obviously, disease is one of the most grievous of these. It is natural, therefore, that the textbook of Christian Science should have much to say on this subject, and the book in fact gives complete instructions for the treatment of disease.

A great number of people testify to healings which they have received simply through the study of these instructions and other portions of the book. Its last chapter, consisting of 100 pages, is made up of such testimonies, and the conditions there referred to as having been overcome include rheumatism, hernia, astigmatism, cataract, tuberculosis, cancer, spinal trouble, dropsy, heart disease, gastric catarrh, neurasthenia, deafness, insanity, liver and kidney diseases, and other ailments. Other healings credited simply to the study of the textbook are continually reported in the Christian Science periodicals and the weekly testimony meetings in Christian Science churches. Mrs. Eddy provided, however, for regularly recognized public practitioners of Christian Science, experienced workers whose help would be available when it was needed. These are now to be found in virtually all sizeable English-speaking communities throughout the world, and in many other centers;

and vast numbers of healings are ascribed to their work.

How do healings through Christian Science occur? The textbook is explicit in its answer to this question. Disease, being unlike God and impossible in the divine allness, is recognized as being "always induced by a false sense, mentally entertained, not destroyed" (*Science and Health,* page 411).

The destruction of an illusory false sense through realization of Truth is therefore all that is required for the cure of disease. An illustration of the specific instructions given in the textbook for such curative work is the following paragraph (page 495): "When the illusion of sickness or sin tempts you, cling steadfastly to God and His idea. Allow nothing but His likeness to abide in your thought. Let neither fear nor doubt overshadow your clear sense and calm trust, that the recognition of life harmonious— as Life eternally is—can destroy any painful sense of, or belief in, that which Life is not. Let Christian Science, instead of corporeal sense, support your understanding of being, and this understanding will supplant error with Truth, replace mortality with immortality, and silence discord with harmony."

An example of such healing from the author's experience is given on pages 184 and 185 of the text-book. "A woman, whom I cured of consumption," Mrs. Eddy writes, "always breathed with great difficulty when the wind was from the east. I sat silently by her side a few moments. Her breath came gently. The inspirations were deep and natural. I then requested her to look at the weathervane. She looked and saw that it pointed due east. The wind had not changed, but her thought of it had and so her difficulty in breathing had gone. The wind had not produced the difficulty. My metaphysical treatment changed the action of her belief on the lungs, and she never suffered again from east winds, but was restored to health."

Much of the chapter entitled Christian Science Practice and many other portions of *Science and Health* are made up of detailed instructions concerning such healing treatment or prayer. Always it is essentially a recognition of spiritual truth, as contrasted with the false, material sense of things; of the nature and allness of God, as contrasted with that which appears to be unlike Him. This recognition dispels the falsity called disease, leaving the spiritually natural evidences of health.

The author does not hesitate to state that this healing work points to the overcoming of death—the fulfillment of Jesus' words, "If a man keep my saying, he shall never see death." She refers to many instances in which imminent death already has been prevented. The patients turned to Christian Science after their physicians had given up hope for their recovery, and were healed. Other instances are on record in which those who were believed to have died were presently restored to life and health through Christian Science. Such results, the author teaches, will multiply and improve as men and women advance in spiritual understanding. Death, like disease, she reasons, is a misrepresentation of true being, in which all is God, eternal divine Life, and man is His image or expression; and the full recognition of this truth must blot out the false sense.

"The great spiritual fact must be brought out that man *is*, not *shall be*, perfect and immortal," Mrs. Eddy writes *(Science and Health,* page 428); and she continues, "We must hold forever the consciousness of existence, and sooner or later, through Christ and Christian Science, we must master sin and death." Elsewhere she writes (page 162): "Christian Science heals organic disease as surely as it heals what is called functional, for it requires only a fuller understanding of the divine Principle of Christian Science to demonstrate the higher rule."

But disease and death are by no means the only unhappy human circumstances to which the teachings of the textbook relate. They relate to all of them. Every unsatisfactory condition, being unlike infinite Life, Truth, and Love, is illusory and something to be overcome, the book teaches. Thus it shows that fatigue is illegitimate, and, as in the case of disease, it shows how this trouble may be both cured and prevented. The author by no means recommends that anyone go beyond his understanding, or beyond the point of reasonable comfort, in foregoing what is considered normal rest. She does teach that through growing understanding one may have less need of rest, and an increasing experience of actual refreshment in his work.

"Constant toil, deprivations, exposures, and all untoward conditions, *if without sin,* can be experienced without suffering," she writes (page 385). She also says (page 218), "The consciousness of Truth rests us more than hours of repose in unconsciousness," and on pages 519 and 520 she adds this striking paragraph: "God rests in action. Imparting has not impoverished, can never impoverish, the divine Mind. No exhaustion follows the action of this Mind, according to the apprehension of divine Science. The highest and sweetest rest, even from a human standpoint, is in holy work."

Loneliness is likewise seen in the light of the teachings of the textbook to be illegitimate and susceptible always of healing. Certain statements of Jesus may be recalled in this connection. "I am not alone," he said on one occasion. And again, "He that sent me is with me." Again, throwing a further light on these assertions, he declared, "I and my Father are one." These are not statements which Jesus alone was entitled to make, the textbook teaches; they are statements about man as God's likeness, and the book clearly implies that in making them, as in all his teaching and healing practice, the Master was setting an example for everyone. He was superbly demonstrating man's oneness with God on his own behalf, but he was also leading others to demonstrate it for themselves.

The real selfhood of anyone, the book teaches, is never separate from the infinite Father, Love, or excluded from happy relationship with His children. Thus Mrs. Eddy writes of man (page 259) that he is "not an isolated idea, for he represents infinite Mind, the sum of all substance." And she further writes on page 444 that "Immortals, or God's children in divine Science, are one harmonious family."

What appears as loneliness, however persistent or distressing it may have been, is, in the light of Christian Science, a false sense of being, and through understanding and consequent exemplification of the truth—the truth of man's unity with God, infinite Mind, Life, and Love—loneliness is healed.

Perhaps everyone has seen how as he expresses more consideration, more love, for others, he loses his sense of loneliness. Such experience points to the scientific process set forth in the Christian Science textbook. Man is in reality the reflection of Love, hence forever one with all good. As the individual recognizes and illustrates to himself and others that this is what he is, he has the actual proof of his true selfhood.

Hatred, likewise, is found to be without basis in spiritual or actual reality, and therefore subject always to healing. In infinite Love, which is God and which is All, there can obviously be no hatred. In the one infinite, harmonious Mind, there can obviously be no mind arrayed against another. There can be nothing to be hated, and nothing to do any hating. Hatred, however stubborn or intense it may have seemed, however apparently armed with power to wound, is thus found to be an illusion of the material senses. It belongs to no one and confronts no one as he really is; and through realization of this fact, and the fact of man's oneness with God, hatred is overcome and thus proved to be nothing.

The realization of man's unity with God, it may be noted, is realization of his oneness with unlimited wisdom and power and perfect rightness of action, for all these belong to God. As the proof of this unity appears through such realization, the devices of hatred and its claims to power are naturally frustrated and annulled.

The Christian Science textbook teaches similarly the illegitimacy of fear, and the means of overcoming it; and it presents such overcoming as even more desirable than it is commonly considered to be. For fear, the book teaches, is at the root of all disease, and of virtually all trouble.

In the allness of God, good—in the infinitude of Love—there is obviously nothing to fear. Fear and all that would seem to produce it are thus seen to be but a false and unreal depiction of the material senses, or of the so-called mentality—designated by Mrs. Eddy as mortal mind—which is one with these illusory senses and expressed by them. And again, as the individual turns in thought to the truth of being, in which God, Spirit, is All, and man is His reflection or likeness, fear and the occasion for it disappear, and its consequences in the form of disease, greed, friction, dishonesty, and so on, vanish with it.

"Christian scientific practice," the textbook declares (page 410), "begins with Christ's keynote of harmony, 'Be not afraid!'" And on the next two pages it adds: "Always begin your treatment by allaying the fear of patients. . . . Watch the result of this simple rule of Christian Science, and you will find that it alleviates the symptoms of every disease. If you succeed in wholly removing the fear, your patient is healed."

What, then, of poverty? Surely it is unlike the affluence of God, and therefore is illegitimate; and proportionally as one realizes the fact of the presence and infinitude of good, lack of what is needful disappears. The true riches, the textbook teaches, are not material but mental, or spiritual; but as one grows in understanding of divine wisdom and Love and man's oneness with them, even the human conditions about him evidence the healing influence of the divine, and what he needs materially is supplied. Many of the most impressive testimonies of help received through Christian Science relate to the overcoming of lack.

So sin, which may be defined as the breaking of divine law, has no incentive and no scope in actual reality, as presented in Christian Science. For in reality man expresses the divine nature or law, and is utterly satisfied in so doing. He can know no inducement for anything else.

The Christian Science textbook follows the example of Jesus in denouncing all wrong procedure, all human action that is unlike God. It urges its unprofitable character, and points to the dissatisfaction and suffering that are inherent in it. It teaches, further, that the true forgiveness of sin is simply its destruction, and that the suffering associated with it ends as the sin is destroyed. But it also shows that in proportion to one's growth in true enlightenment, the supposititious and illusory attraction of sin, and even its

appearance of reality, fade out. Thus the unnaturalness and impossibility in the divine order of sin or error of any sort are demonstrated.

The textbook stresses the importance of self-correction as the means of release from error or evil—the importance, that is, of putting off the false sense of self in favor of the true. Especially does it inculcate watchfulness against those modes of thought and action, such as carelessness, idleness, self-indulgence, self-justification, dishonesty, aggression, oppression, and the like, which may momentarily seem attractive, but are nevertheless always limiting, and disappointing, because of their unlikeness to reality. The book, and particularly the remarkable chapter on Prayer, which follows the Preface, abound in stirring passages on the opportunities which lie before everyone in the way of such watchfulness and self-correction.

The true and effectual prayer, the book teaches, is not mere words, but an actual turning aside from any unscientific concept or procedure. It is the recognition and acceptance of spiritual truth, and its consequent externalization in one's life. Thus the author writes (page 4): "What we most need is the prayer of fervent desire for growth in grace, expressed in patience, meekness, love, and good deeds." And she continues on the same page: "Simply asking that we may love God will never make us love Him; but the longing to be better and holier, expressed in daily watchfulness and in striving to assimilate more of the divine character, will mould and fashion us anew, until we awake in His likeness." She adds, on page 16: "The highest prayer is not one of faith merely; it is demonstration. Such prayer heals sickness, and must destroy sin and death."

The textbook makes it plain that the errors and ills of nations, no less than of individuals, are to be healed by the understanding of spiritual truth. It accepts and explains the vivid words of the Book of Revelation that "the leaves of the tree were for the healing of the nations," and also those of Isaiah: "The Lord shall arise upon thee, and his glory shall be seen upon thee. And the Gentiles shall come to thy light, and kings to the brightness of thy rising." "Neither shall they learn war any more."

It is clear that in the allness of good, the infinite oneness of Mind, there can be no war or occasion for war. Hence war and all that would lead to it—real and bitter as they have seemed in human experience—are without foundation in reality, are illusions of the material senses; and proportionally as individuals and nations realize and evidence their oneness with God, infinite wisdom, Life, and Love, the spectre of war must vanish for them.

"One infinite God, good," the textbook declares (page 340), "unifies men and nations; constitutes the brotherhood of man; ends wars; fulfills the Scripture, 'Love thy neighbor as thyself.' "

While the improvement and removal of afflictive conditions—disease, conflict, want, and the like—are an important part of the work of Christian Science, as set forth by Mrs. Eddy, they are by no means all that is included in this work. It embraces also the improvement of conditions not ordinarily considered afflictive—conditions that are regarded as normal, or even better than normal. The words of Christ Jesus, "I am come that they might have life, and that they might have it more abundantly," are thus construed as being directed not only to those who are in trouble, but to every human being, however happy or unhappy his situation may already be.

Thus men and women who are already capable, successful and happy before learning of Christian Science are assured that they may be more so

through this Science, that they may have a still better experience of freedom, security, capability, and satisfaction; and the assurance is for those in every field of work—in the arts, the professions, business, and elsewhere. The book declares (page 128) "that business men and cultured scholars have found that Christian Science enhances their endurance and mental powers, enlarges their perception of character, gives them acuteness and comprehensiveness and an ability to exceed their ordinary capacity. . . . A knowledge of the Science of being develops the latent abilities and possibilities of man. . . . It raises the thinker into his native air of insight and perspicacity." And in another of her books (*Rudimental Divine Science,* page 2), the author writes: "Healing physical sickness is the smallest part of Christian Science. It is only the bugle-call of thought and action, in the higher range of infinite goodness."

The reason for this teaching becomes patent to the student of the textbook. Man—which term may be taken as signifying the true individuality of every one—is the likeness or expression of infinite Mind and Life, and therefore is himself not limited. He is, as the textbook declares (page 336), "the infinite expression of infinite Mind." Thus what appears to be limitation or frustration, deterioration or insecurity, in any manner or measure, is seen as illusion—no phase or aspect of reality. And in proportion as reality is understood and thereby evidenced by any individual, the contrary evidence disappears for him: he finds himself released from the false beliefs and false evidences of limitation and mortality.

Before the first edition of *Science and Health* was published in 1875, there had been many proofs of these things. Indeed Mrs. Eddy had recognized, as she states in the Preface (page IX), that "this Science must be demonstrated by healing, before a work on the subject could be profitably studied." As editions of the book multiplied, the evidences of the effectiveness of Christian Science continued to accumulate, and on pages 149 and 150 we find these words: "To-day there is hardly a city, village, or hamlet, in which are not to be found living witnesses and monuments to the virtue and power of Truth, as applied through this Christian system of healing disease. To-day the healing power of Truth is widely demonstrated as an immanent, eternal Science, instead of a phenomenal exhibition."

And on pages 348 and 349 the author writes: "I have never supposed the world would immediately witness the full fruitage of Christian Science, or that sin, disease, and death would not be believed for an indefinite time; but this I do aver, that, as a result of teaching Christian Science, ethics and temperance have received an impulse, health has been restored, and longevity increased. If such are the present fruits, what will the harvest be, when this Science is more generally understood?"

In other passages, the book is definite and detailed as to the further results to be expected from Christian Science. It regards the good that has appeared thus far in human experience—all that has been accomplished usefully in science and art, all the health, freedom, abundance, security, and happiness that men have known —as but a meager indication of what is possible for them. In matter of fact terms, the book urges that the kingdom of God, the reign of true intelligence, in which is no evil, and good is ever natural and unlimited, can come "on earth, as it is in heaven," in fulfillment of the Lord's Prayer; and that reality is thus to appear through true enlightenment, through Science.

After quoting from the Revelation of St. John, "And I saw a new heaven and a new earth: for the first heaven and the first earth were passed away," the book continues (page 573): "This is Scriptural authority for concluding that such a recognition of being is, and has been, possible to men in this present state of existence,—that we can become conscious here and now, of a cessation of death, sorrow, and pain." And elsewhere the author declares (page 264), "When we learn the way in Christian Science and recognize man's spiritual being, we shall behold and understand God's creation—all the glories of earth and heaven and man."

TOPICAL INDEX

ANGER

BUDDHISM 133
*Dhammapada: 3; 4; 5; 6; 7; 8; 9; 10;
12; 13.*
One should not give way to anger, but
should control it. He who controls
anger has power far greater than those
who give way to it. The one is master
of his emotion while the other is mastered by it. Hatred is damaging to
mankind and should be eliminated.

CHRISTIANITY 227
*Matthew 5:22; Ephesians 4:26–31;
Colossians 3:8; James 1:19–20; I John
3:14–15.*
God does not sanction anger. One
should be slow to anger and always
ready to forgive. If one hates his
"brother" he is the same as a murderer. The mark of a Christian is love,
not hatred.

CONFUCIANISM 91
Lun Yu: 5.4.2; 15.14.
One should so conduct himself as to
avoid hatred or anger from others.
Mild speech and demanding little of
others are ways to avoid their anger.

HINDUISM 9
Bhagavad Gita: 2.63.
Anger breeds confusion. He who would
be clear and unconfused, must avoid
becoming angry.

JAINISM 119
Uttaradhyayana Sutra: 1.9; 2.26.
Anger is not for the wise or the religious. They will endure persecution
and not be angry. Only the ignorant
and the evil will give way to anger.

JUDAISM 152
*Leviticus 19:17–18; Proverbs 10:12;
14:29; 15:1, 18; Ecclesiastes 7:9.*
Love and not anger is commanded.
Anger causes strife and destruction.
One should respond to anger in others
with love and kindness. In that way
he will turn away the anger of others.
Only fools give way to anger.

TAOISM 79
Tao Teh King: 22.2; 63.1.
No one should be angry with holy men
since they are not angry at anyone. If
one is angry with you, return this with
goodness. Do good to those who hate
you.

ASSOCIATES

BUDDHISM 133
*Maha-Parinibbana Sutta: 1.31; Dham-
mapada: 76; 207–208; 328; 329–330.*
One should pick his associates from
the wise and the good. Evil associates
will corrupt a man. One who reproves
intelligently should be sought out since
his words are needed advice.

CHRISTIANITY 227
I Corinthians 15:33; Ephesians 4:25; 5:6–11; II Thessalonians 3:6; Hebrews 13:3.

"Evil companions corrupt good morals." Shun those who are not good. The wise man will seek out those who will help him to be better and attain greater sanctity. Shun those who are idle and unfruitful and seek out the industrious and the creative.

CONFUCIANISM 91
Shu King: 5.26; Lun Yu: 1.6; 1.13; 1.14; 4.25.

Seek out the company of those who can give good advice and whose example is good. One may be friendly to all men, but he should be discriminating in his choice of associates. Good associates will do you good, therefore cling to the best.

JAINISM 119
Ayaranya Sutra: 1.1.6.6; Sutrakritanga: 1.2.1.20.

Do not allow yourself to be deluded by evil associates. Make your friends those who are considerate both of other people and of animals.

JUDAISM 152
Proverbs 4:14.

Do not follow the pathway of the wicked or associate with those who are evil. Good friends are best.

MOHAMMEDANISM . . . 305
Koran: 11.115; 49.12.

Avoid those who do wrong. To associate with the evil casts suspicion upon one. Therefore, avoid such suspicion by seeking out only the good as associates.

ZOROASTRIANISM . . . 67
Yasna: 33:2; 60:4.

The good should associate with those whom they can help. A virtuous man will radiate his virtue far and wide.

One is fortunate to be the associate of such a good man.

BROTHERHOOD

BUDDHISM 133
Dhammapada: 204; 376.

A friend is a great treasure and should be cherished as a brother. One should make good men his closest friends, his brothers.

CHRISTIANITY 227
Matthew 5:23–24; 12:50; 18:15; 23:8; Acts 10:28; Romans 12:10, 15; Ephesians 2:18–19; 3:14; Hebrews 13:1; I John 3:14.

All men are brothers. If one has anything against a brother, he should make his peace with him before attending to other religious duties. As one treats a brother, so he treats God. To hate one's brother is evil. Brotherly love should rule the world.

CONFUCIANISM 91
Lun Yu: 12:24; 15:9; 16:4.

Friendship, brotherhood, are the cardinal virtues. One should gather about him many friends and should love them as brothers. The wise man will choose good friends who will be worthy of brotherly love.

HINDUISM 9
Rig Veda: 2.28.3; 10.117.4; Bhagavad Gita: 6.9.

The good man makes no distinction between friend and foe, brother or stranger, but regards them all with impartiality. A true friend will be sympathetic with you at all times.

JAINISM 119
Sutrakritanga: 1.2.3.13.

Be fair and impartial to all. Treat all men as brothers at all times. As one treats men, he should also treat all animals. They are our brothers also.

religion of the Wise One takes away the sins of those who confess.

CONTEMPLATION

BUDDHISM 133

Maha-Parinibbana Sutta: 1.12, 14, 18; 3.66; Dhammapada: 36; 327; 372.
Great are the rewards of contemplation. One who trains himself in the art of meditation will penetrate the heart of truth and discover great spiritual riches.

CHRISTIANITY . . . 227

Romans 12:2; I Timothy 4:13–15.
Thinking on the great things of life results in greatness. If one would be good, he must contemplate the good. All virtues will be strengthened by meditation upon them. This, too, is the way to clearer understanding.

CONFUCIANISM 91

Shu King: 5.17.2; 5.18.2; Lun Yu: 2.2.
One should avoid bad, evil thoughts. He should at all times think that which is good. Careful consideration of the end as well as the beginning and middle will save one much trouble.

HINDUISM 9

Rig Veda: 3.62.10; Brihad-Aranyaka Upanishad: 2.4.5; 4.4.21; Chandogya Upanishad: 7.6.1–2; Svetasvatara Upanishad: 1.3; Bhagavad Gita: 2.53, 66; 4.24; 6.14–15, 36; 12.6–8.
Those who do not meditate can have no steadiness nor peace. The great and the wise meditate constantly on the divine. This is the source of strength and the way to knowledge of the Supreme One.

JAINISM 119

Ayaranya Sutra: 1.8.2.12; Uttaradhyayana Sutra: 29.25.
Contemplation is the means of obtain-

ing stability of mind. Even though one is severely persecuted, he must obey the law of silent meditation.

JUDAISM 152

Psalms 19:14; 46:10; 63:1–6; 119:59–60, 97; 143:5–6; Proverbs 23:7.
Meditation brings understanding. One should contemplate God in all His greatness at all times. This is enjoyable and brings the greatest of peace and happiness. To meditate upon the Law of the Lord is the duty of all believers.

MOHAMMEDANISM . . . 305

Koran: 2.199; 13.27–28.
Meditate upon God and you will find peace. Meditation must be in humility and constant if one would reap its true rewards.

ZOROASTRIANISM . . . 67

Yasna: 34:8; 44:8.
Keep the plan and purposes of the Lord always in mind. Meditate upon them day and night. Then you will come to clear understanding.

COURAGE

BUDDHISM 133

Dhammapada: 258.
The wise man is not afraid. He knows his strength and does not fear. Likewise, he knows his weaknesses and does not attempt the impossible.

CHRISTIANITY . . . 227

Matthew 10:28–31; Luke 12:4–7, 31–32; John 14:27; Ephesians 6:10; II Timothy 1:7; Hebrews 13:6; I John 4:17–18.
God is strong, the helper of the good. Therefore, we should not fear, but face life with courage and confidence that the source of all power in the universe is on our side. God watches over even the least of men.

CONFUCIANISM . . . 91

Lun Yu: 2.24.2; 14.5.

The man of principle is courageous. He knows the right and will fight for it at all cost. God is on his side, and he takes courage from the knowledge of this fact.

HINDUISM 9

Brihad-Aranyaka Upanishad: 4.4.15.

To realize that God is all and all is God gives man courage. He does not shrink.

JUDAISM 152

Deuteronomy 31:6; Psalms 27:1–3, 14; 31:24; Isaiah 41:9–13.

Be courageous, for God will not fail you. The Lord is on the side of the righteous man, whom then shall he fear. He will give you needed strength when the time arrives for its use.

MOHAMMEDANISM . . 305

Koran: 2.36, 106, 264; 7.33.

God will guide the good. Therefore they shall have no fear. He will lead them through all the rough spots of life.

SIKHISM 355

Rahiras, Guru Arjan, Rag Gujari.

God gives everyone the food he needs each day. Then, no one should be afraid. Each will be taken care of by the power of God.

TAOISM 79

Tao Teh King: LXVII; Kwang-tze: 1.3; 2.7.

The philosopher is not influenced by praise or blame. He knows the truth and is not afraid, regardless of what happens to him in this world.

DEEDS

BUDDHISM 133

Dhammapada: 163; 173; 236–238; 313.

Deeds determine the place of one in society. He becomes an outcast or a high class person by his deeds. Evil deeds are easy to do; good deeds are hard; but the good deeds pay the highest rewards.

CHRISTIANITY . . . 227

Matthew 7:16–17; John 5:17; I Corinthians 15:58; Ephesians 6:6–7; Philippians 2:12–13; Colossians 1:29; I Thessalonians 4:11–12; II Thessalonians 3:10–12; II Timothy 2:15; Hebrews 6:10; James 1:25; 4:13–15.

Man is known by his deeds, and is judged even so by God. God will reward good deeds and will punish evil ones. To profess goodness is of no value; one must produce good deeds or be condemned.

CONFUCIANISM . . . 91

Shu King: 5.15.1–2; 5.17.2.

Reward will follow every good deed. Only in doing good deeds can man know the true joy of living and have long life.

HINDUISM 9

Brihad-Aranyaka Upanishad: 4.4.5; Bhagavad Gita: 2.47; 3.7–8. 26; 5.2; 6.1–4, 40.

One will become what he does. The doer of good deeds will become good and the doer of evil deeds will become evil. Action, the doing of the good, is superior to renunciation. Thus, at all times one should be doing good.

JAINISM 119

Sutrakritanga: 1.15.9–10; Uttaradhyayana Sutra: 14.25.

The good show the way to others by their good acts. Each day passes never to return. Therefore, do good at all times for you can never call back a day to perform a good deed that was neglected.

JUDAISM 152

Psalms 62:12; Proverbs 10:16; 20:11; Ecclesiastes 5:18–19; 9:10.

Do good at all times, for man will be judged by his works and will be established by the works of his hands.

MOHAMMEDANISM . . . 305
Koran: 4.124; 7.31; 11.116–117; 16.112.
On the day of judgment every soul shall be judged in accordance with his deeds. To do good drives out evil.

SIKHISM 355
Japji: XX; Asa Ki War: Pauri XVI; Pauri XXIV.
Man's deeds are recorded by the divine. He becomes good in the eyes of the divine by good deeds. God is the source of good deeds.

ZOROASTRIANISM . . . 67
Yasna: 38.4–5; Vendidad: 3.33.
We come to the Wise One through good deeds. It is important that one keep himself physically fit to do good deeds at all times.

DUTY

BUDDHISM 133
Dhammapada: 166; 376.
One should be faithful to his duty at all times regardless of the situation. Faithfulness to duty brings the greatest of rewards.

CHRISTIANITY . . . 227
Luke 17:10; Romans 13:7.
One has a duty to God and duties toward his fellows. He should take care to discharge all these. It is one's duty at all times to do the will of God.

CONFUCIANISM . . . 91
Shu King: 5.1.3; Chung Yung: 1:1–2; Meng-tze: 4.1.11.
Man's duty comes from Heaven. Therefore, he fails in his duty at his peril. The wise man makes duty his aim at all times.

HINDUISM 9
Bhagavad Gita: 2.31; 4.7–8; 18.45–48.
Never falter in doing your duty. God has decreed a man's duty, and to fail is to disobey God. It is through duty that man reaches perfection.

JAINISM 119
Uttaradhyayana Sutra: 1.45; 19.25.
A wise man discovers his duty and does it at all cost. It is the duty of all to be impartial and to abstain from the injury of all living things.

JUDAISM 152
Deuteronomy 10:12–13; Ecclesiastes 12:13.
The whole duty of man is to fear God and keep his commandments. This involves love and service to God with the whole heart.

MOHAMMEDANISM . . . 305
Koran: 3.197.
All men who do their duty will receive a fitting reward from the Lord.

TAOISM 79
Kwang-tze: 3.1.
The middle way is the duty of man. He should avoid all excess. In this way he fulfills his duty toward man and God.

EARNESTNESS

BUDDHISM 133
Maha-Parinibbana Sutta: 2.34; 3.66; Dhammapada: 27; 29; 52; 327.
Be not slothful or flippant, but be earnest at all times. Goodness comes from earnestness. God loves the earnest, sincere man.

CHRISTIANITY . . . 227
Matthew 6:1–5; Romans 12:11; II Corinthians 1:12; Philippians 1:9–10; Titus 2:7–8; James 1:8; 3:17; I Peter 2:1–2.

One's religious actions should not be for display but should be done in earnestness. At all times the true Christian is sincere and earnest. He is never the hypocrite who acts merely for show.

CONFUCIANISM 91
Shu King: 4.3.3; 5.5.2; 5.9.2; Lun Yu: 8.13.1; 15.5; Chung Yung: 22.

Whatever you do, you should do with all your heart. Heaven will help the man who is sincere, and one's fellow men will trust him if he is sincere and earnest.

JAINISM 119
Uttaradhyayana Sutra: 29.50–52.

Clear thinking comes through sincere and earnest effort. One will be proficient in religious practices only to the degree that he is earnest and sincere. Through sincere actions one becomes pure.

JUDAISM 152
Joshua 24:14; Psalms 145:18.

The Lord will help those who are earnest. He is near to the sincere and knows man's inner intentions. He is not fooled by outward appearances.

MOHAMMEDANISM . . . 305
Koran: 3.161; 4.107, 141–145.

God is not to be fooled. He knows whether or not a man is earnest in his professions and will deal with all men according to this knowledge. One who repents in earnestness, will be forgiven.

SIKHISM 355
Asa Ki War, Slok XI.

To pretend religion is of no avail. Earnestness is the only basis for true religious acts.

TAOISM 79
Tao Teh King: XIX; Kwang-tze: 4.2.

The manner of heaven is earnestness. If one is sincere and earnest in all his acts, he will attain to the truest sainthood.

ZOROASTRIANISM . . . 67
Yasna: 53.7.

As long as a man is earnest, his reward will be great.

EVIL

BUDDHISM 133
Mahavagga: 6.31.7; Dhammapada: 1–2; 42; 318–319.

Evil actions will be punished inevitably, and good actions will be rewarded with happiness. The good man will loathe evil at all times and will keep himself pure.

CHRISTIANITY 227
Matthew 15:19–20; Romans 6:12–14, 23; 12:9; I Corinthians 15:34; I Thessalonians 5:21–22; James 4:17.

The Christian will hate evil and will keep himself free even from the appearance of evil. To know what is good and not to do it is sin.

CONFUCIANISM 91
Shu King: 4.6.2; Meng-tze: 4.2.9.

Heaven visits punishment or happiness upon man in accord with his good or evil acts. The rewards of good are inevitable just as are the punishments of evil.

HINDUISM 9
Bhagavad Gita: 7.15.

He who is evil cannot hope to attain eternal happiness. Heaven punishes the evil. All pain and suffering comes from evil-doings.

JAINISM 119
Ayaranya Sutra: 1.2.6.1; 1.5.4.5; Sutrakritanga: 1.1.2.26; 1.1.2.29.

Avoid all evil. One may commit evil by doing something wrong or by the approval of another's evil act. Do not cause others to sin.

JUDAISM 152

Genesis 4:7; I Kings 8:46; Psalms 1:6; 19:12–13; 34:13–14; 37:1; 51:4; 66:18; 97:10; Proverbs 14:34; 16:6; Ecclesiastes 9:18; 12:14; Isaiah 1:18.

Evil is the cause of suffering. Everyone is evil and must repent. God will reward those who flee from evil and will seek the good. God is ever ready to pardon.

FAITH

BUDDHISM 133

Mahavagga: 8.22.1; Maha-Parinibbana Sutta: 1.8; Dhammapada: 144; 303.

Faith is necessary for the virtuous life. One's faith will not be unrewarded. Prosperity follows upon faith.

CHRISTIANITY . . . 227

Matthew 9:22–29; Mark 5:34; Romans 1:17; 5:1; 14:23; II Corinthians 1:24; Galatians 3:11; Philippians 1:27–28; I Thessalonians 5:24; II Thessalonians 3:3; Hebrews 10:38; 11:1–6; James 1:6–7; 2:5, 26; I John 5:4; Revelation 2:10.

Faith is necessary, but it must be accompanied by works. One who is faithful even to death, will receive a crown of life. He who asks in perfect faith shall receive. Faith is basic to full understanding.

CONFUCIANISM . . . 91

Lun Yu: 2.22; 15.5.

He who lacks faith will not succeed. One must hold to faith at all times. Heaven makes great demands upon one's faith, but God is with man and he should never waver in his faith.

HINDUISM 9

Rig Veda: 10.151.4; Brihad-Aranyaka Upanishad: 3.9.21; Chandogya Upanishad: 1.1.10; Bhagavad Gita: 4.39–40; 6.47; 12.2, 20; 17.3.

Faith is the pathway to wisdom. This faith will come if one yearns in his heart for it. The most prized of God is the man of faith.

JAINISM 119

Sutrakritanga: 1.2.1.21; Uttaradhyayana Sutra: 18.33.

The man of faith has chosen the right pathway. He should practice his faith at all times.

JUDAISM 152

Deuteronomy 7:9; Psalms 31:23; 62:8; Proverbs 28:20; Isaiah 25:1.

God is faithful and will preserve the faithful. The man of faith can expect great rewards from God.

MOHAMMEDANISM . . . 305

Koran: 2.257; 3.118, 153–154; 5.1, 14; 6.162; 49.7–8.

Man should have faith in God for God will always prove faithful. But God has no patience with the unfaithful.

SHINTO 347

God of Fujiyama.

Even the slightest yielding to doubt is a departing from the natural nature of man. Faith is fundamental to human beings.

TAOISM 79

Tao Teh King: XVII; XLIX.

To have less than enough faith is to have no faith at all. The divine will repay faith with faith and faithlessness with faithlessness.

ZOROASTRIANISM . . . 67

Yasna: 31.21; Vendidad: 3.42.

Good life and immortality are the rewards of the faithful. The religion of the Wise One will cleanse the faithful from all sin.

FAMILY

BUDDHISM 133

Dhammapada: 109.

The aged should be respected and

reverenced. He who does this will receive great rewards and will prosper. Children should give support to their parents. Always honor one's parents.

CHRISTIANITY 227
Matthew 19:19; Mark 10:19; Ephesians 6:1-4.
Children must respect and obey their parents, but the parents must also respect their children. There is to be mutual understanding and appreciation within the family.

CONFUCIANISM 91
Shu King: 4.4.2; Lun Yu: 1.6; 5.25.4; Meng-tze: 1.1.1.5.
Filial piety is highly respected. The virtuous man will never neglect his parents. Love and respect for relations and elders is the beginning of love and respect for all members of the state.

HINDUISM 9
Brihad-Aranyaka Upanishad: 2.4.5.
Love and respect must reign in the home. This is commanded because every member of the home circle is a soul and as a soul he is worthy of love and respect. Faithfulness must mark the relationships of husband and wife.

JAINISM 119
Sutrakritanga: 1.3.2.4; 1.9.5.
The child should support his parents when he is able. Although the family should work together to aid each other, each one must suffer for his own deeds. One's family is of no use to him in the time of judgment. Then he shall be judged in accord with his deeds.

JUDAISM 152
Exodus 20:12; Leviticus 19:3; Deuteronomy 5:16; 11:18-19; 12:12; Proverbs 3:33; 12:4-7; 20:7; 22:6; 23:22-24; 31:11-12, 23, 28, 30; Ecclesiastes 9:9.
Family love and solidarity is basic to Jewish life. The child must honor and respect his parents and obey at all times. The parent must teach the child and rear him in the ways of the Lord.

MOHAMMEDANISM . . . 305
Koran: 31.13.
A child should be grateful both to God and to his parents. The family is a unit, and should beseech God as one.

ZOROASTRIANISM . . . 67
Yasna: 44.7; 60.2, 5.
Obedience, peace, charity, humility, truth, and righteousness should prevail in every home and the children should respect the parents at all times.

FORGIVENESS

CHRISTIANITY 227
Matthew 6:14-15; 18:21-22; Mark 11:25-26; Luke 17:3-4; Ephesians 4:32; James 2:13.
Man should be forgiving. As he forgives his fellows so God will forgive him. God is forgiving and is ready and anxious to forgive those who ask.

CONFUCIANISM 91
Shu King: 2.2.2.
One should forgive if the act is unintentional, but should punish the intended evil act.

HINDUISM 9
Rig Veda: 5.85.7-8.
God will forgive the sinner, if he earnestly casts away his sin. Human forgiveness is the way to happiness among men. A wise man will always be ready to forgive.

JUDAISM 152
Psalms 103:1-4, 10-12; 130:3-4.
The Lord forgives all sins. He is forgiving at all times, if the wicked ones will forsake their ways.

MOHAMMEDANISM . . . 305
*Koran: 2.195; 3.141, 149; 4.106;
5.12, 16; 8.71; 16.120.*

God loves those who forgive their fellows. God is forgiving and is anxious to forgive all those who will come to him with contrite hearts.

FRIENDS

See Associates

FUTURE LIFE

BUDDHISM 133
Dhammapada: 21; 131; 177.

The good and wise will find happiness in the life to come. The evil and thoughtless will die eternally. Heaven is a place of bliss for the good. Here one who has lived earnestly and wisely shall find his reward.

CHRISTIANITY 227
Luke 18:29–30; John 14:2; I Corinthians 15:54.

God has prepared a home after death for the good. All here on earth changes and passes away, but he who obeys the will of God lives forever. Heaven is a place of rewards and hell a place of punishment. Each man shall receive justice after death.

HINDUISM 9
*Brihad-Aranyaka Upanishad: 4.4.4;
Svetasvatara Upanishad: 3.10–13;
4.15–17; Bhagavad Gita: 2:22; 16.7–
16; 18.56–58, 63–71.*

The soul destroys the earthly body in order to make for itself a new and more beautiful body. The wise man will become immortal. Death is the taking off of the robe of life to put on the robe of immortality. The good and just shall live forever.

JAINISM 119
Uttaradhyayana Sutra: 18.25, 27.

There will be a life hereafter. The evil shall go to hell and the good to heaven. In heaven the soul develops to perfection.

JUDAISM 152
*Psalms 23:6; 133:3; Ecclesiastes 12:5–
7; Isaiah 25:8; 26:19.*

The dust will return to dust, and the spirit of man will go to its everlasting home. The Lord will reward the good with eternal life and the spirit of man will dwell forever with God who made it.

MOHAMMEDANISM . . . 305
*Koran: 2.104; 3.163; 4.123; 7.40–41;
10.63–65; 13.20–22; 28.77; 40.1–3.*

The good and those who have died in the service of the Lord shall be rewarded with eternal life. God will gather all his faithful followers to himself after death. Theirs is the reward of Paradise.

SIKHISM 355
Japji: XXI.

The good man dies only to go home. He does not die, but lives forever. Heaven is the company of the saints.

TAOISM 79
Tao Teh King: XVI; LII.

Death is a going home. The good and wise shall suffer no harm even though the body die.

ZOROASTRIANISM . . . 67
Yasna: 30.4; 43.3; 45.7; 60.1.

The righteous shall live happily in the future life while the evil shall suffer great torments. The Lord dwells in the life beyond to receive his followers.

GIVING

BUDDHISM 133
*Mahavagga: 8.1.35; Dhammapada:
177.*

Liberality is a virtue. The wise and good man will share what he has with others. In this way he will save himself. Giving is saving.

CHRISTIANITY 227
Matthew 5:42; 6:3–4; 10:42; Mark 12:41–44; Luke 6:38; Romans 15:1; II Corinthians 9:6–7; Galatians 6:2; James 2:15–16; I John 3:17.

One should give to all who ask, for in giving to the needy one gives to God. The Christian should bear the burdens of others and should share his goods with those in need. The Lord loves a cheerful giver.

CONFUCIANISM 91
Lun Yu: 6.3.2; Meng-tze: 6.1.2.2; 6.1.18.1.

Benevolence is a characteristic of the wise. The superior man gives generously to the needy. He knows that this is the chief element in humanity.

HINDUISM 9
Rig Veda: 10.117.3–6; Bhagavad Gita: 17.20–21.

Giving with cheerfulness is the way to security and happiness. To give is superior to receiving since the giver acquires a friend and protects himself from enemies. The wise man will always share with others.

JUDAISM 152
Deuteronomy 15:7–8; Psalms 41:1; 146:9; Proverbs 14:21; 22:9.

Those who have should give to those who have not. The poor should always be helped. One who gives to the poor gives to the Lord. If one does not give when the poor ask, he will not be aided when he is in need.

MOHAMMEDANISM . . . 305
Koran: 2.104, 172, 191, 269–270, 274; 3.128; 4.40–41; 8.74; 28.77.

The pious man will give alms. His gifts will return to him. God loves the giver. As God has been generous to man, so should he be generous to his fellows.

SHINTO 347
Oracle of Hachiman.

Be generous to all creatures, both human and animal. Long life is the reward for generous giving.

SIKHISM 355
Asa Ki War: Slok VI.

Only what one gives to others will be preserved for him in the future world. The generous will find contentment.

TAOISM 79
Tao Teh King: LXVII.

One should help all those in need, and should not think of his reward. The good will be frugal in order to be liberal to those in need.

ZOROASTRIANISM . . . 67
Vendidad: 8.19; 19.22.

The Wise One was generous. So should all his followers be generous. For one who helps the poor does in so far help to make the Lord King.

GOLDEN RULE

BUDDHISM 133
Dhammapada: 129–130.

Remember that you are like other men. As you fear and suffer, so do they. Therefore, do not do those things which will cause them trouble. As you would not harm yourself, do not harm others.

CHRISTIANITY 227
Matthew 7:12; 19:19; 22:39; Mark 12:31; Luke 6:31; Romans 13:9; Galatians 5:14; James 2:8.

Whatever you would want men to do to you, do even so unto them. One should love his neighbor as himself.

CONFUCIANISM 91
Shu King: 4.2.3; Lun Yu: 5.11; 6.28.3; 12.2; Chung Yung: 13.3.

What one does not like to have done

to himself, he should not do to others. The rule of philanthropy is to draw from one's self a parallel for the treatment of others.

JAINISM 119
Sutrakritanga: 1.10.1–3; 1.11.9–11, 33.
One should treat all beings as he himself would be treated. Since all beings hate pain, he should kill nothing.

JUDAISM 152
Leviticus 19:18; Tobit 4:14–15.
What you hate do to no man. One should love his neighbor as himself.

GUIDANCE

BUDDHISM 133
Mahavagga: 8.15.13.
Trust in the Lord and he will guide you aright. One who has this trust need fear nothing. He can be at perfect peace and happiness, for he will be guided aright.

CHRISTIANITY . . . 227
Mark 9:22–24; John 5:30; I Corinthians 9:26; II Corinthians 1:10.
If we trust in God, he will carry us through all hardships and troubles. One should have complete confidence in God. Even in persecution we should not falter, for God will guide us to our reward.

CONFUCIANISM . . . 91
Lun Yu: 7.22.
God is with the good man. Therefore, he should never fear. God will guide the good aright. Follow the will of God without questioning, for it is true and the end will be success.

HINDUISM 9
Bhagavad Gita: 11.31.
No enemies can overcome the believer.

He trusts in God, knowing that God will guide him through all troubles.

JUDAISM 152
Psalms 23:1–4; 25:4–5, 20; 26:1, 20; 31:1–6, 14; 62:8; 119:18, 27, 140; Proverbs 3:5–6.
Trust in God at all times. He will lead one even through the shadows of death and will protect him in the presence of his enemies.

MOHAMMEDANISM . . . 305
Koran: 3.6–7; 26.77–89.
The Lord has created and will guide man through life. Those who trust in his guidance at all times will find that the Lord will not fail them.

ZOROASTRIANISM . . . 67
Yasna: 28.11; 33.11; 41.6.
God is our protector and guide. In him must we trust and never waver. He is all-powerful and will never fail those who yield to his guiding.

HAPPINESS

BUDDHISM 133
Dhammapada: 18; 23; 132; 197–198; 199; 201; 333.
The wise and good man will be happy in this world and in the next. He has the secret of perfect contentment and joy. One should not seek after happiness, but should find it as a natural result of good deeds.

CHRISTIANITY 227
Matthew 5:4–7, 10–12; 25:21–23; Luke 15:7; Romans 5:2; 14:17; II Corinthians 1:24; I Thessalonians 5:16; James 5:11; I Peter 1:8.
The Christian life is a happy one. Despite persecution and tribulations, the Christian is happy because he has right on his side and his reward will be great in heaven.

CONFUCIANISM 91
Lun Yu: 7.15.

Even in the meagerest of circumstances, the man who lives rightly will be happy. Ill-gotten gains will never bring happiness. Heaven grants happiness to the good.

HINDUISM 9
Bhagavad Gita: 5.21–24; 6.21–28; 10.8–9, 23.

True happiness comes not from external things, but through attachment to things spiritual. It is an inner joy which nothing outside can destroy. It comes from God and is a reward for goodness. Only the wise have real happiness.

JAINISM 119
Ayaranya Sutra: 1.2.2.3; 1.2.3.2.

Happiness comes through self-control. The man who is able to subdue himself will find happiness in this and in the next world.

JUDAISM 152
Psalms 16:7–11; 28:7; 92:4; 97:1–12; 119:111, 162; 126:5–6; 128:1–2; Proverbs 14:21; 15:13; 17:22; Isaiah 41:16.

Judaism is joyous. One who has the Lord on his side should be happy, rejoicing all the time. Happiness results from good works. If a people keep the law, they shall be happy.

MOHAMMEDANISM . . . 305
Koran: 10.58–59.

Happiness will come when one turns to God and seeks union with him. The good will be rewarded greatly for their works and will be happy.

SIKHISM 355
Asa Ki War: Slok III; Pauri XXI.

We shall find happiness in the worship of the Lord. He made everything and is the source of all true happiness.

TAOISM 79
Kwang-tze: 13.2.

Human happiness comes from perfect harmony with one's fellows. The source of divine happiness is complete accord with God. The good shall be truly happy.

ZOROASTRIANISM . . . 67
Yasna: 43.2; 53.6; Vendidad: 19.22.

Holiness is the source of the truest happiness. Only those who live justly shall know happiness. The unrighteousness of man shall bring misery.

HATE

BUDDHISM 133
Dhammapada: 3; 4; 5; 133; 202; 222; 232; 390; 400.

Hatred is damaging to mankind. One who gives way to hating is no longer master of himself.

CHRISTIANITY 227
Matthew 5:22; Ephesians 4:26–31; Colossians 3:8; James 1:19–20; I John 3:14–15.

Love and not hatred should rule. If one has any hatred in his heart, he should cast it out before turning to his religious observances. To hate is to be a murderer.

CONFUCIANISM 91
Lun Yu: 5.4.2; 15.14.

Those who speak harshly will stir up hatred. One should demand much of himself and little of others. By so doing he will avoid hatred.

HINDUISM 9
Bhagavad Gita: 2.63.

Hatred breeds confusion. Clear thinking and careful action can come only when the heart is free from hate.

JAINISM 119
Uttaradhyayana Sutra: 1.9; 2.26.

Hatred will drag down the soul and

defile it. To attain purity of soul, one should avoid hate at all cost.

JUDAISM 152

Leviticus 19:17–18; Proverbs 10:12; 14:29; 15:1, 18; Ecclesiastes 7:9.

It is wrong to hate a brother. Hatred begets strife, and strife destroys a people. Only the fool will give way to hatred.

TAOISM 79

Tao Teh King: 22.2; 63.1.

Return goodness for hatred. The wise man hates not, but seeks always to do good. He will not enter a dispute and thus can have no one disputing and hating him.

HELPING

See Giving

HOME

BUDDHISM 133

Dhammapada: 109.

The home should be a place of mutual understanding and love, of chastity and faithfulness, of reverence for the aged and respect for the young. There should be no selfishness among members of the home.

CHRISTIANITY 227

Matthew 19:19; Mark 10:19; Ephesians 6:1–2, 4.

In the home the child should honor his father and mother and the parents should respect the children. The parent's duty is to teach the children and rear them in the truly religious life.

CONFUCIANISM 91

Shu King: 4.4.2; Lun Yu: 1.6; 5.25.4; Meng-tze: 1.1.1.5.

The home, with its atmosphere of love and respect, should be the model for the entire world. At all times, affection, harmony, and honor should reign in the home. Filial piety, begun in the

home, extends to the state and becomes devotion to the ruler.

HINDUISM 9

Brihad-Aranyaka Upanishad: 2.4.5.

The highest law of the home is fidelity among its members. The wife should be faithful, the children obedient, and the father understanding and industrious. Thus will develop the perfect home.

JAINISM 119

Sutrakritanga: 1.3.2.4; 1.9.5.

The child should support his father and mother when he is able and they are in need. But, in religious matters, the man must stand alone. Home, parents, or family cannot help him here. His right conduct alone is of avail.

JUDAISM 152

Exodus 20:12; Leviticus 19:3; Deuteronomy 5:16; 11:18–19; Joshua 24:15; Proverbs 12:4–7; 20:7; 22:6; 23:22–24; Ecclesiastes 9:9.

The home should be a place of worship. Here all members should serve the Lord and honor and respect should reign. The home in which righteousness rules will stand against the world and the children going out from it shall prosper and receive bounteous rewards.

MOHAMMEDANISM . . . 305

Koran: 21.13.

Prayer should dominate the home. In it the parents and children should serve the Lord at all times. The home is a unit and should approach the Lord as one. Here kindness to parents should dominate the children and the parents should see to it that children are nurtured rightly in all religious matters.

ZOROASTRIANISM . . . 67

Yasna: 44.7; 60.2–5.

The home should be a place where obedience, peace, love, generosity, humility, truth, and righteousness reign. Here children should respect their parents. To such a home will come contentment, knowledge, prosperity, and glory.

IMMORTALITY

See Future Life

JOY

See Happiness

JUDGMENT

See Justice

JUSTICE

BUDDHISM 133
Dhammapada: 256–257; 268.

The wise man will weigh matters carefully so that he may judge justly. Hasty judgment shows a man to be a fool.

CHRISTIANITY 227
John 7:24; Romans 2:2, 16; 14:3–4; I Corinthians 2:15; Colossians 4:1; Hebrews 10:30; James 2:12–13.

All judgments should be made justly. Beware lest you fall into evil judgments. God is just and will judge all men justly, according to their deeds.

CONFUCIANISM 91
Shu King: 5.4.3.5; Lun Yu: 4.11.

The man of honor desires justice and will seek after it in all his actions. Only the fool is unjust.

JUDAISM 152
Psalms 33:4–5; 97:2; Proverbs 4:18–19; Ezekiel 18:5–9.

The Lord loves justice and has erected his throne upon it. The man who deals justly with his fellows at all times shall truly live.

MOHAMMEDANISM . . . 305
Koran: 2.281; 4.2, 44; 5.11; 6.52.

Live a just and honest life. God does not do injustice, and he expects his followers to be just. Act justly at all times and under all conditions.

ZOROASTRIANISM . . . 67
Yasna: 43.9; 45.9.

Injustice shall be overcome by justice. If one has made a promise, he must fulfill it justly even though it be made with the unrighteous. Man should think and act justly at all times.

LOVE

CHRISTIANITY 227
Matthew 19:19; 22:37–40; Mark 12:30–31; Romans 8:28, 38–39; 12:9; 13:7–9; I Corinthians 8:1; 13:1–13; Galatians 5:14; Philippians 2:2; Colossians 3:12–14; I Thessalonians 4:9–10; II Thessalonians 3:5; I Timothy 1:5; James 2:8; I Peter 1:22; 2:17; 3:8; I John 2:5; 3:11–18; 4:7–21.

Love is supreme in Christianity. It is the heart of the religion. God's love for man and man's love for God, the love of man for man, and the love of the Christian for all others are central themes of Christian teaching.

CONFUCIANISM 91
Shu King: 5.1.2; Lun Yu: 1.5; Mengtze: 2.1.6.1–7; 4.1.4.1.

Love is the basis of human understanding. One should love others and, if his love is not returned, he should examine himself to see what the trouble might be. Heaven loves mankind.

HINDUISM 9
Bhagavad Gita: 5.29; 10.1, 10.

The Lord is the lover of all beings, but he especially loves those who keep his laws and are devoted to him. One can best worship the Lord through love.

JAINISM 119
Uttaradhyayana Sutra: 14.32.
One should show compassion to all creatures, do nobly, and obey the Law at all times.

JUDAISM 152
Leviticus 19:18; Deuteronomy 6:6; 10:17–19; 11:1; 30:6, 20; Psalms 18:1–2; 31:23; 66:20; 145:20; 146:8; Proverbs 17:9.
One should love God with all his heart. And he should love his neighbor. The stranger has a claim on one's love. God loves the good man, the righteous. He also loves the sinner and seeks to draw him from his sin and to himself.

SHINTO 347
Oracles of the Gods of Kasuga.
The Lord will visit the home where love reigns. Love is the representative of the Lord.

SIKHISM 355
Japji: XXI.
One who loves God truly will be cleansed of all his impurities. We obtain salvation by loving our fellows and God.

TAOISM 79
Tao Teh King: LXXIX; Kwang-tze: 2.7.
God's love is for the good man at all times. The Wise One taught universal love towards one's fellows, and his followers should follow his teaching.

ZOROASTRIANISM . . . 67
Yasna: 43.16; 49.8.
Everyone should love virtue. Man is the beloved of the Lord and should love him in return.

MAN

BUDDHISM 133
Dhammapada: 1–2.
Man is the product of his thinking. All that he is, all his ideals, likes and dislikes, his very self, is the result of thought.

CHRISTIANITY 227
Matthew 6:26; 19:4; Mark 10:6; 14:38; Romans 8:14–16; I Corinthians 3:17; Hebrews 2:6–8; James 3:9.
Man is a little lower than the angels. He is the measure of all values. It is for him that the world was created and for him Jesus came to earth and died. Man is God's workman on earth. If man fails, all fails.

CONFUCIANISM 91
Shu King: 5.4.1; Lun Yu: 4.15.2; Meng-tze: 6.1.2.2; 6.1.15.1.
Heaven has made man good. His original nature is good, but many depart from it. The earthy in man pulls him down and away from Heaven. Those who follow the Heavenly part of themselves are great, while those who follow the earthy are evil.

HINDUISM 9
Chandogya Upanishad: 3.14.1; Bhagavad Gita:2.23–25.
Man is the highest of the animals. He is an animal with an immortal soul which cannot be hurt by the world. There is nothing nobler than humanity.

JAINISM 119
Uttaradhyayana Sutra: 10.20; 23.38.
Most people are enamored of pleasure and do not reach the moral heights possible for man. Self is the foe to greatness and is as dangerous as pride, anger, and greed. Self is to be subdued.

JUDAISM 152
Genesis 1:27–28; Psalms 8:1–6; Ecclesiastes 7:29.

Man is a creation of God, made in the likeness of God. He has been made a little less than the divine. As sons of the living God, men are clay in the hands of God, the potter, to do with as he wills.

MOHAMMEDANISM . . . 305
Koran: 2.28.

God created man to sit on his throne on earth. Man is God's viceroy on earth.

SIKHISM 355
Rahiras: Guru Arjan, Rag Asa.

Man's body is the dwelling place of God. God is the soul of man, his eternal nature.

TAOISM 79
Kwang-tze: 5.3, 5.

Man is both human and divine. The divine in him is eternal and of infinite worth. The human may pass away, but the divine is everlasting. His goodness comes from God.

ZOROASTRIANISM . . . 67
Yasna: 31.11; 43.15.

The Wise One created man to be like him. The mind of man enclosed in a body comes from the divine. Thus, man should serve only the good and flee from all that is wicked.

MEDITATION

See Contemplation

OBEDIENCE

BUDDHISM 133
Dhammapada: 20; 376.

Those who obey the Law and follow studiously the commandments shall have serenity of mind, joy, and prosperity. Obedience is the way to the good things of this life and of the life to come.

CHRISTIANITY 227
Matthew 19:17; John 14:31; Acts 5:29; Romans 6:17; Hebrews 12:9; James 1:22; I John 3:24; 5:2–3.

The true Christian is known by the fact that he obeys the commandments of God. If one desires true life here and hereafter, he should keep the commandments. The Christian will obey God at all times rather than man. If one keeps God's commandments, God will dwell in him and act through him.

CONFUCIANISM 91
Shu King: 4.3.3; Lun Yu: 20.3.1.

To obtain the favor of Heaven, one should observe all the statutes of Heaven. Those who reverently observe these statutes and are obedient to the will of Heaven shall have happiness and shall become a superior man.

HINDUISM 9
Bhagavad Gita: 18.58, 73.

The laws of God are eternal, lofty, and deep. The man who is obedient to them will be happy and, after death, will experience joy unsurpassable.

JAINISM 119
Sutrakritanga: 1.9.33; Uttaradhyayana Sutra: 5:14–15.

The fool refuses to obey the Law and is sorry when he reaches the hour of death. Man is created to fulfill the law of God. The wise and pious are always obedient to the law of God.

JUDAISM 152
Deuteronomy 7:9; 11:1; I Kings 8:61; Psalms 25:10; 103:17–18; 119:47–48, 70, 77, 97, 101, 112–113, 127, 140–143, 163–167, 174; Proverbs 15:5.

The commandments of the Lord are just and should be obeyed. To disobey God will result in punishment, to obey will result in happiness and blessedness. God will show no mercy to those people or nations who refuse to obey.

MOHAMMEDANISM . . . 305
Koran: 4.124.
It shall be well with the believer who hears the word of the Lord and obeys. The law of the Lord has been set down for men to read and obey. The punishment for disobedience is severe.

SIKHISM 355
Japji: XIII; XIV; XV; Asa Ki War: Pauri 22.
Man is to God as a servant is to his master. Thus, he should obey at all times. If one obeys, he will have honor and happiness and will eventually meet his master.

TAOISM 79
Kwang-tze: 12.2.
The complete and perfect man is the one who obeys the will of the Lord at all times.

ZOROASTRIANISM . . . 67
Yasna: 45.5; 50.6.
The Lord is wise. Thus, what he orders is good for his followers and his commandments should be obeyed. Immortality is the reward which he offers to the obedient.

PEACE

BUDDHISM 133
Mahavagga: 6.31.13; Dhammapada: 194.
True happiness comes to those who live at peace with their fellows. The aim of all should be to learn peace and live peacefully with all men.

CHRISTIANITY 227
Matthew 5:9; Romans 10:15; 12:18; 14:19; II Corinthians 13:11; Ephesians 4:1–3; II Thessalonians 3:16; I Timothy 2:1–4; James 3:18; I Peter 3:10–11.

Jesus is the Prince of Peace. He came to this earth to bring peace to all men. The peacemaker is blessed and shall be a child of God. We should seek the ways of peace and finally come to peace with God.

CONFUCIANISM 91
Shu King: 5.14.2; 5.17.2; Meng-tze: 2.1.3.2.
Seek to live in harmony with all your neighbors and at peace with thy brethren. Peace and love should reign throughout the world. The Most High God seeks peace among his people.

HINDUISM 9
Svetasvatara Upanishad: 4.11; Bhagavad Gita: 1.31–38, 45; 2.65; 9.29–31.
If one would find happiness and security, he must seek for peace. The peaceful mind will become established in wisdom. God is a God of peace and desires peace for all people.

JAINISM 119
Sutrakritanga: 1.3.4.19–20; 1.11.9–11.
The enlightened will make peace the foundation of their lives. All men should live in peace with their fellows. This is the Lord's desire.

JUDAISM 152
Psalms 37:11; 46:9; 119:165; 122:7–8; Proverbs 12:20; 20:3; Ecclesiastes 9:16–18; Isaiah 16:3; 26:12.
Judaism looks forward to an ideal time when peace shall reign throughout the world. God commands peace and urges all His followers to work for peace. The peaceful life offers the greatest opportunity for happiness and prosperity.

MOHAMMEDANISM . . . 305
Koran: 2:10, 257; 5.18; 49.9.
God will guide men to peace. If they will heed him, he will lead them from

the darkness of war to the light of peace.

SHINTO 347
Prayer to the Sun-Goddess.
The earth shall be free from trouble and men shall live at peace under the protection of the divine.

TAOISM 79
Tao Teh King: XXX.
The wise esteem peace and quiet above all else. The good ruler seeks peace and not war, and he rules by persuasion rather than by force.

REPENTANCE

See Confession

SIN

See Evil

SINCERITY

See Earnestness

TRUST

See Guidance

WAR

BUDDHISM 133
Mahavagga: 6.31.13; Dhammapada: 194.
Intentional killing of any living being is condemned. Peace, and not war, is the ideal and should be sought by all who are truly religious.

CHRISTIANITY 227
Matthew 5:9; Romans 10:15; 12:18; 14:19; II Corinthians 13:11; Ephesians 4:1-3; II Thessalonians 3:16; I Timothy 2:1-4; James 3:18; I Peter 3:10-11.
The peacemakers, and not the warmakers, are blessed. Those who take the sword shall perish by the sword.

War is the road to destruction, while peace is the road to happiness and prosperity.

CONFUCIANISM 91
Shu King: 5.14.2; 5.17.2; Meng-tze: 2.1.3.2.
God desires peace, not war. Everyone should strive to dwell in peace with his fellows. The man subdued by force is in his heart still rebellious, but one who is won by love will be loyal forever.

HINDUISM 9
Svetasvatara Upanishad: 4.11; Bhagavad Gita: 1.31-38; 1.45; 2.65; 9.29-31.
Injury to any creature is wrong. The wise man will seek always to avoid strife and will dwell in peace. The ideal for life here on earth is peace, not war. No one should seek to extend his power through war.

JAINISM 119
Sutrakritanga: 1.3.4.19-20; 1.11.9-11.
Never kill anything for any reason whatsoever. The wise live at peace with all men whatever the cost. War is totally condemned.

JUDAISM 152
Psalms 37:11; 46:9; 119:165; 122:7-8; Proverbs 12:20; 20:3; Ecclesiastes 9:16-18; Isaiah 26:3, 12.
Only fools give way to war. The wise seek peace. The peace-loving, the meek, shall inherit the earth. The Lord will judge between nations, and wars are of no avail.

MOHAMMEDANISM . . . 305
Koran: 2.10, 257; 5.18; 49.9.
Peace is to be sought by all. If there is war, the religious man will seek to establish peace. The Lord has ordained peace, and no one can engage in war without endangering the stability of the world.

SHINTO 347
Prayer to the Sun-Goddess.

Let the land under heaven enjoy peace and be free from war. The Sun-Goddess will protect the country so that it may live at peace.

TAOISM 79
Tao Teh King: XXX.

War is always followed by disastrous years. He who truly serves as a ruler of men will not lead his nation into war. Arms are unblessed and are full of sorrow.

WEALTH

BUDDHISM 133
Maha-Parinibbana Sutta: 1.9; Dhammapada: 62; 76; 204.

Wisdom and self-mastery are true wealth. Material possessions are not real wealth, for they can be taken away from a man. Real wealth is everlasting.

CHRISTIANITY 227
Matthew 6:19–24; 16:26; Mark 10:24; Luke 12:15; I Timothy 6:9–10, 17–18; I John 3:17.

Moth and rust will corrupt earthly treasures. Therefore, real treasures are heavenly, where nothing can destroy them. One's heart will be with his treasures. Therefore, turn from mammon to God. Do not count the wealth of this world as valuable. The only true value lies in spiritual wealth.

CONFUCIANISM . . . 91
Lun Yu: 7.15; 8.13.3; 14.1.

Prosperity comes from Heaven. Wealth gained by unrighteousness will not last. The only true wealth is that which comes through right acting. Too often riches are accompanied by pride and other evils.

HINDUISM 9
Rig Veda: 10.117.1–5; Isa Upanishad: 1.

One should work constantly and not seek after wealth. But, if he gains wealth, he should share it with those in need. Beware lest wealth shut the door on the good life. Riches are but means to doing good and should not became the goal of life.

JAINISM 119
Sutrakritanga: 1.2.3.16; 1.9.3; Uttaradhyayana Sutra: 4.2.5.

Wealth is fleeting and will never completely satisfy anyone. To put faith in wealth is to be a fool, for it will cause pain both in this world and in the next.

JUDAISM 152
Psalms 37:16; 62:10; 3:9; 15:16; 16:8; 22:1–2; 23:4–5; 28:6; Ecclesiastes 5:12.

Trust not in wealth. It is fleeting and may be the cause of much evil and suffering. The poverty of a good man is more to be prized than the wealth of the evil man. If one has wealth, he should use it for good and not for evil.

MOHAMMEDANISM . . . 305
Koran: 2.1–4, 184, 263; 3.151; 10.59.

Wealth should be employed at all times for the things of the Lord. He who wastes his wealth in evil actions is condemned. Wealth must not be allowed to turn one from service to God.

TAOISM 79
Tao Teh King: XLIV; Kwang-tze: 14.5.

One's person is of more value than all his wealth. Therefore, one with wealth must beware lest he sacrifice himself for his wealth. Riches acquired unjustly will become poison to the soul.

ZOROASTRIANISM . . . 67
Yasna: 43.1; 52.1–4.

Prosperity and wealth are the rewards of right living and come from the Wise

Lord. Thus, wealth must be employed in the service of the Lord.

WORK

BUDDHISM 133

Dhammapada: 163; 173; 236; 238; 313.

Works, and not birth, determine one's place in the world. At all times one should work diligently and with earnestness. Hard work is praised.

CHRISTIANITY . . . 227

Matthew 7:16–17; John 5:17; I Corinthians 15:58; Ephesians 6:6–7; Philippians 2:12–13; Colossians 1:29; I Thessalonians 4:11–12; II Thessalonians 3:10–12; II Timothy 2:15; Hebrews 6:10; James 1:25; 4:13–15.

God works, and so man should work. The Christian will be diligent in good works all the time, for a man is to be judged by his works. As man works for the good, it is God who worketh in and through him.

CONFUCIANISM . . . 91

Shu King: 5.15.1–2; 5.17.2.

Not ease, but work is the mark of a good man. The superior individual does not indulge in luxurious ease, but works constantly for the good. He is superior in that he does things which the base cannot understand or appreciate.

HINDUISM 9

Brihad-Aranyaka Upanishad: 4.4.5; Bhagavad Gita: 2.47; 3.7–8, 26; 5.2; 6.1–4, 40.

One becomes what he does. The man who does good becomes good, and the man who does evil becomes evil. The motive of one's works should not be the consequences. He should do good despite the results. No one who does good will come to an evil end.

JAINISM 119

Sutrakritanga: 1.15.9–10; Uttaradhyayana Sutra: 14.25.

A day once gone will never return. Therefore, one should be diligent each moment to do good. We reach the goal of the good life by pious works.

JUDAISM 152

Psalms 62:12; Proverbs 10:16; Ecclesiastes 5:18–19; 9:10.

God will judge each man according to his works. All men shall be known by their works. Whatever one undertakes to do, he should do it with all his might. God commands men to work and promises that he will be with them in all good works.

MOHAMMEDANISM . . . 305

Koran: 4.124; 7.31; 11.116–117; 16.112.

Everyone should strive to excel in good works. Work constantly. God will observe your works and judge you according to whether they are good or evil.

SIKHISM 355

Japji: XX; Asa Ki War: Pauri XVI; Pauri XXIV.

God has determined from the beginning the works man must do. No man can escape this determination. Men become saints or sinners by their works only, not by their professions. Good works bring men to a clearer knowledge of the divine.

ZOROASTRIANISM . . . 67

Yasna: 36.4–5; Vendidad: 3.33.

We come to the divine through our good works. Thus, at all times man should strive to work well so that he may gain recognition in the sight of the Wise Lord.

WRATH

BUDDHISM 133

Dhammapada: 3; 4; 5; 133; 202; 232; 357; 390; 400.

A true disciple is free from all passion,

including wrath. To give way to wrath is to bind oneself to a master who will destroy. Happiness lies in freedom from wrath.

CHRISTIANITY 227

Matthew 5:22; Ephesians 4:26–31; Colossians 3:8; James 1:19–20; I John 3:14–15.

Everyone should beware of wrath. Be slow to wrath and do not become angry without cause. Love, and not anger, is the mark of a true Christian. Put away all wrath and malice and seek to dwell in friendliness with all men.

CONFUCIANISM 91

Lun Yu: 5.4.2; 15.14.

Do not deal with your fellows as though you were superior to them. Those who do, will find themselves hated. To avoid the wrath of others, demand little of them and much of yourself.

HINDUISM 9

Bhagavad Gita: 2.63.

Wrath breeds confusion. One who would be master of himself and of all situations, must avoid wrath. The ideal is to live free from hate and anger.

JAINISM 119

Uttaradhyayana Sutra: 1.9; 2.26.

Wrath is a passion which defiles the soul. The wise man will avoid wrath lest he be caught in the toils of the passion as a fly is caught in glue. Even though he is beaten, the religionist will not give way to wrath.

JUDAISM 152

Leviticus 19:17–18; Proverbs 10:12; 14:29; 15:1, 18; Ecclesiastes 7:9.

The wise man is slow to wrath. He gives soft answers and thereby turns away wrath on the part of others. Love, and not wrath, should be the goal of all true believers, for wrath leads to strife.

TAOISM 79

Tao Teh King: XXII; LXIII.

Return goodness for hatred. Do not become angry and do not quarrel with your fellows. The wise man is free from wrath at all times.